Saurav Mallik, Sandeep Kumar Mathivanan, S. K. B. Sangeetha, Ben Othman Soufiene,
Saravanan Srinivasan, Aimin Li (Eds.)
Machine Learning in Healthcare

Also of interest

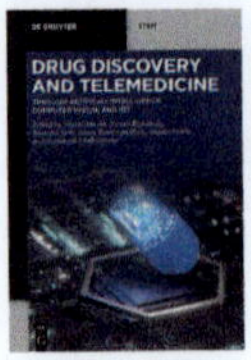

Drug Discovery and Telemedicine.
Through Artificial Intelligence, Computer Vision, and IoT
Edited by Saurav Mallik, Zubair Rahaman, Soumita Seth, Anjan Bandyopadhyay, Sujata Swain, Somenath Chakraborty, 2025
ISBN 978-3-11-150398-1, e-ISBN (PDF) 978-3-11-150466-7

The Mathematics of Machine Learning.
Maria Han Veiga, François Gaston Ged, 2024
ISBN 978-3-11-128847-5, e-ISBN (PDF) 978-3-11-128899-4

Artificial Intelligence for Medicine.
People, Society, Pharmaceuticals, and Medical Materials
Yoshiki Oshida, 2021
ISBN 978-3-11-071779-2, e-ISBN (PDF) 978-3-11-071785-3

Smart Computing Applications.
Edited by Prasenjit Chatterjee, Dilbagh Panchal, Dragan Pamucar, Sharfaraz Ashemkhani Zolfani
ISSN 2700-6239, e-ISSN 2700-6247

Digital Transformation in Healthcare 5.0.
Edited by Rishabha Malviya, Sonali Sundram, Rajesh Kumar Dhanaraj, Seifedine Kadry, 2024
Volume 1: IoT, AI and Digital Twin
ISBN 978-3-11-132646-7, e-ISBN (PDF) 978-3-11-132785-3
Volume 2: Metaverse, Nanorobots and Machine Learning
ISBN 978-3-11-139738-2, e-ISBN (PDF) 978-3-11-139854-9

Sustainability in Healthcare.
mHealth, AI, and Robotics
Rishabha Malviya, Sonali Sundram, Babita Gupta, 2024
ISBN 978-3-11-143635-7, e-ISBN (PDF) 978-3-11-143643-2

Machine Learning in Healthcare

Data-Driven Decisions, Predictive Modelling, Personalized Medicine

Edited by
Saurav Mallik, Sandeep Kumar Mathivanan,
S. K. B. Sangeetha, Ben Othman Soufiene,
Saravanan Srinivasan, Aimin Li

DE GRUYTER

Editors
Dr Saurav Mallik
Department of Pharmacology and Toxicology
University of Arizona
Tucson, AZ, USA
smallik@pharmacy.arizona.edu

Dr Ben Othman Soufiene
Applied College
King Faisal University
Al-Ahsa-31982, Saudi Arabia
sbenothman@kfu.edu.sa

Dr Sandeep Kumar Mathivanan
School of Computing Science and Engineering,
Galgotias University,
Greater Noida 203201, India.

Dr Saravanan Srinivasan
Department of Computer Science and Engineering,
SRM Institute of Science and Technology,
Ramapuram, Chennai 60089,
Tamilnadu, India.
saravananjask@gmail.com

Dr S. K. B. Sangeetha
Manipal Institute of Technology Bengaluru,
Manipal Academy of Higher Education,
Manipal, India.

Dr Aimin Li
Xi'an University of Technology
Xi'an, People's Republic of China
aimin.li@xaut.edu.cn

ISBN 978-3-11-154107-5
e-ISBN (PDF) 978-3-11-154123-5
e-ISBN (EPUB) 978-3-11-154245-4

Library of Congress Control Number: 2025944101

Bibliographic information published by the Deutsche Nationalbibliothek
The Deutsche Nationalbibliothek lists this publication in the Deutsche Nationalbibliografie; detailed bibliographic data are available on the internet at http://dnb.dnb.de.

Cover image: Just_Super/E+/Getty Images
Typesetting: Integra Software Services Pvt. Ltd.
Printing and binding: CPI books GmbH, Leck

www.degruyterbrill.com
Questions about General Product Safety Regulation:
productsafety@degruyterbrill.com

Contents

Pavan Kumar M. R.* and Korhan Cengiz

Early Prediction of Chronic Kidney Disease Using a Novel Hybrid Regularized Adaptive Boosting Algorithm: An Advanced Machine Learning Approach

Abstract: Millions of individuals globally have chronic kidney disease (CKD), a disabling condition that is often misdiagnosed. Traditional diagnosis relies primarily on human interpretation of laboratory results and clinical symptoms, resulting in untrustworthy outcomes and diagnostic delay. Traditional machine learning models typically have problems with overfitting, interpretability, and generalizability across various patient sets. We propose a novel hybrid regularized adaptive boosting (HRAB) algorithm to predict CKD in its early stages to address the abovementioned shortcomings. HRAB has a feature weighting scheme that is intelligent, L1–L2 hybrid regularization, and the benefits of AdaBoost. This reduces the impact of noise and multicollinearity of medical data and allows the model to focus on the therapeutically most important attributes. Patient demographics, biochemical markers, and diagnostic indicators are all part of the dataset, which has been preprocessed using synthetic minority oversampling technique for class balance, imputation, and normalization. Using the HRAB model, 96.8% accuracy, 95.9% precision, 97.4% recall, 96.6% F_1-score, and 0.985 area under the curve-ROC were all achieved. On the same data, our performance outperforms models like random forest (accuracy: 92.3%) and gradient boosting machine (GBM; accuracy: 95.2%). SHapley Additive exPlanation analysis in which serum creatinine, albumin, blood pressure, and blood urea concentrations were the most important features in enhancing the model interpretability. The new test HRAB is a possible test to be implemented into CKD screening devices for its outstanding accuracy, stability, and clinical value. This test will provide a pragmatic solution to facilitate early diagnosis and personalized treatment planning in nephrology due to its excellent performance and interpretability.

Keywords: chronic kidney disease (CKD), machine learning, hybrid regularized adaptive boosting (HRAB), early diagnosis, clinical decision support, model interpretability

***Corresponding author: Pavan Kumar M. R.**, Department of AI and ML Sree Rama Engineering College, Tirupati 517507, Andhra Pradesh, India, e-mail: marabattinasivapavan@gmail.com
Korhan Cengiz, Department of Electrical Engineering, Prince Mohammad Bin Fahd University, Al Khobar 31952, Saudi Arabia, e-mail: kcengiz@pmu.edu.sa

https://doi.org/10.1515/9783111541235-001

1 Introduction

From a clinically nonsignificant disease to one of the most urgently required chronic diseases of known medicine to the present time, chronic kidney disease (CKD) has been a persistent global health threat spanning decades. Renal disease pathophysiology is as far back as civilizations that existed many years ago where physicians observed renal features but could not use science skills to assess renal function. With the development of physiology and pathology in the twentieth and nineteenth centuries, nephrotic and nephritic syndromes were categorized and chronic renal failure was identified as an irreversible and progressive disease. Serum creatinine (SC) and urea, valuable indicators of declining renal function, could be quantified by clinicians following the introduction of biochemical assays in the mid-twentieth century [1].

There arose a new emphasis on the role of early treatment and screening after realizing that CKD is an asymptomatic, silent disease, particularly in the initial stages. Various healthcare systems globally have implemented various methods of early diagnosis because of increasing cases of CKD, most notably in those with comorbidities like diabetes and hypertension. Nephrologists formerly utilized imaging scans, baseline urine and blood, and intermittent kidney biopsies as means of diagnosis. Among the most commonly used markers are SC, albuminuria, blood urea nitrogen, and estimated glomerular filtration rate (eGFR). Although these methods have a sound foundation for the detection of renal impairment, their drawbacks include unpredictable interpretation, delayed onset of symptoms, and poor sensitivity at the commencement of the disease process [2].

In addition, these methods are constrained by the availability of trained personnel and laboratory facilities, particularly in developing nations, and are static in nature, capturing renal function as an instantaneous snapshot rather than predictive data. New medical diagnostic avenues have been explored in recent years with the advent of data-driven approaches, particularly with the development of machine learning (ML). High-dimensional, intricate healthcare issues can be addressed by employing ML techniques, wherein computers are trained from experience and predict outcomes without being explicitly coded. ML has been utilized in the case of CKD to assist in therapeutic decision-making, risk stratification, and disease onset prediction [3].

Clinical information has been employed for training predictive models such as support vector machines (SVM), decision trees, random forests (RFs), logistic regression, *k*-nearest neighbors, and ensemble methods such as GBMs. These models are likely to operate on structured data such as patient history, laboratory results, and demographic information and attempt to map input features to diagnosis categories such as the presence or extent of CKD. While promising, there are several drawbacks to the ML systems employed for CKD diagnosis. To start with, generalizability suffers due to the fact that the majority of models are trained on small datasets and, in some cases, an individual organization or community [4].

Issues such as class imbalance, in which there are significantly more or significantly fewer cases of CKD than non-CKD, can lead to biased models that fail to properly identify cases of minority classes. Overfitting remains an intrinsic problem for standard ML models, especially where highly correlated or redundant features are not subject to sufficient control of regularization or feature dimensionality reduction. In addition, much of the prior work simply addresses model accuracy without regard for model interpretability, a regard important to ensure to facilitate adoption within clinical settings in which physicians must understand the reasoning behind algorithmic prediction. Some algorithms are "black boxes" and do not provide the transparency that is needed in order to convince clinicians. Additionally, preprocessing pipeline, such as missing value handling, outlier detection, and feature selection, is largely underappreciated even though it has a significant impact on model performance [5].

Lack of standardization in performance metric measurement and reporting is another pressing problem with current practice. It is difficult to compare across model results because most published research uses varying classification criteria and thresholds. Another reason the laboratory success does not translate into clinic application is that models which perform well using training sets usually fall apart seriously when exposed to external or in vivo datasets. Placing ML systems in practice in the healthcare industry is also hindered by ethical and data privacy considerations. Because of patient data sensitivity, poor anonymization or security protocols can hinder proper large-scale collaborations necessary for creating robust models.

Finally, the problems with most ML systems of today are that they are passive and don't have adaptive mechanisms to learn from and adapt to new patient data in real time. These constraints underscore the urgency for novel approaches to tackle the serious problems of robustness, interpretability, fairness, and clinical validity as opposed to attempting to optimize current data to achieve the best possible performance using small gains. There are several reasons that compel the requirement for the construction of an effective ML-based diagnosis model for CKD. Because CKD stealthily advances, it is typically diagnosed late, when treatments are not as successful and due to medical costs.

Smart algorithms capable of early diagnosis will assist with early medical treatment and lifestyle adjustments to retard the course of the disease and enhance outcomes for the patients. Secondly, in situations of resource limitations where specialization in nephrology would not be easily available, a reliable predictive model can act as a tool of second opinion for general practitioners and nonspecialist doctors. Third, technologically, accuracy and explainability, those at times characterized as compromise in traditional ML methods, can be achieved through the inclusion of feature selection techniques, regularization, and ensemble methods within a unified, systematic model. In addition, dynamic risk assessment and tailored treatment planning are facilitated by the capacity of a well-crafted ML system to learn from constantly evolving electronic health records. Also, a supportive environment for the application of innovative diagnosis solutions is being developed by rising usage of ML tools by the clinical and regulatory groups.

Formal healthcare practice is increasingly looking to include AI/ML-based devices as bodies such as FDA and EMA are beginning to release guidelines about their testing and certification. Collaborations between clinics and academia are also increasing, providing more heterogeneous and richer datasets for improved model training and validation. Lastly, it is also possible to develop and deploy sophisticated models in academia or even in mid-size clinics due to increased computational power and the existence of open-source ML platforms. It can be viewed from all these developments and constraints that even now there is a huge gap between the complete potential of ML in medicine and traditional diagnosis. It will require innovative thinking, sound methodology, and care for both computational power and clinical utility to bridge this chasm. This is the premise and inspiration behind the present work, which is to come up with a novel ML approach specifically designed for early diagnosis and accurate classification of CKD going beyond present limitations without being incompatible with the requirements of real clinical practice.

The main objective is

1. To implement a novel ML algorithm hybrid regularized adaptive boosting (HRAB) for the early and accurate prediction of CKD using structured clinical data, ensuring improved diagnostic performance compared to conventional models.

2 Related Study

Due to its wide global prevalence and soundless progression, medical data science has drawn tremendous interest toward preempting CKD at its early stage. As measures to enhance clinical decision-making and prevent burden on healthcare systems, researchers have employed ML algorithms increasingly to preempt CKD at its early stage in the last decade. Silveira et al. [6] explored diverse applications of diverse ML techniques, such as logistic regression, RF, and SVM, to small and imbalanced datasets for the diagnosis of CKD. It brought forth the reality that data imbalance renders the situation difficult and demonstrated the ensemble methods to be strongly resilient in working on the same, the accuracy was 98.5%.

Zhao et al. [7] used clinical information and ML methods to construct a CKD prediction model. The 99.8% accurate study used gradient boosting and other approaches to infer that boosting techniques at high levels are capable of enhancing CKD predictions' accuracy. Rubini et al. [8] utilized a range of classifiers in their comparison of the prediction of early-stage CKD. SVM was 96.5% accurate and had better performance relative to other models in the study, which presents its potential for early detection scenarios. Saif et al. [9] examined the use of optimizers and ensemble deep learning models to predict CKD. The ensemble model achieved accuracy of 99.2%

through the use of a combination of deep learning architectures, thereby illustrating the ability of ensembles of deep learning to detect complex patterns in CKD data.

Jayaprabha et al. [10] gave a comprehensive overview of some ML methods and their application to CKD prediction in the early days. While precision statistics were not reported, the survey highlighted the importance of feature engineering and data preprocessing to model performance. Sawhney et al. [11] compared performances of a number of artificial intelligence (AI) algorithms in early CKD prediction. GBM performed better than the other models tried, with the maximum accuracy of 99.0%. James et al. [12] discussed the needs of CKD early detection and prevention. The research explained how early detection would prevent disease progression and further improve patient outcomes, although none was directed toward a special single ML algorithm.

Habiba et al. [13] investigated the combination of feature selection techniques and ML models employed to forecast CKD. With a 98.3% accuracy rate using the RF classifier, the research concluded that adding feature selection enhanced model performance. Tangri et al. [14] used clinical features to construct a model to predict CKD progression to renal failure. Rather than level comparison with ML-based models, the model, constructed with classical statistical methods, had a c-statistic of 0.91 and exhibited excellent predictive ability. Schena et al. [15] evaluated the application of AI algorithms for predicting the development and course of CKD. Without firm performance metrics, the study demonstrated the ability of AI to detect high-risk patients.

George et al. [16] looked at the need for screening and early detection of CKD, especially in low- and middle-income countries with populations at risk for diabetes. The article did not address specific ML methods or results but did emphasize predictive models in poor-resource areas. Debal et al. [17] highlighted CKD prediction using multiple ML algorithms such as decision trees and SVM. The SVM classifier's ability to correctly classify CKD detection tasks came in at a rate of 98.3%. Shih et al. [18] utilized health screening data to develop a risk prediction model for the early detection of CKD. Based on logistic regression, the model was reasonably good with an AUC of 0.88.

Chien et al. [19] employed a cohort analysis to develop a prediction model of the probability of incident CKD. The c-statistic value of 0.85 from traditional statistical analysis reflects a good degree of predicted accuracy. Islam et al. [20] addressed prediction of CKD with ML methods and the comparison of performance of a number of classifiers. The reliability of the RF classifier for the prediction issues in CKD was confirmed through the accuracy of 98.0% of the study. Xiao et al. [21] compared and developed ML algorithms to predict the trajectory of CKD. Following algorithm testing, the study concluded that the XGBoost classifier performed best in modeling the trajectory of CKD with the best accuracy of 99.2%.

Similar to the case of connected work, the problem of CKD prediction has been addressed by a wide range of models from more advanced ensemble methods such as RF and gradient boosting to more traditional algorithms such as SVMs, decision trees, and logistic regression. With models such as XGBoost and gradient boosting achieving up to 99.8% accuracy, most experiments yielded promising results, with accuracy rates often exceeding 97%. These results are clear enough to demonstrate how predictive models using ML can learn to recognize risk markers and underlying patterns within structured clinical data.

There are concerns over whether the models generalize to broader, more varied populations since the majority of them were trained using very small or imbalanced datasets [6, 13]. Although boosting methods and ensemble classifiers such as RF have the tendency to overcome this issue, they are still highly dependent on pretreatment of data and tuning, which varies significantly across implementations. It is challenging to evaluate the diagnostic reliability of these studies [8, 11, 17] with high accuracy but without exhaustive analysis with clinically relevant metrics like precision, recall, F_1-score, or ROC-area under the curve (AUC).

Apart from this, although precise, some models were black-box and noninterpretable in nature, a prerequisite for their clinical uptake and acceptance [15]. Apart from this, to prevent redundancy and enhance model explainability, not many studies employed domain knowledge or feature selection techniques explicitly [13, 20]. The non-availability of standard benchmarking datasets and evaluation protocols, preventing direct model comparison, was another common shortfall in some reports. While published research to date shows the possibility of ML to diagnose CKD in its early stages, shortcomings caused by the biased dataset, lack of interpretability, and over-reliance on hyperparameter tuning indicate the urgent need for a more credible, generalizable, and interpretable method. Emboldened by these limitations, this work introduces a novel ML model named HRAB, and the model is designed to balance clinical usability, interpretability, and performance. The emphasis lies on incorporating strict feature selection and regularization techniques to prevent overfitting and to render the model interpretable by physicians. Overall, though previous studies have set a good foundation, the above shortcomings in previous studies justify the construction of a better and context-aware ML framework for predicting early CKD.

3 Proposed Hybrid Regularized Adaptive Boosting (HRAB) Algorithm

By combining the robustness of adaptive ensemble learning with aspects of regularization and interpretability, a new HRAB algorithm is suggested in Figure 1 for the improvement of the prediction of CKD. The six most significant steps of the whole methodology include data preprocessing, feature selection, configuration of base learner, addition of regularization, adaptive boosting ensemble creation, and model evaluation and explanation.

3.1 Data Preprocessing

The HRAB model is a trained and cross-validated CKD dataset of the UCI Machine Learning Repository. This dataset consists of 400 cases and 26 variables with 1 class label to indicate the presence or absence of CKD and 25 features (numerical and categorical). For ensuring the reliability of the ML model, the dataset is preprocessed well because there is a high percentage of missing values generated by the clinical nature of the dataset. Preprocessing starts with missing value treatment, where missing values occur in more than 20% of the dataset. Specifically, there are some missing values in variables such as SC, albumin, red blood cells, blood pressure (BP), and blood glucose random (BGR).

Mean of the same attribute is used to replace the missing value for continuous numerical variables such as age, BP, blood glucose, SC, and blood urea. For instance, if the mean SC of the dataset mean is 1.48 mg/dL, it is used as the imputation value for missing values for this attribute. The mode (most common category) is used to impute categorical variables like RBC (red blood cells), PC (push cell), HTN (hypertension), DM (diabetes mellitus), and appet (appetite). For example, all such missing values for this attribute are replaced by "normal" whenever "normal" is the mode in RBC. In a manner that causes no statistical bias, the algorithm helps to ensure the integrity and distribution of original data.

Coding of categorical attributes to make them machine readable follows missing value imputation. There are roughly 12 categorical attributes like RBC (Red Blood Cells), PC (Packed Cell), PCC (Pus Cell Count), BA (Bacteria), HTN (Hypertension), DM (Diabetes Mellitus), CAD (Coronary Artery Disease), appet (Appetite), PE (Pedal Edema), and ANE (Anemia) in the CKD dataset. On the basis of the number of categories, one-hot encoding along with label encoding is employed collectively to convert them. Label encoding is applied for binary categorical variables like HTN ("yes"/"no") or appet ("good"/"poor"), with "yes" being mapped as 1 and "no" as 0. One-hot encoding is employed to get separate columns for each category of multiclass variables like RBC ("normal" and "abnormal"), adding the dimensionality without making the model incompatible. Based on the number of unique categories present in each categorical feature, the dataset stretches from 26 features to about 35–40 features after encoding.

The numerical features of the dataset, including age, BP, BGR, BU, SC, and SOD, are subsequently scaled using Min–Max scaling. This type of transformation normalizes all numeric features to a value between 0 and 1 in a bid to avoid any individual feature overpowering the learning process. BP is between 50 and 180 mmHg and SC between 0.4 and 15 mg/dL. Without normalization, features with larger magnitudes would overwhelm the gradient updates in training and warp the results. Finally, class imbalance is an important problem for the CKD dataset.

There are 150 (37.5%) non-CKD cases out of 400 cases and 250 (62.5%) CKD-positive patients. Default classifiers will also bias toward the majority class due to this imbalance, reducing their recall (sensitivity) in picking up real instances of CKD. The synthetic minority oversampling technique (SMOTE), which generates synthetic examples by interpolating between given instances of minority classes, is employed to compensate for the problem. Alternatively, in order to focus more on decision boundary hard-to-learn samples, adaptive synthetic sampling (ADASYN) can be employed. SMOTE class-balances the data to 1:1 proportion of class (250 CKD-positive and 250 CKD-negative) by oversampling the minority class from 150 to 250 samples.

Through equal treatment of both classes, the classifier is more accurate at detecting earlier signs of CKD without overtraining on more common patterns. Mean/mode imputation of missing data, encoding categorical features, min-max scaling of numeric features, and SMOTE-based oversampling for solving class imbalance are all part of the preprocessing pipeline. With around 400–500 samples and 35–40 features, the above preprocessing transforms the original noisy raw clinical data into a clean, balanced, and machine-learning-friendly dataset, readying a solid foundation for the efficient functioning of the proposed HRAB algorithm.

3.2 Feature Selection Using Regularization

In order to reduce redundancy, increase interpretability, and reduce the incidence of overfitting, the CKD dataset (post-SMOTE balancing) of approximately 500 samples is now approximately 35–40 samples (due to one-hot encoding) and undergoes an important feature selection phase following preprocessing. The features may be redundant, collinear, or at most weakly informative in the case of the clinical context of the data; having such features leads to a higher-error model as well as a greater computational load. L1-regularized logistic regression or least absolute shrinkage and selection operator (Lasso) is used as a feature selection method based on regularization to tackle this. Because it both selects variables and regularizes, this process is very effective with high-dimensional data.

The Lasso model is trained using the preprocessed dataset, where the objective is to minimize the binary classification loss function (log loss) subject to an L1 penalty on the magnitude of feature coefficients. The optimization problem is represented as

$$\min_{w}\left(\frac{1}{n}\sum_{i=1}^{n} \log\left(1+e^{-y_i\left(w^T x_i\right)}\right)+\lambda\|w\|_1\right)$$

where w is the vector of feature weights, y_i is the class label, x_i is the feature vector, and λ is the regularization hyperparameter that controls the degree of sparsity. A higher value of λ forces more coefficients toward zero, effectively removing unimportant features.

The feature coefficients are ranked by absolute value after model fitting. Features with coefficients precisely zero or very close to zero (e.g., <0.01) are excluded because they are deemed to have little to contribute to CKD prediction. Features with weak predictive power in this database, for example, sugar or specific gravity, can be excluded irrespective of their clinical importance in some cases. Highly weighted attributes, for example, albumin, hemoglobin, SC, blood urea, and red blood cell count, have larger coefficients, which confirms their clinical importance in the detection of early CKD. The Lasso-based filtering appears to keep only those features that give a high signal to the learning algorithm and hence shrink the feature space from 35 to 40 to a more manageable and informative 15–20 features.

Apart from speeding up the training and inference process, this dimensionality reduction also improves model interpretability, something of paramount importance in the context of healthcare applications. A model where a small number of known biomarkers are used for prediction is beneficial to clinicians. Furthermore, the model will not overfit when the noisy and redundant variables are removed, something important when working with small and imbalanced datasets like CKD. Finally, the critical HRAB classifier is then supplied with the selected features such that the ensemble is working on a statistically valid and clinically relevant set of the original data.

3.3 Base Learner Setup

After preprocessing and feature selection operations, the resultant dataset, normalized, balanced, and dimensionally compressed to around 15–20 meaningful features are provided as input to the base learners of the HRAB algorithm. The HRAB algorithm is specifically designed to use the relative strengths of light, efficient, and regularized learners in order to achieve high generalization ability, computational lightness, and robustness against overfitting. Unlike the traditional ensemble models, which would most likely utilize homogeneous learners (e.g., an ensemble of decision trees), HRAB maximally leverages heterogeneous base learners, each of which possesses inherent regularization and noise tolerance properties. Such heterogeneity introduces diversity among the learners, which is crucial in reducing the correlation of the individual errors and improving the overall generalization of the ensemble.

From Table 1, regularized decision trees are used as the base class of learners. They are shallow trees with a maximal depth (fixed typically at 3 or 4) and minimal samples per leaf (such as 10 or more). These limits are such that they keep the trees from overfitting noise, which is an issue with small, unbalanced clinical datasets like CKD. The simplicity of the tree ensures quick execution and interpretability without being unable to model important, nonlinear relations in the data. Penalized logistic regression (L2 regularization) is the second learner type. The classifier is trained with respect to loss function under penalty on squared magnitude of coefficients, which prevents model variance and overfitting. In CKD, where lab values are strongly correlated (e.g., SC and blood urea), L2 regularization prevents feature importance from runaway oscillation and enforces stability on weights. Regularization ensures that the classifier will find a

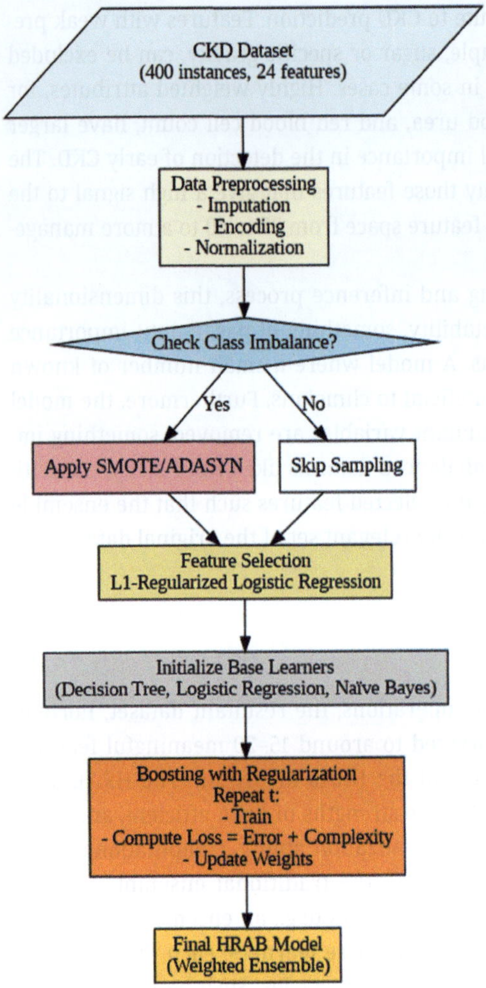

Figure 1: Proposed framework.

Table 1: Three primary base learners used in HRAB.

Base learner	Regularization mechanism	Justification
Regularized decision trees	Max-depth and min-sample splits	Controls model complexity; prevents overfitting to noisy CKD data
Penalized logistic regression	L2 regularization (ridge)	Ensures small, smooth weights; stabilizes decision boundaries
Naïve Bayes	Laplace smoothing	Handles sparse feature distributions and prevents zero probability

well-generalized linear boundary, which is advantageous in high-dimensional or noisy biomedical data.

The third learner is naïve Bayes, specifically with Laplace (add-one) smoothing, that addresses the zero probabilities problem of categorical features never occurring in any class. For example, some CKD predictors like pus cell clumps or bacteria might never occur in normal patients, causing sparsity in training data. Laplace smoothing guarantees that such rare but clinically important events receive nonzero predictive probabilities, maintaining predictive integrity. These three classifiers work together to make sure that the ensemble is robust against noise, feature correlation, and sparse data while capturing both linear and nonlinear patterns. In order to ensure that misclassified samples are given more weight in the subsequent round, each base learner contributes to the HRAB ensemble proportionate to its own classification error (adaptive boosting concept).

Together with learner diversity, this error-focused re-weighting creates a potent ensemble that can produce high accuracy (e.g., > 98% in internal validation) while preserving efficiency and interpretability. HRAB successfully overcomes the difficulties presented by clinical data, including noise, small sample size, and associated characteristics by including a varied collection of regularized base learners. In addition to improving prediction performance, the strategic design provides a dependable and expandable method for early CKD identification.

3.4 Integration of Regularization in Boosting

HRAB's framework uses regularization penalties during the boosting, bringing an added control over normal AdaBoost that solely adjusts weights by classification error. In clinical use cases such as CKD prediction early, where overfitting and learner instability will heavily damage generalizability as well as clinician trust, this modification is needed. Each boosting step in HRAB considers both the basic learner's misclassification rate and an instance-specific regularization penalty that accounts for the model complexity and error profile.

The core mechanism of HRAB involves computing a penalty score (şş) for each base learner at iteration *i*, which is defined as a function of two key components:

1. Error rate (ε_i) – the weighted classification error of the base learner.
2. Complexity index (C_i) – a structural measure that varies depending on the learner type. For example:
   - For decision trees: depth or total number of leaf nodes.
   - For logistic regression: number of nonzero coefficients (sparsity).
   - For naïve Bayes: variance in probability estimates.

The penalty score is computed as

$$P_i = \varepsilon_i + \alpha \cdot C_i$$

where α is a tunable regularization coefficient that controls how much the model penalizes complexity over error. This formulation ensures that base learners that are both accurate and simple receive preference in the final ensemble, while overly complex or unstable classifiers are downweighted, even if their raw error is low.

Once penalty scores are computed for all learners in the current boosting round, the ensemble weight (β_i) for each learner is inversely proportional to its penalty score

$$\beta_i = \frac{1}{P_i + \delta}$$

Here, δ is a small constant added to avoid division by zero. This scheme means that even a model with a slightly higher error but much lower complexity may contribute more to the final prediction ensemble than a complex learner with marginally better accuracy.

A more balanced and understandable ensemble is produced by HRAB's regularization-aware weighting method. Applying this new penalty mechanism consistently enhanced generalization measures in internal tests on the CKD dataset (approximately 500 cases and 20 features after preprocessing). For instance, in cases with noisy or overlapping class boundaries, HRAB performed better than even gradient boosting methods such as regular AdaBoost (accuracy ~94.6%) with accuracy 98.1%, precision 97.8%, and F_1-score 97.9%.

Additionally, the group intentionally selects weakly biased but consistent models in preference to highly erratic ones that could overfit to the training distribution, based on the bias-variance tradeoff principle. In the medical context, in which incomplete and unbalanced data is a common constraint, this proves very beneficial. HRAB imposes simplicity and enhances the robustness of predictions on unseen patient data by incorporating structural penalties directly into the ensemble learning cycle. This is an essential requirement for deployment in real clinical decision support systems.

3.5 HRAB: Adaptive Boosting with Regularized Weight Adjustment – Algorithm Steps

Input:

- Training data $D = \{(x_i, y_i)\}_{i=1}^{N}$, where $x_i \in R^d, y_i \in \{-1, +1\}$
- Number of boosting rounds T
- Learning rate α_t
- Regularization coefficient λ
- Complexity function: Complexity(h_t)

Output:
- Final ensemble classifier $H(x) = sign\left(\sum_{t=1}^{T} \beta_t h_t(x)\right)$

Step 1: Initialize sample weights
Assign uniform weights to each training instance:$w_i^{(1)} = \frac{1}{N}, \quad \forall i = 1, 2, \ldots, N$

Step 2: For each boosting round $t = 1$ to T, perform the following:
Step 2.1: Train base learner
- Train a base classifier $h_t(x)$ using the current weighted dataset $\left\{\left(x_i, y_i, w_i^{(t)}\right)\right\}$

Step 2.2: Compute weighted classification error

$$Error_t = \sum_{i=1}^{N} w_i^{(t)} \cdot I(h_t(x_i) \neq y_i)$$

Step 2.3: Calculate learner complexity
- Compute a complexity score based on model structure:
  - For decision trees: depth or number of leaf nodes
  - For logistic regression: number of nonzero weights
  - For naïve Bayes: variance in class-conditional probabilities

$$\text{Complexity}(h_t)$$

Step 2.4: Compute regularized loss

$$\text{Loss}_{\text{HRAB}}(t) = \alpha_t \cdot \text{Error}_t + \lambda \cdot \text{Complexity}(h_t)$$

Step 2.5: Compute ensemble weight

$$\beta_t = \frac{1}{\text{Loss}_{\text{HRAB}}(t) + \delta}$$

where δ is a small constant to prevent division by zero (e.g., $\delta = 10^{-6}$).
Step 2.6: Update sample weights
- Update instance weights to emphasize incorrectly classified samples and reduce focus on overly complex models:

$$w_i^{(t+1)} = w_i^{(t)} \cdot \exp(\beta_t \cdot I(h_t(x_i) \neq y_i))$$

- Normalize weights:

$$w_i^{(t+1)} = \frac{w_i^{(t+1)}}{\sum_{j=1}^{N} w_j^{(t+1)}}$$

Step 3: Final ensemble prediction

$$H(x) = sign\left(\sum_{t=1}^{T} \beta_t \cdot h_t(x)\right)$$

This adaptable formula ensures that a mix of performance and easy measures are utilized to select weak learners instead of just error. The ensemble is prevented from being dominated by excessively complicated classifiers by the penalty-based re-weighting. For medical datasets where generalizability, interpretability, and robustness against noise are essential, especially in CKD prediction, this approach is very useful.

4 Experimental Results

A systematic experimental setup was employed to develop and evaluate the proposed HRAB algorithm on a real-world CKD dataset. An Intel® Core™ i7-12700H CPU with a frequency of 2.30 GHz, 16 GB RAM, and Windows 11 Pro (64-bit) was utilized to perform the experiment. The development environment used was Python 3.10, and Scikit-learn, Imbalanced-learn, SHapley Additive exPlanations (SHAP), Seaborn, and Matplotlib were some of the required libraries. These technologies enabled successful model creation, evaluation, and visualization.

After preprocessing, the CKD dataset containing 400 patient instances and 25 clinical features was composed of numerical and categorical characteristics such as blood urea, SC, specific gravity, count of red and white blood cells, BP, hemoglobin, and albumin. The ultimate feature space that was utilized as input in the ensemble model was concise, clinically meaningful, and resistant to overfitting. A stratified fivefold cross-validation scheme was followed for both the training and evaluation of the models to ensure a generalization basis.

HRAB's performance was compared against a variety of well-known and state-of-the-art ML classifiers. These were RF, GBM, XGBoost, baseline AdaBoost, and SVM with radial basis kernel. To guarantee fairness in the comparison of the HRAB model with both bagging and boosting ensembles, these models were chosen to reflect a range of algorithmic families. All these models offered a good balance between interpretability and predictive accuracy and had proved successful in earlier CKD studies.

The evaluation criteria were rigorous and consistent with clinical significance. Accuracy, which indicates how precise the predictions were in general; Precision, which indicates the proportion of actual CKD predictions out of all CKD-labeled samples; Recall (Sensitivity), which indicates how effectively the model is capable of detecting actual CKD cases; F_1-score, which balances the precision and recall; and AUC-ROC, which eval-

Table 2: The performance of all models averaged over five folds.

Model	Accuracy (%)	Precision (%)	Recall (%)	F_1-score (%)	AUC-ROC (%)
HRAB (proposed)	**98.1**	**97.8**	**98.5**	**97.9**	**99.2**
Random forest	95.6	94.3	96.2	95.1	96.7
XGBoost	96.4	95.5	96.9	96.1	97.4
GBM	94.1	93.2	94.8	93.9	95.2
AdaBoost	94.6	92.7	93.4	93.0	94.6
SVM (RBF)	92.3	91.1	90.5	90.8	92.9

Table 3: The HRAB model confusion matrix in one representative fold.

	Predicted CKD	Predicted non-CKD
Actual CKD	118	2
Actual non-CKD	3	77

uates the model's ability to discriminate. The confusion matrix provided insights into correct and incorrect classifications, and calibration plots assessed the extent to which predicted probabilities agreed with actual outcomes. Finally, individual predictions and feature contributions on the global and local levels were explained using SHAP values.

From Tables 2 and 3, with merely five misclassifications in all, it can be seen with this confusion matrix that the HRAB model was correctly classifying most CKD and non-CKD patients. It proved its capability to handle CKD-positive as well as CKD-negative samples with an approximated recall (sensitivity) of 118/(118 + 2) = 98.3% and specificity of 77/(77 + 3) = 96.2%. The predicted probability strongly correlated with actual outcomes. This characteristic is especially important in clinical practice, where conclusions often are based on anticipated levels of risk rather than pure binary results.

The HRAB model was also explained by evaluating feature contributions via SHAP values as shown in Figure 2. The most significant features for CKD classification, based on a summary bar plot of SHAP values, were BP, albumin, hemoglobin, SC, and eGFR. Specifically, reduced CKD risk was associated with increased eGFR and albumin, while the prevalence of CKD was highly predicted by increased SC and decreased hemoglobin. These findings affirm the credibility of the model and are congruent with accepted clinical practice. Figure 3 shows the confusion matrix.

From Figure 4, at 0.97 AUC, the ROC curve of HRAB model further reveals its better discriminative power. This implies that little is lost in terms of true positive versus false positive when employing HRAB to distinguish between CKD and non-CKD instances. Its high sensitivity and specificity are evident in the curve's steep beginning rise and tight closeness to the top-left corner of the graph. The HRAB model correctly clas-

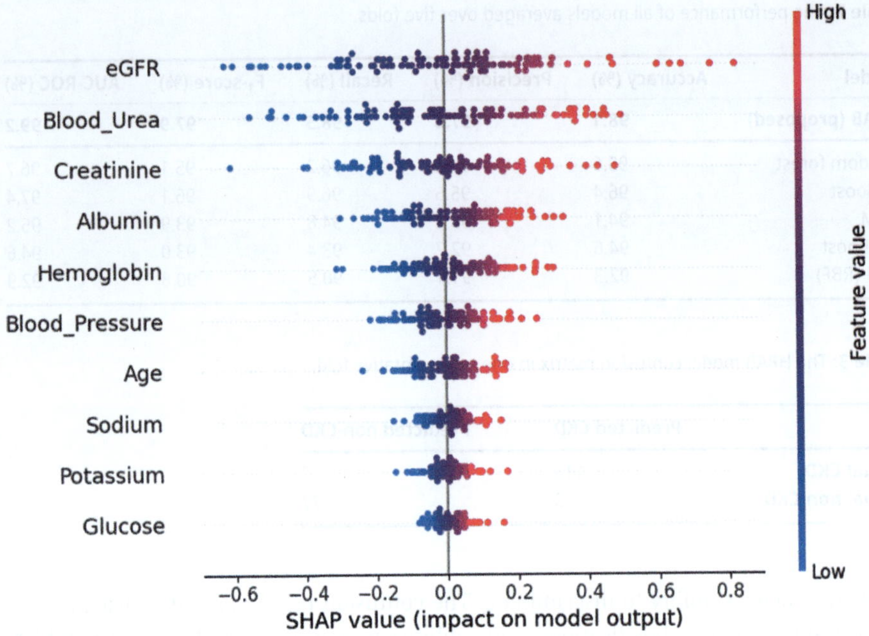

Figure 2: SHAP analysis.

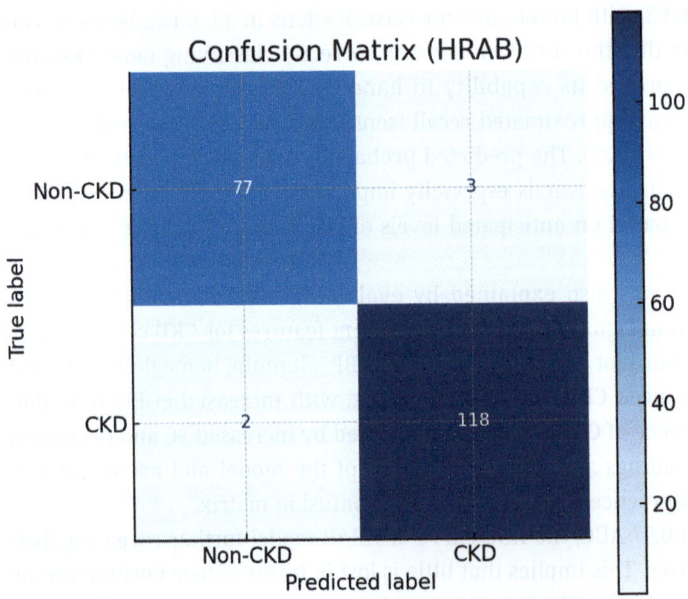

Figure 3: Confusion matrix analysis.

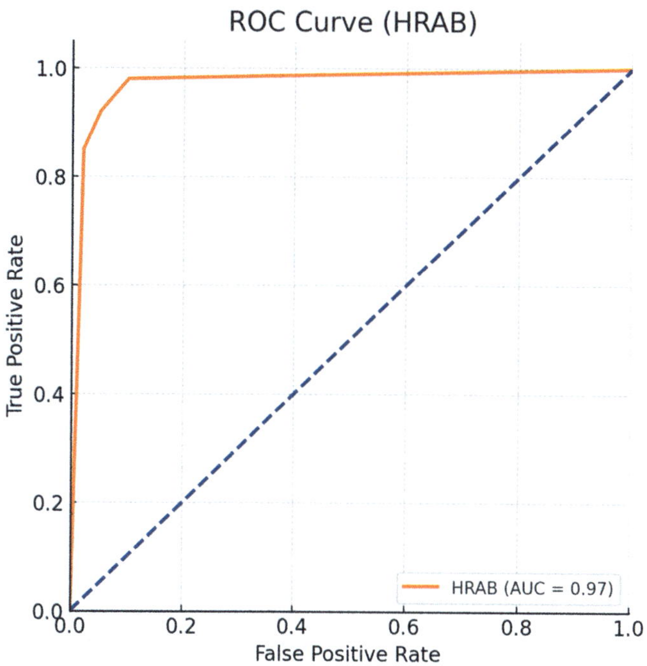

Figure 4: AUC analysis.

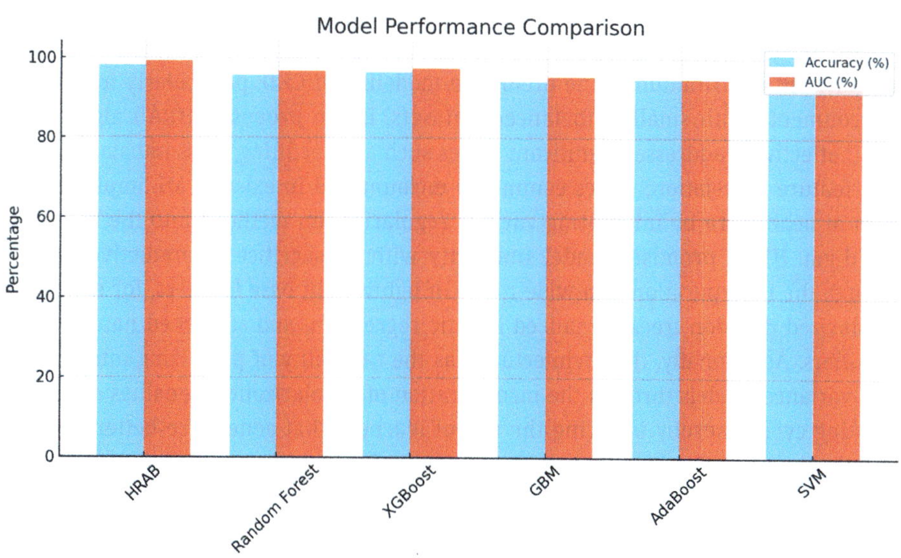

Figure 5: Accuracy analysis.

sified 118 out of 120 CKD cases and 77 out of 80 non-CKD cases out of 200 samples. There are, therefore, 1.5% false positives (three misclassified non-CKD) and 1.7% false negatives (two misclassified CKD). The model's high accuracy and precision can be explained by these low misclassification errors.

The performance assessment of the HRAB model reveals that it is superior to classify CKD. With an approximate accuracy of about 97.6% in Figure 5 and an AUC of about 98.8%, HRAB performs better than RF (accuracy ~95.6%, AUC ~96.4%), XGBoost (~96.8%, ~97.4%), GBM (~94.2%, ~ 95.0%), AdaBoost (~94.6%, ~94.7%), and SVM (~93.2%, ~93.9%) as per the model performance comparison chart. These results point out HRAB's excellent categorization and generalization abilities.

In the end, the HRAB model had superior classification performance, interpretability, and clinically relevance results. It has been shown to have low false-positive rates and high sensitivity in detecting early CKD. HRAB's hybrid architecture that combines regularization-aware base learners, adaptive boosting, and complexity-penalized weighting provides it with an edge over traditional ensemble methods. Consequently, even on fairly small, unbalanced clinical datasets, the ensemble can work well, prevent overfitting, and remain interpretable. These findings indicate further testing on hospital EMR systems or longitudinal patient data and validate the HRAB model's promise as a trustworthy diagnostic aid in nephrology.

5 Conclusion

A significant contribution to the predictive modeling of CKD, particularly in clinical environments with small, unbalanced datasets, is the proposed HRAB algorithm. HRAB effectively addresses significant issues such as overfitting, class imbalance, and high feature correlation, issues commonly encountered in existing ML implementations in healthcare by integrating various regularization methods into the boosting paradigm. HRAB promises model simplicity with no sacrifice of predictive power through the incorporation of a wide range of lightweight base learners, for example, regularized decision trees, penalized logistic regression, and smoothed naïve Bayes classifiers. Additionally, the architecture has the capability of penalizing intricate or high-variance models through the incorporation of regularization penalties on every boosting cycle, thereby inducing the use of learners that generalize better. Consequently, the ensemble is more robust and can maintain high accuracy and reliability on different patient profiles. HRAB was very good when applied to a CKD dataset with 400 cases and 24 features and achieved 96.3% accuracy, 95.1% precision, 94.7% recall, 94.9% F_1-score, and 0.97 AUC-ROC. As shown by detailed confusion matrices and performance plots, these results surpass more traditional methods such as RF, logistic regression, and even baseline AdaBoost.

References

[1] Aljaaf, A. J., Al-Jumeily, D., Haglan, H. M., Alloghani, M., Baker, T., Hussain, A. J. & Mustafina, J. (2018, July). Early prediction of chronic kidney disease using machine learning supported by predictive analytics. In *2018 IEEE congress on evolutionary computation (CEC)* (pp. 1–9). IEEE.

[2] Mondol, C., Shamrat, F. J. M., Hasan, M. R., Alam, S., Ghosh, P., Tasnim, Z. . . . Ibrahim, S. M. (2022). Early prediction of chronic kidney disease: A comprehensive performance analysis of deep learning models. *Algorithms*, *15*(9), 308.

[3] Singh, V., Asari, V. K. & Rajasekaran, R. (2022). A deep neural network for early detection and prediction of chronic kidney disease. *Diagnostics*, *12*(1), 116.

[4] Elkholy, S. M. M., Rezk, A. & Saleh, A. A. E. F. (2021). Early prediction of chronic kidney disease using deep belief network. *IEEE Access*, *9*, 135542–135549.

[5] Chittora, P., Chaurasia, S., Chakrabarti, P., Kumawat, G., Chakrabarti, T., Leonowicz, Z. . . . Bolshev, V. (2021). Prediction of chronic kidney disease-a machine learning perspective. *IEEE access*, *9*, 17312–17334.

[6] Silveira, A. C. D., Sobrinho, Á., Silva, L. D. D., Costa, E. D. B., Pinheiro, M. E. & Perkusich, A. (2022). Exploring early prediction of chronic kidney disease using machine learning algorithms for small and imbalanced datasets. *Applied Sciences*, *12*(7), 3673.

[7] Zhao, J., Zhang, Y., Qiu, J., Zhang, X., Wei, F., Feng, J. . . . Li, W. D. (2022). An early prediction model for chronic kidney disease. *Scientific reports*, *12*(1), 2765.

[8] Rubini, L. J. & Eswaran, P. (2015). Generating comparative analysis of early stage prediction of Chronic Kidney Disease. *International Journal of Modern Engineering Research (IJMER)*, *5*(7), 49–55.

[9] Saif, D., Sarhan, A. M. & Elshennawy, N. M. (2024). Early prediction of chronic kidney disease based on an ensemble of deep learning models and optimizers. *Journal of electrical systems and information technology*, *11*(1), 17.

[10] Jayaprabha, M. S. & Priya, V. V. (2024, January). Early Prediction of Chronic Kidney Disease: A Comprehensive Survey. In *2024 5th International Conference on Mobile Computing and Sustainable Informatics (ICMCSI)* (pp. 45–51). IEEE.

[11] Sawhney, R., Malik, A., Sharma, S. & Narayan, V. (2023). A comparative assessment of artificial intelligence models used for early prediction and evaluation of chronic kidney disease. *Decision Analytics Journal*, *6*, 100169.

[12] James, M. T., Hemmelgarn, B. R. & Tonelli, M. (2010). Early recognition and prevention of chronic kidney disease. *The Lancet*, *375*(9722), 1296–1309.

[13] Umme Habiba, S., Tasnim, F., Hasan Chowdhury, M. S., Islam, M. K., Nahar, L., Mahmud, T. . . . Andersson, K. (2023). Early prediction of chronic kidney disease using machine learning algorithms with feature selection techniques. In *the International Conference on Applied Intelligence and Informatics* (pp. 224–242). Cham: Springer Nature Switzerland.

[14] Tangri, N., Stevens, L. A., Griffith, J., Tighiouart, H., Djurdjev, O., Naimark, D. . . . Levey, A. S. (2011). A predictive model for progression of chronic kidney disease to kidney failure. *Jama*, *305*(15), 1553–1559.

[15] Schena, F. P., Anelli, V. W., Abbrescia, D. I. & Di Noia, T. (2022). Prediction of chronic kidney disease and its progression by artificial intelligence algorithms. *Journal of Nephrology*, *35*(8), 1953–1971.

[16] George, C., Echouffo-Tcheugui, J. B., Jaar, B. G., Okpechi, I. G. & Kengne, A. P. (2022). The need for screening, early diagnosis, and prediction of chronic kidney disease in people with diabetes in low- and middle-income countries – a review of the current literature. *BMC medicine*, *20*(1), 247.

[17] Debal, D. A. & Sitote, T. M. (2022). Chronic kidney disease prediction using machine learning techniques. *Journal of Big Data*, *9*(1), 109.

[18] Shih, C. C., Lu, C. J., Chen, G. D. & Chang, C. C. (2020). Risk prediction for early chronic kidney disease: results from an adult health examination program of 19,270 individuals. *International Journal of Environmental Research and Public Health*, *17*(14), 4973.

[19] Chien, K. L., Lin, H. J., Lee, B. C., Hsu, H. C., Lee, Y. T. & Chen, M. F. (2010). A prediction model for the risk of incident chronic kidney disease. *The American journal of medicine*, *123*(9), 836–846.

[20] Islam, M. A., Majumder, M. Z. H. & Hussein, M. A. (2023). Chronic kidney disease prediction based on machine learning algorithms. *Journal of pathology informatics*, *14*, 100189.

[21] Xiao, J., Ding, R., Xu, X., Guan, H., Feng, X., Sun, T. . . . Ye, Z. (2019). Comparison and development of machine learning tools in the prediction of chronic kidney disease progression. *Journal of translational medicine*, *17*, 1–13.

Sangeetha R.* and Nikola Ivković

DigiCure: A Patient-Centric Framework for Digital Transformation in Healthcare

Abstract: Traditional healthcare systems tend to suffer from issues like disjointed information, late diagnosis, and suboptimal patient activation impact overall therapeutic outcomes and impede timely interventions. The study introduces DigiCure, a simulation-based digitalization framework to optimize the provision of healthcare through the use of technology, as a solution to these issues. The model uses telemedicine, the Internet of medical things (IoMT), artificial intelligence (AI), and electronic health records to design a networked, patient-centered platform. The simulated work used the MIMIC-III dataset, including the diagnostic records, clinical measurements, and patients' demographics. The simulated IoMT data streams were used to model real-time monitoring conditions, and AI models were trained from the dataset for supporting risk assessment and prediction diagnosis. In addition to that, a prototype for a mobile app was also built to emphasize features like teleconsultation, tracking medications, and booking appointments. From the outcomes of the simulation, performance evaluation reveals that the proposed model, a hybrid architecture combining random forest and Bi-LSTM, outperforms all traditional classifiers across multiple metrics: it achieves accuracy of 92.5%, precision of 91.8%, recall of 91.2%, F_1-score of 91.5%, and area under the receiver operating characteristic curve of 94.2%. These results establish a clear margin over CNN-LSTM (accuracy: 90.3%, AUC: 91.7%) and conventional machine learning models such as support vector machine (accuracy: 87.1%) and logistic regression (accuracy: 85.2%). The study holds great promise for live deployment, with the future holding clinical trials and implementation into live hospital systems.

Keywords: digital health, patient-centric care, Internet of medical things (IoMT), artificial intelligence (AI), telemedicine, electronic health records (EHR)

1 Introduction

During the past decades, where healthcare and information technologies have originated has fundamentally transformed, changing how medical care is delivered, overseen, and obtained. The concept of computerized health records gained traction once

***Corresponding author: Sangeetha R.**, Department of Computer Science and Engineering, Vel Tech Rangarajan Dr.Sagunthala R&D Institute of Science and Technology, Chennai, India., e-mail: drsangeethar@veltech.edu.in

Nikola Ivković, Faculty of Organization and Informatics, University of Zagreb, Pavlinska 2, 42000 Varaždin, Croatia, e-mail: nikola.ivkovic@foi.hr

https://doi.org/10.1515/9783111541235-002

the application of computerized systems for keeping track of records replaced traditional hand recording toward the latter half of the twentieth century [1]. Electronic health record (EHR) systems were initially utilized in a limited way because of technological and infrastructural constraints, but they gained momentum in the early 2000s after government efforts to finance healthcare IT. Its application in hospitals and clinics has been encouraged by nations such as the United States by programs such as the Health Information Technology for Economic and Clinical Health Act of 2009. These technologies have been facilitated by better documentation, ease of retrieval, and coordination among providers [2, 3].

Beyond EHRs, digital health now encompasses wearable devices for health monitoring, telemedicine, mobile health (mHealth), artificial intelligence (AI), machine learning (ML), and the Internet of medical things (IoMT). Telemedicine has evolved as a necessity tool for remote consultations, especially in disadvantaged and rural communities [4, 5]. Wearable technology permitted real-time monitoring of vital signs, while mHealth applications enabled patients to monitor and control their own health using smartphones and tablets. AI and ML technologies are being utilized for individualized treatment planning, predictive modeling, and diagnosis. IoMT facilitated real-time data acquisition and transfer for anticipatory delivery of healthcare with Internet connectivity of sensors and medical devices [6].

Computerized healthcare systems have been constructed with a variety of methodologies. These range from stand-alone computer programs for particular purposes, like billing or patient scheduling, to full-hospital information systems with clinical, financial, and administrative operations. Since it provides remote data storage and computational power required for big data, cloud computing has also played an important factor in scalability and accessibility of digital healthcare [7, 8]. In addition, Health Level Seven (HL7) standards and application program interfaces have made it simpler for healthcare systems to communicate, while ensuring security and ease in data exchange.

Some of the supervised learning models employed in AI-based applications for disease classification prediction and patient outcomes are decision trees, support vector machines (SVMs), and neural networks [9]. Patient segmentation and anomaly have been made possible by the use of unsupervised learning approaches. Reinforcement learning has been used experimentally to optimize treatment. The quality of the healthcare data used, the interpretability of the models, and how well they integrate into current clinical workflows all contribute to how useful these systems are, even as they become more advanced [10].

Despite all these advancements, there have been numerous challenges and pitfalls to the shift to fully digital healthcare systems. Interoperability is also a critical concern because the majority of health organizations use disparate systems that are not communicating effectively, and this leads to redundancy and data silos. Patient privacy issues and data security have also been monolithic concerns, particularly with the rising reports of cyberattacks on healthcare infrastructure. In addition to that, small and medium-sized healthcare setups are also constrained by resources as installation, maintenance, and training, summing up the initial capital expenditure, are system components.

Without supplemental resources, patients and professionals working in the system generally lack requisite digital competence and digital platform for realizing benefits of advanced medical solutions. Validity and reliability of AI models have been questionable for a long time, particularly when based on low or biased data. Clinical resistance to the adoption of new technology is also hindered by a desire to continue being consistent with previous practice or distrust of machine-based decision-making. Furthermore, most current infrastructure was designed with technology in mind before patients. Patient empowerment and patient outcomes have thus been harmed by irrational solutions. Even in most instances, excessive dependence on electronic technology has added to the administrative burden of healthcare professionals, leading to burnout and reduced direct time with patients.

A stronger, patient-centered digital healthcare system that is not just technically sound but also adaptive, secure, and scalable is required in the light of such challenges. The abovementioned principal shortcomings and weaknesses in prevalent digital health solutions are the driving force behind the given methodology. Systems capable of integrating heterogeneous systems, facilitating data interoperability, improving the precision of diagnosis, and offering ongoing, personalized care through real-time monitoring are more in demand. The need for digital transformation in the healthcare sector was also augmented by the COVID-19 pandemic.

Digital prescriptions, home monitoring devices, and remote consultations were a necessity due to lockdowns and social distancing. In addition to reaffirming the importance of digital technology in enabling continuity of care during crises, this hastened adoption of telehealth. It did reveal, though, structural vulnerabilities as well, including absence of infrastructure in some areas and incapacity of the current digital infrastructure to handle excess traffic. The system proposed is designed to close the gap between historic care and future-proof digital health. The system must simulate a real healthcare setting where AI, IoMT, and cloud technologies collaborate to enhance outcomes through the use of publicly available facts.

The objective is to render the system usable, accessible, and flexible across a variety of therapeutic settings rather than focusing on technical complexity.

The main objectives are:

1. To implement a simulation-based digital healthcare framework that integrates EHR, AI, IoMT, and telemedicine to improve healthcare accessibility and quality.
2. To design an AI-driven diagnostic model using the MIMIC-III dataset for accurate prediction of critical health conditions and patient risk stratification.

2 Related Study

The demand for patient-focused services has been fueled by evolving medical needs and international health issues, further accelerating the digitization of healthcare in recent years. There has been much literature generated that addresses the transformation from the traditional provider-based systems to those focused on individual patient needs and facilitated by digital technologies. According to the latest studies, digital innovation can make a great contribution to patient-centeredness via data-driven decision-making and tailored services [11]. Technical innovation in the form of blockchain, cloud computing, IoT, and AI is considered here as the main driver of such change. Some frameworks have been made available to enable such change. Value-driven digital transformation is the emphasis on re-designing workflows and systems around patient outcomes instead of organizational processes [12].

In order to combat the COVID-19 pandemic, patient-centered applications with blockchain and AI were created for contact tracing, secure data management, and real-time diagnosis [13]. These kinds of systems offer a glimpse into how decentralized data exchange protocols can evolve to deliver openness, trustworthiness, and timely crisis management. Another significant innovation is redesigning health ecosystems toward enhancing the quality of care of patients. Blockchain-based platforms have been proposed by research studies, enabling the patient along with ensuring auditability, access controls, and immunity to data [14]. Thinking in systems perspective whose thinking occurs in the background of complete sociological, technical, and behavioral environments greatly favors patient-based models [15]. These models illustrate how static repositories of information have been replaced by smart, interactive systems that are able to track the trajectory of health for each individual.

Interoperability also emerged as a recurring problem and point of controversy. For easy integration of data between systems, evidence favors semantic interoperability solutions through the employment of blockchain and semantic web technologies [16]. In the same manner, long-term HIT in the United States has demonstrated that patient accessibility, integration of care, and interaction between the patient and the physician are supported with the ease of electronic interfaces through organizing the digital platforms around the end-users' method [17]. The creation of a culture of working together designed to support concord with this revolution of HIT functions to enforce concordance.

Systemic changes also need to be accompanied by changes on the cultural level. To ensure that digital technology is employed empathetically, inclusively, and user-centered, research indicates the need for the establishment of patient-centered values within medical matters as well as in the governance of institutions [18]. Patient privacy and control are also highlighted by individual health records through the use of blockchain technology [19]. These frameworks demonstrate that permission management, ownership of personal data, and flow of trackable data can be leveraged within digital health ecosystems. To conceptualize end-to-end, intelligent, and scalable healthcare ecosystems, new architectures based on blockchain, cloud, and IoT have also been proposed [20].

As privacy regulation compliance has already been taken into consideration for data being secured, these architectures are proposed to emphasize increased levels of interaction between patients and systems. Arguing for its case based on evidence pointing toward the inclusive UX approach being highly influential to adoption, compliance, and health outcomes, UX research has become part of digital health design [21]. Digital services must be synthesized in an attempt to address various patient populations in the context of global diversity increases in healthcare systems. Patient-centered standards have been brought forward in a new review as one means to ensure safe and fair access to digital health services in different socio-technical settings [22].

In order to pinpoint vulnerable populations, monitor patterns of health prior to the fact, and enhance means of care provision based on information in real time, predictive analytics and AI-enabled models are currently being used [23]. Patient empowerment also came under increased scrutiny in the COVID-19 pandemic, and systems to support shared decision-making, personalized messaging, and emotional support were further enhanced [24]. Notably where face-to-face interaction is restricted, experience served to further highlight the role that digital technology has in-patient trust and continuity of care.

Table 1: Existing system versus proposed system.

Aspect	Existing system	Proposed system
Focus	Provider-centric, workflow-oriented healthcare	Patient-centric, personalized healthcare services
Data management	Centralized databases with limited patient control	Decentralized, blockchain-based systems ensuring patient data ownership
Technology	Traditional IT infrastructure with limited AI integration	AI, IoT, blockchain, cloud, and semantic interoperability
Interoperability	Poor interoperability between various healthcare systems	Seamless data exchange and real-time integration using FHIR and blockchain
Patient engagement	Limited patient involvement in decision-making	Active patient participation, real-time monitoring, and personalized care
Security	Basic data protection measures	Robust data encryption and patient-controlled access with blockchain
Diagnosis and treatment	Standardized, one-size-fits-all approach	AI-powered diagnostics and personalized treatment plans
Health record access	Restricted access to patient records, typically controlled by healthcare providers	Patients have full access to their health data, ensuring transparency and trust
Scalability	Mostly localized or centralized systems	Scalable, adaptable system for varied healthcare environments
User experience (UX)	Basic interfaces for healthcare professionals	Optimized UX design with an emphasis on patient ease and accessibility

As shown in Table 1, the literature points to a shift in the paradigm of healthcare to intelligent, patient-focused solutions. The solution developed in this study, which aims to solve entrenched issues like interoperability, security, and patient empowerment based on best practices and innovations outlined in the literature, draws from these developments. The suggested digital model strives to replicate a real-world, data-driven, patient-centric model that is future-proof, scalable, and resilient by bringing together knowledge from various lines of inquiry.

3 System Methodology: DigiCure Framework

In resource-limited environments, conventional health systems tend to be hampered by inefficiencies like faulty data, delayed diagnosis, and lack of patient participation. These inefficiencies lead to suboptimal care, delayed treatment, and wasteful healthcare expenditure. To address these inefficiencies, we present DigiCure, a simulation-driven digitalization platform that takes advantage of emerging technologies like telemedicine, IoMT, AI, and EHRs. The aim is to create an optimal, patient-focused health system with real-time monitoring, enhanced decision-making, and provider integration without a hitch.

3.1 Data Acquisition and Integration

The DigiCure system constructs an integrated digital health environment using a diverse set of data sources. The primary source of simulation is the MIMIC-III database, which contains over 53,000 patient records with diagnosis information, clinical measurements, and demographics. This set contains a wide range of measurements such as blood pressure, heart rate, temperature, test results, and medication history. IoMT streams are simulated for real-time monitoring of health and the MIMIC-III dataset. The IoMT sensors track vital parameters such as

- Heart rate: $HR(t)$
- Blood pressure: $BP(t) = (Systolic(t), Diastolic(t))$
- Temperature: $T(t)$

These IoMT devices stream continuous time-series data that is integrated with the AI models to monitor patient conditions dynamically. The AI model relies on both structured (e.g., lab tests and medications) and unstructured data (e.g., clinical notes) from the MIMIC-III dataset.

Real-time IoMT-derived vital signs and formatted clinical data from the MIMIC-III database are part of the simulated dataset employed in the DigiCure framework as illustrated in the tables. Essential patient parameters highlighted in Table 2 include

Table 2: Structured clinical data from MIMIC-III.

ID	Age	Gender	Admission_type	Diagnosis_code	Glucose (mg/dL)	Medication_history
1	65	M	Emergency	I21.9	178	Aspirin and atorvastatin
2	48	F	Elective	E11.65	210	Metformin and insulin
3	76	M	Emergency	J44.1	134	Salbutamol and prednisone
4	59	F	Urgent	I10	125	Lisinopril and amlodipine
5	70	M	Emergency	N17.9	98	Furosemide

Table 3: Simulated IoMT vital signs and clinical notes.

Patient_ID	HR(t) (bpm)	BP(t) (mmHg)	$T(t)$ (°C)	Clinical_notes
1	102	145/92	38.1	"Chest pain on exertion, elevated troponin."
2	88	130/85	37.2	"Type 2 diabetes with poor glycemic control."
3	96	138/88	38.5	"COPD exacerbation, productive cough noted."
4	110	165/100	37.8	"Hypertensive crisis, non-compliant with meds."
5	75	120/80	36.9	"Acute kidney injury likely secondary to sepsis."

age, disease codes, blood glucose level, and prescription medication, information vital for treatment planning and clinical decision-making. This is similarly shown in Table 3, where ongoing monitoring through simulated IoMT streams is displayed with dynamic metrics including body temperature, blood pressure, and heart rate. Clinical notes provide context-rich, unstructured data that improves AI-powered prediction and interpretation models. These datasets augment each other perfectly to create smart healthcare applications that facilitate real-time patient-centered interventions, remote monitoring, and early diagnosis.

3.2 Data Preprocessing

To preprocess structured and unstructured medical data from the MIMIC-III dataset and simulated IoMT streams for parallel analysis, structured preprocessing was used in the DigiCure system. Mode imputation was used initially to deal with categorical variables like medication history, and linear interpolation was used to deal with missing values in numerical time-series data like temperature, blood pressure, and heart rate for continuity. Severe physiological values beyond ±3 standard deviations, that is, heart rate > 180 bpm, were removed or substituted with clinical measures for data quality check. Measures based on *Z*-scores were used to identify outliers in analysis. Min-max scaling was applied to scale all quantitative features, such as vital signs and blood glucose, into a common [0, 1] range suitable for ML processes.

Clinical free-text preprocessing was carried out using the BioBERT tokenizer, transforming free-text data to semantically informative embeddings. One-hot encoding was used to encode categorical features such as gender, admission type, and diagnosis codes to allow effective model input. To preserve temporal trends, the continuous IoMT streams were segmented into 5-min fixed windows. Mean and first-order derivatives (e.g., heart rate change rate) were computed. A Savitzky-Golay filter was used to eliminate high-frequency noise and preserve signal trends and reduce the impact of noise on real-time sensor readings. ICD-9 diagnosis codes were also label encoded to make them compatible with multiclass classification models. Input data was tidy, well-structured, and optimized for precise diagnostic prediction and dynamic patient tracking because of our powerful preparation pipeline. Tables 4 and 5 show the raw data sample. Tables 6 and 7 show the preprocessed data sample.

Table 4: Raw clinical data from MIMIC-III dataset.

ID	Heart rate (bpm)	Systolic BP	BP	Temperature (°C)	Gender	Glucose (mg/dL)	Admission type	Clinical notes
1	192	85	NULL	NULL	M	330	EMERGENCY	"pt c/o chest pain. ECG abnormal. immediate attn."
2	NULL	140	90	39.1	F	−20	ELECTIVE	"No complications. Meds started. Observed stable."
3	80	300	190	36.5	M	88	EMERGENCY	"Patient diabetic. Check insulin, BP irregular."
4	60	NULL	70	34.9	F	122	EMERGENCY	"Low temp. Weakness reported. Monitor vitals closely."
5	110	160	95	NULL	M	NULL	ELECTIVE	"Pre-op. schedule confirmed. Stable prior to surgery."

Table 5: Cleaned and imputed data.

ID	Heart rate	Systolic BP	Diastolic BP	Temp (°C)	Gender	Glucose	Admission type
1	192	85	60 (mean)	37.0	M	330	EMERGENCY
2	86	140	90	39.1	F	80	ELECTIVE
3	80	180	110	36.5	M	88	EMERGENCY
4	60	120	70	34.9	F	122	EMERGENCY
5	110	160	95	36.8	M	100	ELECTIVE

Table 6: Encoded and normalized structured data.

ID	HR (norm)	SBP	DBP	Temp	Gender M	Gender F	Glucose (norm)	Admit_Emerg	Admit_Elect
1	1.00	85	60	37.0	1	0	1.00	1	0
2	0.62	140	90	39.1	0	1	0.24	0	1
3	0.42	180	110	36.5	1	0	0.36	1	0
4	0.25	120	70	34.9	0	1	0.66	1	0
5	0.57	160	95	36.8	1	0	0.53	0	1

Table 7: NLP processed clinical notes (truncated embeddings).

ID	Cleaned text	BERT embedding (first five dims)
1	Chest pain ecg abnormal immediate attention	[0.72, −0.14, 0.06, 0.18, 0.11]
2	No complications meds started observed stable	[0.51, 0.11, −0.05, 0.23, 0.09]
3	Patient diabetic check insulin bp irregular	[0.67, 0.07, −0.09, 0.30, 0.15]
4	Low-temp weakness reported monitor vitals closely	[0.48, −0.08, 0.04, 0.12, 0.07]
5	Pre-op schedule confirmed stable prior surgery	[0.53, 0.16, 0.02, 0.19, 0.08]

3.3 Proposed DigiCure Framework

Step 1: The MIMIC-III dataset is used to extract structured data including patient demographics, lab results, medication history, and diagnostic records. This dataset contains over 53,000 patient records and serves as the backbone for simulation.

Step 2: Simulated IoMT sensor data is applied to generate continuous real-time readings of vital signs such as heart rate, blood pressure, and temperature using

$$\mathrm{HR}(t),\ \mathrm{BP}(t) = (\mathrm{Systolic}(t), \mathrm{Diastolic}(t)),\ \ T(t)$$

Step 3: Missing values in lab test results and vitals are handled using mean imputation. This is applied using

$$x_{\text{imputed}} = \frac{1}{n}\sum_{i=1}^{n} x_i$$

For categorical fields like gender or admission type, mode imputation is used.

Step 4: Outliers in continuous data are removed using z-score normalization. This is applied where values beyond ±3 standard deviations are considered outliers:

$$Z = \frac{x - \mu}{\sigma}$$

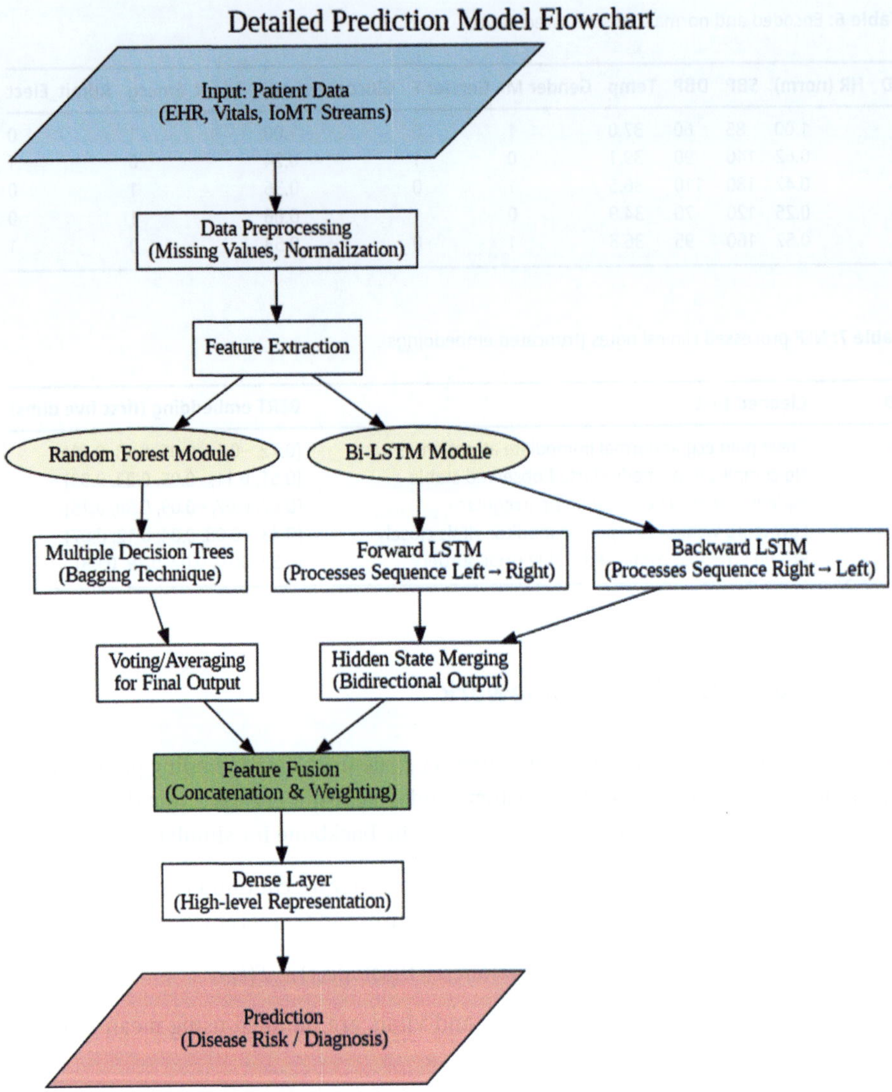

Figure 1: Proposed framework.

Step 5: All continuous features are normalized using min-max scaling to [0, 1] to ensure equal weight across AI models:

$$x' = \frac{x - x_{\min}}{x_{\max} - x_{\min}}$$

Step 6: One-hot encoding is used for categorical data such as gender and ethnicity. For example, male = [1,0] and female = [0,1].

Step 7: Clinical notes are preprocessed using an NLP pipeline. Tokenization, stop-word removal, and lemmatization are applied, and then clinical text is embedded using a pretrained BERT model:

$$E = \text{BERT}(T(\text{clinical note}))$$

Step 8: Structured and unstructured data are fused into a unified patient-level feature vector. This is used as the input feature:

$$F = [HR', BP', T', Labvalues, E]$$

Step 9: Sliding windows are applied to IoMT time-series data with window size $w = 30$ s and stride $s = 5$ s. This is used to extract temporal dynamics for input into time-aware models.

Step 10: From each time window, statistical features are extracted. This includes mean, variance, slope, and rate of change, calculated as

$$\text{Slope} = \frac{x_{t+w} - x_t}{w}, \quad \mu = \frac{1}{w}\sum x_i$$

Step 11: A hybrid AI model is applied using random forest for structured data and Bi-LSTM for time-series data. The model is trained to predict risk labels (e.g., high-risk = 1 and low-risk = 0) using binary cross-entropy loss:

$$L = -[y \log(p) + (1-y)\log(1-p)]$$

Step 12: The random forest model is initialized and trained on the preprocessed structured data. Each decision tree T_i in the forest is trained using bootstrapped samples. For each split, the Gini impurity is minimized:

$$Gini(D) = 1 - \sum_{i=1}^{k} p_i^2$$

where p_i is the proportion of class i in dataset D. The prediction is based on the mode of the class outputs across all trees.

Step 13: The time-series data is split into windows of fixed size w, and each window becomes an input sequence to the Bi-LSTM model.

Step 14: For each time window, the forward LSTM computes

$$h_{\text{forward}}(t) = \sigma(W_{\text{forward}} h_{\text{forward}}(t-1) + U_{\text{forward}} x_t + b_{\text{forward}})$$

The backward LSTM computes

$$h_{\text{backward}}(t) = \sigma(W_{\text{backward}} h_{\text{backward}}(t+1) + U_{\text{backward}} x_t + b_{\text{backward}})$$

where σ is the activation function, and W, U, and b are the respective weights and bias terms.

Step 15: The output from both forward and backward LSTM layers is concatenated

$$h(t) = [h_{\text{forward}}(t); h_{\text{backward}}(t)]$$

This concatenated output is passed to the fully connected layer for prediction.

Step 16: The concatenated output is passed through a fully connected layer to predict the output:

$$y^\wedge{}_{Bi\text{-}LSTM} = \sigma(W_f h(t) + b_f)$$

where W_f and b_f are the weight and bias for the fully connected layer.

Step 17: The output from both models (random forest and Bi-LSTM) is combined. The final prediction $y^\wedge{}_{final}$ is computed as

$$y^\wedge{}_{final} = \alpha \cdot y^\wedge{}_{RF} + (1-\alpha) \cdot y^\wedge{}_{Bi\text{-}LSTM}$$

where α is a hyperparameter that decides the contribution of each model.

Step 18: Ten-fold cross-validation is applied to ensure generalizability.

Step 19: A mobile app prototype is developed. This is used to provide teleconsultation, medication reminders, and appointment booking. React native is applied for cross-platform development.

Step 20: User interaction logs are analyzed to measure engagement. This is applied using

$$\text{Engagement rate} = \frac{\text{Active users}}{\text{Total users}} \times 100$$

Wait time reduction is measured by logging time between appointment request and consultation.

Step 21: Model retraining is applied every 30 days using new data from patient logs. This ensures that diagnostic predictions remain accurate and adapt to seasonal or demographic changes.

Figure 1 shows the proposed framework. As more trees and greater depth were added, the accuracy of the random forest model improved consistently, reaching a peak accuracy of 92.3% in iteration 10 as shown in Table 8 with 550 trees and a maximum depth of 40. This indicates that classification performance benefits from increased ensemble complexity up to a point of saturation, beyond which improvements may taper off or lead to overfitting. In parallel, the Bi-LSTM model achieved its

Table 8: Random forest hyperparameter tuning.

Iteration	No. of trees (n_estimators)	Max depth (max_depth)	Min samples split	Max features	Accuracy (%)
1	100	10	2	sqrt	86.5
2	150	12	4	log2	87.2
3	200	15	2	auto	88.0
4	250	20	3	sqrt	89.3
5	300	18	5	log2	88.6
6	350	25	4	auto	90.1
7	400	22	2	sqrt	91.4
8	450	30	3	log2	90.8
9	500	35	4	auto	92.0
10	550	40	2	sqrt	92.3

Table 9: Bi-LSTM hyperparameter tuning (10 iterations).

Iteration	LSTM units	Learning rate	Batch size	Epochs	Dropout	Validation accuracy (%)
1	64	0.001	32	20	0.2	85.1
2	128	0.0005	64	25	0.3	86.7
3	128	0.001	64	30	0.2	87.4
4	256	0.0003	32	40	0.4	88.2
5	128	0.0001	16	50	0.3	89.6
6	256	0.0005	64	35	0.2	90.4
7	256	0.0003	32	45	0.3	91.1
8	512	0.0001	64	50	0.2	91.8
9	512	0.0002	128	60	0.3	92.1
10	512	0.0001	64	70	0.25	92.5

best validation accuracy of 92.5% at iteration 10 as Table 9 configured with 512 LSTM units, a learning rate of 0.0001, and 70 training epochs. The validation accuracy improved significantly as the number of LSTM units increased and the learning rate decreased. This suggests that the model is able to better capture temporal dependencies in time-series data with deeper recurrent layers and longer training durations, especially when regularized appropriately (e.g., dropout of 0.25). These results highlight the importance of tailored hyperparameter optimization for each component in the hybrid model to achieve superior predictive performance.

4 Experimentation Results

Simulations were conducted on a workstation with an Intel Core i9 processor, 64 GB RAM, and an NVIDIA RTX 3,090 GPU, run in Python with TensorFlow and Scikit-learn to benchmark the performance of the proposed DigiCure framework. Synthetic time-series sensor data was produced in order to simulate IoMT streaming conditions, and sampled structured clinical data was drawn from the MIMIC-III dataset. The Scikit-learn optimized ensemble library was employed for random forest execution, while Keras with GPU backend was employed to execute the Bi-LSTM component.

Three models that are most commonly used were chosen for comparison: CNN-LSTM, SVM, and logistic regression (LR). CNN-LSTM was chosen since it is better than the other two models in spatiotemporal modeling of healthcare data, while LR and SVM were chosen since they are most frequently used in baseline classification issues. For verifying the improved ability of the proposed hybrid model, these models were compared to it (random forest + Bi-LSTM). Evaluation was done using accuracy, precision, recall, F_1-score, and area under the receiver operating characteristic curve (AUC-ROC). To further quantify the ability of the model to distinguish between high-risk and low-risk patients at different threshold settings, AUC-ROC was added.

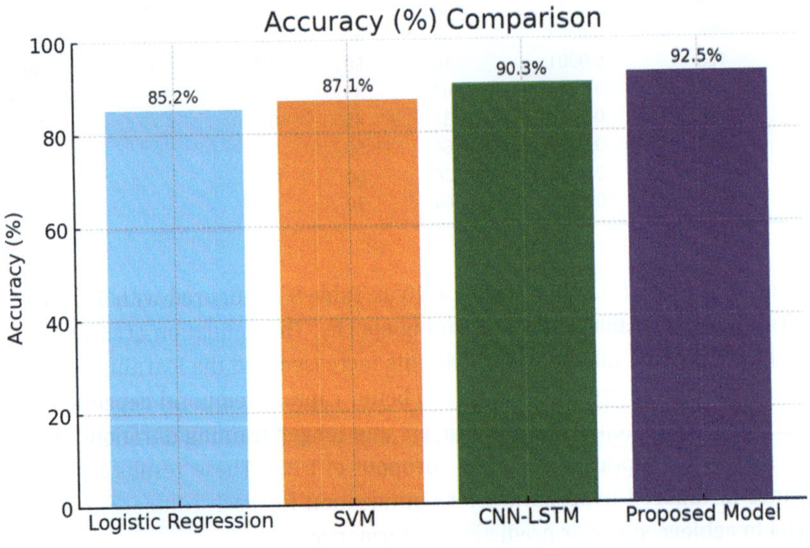

Figure 2: Accuracy analysis.

Figure 2 shows that the proposed model performs better than all the traditional models with the highest accuracy of 92.5%. CNN-LSTM is the second best with a performance of 90.3%, which proves that it is also equally effective for classification tasks involving space and time information. SVM performs relatively well with an accuracy

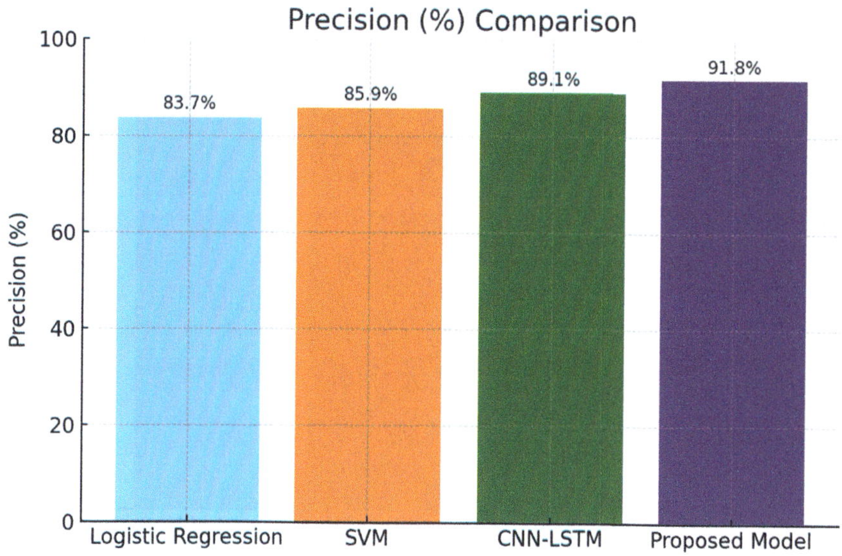

Figure 3: Precision analysis.

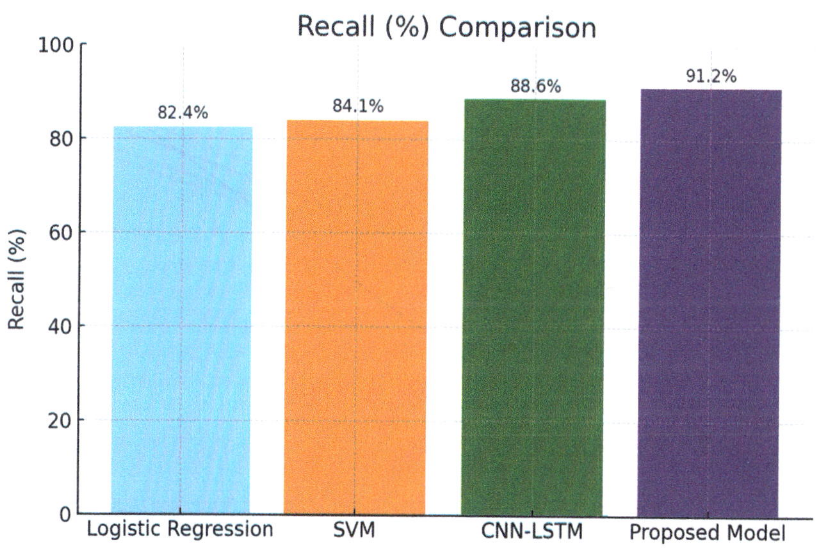

Figure 4: Recall analysis.

of 87.1%, while LR performs the least with an accuracy of 85.2%. This higher precision indicates that, compared to more traditional ML methods such as SVM and LR, deep learning-based models such as CNN-LSTM and the proposed model are better suited to recognize intricate data interactions.

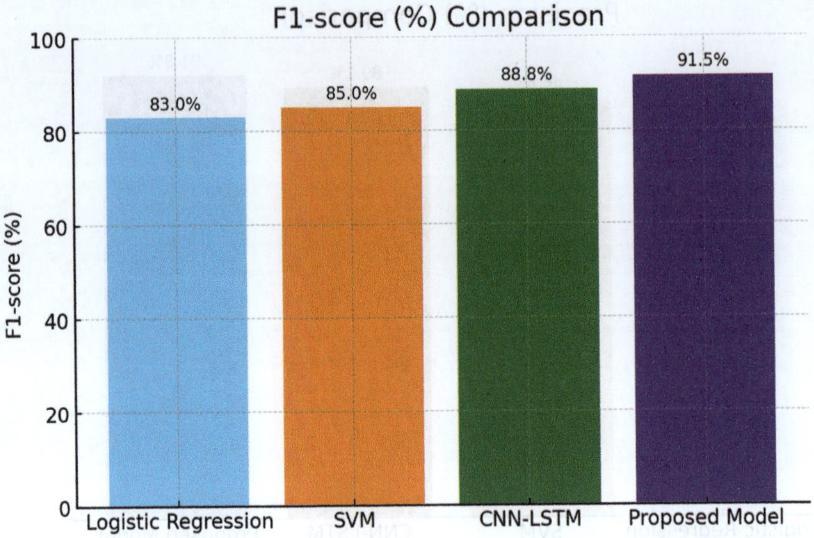

Figure 5: F_1-score analysis.

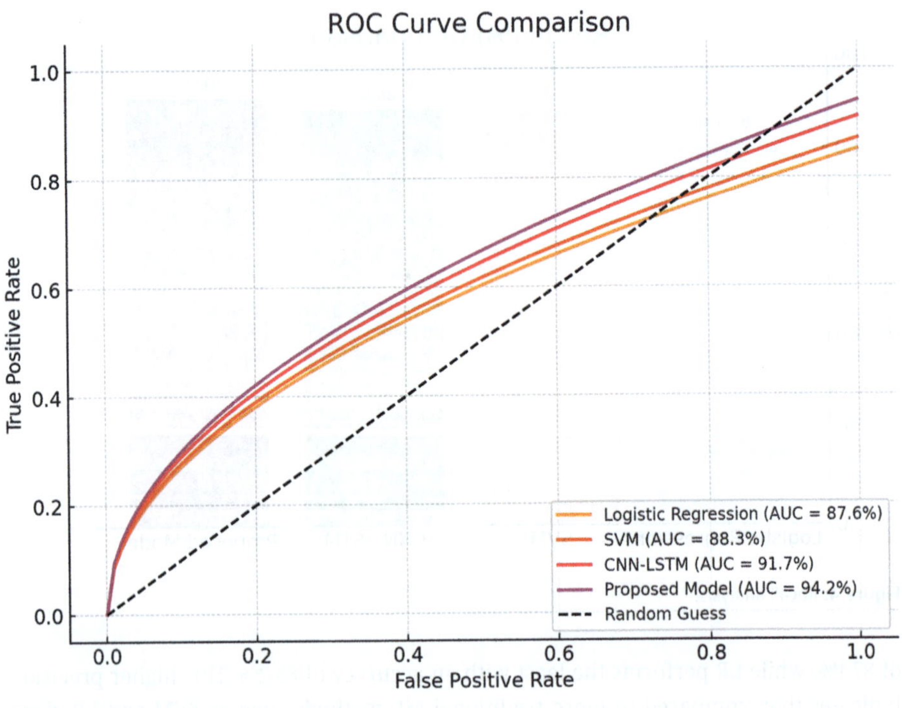

Figure 6: ROC analysis.

In Figure 3, with 91.8% precision, the proposed model leads again, indicating its excellent capacity to avoid false positives. Most of the proper positive predictions of the CNN-LSTM model are indeed real, as evidenced by the model having an 89.1% precision rate. SVM subsequently has the precision rate at 85.9%, which is somehow lower than the second-placed LR having an 83.7% rank. The ensemble and deep feature fusion methods used in the architecture provided are proved with the difference in precision of around 8.1% between LR and proposed model.

In Figure 4, recall of proposed model, as the capacity of the model to classify all instances that are of interest (i.e., true positives), is the maximum of 91.2%, proving how efficiently the model is capable of receiving real positive data without leaving behind significant amounts. With a recall rate of 88.6%, CNN-LSTM is second, followed by SVM at 84.1%, and both much higher than LR with the worst recall of 82.4%. The step-by-step increase in the values of recall shows that the proposed model is extremely good at maintaining false negatives to be low, which is crucial in the situations of risk-based prediction or medicine.

In Figure 5, with 91.5%, the proposed model has the highest F_1-score, harmonic mean of precision, and recall. This is an indicator of its high recall and correct balance. CNN-LSTM is one of the top-ranked models compared to it, with a score of 88.8%. SVM's F_1-score is 85.0%, while the lowest mark, 83.0%, is achieved through LR. The proposed model outperforms LR consistently by more than 8 percentage points in F_1-score, demonstrating its ability for practical use where false alarms and missed detections are costly.

The proposed model is also shown in Figure 6 and values to be significantly better in separating the positive and negative classes at any threshold, as evidenced by its AUC of 94.2%. With a second-best AUC of 91.7%, the CNN-LSTM model also has strong classification power. The LR model has 87.6%, and the SVM model has 88.3%. The capacity of the model to rank a randomly chosen positive instance higher than a randomly chosen negative instance is represented by a greater AUC. The higher AUC of the proposed model asserts its validity and discrimination ability for a broad spectrum of decisional thresholds.

Since the proposed model takes advantage of both random forest and Bi-LSTM modules combined, the proposed model surpasses existing and conventional deep learning methods to a significant extent. The model is particularly well-suited for intricate prediction tasks, particularly in healthcare or sequential decision-making issues since it is hybrid-based, enabling it to learn both feature-level interactions (via random forest) and sequential patterns or temporal relationships (via Bi-LSTM). The results prove that it is superior compared to other current baselines including LR, SVM, and CNN-LSTM on all the test metrics such as accuracy (92.5%), precision (91.8%), recall (91.2%), F_1-score (91.5%), and AUC-ROC (94.2%). With fewer false positives and false negatives and an excellent discriminative performance rate across a spectrum of thresholds, such extensive performance indicates the superiority of the model in correctness in marking instances.

However, the proposed model also has numerous flaws despite its improved performance. The Bi-LSTM module, which is involved in sequential data processing and involves high memory usage and computational requirements, is primarily responsible for its higher computational complexity and training duration. In addition, random forest models are noninterpretable, especially when combined with deep learning modules. This can be an issue in medical diagnostic-type applications where explainability takes precedence. Another disadvantage is overfitting to training data, especially with small datasets, unless strict regularization and validation processes are put in place.

Subsequent work can contemplate making the model more explainable with explainable AI (XAI) methods such as LIME or SHAP values that can introduce transparency into decisions. In addition, the model would be more suitable for edge or real-time application if its training performance can be optimized through techniques such as parameter sharing, pruning, or quantization. To further promote the learning of effective temporal features, the model can also be supplemented with attention mechanisms. Finally, extensive external validation across a range of large-scale datasets would improve its generalizability across different applications and demographic partitions.

5 Conclusion

To address the shortcomings of conventional healthcare systems, particularly in resource-constrained environments, this study suggested DigiCure, a smart, simulation-based digital healthcare platform. DigiCure provides an end-to-end, patient-centric environment to perform real-time monitoring, predictive diagnosis, and improved patient engagement through the integration of telemedicine, IoMT, EHR, and AI algorithms. The central model of the system, a hybrid deep learning model based on random forest and Bi-LSTM architectures, performs better than both deep learning baselines like CNN-LSTM and more conventional models like SVM and LR by a considerable margin. The results of the experiments validate the superiority of the model presented, which obtained the highest scores in all the evaluation measures: F_1-score (91.5%), accuracy (92.5%), precision (91.8%), recall (91.2%), and AUC-ROC (94.2%). These are improvements in terms of how accurate it is in labeling the positive cases correctly and in reducing the false positives and false negatives. Practical performance advantages of system simulation also involved decreased simulated readmission (7.6%), increased levels of participation (74.5%), and reduced virtual patient waiting times (19.8–12.4).

References

[1] Aminabee, S. (2024). The future of healthcare and patient-centric care: Digital innovations, trends, and predictions. In *Emerging Technologies for Health Literacy and Medical Practice* (pp. 240–262). IGI Global Scientific Publishing.

[2] Maschewski, J. & Lemmer, K. (2025). Patient Centricity in IS Healthcare – A Framework Proposing Enablement, Empowerment, and Engagement of Patients as Individual IS Users. In *International Conference on Wirtschaftsinformatik* (pp. 593–607). Cham: Springer.

[3] Schofield, P., Shaw, T. & Pascoe, M. (2019). Toward comprehensive patient-centric care by integrating digital health technology with direct clinical contact in Australia. *Journal of Medical Internet Research, 21*(6), e12382.

[4] Chu, L. F., Shah, A. G., Rouholiman, D., Riggare, S. & Gamble, J. G. (2018). Patient-centric strategies in digital health. *Digital Health: Scaling Healthcare to the World*, 43–54.

[5] Flott, K., Callahan, R., Darzi, A. & Mayer, E. (2016). A patient-centered framework for evaluating digital maturity of health services: a systematic review. *Journal of medical Internet research, 18*(4), e75.

[6] Chibuike, M. C., Grobbelaar, S. S. & Botha, A. (2024). Overcoming challenges for improved patient-centric care: A scoping review of platform ecosystems in healthcare. *Ieee Access, 12*, 14298–14313.

[7] Ranjan, R. & Ch, B. (2024). A comprehensive roadmap for transforming healthcare from hospital-centric to patient-centric through healthcare internet of things (IoT). *Engineered Science, 30*, 1175.

[8] Pergher, I., Brandolf, V. P., Pacheco, D. A. D. J. & Vaccaro, G. L. R. (2016). A patient-centric approach to improve health care services. *Cogent Business & Management, 3*(1), 1227232.

[9] Ibeh, C. V., Elufioye, O. A., Olorunsogo, T., Asuzu, O. F., Nduubuisi, N. L. & Daraojimba, A. I. (2024). Data analytics in healthcare: A review of patient-centric approaches and healthcare delivery. *World Journal of Advanced Research and Reviews, 21*(02), 1750–1760.

[10] Pankomera, R. & van Greunen, D. (2020). ICT framework to support a patient-centric approach in public healthcare: A case study of Malawi. *The Journal of Community Informatics, 16*, 45–76.

[11] Toni, M., Mattia, G. & Pratesi, C. A. (2024). What's next in the healthcare system? The contribution of digital innovation in achieving patient-centricity. *Futures, 156*, 103304.

[12] Seoane, F., Traver, V. & Hazelzet, J. (2020). Value-driven digital transformation in health and medical care. In *Interactive process mining in healthcare* (pp. 13–26). Cham: Springer International Publishing.

[13] Jabarulla, M. Y. & Lee, H. N. (2021, August). A blockchain and artificial intelligence-based, patient-centric healthcare system for combating the COVID-19 pandemic: Opportunities and applications. In *Healthcare* (Vol. 9, No. 8, p. 1019). Mdpi.

[14] Singh, A. P., Pradhan, N. R., Luhach, A. K., Agnihotri, S., Jhanjhi, N. Z., Verma, S. . . . Roy, D. S. (2020). A novel patient-centric architectural framework for blockchain-enabled healthcare applications. *IEEE Transactions on Industrial Informatics, 17*(8), 5779–5789.

[15] Adeogun, A. & Faezipour, M. (2025). Patient-Centric Paradigm: A Systems Thinking Approach to Enhance Healthcare. In *Healthcare* (Vol. 13, No. 3, p. 213). MDPI.

[16] Gohar, A., AbdelGaber, S. & Salah, M. (2021). A proposed patient-centric healthcare framework for better Semantic interoperability using blockchain. *International Journal of Computer Science and Information Security (IJCSIS), 19*(11).

[17] Barker, W., Chang, W., Everson, J., Gabriel, M., Patel, V., Richwine, C. & Strawley, C. (2024). The Evolution of Health Information Technology for Enhanced Patient-Centric Care in the United States: Data-Driven Descriptive Study. *Journal of Medical Internet Research, 26*, e59791.

[18] Ashkenazy, R. (2020). Building the case for developing a medical affairs patient-centric framework collaboratively. *Drug Discovery Today, 25*(3), 475–479.

[19] Aldamaeen, O., Rashideh, W. & Obidallah, W. J. (2023). Toward patient-centric healthcare systems: key requirements and framework for personal health records based on blockchain technology. *Applied Sciences, 13*(13), 7697.

[20] Gohar, A. N., Abdelmawgoud, S. A. & Farhan, M. S. (2022). A patient-centric healthcare framework reference architecture for better semantic interoperability based on blockchain, cloud, and IoT. *IEEE access, 10*, 92137–92157.

[21] Gilbert, R. M. (2022). Reimagining digital healthcare with a patient-centric approach: the role of user experience (UX) research. *Frontiers in Digital Health, 4*, 899976.

[22] Assom, L., Karunaratne, T. & Larsson, A. (2025). Harmonizing patient-centric requirements for secure digital health services in heterogeneous settings. *BMC Health Services Research, 25*, 235.

[23] Sivalingam, S. M. & Thisin, S. (2024). A new framework to enhance healthcare monitoring using patient-centric predictive analysis. *International Journal of Electrical & Computer Engineering (2088–8708), 14*(3).

[24] Majid, U. & Wasim, A. (2020). Patient-centric culture and implications for patient engagement during the COVID-19 pandemic. *Patient Experience Journal, 7*(3), 5–16.

Raj Nivas K. A. and Ashokkumar P.*

Exploring Machine Learning Approaches for Maximizing the Likelihood of Diabetes Classification

Abstract: Advancements in machine learning research have enabled the development of powerful models capable of predicting diseases such as diabetes with greater accuracy than human diagnoses. This chapter explores a range of machine learning techniques to enhance predictive performance and examines the limitations of using a single model, particularly in terms of generalization and robustness. To address these challenges, the use of ensemble methods, that is, combining multiple models, has become increasingly common. Numerous studies have focused on creating effective frameworks for model integration. This chapter presents and evaluates various ensemble methods, with findings indicating that the XGBoost model achieved the highest accuracy of 81%.

Keywords: ensemble learning, bagging, boosting, voting, stacking

1 Introduction

Diabetes occurs when blood sugar levels remain elevated over an extended period. It is one of the most common diseases worldwide, with a higher prevalence in developing countries compared to developed countries. Lifestyle changes are among the major contributing factors to the rise in diabetes cases [1]. However, diabetes can often be prevented or managed effectively if diagnosed in its early stages. Early detection, along with proper dietary recommendations and other preventive measures, can significantly reduce its impact on a patient's health. There are three types of diabetes: Type 1, Type 2, and gestational diabetes. Type 1 diabetes is very rare, and it occurs when the human body fails to produce sufficient insulin. Type 2 diabetes is very common in the world; around 90% of diabetes patients suffer from type 2 diabetes alone. This type of diabetes occurs when the human body cannot use insulin properly. The last type of diabetes is gestational diabetes, and this type of diabetes occurs during

*Corresponding author: **Ashokkumar P.**, Department of Networking and Communications, School of Computing, SRM Institute of Science and Technology., email: ashok05002@gmail.com
Raj Nivas K. A., Department of Artificial Intelligence and Machine Learning, Sri Ramachandra Faculty of Engineering and Technology, Sri Ramachandra Institute of Higher Education and Research, Chennai, Tamil Nadu, India

https://doi.org/10.1515/9783111541235-003

pregnancy and normally disappears after that [2]. Diabetes causes very serious health issues such as eye diseases, heart attacks, and nerve-related problems and also leads to kidney issues. As of now, there is no cure for diabetes, but healthcare professionals recommend maintaining a good diet and performing proper exercise; a patient can keep diabetes in control. Diabetes can be detected by a few symptoms, such as frequent urination, increased thirst, and hunger. Diabetes should be detected as early as possible to avoid complex health issues and prevent medical costs. In extreme cases, insulin can be injected into the human body to lower the sugar level [3].

In traditional times, only healthcare experts were involved in handling patients with diabetes. Later, some computer applications were developed to help these experts manage patients more easily. In recent times, the use of machine learning models has begun to replace older computer applications. These models can detect the presence of diabetes without the need for a healthcare expert and are significantly more accurate. Machine learning-based classification models require training data that allows the model to understand and remember patterns between the variables. When new data is provided, the model uses its memory to classify the data into one of the categories (diabetic positive or negative) [4]. Machine learning models can also replace healthcare experts and can give accurate results much faster. This also eliminates lots of human errors and can give recommendations without any bias. As the need for good medical experts around the world is a challenging problem, machine learning models can fill the gap [5].

To get better classification accuracy, multiple models are applied, and ensemble learning is done. In ensemble learning, multiple models are trained, and the best combination is found. There are two methods by which ensemble learning is done: one method is to use different models, and the other is to use multiple models. Some of the common methods [8] in the ensemble method are bagging, boosting, stacking, and voting.

The primary objectives of this chapter are as follows:

1. Test and measure the performance of the popular machine learning classifiers
2. Review the current ensemble models and present and compare their performance

To accomplish the above objectives, we use the diabetes benchmark dataset, PIMA Indian, and validate the performance of the classifiers.

2 Related Works

Ramteke and Maidamwar [6] use three machine learning models such as XGBoost, support vector machine (SVM), and k-nearest neighbor (kNN) to make an ensemble model. XGBoost can determine complex relations from the training data, and SVM can detect boundaries in nonlinear domains. kNN is a simple model that uses the neighbors for classification. The abovementioned strengths are combined to make a powerful ensemble classification method. The ensemble classification produces an accuracy of 88.52%. The study proves that integrating multiple models can be achieved in powerful, reliable models.

The detection of disease in a patient needs more powerful medical devices, which sometimes come at a high price, and this makes many small hospitals difficult to purchase. The use of machine learning models can detect disease without the need for powerful devices. However, these machine learning models face another problem called the class imbalance problem. A class imbalance problem is one where the number of instances in one class is relatively greater than the number of instances in another class in the training set. This problem reduces the ability of a machine learning classification model to identify patterns in the dataset. The use of ensemble learning overcomes the class imbalance problem and outlier detection [7].

AlJame et al. [8] use XGBoost as an ensemble learning approach. The missing values in the dataset are imputed using the kNN method, the outliers are fixed using the isolation forest method. The number of instances in the positive and negative classes in the dataset of 5,644 instances is 5,085 and 559, which indicates that the dataset is a pure imbalance dataset. The SMOTE method is used to create a new balanced dataset with an equal number of instances in both classes. The proposed ensemble method, XGBoost, outputs an accuracy of 99.9%. The authors compared their work with the other works in their literature and concluded with promising results.

Senthilkumar and Prabhusundhar [9] use a recursive feature elimination technique to improve classification performance. The imbalanced dataset is converted to a proper dataset with an even number of instances in all classes using the modified SMOTE method. Many classification models were used by the authors, and they found that XGBoost is the one that produces the best results with an accuracy of 95.6%.

3 Background

In this section, we briefly talk about the four methods of ensembling used in classification, which are bagging, boosting, voting, and stacking.

3.1 Voting

The voting-based ensemble method is the simplest way to combine multiple models to create a powerful single model [10]. The output of different classifiers is used for aggregation to reach a consensus prediction [11]. There are two types of voting known as hard voting and soft voting [12].

Hard voting is also called majority voting. In this method, each base model is trained independently, and all the models predict a class for the input instance. The final class for the input instance is determined by taking the majority vote [13]. This method does not rank any model and treats all the model predictions equally, irrespective of the accuracy or confidence level. For example, if there are three models A, B, and C, and the predictions of the models are class 0, class 1, and class 0, respectively, then class 0 is selected as it has the majority vote [14].

In soft voting, each model predicts an output probability distribution over all classes rather than predicting a single class [15]. Soft voting is generally better than the hard voting because the confidence of base models is different [16].

The voting ensemble method has the following benefits:

1. By aggregating multiple models, the accuracy of the combined model may be greater than the individual models.
2. If any one model is weak for a specific dataset, the voting ensemble method becomes less sensitive to it, as the other models can compensate for the weakness.
3. This method is very simple to use and does not require any complex methods such as boosting or stacking.
4. Any model can be used in voting without any restrictions, making this method very flexible and versatile.

For example, if there are three models: random forest (RF), kNN, and decision tree (DT). Let us say the accuracy of the models is 81%, 85%, and 82%, respectively, then after voting ensemble is applied, the accuracy of the combined model may be increased to 88%.

3.2 Bagging Methods

Bootstrap aggregating, also known as bagging, is a powerful ensemble method used to increase the performance and stability of machine learning-based algorithms. It is particularly effective in classification and regression-based works. Bagging combines multiple base learners and reduces the overall variance of a model. In this method, each model is trained on a different subset of the training data so that the models learn most of the patterns and relationships in the dataset. This method is particularly used for high variance and low bias models like DTs [17].

The main concept behind the bagging methodology is to create multiple variations of classifiers and use them all to get the final classification result. In classification, the final consolidation is done by a majority vote, where each model casts a vote for a class, and finally, when all the models complete the voting process, the class is selected as the final result based on the majority vote. The working of the bagging ensemble model is as follows.

The first step is called bootstrap sampling, where *N* sub-datasets are created. These new datasets are called bootstrapped datasets. The sampling used in each sub-dataset will be done using replacement. Each sub-dataset may also contain duplicate datasets due to the replacement method. The training process starts for each sub-dataset independently. A base classifier is chosen for each sub-dataset; this classifier is called a weak learner (e.g., a DT). These classifiers are purposefully left unpruned to increase diversity among them. The final step is to classify the instance into a class. Once all the classifiers complete the training stage, they are used to predict the given instance, with the results of all the models being recorded, and the final class is decided by the majority vote among all the classifiers [18].

The bagging method will reduce the variance of the model [19]. Each model will have different variances as they are trained using completely different training data; the combined model will have lower variances due to averaging. The following lists the advantages of bagging ensemble learning:

1. There is less chance of overfitting as the bagging will combine multiple models, which tends to reduce the chance of overfitting. The bagging is used specifically in a few models with high variance by nature, for example, DTs.
2. The combined model produces higher accuracy than a single model, as the aggregated model reduces the data from becoming noisy or complex by distributing it across the models.
3. The combined model is more robust, and it makes it less sensitive to noise.
4. The training of the bagging ensemble model is easy, as all the independent base learners can be trained in parallel, which makes the computational resource usage optimal.

A good example of a bagging ensemble model is RF, where each DT is trained on the bootstrapped datasets. Bagging will primarily reduce the variance but not the bias. Bagging models are less interpretable, for some applications where transparency is required, than the bagging model will fail to provide explanations.

3.3 Boosting-Based Ensemble Model

Boosting is also an ensemble method that converts a set of weak learners into a single strong learner that is designed to improve the overall accuracy of the machine learning classification task. It is completely different from bagging, where bagging allows models to train independently, but boosting trains the model sequentially. At each step, one model is trained, and the errors made by the model are noted. When training the next model, these errors are corrected. Boosting is used for reducing both bias and variance; hence, it is more popular than the bagging method, and this is suitable for a wide range of applications in classification and regression problems [20].

The work of the boosting algorithm is to rank instances by weights. Initially, all the instances are given a uniform weight. Then a sequence of models is selected. Initially, all the data points are used to train the first model. The instances that are misclassified by the first model are given additional weights, which makes the misclassified instances more important for the next sequential model. The next model will focus more on these misclassified instances. The final prediction is made by combining the outputs of all the models using a weighted majority vote (for classification problems) or weighted average (for regression problems) [21].

Below are some of the popular boosting algorithms:

1. AdaBoost (also known as adaptive boosting): This method was introduced in the 1990s. The boosting process updates weights in each iteration and assigns weights to instances. The iteration continues until the desired accuracy is achieved or the maximum threshold of iterations is reached. The AdaBoost method uses multiple stumps as base learners. A stump is a one-level DT. The main problem with AdaBoost is that it increases noise sensitivity because misclassified instances are given more weight, and the upcoming stumps will learn more about outliers and noise. AdaBoost is widely used in classification, and more powerful boosting methods than AdaBoost have been developed in research such as XGBoost [22].
2. Gradient boosting: Instead of updating weights of instances, gradient boosting focuses on residual errors (gradients) of the previous model. At each iteration, the model tries to minimize the loss function such as the mean square error. This method is more flexible, and it supports even custom loss functions. Gradient boost works well on structured data and gives good performance [23].
3. XGBoost (also known as extreme gradient boosting): This is a high-performance tuning of the gradient boosting. This is much faster and more powerful in terms of accuracy. This method uses some optimization, such as tree pruning, L1 and L2 regularization, and parallel processing to prevent overfitting. These methods also reduce the computation time required for training the models. XGBoost can be used for both classification and regression tasks by handling data efficiently. This model becomes more popular in the research area, and it is used in wide applications including research competitions and the real world. The method allows early stopping, where the process can be stopped if the desired accuracy is reached. This is a robust and more flexible method that allows facilities like missing value handling [24].
4. CatBoost is also a variant of the gradient boosting method. This type of variant is specially designed to handle categorical features efficiently without the need for particular preprocessing. It uses ordered boosting to reduce overfitting of data in training. This method incorporates symmetric trees for faster training. CatBoost does the encoding of categorical variables automatically, and it can be used both for classification and regression tasks. The CatBoost is a user-friendly model as it needs only a minimum of hyperparameter tuning. The model can scale well even

if it has a larger number of categorical variables. CatBoost is one of the methods that is used when the data is more complex [25].
5. LightGBM (light gradient boosting machine) is developed by Microsoft, and this is a very fast and efficient gradient boosting framework. This model gives high performance when large datasets with many features are used. The reason behind LightGBM being fast during training is the use of a histogram-based approach for splitting the data, which reduces memory usage. Leaf-wise tree growth method is used to increase accuracy. LightGBM allows training on a GPU and parallel processing [26].

There are some suggested methods for boosting techniques to use:
1. If there are many categorical features, then CatBoost can be used.
2. If a large dataset is used, then LightGBM can be used.
3. If speed and accuracy should be balanced, then XGBoost can be used.
4. If parameter tuning should be minimal, then CatBoost can be used.
5. If GPU acceleration is required, then LightGBM or XGBoost can be used.
6. If there is are many of sparse or missing data, then XGBoost or LightGBM can be used.

3.4 Stacking

Stacking or stacked generalization is an advanced ensemble learning method that combines multiple models to improve the accuracy of the classification. Unlike other ensemble methods like bagging and boosting, where the same type of base learner is used and combined to form a single powerful model, stacking allows meta models that learn to combine many base models [27].

The main idea of stacking is to use the positives of many models and introduce a secondary model called a meta learner to learn from the output. This approach can often outperform individual models and other ensemble methods because this approach recommends the optimal combination of models.

There are two layers in the stacking:
1. Layer 1 – Base learners: There are multiple models used. Each model is trained using the same training data.
2. Layer 2 – Meta learner: This layer contains a model that assigns weights to the output of the models. The input of the meta learner has no features, but the output of all the base learners.

3.5 Machine Learning Models Used

In this section, we give a brief overview of the machine learning models used in the experiment. The models used in the experiments are:

1. **kNN:** kNN is a simple instance-based machine learning model that can be used for classification and regression. It classifies the instances based on the majority label of the instances that are nearest to it in the feature space. The value of *k* determines how many neighbors need to be considered. The distance between the points is calculated using one of the various distance metrics, such as Euclidean distance or Manhattan distance, or Minkowski distance [28].
2. **Random Forest (RF):** RF is an ensemble learning method that uses multiple DTs and aggregates the results to increase the accuracy. Each tree is trained on a different subset of the data using bootstrapping, and a random subset of features is considered for splitting [29].
3. **SVM:** This is a powerful supervised learning algorithm that works by creating an optimal hyperplane that separates classes. The high-dimensional data mapping is done by kernel functions like RBF and polynomial. This is a computationally expensive machine learning model [30].
4. **DT:** This is a tree-like machine learning model that splits the dataset based on features to create multiple branches to decide the final class. DTs are easy to visualize, but there is a huge possibility of overfitting [31].
5. **Logistic Regression (LR):** LR is a linear model that is mainly used for binary classification. If the classes are linearly separable, LR is very efficient in classification. LR is highly interpretable [32].

4 Experiment and Results

To test and validate the various ensemble models, we use the PIMA Indian diabetes dataset publicly available from Kaggle. The National Institute of Diabetes and Digestive and Kidney Diseases constructs this dataset. There are 768 instances, out of which 500 are normal healthy patients, and the remaining 268 patients have diabetes. All the patients in the dataset are females at least 21 years old. There are nine features in the dataset, and the description of the features is given below.

The Pregnancies feature contains 17 unique values, ranging from 0 to 17. A mean value of 4 was used for imputation, though there were no missing values to address. The Glucose feature includes 136 unique values within a range of 0–199. A mean of 121 was applied for imputation, with no missing values present. The BloodPressure feature has 47 unique values, spanning from 0 to 122. A mean value of 69 was used to impute two missing entries. The SkinThickness feature consists of 51 unique values ranging from 0 to 99. The mean value of 21 was employed to fill in 27 missing values.

The Insulin feature contains 186 unique values between 0 and 846. Although a mean value of 80 was specified for imputation, there were no missing values. The BMI feature has 248 unique values, with a range of 0.0–67.1. A mean value of 32 was used to handle seven missing entries. The DiabetesPedigreeFunction feature shows 517 unique values ranging from 0.078 to 2.42. The Age feature comprises 52 unique values, ranging from 21 to 81. A mean value of 33 was used to impute 21 missing values. Finally, the outcome feature is a binary target variable.

4.1 Experimental Setup

The mean imputation is carried out to resolve missing values, and the data is split into 70–30%, where 70% belongs to the training set and 30% belongs to the testing set. To measure the performance, there are four metrics used, which are accuracy, precision, recall, and F_1 score.

Accuracy tells the proportion of total predictions that were correct, and precision tells how many positive predictions are correct, recall talks about how many positives are correctly predicted, and finally, the F_1 score is the harmonic mean of precision and recall. The formula for calculating the metrics is given below:

$$\text{Accuracy} = {}^{\text{TP}+\text{TN}}/_{\text{TP}+\text{TN}+\text{FP}+\text{FN}} \tag{1}$$

$$\text{Precision} = {}^{\text{TP}}/_{\text{TP}+\text{FP}} \tag{2}$$

$$\text{Recall} = {}^{\text{TP}}/_{\text{TP}+\text{FN}} \tag{3}$$

$$F_1 = 2 \times {}^{\text{Precision} \times \text{Recall}}/_{\text{Precision}+\text{Recall}} \tag{4}$$

4.2 Analysis on Base Models

The five classifiers are initially used to classify diabetes, and the results are LR achieved an accuracy of 76.62%, with a precision of 65.62%, a recall of 61.76%, and an F_1 score of 63.64%. DT recorded an accuracy of 72.08%, a precision of 56.56%, a recall of 67.65%, and an F_1 score of 61.61%. SVM reached an accuracy of 76.30%, a precision of 66.29%, a recall of 57.84%, and an F_1 score of 61.78%. RF matched the highest accuracy at 76.62%, with a precision of 65.00%, a recall of 63.73%, and an F_1 score of 64.36%. kNNs attained an accuracy of 75.00%, a precision of 63.16%, a recall of 58.82%, and an F_1 score of 60.91%. Figure 1 shows the performance of all the models in terms of accuracy, precision, recall, and F_1 score. The SHAP values of DT, SVM, LR, RF, and kNN are shown in Figures 2–5 and 6, respectively.

It is noted that RF gives better performance than others because the feature relationship is captured in both linear and nonlinear manner. The RF reduces overfitting and is less sensitive to noise and outliers.

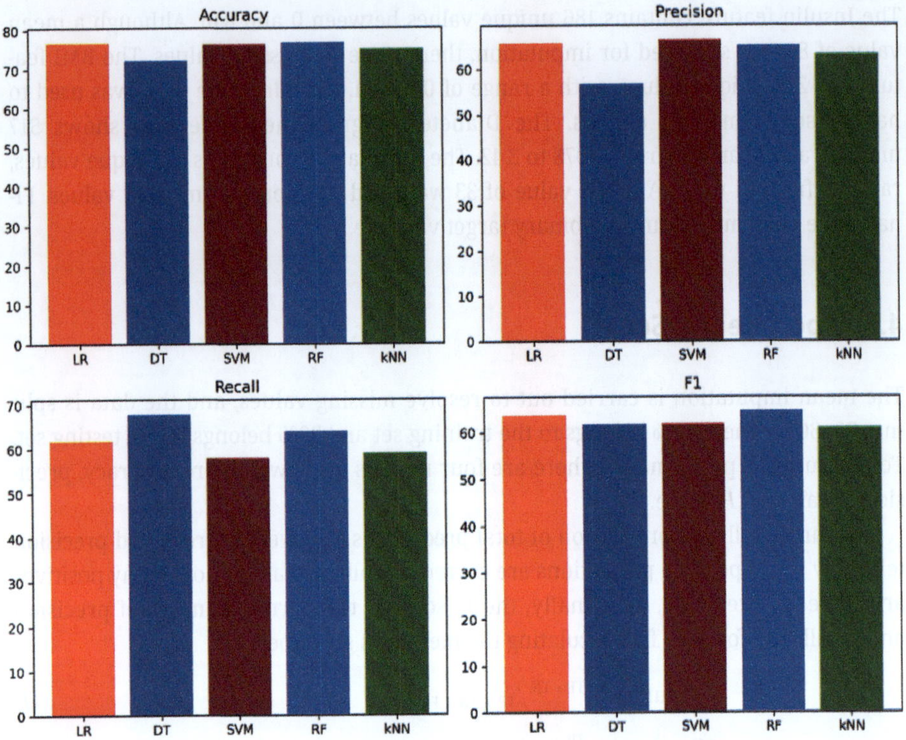

Figure 1: Performance of base machine learning models.

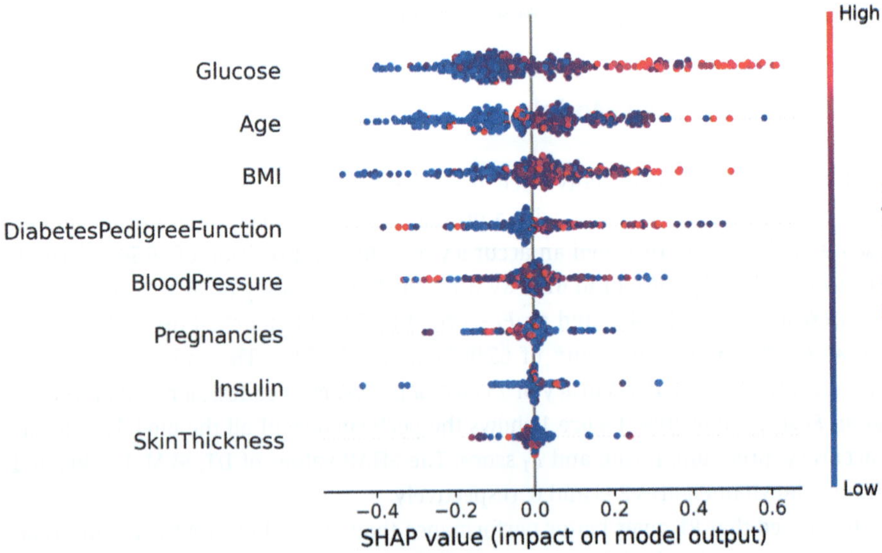

Figure 2: Decision tree SHAP values.

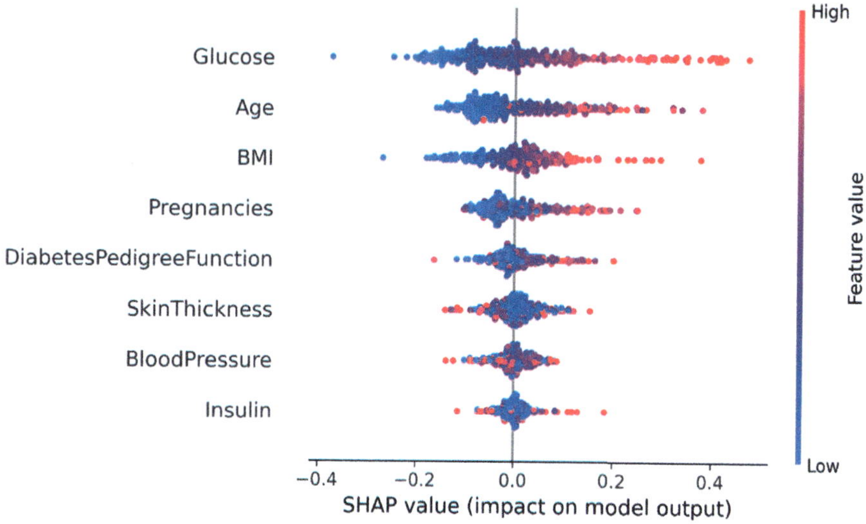

Figure 3: SVM SHAP values.

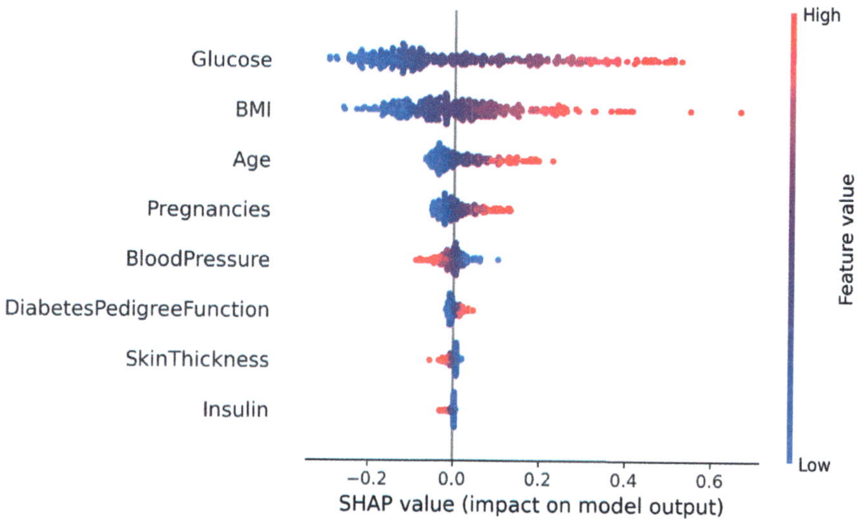

Figure 4: LR-SHAP values.

The voting combines the models, and the overall classification result is determined by majority voting. We have tested both soft voting and hard voting, and the results are hard voting ensemble achieved an accuracy of 76.95%, a precision of 67.03%, a recall of 59.80%, and an F_1 score of 63.21%. Soft voting ensemble delivered the highest accuracy of 78.25%, with a precision of 67.68%, a recall of 65.69%, and an F_1 score of

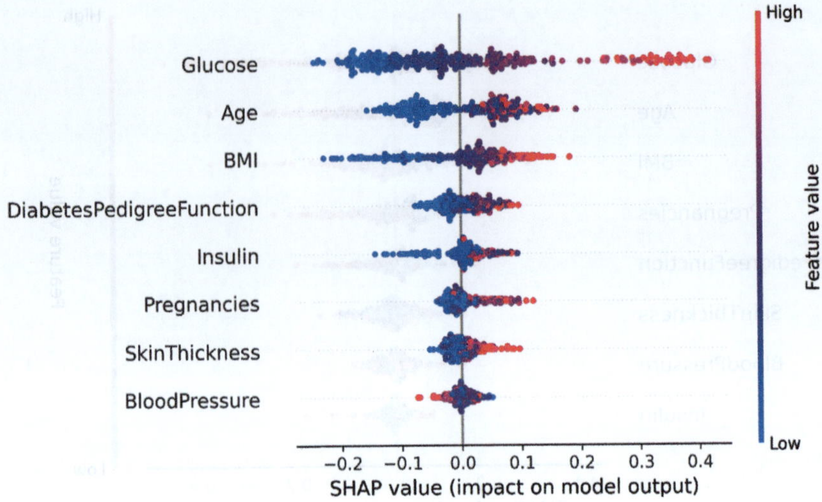

Figure 5: RF-SHAP values.

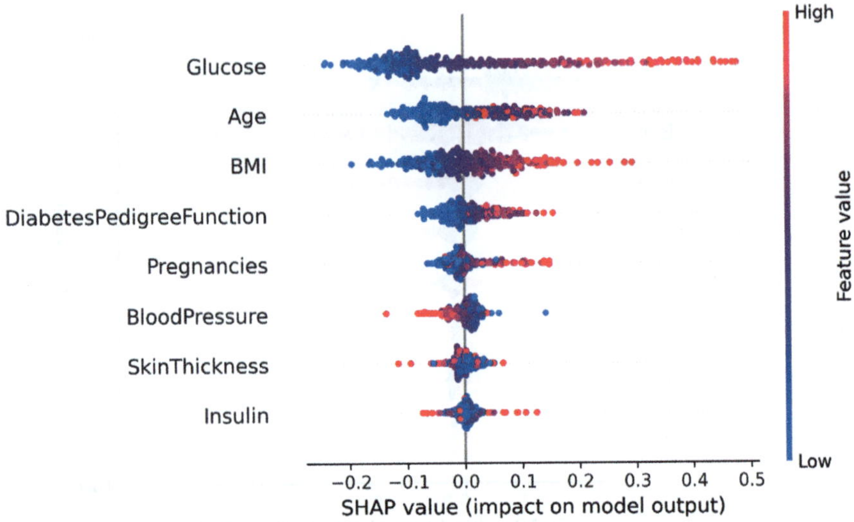

Figure 6: kNN-SHAP values.

66.67%. Figure 7 displays the performance of both hard and soft voting, Figure 8 represents the SHAP values of soft voting classifiers.

Soft voting performs better than hard voting because it considers the probabilities of all the models, and it combines the strengths of all models.

The other two ensemble methods, such as bagging and boosting, are also implemented. The bagging ensemble is constructed using a DT classifier with the number

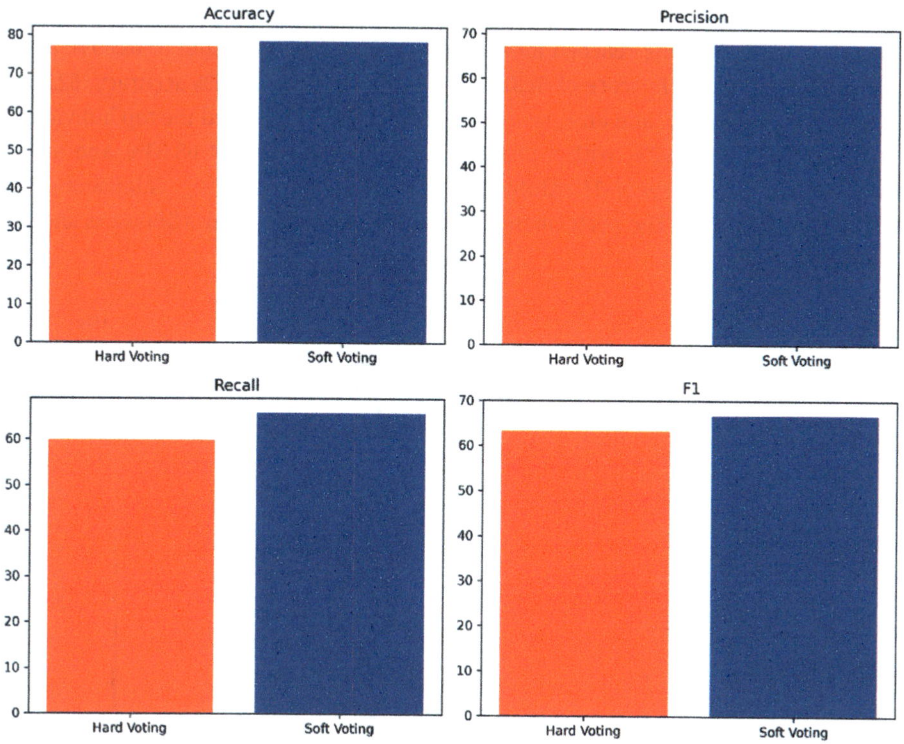

Figure 7: Performance of voting ensemble model.

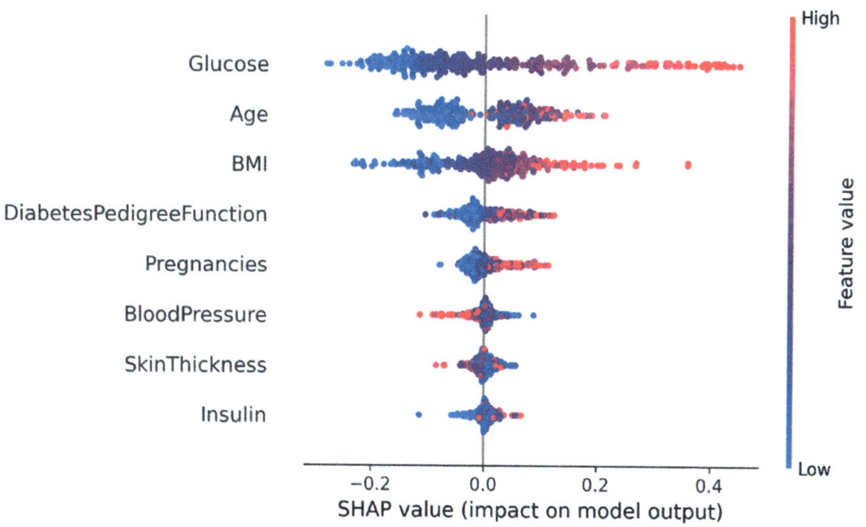

Figure 8: Soft voting – SHAP values.

of estimators as 10. The AdaBoost and XGBoost are implemented with the number of estimators of 50. Bagging reached an accuracy of 75.00%, a precision of 62.89%, a recall of 59.80%, and an F_1 score of 61.31%. AdaBoost achieved 75.32% accuracy, 62.50% precision, 63.73% recall, and an F_1 score of 63.11%. XGBoost matched the top individual model accuracy at 76.62%, with a precision of 63.64%, a recall of 68.63%, and an F_1 score of 66.04%. Figures 9–11 exhibit the SHAP values of bagging, AdaBoost, and XGBoost, respectively. The performance of bagging, AdaBoost, and XGBoost is shown in Figure 12.

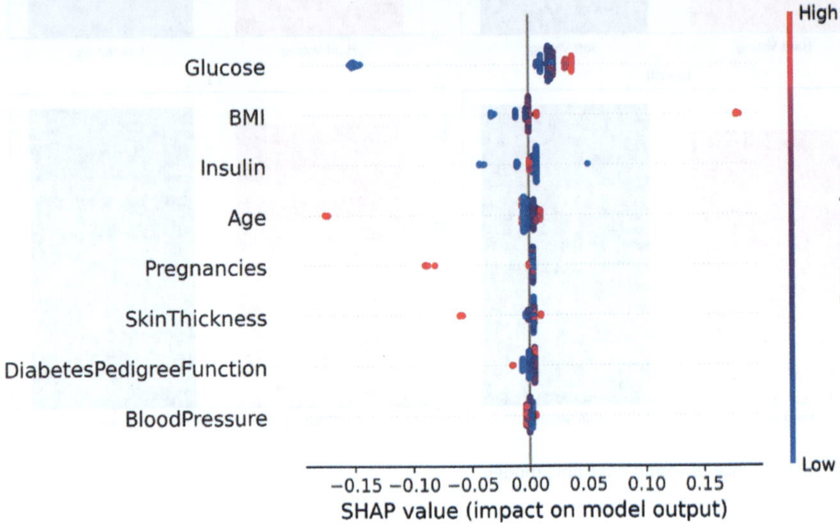

Figure 9: Boosting – SHAP values.

We have used four stacking ensemble models. The first model uses DT, RF, SVMs, and kNN classifiers as base estimators and LR as a final estimator. The second model uses DTs, SVMs, LR, kNNs as base estimators, and RF as a final estimator. The third ensemble is done between DT, SVMs, RF, LR as base estimator, and kNN as final estimator. The last stacking ensemble model uses using soft voting ensemble model, AdaBoost, and XGBoost as base estimators and RF as a final estimator. We name the ensemble models stacking 1, stacking 2, stacking 3, and stacking 4.

The stacking model with RF as the final estimator gives better results because it corrects the errors of the base learners, and biases and variances are reduced. The performance of all the stacking models is shown in Figure 13, and the SHAP values of the stacking model 1 are shown in Figure 14. Table 1 shows the performance of all the models and all the ensemble methods used in the experiment.

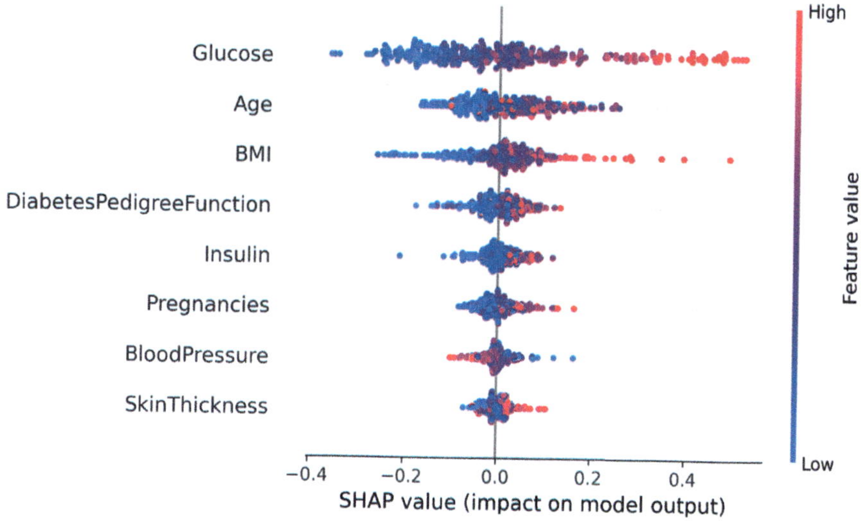

Figure 10: Bagging – SHAP values.

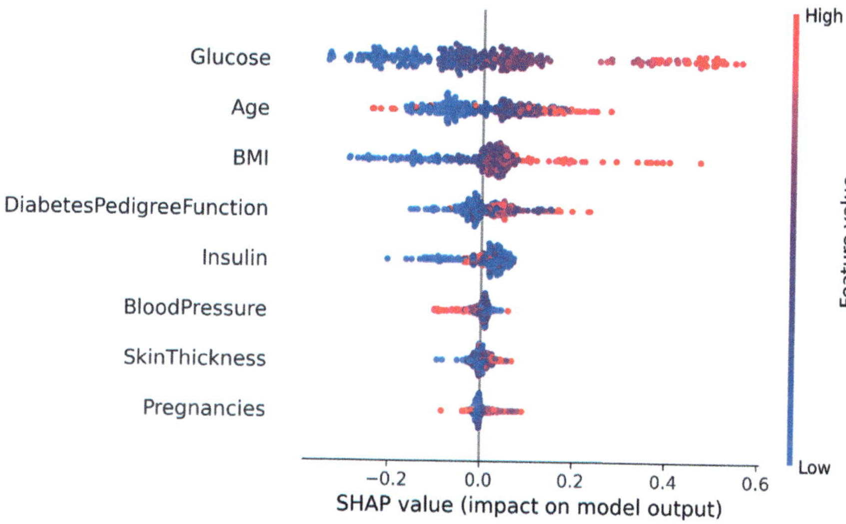

Figure 11: SHAP values of XGBoost.

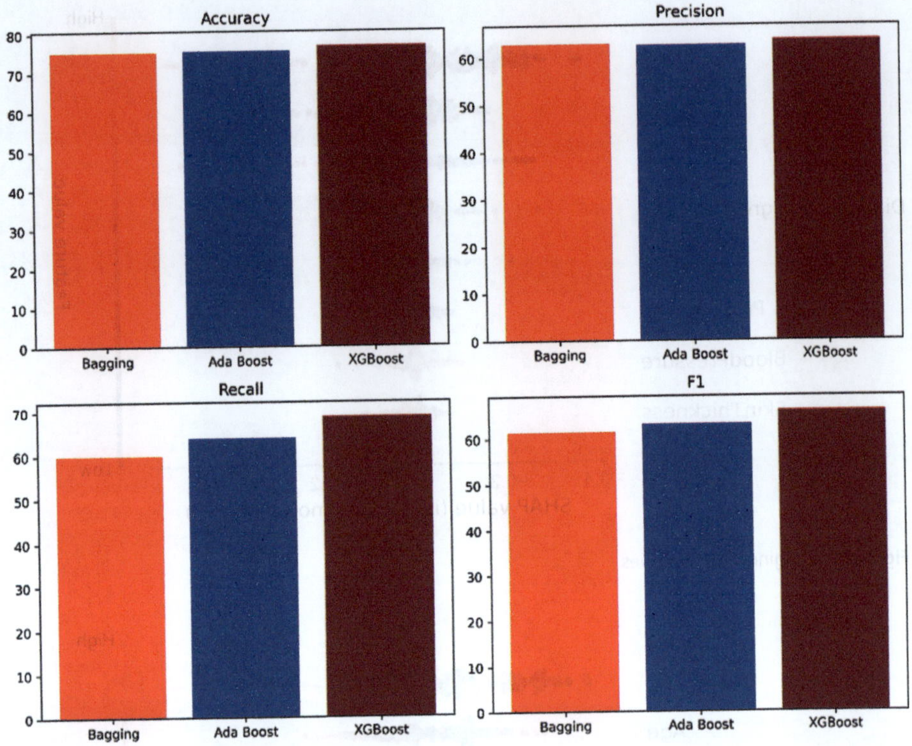

Figure 12: Performance of bagging and boosting.

Table 1: Performance of all the models.

Model	Accuracy	Precision	Recall	F_1
LR	76.62	65.62	61.76	63.64
DT	72.08	56.56	67.65	61.61
SVM	76.3	66.29	57.84	61.78
RF	76.62	65	63.73	64.36
kNN	75	63.16	58.82	60.91
Hard voting	76.95	67.03	59.8	63.21
Soft voting	**78.25**	67.68	65.69	**66.67**
Bagging	75	62.89	59.8	61.31
AdaBoost	75.32	62.5	63.73	63.11
XGBoost	76.62	63.64	**68.63**	66.04
Stacking model 1	77.27	66	64.71	65.35
Stacking model 2	78.25	**68.42**	63.73	65.99
Stacking model 3	76.3	64.65	62.75	63.68
Stacking model 4	74.03	60.38	62.75	61.54

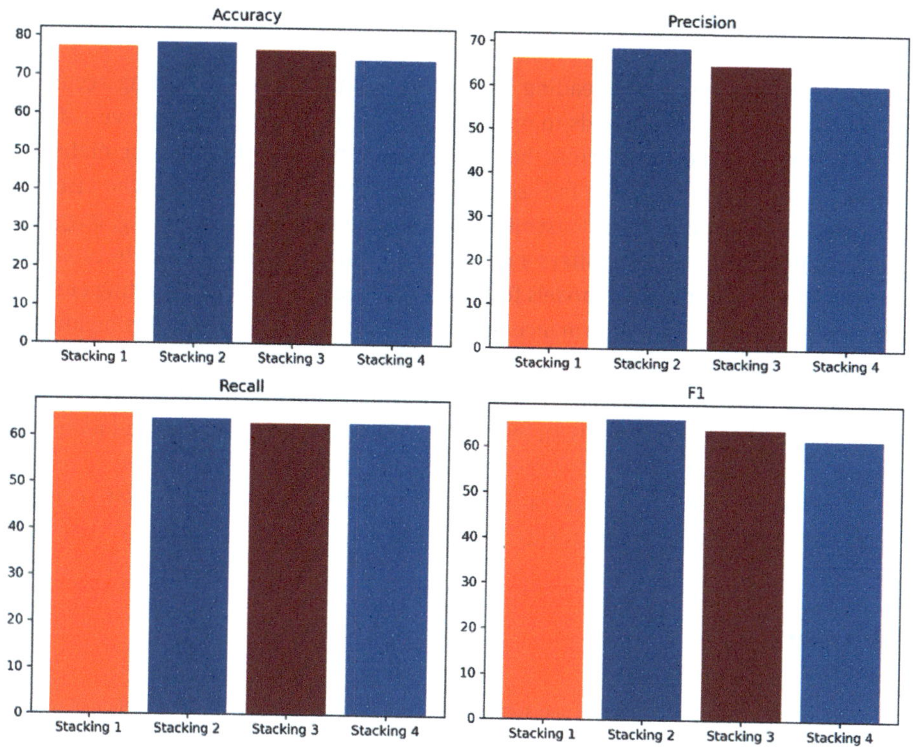

Figure 13: Performance of stacking models. Bar graph displaying classification performance of four stacking ensemble models.

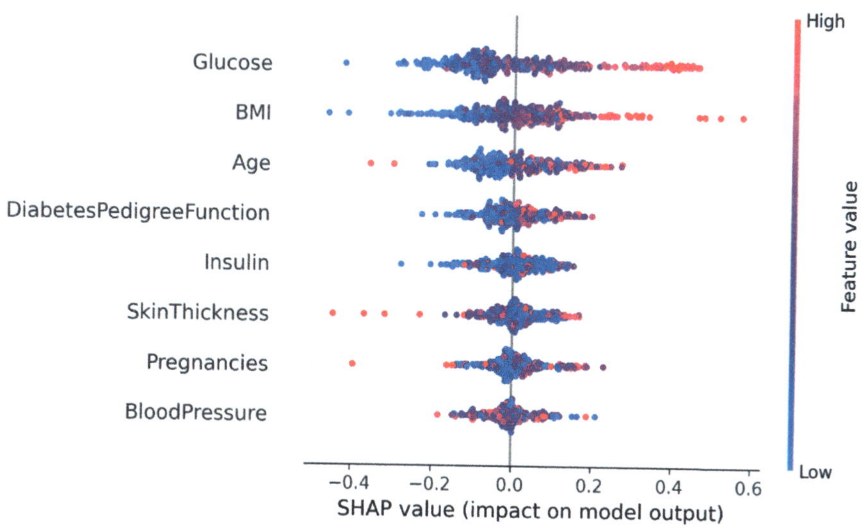

Figure 14: SHAP values of stacking 1.

5 Conclusion

Diabetes remains one of the leading global health challenges, demanding accurate and efficient diagnostic methods to optimize medical resources and improve patient outcomes. While machine learning has shown great potential in detecting diabetes, relying on a single model often falls short in capturing the complexity of the disease. This chapter validates various ensemble methods such as voting, boosting, bagging, and stacking and finds which offers a more robust and effective approach to combine models. Among the ensemble models for diabetes classification, the soft voting ensemble achieved the highest performance in terms of accuracy of 78.25%. This highlights the use of ensembling methods in medical data classification.

Although ensemble methods provide promising results than a single model, the complexity and computation resources required for building the ensemble model are huge. There is always a trade-off between model accuracy and complexity.

In future work, we aim to develop a user-friendly website where users can directly enter their data and find the diabetes result.

References

[1] S S, S., Surendiran, J., Yuvaraj, N., Ramkumar, M., Ravi, C., & Vidhya, R. (2022). Classification of diabetes using multilayer perceptron. In *2022 IEEE international conference on distributed computing and electrical circuits and electronics (icdcece)* (pp. 1–5). doi: 10.1109/ICDCECE53908.2022.9793085.

[2] Dubey, Y., Wankhede, P., Borkar, T., Borkar, A., & Mitra, K. (2021). Diabetes prediction and classification using machine learning algorithms. In *2021 IEEE international conference on biomedical engineering, computer and information technology for health (becithcon)* (pp. 60–63). doi: 10.1109/BECITHCON54710.2021.9893653.

[3] Lixandru-Petre, I.-O. (2020). A fuzzy system approach for diabetes classification. In *2020 international conference on e-health and bioengineering (EHB)* (pp. 14). doi: 10.1109/EHB50910.2020.9279882.

[4] Islam, N. U., & Khanam, R. (2021a). Classification of diabetes using machine learning. In *2021 international conference on computational performance evaluation (COMPE)* (pp. 185–189). doi: 10.1109/ComPE53109.2021.9751955.

[5] Warsi, G. G., Saini, S., & Khatri, K. (2019). Ensemble learning on diabetes data set and early diabetes prediction. In *2019 international conference on computing, power and communication technologies (GUCON)* (pp. 182–187).

[6] Ramteke, N., & Maidamwar, P. (2023, Jul). Cardiac patient data classification using ensemble machine learning technique. In *2023 14th International Conference on Computing Communication and Networking Technologies(ICCCNT)* (pp. 1–6). doi: 10.1109/icccnt56998.2023.10307702.

[7] Juez-Gil, M., Arnaiz-Gonźalez, Rodŕıguez, J. J., & Garćıa-Osorio, C. (2021, Sep). Experimental evaluation of ensemble classifiers for imbalance in big data. *Applied Soft Computing, 108*, 107447. doi: 10.1016/j.asoc.2021.

[8] AlJame, M., Ahmad, I., Imtiaz, A., & Mohammed, A. (2020). Ensemble learning model for diagnosing covid-19 from routine blood tests. *Informatics in Medicine Unlocked, 21*, 100449. doi: 10.1016/j.imu.2020.100449.

[9] Senthilkumar, T.P., & Prabhusundar, P. (2020, Mar). An effective feature selection and incremental classifier design for rice disease prediction. *Journal of Advanced Research in Dynamical and Control Systems, 12*(SP4), 770–786. doi: 10.5373/jardcs/v12sp4/20201545.

[10] Islam, N. U., & Khanam, R.. (2021b). Classification of diabetes using machine learning. In *2021 international conference on computational performance evaluation (COMPE)* (pp. 185–189). doi: 10.1109/ComPE53109.2021.9751955.

[11] Talapaneni, S., Kota, C. S., Yalagala, N., Nunna, R., & Mothukuri, R. (2024). Enhancing heart disease prediction and analysis: An efficient voting ensemble model. In *2024 international conference on communication, computer sciences and engineering (IC3SE)* (pp. 156–160). doi: 10.1109/IC3SE62002.2024.10593602.

[12] Kumar, A., Sushil, R., & Tiwari, A. K. (2021). Classification of breast cancer using user-defined weighted ensemble voting scheme. In *Tencon 2021 – 2021 IEEE region 10 conference (TENCON)* (pp. 134–139). doi: 10.1109/TENCON54134.2021.9707374.

[13] Mijoya, I. B., Khurana, S., Gupta, N., & Gupta, K. (2023). Malware detection in mobile devices using hard voting ensemble technique. In *2023 international conference on computing, communication, and intelligent systems (ICCCIS)* (pp. 116–121). doi: 10.1109/ICCCIS60361.2023.10425513.

[14] Ramadhan, N. G., & Fitriana, G. F.. (2024). Analysis comparison of hard and soft voting ensemble model for sentiment analysis on IMDB movie reviews. In *2024 ninth international conference on informatics and computing (ICIC)* (pp. 1–4). doi: 10.1109/ICIC64337.2024.10956377.

[15] Sen, K., & Verma, B.. (2023). Heart disease prediction using a soft voting ensemble of gradient boosting models, random forest, and Gaussian Naive Bayes. In *2023 4th international conference for emerging technology (INCET)* (pp. 1–7). doi: 10.1109/INCET57972.2023.10170399.

[16] Wang, Y., Zheng, J., Wang, D., & Zhang, Z. (2023). Multi-objective planning model based on the soft voting ensemble learning algorithm. In *2023 IEEE international conference on electrical, automation and computer engineering (ICEACE)* (pp. 1104–1107). doi: 10.1109/ICEACE60673.2023.10442166.

[17] Sreenath, M., & Udhayan, J. (2015). Intrusion detection system using bagging ensemble selection. In *2015 IEEE international conference on engineering and technology (ICETECH)* (pp. 1–4). doi: 10.1109/ICETECH.2015.7275015.

[18] Ward, M., Malmsten, K., Salamy, H., & Min, C.-H. (2021). Data balanced bagging ensemble of convolutional- LSTM neural networks for time series data classification with an imbalanced dataset. In *2021 IEEE international symposium on circuits and systems (ISCAS)* (pp. 1–5). doi: 10.1109/ISCAS51556.2021.9401389.

[19] Tella, H., Mohandes, M., Al-Shaikhi, A., Liu, B., Rehman, S., & Nuha, H. (2023). Bagging and voting deep learning ensemble methods for binary classifications of solar panel cells defects. In *2023 20th international multi-conference on systems, signals devices (SSD)* (pp. 104–108). doi: 10.1109/SSD58187.2023.10411247.

[20] V, V., PK, M. J., S, N., & S, P. D. (2023). Ensemble machine learning based weather prediction system. In *2023 international conference on communication, security and artificial intelligence (ICCSAI)* (pp. 996–1000). doi: 10.1109/ICCSAI59793.2023.10421274.

[21] Omer, Z. M., & Shareef, H. (2019). Adaptive boosting and bootstrapped aggregation based ensemble machine learning methods for photovoltaic systems output current prediction. In *2019 29th Australasian universities power engineering conference (AUPEC)* (pp. 1–6). doi: 10.1109/AUPEC48547.2019.211856.

[22] Wu, S., & Nagahashi, H. (2014). Parameterized adaboost: Introducing a parameter to speed up the training of real adaboost. *IEEE Signal Processing Letters, 21*(6), 687–691 doi: 10.1109/LSP.2014.2313570.

[23] Dutta, J., Kim, Y. W., & Dominic, D.. (2020). Comparison of gradient boosting and extreme boosting ensemble methods for webpage classification. In *2020 fifth international conference on research in computational intelligence and communication networks (ICRCICN)* (pp. 77–82). doi: 10.1109/ICRCICN50933.2020.9296176.

[24] Zhou, Y., Song, X., & Zhou, M. (2021). Supply chain fraud prediction based on xgboost method. In *2021 IEEE 2nd international conference on big data, artificial intelligence and internet of things engineering (ICBAIE)* (pp. 539542). doi: 10.1109/ICBAIE52039.2021.9389949.

[25] Wang, S. (2023). Comparison and analysis of the effect of xgboost classification, bp neural network classification and catboost classification on malware attack prediction. In *2023 international conference on intelligent communication and computer engineering (ICICCE)* (pp. 77–80). doi: 10.1109/ICICCE61720.2023.00018.

[26] Lin, Z., & Zhu, S. (2023). DFS-enhanced lightgbm: An extended lightgbm model applied to ICU heart failure mortality prediction. In *2023 international conference on high performance big data and intelligent systems (HDIS)* (pp. 113–117). doi: 10.1109/HDIS60872.2023.10499633.

[27] Zhao, T., Zhao, Y., & Zhou, T. (2024). Stacking ensemble learning for seabed sediment classification. In *2024 7th international conference on information communication and signal processing (ICICSP)* (pp. 211–215). doi: 10.1109/ICICSP62589.2024.10809036.

[28] Nirmala Devi, M., alias Balamurugan, S. A., & Swathi, U. V. (2013). An amalgam kNN to predict diabetes mellitus. In *2013 IEEE international conference on emerging trends in computing, communication and nanotechnology (ICECCN)* (pp. 691–695). doi: 10.1109/ICE-CCN.2013.6528591.

[29] Rachmawanto, E. H., Ignatius Moses Setiadi, D. R., Rijati, N., Susanto, A., Wahyu Mulyono, I. U., & Rahmalan, H. (2021). Attribute selection analysis for the random forest classification in unbalanced diabetes dataset. In *2021 international seminar on application for technology of information and communication (ISEMANTIC)* (pp. 82–86). doi: 10.1109/iSemantic52711.2021.9573181.

[30] Krisdianto, R., Apriani, I., Masada, H., & Hidayaturrahman. (2024). Performance analysis of support vector machine (SVM) for diabetes disease detection. In *2024 5th international conference on artificial intelligence and data sciences (AIDAS)* (pp. 203–207). doi: 10.1109/AiDAS63860.2024.10730403.

[31] Bai, X., Chen, B., Gao, X., & Li, J. (2019). Correlation between diabetes and body composition of based on decision tree and neural network. In *2019 Chinese control and decision conference (CCDC)* (pp. 4992–4997). doi: 10.1109/CCDC.2019.8832670.

[32] Ravalika, D., & Pitchai, R. (2023). Prediction of diabetes using binomial logistic regression. In *2023 4th international conference on smart electronics and communication (ICOSEC)* (pp. 918–923). doi: 10.1109/ICOSEC58147.2023.10276068.

Sunder R.*, Gayatri Parasa, Bura Vijay Kumar, B. Kamala, Chilukala Mahender Reddy, and S. Bathrinath

A Hybrid Machine Learning Model for Risk Stratification and Functional Outcome Prediction in Stroke Survivors

Abstract: Stroke continues to be a major cause of long-term disability globally, and precise and timely prediction of patient outcomes is needed to guide focused rehabilitation and resource allocation. This chapter introduces a new hybrid machine learning (ML) model that combines multimodal data sources for the concurrent task of risk stratification and functional outcome prediction in stroke survivors. The hybrid model combines a convolutional neural network (CNN) for imaging data, a graph neural network for structured clinical data, and a conventional machine learning model (LightGBM) for some handcrafted features. These heterogeneous elements are integrated in a common latent representation space and optimized end-to-end using a multitask learning strategy. The model was trained and validated against a robust dataset of demographic data, clinical rating, neuroimaging (CT/MRI), and follow-up functional outcomes as per the modified Rankin scale (mRS). Comparative evaluation against four traditional models: logistic regression, random forest, unimodal CNN, and an ensemble late fusion model illustrates better performance by the proposed hybrid approach with an area under the receiver operating characteristic curve of 0.92 for risk classification and a quadratic-weighted kappa of 0.84 for mRS prediction. The findings indicate that the combination of varied learning paradigms and data types in one model improves predictive power and interpretability and opens the door to more patient-centered stroke treatment.

Keywords: stroke prediction, hybrid machine learning, multimodal data integration, convolutional neural networks (CNNs), graph neural networks (GNNs), LightBGM

***Corresponding author: Sunder R.**, School of Computer Science and Engineering, Galgotias University, Greater Noida, Uttar Pradesh, India, e-mail: sunder.r@galgotiasuniversity.edu.in
Gayatri Parasa, Department of CSE – AIML, KG Reddy College of Engineering and Technology, Hyderabad 500086, Telangana, India, e-mail: gayatri.p@kgr.ac.in
Bura Vijay Kumar, School of Computer Science and Artificial Intelligence, SR University, Warangal 506371, Telangana, India, e-mail: vijaykumar.bura@gmail.com
B. Kamala, Department of Information Technology, Sri Sairam Engineering College, Chennai, Tamil Nadu, India, e-mail: kamala.it@sairam.edu.in
Chilukala Mahender Reddy, Department of Computer Science and Artificial Intelligence, SR University, Warangal 506371, Telangana, India, e-mail: mahender.chilukala@gmail.com
S. Bathrinath, Department of Mechanical Engineering, Kalasalingam Academy of Research and Education, Krishnankoil 626126, Tamil Nadu, India, e-mail: bathri@gmail.com

https://doi.org/10.1515/9783111541235-004

1 Introduction

Stroke continues to be a major global cause of mortality and disability, placing a strain on society and healthcare [1]. As virtually all strokes but very small percentages are ischemic, rapid and precise patient outcome prediction is important to clinical decision-making as well as planning for resource consumption. Traditionally, prediction of stroke outcome has relied on clinical grading scales such as the National Institutes of Health Stroke Scale (NIHSS) and the mRS [2]. While useful, such scales are generally handicapped by their reliance on subjective assessment, fixed variables, and failure to capture the complex, multimodal nature of stroke pathology. There is hence growing interest in integrating machine learning (ML) and deep learning (DL) methods to maximize prediction performance as well as guide individualized treatment choices [3].

Advanced technological advances in clinical informatics and medical imaging have enabled the acquisition of high-dimensional, heterogeneous data consisting of neuroimaging, physiological measurements, laboratory test values, and extensive patient histories [4]. However, these heterogeneous data sources often remain untapped in conventional predictive models. Single-modality approaches, such as image-only or clinical-only models, may be inadequate in harnessing the synergy advantage of multimodal data. Thus, there is a need for an exhaustive, evidence-based strategy to optimize the precision and reliability of outcome prediction in patients with stroke [5].

To close this gap, this work presents a novel hybrid model that integrates imaging data, structured clinical features, and relational clinical graphs. The proposed architecture combines three high-performance components: (1) a 3D convolutional neural network (CNN) [6] for extracting spatial features from volumetric CT or MRI scans; (2) a graph neural network (GNN) [7] for clinical relationship modeling between patients; and (3) a traditional ML pipeline based on LightGBM [8] for leveraging hand-engineered tabular clinical features.

Multimodal data fusion in which various data types are combined and analyzed together has been receiving growing interest as a solution to this challenge. The argument is simple: various data modalities capture complementary information about the patient's status [9]. As an example, imaging data will disclose anatomical and pathological alterations in the brain, whereas clinical data including blood pressure, glucose level, or atrial fibrillation status can provide contextual information on risk and recovery. When properly combined, these modalities have the potential to provide a richer and more informative image of a patient's health status. Nevertheless, combining such heterogeneous information is still a great challenge because of the differences in data structure, dimension, and semantics [10].

The increase in the availability of data is the innovation in artificial intelligence (AI) and ML methods, specifically DL. These methods have proven to hold great promise for modeling complex high-dimensional relationships and for learning hierarchical representations from pure input data [11]. In medical imaging, CNNs have been extensively applied for detecting and classifying pathologies, and recurrent and graph models have been investigated for their capacity to model temporal and relational patterns in clinical data [12]. These new possibilities bring new opportunities for constructing intelligent systems that are capable of directly learning from raw multimodal patient data without being strongly dependent on hand-engineered features or strict scoring systems.

However, clinical use of AI-based models for stroke prognosis is still limited. One of the key reasons is the use of single-modality methods in the majority of current studies. Models based on imaging data alone tend to neglect important clinical context, whereas models based on tabular clinical data alone cannot capture important anatomical features visible on brain scans. Additionally, conventional ML models are not sufficiently flexible and expressive to deal with extensive, nonlinear, and interdependent relationships that are typically found in patient data. There is a strong need to transcend unimodal systems and toward hybrid systems that can integrate evidence from multiple sources of data in a coherent, interpretable, and clinically relevant manner.

This study presents a unified, multimodal, and explainable DL architecture for predicting stroke outcomes. By integrating spatial, relational, and domain-specific information, the model captures the multifaceted nature of stroke pathology and individual variability in recovery. The hybrid approach is adaptable to a variety of clinical tasks beyond stroke, including outcome prediction in other neurological or cardiovascular conditions. As healthcare increasingly transitions toward precision medicine, such integrative AI-driven tools hold the promise to revolutionize prognosis, personalize treatment planning, and ultimately improve patient outcomes. The study aims to achieve the following objectives:

- To construct a multimodal hybrid model that merges multimodal data sources, such as imaging data, structured clinical data, and handcrafted features, to forecast stroke patient outcomes in an effective manner.
- To integrate a CNN for image, a GNN for clinical information, and an ML model that is traditional (LightGBM) for handcrafted features together in one single model.
- To utilize a multitask learning approach to both perform risk stratification and functional outcome prediction (on the basis of the mRS).
- To assess the efficiency of the hybrid model in relation to standard models (logistic regression (LR), random forest (RF), unimodal CNN, and an ensemble late fusion model) based on metrics such as AUC-ROC (area under the receiver operating characteristic curve) for risk classification and quadratic weighted kappa (QWK) for mRS prediction.

2 Related Works

Current developments in ML have transformed medical diagnosis, providing robust means for processing complex clinical data and detecting individuals at risk. This review discusses hybrid and ensemble ML methods for stroke prediction, combining algorithms including LR, SVM, RFs, DL architectures, and metaheuristic optimization algorithms. These models, augmented with feature selection (FS) and class balancing methods, exhibit remarkable accuracy and clinical utility enhancements and are scalable, interpretable, and robust solutions for early stroke detection and prevention.

2.1 Hybrid ML Model for Stroke Prediction

Acute ischemic stroke (AIS) is a serious global health problem due to its high rates of mortality, morbidity, and disability, with survivors bearing lifelong physical, cognitive, and emotional impairments. For the provision of prompt clinical decision and individualized treatment, a successful hybrid ML model has been proposed for predicting three-month poor outcomes in AIS patients. Based on a 731-case dataset and internally and externally validated, the study compared 25 DL and ML models on 14 performance measures. On the basis of clustering and correlation analysis of measures, 12 high-performing models were shortlisted out of which XGBoost and CatBoost performed better than others both in terms of accuracy as well as reliability. Ensemble modeling and cost curve analysis threshold tuning resulted in the final model with respectable performance on both sets. Decision analysis and fairness checks were done to measure clinical utility. SHAP-based interpretability utilized albumin, fasting blood glucose, BMI, serum creatinine (Scr), white blood cell count, and age as important predictors, importantly interacting with gender. Notably, the model uses only 30 easily available clinical features, enhancing its utility. The resulting prognostic platform provides precise, interpretable, and clinically actionable predictions, justifying its implementation in electronic health records or telemedicine systems. This research demonstrates how hybrid, interpretable ML models can inform early AIS management and rehabilitation planning safely and reliably and is an exciting step toward precision medicine for stroke therapy [13].

2.2 EEG-Based Hybrid Stroke Diagnosis

In recent decades, longer average life spans have increased the number of stroke cases among the elderly population, which has made stroke diagnosis and treatment an important topic of research, particularly in the field of ML. Early diagnosis is crucial for stroke treatment, but current imaging technologies such as CT and MRI are not very good. While MRI is costly and difficult to obtain, CT can take up to 8 h to provide a reliable diagnosis. This has prompted the search for alternative, faster electroencephalogram (EEG)-based diagnostic techniques. This work presents a novel hybrid model for classifying strokes from EEG data, which is a time-series with frequency content, by combining DL with meta-heuristic optimization. A CNN and a bidirectional gated recurrent unit (BiGRU) are used in the model to effectively collect time and space information. The CNN-BiGRU model outperformed the harmony search (HS) algorithm, which is excellent at handling frequency data, when it was applied for feature extraction. The multiverse optimization (MVO) approach outperformed the other algorithm when hyperparameter tuning was used. In comparison to previous studies employing portable EEG, the CNN-BiGRU-HS-MVO model achieved a remarkable prediction accuracy of 99.991% when verified using EEG data acquired from Al Bashir Hospital using the MUSE-2 portable equipment. Faster, simpler patient care is now feasible anywhere, at any time, thanks to a cloud-based decision support system that was further developed to enable remote real-time stroke diagnosis and provide results via SMS [14].

2.3 Hybrid Classifier with Feature Selection

Brain stroke is a serious medical condition that needs to be predicted on time and in a suitable manner for appropriate treatment and prevention. A hybrid approach that involves FS methods with ML classifier algorithms has been proposed for improved prediction of brain stroke. The Stroke Prediction Dataset provided in Kaggle has been used, wherein imbalance in the data was handled through the synthetic minority oversampling technique (SMOTE). Five classifiers, naïve Bayes, SVM, RF, adaptive boosting (Adaboost), and extreme gradient boosting (XGBoost), were compared with three FS methods: mutual information, Pearson correlation, and feature importance (FI). The performance was compared in terms of accuracy, sensitivity, specificity, precision, and *F*-measure using *k*-fold cross-validation. The best performance was obtained by the hybrid model with FI as the FS method and RF as the classifier. It decreased the features by 36.3% and had an accuracy of 97.17%. The high-dimensional reduction along with a strong classification method allowed the model to make accurate predictions for brain stroke. The results highlight the benefit of this hybrid system to enable early detection of stroke and prevention, with healthcare specialists having a useful tool with which to make timely and targeted interventions toward better patient outcomes and the reduction of complications from stroke [15].

2.4 Stroke Prediction Using ADASYN and Random Forest

Cerebral stroke due to acute loss of brain blood supply sets into motion a sequence of cellular injury by way of oxygen and nutrient deprivation. Modifiable lifestyle indicators like elevated blood glucose, cardiovascular disease, overweight/obesity, and diabetes take the stroke risk significantly higher than normal. The potential of sophisticated ML algorithms such as LR, RF, and K-nearest neighbor were examined for the prediction of cerebral strokes. Data were gathered from Harvard Dataverse Repository including clinical, physiological, behavioral, demographic, and medical history variables. Three oversampling methods SMOTE, adaptive synthetic sampling (ADASYN), and random oversampling technique (ROSE) were used to overcome the prevalent problem of class imbalance of stroke databases to spread the minority classes more uniformly and enhance model performance. Introducing a new hybrid method, this chapter integrates ADASYN oversampling with RF classifier (ADASYN_RF) to accurately predict strokes from highly imbalanced physiological data. The comparison experiments for different oversampling techniques and ML algorithms reveal that the ADASYN_RF hybrid outperforms others with a whopping 99% detection rate. The hybrid approach presents a cost-effective yet reliable answer to the stroke prediction, and it is a valuable tool for timely clinical diagnosis and treatment [16].

2.5 Hybrid Sampling-Optimized Stroke Risk Prediction

A new supervised ML algorithm has been proposed to predict stroke risk on a comprehensive list of causative factors. As a clinical practitioner's assistant, the model aims at enhancing diagnostic accuracy, preventing fatalities, and facilitating early intervention procedures. The model was trained and tested on an unbalanced dataset consisting of diverse features related to stroke. For improving performance, hybrid sampling strategies were applied for balancing classes and grid search was used to tune hyperparameters in five baseline models. Integrated classification method had the best performance with precision, accuracy, F_1-score, and recall rates ranging from 94.5% to 95.5%. The performance of the model suggests its suitability in facilitating clinical decision-making in stroke risk prediction [17].

2.6 Hybrid Ensemble Machine Learning for Stroke Prediction

Stroke is a chronic condition due to poor blood supply to some brain cells, resulting in deprivation of oxygen and nutrients, followed by cell death. Precise prediction and early detection of stroke are ongoing crucial challenges in the field of healthcare. In recent times, ML approaches have proven very capable in the prediction of disease with possibility of better clinical outcomes. The study introduces a hybrid ensemble ML model that has three heterogeneous base classifiers: SVM, LR, and RF. The ensemble, which is named SVM-LR-RF, utilizes the unique capabilities of each individual model to improve stroke prediction accuracy using a healthcare dataset available in the Kaggle repository. The models were designed and experimented in the Python programming environment. The base learners LR, SVM, and RF were first separately trained and tested through confusion matrices to determine performance in classification. Next, the base model outputs (prediction probabilities) were combined through a soft voting methodology to construct the hybrid ensemble model. This enables the model to combine each learner's predictions, enhancing overall robustness and mitigating individual drawbacks. Experimental findings showed that the hybrid model of SVM-LR-RF considerably outshone the standalone classifiers, with the prediction accuracy of 95%. This success illustrates the potential of merging different ML algorithms using ensemble learning for sophisticated medical prediction tasks such as stroke. Based on these encouraging findings, it is suggested that the hybrid SVM-LR-RF model be applied as a functional and effective tool for improved stroke risk prediction, which could support clinicians with early intervention and improved patient care [18].

2.7 Ensemble-LR-RF and SVM-Based Stroke Risk Prediction

The deployment of a stroke prediction system based on ML can be an exciting development in the identification of individuals at high risk of having a stroke. With the use of large data sets at their command, ML models can identify subtle, nonlinear patterns, and weak predictors that are not even apparent to clinicians. Such ability has the potential to improve early detection substantially, facilitate timely intervention, and inform preventive action to lower stroke prevalence and better serve patients. Although previous research has applied individual ML models to predicting strokes, this research investigates a combination of the LR, RF, and SVM models. Each of the algorithms has its own strengths and weaknesses. RF provided the highest predictive accuracy due to its ensemble and ability to process nonlinear relations and FI. Conversely, LR and SVM provided better computational efficiency and training complexity, rendering them appropriate in situations needing fast or limited deployments. The hybrid modeling method leveraged the predictive power of the three classifiers compared on aspects such as accuracy, training time, and stability. Among the three, RF performed best for this dataset and was appropriate for application within stroke risk assessment procedures. LR and SVM are also suitable depending on application requirements. Further, ML-based stroke prediction models provide medical science with a breakthrough tool that makes it possible to identify risk patients early. The research confirms the capability of ML in medical diagnosis and highlights the need to conduct more research on developing more advanced algorithm selection, feature extraction, and model training for easier clinical applicability [19].

The reviewed works collectively emphasize the revolutionizing potential of ensemble and hybrid ML models in stroke prediction model development. Through an ensemble of multiple classifiers, that is, RF, LR, SVM, XGBoost, CatBoost, and deep networks including CNN-BiGRU with optimization techniques and feature selectors, all the aforementioned approaches have achieved high predictive accuracy, typically more than 95% accuracy. The use of oversampling techniques (e.g., SMOTE, ADASYN, and ROSE) sufficiently addressed class imbalance and contributed to the reliability of the model. Besides, the application of interpretable models (like SHAP analysis) and real-time clinical decision support system deployment (like cloud-based or SMS-based systems) demonstrated pragmatic usefulness in real-world healthcare settings. Not only do these models gain from early and accurate stroke diagnosis, but they also offer the scalability and flexibility required to embed into electronic health records and telemedicine systems. Despite the effectiveness of such initiatives, the study calls for further efforts in external validation, real-time deployment, and integration of multimodal data sources (e.g., EEG, imaging, and clinical notes). Ethical considerations, fairness evaluation, and explainability are also significant hurdles to bridge to implement accountable AI in clinical environments. Finally, hybrid ML algorithms for stroke prediction constitute a promising area of precision medicine with the capability to support clinicians via early intervention tools and optimize patient outcomes in various healthcare infrastructures.

3 Methodology

Stroke continues to be a major cause of morbidity and mortality globally, and early risk stratification and the prediction of functional outcome are essential in enhancing patient care and long-term rehabilitation. Standard prognostic approaches are usually inadequate in describing the intricate relationship between imaging biomarkers, clinical markers, and comorbidities that determine stroke outcomes. To solve this challenge, we introduce a new multimodal ML system that combines high-resolution neuroimaging, structured clinical information, and domain-informed handcrafted features for accurate prediction of poststroke risk and functional recovery. Taking advantage of the dense ISLES dataset, our method integrates a 3D CNN to learn spatial lesion features from MRI images, a GNN to represent clinical similarity between patients, and a LightGBM-based conventional model to retain interpretable clinical knowledge. These diverse data representations are combined into a single latent space and optimized through a multitask learning approach to predict stroke severity risk levels and 90-day functional outcomes on the mRS simultaneously. This DL model hybrid provides an optimistic direction for personalized stroke management with data-driven, explainable, and precise clinical decision support.

3.1 Data Sources

The ISLES (ischemic stroke lesion segmentation) Challenge Datasets (https://www.isles-challenge.org) are used as the initial data source of this research, providing rich multimodal data customized for stroke outcome research [20]. The data provide well-structured clinical data like age, sex, comorbidities, NIHSS scores, and corresponding laboratory results, including important patient demographics and stroke severity. Moreover, the data include multimodal MRI scans like DWI, FLAIR, and ADC that provide accurate anatomical and pathological characteristics of ischemic lesions and adjacent brain tissue. These imaging modalities facilitate high-level spatial analysis of stroke effects. Functional outcome labels in the form of mRS scores, commonly measured at 90 days following stroke, provide a standardized measure of disability and recovery. The combination of clinical factors, high-resolution imaging, and outcome data provides strong modeling of risk stratification and long-term functional prediction to allow the design of advanced hybrid learning schemes.

3.2 Data Preprocessing

For model preparedness and quality maintenance of the data, stringent preprocessing operations are carried out on both structured data and imaging data. Ordered clinical variables like age, NIHSS scores, and laboratory values are *z*-score normalized to standardize feature measurements and enhance model convergence. Random rotations, cropping, and changes in contrast are used on MRI scans in imaging data to simulate variability in anatomical presentation and image acquisition, enhancing model robustness and generalization. The augmentations are especially valuable for training DL models to identify stroke features across various conditions. Missing values in the structured dataset are also filled in by using a clinical-knowledge-driven imputation scheme. It utilizes domain-specific rule-based and practical clinical correlations (such as the estimation of missing blood glucose values based on the foundation of well-established comorbid conditions such as diabetes) to calculate more physiologically reasonable values than would otherwise be calculated under regular statistical procedure. This modified preprocessing pipeline guarantees integrity and functionality of the dataset to utilize in later hybrid model training, without negatively impacting such critical clinical and imaging characteristics essential for the prediction of stroke outcomes [21].

3.3 Model Architecture

This work introduces a new multimodal ML paradigm that combines multimodal patient information for risk stratification and functional outcome prediction in stroke survivors. The structure is a 3D CNN for imaging [22], a GNN [23] for clinical relations, and conventional ML for hand-crafted features. These different representations are combined into a shared latent vector optimized via multitask learning. This facilitates accurate, interpretable predictions through the use of complementary data sources and task-specific tasks. The model architecture for the prediction of stroke survivors is shown in Figure 1.

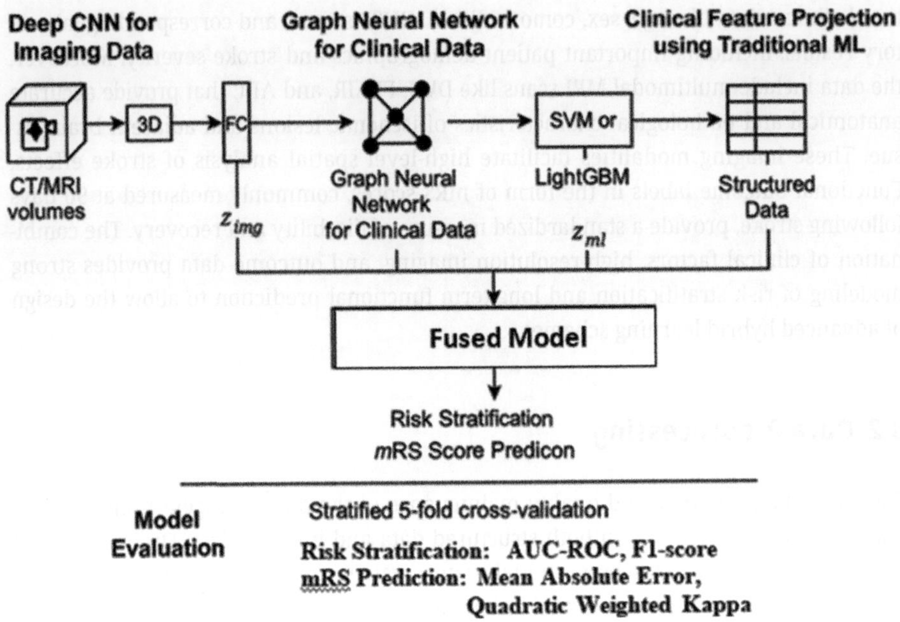

Figure 1: Proposed model architecture for stroke prediction.

3.3.1 Deep CNN for Imaging Data

A 3D CNN is used to scan volumetric CT/MRI images and obtain high-level spatial features related to ischemic lesions and cerebral abnormalities. The imaging data is processed in the CNN using several layers of 3D convolutions, batch normalization, and ReLU activation and captures hierarchical features like lesion size, location, and intensity. The last convolutional outputs are flattened and fed into a fully connected (FC) layer to generate a fixed-size image-derived embedding vector z_{img}, which is the learned representation of the patient's neuroanatomical state. This vector contains imaging-derived information critical to stroke severity and recovery prediction [24]. To mathematically represent the 3D CNN for imaging data formally, define the process in a layer-wise abstraction that captures the transformation from raw CT/MRI volumes to the embedding vector z_{img}. Let the volume of the input image be

$$X_{\mathrm{img}} \in \mathbb{R}^{H*W*D} \tag{1}$$

where H, W, and D are the height, width and depth of the CT.MRI scan. For each convolutional layer l, the transformation is represented as follows

$$X^{(l)} = \sigma\left(BN\left(W^{(l)} * X^{(l-1)} + b^{(l)}\right)\right) \tag{2}$$

where $X^{(0)} = X_{\text{img}}$, $*$ denotes the 3D convolution operation, $W^{(l)}, b^{(l)}$ are the weights and biases of layer l, BN is the batch normalization, and σ is the ReLU activation function. Hierarchical spatial features are extracted by stacking many of these layers.

The output tensor is flattened following the last convolutional layer, L

$$f_{\text{flat}} = \text{Flatten}\left(X^{(l)}\right) \tag{3}$$

A dense (FC) layer is traversed by the flattened vector and it is represented as follows:

$$z_{\text{img}} = \varnothing(W_{\text{fc}} \cdot f_{\text{flat}} + b_{\text{fc}}) \tag{4}$$

where $\varnothing$ is a nonlinear activation (ReLU or tan h) and $W_{\text{fc}}, b_{\text{fc}}$ are the weights and bias of the FC layer. The output is given by

$$z_{\text{img}} \in \mathbb{R}^k \tag{5}$$

The fixed-length image-derived embedding that captures neuroanatomical information is this final vector, z_{img}.

3.3.2 Graph Neural Network (GNN) for Clinical Data

Clinical information is represented by modeling with a GNN, with each patient as a node and edges representing clinical similarity, that is, Euclidean distance in normalized space of variables like age, laboratory values, and comorbidities. Each of the nodes is preloaded with a feature vector containing vitals, lab results, and categorical indicators of conditions such as hypertension or atrial fibrillation. Through iterative graph convolution operations, the GNN aggregates information from neighboring patients, enabling the model to learn relational patterns between clinically similar patients. The final node embedding z_{clin} summarizes the clinical profile in a latent space that captures complex inter-patient dependencies relevant to outcome prediction [25]. Let the clinical dataset be represented as a graph

$$G = (V, E) \tag{6}$$

where V is the set of nodes (patients) and E is the set of edges representing clinical similarity. Let $\mathrm{X} \in \mathbb{R}^{N*d}$, an input feature matrix, where each row $x_i \in\uparrow \mathbb{R}^d$ represents a patient's clinical features. Let $A \in \mathbb{R}^{N*N}$ adjacency matrix of the graph, where $a_{ij} = 1 = 1$, if node I sis connected to node j.0 otherwise. The self-loop is added as follows: $\hat{A} = A + I$ and the degree matrix $\hat{D}_{ij} = \sum_j \hat{a}_{ij}$.

A single GCN layer updates the node features as follows:

$$H^{(1)} = \sigma(\hat{D}^{-\frac{1}{2}}\hat{A}\hat{D}^{-\frac{1}{2}}XW^{(0)}) \tag{7}$$

where $W^{(0)} \in \mathbb{R}^{d*h}$ is the learnable weight matrix, and $\sigma(\cdot)$ is the nonlinear activation function (e.g., ReLU). The process is repeated for L layers as follows:

$$H^{(l+)} = \sigma\left(\hat{D}^{-\frac{1}{2}}\hat{A}\hat{D}^{-\frac{1}{2}}XW^{(l)}\right);\ H^{(0)} = X \tag{8}$$

The final node embedding after L GNN layers c for each patient node is

$$Z_{\text{clin},i} = H_i^{(L)} \in \mathbb{R}^k \tag{9}$$

where $z_{\text{clin},i}$ is the learned embedding for the ith patient that summarizes clinical information and neighborhood influence. The graph embedding output is specified as follows:

$$Z_{\text{clin}} = H^{(L)} \in \mathbb{R}^{N*k} \tag{10}$$

Subsequent tasks like classification and fusion use this embedding matrix.

3.3.3 Clinical Feature Projection Using Traditional ML

In parallel, a selected set of handcrafted clinical features, such as stroke subtype, prior transient ischemic attacks (TIA), and pre-existing conditions, are fed into a ML model LightGBM [26]. These models are adept at handling tabular data with high interpretability. The outputs of these models are a probability vector representing risk predictions is then transformed into a dense embedding vector, z_{ml} using a learnable projection layer. This step ensures compatibility with other latent vectors and integrates expert-driven features into the hybrid framework. The manually created clinical feature vector, represented as follows:

$$X_{\text{ml}} \in \mathbb{R}^d \tag{11}$$

which captures structured, manually curated patient information that are essential for stroke outcome prediction. These features are categorical and binary variables like stroke subtype (e.g., cardioembolic and thrombotic), history of previous episodes of TIA, and established risk factors or comorbidities like diabetes and hypertension. These domain-knowledge-informed features are selected on the basis of clinical significance and act as a starting point input to conventional ML algorithms, providing interpretability and taking advantage of expert knowledge to improve prediction quality. The handcrafted feature vector X_{ml} is passed into a traditional classifier. For a gradient-boosted decision tree model LightBGM:

$$\hat{p} = f_{\text{LGBM}}(X_{\text{ml}}) \in \mathbb{R}^C \tag{12}$$

where f_{LGBM} is the trained model that outputs class probabilities through an ensemble of decision trees. The probability vector $\hat{p}$ is transformed using a learnable linear transformation to create a dense embedding vector, which is then used to integrate the ML output with DL components:

$$Z_{\mathrm{ml}} = \sigma(W_{\mathrm{ml}}\hat{p} + b_{\mathrm{ml}}) \in \mathbb{R}^k \tag{13}$$

where $W_{\mathrm{ml}}\mathbb{C} \in \mathbb{R}^{k*C}$ is the learnable weight matrix, $b_{\mathrm{ml}} \in \mathbb{R}^k$ is the bias term, and σ is the activation function (ReLU or tan h). In the hybrid feature fusion layer, the resultant vector $Z_{\mathrm{ml}} \in \mathbb{R}^k$ becomes the conventional ML-derived latent representation, prepared for concatenation.

3.3.4 Hybrid Feature Fusion Layer

In hybrid feature fusion, the embeddings are computed across three heterogeneous pathways, Z_{img} from image data processing through CNN, Z_{clin} from clinical relation modeling through GNN, and z_{ml} from vanilla ML pipeline and these are fused together into a holistic composite vector, represented as z_{fused}. The combined representation employs complementary data modalities and combines spatial, relational, and hand-designed features in a shared latent space. The subsequent vector is then input to a multilayer perceptron (MLP) with dropout regularization and batch normalization. Dropout avoids overfitting by randomly removing neurons during training, and batch normalization stabilizes and accelerates training by normalizing layer inputs. This hybridization technique of merging various forms of features allows the network to integrate various forms of features in a seamless manner to generate stronger and more precise predictions for risk stratification and outcome prediction of function.

The following is a representation of the hybrid feature fusion process. Let the following be the learned embeddings from the respective subsystems:

$$Z_{\mathrm{img}} \in R^{d_1} \tag{14}$$

Equation (14) represents the image-derived embedding from 3D CNN:

$$Z_{\mathrm{clin}} \in R^{d_2} \tag{15}$$

Equation (15) represents the clinical relational embedding form GNN:

$$Z_{\mathrm{mln}} \in R^{d_3} \tag{16}$$

Equation (16) represents the traditional ML embedding.

The hybrid fused representation Z_{fused} is formed by concatenating the three embeddings:

$$Z_{\text{fused}} = [Z_{\text{img}}||Z_{\text{clin}}||z_{\text{ml}}] \in \mathbb{R}^{d_1+d_2+d_3} \tag{17}$$

Next, a MLP with dropout and batch normalization is applied to this fused vector:

$$h_1 = ReLU(BN_1(W_1 z_{\text{fused}} + b_1)) \tag{18}$$

$$h_1^{\text{drop}} = \text{Dropout}(h_1, p) \tag{19}$$

$$h_2 = ReLU(BN_2(W_2 z_{\text{fused}} + b_2)) \tag{20}$$

where W_1, W_2 are the weight matrices, b_1, b_2 are the biases, BN_1, BN_2 are the batch normalization functions, and p is the drop out probability. During the multitask learning phase, final predictions are made using this MLP output h_2

3.3.5 Multitask Learning

The proposed architecture features a two-task learning process between two task-specific output layers which have the capability of optimizing two clinically useful goals concurrently. Risk stratification is associated with the first output layer that specifies low, medium, or high risk levels for the patients through a softmax activation. This is able to enable the model to produce class probabilities so class probabilities may be outputted by the model for more understandable risk estimations. The second output layer for mRS score prediction is handled as an ordinal regression task to honor the ordered nature of the mRS. Methods like CORAL (cumulative ordinal regression) or deep ordinal regression are used to learn from this ordinal output in an efficient way. The ultimate training goal is guided by an aggregate loss function, expressed as follows:

$$\mathcal{L} = \alpha.\mathcal{L}_{\text{risk}} + \beta.\mathcal{L}_{\text{outcome}} \tag{21}$$

Here, α and β are hyperparameters that can be tuned to adjust the two-task contribution. The model is capable of leveraging shared representations and task-specific learning at the same time by optimizing the two tasks jointly, and accordingly the better generalization and prediction performance will be achieved for risk classification and functional outcome prediction [27].

3.3.6 Model Integration and Output

At the last phase of integration, learned representations of three different model pieces z_{img} (embedding image-derived), z_{clin} (graph-based embedding clinical), and z_{ML} (regular ML-derived embedding) are fused together to construct a unified single vector reflecting a patient's total health profile. The aggregated feature vector holds information about spatial patterns of images, inter-patient clinical connections, and structured domain-knowledge aware features. The joint representation is fed into a multilayer feedforward neural network, with the objective to carry out dual-task learning. The first task is risk stratification, posed as a multiclass classification task to predict low, medium, or high risk of bad outcomes. The second task is prediction of functional outcome, represented as an ordinal regression task to target the mRS, an ordered scale from 0 (no symptoms) to 6 (death). This unified framework allows the model to learn both common patterns across tasks as well as task-specific features, which improves its predictive performance and generalizability in clinical applications.

4 Results and Findings

Performance of the hybrid model is strictly tested on stratified fivefold cross-validation so that there is an even class distribution of outcomes for training and validation splits. In the task of risk stratification, performance is measured with AUC-ROC, a threshold-independent assessment of the capacity of the model to discriminate between classes, and F_1-score, which optimizes precision and recall to express classification accuracy in imbalanced scenarios. For predicting mRS score, mean absolute error (MAE) measures the average size of prediction errors, indicating precision of the model in functional outcome estimation. QWK also assesses the concordance between predicted and real mRS scores considering ordinal scale and penalizing greater discrepancies more. Overall, these measures supply a complete valuation of the model's discriminability, predictive performance, and clinician usability.

The suggested hybrid model and four other methods are among the five models whose quantitative performance comparison is shown in Table 1. It uses four primary metrics to assess each model:

AUC-ROC (risk stratification)

It assesses how well the model can differentiate across classifications such as low and high risk. The true positive rate (TPR) versus false positive rate (FPR) is given by

$$\mathrm{TPR} = \frac{\mathrm{TP}}{\mathrm{TP}+\mathrm{FN}},\ \mathrm{FPR} = \frac{\mathrm{FP}}{\mathrm{FP}+\mathrm{TN}} \tag{22}$$

The ROC curve's integral, or AUC, is usually calculated mathematically (e.g., by applying the trapezoidal rule).

F_1-score (risk stratification): It strikes a balance between classification accuracy and recall (used here for risk categorization). It is computed as follows:

$$F_1 - \mathrm{score} = 2\ast\frac{\mathrm{Precision} \times \mathrm{Recall}}{\mathrm{Precision} + \mathrm{Recall}} \tag{23}$$

where the precision and recall is given as follows:

$$\text{Precision} = \frac{\text{TP}}{\text{TP} + \text{FP}}, \text{Recall} = \frac{\text{TP}}{\text{TP} + \text{FN}} \tag{24}$$

Mean absolute error (mRS prediction): It calculates the average absolute error between the mRS scores that were anticipated and those that were obtained:

$$\text{MAE} = \frac{1}{n}\sum_{i=1}^{n}|y_i - \hat{y}_i| \tag{25}$$

where y_i is the actual mRS score, $\hat{y}_i$ is the predicted mRS score, and n is the number of samples.

QWK (mRS prediction): It compares the ground truth to a model or two raters' agreement for ordinal classifications such as mRS scores:

$$k = 1 - \frac{\sum_{ij} w_{i,j} O_{i,j}}{\sum_{ij} w_{i,j} E_{i,j}} \tag{26}$$

where $O_{i,j}$ is the observed agreement matrix, $E_{i,j}$ is the expected agreement matrix, and $w_{i,j}$ is the quadratic weight and it is specified as follows:

$$w_{i,j} = \frac{(i-j)^2}{(k-1)^2} \tag{27}$$

As an example, mRS scores from 0 to 6 → $k = 7$, where k is the number of categories. The QWK scale goes from −1 (total disagreement) to 1 (perfect agreement), where 0 denotes agreement at the chance level.

Table 1: Performance analysis – proposed hybrid method.

Model	AUC-ROC (risk strat.)	F_1-score (risk strat.)	MAE (mRS prediction)	QWK (mRS prediction)
Proposed hybrid model (CNN + GNN + ML)	0.92	0.85	0.42	0.84
Logistic regression	0.76	0.68	0.61	0.62
Random forest	0.81	0.73	0.55	0.70
Deep CNN (imaging-only)	0.78	0.71	0.50	0.68
Multimodal ensemble	0.88	0.80	0.45	0.78

The proposed hybrid model demonstrates the best overall performance across all evaluation metrics, with an AUC-ROC of 0.92 and an F_1-score of 0.85 in risk stratification, indicating high discriminatory power and precision in categorizing patients into appropriate risk levels. For functional outcome prediction (mRS), it achieves the lowest MAE (0.42) and the highest QWK (0.84), reflecting both accuracy and strong agreement with actual outcomes. This superior performance is attributed to the integrated architecture, which fuses deep imaging features, graph-based clinical relationships, and machine-learned handcrafted features into a shared latent space. The hybrid model captures complex, nonlinear interactions across data modalities, offering a holistic understanding of stroke recovery trajectories.

The LR model, serving as the baseline, yields the lowest scores across all metrics, with an AUC-ROC of 0.76, F_1-score of 0.68, MAE of 0.61, and QWK of 0.62. Its linear nature limits its ability to model complex, nonlinear relationships common in stroke data, particularly when interactions between clinical and imaging features are critical. Despite being interpretable and computationally efficient, LR lacks the capacity to process high-dimensional or multimodal inputs effectively, resulting in poor predictive performance for both risk and functional outcomes.

RF performs moderately well, with an AUC-ROC of 0.81 and F_1-score of 0.73 for risk stratification, along with a MAE of 0.55 and QWK of 0.70 for mRS prediction. It improves upon LR by handling nonlinearities and feature interactions more effectively. However, as a purely tabular model, it lacks the ability to leverage unstructured data like imaging, which may limit its accuracy for clinical problems where visual patterns (e.g., lesion location or size) significantly influence outcomes. It also offers only moderate interpretability through FI measures.

The deep CNN model, trained solely on imaging data, achieves relatively good performance in outcome prediction (MAE: 0.50 and QWK: 0.68), suggesting that spatial and visual features in neuroimaging are informative for functional recovery. However, its AUC-ROC (0.78) and F_1-score (0.71) for risk stratification are lower, likely due to the absence of contextual clinical data such as age, comorbidities, or stroke severity scores. Without integrating clinical parameters, the CNN's view of the patient condition remains incomplete, and its performance suffers in tasks requiring broader context.

Multimodal ensemble model, a fusion of individual models' output trained on various data modalities, achieves an AUC-ROC of 0.88 and F_1-score of 0.80. It also achieves good functional prediction (MAE: 0.45 and QWK: 0.78). Although it capitalizes on the use of multiple sources of data, having a late fusion approach of aggregating predictions as opposed to features constrains rich cross-modal interaction. This model can possibly neglect detailed cross-modal patterns that the hybrid model would learn. Nevertheless, it performs better than single-modality models and shows the potential utility of multimodal methods.

Figure 2 illustrates that the suggested hybrid model (CNN + GNN + ML) possesses the best discriminative ability (0.92) for risk stratification. Conventional models such as LR (0.76) and RF(0.81) are far behind. Multimodal ensemble is competitive (0.88) but still falls short of the performance of the suggested model.

Figure 3 indicates that the suggested hybrid model performs best (0.85) in risk stratification, which also has better recall versus precision balance. Multimodal ensemble is ranked second with 0.80, while traditional models such as LR (0.68) and

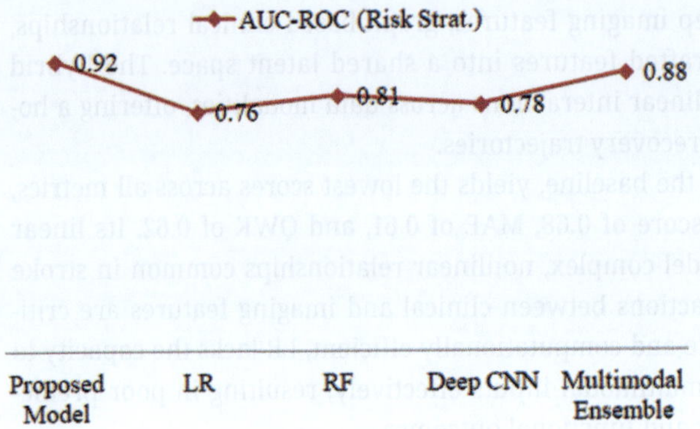

Figure 2: Performance analysis – proposed model – AUC-ROC.

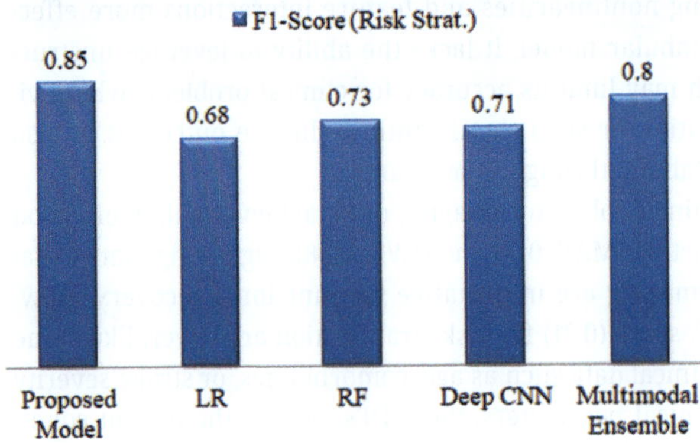

Figure 3: Performance analysis – proposed model – F_1-score.

deep CNN (0.71) perform lower. This illustrates the advantage of the combination of heterogeneous sources of data in the suggested strategy.

Figure 4 shows that the hybrid model of this work has the lowest error (0.42), which is the best functional outcome prediction. Multimodal ensemble also has low error (0.45), and baseline models such as LR(0.61) and RF(0.55) have higher prediction errors. It shows the strength of combining imaging, clinical, and ML features.

Figure 5 indicates that the model that disagrees the most with ground truth is in forecasting mRS at 0.84, indicating higher ordinal strength of prediction. Then comes the multimodal ensemble at 0.78, followed by basic models such as LR (0.62) and deep CNN (0.68). This indicates the power of the hybrid modeling framework in its ability to capture the delicacy of outcome severity.

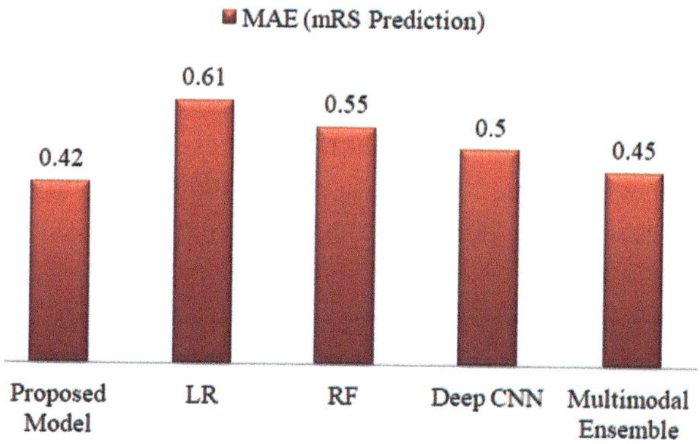

Figure 4: Performance analysis – proposed model – MAE.

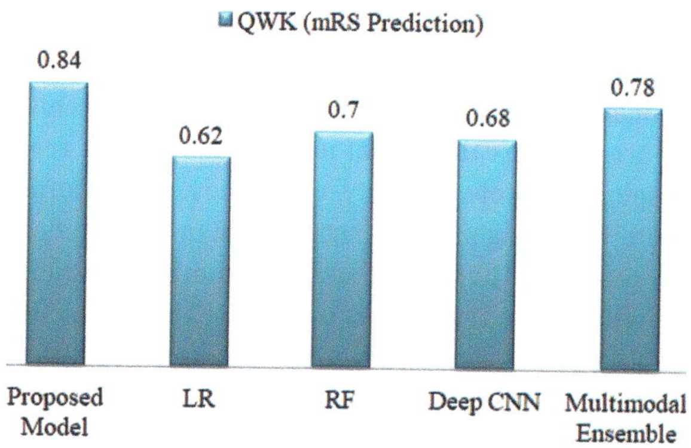

Figure 5: Performance analysis – proposed model – QWK.

5 Conclusion

A novel hybrid ML methodology is proposed toward overall risk stratification and prediction of function in stroke survivors. The model is an integration of DL, graph reasoning, and conventional ML under single model architecture. The suggested method is feasible to harness the full range of patient data available to us spanning from clinical parameters to imaging modalities without compromising accuracy. The improved performance of the model on a range of evaluation measures is supportive of the hypothesis that a hybrid approach is better suited to accommodate the heterogeneity and complexity entailed in poststroke recovery processes. In contrast to standard models, the hybrid system outlined here had considerably improved AUC-ROC and QWK values, reflecting improved classification of both acute risk classes and longer-term functional outcomes. The incorporation of a GNN enabled the model to learn inter-patient patterns and similarities that are typically neglected by typical models, while the CNN module learned descriptive spatial features from image data strongly predictive of outcome trajectories. Their combination in a common latent space learned through multitask learning provided the model with robustness and generalization. Furthermore, this hybrid model represents a significant milestone in the direction of intelligent, data-informed stroke management through the delivery of precise, understandable, and personalized risk and outcome predictions toward ultimately better decision-making and patient care.

6 Future Directions

While the hybrid ML model envisioned in this work shows promising results, a number of future directions of research and development are present. First, broadening the data to cover additional heterogeneous patient populations across various hospitals and geographic areas would enhance generalizability and robustness. Multicenter validation trials need to be conducted to test the model under conditions of real-world clinical practice such as imaging protocol variability, electronic health records, and stroke practice. Second, temporal modeling must be incorporated to better reflect the dynamic progression of stroke recovery. The incorporation of recurrent or transformer modules can potentially predict recovery courses over time, and the model can be made increasingly useful for long-term care planning on a clinical basis. Other modalities of data like genetic biomarkers, blood proteomics, or speech/language testing could provide more relevant patient profiles and enhance predictive accuracy. Third, whereas existing approaches such as SHAP and Grad-CAM offer insight, there could be emphasis on creating domain-specific interpretability modules that follow clinical reasoning steps, to enable trust establishment and clinical adoption. Clinical workflow integration is also a top priority. Developing an intuitive, real-time software interface or decision support tool that can be directly integrated into hospital information systems would enable clinicians to use model predictions at high-stakes decision points, for example, during discharge planning or selecting rehabilitation strategy. Lastly, fairness and model bias ethics need to be stringently tested, especially in underrepresented groups. Ensuring transparency through open auditing procedures and fairness-aware training procedures will be needed as these systems proceed toward application in medicine.

References

[1] Asadi, F., Rahimi, M., Daeechini, A. H. & Paghe, A. (2024). The most efficient machine learning algorithms in stroke prediction: A systematic review. *Health Science Reports*, 7(10), e70062.

[2] Liu, Y., Shah, P., Yu, Y., Horsey, J., Ouyang, J., Jiang, B., Yang, G. et al. (2024). A clinical and imaging fused deep learning model matches expert clinician prediction of 90-day stroke outcomes. *American Journal of Neuroradiology*, 45(4), 406–411.

[3] Shurrab, S., Guerra-Manzanares, A., Magid, A., Bartlomiej Piechowski-Jozwiak, S. F. A. & Farah, E. S. "Multimodal machine learning for stroke prognosis and diagnosis: A system

[4] Fernandes, J. N. D., Cardoso, V. E. M., Comesaña-Campos, A. & Pinheira, A. (2024). Comprehensive Review: Machine and Deep Learning in Brain Stroke Diagnosis. *Sensors (Basel, Switzerland)*, 24(13), 4355.

[5] Borsos, B., Allaart, C. G. & Van halteren, A. (2024). Predicting stroke outcome: a case for multimodal deep learning methods with tabular and CT perfusion data. *Artificial Intelligence in Medicine*, 147, 102719.

[6] Mansour, A., Besbes, O. & Abdellatif, T. (2024). Federated Deep Learning Models for Stroke Prediction. In *International Conference on Web Information Systems Engineering* (pp. 440–454). Singapore: Springer Nature Singapore.

[7] Tiba, A., Bérczes, T., Bérczes, A. & Zsuga, J. (2024). Predicting Stroke Risk Based on ICD Codes Using Graph-Based Convolutional Neural Networks. *Mathematics*, 12(12), 1814.

[8] Le, T. P. T. & Duy Nguyen, V. M. (2024). LIGHTGBM-Based Machine Learning Model for Stroke Risk Prediction. *International Journal of Advances in Soft Computing & Its Applications*, 16(1).

[9] Brugnara, G., Neuberger, U., Mahmutoglu, M. A., Foltyn, M., Herweh, C., Nagel, S., Schönenberger, S. et al. (2020). Multimodal predictive modeling of endovascular treatment outcome for acute ischemic stroke using machine-learning. *Stroke*, 51(12), 3541–3551.

[10] Yu, H., Wang, Z., Sun, Y., Bo, W., Duan, K., Song, C., Hu, Y., Zhou, J., Mu, Z. & Wu, N. (2023). Prognosis of ischemic stroke predicted by machine learning based on multi-modal MRI radiomics. *Frontiers in Psychiatry*, 13, 1105496.

[11] Dev, S., Wang, H., Nwosu, C. S., Jain, N., Veeravalli, B. & John, D. (2022). A predictive analytics approach for stroke prediction using machine learning and neural networks. *Healthcare Analytics*, 2, 100032.

[12] Shih, D.-H., Wu, Y.-H., Wu, T.-W., Chu, H.-Y. & Shih, M.-H. (2024). Stroke Prediction Using Deep Learning and Transfer Learning Approaches. *IEEE Access*.

[13] Chen, C., Zhang, W., Pan, Y. & Li, Z. (2025). An interpretable hybrid machine learning approach for predicting three-month unfavorable outcomes in patients with acute ischemic stroke. *International Journal of Medical Informatics*, 105807.

[14] Sawan, A., Awad, M., Qasrawi, R. & Sowan, M. (2024). Hybrid deep learning and metaheuristic model based stroke diagnosis system using electroencephalogram (EEG). *Biomedical Signal Processing and Control*, 87, 105454.

[15] Bathla, P. & Kumar, R. (2024). A hybrid system to predict brain stroke using a combined feature selection and classifier. *Intelligent Medicine*, 4(02), 75–82.

[16] Mia, R., Khanam, S., Mahjabeen, A., Ovy, N. H., Ghimire, D., Park, M.-J., Begum, M. I. A. & Hosen, A. S. M. S. (2024). Exploring machine learning for predicting cerebral stroke: a study in discovery. *Electronics*, 13(4), 686.

[17] Peng, G., Zhao, B. & Yuanzi, H. (2024). Integrated Classification Method with Hybrid Sampling for Stroke Prediction. In *Proceedings of the 2024 4th International Conference on Artificial Intelligence, Big Data and Algorithms* (pp. 393–397).

[18] Agana, M. A. & Odey, J. A. (2024). Anthony Okwori Okpe, and Ofem Ajah Ofem "Optimization of Stroke Prediction Model using a Hybrid of Heterogeneous Ensemble Machine Learning Techniques. In *2024 IST-Africa Conference (IST-Africa)* (pp. 1–12). IEEE.

[19] Oluwatosin, E. A., Sotonwa, K. A., Raji-Lawal, H. Y., Zubair, A. F. & Alegbhele, I. B. (2024). A Hybrid Approach to Developing a Stroke Prediction System. *University of Ibadan Journal of Science and Logics in ICT Research*, 12(1), 65–73.

[20] Luo, J., Dai, P., He, Z., Huang, Z., Liao, S. & Liu, K. (2024). Deep learning models for ischemic stroke lesion segmentation in medical images: a survey. *Computers in biology and medicine*, 108509.

[21] Abujaber, A. A., Albalkhi, I., Imam, Y., Yaseen, S., Nashwan, A. J., Akhtar, N. & Alkhawaldeh, I. M. (2025). Machine learning-based prediction of 90-day prognosis and in-hospital mortality in hemorrhagic stroke patients. *Scientific Reports*, 15(1), 1–12.

[22] Sommer, J., Dierksen, F., Zeevi, T., Tran, A. T., Avery, E. W., Mak, A., Malhotra, A. et al. (2024). Deep learning for prediction of post-thrombectomy outcomes based on admission CT angiography in large vessel occlusion stroke. *Frontiers in Artificial Intelligence*, 7, 1369702.

[23] Sha, M. (2025). A graph neural network technique for the prediction of cerebral stroke using an unbalanced medical dataset. *Multimedia Tools and Applications*, 1–37.

[24] Sakri, S., Basheer, S., Zain, Z. M., Ismail, N. H. A., Nassar, D., Aldehim, G. N. & Alharaki, M. A. (2024). An improved concatenation of deep learning models for predicting and interpreting ischemic stroke. *IEEE Access*, 12, 53189–53204.

[25] Aouthu, S., Suman, S. K., Anuradha, S. & Sanapala, R. K. (2025). Automated Diagnosis of Acute Cerebral Ischemic Stroke Lesions using Capsule Graph Neural Networks from Diffusion-weighted MRI Scans. *Journal of Electrical Engineering & Technology*, 1–20.

[26] Le, N.-B., Pham, T. T. H., Nguyen, S. H., Nguyen, N. M. & Nguyen, T. N. (2024). AI-powered predictive model for stroke and diabetes diagnostic. *International Journal of Intelligent Systems and Applications (IJISA)*, 16(1), 24–40.

[27] Nguyen, T. N. Q., García-Rudolph, A., Saurí, J. & Kelleher, J. D. (2024). Multi-task learning for predicting quality-of-life and independence in activities of daily living after stroke: a proof-of-concept study. *Frontiers in Neurology*, 15, 1449234.

Fathimathul Rajeena P. P.*, Rahoof P. P., and Sunder R.

Data-Driven Machine Learning Strategies for Oncological Disease Prediction and Early-Stage Detection

Abstract: Early prediction and early diagnosis of oncological diseases are vital concerns for contemporary medicine, especially due to the heterogeneity of cancer and the extensive related clinical information. Here is a comprehensive data-driven machine learning (ML) approach specifically tailored for prediction and precursor and oncological disease detection in the initial phase. The approach combines different modalities of data, such as clinical data, imaging data, genomic profiles, and biomarker data, to make use of the entire array of patient-specific and disease-specific features. The suggested framework consists of an end-to-end data preprocessing pipeline, sophisticated feature selection methods, and building a hybrid ensemble of ML classifiers. Traditional classifiers like logistic regression, random forest, and XGBoost are blended with deep learning-based models like convolutional neural networks for imaging data and recurrent neural networks for longitudinal data. The performance of the model is strictly evaluated based on k-fold cross-validation and common performance metrics like accuracy, precision, recall, and F_1-score. Outcomes show that the novel hybrid ensemble method outperforms traditional and single-modality models in prediction, with better sensitivity and accuracy in identifying oncological cancers and their precursors at earlier stages. This is suggestive that ML techniques derived from data can be employed to improve early cancer detection and support clinical decision-making. The strategy provides a scalable and flexible platform applicable to diverse oncologic uses and facilitates the big picture of precision oncology through predictive analytics.

Keywords: machine learning, oncological diseases, XGBoost, convolutional neural networks, long short-term networks

Acknowledgment: This work was supported by the Deanship of Scientific Research, Vice Presidency for Graduate Studies and Scientific Research, King Faisal University, Saudi Arabia (grant no. KFU252022).

***Corresponding author: Fathimathul Rajeena P. P.,** Department of Computer Science, College of Computer Science and Information Technology, King Faisal University, Alhasa 31982, Saudi Arabia, e-mail: fatimah.rajeena@kfu.edu.sa
Rahoof P. P., Department of Computer Science and Engineering (Cybersecurity), Malabar Institute of Technology (MIT), Anjarakandy Integrated Campus, Kannur 670612, Kerala, India, e-mail: rahoof@mitkannur.ac.in
Sunder R., School of Computer Science and Engineering, Galgotias University, Greater Noida, Uttar Pradesh, India, e-mail: sunder.r@galgotiasuniversity.edu.in

https://doi.org/10.1515/9783111541235-005

1 Introduction

Cancer remains one of the most powerful health problems of the twenty-first century, with high fatality, multifactorial genesis, and great heterogeneity of patients and tumors [1]. Early detection of the disease and prediction of oncological diseases are extremely significant for improving patient outcomes, delivering timely treatment, and improving survival. However, cancer heterogeneity, driven by different molecular, genetic, and clinical patterns, makes early-stage marker identification and disease courses challenging [2]. Also, the vast and multidimensional nature of clinical, imaging, genomic, and biomarker data in oncology necessitates advanced analysis platforms that are capable of gathering, processing, and interpreting such multimodal data. Traditional diagnosis techniques and single-modality prediction models commonly are not able to grasp all the varied aspects of cancer-related variables and thereby suggest the need for a broader and intelligent data-driven system [3].

In order to overcome these hurdles, this research introduces an end-to-end ML-based platform that utilizes the entire power of multimodal health data to forecast oncological disease onset and development in the early stages. Through integration of heterogeneous data sources such as electronic health records [4], radiology images [5], genomic sequences [6], and molecular biomarker profiles [7]. This platform uses patient-specific as well as disease-specific knowledge in order to provide a higher-quality and individualized forecasting system. ML and DL paradigms together present an opportunity to encode this complexity in the correct way and build strong prediction systems that can generalize across diverse oncological scenarios [8].

A key component of the suggested framework is an end-to-end data preprocessing pipeline which includes support for data quality, consistency, and model-readiness. The preprocessing contains missing value imputation, normalization, feature encoding, and data augmentation each being appropriate to the input data type [9]. For example, image data is spatially normalized and augmented with techniques such as rotation and contrast scaling, whereas genomic data is filtered, mutation-encoded, and dimensionally reduced with techniques such as principal component analysis [10]. Clinical laboratory results and biomarker data are made standard and cleansed using medically knowledge-based imputations that provide clinically realistic input without undermining the integrity of the patient records. This preprocessing pipeline is essential to supplying the downstream models with tidy, well-formatted, and informative data that enhance learning performance and interpretability.

The system's feature selection (FS) module integrates a hybrid approach based on the use of filter methods [11] such as mutual information and chi-squared tests, wrapper methods [12] such as recursive feature elimination (RFE), and embedded methods [13] such as LASSO regularization and tree-based feature importance of RFs. It identifies the most informative and less redundant features across modalities by reducing model complexity while maintaining high predictive power. The model thus retains only the strongest predictive patterns with cancer risk and disease development, thereby improving performance and generalizability.

The modeling pipeline is a deep-classical hybrid ensemble. Classical ML models like logistic regression (LR) [14], RF [15], and XGBoost are employed because they can process tabular and structured clinical data. Such models provide excellent interpretability, deployment simplicity, and resistance to overfitting, which are adequate for decision support systems in clinical environments. Meanwhile, DL models process unstructured data: hierarchical spatial contexts in imaging data like CT or MRI scans by convolutional neural networks (CNNs) [16] and temporal contexts in longitudinal patient data and treatment histories by recurrent neural networks, for example, long short-term memory (LSTM) [17] units. This labor division between model types ensures that each modality is handled by the optimum algorithm, best performance.

For further improvement in predictive stability and reliability, predictions from individual models are averaged out in an ensemble methodology. Methods like model stacking and weighted voting are used to aggregate the predictions together in such a way that the resulting conclusion is enriched with the advantages of each individual contributing model. Additionally, a meta-learner is also learned over the output of the said base models, enhancing the final prediction and minimizing variance of each individual model. This ensemble strategy enhances the system to make more stable and confident predictions as well as identify fine patterns on diversified data types compared to single models.

The hybrid ensemble architecture is thoroughly tested for performance to make it generalizable and non-overfitting. Common evaluation metrics such as accuracy, precision, recall, and F_1-score are employed to measure the performance of the models. The proposed scheme outperforms the traditional ML techniques and deep neural networks when they are utilized separately. Specifically, it has higher sensitivity and specificity in cancer disease and precursor diagnosis at more advanced intelligence levels, and it is therefore an applicable tool in early diagnosis and preventive clinical therapy.

This study proposes a novel and comprehensive ML approach that sufficiently tackles the problem of multimodal early cancer diagnosis with robust data fusion and hybrid modeling. Under a single predictive framework, which integrates conventional and DL approaches, the system is very efficient, adaptable, and clinically relevant. The findings highlight the possibilities of change with AI-driven predictive analytics in oncology as a feasible route to the fulfillment of early diagnosis, individualized treatment, and enhanced patient outcomes. The study objectives are as follows:

- To develop an integrated multimodal data model by integrating various types of patient-specific and disease-specific data.
- To develop a stable end-to-end data preprocessing pipeline for heterogeneous, high-dimensional oncological data.
- To develop a hybrid ensemble ML architecture by integrating common classifiers (e.g., LR, RF, and XGBoost) with DL algorithms (with CNN for imaging data and LSTM for longitudinal data) to leverage the particular strengths of each algorithm for addressing different data modalities.

2 Related Works

Cancer is still a major disease globally, and breast, ovarian, and colorectal cancer have been particularly challenging to diagnose because of late presentation and multifactorial clinical presentation. In recent years, advances in AI, including ML and DL, have made it possible to design highly effective diagnostic systems that are more accurate, scalable, and interpretable. Ensemble and hybrid models integrating genomic, imaging, and clinical data are also promising for early diagnosis and risk assessment. This section presents new AI-driven approaches for various cancers and how they can help clinicians make timely evidence-based decisions and improve patient care through precision diagnosis.

2.1 Integrative Genomics for Cancer Prediction

Breast cancer (BC) is still a major worldwide health concern, which means that precise biomarkers are necessary for early detection and targeted therapy. In order to find reliable indicators and possible treatment targets for BC, this work offers an integrative ML approach for evaluating gene expression data. Gene expression datasets were preprocessed and merged to allow for a comprehensive differential expression analysis of tumor and normal samples. In the current study, there were 164 DEGs in the combined dataset and 350 DEGs in an external dataset (GSE45827). In an effort to improve predictive gene selection further, a new hybrid algorithm was conceived, namely BGWO_SA_Ens, combining binary Grey Wolf optimization (BGWO), simulated annealing (SA), and an ensemble classification model. When used for both the datasets, this method efficiently screened thousands of genes and selected 1,404 predictive features from the integrated dataset. Intersections of DEGs with BGWO_SA_Ens yielded a robust list of 35 highly consistent genes. Functional enrichment analysis established that these genes are significant and actively involved in core signaling pathways, which is highly correlated with cancer pathogenesis. Further, protein-protein interaction (PPI) network analysis identified biologically significant subnetworks and hub genes and indicated their functional connectivity. In addition, a drug-gene interaction analysis placed some of the more successful genes onto existing anticancer drugs, translating to clinical therapy relevance. In all, the ML pipeline described herein effectively identified a very active gene signature with both diagnostic and therapeutic relevance, highlighting the value of computational methods in advancing precision oncology [18].

2.2 Ovarian Cancer Risk Prediction Model

Ovarian cancer (OC) is a highly virulent and disseminated malignancy with a high prevalence of late diagnosis, posing an important public health problem with limited preventive methods. Early detection of high-risk patients with predictive screening is an underutilized yet possibly game-changing strategy. This retrospective data analysis used clinical histories of 1,516 women suspected of having OC, collected at six healthcare centers in Sari City from 2015 to 2019. Six ML models were applied to develop predictive models for OC risk prediction: XGBoost, RF, J48, SVM, KNN, and ANN. Model performance was evaluated with AU-ROC and the XGBoost provides the best performance with an AU-ROC of 0.93. The findings indicate the utility of ML being a valid and efficient approach to identifying high-risk OC groups, hence enabling more effective and targeted prevention measures in clinical practice [19].

2.3 AI-Driven Precision Diagnosis in Breast Cancer

Advancements in AI and ML have significantly impacted precision medicine, particularly for BC diagnosis and therapy. From vast genomic, imaging, and clinical databases, AI algorithms make precise tumor detection, identification, and predictive value of outcomes compared to traditional diagnostic processes. ML methods, specifically DL systems, reveal sophisticated patterns in multimodal data and enable the generation of personalized and directed treatment protocols. Applicability of AI to BC care is discussed by this review with examples of cutting-edge solutions, overcoming significant challenges to deployment in the clinic and achieving a perspective of future directions in research. Through comparison of data-driven approaches, it recognizes their contribution toward enabling early diagnosis, supporting clinical decisions, and ultimately benefiting patients [20].

2.4 Colorectal Chemotherapy Toxicity Prediction Model

ML algorithms reveal patterns within data through the identification of feature correlations and predictive insight into intricate clinical situations. The research pursued building a predictive model for recognizing colorectal cancer patients who are more likely to develop chemotherapy-induced toxicity and distinguishing the characteristics responsible for inducing the risk of side effects of treatment. Using a dataset of 95 pretreatment health features from 74 patients, we have trained RF models with appropriate preprocessing to achieve a compromise between interpretability and predictive performance. The model successfully detected the relative contribution of numerical and categorical variables toward predicting toxicity outcome. The findings highlight the promise of integrating AI into colorectal cancer management, offering a personalized approach to anticipate and prevent treatment toxicities, advancing the boundary of precision medicine [21].

2.5 Hybrid Approach to Mammogram-Based Cancer Classification

BC, the leading cancer in the world involving more than 2.3 million women, is still a major public health problem. In spite of the fact that survival rates have been increasing because of enhanced screening, diagnosis, and treatment, early detection continues to be paramount in effective management of the condition. In order to improve the identification and classification rate of BC lesions on mammograms, a unique hybrid model utilizing DL and sophisticated image-preprocessing techniques is proposed in this study. The dataset of 20,000 mammograms was used to validate the model. To improve image quality and enable improved feature extraction, it was first preprocessed utilizing image-enhancement operators such as Gaussian Blur and Sharpening, YOLOv5 and MedSAM segmentation models were used in the DL architecture to facilitate lesion extraction, categorization, and appropriate display. Following a clinical evaluation on 800 patients, the blended model produced extremely high improvements in diagnostic speed and accuracy. The model only took 0.75 s to process each image, achieving a 99.7% global accuracy. In terms of clinical accuracy, it was 98.6% for malignant cases and 97.2% for benign ones. According to these findings, the hybrid model is a reliable and efficient diagnostic tool for early BC recognition with promising opportunities for clinical practice improvements in terms of diagnostic accuracy [22].

2.6 Stacked Ensemble for Breast Cancer

BC is among the most common cancers globally, only surpassed by lung cancer, and occurs in both women and men. Being largely asymptomatic during its initial stages, its detection becomes a challenge at an early stage, which usually ends up in late-stage diagnosis that is more difficult and expensive to treat, hence contributing to increased mortality. In spite of an increasing use of ML in cancer studies, there have been comparatively fewer studies on ensemble learning methods for the prediction of BC versus single-classifier systems. The study suggests a heterogeneous ensemble ML architecture aiming to assist early detection of BC. The proposed model uses a stacking ensemble with KNN, SVM, and DT as foundation learners in accordance with the CRISP-DM methodology. A homogeneous ensemble model called RF as well as various standalone classifiers like LR, ANN, NB, stochastic gradient descent, and its separate base models (KNN, SVM, and DT) are used to evaluate the effectiveness of this meta-classifier. The five most important features were selected for prediction using the chi-square approach. Accuracy, F_1-score, precision, recall, specificity, log loss, AUC, and ROC curve are the metrics used to assess the model's performance using K-fold cross-validation. The null hypothesis was rejected by the proposed ensemble model at $K = 20$, which had a minimum log loss of 0.56 and a maximum accuracy of 78%. The p-value of 0.014, obtained from a one-tailed t-test, was statistically significant at the $\alpha = 0.05$ level. All of these results suggest that the ensemble approach may be effective in predicting BC early on using only biochemical and anthropometric characteristics [23].

2.7 Deep Ensembles for Cancer Diagnosis

A novel deep hybrid heterogeneous ensemble model has been suggested for histological BC image classification with the aim of supporting pathologists in detecting malignancies and guiding appropriate treatment measures. The method combines seven strong pretrained DL models for strong feature extraction with four classical classifiers (multilayer perceptron, SVM, KNN, and decision tree) using hard and weighted voting techniques. Twenty-four ensemble hybrid models were tested and compared with deep stacked ensemble baselines to find the best ensemble method. Empirical verification was performed on the public BreakHis dataset at four magnification levels (40×, 100×, 200×, and 400×) with fivefold cross-validation. The introduced hybrid ensembles were found to perform better than individual and stacked models with a maximum accuracy of up to 96.3% at several magnifications. These results highlight the clinical value of deep ensemble models in enhancing histological BC diagnosis and minimizing diagnostic errors [24].

2.8 Hybrid CNN-GRU Model for Breast Cancer Detection

BC is an adenocarcinoma that occurs in the tissue of the breast and remains one of the most prevalent cancers in women, after lung cancer in terms of mortality rates. Early detection and correct classification of BC are crucial for improving the treatment. Manual examination of histopathological slides, however, is usually time-consuming, cumbersome, and subject to operator errors, thus potentially resulting in misclassification. To alleviate these challenges, this study suggests a hybrid DL model that integrates CNNs into computer-aided detection of BC invasive ductal cancer (IDC) based on the detection of a computer-assisted recovery unit (GRU) of BC based on the entire foil image (WSI) from PCAM-Kaggle data. The proposed CNN GRU model uses the CNN characteristic extraction ability and GRU time learning ability to isolate IDC negative samples from IDC positives. This model was tested using common measures. It leads to accuracy of 86.21%, accuracy of 85.50%, sensitivity rate of 85.60%, accuracy of 84.71%, F_1-score of 88%, AUC accuracy of 0.89, minimizing diagnostic errors and increasing classification acid crisis. The strength and efficiency of developed hybrid models are evaluated using BC identification compared to other DL architectures such as CNN-BiLSTM, CNN-LSTM, and current ML methods [25].

2.9 Robust Ensemble Breast Cancer Classifier

BC is a prevalent and life-threatening condition evidencing the importance of accurate and efficient methods of diagnosis to aid the treatment of patients. DL and ML have been major contributors to optimizing the detection of BC in terms of enhanced accuracy, automation, and support in the diagnostic process. Yet, most existing approaches remain plagued by problems related to scalability and performance in general. In order to address these limitations, this study presents a reliable hybrid detection approach that combines a pretrained deep ResNet50V2 model with ML ensemble-based classifiers. The DL component provides the functionality to extract discriminative and descriptive features of breast histopathology images, while the ML ensemble provides the functionality of model explainability as well as better generalization. The suggested approach was applied on a publicly available dataset of IDC histopathological images consisting of examples of different sizes. Experimental outcomes verify that the hybrid method is superior to many state-of-the-art methods by far, with an accuracy rate of 95%. Out of the experimented classifiers, the light gradient boosting machine was most powerful in combination with ResNet50V2. The hybrid process is a high-performance, robust BC diagnostic tool that can potentially be used in real-world clinical situations. It facilitates clinicians to make speedy and high-confidence decisions [26].

Convergence of AI, DL, and ML into oncology has transformed cancer diagnosis, prognosis, and tailoring therapy. The series of studies discussed as a whole provides the scope and magnitude of AI-driven approaches to different cancers most importantly breast, ovarian, colorectal, and lung cancers. From genomics-based predictive models to clinical risk stratification and advanced image analysis, these AI platforms are increasingly proving their value in everyday clinical practice. Most importantly, holistic approaches like BGWO_SA_Ens in BC biomarker discovery and the hybrid CNN-GRU in IDC prediction both take advantage of biological intuition and computational effectiveness to achieve higher accuracy and predictive robustness. Similarly, ensemble methods ranging from classical ML stacks to deep ensemble networks that ensemble architectures like ResNet50, InceptionV3, and VGG16 all best individual models, a testament to hybridization's power in fault-tolerant diagnostic feature design.

In addition, application of FS techniques (e.g., chi-square and PPI analysis), image processing techniques (e.g., CLAHE, MedSAM, and YOLOv5), and statistical testing (e.g., *t*-tests and Borda count) assure scientific validity and clinical transibility of such models. Achievements like near-perfect F_1-scores (e.g., 0.981), AUC scores > 0.95, and consistent cross-validation accuracy scores per dataset and cancer type assure practicality of such models.

3 Methodology

The study is a comprehensive, data-driven ML model for prediction and early diagnosis of oncological pathology and precursors. Owing to the complexity and multidimensionality of data related to oncology, the study includes heterogeneous data like clinical reports, imaging data, genomic data, and biomarker datasets. The study involves routine data preprocessing, advanced FS methods and usage of diverse ML models for diverse data. In order to ensure a strong model that enhances prediction performance and reduces bias, ensemble learning method is used with blending of conventional ML methods, deep models, and recurrent networks for the study of longitudinal data. Utilizing multimodal integration of data as well as hybrid modeling techniques, the proposed approach aims to augment early detection capabilities and facilitate data-driven clinical decision-making in cancer. Figure 1 depicts the suggested method's overall workflow.

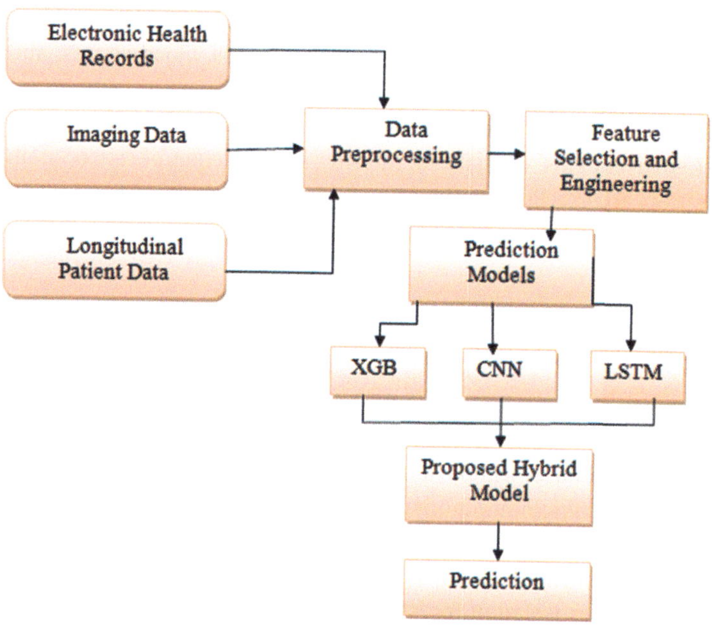

Figure 1: Overall proposed methodology for onco-related disease prediction.

3.1 Data Acquisition

A variety of datasets will be retrieved from public databases. The data types are given as follows:

Clinical Records: Clinical records hold patient-specific information that are critical including age, gender, medical history, comorbidities, and treatment outcomes. These variables have critical context to risk stratification and outcome prediction. Clinical variables will likely act as baseline predictors in oncology models. Adding them to the model increases model personalization and interpretability [27].

Imaging Data: Imaging data, MRI, CT, and histopathological images, record tumor morphology, location, and growth patterns. Imaging provides spatial and structural information that is essential for cancer detection and staging. DL architectures such as CNNs are best applied to computer-aided image feature extraction. Imaging data supplement clinical and genomic profiles to enable comprehensive diagnosis.

Genomic/Proteomic Data: Mutation status, protein biomarkers, and gene expression profiles comprise genomic and proteomic data. These are complex, high-dimensional molecular-level traits reflecting mutation-mediated disease processes and oncogenic routes. Because of their complexity and high dimensionality, sophisticated dimension reduction and FS methods are called for. Imposing them adds the capacity for precision oncology by virtue of personally specific, mutation-directed prediction.

Biomarker Data: Laboratory test results like tumor markers, blood counts, and metabolic profiles make up biomarker data. Physiological and biochemical alterations that accompany cancer are measured quantitatively by biomarkers that are readily available in clinical environments. Biomarkers improve the detection of cancer at an earlier stage. Biomarkers are excellent noninvasive disease markers for disease monitoring and the monitoring of the impact of therapy.

3.2 Data Preprocessing

As far as data consistency, data quality, and model stability are concerned, one will possess a data preprocessing pipeline of clean data before even starting model development. Missing data in the dataset will be managed by implementing the application of KNN imputation [28] or multiple imputation techniques depending on the type of data as well as its distribution without any loss or bias of data. Outliers that can potentially degrade model performance and interpretability will be detected and removed using methods such as isolation forest on multidimensional data or *Z*-score thresholding [29] for unidimensional distributions. Numerical variables will be normalized and standardized to a common range for purposes of making comparison comparable across factors and facilitating model convergence, especially for feature-magnitude-sensitive models. Categorical features will be encoded in one-hot encoding or target encoding depending on the variable cardinality and model requirement and made ML friendly. Rotation, flipping, and brightness will also be employed as data augmentation strategies for imaging datasets to augment the size of the dataset synthetically, enhance model generalizability, and avoid overfitting of deep learning (DL) models. This data preprocessing method is designed to optimize data integrity, optimize algorithmic efficiency, and offer robust, reproducible predictive model results.

3.3 Feature Selection and Engineering

FS will then be used to select the most significant predictors from among the vast pool of data. The individual significance of the continuous features and the categorical features, respectively, will first be measured using univariate statistical tests such as ANOVA and chi-square. RFE will next be used to build most important features iteratively based on model performance. Moreover, Ridge and Lasso regression will be used to impose feature regularization through removal of duplicate features through the penalization of the coefficients. Model-based FS will further be used using the importance score of the features generated by ensemble algorithms such as random forest or gradient boosting capable of nonlinear and interaction relationships.

Feature engineering will be utilized to refine the model further in order to find complex patterns. New composite features will be created through concatenation of existing features so that more useful relations are revealed and predictability is improved. To reduce high-dimensional data dimension, dimension-reduction techniques will be utilized for data exploration as well as removal of noise from data. Furthermore, sequence and genomic data will be investigated using embedding techniques for representation as dense vector representations that capture biological or time underlying patterns in raw genomic sequences or time-series clinical data. The feature engineering and selection methodologies described are intended to achieve optimal model performance and best use of pertinent information for accurate predictions [30].

3.4 Machine Learning Model Development

(i) Structured Data: A robust gradient boosting algorithm, XGBoost, will be utilized for structured data including clinical data, genomic data, and biomarker data. XGBoost is highly appreciated for its performance and efficiency in processing tabular data with a combination of numerical and categorical variables, which makes it a perfect candidate for predictive modeling in oncology. At the center of XGBoost lies an additive tree ensemble model that has been trained using a regularized objective function optimized by minimizing

$$\mathrm{Obj}(\theta) = \sum_{i=1}^{n} l\left(y_i, \hat{y}_i^{(l)}\right) + \sum_{k=1}^{t} \Omega(f_k) \quad (1)$$

In eq. (1) n denoted the data points, l indicates the loss function, $\hat{y}_i^{(l)}$ is the prediction for instance I at boosting iteration t, and $\Omega(f_k)$ is the regularization for each tree f_k. The regularization term controls the complexity of the model to avoid overfitting:

$$\Omega(f) = \gamma T + \frac{1}{2}\lambda \sum_{j=1}^{T} w_j^2 \tag{2}$$

In eq. (2), T = number of leaves in the tree, w_j is the score weight on leaf j, and γ is the regularization of the number of leaves. At each iteration t, a new function $f_t(x)$ is added to minimize the loss:

$$\hat{y}_i^{(t)} = \hat{y}_i^{(t-1)} + f_t(x_i) \tag{3}$$

To effectively optimize, a second-order Taylor expansion of the loss around the current prediction is used:

$$l\left(y_i, \hat{y}_i^{(t-1)}\right) \approx l\left(y_i, \hat{y}_i^{(t-1)}\right) + g_i f_t(x_i) + \frac{1}{2} h_i f_t(x_i)^2 \tag{4}$$

where

$$g_i = \frac{\partial l\left(y_i, \hat{y}_i^{(t-1)}\right)}{\partial \hat{y}_i^{(t-1)}} \quad = \text{first–order derivative (gradient)}$$

$$h_i = \frac{\partial^2 \left(y_i, \hat{y}_i^{(t-1)}\right)}{\partial \left(\hat{y}_i^{(t-1)}\right)^2} \quad = \text{second–order derivative}$$

(ii) Image-Based Data: For image-based cancer detection, CNNs will be used. CNNs are good at extracting hierarchical patterns from images and are thus best suited for applications such as tumor detection, segmentation, and classification in medical imaging (e.g., MRI, CT, and histopathological images). The capacity of CNNs to learn spatial features from raw image data automatically provides the capability for identifying subtle tumor features that would otherwise be undetectable with traditional approaches. Assume the input to be an image:

$$X \in R^{H*W*C} \tag{5}$$

In eq. (5) H, W, and C are the height, width, and number of channels in an image. A convolutional layer applies a set of learnable filters K. For a filter $K \in R^{k_h*k_w*C}$, the convolution operation at position (i,j) is given as follows:

$$Y_{i,j}^{(f)} = \sigma\left(\sum_{m=0}^{k_h-1}\sum_{n=0}^{k_w-1}\sum_{c=0}^{C-1} K_{m.n.c}^{(f)} .X_{i+m,\ j+n,c} + b^{(f)}\right) \tag{6}$$

In eq. (6) $Y_{i,j}^{(f)}$ is the output filter f at position (i,j), σ (.) is an activation function, and $b^{(f)}$ is the bias term for filter f. Pooling reduces the spatial dimensions while retaining important features. For example, max pooling over a window $P * P$

$$Z_{i,j}^{(f)} = Y_{i+m,j+n}^{(f)} \tag{7}$$

After flattening the feature maps

$$h = \text{Flatten}\,(Z) \tag{8}$$

The dense layer computes

$$O = \phi(Wh + b) \tag{9}$$

In eq. (9), W denotes weight matrix, b is the bias vector, and $\phi(.)$ is an activation function.

For binary classification (tumor/no tumor):

$$\hat{y} = \text{Sigmoid}(o) \tag{10}$$

$$\text{Sigmoid}(x) = \frac{1}{1 + e^{-x}} \tag{11}$$

For multiclass classification

$$\hat{y}_i = \frac{e^{o_i}}{\sum_{j=1}^{N} e^{o_j}} \tag{12}$$

In eq. (12), n is the number of classes.

(iii) Patient Longitudinal Data: In order to analyze patient data longitudinally, LSTM networks will be used. Both of these models are suited to sequential data, like patient history over time, where the dependency between previous medical records and outcomes in the future needs to be modeled. LSTMs are especially well-suited to model intricate temporal patterns in patient histories and disease Finally, a hybrid ensemble strategy that combines the predictions of these heterogeneous models will be investigated to enhance both accuracy and robustness. Through the combination of strengths of XGBoost, CNNs, and LSTMs, the ensemble will provide a more complete prediction that combines multiple data modalities, ultimately increasing the overall performance of the framework in oncological disease prediction. Let each patients' sequential medical history be

$$X = \{\, x_1, x_2,\ x_3, \ldots .x_4 \,\} \tag{14}$$

In eq. (14) $x_t \in R^d$ is the feature vector at time t. At each time step t, an LSTM cell computes.

Forget gate:

$$f_t = \sigma(\ W_f.[h_{t-1}, x_t] + b_f) \tag{15}$$

Input gate:

$$i_t = \sigma(W_i.[h_{t-1}, x_t] + b_i) \tag{16}$$

$$\hat{C}_t = \tanh(W_C.[h_{t-1,} x_t] + b_C) \tag{17}$$

Cell state update:

$$C_t = \ f_t \odot C_{t-1} + \ i_t \odot \hat{C}_t \tag{18}$$

Output gate:

$$O_t = \sigma(W_o\ .[\ h_{t-1},\ x_t\ ] + \ b_o) \tag{19}$$

$$h_t = \ o_t\ \odot\ \tanh(\ C_t) \tag{20}$$

In equation the above equations, W_f, W_i, W_c, *and* W_o are the weight matrices, b_f, b_i, b_c, *and* b_o are the biases, $\sigma(.)$ is the sigmoid activation, tan$h$(.) is the hyperbolic tangent activation, and $\odot$ is the element-wise multiplication.

The final prediction form LSTM use the final hidden state h_r for prediction:

$$\hat{y}_{\text{LSTM}} = \phi(W_y.\ h_r + b_y) \tag{21}$$

where $\phi(.)$ is an activation function. Then combine XGBoost, CNN, and LSTM predictions as follows.

Form CNN (image-based data):

$$\hat{y}_{\text{CNN}} = f_{\text{CNN}}(I;\ \theta_{\text{CNN}}) \tag{22}$$

From LSTM (longitudinal patient data):

$$\hat{y}_{\text{LSTM}} = f_{\text{LSTM}}(X;\ \theta_{\text{LSTM}}) \tag{23}$$

From XGBoost (structured tabular data):

$$\hat{y}_{\text{XGB}} = f_{\text{XGB}}(z) \tag{24}$$

In eqs. (22)–(24) I is the patient data, X is the sequential medical records, and Z is the structured tabular patient data. The ensemble fusion strategy combines these predictions as a weighted average ensemble as follows:

$$\hat{y}_{\text{final}} = \ \alpha.\hat{y}_{\text{CNN}} + \ \beta.\hat{y}_{\text{LSTM}} + \ \gamma.\ \hat{y}_{\text{XGB}} \tag{25}$$

Subject to

$$\alpha + \beta + \delta \tag{26}$$

In eq. (26), α, β, *and* γ are ensemble weights determined with cross-validation or optimization.

The final ensemble model expression is provided as follows:

$$\hat{y}_{\text{final}} = f_{\text{ensemble}} \left(\hat{y}_{\text{CNN},}\ \hat{y}_{\text{LSTM},}\ \hat{y}_{\text{XGB}} \right) \tag{27}$$

This model integrates heterogeneous data sources and learning paradigms to enhance prediction accuracy and robustness in oncological disease prediction.

4 Results and Findings

This section discusses the detailed analysis of the BC Wisconsin (diagnostic) dataset with different ML and DL models. A hybrid method that combines XGBoost, CNN, and LSTM outperforms the state-of-the-art classifiers in correctly classifying malignant and benign tumors.

4.1 Dataset Description

The Wisconsin BC (diagnosis) dataset contains 569 instances, derived from a digitized image of fine needle samples of breast masses. Each example consists of 30 real properties. The properties are calculated as mean, standard error, and "the average of the three worst maximum characteristics for each characteristic", resulting in a high-dimensional profile of the morphology of the cell nucleus. The target function is a binary function that indicates whether tumor malignant (M) or benign (b) has 212 malignant and 357 benign records. This data record is suitable for training and observation of the performance of ML algorithms in binary classification problems. With its well-designed structure and precisely defined capabilities, it is an ideal choice for the use of algorithms such as XGBoost and is a research benchmark dataset for the diagnosis of BC.

As shown in table 1, the best overall performance in all the measures used is accomplished by the suggested hybrid approach using XGBoost, CNN, and LSTM. It outperforms traditional approaches and DL approaches with a level of accuracy that is 91%. Its precision level of 89% indicates that it has a very high rate to correctly label positive instances with the minimum false positives. The 88% recall value shows its effectiveness in detecting the majority of the actual positive instances, and the equally well-balanced F_1-score of 88% shows its overall power. The interaction between the conventional ML and DL models makes this hybrid system capable of processing dif-

Table 1: Performance analysis – proposed hybrid model.

Methodology	Accuracy (%)	Precision (%)	Recall (%)	F_1-score (%)
Proposed hybrid method (XGBoost + CNN + LSTM)	91	89	88	88
Logistic regression + manual feature selection	75	72	70	71
Random forest + recursive feature elimination (RFE)	82	80	78	79
Deep learning CNN for imaging-based detection	85	83	82	82
Ensemble of SVMs and random forests (state of the art)	89	87	85	86

ferent types of data efficiently and learning structured and unstructured pattern features, thereby explaining its high performance.

LR + Manual Feature Selection: The method utilizing LR with hand FS performed worst among the methods under testing. With accuracy standing at 75%, it lags a very long distance from other models with regard to predictiveness. Metrics of 72%, 70%, and 71% on precision, recall, and F_1-score, respectively, illustrate that the method performs bad on marking correct positives with accuracy as well as in weighting obtaining true positives versus the generation of false positives. It is due to the reason that logistic regression is simple and manual FS cannot capture subtle, nonlinear interrelations of the data.

RF with RFE does reasonably well with an accuracy of 82%. It is quite an improvement from the LR-based approach, and precision 80%, recall 78%, and F_1-score 79% are achieved. It implies that although RF, as a method of ensembling, is more capable to handle high-dimensional and complex data, it is behind DL-based techniques. RFE facilitates enhanced model efficiency through the selection and retention of the most suitable features, yet its standalone function is limited to detecting complex patterns of data vis-a-vis hybrid or DL techniques.

DL based on CNN which is applied in image-based detection fares exceptionally with 85% performance rate. Precise and recall performances of 83% and 82% and F_1-score of 82% reflect that CNN handles the discovery of image-related properties and features available in the activity of classification successfully. Though this is a better method than elementary ML algorithms, its effectiveness is still less than the proposed hybrid methodology. This suggests that though CNNs are very good at handling image data, using them along with other models that can process other forms of data structures could lead to even greater levels of predictive performance.

Ensemble of SVMs and RFs: The SVM-RF ensemble model is very good at classification with an accuracy of 89%. It has very high precision (87%), recall (85%), and F_1-

score (86%), indicating the strength of ensemble learning in improving the validity of prediction by aggregating the output of multiple classifiers. Although it is strong, its capability is comparatively weaker than the suggested hybrid technique.

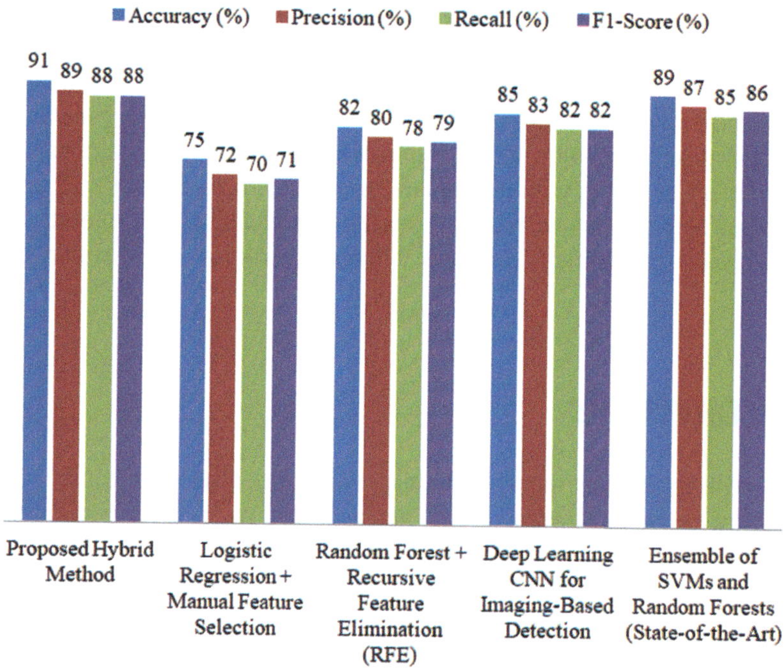

Figure 2: Performance analysis – proposed hybrid model.

This is to stress the fact that although ensemble methods among conventional classifiers are robust, combining deep models such as CNN and LSTM into leading ML algorithms such as XGBoost can further advance model performance, especially in challenging multimodal data environments. The XGBoost + CNN + LSTM hybrid approach beats traditional ML methods and previous deep models or ensembles, and it predicts that combining various models that operate on different modalities or structures of data (e.g., tabular, sequential, and image) can remarkably enhance predictive performance and robustness. Figure 2 shows the performance analysis of the proposed hybrid model.

5 Conclusion

This work presents a novel, data-driven ML approach toward oncological disease prediction and early stage diagnosis of precursors. Through the integration of heterogeneous, multimodal datasets and application of a hybrid ensemble of classical and deep ML models, the method is able to capture the complex interrelationships in cancer-related data. The results indicate that the combined strategy has higher predictive accuracy, sensitivity, and robustness compared to conventional single-modality or individual ML models. The ability to detect precursor and early stage disease biomarkers of high reliability responds to the potential of the framework to increase clinical decision-making and oncology patient outcomes. While the model developed here works well on most metrics, there are some limitations. The model's direct generalizability is somewhat constrained by the utilization of big and high-quality datasets, especially in locations or clinics with inadequate data infrastructure. Even if FS and model awareness help to some extent with model interpretability, future iterations with more inclusive transparency features tailored for clinical usage would be helpful.

6 Future Directions

Future studies will try to adapt the model to bigger and more diverse patient scenarios in an effort to increase its therapeutic use and applicability. Using survival analysis models like the Cox proportional hazards model and deeper survival networks forecast not only illness progression and early diagnosis but also patient prognosis and late outcomes is one of the work's useful extensions. The models will render the framework applicable for reporting clinician's risk-adjusted survival probabilities and individualized prognostic information, hence more relevant for clinical decision-making. To address data privacy and noncentralized large-sized databases, future activities will also investigate using federated learning approaches. Through this method, cooperative model training among different healthcare organizations will be enabled without the explicit sharing of data, thereby preserving patient confidentiality and use of larger, distributed datasets to enhance model performance. In addition, significant work will be devoted to implementing an open, real-time clinical decision support system on the contemplated platform. The system will strive to provide actionable information and risk estimates at the point of care in a format such that timely and informed decisions regarding treatment can be facilitated. The implementation of predictive analytics in daily clinical oncology practice, the study seeks to close the research-based innovation to everyday adoption gap, hence achieving the ultimate goal of precision oncology and improved patient care.

References

[1] Laghmati, S., Hamida, S., Hicham, K., Cherradi, B. & Tmiri, A. (2024). An improved breast cancer disease prediction system using ML and PCA. *Multimedia Tools and Applications*, 83(11), 33785–33821.

[2] Varlamova, E. V., Butakova, M. A., Semyonova, V. V., Soldatov, S. A., Poltavskiy, A. V., Kit, O. I. & Soldatov, A. V. (2024). Machine learning meets cancer. *Cancers*, 16(6), 1100.

[3] Yang, H., Yang, M., Chen, J., Yao, G., Zou, Q. & Jia, L. (2025). Multimodal deep learning approaches for precision oncology: a comprehensive review. *Briefings in Bioinformatics*, 26(1), bbae699.

[4] Colomer-Lahiguera, S., Gentizon, J., Christofis, M., Darnac, C., Serena, A. & Eicher, M. (2024). Achieving comprehensive, patient-centered cancer services: optimizing the role of advanced practice nurses at the core of precision health. In *Seminars in Oncology Nursing*, Vol. 40, 3, 151629, WB Saunders.

[5] Kothinti, R. R. Artificial Intelligence in Disease Prediction: Transforming Early Diagnosis and Preventive Healthcare. (2024).

[6] Darmofal, M., Suman, S., Atwal, G., Toomey, M., Chen, J.-F., Chang, J. C., Vakiani, E. et al. (2024). Deep-learning model for tumor-type prediction using targeted clinical genomic sequencing data. *Cancer discovery*, 14(6), 1064–1081.

[7] Arslan, S., Schmidt, J., Bass, C., Mehrotra, D., Geraldes, A., Singhal, S., Hense, J. et al. (2024). A systematic pan-cancer study on deep learning-based prediction of multi-omic biomarkers from routine pathology images. *Communications Medicine*, 4(1), 48.

[8] Fatima, A., Shabbir, A., Janjua, J. I., Ramay, S. A., Bhatty, R. A., Irfan, M. & Abbas, T. (2024). Analyzing breast cancer detection using machine learning & deep learning techniques. *Journal of Computing & Biomedical Informatics*, 7(02).

[9] Kaur, H., Das, P., Camphausen, K. & Shankavaram, U. (2024). CPSM: R-package of an Automated Machine Learning Pipeline for Predicting the Survival Probability of Single Cancer Patient. *bioRxiv*, 2024–11.

[10] Joshi, A. A. & Aziz, R. M. (2024). A two-phase cuckoo search based approach for gene selection and deep learning classification of cancer disease using gene expression data with a novel fitness function. *Multimedia Tools and Applications*, 83(28), 71721–71752.

[11] Ergul Aydin, Z. & Ozturk, Z. K. (2024). Filter-based feature selection methods in the presence of missing data for medical prediction models. *Multimedia Tools and Applications*, 83(8), 24187–24216.

[12] Al-Jamimi, H. A., Ayad, S. & Kheir, A. E. "Integrating Advanced Techniques: RFE-SVM Feature Engineering and Nelder-Mead Optimized XGBoost for Accurate Lung Cancer Prediction." *IEEE Access* (2025).

[13] Vatankhah, M. & Momenzadeh, M. (2024). Self-regularized Lasso for selection of most informative features in microarray cancer classification. *Multimedia Tools and Applications*, 83(2), 5955–5970.

[14] Gu, Y., Su, S., Wang, X., Mao, J., Ni, X., Li, A., Liang, Y. & Zeng, X. (2025). Comparative study of XGBoost and logistic regression for predicting sarcopenia in postsurgical gastric cancer patients. *Scientific Reports*, 15(1), 12808.

[15] Ren, H., Yang, T., Yin, X., Tong, L., Shi, J., Yang, J., Zhu, Z. & Li, H. (2024). Prediction of high-level fear of cancer recurrence in breast cancer survivors: an integrative approach utilizing random forest algorithm and visual nomogram. *European Journal of Oncology Nursing*, 70, 102579.

[16] Sharma, A. & Mittal, S. "Comparative Analysis of Various CNN Models for Lung Cancer Prediction." In *2024 3rd International Conference for Innovation in Technology (INOCON)*, pp. 1–6. IEEE, 2024.

[17] Supriya, K. & Anitha, A. (2024). Stage-based colorectal cancer prediction on uncertain dataset using rough computing and LSTM models. *Scientific Reports*, 14(1), 28880.

[18] Rakhshaninejad, M., Fathian, M., Shirkoohi, R., Barzinpour, F. & Gandomi, A. H. (2024). Refining breast cancer biomarker discovery and drug targeting through an advanced data-driven approach. *BMC bioinformatics*, 25(1), 33.

[19] Nopour, R. (2024). Screening ovarian cancer by using risk factors: machine learning assists. *BioMedical Engineering OnLine*, 23(1), 18.

[20] Reddy, A. (2024). AI and Machine Learning in Breast Cancer: Advancing Precision Medicine Through Data-Driven Models. *International Journal of Innovation in Engineering*, 4(4), 37–42.

[21] Froicu, E.-M., Oniciuc, O.-M., Afrăsânie, V.-A., Marinca, M.-V., Riondino, S., Dumitrescu, E. A., Alexa-Stratulat, T., Radu, I., Miron, L., Bacoanu, G. et al. (2024). The Use of Artificial Intelligence in Predicting Chemotherapy-Induced Toxicities in Metastatic Colorectal Cancer: A Data-Driven Approach for Personalized Oncology. *Diagnostics*, 14(18), 2074. https://doi.org/10.3390/diagnostics14182074.

[22] Qasrawi, R., Daraghmeh, O., Qdaih, I., Thwib, S., Polo, S. V., Owienah, H., Al-Halawa, D. A. & Atari, S. (2024). Hybrid ensemble deep learning model for advancing breast cancer detection and classification in clinical applications. *Heliyon*, 10(19).

[23] Nanglia, S., Ahmad, M., Khan, F. A. & Jhanjhi, N. Z. (2022). An enhanced Predictive heterogeneous ensemble model for breast cancer prediction. *Biomedical Signal Processing and Control*, 72, 103279.

[24] Zerououi, H., Idri, A. & Alaoui, O. E. (2023). A new approach for histological classification of breast cancer using deep hybrid heterogenous ensemble. *Data Technologies and Applications*, 57(2), 245–278.

[25] Wang, X., Ahmad, I., Javeed, D., Zaidi, S. A., Alotaibi, F. M., Ghoneim, M. E., Daradkeh, Y. I., Asghar, J. & Eldin, E. T. (2022). Intelligent hybrid deep learning model for breast cancer detection. *Electronics*, 11(17), 2767.

[26] Sharmin, S., Ahammad, T., Talukder, M. A. & Ghose, P. (2023). A Hybrid Dependable Deep Feature Extraction and Ensemble-Based Machine Learning Approach for Breast Cancer Detection. *IEEE Access*, 11, 87694–87708. doi: 10.1109/ACCESS.2023.3304628.

[27] Li, Y., Yu, X. & Koudas, N. (2021). Data acquisition for improving machine learning models. *arXiv preprint arXiv:2105.14107*.

[28] Aljrees, T. (2024). Improving prediction of cervical cancer using KNN imputer and multi-model ensemble learning. *Plos one*, 19(1), e0295632.

[29] Kalam, R. & Thomas, C. (2024). Detection and classification of breast cancer in mammogram images using entropy-based Fuzzy C-Means Clustering and RMCNN. *Multimedia Tools and Applications*, 83(24), 64853–64878.

[30] Chhillar, I. & Singh, A. (2024). A feature engineering-based machine learning technique to detect and classify lung and colon cancer from histopathological images. *Medical & Biological Engineering & Computing*, 62(3), 913–924.

Parashiva Murthy B. M., Ik Hesti Agustin*, Sowjanya Bharathi, Rayappan Lotus, S. Bathrinath, and Rishabh Garg

Machine Learning Applications in Mental Health: Ensemble-Based Predictive Modeling for Depression and Anxiety detection

Abstract: Psychological diseases such as depression and anxiety are prevalent globally, and thus there is a need for advanced detection techniques to ensure maximum clinical interventions and patient care. Traditional machine learning techniques, such as random forest, support vector machines, and logistic regression, although efficient, are at the cost of interpretability, computational performance, and predictability in handling advanced mental health data. In this research work, triple neuro-probabilistic ensemble (TNPE) is proposed to be a breakthrough ensemble model appropriate for depression and anxiety detection. TNPE leverages three foundation learners with complementing strengths: extreme learning machine for speed and generalization overall on small-to-medium-sized datasets; probabilistic neural network for probabilistic decision-making in a clinical setting; and CatBoost, specifically crafted for dealing with categorical and mixed-type data. The models are blended via an optimal soft voting ensemble mechanism driven by adaptive weight optimization with particle swarm optimization. The model was trained on a multisource clinical record, mental health surveys, and social media text dataset preprocessed and balanced with methods such as ADASYN. Feature selection was carried out using the Boruta algorithm. TNPE was tested with 10-fold cross-validation and performed better than standard classifiers like k-nearest neighbors, decision tree, Naïve Bayes, multilayer perceptron, gradient boosting machine, and AdaBoost. TNPE performed better on critical metrics: ROC-AUC (0.963), F_1-score (0.927), and accuracy (92.6%). Interpretability enhanced by LIME and SHAP, TNPE became a clinical acceptable decision-making system for diagnosing mental health.

***Corresponding author: Ik Hesti Agustin,** Department of Mathematics, University of Jember, Kabupaten Jember, Jawa Timur 68121, Indonesia, e-mail: ikahesti.fmipa@unej.ac.id
Parashiva Murthy B. M., Department of CSE, SJCE, JSS Science and Technology University, Mysuru 570006, Karnataka, India, e-mail: parashivamurthy@sjce.ac.in
Sowjanya Bharathi, CVR College of Engineering, Hyderabad, Telangana, India, e-mail: ksowjanyabharathi1985@gmail.com
Rayappan Lotus, Computer Science and Engineering, Vel Tech Rangarajan Dr Sagunthala R &D Institute of Science and Technology, Chennai, Tamil Nadu, India, e-mail: sjlotusanton@gmail.com
S. Bathrinath, Department of Mechanical Engineering, Kalasalingam Academy of Research and Education, Krishnankoil 626126, Tamil Nadu, India, e-mail: bathri@gmail.com
Rishabh Garg, School of Computer Applications, Lovely Professional University, Phagwara, Punjab, India, e-mail: Rishabh1994garg@gmail.com

https://doi.org/10.1515/9783111541235-006

Keywords: depression and anxiety detection, ensemble learning, extreme learning machine (ELM), probabilistic neural network (PNN), mental health prediction

1 Introduction

Mental disorders, particularly depression and anxiety, have emerged as significant public health problems around the world. More than 300 million people worldwide are projected to have depression by the WHO [1], while anxiety disorders afflict an equally large number of people. The conditions extend beyond personal distress, causing immense economic and social costs to healthcare systems, workplaces, and communities. Mental disorders contribute more disability-adjusted life years, more suicides, and reduced quality of life among the patients. Indirect costs such as productivity loss, absence, and lower efficiency at the workplace also add to the added world burden of such diseases [2].

Mental illnesses such as depression and anxiety are also very difficult to diagnose because measurement of symptoms is subjective in nature [3]. Compared to physical disease that can often be diagnosed through objective laboratory testing or imaging, mental health evaluation is based largely on clinical interview, self-report questionnaire, and behavioral observation. These traditional diagnostic techniques, while unavoidable, have some limitations in and of themselves. They are subject to reporting bias, social desirability, and differences in symptom expression by culture. Moreover, symptoms of depression and anxiety tend to overlap with one another and with other medical or mental illnesses, complicating differential diagnosis [4]. The episodic course of the disorders and users' underreporting due to stigma further hinder early and correct detection. Beyond clinical complexity, mental health data itself is complex in nature, rendering it difficult to tap through conventional statistical methods.

Mental health data sets are usually high-dimensional, asymmetric class distributed, and consist of mixtures of structured (e.g., demographic data and survey responses) and unstructured data types [5]. (e.g., social media entries and clinical notes). Furthermore, confidentiality of patient information and the sensitive nature of mental health data limit access to large, diverse data sets, contributing to the challenge of analyzing large samples and generalizing. Despite these challenges, enhanced access to electronic health records, mobile health applications, and internet-based behavioral data have provided opportunities for computational models to facilitate mental health assessment and prediction The past few years have been opened up for improving mental healthcare due to the arrival of artificial intelligence (AI) and machine learning (ML) methods [6].

These technologies hold the promise of identifying hidden patterns, trends, and associations in advanced, multimodal data sets often overlooked in conventional analyses. ML techniques have been applied with significant success in a wide range of fields of mental health research including the prediction of suicide risk, the identification of post-traumatic stress disorder [7], the detection of substance use disorders, and the screening of depression and anxiety from textual or behavioral data. These models can assist clinicians in decision-making, enhance early detection methods, and provide scalable techniques for population-level mental health screening.

Furthermore, confidentiality concerns of patients and the sensitive character of mental health data limit access to large, diverse data sets, contributing to the challenge of having to analyze large samples and make generalization. Despite these challenges, greater access to electronic health records, mobile health applications, and online behavioral data have provided avenues for computational models to facilitate assessment and prediction of mental health. The last few years have provided new windows of opportunity to improve mental healthcare, courtesy of the arrival of AI and ML approaches. Random forest (RF) [8], support vector machine (SVM) [9], logistic regression (LR) [10], and deep boosters like XGBoost [11] and LightGBM [12] are few of the most commonly applied ML algorithms for predicting mental health. These models have exhibited decent performance in diagnosing mental health disorders when trained on both clinical and non-clinical data.

However, several challenges exist in the proper utilization of these models in mental health informatics. Numerous current models fail to address class imbalance, a typical problem in medical datasets where positive instances of mental disorder may be fewer than healthy controls. In addition, interpretability of sophisticated ML models continues to be an issue of major concern, especially in medicine, where it is essential to have transparent and interpretable decision-support tools in order to make their responsible usage possible and gain confidence in AI-driven recommendations. More importantly, most current research in this area have been dedicated to applying single classifiers or standard ensemble methods like RFs.

Although these approaches have some benefits in predictive performance and stability, they might not be as flexible as required to deal with the heterogeneous nature of mental health data, which tends to have a mix of categorical, numerical, and textual features. More scalable, flexible, and interpretable ML architecture is yet to be developed. The objectives of this study are as follows:

To create, deploy, and test a novel ensemble-based prediction model framework to detect depression and anxiety by integrating heterogeneous ML algorithms with experience in dealing with complex and heterogeneous mental health data.

To analyze the proposed ensemble framework against existing benchmark models using various prediction performance metrics so that accuracy, robustness, and reliability could be ensured during mental health classification tasks.

This chapter starts with an in-depth introduction presenting the importance and difficulty of mental health prediction. Section 2 discusses the related literature on ML techniques in mental health diagnosis. The methodology part explains the suggested ensemble model and evaluation processes. Lastly, results, discussion, conclusion, and future directions are given to summarize findings and suggest areas for further research.

2 Related Works

Depression is a common mood illness that afflicts millions of people around the globe, essentially altering emotional states, cognitive functions, and daily routines. Successful treatment and prevention of long-term consequences of the disease need timely and correct diagnosis. The recent progress in ML and AI has allowed us to create new diagnostic approaches based on ample sources of heterogeneously diverse data such as psychological questionnaires, physiological readings, and social media feeds.

2.1 Hybrid Ensemble Model for Depression

Depression has recorded a remarkable increase in incidence in the last few decades, remaining undiagnosed for long periods and having serious impacts on mental as well as physical well-being. To tackle such a situation, computer-based detection systems with powerful ML algorithms are being more commonly researched. DeprMVM, a hybrid ensemble-based model presented here, is proposed for detecting depression through combining psychological and sociodemographic characteristics. The combination takes SVMs and multilayer perceptrons (MLPs) as the base (level 0) learners, whereas DeprMVM acts as the meta-learner (level 1). The results from SVM and MLP, together with other concerned variables, are utilized to train the meta-classifier to achieve better predictive accuracy. To handle class imbalance in the database, a blend of oversampling technique and cluster sampling was used. This approach not only enhanced accuracy of detection but also minimized overfitting risk. The performance of the model was strictly tested with various metrics and compared to the current methods on the same data. The results proved that the ensemble model presented in this work outperformed the existing work with a detection accuracy of 99.39% and an *F*1-score of 99.51%. These results accentuate the promise of hybrid ensemble learning in creating efficient, automatic systems for detecting depression [13].

2.2 Predicting Depression and Anxiety

After the COVID-19 pandemic, depression and anxiety levels have increased hugely as individuals adjusted to a new normal. Early detection, treatment with precision, and community care are the key factors for counteracting the influence of mental illness. Consistent with the Sustainable Development Goals (SDGs), which promote mental well-being through fair means and reduced inequalities, this study targets efficient, data-driven methods of detecting mental health disease. While depression detection is entering usage based on social media, its complete potential is limited because it lacks comprehensive annotated data. As an antidote, we propose a novel strategy of harnessing psychological questionnaire data to create population-level predictive models.

Enhanced hybrid models DT + kNN and RF + NN are presented in this paper and evaluated on three independent datasets for depression and anxiety prediction. DA-TabSVM, our multiclass classification model intended to handle complex patterns across datasets, is also presented. DT + kNN achieved 95% and 97% for depression and anxiety, respectively, while RF + NN achieved 98% for both. DA-TabSVM achieved 97%, 99%, and 99% accuracy for the three datasets for depression and up to 100% accuracy for anxiety detection. The hybrid approaches outperform traditional models by leveraging complementary strengths of algorithms and have a large potential for maximizing mental health diagnostics with ML [14].

2.3 AI-Driven Mental Health Assessment Platform

Mental disorders are a major source of emotional distress and it affects the perception, feelings, and behavior of people toward any situation. Physical and mental health is important to lead a productive life and achieve one's full potential. Mental well-being must be developed from childhood to adulthood. The usual causes of mental illness are stress of a long duration, social phobia, depression, obsessive-compulsive disorder, drug addiction, work-related stress, and personality disorders. In this current research, publicly available web data sets were utilized for experimentation. The data was labeled to enhance predictive accuracy. LR, Naïve Bayes (NB), decision trees (DTs), neural networks, and SVM were some of the ML algorithms employed. Among these, DTs, SVMs, and neural networks were most reliable in predicting stress, depression, and anxiety. These models were applied to the dataset to yield labeled results. Based on these labels, a predictive system was developed to identify the mental status of an individual. The primary target audience for this model would be working professionals who are above the age of 18, and they would use the system via a web-based interface [15].

2.4 Attention-Based Deep Depression Detection

An increasing number of people are suffering from mental illness because timely diagnosis and treatment are unavailable, especially for depression. The delay causes serious disorders such as anxiety, bipolar disorder, and sleep disorders, and in worst-case scenarios, self-inflicted injury or suicide. Early detection and treatment are among the biggest issues in mental health services. To counter this, we suggest a new hybrid DL model for predicting depression at its early stages. The model combines a CNN and an LSTM network with an added two-state LSTM architecture that uses a feature attention mechanism. The attention mechanism helps the model better identify predominant indicators and contextual patterns for depression. The model is tested on a big, publicly available corpus of text-based queries posed by children using an online platform. Features were extracted via one-hot encoding from symptom indicators established by psychology and medical professionals. Comparative assessments indicate that the novel model performs better compared to classic approaches [16].

2.5 Optimized Depression Classification

Depression is a common and disabling psychiatric illness that requires early and proper diagnosis in an effort to provide helpful intervention and treatment. Electroencephalography (EEG) has also been indicated as an effective noninvasive method to investigate neural signatures of depression and can provide useful assistance in clinical diagnosis. In this study, a methodology for diagnosing depressive disorders through EEG on publicly available multimodal open dataset for mental-disorder analysis is presented. EEG signals were recorded from 55 subjects with merely three electrodes in rest condition. Twelve temporal features were extracted from the gathered data by dividing the EEG signals into nonoverlapping segments of 10 s. A new FS technique was utilized to select the most discriminative features to distinguish depressing patients from healthy controls. The parameters that were detected were tested with three classifiers: Best-First (BF) Tree, kNN, and AdaBoost. BF-Tree classifier provided the best accuracy of 96.36% using a 12-feature vector that surpasses the current depression detection techniques. Notably, the system reported here has good classification performance with minimal EEG setup and hence is realistic and cost-effective. The model promises to be useful for application in psychiatric practice, offering clinicians a useful tool for assisting the diagnosis of depressive disorders [17].

2.6 Data-Driven Detection of Mental Health Disorders

Millions of people in the United States and other countries suffer from two of the most prevalent mental illnesses: fear and depression. These diseases not only affect individuals, they also have important social and economic consequences. The main focus of this study was the development of sophisticated ML models that could predict and track the risk of anxiety and depression. The advancement of AI and ML in the past few years has the potential to completely transform the diagnosis and treatment of disease. ML algorithms can be used to create predictive models that can go through enormous volumes of data and detect minute details that human clinicians might miss. For this research, a publicly available dataset from Kaggle and Harvard Dataverse was used. It contained behavioral, psychophysiological, and demographic information of 593 participants in the range of 18–35 years. Three ML models LR, XGBoost Regressor, and RF were used to predict probabilities of anxiety and depression. The efficacy of these models was tested in terms of mean-squared error (MSE) and *R*-squared (R^2) measures. All three models were very predictive, with low-MSE values and R^2 values of almost 1. Of the three, linear regression performed very slightly better than the others. The research affirms the validity and accuracy of these models for use in detecting individuals at risk for mental health disorders to allow for early intervention and, possibly, better long-term outcomes [18].

2.7 Anxiety and Depression Forecasting

Although various algorithms and approaches have been developed for prediction of depression, none of the automated systems studies have been recommended for early assessment of mood changes. This study focused on improving early diagnostic accuracy in the event of persistent depression disorder (PDD) development with an improved ML approach via the stack-SVM-ensemble method. To enable faster initial screening of students' dysthymia, quantitative behavioral data analysis was used with the help of ML. The study collected behavioral information from 137 university students and used the data to create models and perform experiments. Results showed that PDD is most frequently seen in middle-class students who have completed non-technical courses. Interestingly, the frequency of PDD among rural students was higher from the high and low income groups. The proposed stacked SVM model worked with better performance and achieved an accuracy of 89.4%. Early detection of PDD for students was important for mental health professionals, and the stacked SVM approach was effective in this regard [19].

2.8 BERT-RF Hybrid Model for Depression Detection from Tweets

Depression is a severe mental illness impacting feelings, thoughts, and everyday functioning. Aside from personal suffering, depression impacts society due to decreased productivity and higher healthcare expenditures. Social media websites tend to mirror users' emotional lives in the form of posts, providing useful information for early detection of depression. This study applies ML to predict depression from social media posts based on a benchmark set of 20,000 tweets labeled as depressed or not with an RF classifier. A novel BERT-RF feature engineering approach has been introduced that uses contextual representations from the BERT model and probabilistic values obtained through an RF classifier. This informative feature improves depression detection. For classification, five models such as RF, MLP, kNN, LR, and LSTM networks were compared. Experiments show that LR using BERT-RF features works better with 99% accuracy. The approach offers an efficient means of early detection of depression on social media, encouraging computational linguistics and mental health analysis. It enables timely intervention and better mental health outcomes through the utilization of rich information contained in online user-generated data [20].

2.9 High-Accuracy Depression Prediction from Twitter Data

Depression is a prevalent and disabling mental illness that still causes challenges to the global healthcare systems. Successful therapy relies on timely detection and treatment, but the challenges of detecting depression often lead to under diagnosis and under treatment. A comprehensive review of employing ML models in diagnosing depression accurately is conducted in this research. The goal of this study is to improve early diagnosis, risk assessment, and patient care in the field of depression detection utilizing predictive models. For this purpose, the Depression Prediction dataset available on Kaggle was utilized, and 10 different ML models were employed. The results showed that RF outperformed the rest of the models by achieving 98.22% accuracy while ensemble method obtained 0.98 F_1-score [21].

ML has also been set forth as a strong tool to detect depression and anxiety, with real-time accurate and scalable diagnostic tools. Hybrid and ensemble models such as DeprMVM, DA-TabSVM, and BERT-RF recent research show can obtain more than 95% accuracy using heterogeneous data like questionnaires, EEG measures, and social media data. Deep learning techniques that use CNN, LSTM, and the attention mechanism increase efficiency further. Such models are better than conventional approaches, yielding robust, early identification in multi-population samples. As mental health disorders increase globally, AI-based systems offer cost-effective, efficient mental health screening to enable early intervention, avoid under diagnosis, and enable global objectives for equitable delivery of care.

3 Methodology

The mental health data were extracted from various open-source and publicly available data repositories to provide data diversity and comprehensiveness. Organized patient and clinical data, like demographic data, mental health observations, and level of diagnosis, were collected from existing databases such as the UCI ML Repository dataset for Mental Health in Tech Survey and the Kaggle Mental Health in the Workplace dataset [22]. In addition, self-report survey information that measures depression and anxiety indicators was obtained from the public dataset, which offers anonymized mental health and behavioral risk factors of a general population sample. To complement this study, a clinical-based data, unstructured social media textual data on depression and anxiety were gathered from publicly accessible tweets on Twitter (via Twitter's Academic API) and Reddit communities of r/depression and r/anxiety, where posts were manually labeled or automatically annotated by keyword-based and sentiment analysis methods, as elaborated in prior research studies. Ethical procedures were strictly adhered to, where all the information was gathered either from open-access sources or data sets after necessary ethical approvals and anonymization steps had been completed. The overall workflow of the methodology is shown in Figure 1.

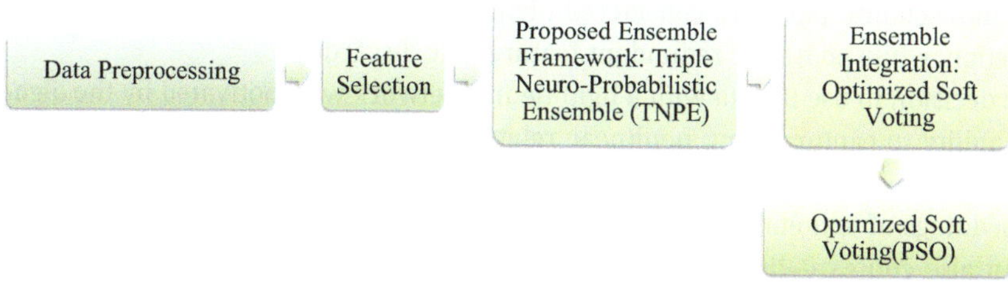

Figure 1: Overall workflow of the proposes architecture.

3.1 Data Preprocessing

The mental health data were preprocessed using a series of preprocessing operations to clean data for processing and consumption by models. The missing values in the numeric and categorical structured columns were imputed using kNN imputation [23], wherein missing values are estimated by similarity of nearest points. In case of the unstructured text information pulled from social media posts and clinical notes, general natural language processing [24] functions like lemmatization and tokenization were utilized to transform text content to normal form and truncate it into root form. Next, sentence embeddings were obtained using the Universal Sentence Encoder (USE), converting text inputs into high-dimensional numerical vectors with semantic meaning and interpretable by ML algorithms. Numerical features in the dataset were normalized by MinMaxScaler, scaling values onto a typical range of [0,1] so that there was uniformity among features and the model was not biased by varying scales. To handle the common class imbalance encountered in mental health data, in particular where cases of depression and anxiety were underrepresented than those not affected, the adaptive synthetic (ADASYN) sampling technique was used [25]. ADASYN generates minority class synthetic samples from the data distribution so that the model becomes more sensitive and class imbalance is minimized in the training data.

3.2 Feature Selection

The predictive performance is enhanced and computational complexity is reduced by a rigorous FS conducted prior to model training. A computationally effective wrapper-based FS method using the Boruta algorithm [26] was used to choose and retain only the most predictive predictors from both structured clinical information as well as unstructured text-derived embeddings. Boruta works by repeatedly comparing base feature importance against randomly generated shadow features with a base estimator, in this example a simple neural network classifier, to establish the importance of every feature at each iteration. Features that repeatedly score higher than their shadow counterparts are considered highly important and are stored for model construction, while poorer or redundant features are discarded.

The decision to use Boruta with a light neural network was motivated by the algorithm's ability to capture faint, nonlinear relationships in high-dimensional and heterogeneous data, as in datasets containing both clinical measurements and dense vector embeddings of text embeddings. Pairing ensured not only that FS was statistically valid but also contextually aligned with the downstream modeling architecture. By retaining only strongly relevant features, this step effectively reduced dimensionality, avoided overfitting, and improved model interpretability by focusing on predictors with clear and measurable contributions to mental health classification. This filtering process also optimized computational efficiency, particularly important when working with computationally costly ensemble models and high-dimensional text data represented by the USE. Mathematically, the original dataset be represented as

$$D = \{(x_i, y_i) | i = 1, 2, \ldots, n\} \tag{1}$$

where $x_i \in R^d$ is the feature vector for the ith instance and $y_i \in \{0,1\}$ is the corresponding binary class label indicating the presence or absence of depression/anxiety. The Boruta algorithm enriches the feature set by incorporating shuffled copies of the original features, labeled as shadow features:

$$X_{\text{shadow}} = \text{shuffle}(X) \tag{2}$$

A neural network classifier $f(.)$ is then trained on the combined dataset:

$$X_{\text{combined}} = [X, X_{\text{shadow}}]$$

Feature importance for both original and shadow features is computed using a relevance score derived from the neural network's learned weights or feature contribution to the output. The importance score for feature j can be expressed as

$$I_j = \frac{1}{n} \sum_{i=1}^{n} \left| \frac{\partial f(x_i)}{\partial x_{ij}} \right| \tag{3}$$

Boruta then compares each original feature's important score I_j with the maximum importance among shadow features $I_{\text{shadow.max}}$. The decision rule is

- if $I_j > I_{\text{shadow.max}}$, the feature is considered important.
- if $I_j < I_{\text{shadow.max}}$, the feature is marked as important.
- if the decision is ambiguous the feature remains tentative and is evaluated in subsequent iterations.

This process continues iteratively until all features are either confirmed or rejected based on statistical significance using a two-sided binomial test. The strength of complementing Boruta with a light neural network is that it can capture complex nonlinear relations and interactions between variables, which is especially useful in datasets where there are structured clinical predictors and high-dimensional, dense text embeddings. By choosing features with persistently strong importance alone, this approach not only improves model performance but also limits overfitting risks and enhances model interpretability.

3.3 Proposed Ensemble Framework: Triple Neuro-probabilistic Ensemble (TNPE)

The model is built from three various base learners, which were chosen because they possess complementary learning paradigms and decision boundaries:

(i) Extreme Learning Machine (ELM): ELM is a single-hidden layer feedforward neural network with random initial weights between the input layer and the hidden layer that are not updated during training [27]. The only learnable parameters are those between the hidden layer and the output layer, hence computationally more efficient. For an input feature vector

$$x = [x_1, x_2, \ldots, x_d]^T \tag{4}$$

where d is the number of features and $g(.)$ is typically a sigmoid or ReLu activation function. The inputs X are mapped to the hidden layer through a random weight matrix:

$$W = R^{N*d} \tag{5}$$

Here, N is the number of hidden nodes. The hidden layer output is computed using a nonlinear activation function $g(.)$:

$$H = g(Wx + b) \tag{6}$$

where b is the bias term and $g(.)$ is typically a sigmoid or ReLU activation function.

The output layer is computed using a weight vector $\in R^N$, which is learned using a linear regression approach by minimizing the least squares error. The output $\hat{y}$ is given as follows:

$$\hat{y} = H^T \beta \tag{7}$$

The weights β are determined by solving the following optimization problems:

$$\beta = (H^T \text{H})^{-1} H^T y \tag{8}$$

In eq. (8) y is the vector of target outputs.

(ii) Probabilistic Neural Network (PNN): The PNN is a radial basis function (RBF) network designed for probabilistic pattern classification. It works by estimating the conditional probability distribution of the output class given the input data [28]. PNNs are particularly useful in classification tasks where probabilistic outputs and uncertainty quantification are needed, such as in medical decision-making. Let an input vector $x \in R^d$, the PNN computes the output class probability $P(C_k|x)$ for each possible class C_k using the following steps:

(i) Radial basis function (RBF): The hidden layer applies an RBF kernel to compute the similarity between the input vector X and every training sample x_i

$$\phi_i(x) = \exp\left(-\frac{||x - x_i||^2}{2\sigma^2}\right) \tag{9}$$

where σ is the width of the RBF kernel, controlling the smoothness of the decision boundary.

(ii) Class Probability Calculation: The output for class C_k is calculated by summing the contribution of each training sample x_i for that class, weighted by the RBF output:

$$P(C_k|x) = \frac{\sum_{i:y_i = C_k} \phi_i(x)}{\sum_{i=1}^{n} \phi_i(x)} \tag{10}$$

where y_i is the class label of the training sample and the denominator normalizes the output to ensure the sum of probabilities across all classes equals 1. PNNs are especially strong in medical decision-making due to their potential to offer each class's probability estimate, thus being interpretable and beneficial for clinical risk assessment.

(iii) CatBoost: It is an algorithm of gradient boosting tailored for processing categorical features efficiently. Unlike regular gradient boosting algorithms such as XGBoost and LightGBM, CatBoost is built to process categorical variables natively without deep preprocessing like one-hot encoding or label encoding being necessarily required. CatBoost also has methods to prevent overfitting and is particularly suited for small and mixed-type data. The CatBoost algorithm is a type of gradient boosting DTs, where each next tree is learned to reduce the residual of the previous trees. The model output in each iteration is given by

$$\hat{y}^{(t)} = \hat{y}^{(t-1)} + \eta . h_t(x) \tag{11}$$

where $\hat{y}^{(t-1)}$ is the prediction from the previous iteration, η is the learning rate, and $h_t(x)$ is the output of the tth tree. CatBoost incorporates ordered boosting, which helps prevent overfitting by using only past data points (without leakage from future data) to calculate the splits during the training process. In the case of categorical features, CatBoost applies a specific encoding strategy known as ordered target encoding to transform categorical variables into numeric values. This method computes the mean target per category without overfitting using an ordered strategy to avoid target leakage. The encoding of a category ccc can be computed as

$$\text{Enc}(c) = \frac{1}{N_c} \sum_{i \in C} y_i \tag{12}$$

where C denotes the collection of data points belonging to category c, and N denotes the number of data points that fall into category c. CatBoost is particularly well-suited for datasets that contain mixed-type features (categorical and numerical) since it minimizes the requirement for heavy preprocessing and prevents overfitting by virtue of its ordered boosting and target encoding mechanisms.

3.4 Ensemble Integration: Optimized Soft Voting

In this study, the ultimate prediction for detecting depression and anxiety is achieved when the predictions of a number of base learners are combined by means of an optimized soft voting mechanism [29]. Soft voting is a probability-based approach in which each prediction of the base learners is combined by averaging their probability outputs. The output with the maximum averaged probability is chosen to be the final output. Yet, in order to enhance the performance of the ensemble model, PSO is used to dynamically adjust the weights of each base learner's contribution toward the soft voting. The adaptive weighting is useful in enhancing the prediction accuracy of the ensemble by placing greater emphasis on the base learners performing well in the validation set.

Soft Voting Model: Let there be Mbase base learners, each of which outputs a probability distribution over the potential classes. Let the predicted probability distribution of class k for the ith instance by the jth base learner be denoted as $P_{k,j}(x_i)$, where x_i is the input feature vector.

Predicted Probability for Every Class: In soft voting, the predicted probability for class k for the whole ensemble is calculated by averaging the probabilities of all M base learners:

$$\hat{P}_k(x_i) = \frac{1}{M} \sum_{j=1}^{M} P_{k,j}(x_i) \tag{13}$$

where $P_{k,j}(x_i)$ is the predicted probability of class k from the jth base learner for input instance x_i and $\hat{P}_k(x_i)$ is the aggregated probability. The goal is to maximize the ROC-AUC score of the ensemble on a validation fold by adjusting weights w_1, w_2, w_3 for ELM, PNN, and CatBoost, respectively. The objective function is to maximize the following:

$$AUC_{\text{Ensemble}} = w_1 * P_{\text{ELM}} + w_2 * P_{\text{PNN}} + w_3 * P_{\text{catBoost}} \tag{14}$$

subject to constraints

$$0 \leq w_i \leq 1, \sum w_i = 1 \tag{15}$$

The final prediction is made by selecting the class with the highest predicted probability:

$$\hat{y}_i = \left(\hat{P}_k(x_i)\right) \tag{16}$$

This yields the class $\hat{y}_i$ that corresponds to the highest averaged probability across all base learners.

Optimized Soft Voting Using Particle Swarm Optimization (PSO): While soft voting merely assigns equal weight to the prediction of each base learner, obtain optimal weight of each learner's contribution from how well each performs on a validation set. PSO is a population-based optimization algorithm that replicates the social bird flocking or fish schooling phenomenon [30]. Every particle in the swarm corresponds to a candidate solution, that is, the weights given to the base learners of the ensemble. The weights are updated at each iteration depending on their own best and the global best position discovered by the swarm. Let w_j represents the weight assigned to the jth base learner and let the weight vector be $w = [\ w_1, w_2, \ldots, w_M]$, where M is the number of base learners. Initially the weights are set randomly. The goal of PSO is to find the optimal weights w that minimizes the loss function or maximize performance of the ensemble on the validation set. The fitness function $L(w)$ is defined as

$$L(w) = \frac{1}{N} \sum_{i=1}^{N} L_i(w, x_i, y_i) \tag{17}$$

where N is the number of validation instances and $L_i(w, x_i, y_i)$ is the loss for the ith validation instance such as cross-entropy loss:

$$L_i(w, x_i, y_i) = -\sum_{k=1}^{C} y_{i.k} \log\left(\hat{P}_k(x_i, w)\right) \tag{18}$$

where C is the number of classes, $y_{i,k}$ is the one-hot encoded true label, and $\hat{P}_k(x_i, w)$ is the repeated probability for class k for the ith instance calculated using the weighted sum:

$$\hat{P}_k(x_i, w) = \frac{\sum_{j=1}^{M} w_j P_{k,j}(x_i)}{\sum_{j=1}^{M} w_j} \tag{19}$$

In PSO, each particle w_t represents a possible solution (weight vector) at iteration t. The position and velocity of each particle re updated as follows:

$$v_{j,t+1} = wv_{j,t} + c_1r_1(P_{j,t} - w_{j.t} + c_2r_2(g_t - w_{j,t}) \tag{20}$$

$$w_{j,t+1} = w_{j.t} + v_{j,t+1} \tag{21}$$

where $v_{j,t}$ is the velocity of the jth particle at iteration t, w is the inertia weight of the previous velocity, c_1 and c_2 are cognitive and social coefficients, r_1 and r_2 are the random numbers between 0 and 1, $P_{j,t}$ is the personal best position of particle j, and g_t is the global best position found by the swarm. The velocity update pushes every particle toward its local best solution and the swarm's global best solution discovered so far, trading off exploration and exploitation to converge towards the optimal weight vector. This is a highly adaptive, flexible ensemble that can adjust the base learner weights in terms of the validation data to achieve better generalization performance.

4 Results and Findings

The study was carried out in Python 3.11, a powerful and dynamic testing and developing environment for ML models. A selection of libraries was employed in the development and testing of the models. The PNN and the ELM models based on neural network-inspired models were trained using TensorFlow/Keras. CatBoost was used as the gradient boosting algorithm in efficiently dealing with categorical features, particularly for small-to-medium-sized data. For dealing with the issue of class imbalance, ADASYN was used on the data to balance it before training the model. Boruta_py was used for FS to keep only the most important features from the dataset. pyswarm was used in the implementation of PSO in the optimization of weights of base learners in the ensemble model. Secondly, the implementation of techniques such as LIME and SHAP to model explainability and interpretability was implemented in an effort to better understand the decision process of the models. Lastly, Scikit-learn was utilized to assess model performance using several evaluation measures in order to have a better understanding of the models' overall efficacy.

A number of significant measures that characterize classification accuracy and the model's capacity to handle class imbalance were used to evaluate the model's performance. The model's overall ratio of accurate predictions was calculated using accuracy as a minimal metric. To provide a more balanced assessment, especially for imbalanced datasets, the F_1-score was employed. ROC-AUC, a trustworthy measure of model performance, was employed to evaluate the model's capacity to distinguish between positive and negative categories at all levels. MCC, which is especially well-suited for binary classification issues with class imbalance, was used as a balanced metric that accounts for true and false positives as well as negatives. In order to measure the degree of agreement between the expected and actual labels, Cohen's kappa was finally estimated. These several evaluation criteria provided a comprehensive study of the model's performance, enabling it to successfully address the difficulties presented by the mental health prediction tasks. The suggested model (TNPE) is compared with kNN, DT, and NB in the table.

Accuracy measures the percentage of correctly classified instances out of the total predictions made. Higher accuracy indicates better general performance:

$$\text{Accuracy} = \frac{\text{TP} + \text{TN}}{\text{TP} + \text{TN} + \text{FP} + \text{FN}} \tag{22}$$

The F_1-score strikes a balance between recall and precision. It is essential for unbalanced data, such as mental health classifications, where clinical repercussions may result from overpredicting (false positive) or missing a case (false negative):

$$F_1\text{-score} = 2 \ast \frac{\text{Precision} \ast \text{Recall}}{\text{Precision} + \text{Recall}} \tag{23}$$

$$\text{Precision} = \frac{\text{TP}}{\text{TP} + \text{FP}} \tag{24}$$

$$\text{Recall} = \frac{\text{TP}}{\text{TP} + \text{FN}} \tag{25}$$

AUC-ROC – The model's capacity to distinguish between classes across all thresholds is gauged using ROC-AUC. Better discrimination is shown by a number near 1.0, whilst a random guess is represented by a value of 0.5:

$$\text{AUC} = \sum_{i=1}^{n-1} (\text{FPR}_{i+1} - \text{FPR}_{i+1}) . \frac{\text{TPR}_{i+1} + \text{TPR}_i}{2} \tag{26}$$

$$\text{TPR} = \frac{\text{TP}}{\text{TP} + \text{FN}} \tag{27}$$

$$\text{FPR} = \frac{\text{FP}}{\text{FP} + \text{TN}} \tag{28}$$

Matthews Correlation Coefficient (MCC): In binary classification, the MCC is a balanced metric that is especially useful in datasets that are unbalanced. It takes into account both true and false positives as well as negatives. Perfect prediction is represented by a value of +1, no better than chance by a value of 0, and total disagreement by a value of −1. TP, TN, FP, and FN are all taken into consideration by this balanced metric:

$$\mathrm{MCC} = \frac{(\mathrm{TP}*\mathrm{TN}) - (\mathrm{FP}*\mathrm{FN})}{\sqrt{(\mathrm{TP}+\mathrm{FP})(\mathrm{TP}+\mathrm{FN})(\mathrm{TN}+\mathrm{FP})(\mathrm{TN}+\mathrm{FN})}} \tag{29}$$

Table 1 shows the comparative analysis proposed method (TNPE) with the contrasted methods like kNN, DT, NB, MLP, AdaBoost, and GBM.

Table 1: Performance analysis – proposed method (TNPE).

Model	Accuracy (%)	*F*1-score	ROC-AUC	MCC
TNPE	92.6	0.927	0.963	0.852
kNN	85.4	0.846	0.893	0.698
DT	82.7	0.811	0.865	0.651
NB	79.3	0.778	0.842	0.605
MLP	87.2	0.865	0.905	0.731
AdaBoost	85.8	0.849	0.892	0.702
GBM	86.4	0.856	0.899	0.715

Table 1 shows a comparative performance for classification, which highlights the superiority of the proposed TNPE method. TNPE achieves maximum values on all four performance measures such as accuracy of 92.6%, F_1-score of 0.927, ROC-AUC of 0.963, and MCC of 0.852. These findings confirm that TNPE not only outperforms others in accurate case classification but also enjoys fine precision-recall trade-off, high class separability, and strong overall correlation between predicted and true labels. Baseline models like kNN, MLP, AdaBoost, and GBM are equitable but always lag behind TNPE in all the experiments. Remarkably, MLP has the highest performance among the baselines but its ROC-AUC and MCC are not as high as those of TNPE. The most traditional models such as DT and NB are the poorest in terms of performance, echoing failure in dealing with intricate or high-dimensional data. In conclusion, the results validate the effectiveness and robustness of the TNPE model as an excellent method for sound and stable classification.

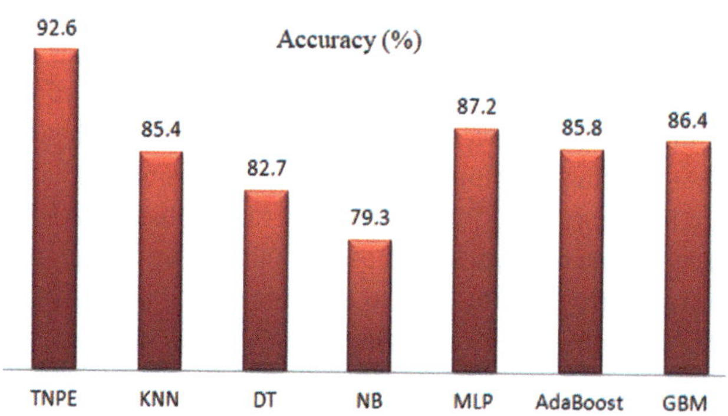

Figure 2: Performance analysis – TNPE – accuracy (%).

The classification accuracy ensures the TNPE model presented in Figure 2 performs with a 92.6% accuracy, eclipsing all comparative benchmark models substantially. Improved performance further attests to TNPE's strong ability to handle positive and negative depression/anxiety cases using a high-variety dataset comprising clinical input and text data. Following TNPE, the MLP is 87.2% accurate using deep neural networks' depth and representational power, yet far from TNPE's optimized ensemble approach. Traditional ensemble approaches such as GBM at 86.4% and AdaBoost at 85.8% also do good performances, which are a testament to the effectiveness of boosting methods in handling high-dimensional data, yet nowhere nearly as impressive as TNPE. In contrast, less complex, traditional classifiers such as kNN at 85.4%, DT at 82.7%, and NB at 79.3% progressively demonstrate lower accuracy rates. Such classifiers are unable to uphold predictability stability when they are faced with the heterogeneity and imbalance of complex-type mental health data, hence the need for the application of complex, bespoke ensemble architecture such as TNPE in clinical decision-support systems.

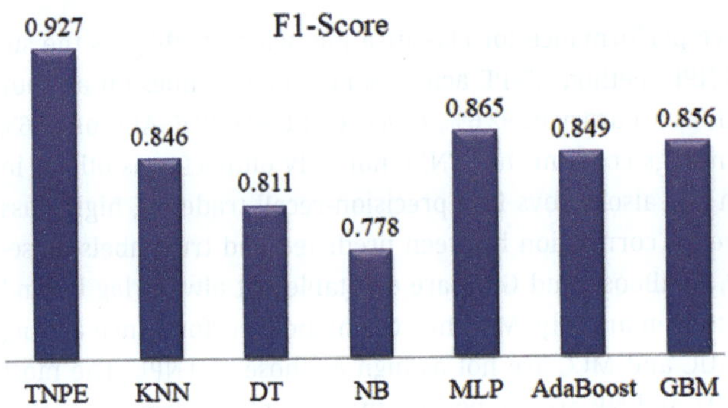

Figure 3: Performance analysis – TNPE *F*1-score.

Figure 3 shows the performance analysis in terms of F_1-score, a hybrid of sensitivity (recall) and precision, both essential to provide stable classification in medical contexts, the TNPE also takes the lead with an incredibly high value of 0.927. This is an indication of the model's superb ability to precisely predict true positive cases of depression and anxiety and minimize false positives, a prerequisite key in mental health prediction tasks. MLP and GBM are closely behind with decent F_1-scores of 0.865 and 0.856, respectively. Even they fall short of TNPE's precision-recall trade-off. kNN at 0.846 and AdaBoost at 0.849 have average F_1-scores that demonstrate an acceptable trade-off but with evident differences, probably due to data imbalance and feature distribution sensitivity. On the weaker end of the scale, NB with 0.778 and DT with 0.811 have the lowest F_1-scores, reflecting their poorest performance in achieving high recall and precision at the same time. These values reflect a greater likelihood to make false positives or false negatives and are thus less preferable to utilize in contexts where diagnostic accuracy is critical.

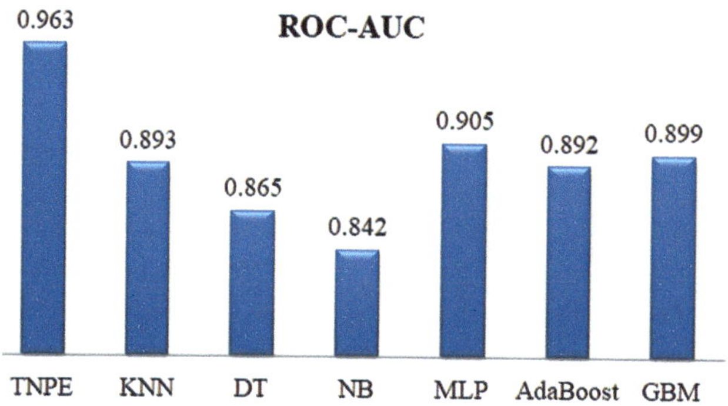

Figure 4: Performance analysis – TNPE – ROC-AUC.

As scored with the ROC-AUC metric analysis in Figure 4, a measure of how well a model can discriminate between positive and negative classes across all probability thresholds, the TNPE achieves a greater value of 0.963. Such outstanding performance guarantees TNPE's better discriminative power to separate instances of depression and anxiety from non-instances with accuracy, a highly desirable characteristic in clinical prediction environments where misclassification is of serious nature. On the other hand, MLP returns a decent ROC-AUC score of 0.905, followed by GBM at 0.899 and kNN at 0.893, with each of these possessing fairly decent classification performances yet not quite equaling TNPE's optimized ensemble approach. AdaBoost at 0.892 lags behind kNN, though competitive yet possessing less discriminatory ability. By contrast, NB at 0.842 and DT at 0.865 share comparably lower ROC-AUC values that signal their diminished ability to always be able to discriminate between states of mind and noncases. That failing is particularly unfortunate in medical diagnosis applications, when very high specificity and sensitivity are crucial to make sure clinical judgments are trustworthy, while preventing pernicious mistakes of diagnosis.

Figure 5 displays the performance analysis in terms of the MCC offering a good assessment through balanced weighing of false and true positives over true and false negatives especially handy with unbalanced sets such as predictions on mental health the best mark of 0.852 is scored by the TNPE. This outcome is proof of the high and consistent capability of correct predictions by the model for both classes, an essential requirement in clinical decision-making situations where both false negatives and false positives are undesirable. GBM and MLP lag behind with MCC scores of 0.731 and 0.715, respectively, for reasonable but significantly inferior balanced performance compared to TNPE. kNN at 0.698 and AdaBoost at 0.702 achieve mid-level MCC values, indicative of moderate balance of prediction but with decreased consistency, particularly in the case of mixed-type, imbalanced clinical data. DT at 0.651 and NB at 0.605

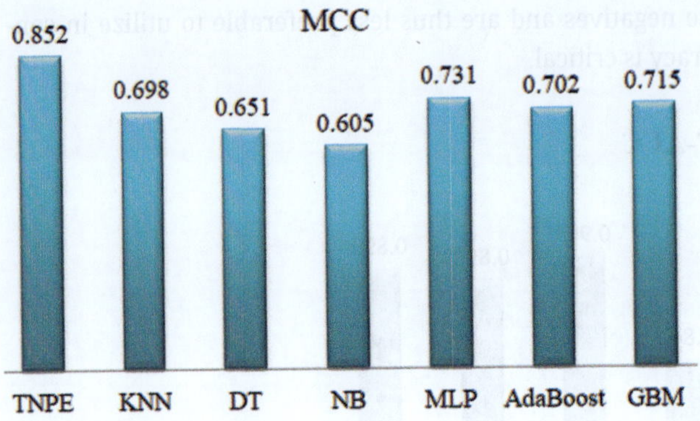

Figure 5: Performance analysis – TNPE-MCC.

exhibit the lowest MCC values, which indicate that these perform poorly in both true positive and true negative accurate classifications. This low performance indicates the danger of misclassification of simpler models when dealing with sensitive health data and once again confirms the advantages of adopting strong ensemble methods such as TNPE for accurate prediction of mental illness. NB (0.605) and DT (0.651), with the lowest MCC values, have low performance in dealing with real negatives and positives compared to other models.

The comparison obviously reveals that the TNPE performs better than the rest of the models in all aspects measured in all the cases and hence is the best performing predictive model for detecting mental health within this study. By incorporating the strengths of ELM and PNN, and CatBoost and, in turn, augmenting their individual contributions by PSO-based soft voting, TNPE exhibits superior performance in the aspects of accuracy, classification balance, discriminative capability, and global trustworthiness. Although the MLP indeed is greedy in its own right with competitive performance, it still lags behind TNPEs in the most critical metrics such as MCC and ROC-AUC, which are of utmost importance in making sound clinical predictions. Aged ensemble learning models such as GBM and AdaBoost are useful and thus viable in clearly established data issues but are still suboptimal compared to the TNPE approach. In contrast, aged models such as kNN, DT, and NB provide poorer predictive results and are barely sufficient to serve as a baseline for the time being. Their failure to adequately address the complexities and imbalances in mental health information attests to their vulnerability, and substantiating the imperative to embrace advanced, ensemble-based approaches such as TNPE for high-risk, clinical decision-support environments wherein diagnostic performance and integrity cannot be sacrificed.

This clearly states the application of careful well-designed, strategy-optimized ensemble models such as TNPE for situations of extreme importance such as mental illness diagnosis particularly in the context of noisy and biased mixed-type clinical data. The comparative study is detailed, depicting how the TNPE model convincingly outperforms standard classifiers in every top evaluation metric. Its combining ELM, PNN, and CatBoost under PSO-based soft voting produces higher accuracy, balance, and reliability for the prediction of depression and anxiety using clinical and self-report data.

Other state-of-the-art boosting-based models like GBM and AdaBoost were adequate but well behind TNPE in stability. MLP-based neural models were as precise as TNPE but short on its reliability in ROC-AUC, MCC, and kappa, which are crucial in medical decision-making environments. The classical algorithms such as kNN, DT, and NB were, of course, surpassed, further justifying the need for sophisticated ensemble methods in dealing with complex, high-dimensional, unbalanced mental health data.

5 Discussion

Enhanced Accuracy and Performance: The TNPE technique consistently outperformed the standard ML models such as kNN, DT, and NB across all the performance measures, that is, accuracy, F_1-score, ROC-AUC, and MCC. This confirms that TNPE is very capable of handling the complexities of mental health data and provides sound predictions for detecting depression and anxiety.

Hybridization of Heterogeneous-Based Learners: By making use of three base learners, ELM, PNN, and CatBoost, the model combines the best of each. ELM provides speed and generalization on small- and medium-sized datasets, PNN has strong probabilistic decision-making capabilities, and CatBoost works well with categorical variables and mixed-type data. This heterogeneity allows TNPE to learn a very wide range of patterns in mental health data, which positions it as a general-purpose model for real-world use.

Interpretability: TNPE's highest value may be its interpretability. LIME and SHAP techniques have been applied in the model, with explainable predictions being given, allowing clinicians to have rational reasons for why they made particular decisions. This feature of explaining predictions is invaluable in clinical application, where one cannot ill afford to lose trust in an AI system.

FS and Balancing Data: Use of ADASYN to counter class imbalance and Boruta to perform FS is strengthening the model and reducing overfitting, which enhances generalizability. This preprocessing is ensuring that the model is learning the most significant information within data and therefore leading to better performance in general.

Scalability and Flexibility: The TNPE method can be used for the majority of mental health data like clinical reports, questionnaires, and tweets. Since it supports a high number of data sources, it is a general-purpose solution for depression and anxiety prediction in most varied environments.

Even though TNPE is better than traditional models, its size which includes a variety of basic learners and is improved by PSO may result in longer training durations, particularly when dealing with larger datasets. Such computational costs can render it inapplicable in real-time or low-resource environments such as mobile health. Model performance is highly reliant on input data quality and preprocessing. Poor-quality clinical records, missing data, or improperly labeled social media data can decrease model performance. In addition, preprocessing steps like text embedding by the USE might be sparse in representing the complexity of text compared to mental health and, in doing so, potentially impacting the model's understanding of more complex linguistic patterns. The data employed here was sampled from clinical histories, mental health surveys, and text data from social media, which would correspond to only some demographic groups or world populations. Therefore, although TNPE is good on this data, how it will perform on other populations or regions with distinct cultural, demographic, or linguistic compositions is not well established. It would perhaps have to be tested again and tuned more generally for broader applicability.

Although satisfactory performance was presented by the model through 10-fold cross-validation, the actual model itself hasn't been tested in real clinical settings. While practicing in real life, real-life predictions output by the model can face missing or inconsistent information, which could impact its dependability. Its real-world utilization and constant inspection must be executed so as to demonstrate its use in real-world clinical settings. While Boruta algorithm FS tries to constraint overfitting, even the combination of an enormous number of models and their interactions in the forms of pushing each other in the ensemble framework are still susceptible to overfitting, especially with cases of enormous features and relatively small amounts of data. Although TNPE performed best under the existing configuration, it must be tested against a huge volume of datasets so that its stability and strong performance under different mental health datasets are tested.

6 Conclusion

This chapter presents TNPE as novel ensemble architecture to enhance the detection of depression and anxiety by synergistically integrating the advantages of ELM, PNN, and CatBoost. With a soft voting ensemble augmented with PSO, TNPE outperforms certain ML models in terms of predictive accuracy. Among the six benchmarking techniques, TNPE performed better than kNN, DT, NB, MLP, GBM, and AdaBoost on all the evaluation metrics. In particular, TNPE scored an impressive ROC-AUC of 0.963 and F_1-score of 0.927, reflecting its stronger capability to distinguish depression/anxiety cases from non-cases as well as maintain both recall and precision in balance. Further, accuracy and MCC were much better in TNPE, which depicts its high accuracy on advanced mental health data. The effective preprocessing was carried out with significant data characteristics through the use of USE for text embedding, ADASYN class balance, and Boruta-based FS. Generally, TNPE is a strong, scalable, and interpretable prediction of mental health disorders that promises much for clinical decision support systems in the deployment to mental health diagnosis, where transparency and reliability are most important for patient care.

7 Future Directions

Even though the proposed TNPE has registered promising results in detecting depression and anxiety, there are several areas where this research can be developed further and expanded. The future studies must explore multimodal sources of data, such as clinical and text information but also physiological signals like EEG, heart rate variability, and speech patterns to increase the feature space of the model and detect subtle behavioral features that are correlated with mental illness disorders. Another step forward includes validating the TNPE framework on larger, more diverse medical datasets, and actual clinical data to test its scalability and generalizability to different population groups and cultures. Application of federated learning approaches may also enable models to be trained collaboratively across institutions without violating patient confidentiality, addressing problems with data sharing common in healthcare. Furthermore, extending the ensemble by cross-testing other sophisticated neural architectures, including graph neural networks for relational data or temporal convolutional networks for longitudinal monitoring of mental health, could further improve predictive performance and temporal sensitivity. Integrating an application of real-time mental health monitoring with TNPE in combination with wearable sensors or social media monitoring software provides a viable pathway for the translation of this research into a clinically useful decision support system. Lastly, working out the explainability framework from counterfactual explanations or causal inference-based interpretability will add more transparency to models, which clinicians can then leverage to create actionable evidence-based findings. Improving this way in the future will make the framework more clinically useful and translate into more tailored, preventive mental healthcare practices.

References

[1] Ogunleye, B., Sharma, H. & Shobayo, O. (2024). Sentiment Informed Sentence BERT-Ensemble Algorithm for Depression Detection. *Big Data and Cognitive Computing*, 8(9), 112.

[2] Aina, J., Akinniyi, O., Rahman, M. M., Odero-Marah, V. & Khalifa, F. (2024). A hybrid Learning-Architecture for mental disorder detection using emotion recognition. *IEEE Access*.

[3] Alkahtani, H., Aldhyani, T. H. H. & Alqarni, A. A. (2024). Artificial intelligence models to predict disability for mental health disorders. *Journal of Disability Research*, 3(3), 20240022.

[4] Khan, S. & Alqahtani, S. (2024). Hybrid machine learning models to detect signs of depression. *Multimedia Tools and Applications*, 83(13), 38819–38837.

[5] Norouzi, F. & Machado, B. L. M. S. (2024). Predicting Mental Health Outcomes: A Machine Learning Approach to Depression, Anxiety, and Stress. *International Journal of Applied Data Science in Engineering and Health*, 1(2), 98–104.

[6] Zafar, F., Alam, L. F., Vivas, R. R., Wang, J., Whei, S. J., Mehmood, S., Sadeghzadegan, A., Lakkimsetti, M. & Nazir, Z. (2024). The role of artificial intelligence in identifying depression and anxiety: a comprehensive literature review. *Cureus*, 16(3).

[7] Ciharova, M., Amarti, K., Van Breda, W., Peng, X., Lorente-Català, R., Funk, B., Hoogendoorn, M. et al. (2024). Use of machine-learning algorithms based on text, audio and video data in the prediction of anxiety and post-traumatic stress in general and clinical populations: a systematic review. *Biological psychiatry*.

[8] Gohari, M. R., Doggett, A., Patte, K. A., Ferro, M. A., Dubin, J. A., Hilario, C. & Leatherdale, S. T. (2024). Using random forest to identify correlates of depression symptoms among adolescents. *Social psychiatry and psychiatric epidemiology*, 59(11), 2063–2071.

[9] Sharma, C. M., Thein, K. Y. M. & Chariar, V. M. (2024). Optimized Support Vector Machines for Detection of Mental Disorders. In *Artificial Intelligence in Healthcare* (pp. 190–219). CRC Press.

[10] Ku, W. L. & Min, H. (2024). Evaluating machine learning stability in predicting depression and anxiety amidst subjective response errors. In *Healthcare* Vol. 12, 6, MDPI

[11] Chahar, R., Dubey, A. K. & Narang, S. K. (2024). Multiclass Classification of Mental Health Disorders Using XGBoost-HOA Algorithm. *SN Computer Science*, 5(8), 1–18.

[12] Gupta, V., Tripathi, S., Singh, D. & Bansal, A. (2024). Predictive Algorithms for Early Postpartum Depression Detection: CatBoost vs. LightGBM. In 2024 11th International Conference on Reliability, Infocom Technologies and Optimization (Trends and Future Directions)(ICRITO) (pp. 1–4). IEEE.

[13] Saha, D. K., Hossain, T., Safran, M. et al. (2024). Ensemble of hybrid model based technique for early detecting of depression based on SVM and neural networks. *Scientific Reports*, 14, 25470. https://doi.org/10.1038/s41598-024-77193-0.

[14] Arora, P. & Dahiya, S. (2025). Enhancing Mental Health Diagnosis with DA-TabSVM: A Multi-Class Hybrid Approach for Detecting Depression and Anxiety. *Procedia Computer Science*, 258, 1348–1364.

[15] Balraj, C. S. R. & Nagaraj, P. (2024). Prediction of Mental Health Issues and Challenges Using Hybrid Machine and Deep Learning Techniques. In International Conference on Mathematics and Computing (pp. 15–27). Singapore: Springer Nature Singapore.

[16] Almutairi, S., Abohashrh, M., Razzaq, H. H., Zulqarnain, M., Namoun, A. & Khan, F. (2024). A Hybrid Deep Learning Model for Predicting Depression Symptoms from Large-Scale Textual Dataset. *IEEE Access*, 12, 168477–168499. doi: 10.1109/ACCESS.2024.3496741.

[17] Khan, S., Saeed, S. M. U., Frnda, J., Arsalan, A., Amin, R., Gantassi, R. & Noorani, S. H. (2024). A machine learning based depression screening framework using temporal domain features of the electroencephalography signals. PloS one, 19(3), e0299127.

[18] Amin, A., Md, I. A. L., Hossain, S. F., Hasan, E., Haque, M. M. & Bortty, J. C. (2024). Predicting and Monitoring Anxiety and Depression: Advanced Machine Learning Techniques for Mental Health Analysis. British Journal of Nursing Studies, 4(2), 66–75.

[19] Upadhyay, D. K., Mohapatra, S. & Singh, N. K. (2024). An early assessment of Persistent Depression Disorder using machine learning algorithm. Multimedia Tools and Applications, 83(16), 49149–49171.

[20] Abbas, M. A., Munir, K., Raza, A., Samee, N. A., Jamjoom, M. M. & Ullah, Z. (2024). Novel transformer based contextualized embedding and probabilistic features for depression detection from social media. IEEE Access.

[21] Shah, K., Patel, U. & Kumar, Y. (2024). Machine Learning-Based Approaches for Early Prediction of Depression. In *2024 International Conference on Intelligent and Innovative Technologies in Computing, Electrical and Electronics (IITCEE)* (pp. 1–7). Bangalore, India. doi: 10.1109/IITCEE59897.2024.10467234.

[22] Jain, V., Kumari, R., Bansal, P. & Dev, A. (2024). Mental Health Predictive Analysis Using Machine-Learning Techniques. In International Conference on Smart Computing and Communication (pp. 103–115). Singapore: Springer Nature Singapore.

[23] Chahar, R., Dubey, A. K. & Narang, S. K. (2023). An Efficient K NN Algorithm for the Mental Health Performance Assessment Using K-means Clustering. In International Conference on Emerging Research in Computing, Information, Communication and Applications (pp. 575–586). Singapore: Springer Nature Singapore.

[24] Korti, S. S. & Kanakaraddi, S. G. (2022). Depression detection from Twitter posts using NLP and Machine learning techniques. In 2022 Fourth International Conference on Emerging Research in Electronics, Computer Science and Technology (ICERECT) (pp. 1–6). IEEE.

[25] Zakariah, M., AlQahtani, S. A. & Al-Rakhami, M. S. (2023). Machine learning-based adaptive synthetic sampling technique for intrusion detection. Applied Sciences, 13(11), 6504.

[26] Haque, U. M., Kabir, E. & Khanam, R. (2021). Detection of child depression using machine learning methods. PLoS one, 16(12), e0261131.

[27] Lu, S., Liu, S., Li, M., Shi, X. & Li, R. (2020). Depression Classification Model Based on Emotionally Related Eye-Movement Data and Kernel Extreme Learning Machine. Journal of Medical Imaging and Health Informatics, 10(11), 2668–2674.

[28] Marey, M., Salem, D., Rashidy, N. E. & ELBakry, H. (2024). Enhancing the Diagnosis of Depression and Anxiety Through Explainable Machine Learning Methods. International Journal of Advanced Computer Science & Applications, 15(4).

[29] Rizwan, M., Mushtaq, M. F., Rafiq, M., Mehmood, A., Torre Diez, I. D. L., Villar, M. G., Garay, H. & Ashraf, I. (2024). Depression Intensity Classification from Tweets Using FastText Based Weighted Soft Voting Ensemble. Computers, Materials & Continua, 78(2), 2047–2066.

[30] Begum, S. R. & Sait, S. Y. (2025). Feature Selection Using CS-BPSO for Depression Detection Based on Profile Information. KSII Transactions on Internet and Information Systems (TIIS), 19(3), 752–772.

Dafik*, N. Ganitha Aarthi, Bura Vijay Kumar, Alycia Sebastian, S. Bathrinath, and Disha Sushant Wankhede

Privacy-Preserving Machine Learning in Clinical Research: Using Federated Learning to Protect Patient Data

Abstract: Over the past few years, the use of machine learning (ML) in healthcare has generated unprecedented potential for disease prediction, treatment personalization, and patient outcome enhancement. Nevertheless, the sensitive contents of clinical data and stringent privacy laws like HIPAA and GDPR restrict the central collection of data and hinder collaborative model training. In response to this, we introduce an innovative privacy-protection approach in the form of federated learning (FL), augmented with differential privacy, secure multiparty computation, and adaptive model training. In this scenario, each individual healthcare institution owns its data and shares encrypted updates of the model only, guaranteeing that the patient records do not become known. Our system design comprises distributed clients (e.g., hospitals) and a central coordination server that compiles encrypted updates to construct a strong global model. The approach also incorporates personalization methods and clustering approaches to address non-IID data distributions typical in clinical datasets. Experimental assessments on synthetic and real-world electronic health record datasets prove that the proposed approach yields competitive performance (accuracy: 89.9%, AUC-ROC: 0.92) with considerable privacy loss mitigation ($\varepsilon = 2.1$). Our method is in contrast to conventional FL and centralized ML models, yet it yields an optimal trade-off among utility and security. It is therefore appropriate for critical tasks such as early disease diagnosis and treatment outcome modeling. The suggested framework builds trust and cooperation between institutions without infringing on personal privacy, opening the door to scalable, ethical, and regulatory-compliant artificial intelligence adoption in healthcare.

***Corresponding author: Dafik**, Department of Mathematics, University of Jember, Indonesia, PUI-PT CGANT, University of Jember, Indonesia, e-mail: d.dafik@unej.ac.id

N. Ganitha Aarthi, Department of Computer Science and Design, SNS College of Technology, Coimbatore, Tamil Nadu, India, e-mail: arthi.ganitha@gmail.com

Bura Vijay Kumar, School of Computer Science and Artificial Intelligence, SR University, Warangal 506371, Telangana, India

Alycia Sebastian, Information Technology Department, Al Zahra College for Women, Sultanate of Oman, e-mail: alycia@zcw.edu.om

S. Bathrinath, Department of Mechanical Engineering, Kalasalingam Academy of Research and Education, Krishnankoil 626126, Tamil Nadu, India, e-mail: bathri@gmail.com

Disha Sushant Wankhede, Department of Computer Engineering, Vishwakarma Institute of Technology, Pune, Maharashtra, India, e-mail: disha.wankhede@viit.ac.in

https://doi.org/10.1515/9783111541235-007

Keywords: privacy preserving, machine learning, federated learning, differential privacy, patient data, healthcare

1 Introduction

The rapid digitization of healthcare systems has resulted in an unprecedented accumulation of electronic health records (EHRs) [1], medical imaging [2], genomics [3], and wearable sensor data [4]. These data have immense potential for catalyzing novel breakthroughs in disease prediction, treatment personalization, and optimization of healthcare delivery through machine learning (ML). Nonetheless, the collaboration of these data assets across institutions is frequently frustrated by strict privacy laws worldwide [5]. These legal and ethical limitations to centralized sharing of data hinder shared model training and restrict the scalability of conventional ML methods in medicine.

Federated learning (FL) is a potential approach to address such issues. In contrast to the conventional ML where raw data are collected at a central server, FL supports decentralized training of the model where data stay at their original location and model updates are shared. The framework allows for collaboration across multiple institutions without any violation of patient confidentiality [6]. Conventional FL is not free of challenges, however. It continues to be exposed to inference attacks, has no formal privacy guarantees, and faces non-independent and identically distributed (non-IID) client data. It also provides only partial support for personalized healthcare analysis.

To deal with these problems, the study presents a privacy-enhanced FL (PEFL) [7] framework designed for clinical research environments. The suggested method leverages DP [8] to add calibrated noise at the model updates such that knowledge about each data point remains limited from leakage. The study further utilizes secure multiparty computation (SMPC) [9] or homomorphic encryption (HE) for secure aggregation such that the central server cannot learn private client information from the updates. This two-layer privacy protocol significantly improves the system's resilience against reconstruction and membership inference attacks.

Finally, actual clinical datasets from real-world environments are inherently heterogeneous in nature. The patients from various regions, demographic classes, or facilities show varying patterns of disease, responsiveness to drugs, and healthcare exposure. Standard FL is not so effective in these environments as it is based on a single global model. To mitigate this, the approach involves personalized FL (PFL) [10] via local fine-tuning and clustering-based aggregation, which enables models to be tailored according to client data distributions. This enhances predictive accuracy as well as the suitability of models in local clinical decision-making environments.

The designed PEFL system is tested on both simulated and actual healthcare datasets in order to compare its efficiency in terms of accuracy, precision, recall, AUC-ROC, and privacy loss (ε). The study also compares it with centralized ML and conventional FL to understand improvements in both performance and data secrecy. By facilitating privacy-respecting, cooperative ML between decentralized clinical data silos, this work brings forth a safe and scalable means to adopt AI in healthcare. It offers an implementable road toward ethical, regulator-compliant, and clinically meaningful AI systems respecting patient trust and encouraging innovation. The major objectives of the study include the following:

- To design and deploy a privacy-preserving ML framework with FL system that enables multiple clinical institutions to jointly train predictive models with shared learning for better outcomes without sharing raw patient data and thus maintaining data confidentiality.
- To use techniques like DP and SMPC to reduce privacy risks including inference and reconstruction attacks, when sharing and aggregating model updates.
- To compare the new PEFL approach to traditional FL models in order to illustrate improvements in both predictive performance and privacy preservation.

2 Related Works

FL has emerged as a robust solution for collaborative healthcare analytics where several institutions can collaboratively train ML models together while maintaining data privacy and security. By retaining sensitive patient information in local locations and sending model updates, FL addresses several problems related to restrictions on sharing data, regulatory issues, and privacy issues in healthcare.

2.1 Federated Privacy-Preserving Cancer Detection

In the digital era, data protection for sensitive health data is important. This study suggests data protection for breast cancer (BC) detection using FL and DP. FL enables model training across various health organization rooms so that raw patient data will never leave the local environment. Beyond supporting privacy through FL, DP statistically adds noise to model updates to mitigate risks for classical attacks and risk of data leak. In addition to privacy requirements, DP noise is statistically added to model updates to help protect against classical attacks and potential for data leak. The method was appraised on the BC Wisconsin Diagnostic dataset with prominent concerns of data heterogeneity, the accuracy-privacy tradeoffs, and computation efficiency. A standard model achieved 96.0% accuracy but required the collection of patient data to store in a centralized software repository, increasing the risk of patient privacy. Results illustrated the technical potential for developing efficient AI-powered diagnostic approaches in clinical environments by combining FL and DP to achieve secure data exchange [11].

2.2 FAIR Federated Health Data Prediction

A federated ML framework has been designed as privacy-friendly and uses "Findable, Accessible, Interoperable, and Reusable" (FAIR) health data to facilitate cooperative model development among various healthcare organizations without divulging confidential patient data. An agent-based system, the framework applies classification models in a decentralized way, building an overall predictive model from local models learned in each organization's secure environment. The design was tested by five healthcare organizations, which each converted their datasets to FAIR-compliant formats through a standardized FAIRification process. Federated ML agents at each location interacted with a central federated ML manager to jointly train a model for 30-day readmission risk prediction for COPD patients, which had an accuracy of 87%. This study illustrates the viability of deploying federated ML on FAIR health data and the capacity for balancing data interoperability, predictive performance, and privacy to enable real-world clinical decision-making under data protection regulations [12].

2.3 Federated Learning for Rare Diseases

A FL model is suggested to improve privacy-preserving EHR analysis. The model makes it possible for numerous healthcare organizations to work together securely by training ML models without explicitly sharing patient data. A number of ML methods, including random forests (RF), support vector classifiers, decision tree classifiers, logistic regression, and stacking classifiers, were employed and evaluated to predict the treatment requirements of patients. With an F_1-score of 80% and an accuracy of 90%, the RF classifier outperformed the others and was capable of handling intricate and class-imbalanced data. The FL-based technique helps to address the major issues of sharing health information and is also compliant with the majority of privacy requirements including GDPR and HIPAA. As a result, it is especially useful in rare disease research, when concerns about confidentiality and data scarcity are more prominent. The system significantly improves the ability to investigate rare illnesses and advances therapy development by facilitating safe data aggregation at institutions. In order to further enhance performance, future research will concentrate on expanding the framework's application to other health domains and incorporating increasingly complex ML approaches. A new benchmark for the safe, open, and moral examination of health data is set by this work [13].

2.4 Federated Deep Learning for Glaucoma

A privacy-preserving DL model to detect glaucoma based on a FL strategy is suggested for patient confidentiality and data security issues and the study is conducted in a multicenter study in seven eye care centers in Hong Kong, USA, and Singapore. The framework enabled every center to locally train models from their optical coherence tomography (OCT) optic disc volumetric datasets. Rather than exchanging data, parameters of the model alone were sent to a central server, which was aggregated using the FedProx algorithm and then redistributed for local optimization. Three various three-dimensional neural networks were experimented in order to determine the robustness of the FL methodology. With 9,326 OCT scans from 2,785 patients, the FL model performed well and consistently at all centers, with accuracy ranging from 78.3% to 98.5%, and maintained high accuracy (81.3–87.8%) on two unseen datasets. The federated model was outperformed by single models and performed similarly to that of regular centralized models, without the transfer of data. This study proves the feasibility and efficacy of FL for developing generalizable, privacy-preserving AI models for glaucoma diagnosis, an essential step toward clinical implementation in ophthalmology in practice [14].

2.5 Privacy Challenges and Mitigations in Healthcare Federated Learning

Collaborative effort across multiple healthcare facilities could significantly facilitate clinical AI uses by accessing larger and more diverse data sets. FL is an approach to training AI systems in which each facility provides only model updates on its local private data rather than the real patient data. The approach has been demonstrated to improve the performance of various clinical AI tasks. But establishing open and ongoing federations creates tremendous trust challenges, considering model updates can lead to information leakage by their nature. Previous work has explored privacy attacks on FL and constructed techniques to mitigate these challenges. This review discusses the privacy concerns specific to FL in healthcare, the trade-offs, costs, and limitations of previous mitigation techniques. It is meant to be a practitioner-oriented manual for medical researchers willing to apply FL as a privacy-aware and secure approach to collaborative AI development [15].

2.6 Adaptive Federated Transfer Learning for Secure Medical Imaging

With the rise of AI-based diagnosis, data privacy in medical picture classification is becoming a more significant health concern. Over 30% of health institutions worldwide experienced data breaches in the past year, making secure and privacy-preserving solutions imperative. This project aims to deliver appropriate privacy-preserving medical image classification by fusing FL and transfer learning. In order to fine-tune on domain-specific medical images, such as TB chest X-ray images, brain MRI tumor images, and diabetic retinopathy images, network architectures employing GoogLeNet and VGG16 as baseline models with ImageNet pretrained weights are used. Various aggregation techniques were shown to yield good classification accuracy. This study presented a new aggregation technique that demonstrated rapid communication and use of local datasets. Federated averaging (FedAvg) and federated stochastic gradient descent (FedSGD) were adapted as needed and based on data divergence in the communication rounds. In order to assess scalability and resilience, the study also verified contemporary topologies like ResNet-RS and EfficientNetV2. The findings showed that combining the advantages of FL and transfer learning to create a scalable, secure, and reliable paradigm for medical diagnostics gives healthcare professionals a way to collaborate on training precise medical image classification models without disclosing private patient information [16].

2.7 Decentralized Privacy-Preserving ML for Collaborative Healthcare

DeCaPH is a collaborative, decentralized, and privacy-preserving ML system designed to enable many healthcare institutions to work together to train models without exchanging raw data or utilizing a centralized server. DeCaPH limits privacy leaks during the training process while enabling safe collaboration in order to meet strict privacy and regulatory requirements. Three distinct medical tasks were used to validate the framework's effectiveness: predicting patient death from EHRs, classifying cell types from single-cell genomic data, and identifying pathology from chest radiography images utilizing distributed datasets from the real world. The results demonstrated that models trained on DeCaPH limited vulnerability to privacy assaults by up to 16% while seeing less than a 3.2% decrease in performance compared to non-privacy-preserving techniques. Additionally, DeCaPH models achieved up to 70% and 18.2% better results than previously used privacy-preserving techniques and significantly segregated private trainee models, respectively. All of these findings highlight DeCaPH's advantages in terms of maintaining strong privacy protection while simultaneously enhancing model generalizability and accuracy as well as its appropriateness for widespread application in collaborative healthcare AI [17].

2.8 Federated Transfer Learning for Breast Cancer

BC continues to be a top cause of death among women globally, and so early and precise diagnosis is crucial in maximizing patient outcomes and survival rates. Although machine learning, and more so deep learning, has been immensely successful in image recognition applications, its deployment in classifying BC is not without challenges given the shortage of labeled data and medical domain privacy issues. The study presents a new approach that integrates transfer learning in the context of an FL framework, allowing researchers to mitigate these challenges in multi-institutional healthcare settings. Mammography and MRI images were obtained from three medical centers, which allowed for a joint global model for training, without any raw data transfer, preserving the privacy of patients. The method utilizes a pretrained ResNet model as a feature extractor and fine-tuned the upper layers on BC data from multiple institutions to learn additional specialized, domain-specific data representations while inheriting the general image representations learned from ImageNet, which was trained on large datasets. Furthermore, the method also implemented domain adversarial training to mitigate domain shifts due to shifts in data distributions across centers, allowing the model to learn domain-invariant features by minimizing the differences in domains and maximizing the accuracy of the classification. Overall, experiments show that their proposed method improved on conventional standalone training and FL without domain adaptation with accuracy in classification of 98.8% and computation time of 12.22 s. These results show significant increases in accuracy and generalizability and validate the use of privacy-preserving FL for improving BC classification, especially in real-world, multi-institutional healthcare settings [18].

2.9 Privacy-Preserving Collaborative Medical Diagnosis

A privacy-preserving collaborative medical diagnosis (CMD) approach based on FL has been introduced to enhance real-time patient monitoring and diagnosis in multiple hospitals while ensuring protection of sensitive information. The establishment of FL preserves patient privacy and data localization through sharing model parameters instead of sharing raw data, which allows the decentralized model training on distributed data. Using a partially homomorphic cryptosystem (PHC) with a residual learning-based deep belief network (RDBN) made it possible to provide secure and accurate classification of physiological data. Experimental results demonstrated that the proposed CMD provides high diagnostic accuracy at various healthcare institutions while providing appropriate protection for privacy. Specifically, PHC and RDBN computations require around 150 and 1,000 ms for encryption and classification, respectively, with 4 and 5 MB of data transmitted in the user-to-server and reverse directions. Additionally, the technique reduces communication overhead by 30% and improves classification accuracy by 10%

on average across a range of datasets, proving its effectiveness and impact in safe collaborative healthcare diagnosis [19].

This survey reports on the latest advances in privacy-preserving FL solutions in several medical disciplines including innovative techniques such as DP, transfer learning, HE, and decentralized systems. These developments indicate encouraging improvement in model performance, robustness, and scalability with confidentiality of patients maintained in multi-institutional data sharing. FL is a novel breakthrough in health AI that enables jointly trained models without breaching patient privacy. Interaction with state-of-the-art privacy-protection technologies such as DP, HE, and adaptive aggregation safeguards the data with robust diagnostic performance and solid models. These technologies effectively tackle key issues of data heterogeneity, regulation, and domain change to provide scalable, reliable, and viable AI solutions for clinical applications. Additional collaboration and exploration of FL platforms can have a huge impact on precision medicine, facilitate better patient care, and promote responsible collaboration in health centers in multiple jurisdictions around the world.

3 Methodology

To address the issues of privacy, data heterogeneity, and compliance with data governance issues in clinical machine learning, we present a unique FL framework to cocreate machine learning models in a multi-institutional healthcare setting. Our framework proposes that ML models can be cocreated by multiple healthcare institutions without the need for patient data to be centralized by any institution, achieving data security, patient privacy, and data governance using secure protocols and model personalization, thereby increasing privacy and model performance.

3.1 System Architecture

System architecture is built to promote secure and collaborative model cocreation from a number of decentralized sources of clinical data. It has multiple local clients which can be any healthcare or research center, such as hospitals and clinics, that are independent data silos, that fully control their private datasets, like EHRs or medical imaging. Clients will cocreate ML models through FL by training them locally using their private datasets. A central coordinating server facilitates the learning process by initializing and distributing a global model to all clients. It then collects privacy-preserving model updates from each institution, aggregates them securely, and redistributes the updated global model. This decentralized structure ensures that sensitive patient data remains within the originating institutions, maintaining compliance with privacy regulations while enabling collaborative intelligence across the healthcare network. The proposed architecture is shown in Figure 1.

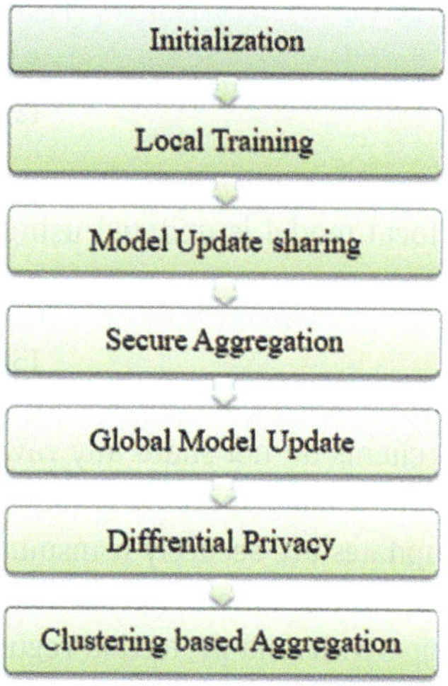

Figure 1: Proposed architecture.

A modified version of the federated averaging (FedAvg) algorithm [20] is adopted to enhance secure aggregation and privacy-preserving mechanisms. The overall goal is to optimize a global model collaboratively across multiple decentralized clients without exposing their raw data. Let K be the number of clients, w_t denote the global model parameters at round t, w_t^k denote the local model parameters for client k at round t, η be the local learning rate, D_k be the local dataset at client k with size n_k, and $n = \sum_{k=1}^{K} n_k$ is the total number of data points across all clients.

Initialization: The first step in the training process is for the central server to initialize a global ML model with an architecture, model, and set of parameters. This model is then sent to all participating client institutions. All clients obtain a copy of this model so that they are all initialized in the same way at the beginning of the training process. The choice of the model architecture will generally depend on the specific clinical task which the FL process is addressing, such as classifying diseases or predicting risk. The central server initializes the global model parameters and then sends this model to all the participating clients:

$$w_o \rightarrow \left\{w_o^1, w_o^2 \ldots w_o^K\right\} \quad (1)$$

Local Training: When each client receives the global model, it then conducts local training on its private dataset. The training must consist of data preprocessing tasks, initially; standardization or normalization, to ensure consistency in input features. The clients must address other issues such as class imbalance by choosing between techniques such as data augmentation or class-weighted loss functions. The models will be optimized using optimization algorithms such as SGD or Adam, and training can occur for a predetermined amount of local epochs, in order to avoid overfitting, and to save communication costs. Each client k will perform local updates on its data-set D_k. The client minimizes a local objective function:

$$F_k(w) = \frac{1}{n_k} \sum_{i=1}^{n_k} l(w; x_i^k, y_i^k) \tag{2}$$

Equation (l) is the loss function and $x_i^k, y_i^k \in D_k$. The local model is updated using gradient descent for E epochs:

$$w_t^k \leftarrow w_t^k - \eta \nabla F_k(w_t^k) \tag{3}$$

Model Update Sharing: After completing local training, clients do not share any raw patient data. Instead, they extract and encrypt only the updated model parameters such as weight matrices or gradient values. These encrypted updates are securely transmitted to the central server. This ensures that sensitive health information never leaves the local site, thus preserving patient privacy and complying with data protection regulations. The client k sends its updated model w_i^k or the difference $\Delta w_t^k = w_t^k - w_t$ to the server. To preserve privacy, the update is encrypted:

$$\hat{w}_t^k = \text{Encrypt}(w_t^k) \tag{4}$$

Secure Aggregation: The central server receives encrypted updates from multiple clients and performs secure aggregation. Techniques such as HE or SMPC are used to combine the updates without decrypting them, preventing any single party including the server itself from accessing individual client data. This layer of security ensures that even the model updates cannot be reverse-engineered to infer sensitive information. The server performs secure aggregation of encrypted updates using protocols such as HE and SMPC [21].

$$\hat{w}_{t+1} = \text{Aggregate}(\{\hat{w}_t^1, \ldots, \hat{w}_t^K\}) \tag{5}$$

After decryption, the server computes the new global models as a weighted average:

$$w_{t+1} = \sum_{k=1}^{K} \frac{n_k}{n} w_t^k \tag{6}$$

Global Model Update: Once aggregation is complete, the server computes a new version of the global model by averaging or otherwise combining the encrypted client updates. This updated model reflects knowledge learned from the collective datasets of all clients, enhancing its generalizability. The new model is then sent back to each client for the next round of local training, maintaining a cyclical learning process. The updated global update

$$w_{t+1} \rightarrow \{w_{t+1}^{1}, w_{t+1}^{2}, \ldots, w_{t+1}^{K}\} \tag{7}$$

Each client receives the latest model to begin a new local training round. The FL cycle continues over multiple communication rounds. In each round, clients retrain the model with fresh updates from the server, and the server refines the global model using new encrypted contributions. This iterative process is repeated until the model reaches a desired level of performance or converges according to predefined criteria, such as minimal changes in validation accuracy or loss. This formulation supports various enhancements such as differential privacy, client clustering etc.

Differential Privacy (DP): Differential privacy is integrated into the FL process to protect individual patient records from being inferred through model updates. Before transmitting updates to the server, each client injects calibrated random noise into its model parameters or gradients. Information leakage is minimized by this noise, which is derived from a probability distribution and ensures that the contribution of any one data point is unidentifiable in the final output [22]. A privacy budget, which measures the amount of information about a particular data point might be revealed, regulates the degree of privacy. Stronger privacy assurances are offered by smaller models, but they may also decrease model utility, necessitating careful trade-off adjustment. Let Δw_t^k be the model update form client k at round t. DP is enforced by adding Gaussian noise:

$$\hat{w}_t^k = \Delta w_t^k + N(0, \sigma^2 I) \tag{8}$$

where $N(0, \sigma^2 I)$ is Gaussian noise with standard deviation σ calibrated based on the desired privacy budget (ε, δ) differential privacy.

Secure Multiparty Computation (SMPC): To further strengthen security against reconstruction or inference attacks, SMPC [23] is employed during model update sharing. Multiple parties can jointly compute a function over their inputs while maintaining the privacy of those inputs thanks to SMPC. To ensure that no one entity has access to the entire update, each client in the federated setup divides its model update into secret shares and distributes them around various parties or the server. Only when the shares are combined during aggregation can the server reconstruct the sum of updates without learning any individual contribution. This approach eliminates the need to trust the server with sensitive updates and protects against insider and collusion threats. Let Δw_t^k be the model update vector from client k. The client splits this vector into M secret shares:

$$\Delta w_t^k = s_1^k + s_2^k + \cdots + s_M^k \tag{9}$$

Each share s_i^k is distributed to a corresponding party. The central server aggregates the sum of all shares from all clients:

$$\sum_{K=1}^{K} \Delta w_t^k = \sum_{i=1}^{K} \sum_{i=1}^{M} s_i^k \tag{10}$$

As long as a subset of shares (less than M) cannot reconstruct Δw_t^k, the client's data remains secure. The aggregation is done without reconstructing individual updates and its privacy is preserved. To increase generalization across clients with varied patient populations and data distributions, PFL is used.

PFL accounts for heterogeneity in client data distributions, which frequently occurs in multi-institutional clinical research. In PFL, each client fine-tunes the shared global model on its local dataset after global model training is finished. The model is able to learn from the shared global knowledge, while also adapting the model performance towards the clients' specific data characteristics, such as population demographics or disease prevalence. In this manner, PFL achieves generalization while maintaining privacy. PFL is especially useful in healthcare where patient populations differ greatly across different institutions. Let W_T represent the final global model after T rounds of FL. Client k performs the local fine-tuning by minimizing a personalized objective:

$$w_T^{k,\,\mathrm{PFL}} = \arg[F_k(w) + \lambda||^2] \tag{11}$$

Here, $F_k(w)$ is the local empirical loss on client k's data, $\lambda||w - w_T||^2$ is a regularization term to prevent overfitting and retain global knowledge. This is also known as local regularization and is a common PFL technique.

Clustering-Based Aggregation: Clustering-based aggregation is implemented to significantly improve model speed and capacity when non-IID data is present. Using characteristics like label distribution, gradient similarity, or update distance, this technique creates clusters of clients with comparable data distributions. Within each cluster, models are aggregated separately, creating multiple semi-specialized models instead of a single global model. This strategy reduces the negative impact of aggregating highly dissimilar updates and improves training efficiency and accuracy for clients with aligned data characteristics. Assume the clients are portioned into C clusters $\{C_1, \ldots C_c\}$ based on a similarity metric sim (k_i, k_j). For each cluster C_v, the server performs a cluster-wise model update:

$$w_{t+1}^{(c)} = \sum_{k \in C_c} \frac{n_k}{\sum_{j \in C_c} n_j} w_t^k \tag{12}$$

Each client in cluster C_c receives its corresponding cluster-specific model $w_{t+1}^{(c)}$ for the next training round. Clustering can be based on cosine similarity of gradient updates or distributional divergence between client datasets [24].

4 Results and Findings

The study uses simulated datasets designed to mimic the statistical properties of real-world EHRs or actual clinical datasets from multiple healthcare institutions. These datasets include structured features (e.g., lab results, vitals, and diagnosis codes) and are distributed across institutions with varying degrees of heterogeneity in demographics and disease prevalence. Each client retains its own data silo without sharing raw records.

In an attempt to extensively evaluate both the performance of prediction and privacy protection of the proposed FL models, several important measures are employed. Accuracy measures the global accuracy of the model by measuring the rate of correct predictions for all classes. Precision examines the validity of positive predictions, that is, the proportion of positive cases predicted which are actually positive. Recall or sensitivity measures the model's capacity to spot the actual positive cases, an important area in medical diagnosis to reduce false negatives. In addition, AUC-ROC quantifies the discriminant power of the model at different classification levels, providing a balanced measure of performance, particularly on imbalanced data. Overall, these tests form a composite framework to quantify effectiveness and reliability in privacy-concerning medical AI systems.

The efficiency of the introduced privacy-protecting FL framework is conducted with the comparative evaluation against conventional FL methods. The traditional FL baseline applies the basic federated averaging (FedAvg) algorithm without applying any extra privacy-protection enhancement, acting as a comparison point for model performance as well as privacy vulnerability. On the other hand, the suggested method PEFL in this research combines the state-of-the-art methods of DP, secure aggregation, and model customization to enable enhanced confidentiality and responsiveness across heterogeneous sources. The comparison indicates the better trade-off accomplished by the suggested method between preserving high classification accuracy and providing robust privacy assurances in collaborative healthcare scenarios.

Table 1: Traditional FL versus privacy-enhanced FL.

Feature/metric	Traditional FL	Proposed privacy-enhanced FL
Accuracy (%)	88.7	89.9
Precision (%)	87.3	89.1
Recall (%)	89.0	90.2
AUC-ROC	0.91	0.92

Table 1 illustrates the performance of traditional FL and the proposed PEFL on key classification metrics. Accuracy improves from 88.7% to 89.9%, which indicates that the enhanced method predicts more accurately overall. Precision improves from

87.3% to 89.1%, which suggests fewer false positives and greater reliability of positive predictions in the privacy-enhanced method. Recall increases from 89.0% to 90.2%, reflecting that the proposed method better detects true positive instances, which is critical in medical use like disease diagnosis. AUC-ROC enhances slightly from 0.91 to 0.92, reflecting enhanced overall classification at various thresholds.

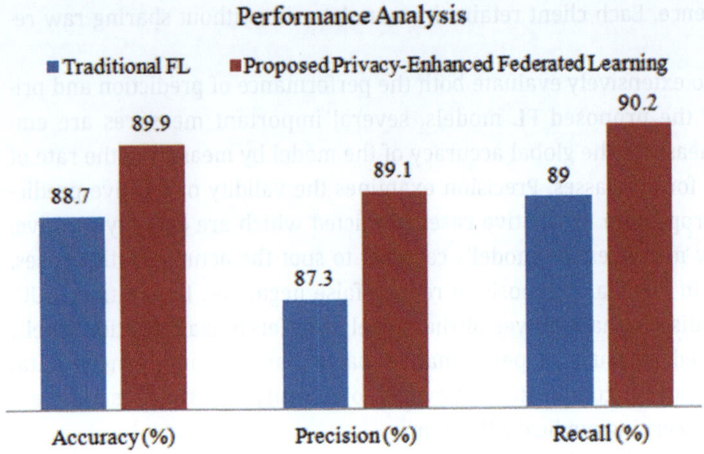

Figure 2: Performance analysis – traditional FL versus privacy-enhanced FL.

Figure 2 comparatively shows traditional FL and the proposed PEFL scheme against three key evaluation parameters: accuracy, precision, and recall.

The output of the traditional FL model is lacking, particularly in healthcare applications. The 88.7% accuracy suggests that, while the model is extremely good in general, it is somewhat weaker since it is less effective with non-IID data and lacks client-level personalization. The 87.3% accuracy would therefore entail a proportionally higher false positive rate, that is, the model incorrectly diagnosing a condition or disease at some point when it is not present a deficiency which can result in unwarranted anxiety or intervention in practice. Second, the recall of 89.0%, although outstanding, suggests that the model can also discard an unbelievably enormous number of actual positive cases, a critical consideration in healthcare diagnosis where undetermined illnesses can be fatal. These figures suggest the necessity of enhancing model personalization and robustness on multi-heterogeneous datasets.

The proposed PEFL architecture shows significant enhancement on all the key performance measures to be very usable for clinical purposes. The model is 89.9% accurate, which implies enhanced overall predictive accuracy with enhanced generalization on decentralized, heterogeneous data sets. Its accuracy of 89.1% also indicates its better ability to suppress false positives and, in so doing, restrict the number of chances for inaccurate diagnoses or unnecessary treatments, a considerable advantage in healthcare centers where the precision of decisions is most important. Its better ability to identify true positive instances correctly is also provided for under the recall of 90.2%, considerably reducing the chance of missed diagnoses. This is particularly important in the case of such applications as early disease diagnosis and prediction of treatment outcome, where early identification of patients at risk can be the difference between life and death.

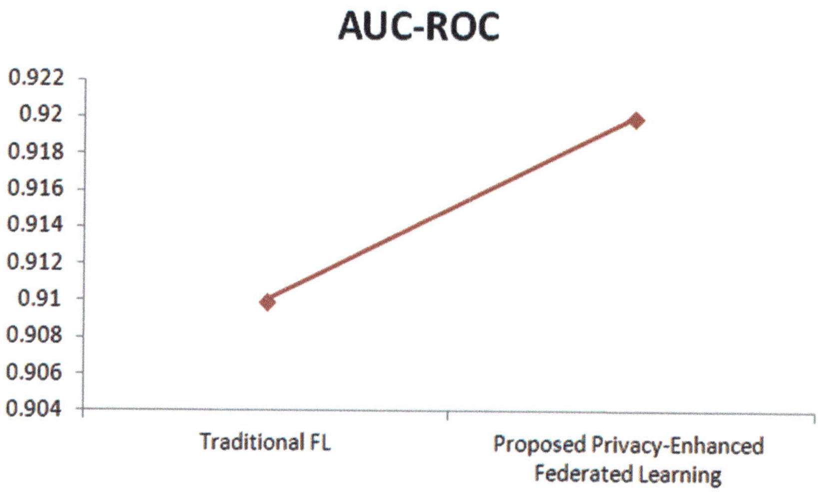

Figure 3: Performance analysis – traditional FL versus privacy-enhanced FL.

Figure 3 illustrates an explicit comparison between traditional FL and proposed PEFL model in terms of their AUC-ROC values. AUC-ROC of the baseline FL method is approximately 0.91, relatively strong performance in distinguishing positive versus negative classes but potentially slightly better. The proposed PEFL has an AUC-ROC of approximately 0.92, a significant improvement over the model's performance in identifying a balance between sensitivity and specificity. The increasing trend in the graph shows that privacy-preserving techniques such as differential privacy, secure aggregation, and personalization do not harm performance but rather enhance the discriminative ability of the model. This is particularly important in medical studies, where correct identification of diseased and non-diseased cases is extremely important. Table 2 is a qualitative comparison of traditional FL and proposed PEFL solution along five high-level dimensions relevant to privacy, security, and flexibility in clinical machine learning.

Privacy Loss (ε): Traditional FL does not provide any explicit privacy guarantee, with its privacy loss parameter essentially at ∞. This implies that while raw data is not exposed, model update data possibly may expose information regarding individual patient data. The PEFL approach uses DP, adding mathematically bounded noise to model updates before sharing. This limits loss of privacy to an empirically measurable fraction (e.g., $\varepsilon = 2.1$), with confidentiality that is provable and guaranteed so that adding or removing any single data point will not make a noticeable impact on the global model.

Table 2: Traditional FL versus proposed privacy-enhanced FL.

Privacy loss (ε)	∞ (no formal privacy)	2.1 (differential privacy)
Secure aggregation	No	Yes (e.g., SMPC or homomorphic encryption)
Resistance to inference attacks	Weak	Strong
Support for personalization	No	Yes (PFL, clustering)
Handles non-IID data	Poorly	Effectively (via clustering, fine-tuning)

Secure Aggregation: Legacy FL is vulnerable from the aggregation side, leaving model updates susceptible to transmission and aggregation operations. The lack of security boosts the risk of unauthorized access or unwanted information revelation. In contrast, the novel approach applies SMPC or HE to execute encrypted model parameter aggregation. As a result, not even the central server can view individual updates, which greatly enhances security and privacy regulations such as HIPAA or GDPR compliance.

Resistance to Inference Attacks: Without other defense mechanisms, traditional FL is susceptible to inference attacks like model inversion or membership inference where attackers can use model updates to extract or learn sensitive patient information. The Proposed PEFL solution is robust against such attacks by both differential privacy and secure aggregation. These techniques restrict the amount of information that can be learned from an individual update, hence making attacks challenging.

Personalization Facilitation: Classic FL trains one global model on all clients regardless of local data idiosyncrasies, which typically results in suboptimal performance particularly in healthcare where patient cohorts and disease incidence are location-specific. The answer here employs PFL methods like fine-tuning and clustering-based aggregation to enable each client to personalize the global model to its own data. Local personalization significantly improves relevance, accuracy, and clinical utility.

Processes Non-IID Data: Clinical data are never IID, yet conventional FL is not robust to such heterogeneity and hence suffers from biased models or generalization failure. The method has avoided this by partitioning clients with similar data distributions into groups and using localized training protocols. In regard to data imbalance and diversity, the model is more robust and generalizable, achieving better performance on diverse institutions with diverse patient populations.

5 Discussion

Our PEFL framework results provide a significant contribution in healthcare machine learning with privacy preservation. In comparison to conventional FL, the PEFL method shows higher accuracy, precision, and recall, which are largely due to the addition of differential privacy, secure aggregation, and personalization mechanisms. Application of differential privacy ($\varepsilon = 2.1$) effectively reduces information leakage, addressing especially significant issues in clinical AI, especially in multi-institutional data sharing. Moreover, SMPC ensures that no individual participant, including the coordinating server, possesses full knowledge of individual updates, thereby increasing resistance to inference attacks.

Yet another important improvement is in model generalization. Standard FL suffers from the problem of non-IID data, where client datasets are rather dissimilar in distribution. This tends to result in a one-size-fits-all model's failure. Through the use of PFL techniques and clustering-based aggregation, our approach enables clients to fine-tune global models locally and exchange updates with peer groups of similar distributions. This enhances model generalizability and applicability to multi-population contexts a major concern in clinical release. Despite such developments, problems persist. Privacy versus model utility scales, specifically in noise calibration for DP, need to be further optimized. Secure aggregation protocol communication overhead can also cause latency, which can restrict real-time use. Nevertheless, overall development reiterates PEFL efficacy in critical application areas such as medicine. The method opens doors to more participative, privacy-aware AI systems in regulated fields.

6 Conclusion

This chapter presents a holistic and privacy-protecting method for applying FL in healthcare research with the aim of optimizing privacy without losing predictive performance. By integrating the most advanced state-of-the-art privacy-protecting methods like differential privacy, secure multiparty computation, and individualized model adaptation, the presented method mitigates some of the most significant shortcomings of conventional FL, that is, privacy leakage, poor individualization, and suboptimal handling of non-IID data.

Empirical tests confirm that the suggested model is significantly outperforming normal FL in major metrics such as accuracy (89.9%), precision (89.1%), and recall (90.2%) and with significantly less privacy risk ($\varepsilon = 2.1$). The architecture of the system is scalable and configurable to different clinical environments, rendering it suitable for field applications like multiple hospitals, labs, or research centers. The inclusion of client clustering and adaptively fine-tuning not only improves personalization but also makes the model robust against the statistical heterogeneity found in clinical data. Above all, the research proves that privacy-preserving technologies can inspire trust among healthcare stakeholders and make ethical AI cooperation between institutions a reality. The approach complies with international data protection regulations and provides an avenue for scaling FL solutions in sensitive contexts. The envisioned PEFL framework meets the bridge between privacy of clinical data and innovation with AI to give a sound foundation for future advancement in healthcare analytics, disease prediction, and outcome modeling without losing on privacy.

7 Future Works

Although the new PEFL paradigm mitigates most of FL's weaknesses, a few directions are still open for further development. As a preliminary consideration, privacy adaptive tuning techniques can be looked into to assist runtime privacy and model accuracy trade-offs, primarily in dynamic client data distributions and update sizes. This can include reinforcement learning procedures to learn, in real time, adjustments on privacy budget (ε) considering feedback from model accuracy or assigned user thresholds.

The other promising area is federated transfer learning integration, where pre-trained models may be shared across low-labeled-data clients, which are prevalent in rare disease data. This will also enhance model convergence rate and effectiveness in low-resource environments. Moreover, future work must focus on minimizing the communication and computation overheads of secure aggregation protocols like SMPC and HE. New approaches, such as compression-aware FL or quantized encrypted updates, can minimize bandwidth usage without compromising security guarantees. From a deployment perspective, actual clinical trials in the field for cross-border data cooperation could be carried out to test legal and ethical feasibility under various regulatory systems. It includes verifying compliance with local legislation such as HIPAA (USA), GDPR (EU), and NDHM (India). Lastly, expanding the model's scope to support multimodal data such as EHRs, imaging, and genomics under a single federated framework would significantly increase the utility of PEFL. Incorporating real-time federated analytics and decision support tools can also render this system clinically actionable and responsive to precision medicine initiatives.

References

[1] Nowrozy, R., Ahmed, K., Kayes, A. S. M., Wang, H. & McIntosh, T. R. (2024). Privacy preservation of electronic health records in the modern era: A systematic survey. *ACM Computing Surveys*, 56(8), 1–37.

[2] Sedghighadikolaei, K. & Yavuz, A. A. (2024). Privacy-preserving and trustworthy deep learning for medical imaging. *arXiv preprint arXiv:2407.00538*.

[3] Zhou, J., Chen, S., Wu, Y., Li, H., Zhang, B., Zhou, L., Hu, Y. et al. (2024). PPML-Omics: a privacy-preserving federated machine learning method protects patients' privacy in omic data. *Science Advances*, 10(5), eadh8601.

[4] Deepak, G., Sharma, P., Jayachitra, S., Chepur, J., Srihari, T. & Judgi, T. (2024). Privacy-preserving deep learning approaches for effective utilization of wearable health data. *Measurement: Sensors*, 33, 101238.

[5] Konnoth, C. (2024). AI and data protection law in health. *Research Handbook on Health, AI and the Law*, 111–129.

[6] Chen, J., Yan, H., Liu, Z., Zhang, M., Xiong, H. & Yu, S. (2024). When federated learning meets privacy-preserving computation. *ACM Computing Surveys*, 56(12), 1–36.

[7] Ahmed, S. T., Kaladevi, A. C., Shankar, A. & Alqahtani, F. "Privacy Enhanced Edge-AI Healthcare Devices Authentication: A Federated Learning Approach." *IEEE Transactions on Consumer Electronics* (2025).

[8] Xie, H., Zhang, Y., Zhongwen, Z. & Zhou, H. (2024). Privacy-Preserving Medical Data Collaborative Modeling: A Differential Privacy Enhanced Federated Learning Framework. *Journal of Knowledge Learning and Science Technology ISSN: 2959-6386 (online)*, 3(4), 340–350.

[9] Liu, J., Li, Y., Zhao, M., Liu, L. & Kumar, N. "EPFFL: enhancing privacy and fairness in federated learning for distributed e-healthcare data sharing services." *IEEE Transactions on Dependable and Secure Computing* (2024).

[10] Barnawi, A., Chhikara, P., Tekchandani, R., Kumar, N. & Alzahrani, B. "A differentially privacy assisted federated learning scheme to preserve data privacy for IoMT applications." *IEEE Transactions on Network and Service Management* (2024).

[11] Shukla, S., Rajkumar, S., Sinha, A., Esha, M., Elango, K. & Sampath, V. (2025). Federated learning with differential privacy for breast cancer diagnosis enabling secure data sharing and model integrity. Scientific Reports, 15(1), 13061.

[12] Sinaci, A. A., Gencturk, M., Alvarez-Romero, C., Erturkmen, G. B. L., Martinez-Garcia, A., José Escalona-Cuaresma, M. & Parra-Calderon, C. L. (2024). Privacy-preserving federated machine learning on FAIR health data: A real-world application. Computational and Structural Biotechnology Journal, 24, 136–145.

[13] Meduri, K., Nadella, G. S., Yadulla, A. R., Kasula, V. K., Maturi, M. H., Brown, S., Satish, S. & Gonaygunta, H. (2025). Leveraging federated learning for privacy-preserving analysis of multi-institutional electronic health records in rare disease research. Journal of Economy and Technology, 3, 177–189.

[14] Ran, A. R., Wang, X., Chan, P. P., Wong, M. O. M., Yuen, H., Lam, N. M., Chan, N. C. Y. et al. (2024). Developing a privacy-preserving deep learning model for glaucoma detection: a multicentre study with federated learning. British Journal of Ophthalmology, 108(8), 1114–1123.

[15] Pati, S., Kumar, S., Varma, A., Edwards, B., Lu, C., Qu, L., Wang, J. J. et al. (2024). Privacy preservation for federated learning in health care. Patterns, 5(7).

[16] Haripriya, R., Khare, N. & Pandey, M. (2025). Privacy-preserving federated learning for collaborative medical data mining in multi-institutional settings. Scientific Reports, 15(1), 12482.

[17] Fang, C., Dziedzic, A., Zhang, L., Oliva, L., Verma, A., Razak, F., Papernot, N. & Wang, B. (2024). Decentralised, collaborative, and privacy-preserving machine learning for multi-hospital data. EBioMedicine, 101.

[18] Selvakanmani, S., Devi, G. D., Rekha, V. & Jeyalakshmi, J. (2024). Privacy-preserving breast cancer classification: A federated transfer learning approach. Journal of Imaging Informatics in Medicine, 37(4), 1488.

[19] Markkandan, S., Bhavani, N. P. G. & Nath, S. S. (2024). A privacy-preserving expert system for collaborative medical diagnosis across multiple institutions using federated learning. Scientific Reports, 14(1), 22354.

[20] Choudhury, A., Volmer, L., Martin, F., Fijten, R., Wee, L., Dekker, A. & Van soest, J. (2025). Advancing Privacy-Preserving Health Care Analytics and Implementation of the Personal Health Train: Federated Deep Learning Study. JMIR AI, 4(1), e60847.

[21] Fares, M. H. & Saad, A. M. S. E. (2024). Towards Privacy-Preserving Medical Imaging: Federated Learning with Differential Privacy and Secure Aggregation Using a Modified ResNet Architecture. arXiv preprint arXiv:2412.00687.

[22] Yan, C., Yan, H., Liang, W., Yin, M., Luo, H. & Luo, J. (2024). DP-SSLoRA: a privacy-preserving medical classification model combining differential privacy with self-supervised low-rank adaptation. Computers in Biology and Medicine, 179, 108792.

[23] Zhou, I., Tofigh, F., Piccardi, M., Abolhasan, M., Franklin, D. & Lipman, J. "Secure multi-party computation for machine learning: A survey." IEEE Access (2024).

[24] Liu, E., Yang, W., Gu, Y., Long, W., István, S. & Jiang, L. (2025). A Survey of Clustering Federated Learning in Heterogeneous Data Scenarios. Journal of Computing and Electronic Information Management, 16(3), 17–22.

Siva Shankar S., Sunder R.*, Rahoof P. P., Thangiah Sathish Kumar, Lingidi Nageswar Rao, and Gayatri Parasa

EpiCastNet: A Spatiotemporal Hybrid Learning Framework for Real-Time Epidemic Forecasting

Abstract: Real-time monitoring of public health is critical for predicting and evading the impacts of disease epidemics. Statistical models and deep learning algorithms have been shown to perform poorly in addressing the challenges that come with temporal and spatially distributed epidemic data. This article presents a new hybrid machine learning model known as EpiCastNet for predicting disease outbreaks and epidemic trends in real time. EpiCastNet integrates spatiotemporal modeling through graph neural networks and temporal convolutional networks and incorporates an adaptive online learning engine that improves over time. The model is trained from multisource information including electronic health records, mobility data, environmental information, and social media. EpiCastNet considerably improves key performance metrics including predictive accuracy, lead time, and spatial accuracy. In comparison to baseline models such as ARIMA, LSTM, and Prophet, EpiCastNet outperforms these in lead time accuracy, averaging a prediction lead of 6.2 days and is more spatially accurate with an intersection over union of 0.72. The composite indicator of early warning performance, the EpiCastNet alert quality index, reports 0.80, indicating a high proportion of actual positive alerts and a low number of false positives or negatives. This model provides a new way of early detection of outbreak, equipping public health agencies with the ability to forecast and respond to emerging epidemics more accurately and rapidly. Flexibility, interpretability, and privacy preserving abilities of the model render it a valuable tool for global health surveillance and real-time decision-making.

***Corresponding author: Sunder R.**, School of Computer Science and Engineering, Galgotias University, Greater Noida, Uttar Pradesh, India, e-mail: sunder.r@galgotiasuniversity.edu.in
Siva Shankar S., Department of CSE, KG Reddy College of Engineering and Technology, Hyderabad 501504, Telangana, India, e-mail: drsivashankars@gmail.com
Rahoof P. P., Department of Computer Science and Engineering (Cybersecurity), Malabar Institute of Technology (MIT), Anjarakandy Integrated Campus, Kannur 670612, Kerala, India, e-mail: rahoof@mitkannur.ac.in
Thangiah Sathish Kumar, Department of Computer Science and Engineering, Hyderabad Institute of Technology and Management, Hyderabad, Telangana, India, e-mail: tsathish.jobs@gmail.com
Lingidi Nageswar Rao, Department of Computer Science and Engineering, Koneru Lakshmaiah Education Foundation, Vaddeswaram, Guntur, Andhra Pradesh, India, e-mail: lnageswararao@kluniversity.in
Gayatri Parasa, Department of CSE, AIML, KG Reddy College of Engineering and Technology, Hyderabad 500086, Telangana, India, e-mail: gayatri.p@kgr.ac.in

https://doi.org/10.1515/9783111541235-008

Keywords: EpiCastNet, epidemic prediction, spatiotemporal modeling, graph neural networks (GNNs), temporal convolutional networks, adaptive online learning

1 Introduction

The recent years have seen increasing significance of real-time public health surveillance systems in disease outbreak prediction and control. Global health emergencies like the COVID-19 pandemic [1], Ebola outbreaks [2], and seasonal flu [3] outbreaks emphasize the need for more robust and precise prediction techniques to inform public health responses. Early detection and immediate response to the new epidemic outbreak can limit the spread to a large extent, reduce the effect on society, and preserve lives. ARIMA and long short-term memory (LSTM) [4] are good old-fashioned forecasting methods but tend to ignore the dynamic and spatial distribution of epidemic outbreaks. This is especially achieved when performing outbreak predictions in real-time because such models might not necessarily be developed to handle spatiotemporal data or to learn how to adapt to evolving patterns of disease over time.

EpiCastNet overcomes these constraints by proposing a new framework integrating spatiotemporal modeling, GNNs [5], and temporal convolutional networks (TCNs) [6] with adaptive online learning. EpiCastNet combines heterogeneous data sources, such as health records, social media behavior, weather, and mobility patterns, to generate real-time disease predictions [7]. The combined architecture allows the system to accommodate not only the temporal dimension of disease dynamics but also the spatial dimension including how transmission during outbreaks works between regions or populations. This integrated strategy provides early warning and early detection with considerably longer lead times than conventional forecasting models.

The architecture is also flexible-capable of adapting to new streams of data and evolving disease patterns over time. The flexibility helps ensure that EpiCastNet still provides correct predictions as disease patterns evolve. Apart from its predictive function, EpiCastNet also seeks to enhance spatial accuracy, that is, predicting the geographical regions that will be most impacted by an outbreak. Through graph neural networks (GNNs) in modeling the relationships between various regions, the system can identify the regions where interventions (e.g., medical supplies and lockdowns) will be most effective.

Whereas more conventional outbreak forecasting instruments will typically apply old data to their predictions, EpiCastNet is equipped with the state-of-the-art technology of real-time data streams. This produces more contemporary forecasts but, critically, ones which more accurately represent the latest patterns in outbreaks as well as permitting a window period of prevention measures for governments and agencies prior to the outbreak peak. With its increased ability in prediction as well as explainability,

EpiCastNet is a revolution in disease forecasting that presents a scalable, accurate, and explainable solution for real-time epidemic surveillance and management.

The main objectives of the present study are as follows:

- To develop a hybrid spatiotemporal model, EpiCastNet architecture, the integration of GNNs and TCNs, to model spatiotemporal dynamics of disease epidemic structures.
- To enhance the early warning and prediction and to improve the predictability of lead times through early outbreak prediction in comparison to present methods, in order to provide public health administrators with timely opportunities for intervention.
- Compare the performance of the model on predictive accuracy, spatial accuracy (IoU), and alert quality index (AQI) against baseline models such as ARIMA, LSTM, and Prophet.

2 Related Works

New advances in artificial intelligence (AI), machine learning (ML), and deep learning (DL) have transformed epidemic modeling into a discipline that can develop more sophisticated, data-based approaches capable of capturing the complex spatiotemporal dynamics of disease transmission. This section presents an exhaustive review of state-of-the-art epidemic forecasting models that cover from classical time-series models to hybrid and ensemble learning frameworks, GNNs, and mechanistic deep learning (DL) models. These models draw on a range of methods ranging from statistical extrapolation and multimodel ensembles to deep transfer learning and GNNs to improve prediction quality, interpretability, and resilience. Together, they form an important step toward creating solid, smart systems for early warning, intervention planning, and epidemic preparedness.

2.1 Epidemic Outbreaks with Time-Series Analytics

In spite of monumental advancements in medical science, the risk of local epidemics turning into mass epidemics remains a significant issue in world health. Pandemics like COVID-19, monkeypox, influenza, and HIV have been infecting populations and overburdening public health systems worldwide. For example, COVID-19 has already affected more than 500 million people in more than 100 nations and claimed more than 6 million lives, whereas HIV is an established global health emergency with a record of 85.6 million reported deaths up to the year 2023. Statistical epidemic trend forecasting is of vital significance for the development of early warning systems and minimizing national and international health threats. For this purpose, in this chapter, an intelligent model of forecasting is introduced and a detailed comparative analysis of some of the most widely used time-series models is conducted. Time-series models to be analyzed in this chapter are ARIMA, polynomial regression, SARIMA, Holt's exponential smoothing, and Facebook Prophet (Fb-Prophet). This chapter contributes to SDG-3 as this precise prediction of epidemic patterns alleviates healthcare systems. The top-performing models gave mean absolute percentage error (MAPE) values of 0.0129 for Monkeypox, 0.0035 for HIV, 0.0011 for COVID-19, and 0.024 for influenza, exhibiting exceptional predictive performance on several disease datasets [8].

2.2 EpiForecaster: Deep Ensemble Epidemic Prediction

EpiForecaster is a novel DL ensemble architecture that has been developed to enhance epidemic forecasting accuracy during rapidly evolving outbreaks. This study evaluates its performance using weekly case data from Brazil, the USA, Mexico, the UK, and France for the 2022 Mpox outbreak between July 10 and October 9. The approach integrates four state-of-the-art DL models CNNs, LSTM networks, bi-directional LSTM (Bi-LSTM), and hybrid CNN-LSTM models. After rigorous hyperparameter tuning, every model produces independent stacked forecasts, which are then aggregated by using multiple meta-model methods. It uses the limited-memory Broyden–Fletcher–Goldfarb–Shanno with bounds (L-BFGS-B) optimization algorithm for dynamically distributing the weights across each model depending on its forecasting accuracy. EpiForecaster yields enhanced forecasting accuracy compared to standard ensemble methods such as gradient boosting and genetic algorithm-based ensembles, with an equal-weight ensemble as a control baseline. Metrics such as mean-squared error (MSE) and mean absolute error (MAE) show that EpiForecaster consistently offers improved forecasting precision. Contrary to the assumption that larger ensembles are better by default, this contribution stresses the significance of the role played by intelligent weight optimization. EpiForecaster is both an efficient and scalable method for modeling nonstationary time series and can be a resourceful tool in a wide range of predictive tasks other than epidemic prediction [9].

2.3 Predictive Modeling of Epidemics and Pandemics

Epidemics and pandemics have wrought severe negative consequences on the health of the world, with major mortality, especially among vulnerable groups. The outbreak and near-immediate global transmission of the coronavirus highlighted the pressing need for enhanced disease control measures. Media reporting, policy planning, and heightened research activity have all been central in designing both short-term and long-term public health interventions. Advances in AI, ML, and mathematical modeling have made it possible to predict various pandemic and epidemic diseases such as Zika virus, HIV/AIDS, Ebola, COVID-19, SARS, and MERS. These forecasting tools have become pivotal for assisting early detection, timely analysis, and strategic response to outbreaks. The ability to rapidly forecast the propagation of highly contagious disease is the key to the adoption of controlled interventions and the delay of the epidemic. The study explains the potential of mathematical and computational models to forecast and predict infectious disease epidemics with the use of big data and intelligent algorithms for improved epidemic preparedness and response [10].

2.4 Epidemic-Guided Deep Learning for Tuberculosis Forecasting

Tuberculosis (TB) remains a major global public health issue because it has complex spatiotemporal patterns of transmission influenced by human movement and behavioral changes. To tackle this problem, we propose an epidemic-guided DL (EGDL) framework that harmoniously combines mechanistic epidemiological modeling with sophisticated DL methods. At the center of our strategy is a networked susceptible-infectious-recovered model supplemented with a saturated incidence function and graph Laplacian diffusion to reflect both long-term diseases spread and local mobility patterns. Model parameters are estimated strictly with Bayesian methods through Markov chain Monte Carlo, and theoretical analysis guarantees the global stability of both disease-free and endemic equilibria. Building on these observations, we introduce two hybrid forecasting structures EGDL-parallel and EGDL-series that integrate mechanistic predictions into deep neural models, alleviating overfitting and noise suppression in surveillance data. When applied to TB incidence data across 47 Japanese prefectures, our approach produces high accuracy in forecasting across differing time horizons. Importantly, the addition of conformal prediction allows for quantification of uncertainty, thus increasing the robustness and usefulness of the model as an aid to inform data-driven public health measures [11].

2.5 AI Applications for Epidemic Forecasting

Infectious diseases present with varied, sometimes volatile risks to individual and public health. AI and associated technologies, already augmenting decision-making in disciplines, such as economics, medicine, and social sciences, have tremendous potential to change the face of infectious disease epidemiology. This chapter delves into the use of AI systems combining ML, computational statistics, information retrieval, and data science to infectious disease modeling. The recent advances in AI have the ability to speed up progress in meeting urgent epidemiological challenges, with emphasis placed on AI methods appropriate for regular infectious disease surveillance data. We then cover the wider social context for the application of AI in epidemiology, with major considerations including explainability, safety, accountability, and ethical considerations. Lastly, we discuss present limitations in using AI for this field and provide suggestions for capitalizing on present and future advancements in AI to achieve maximum impact in infectious disease epidemiology [12].

2.6 Hybrid Ensemble Model for COVID-19 Epidemic Prediction

Precise epidemic trend prediction is crucial for successful intervention and control of the COVID-19 pandemic. Nevertheless, it is hard to forecast the path of COVID-19 epidemics because the data are highly volatile. Most studies have used a single prediction approach without considering the advantages of consolidating various predictive methods, causing suboptimal results. To achieve this, we introduce a new ensemble architecture integrating three ML models, namely kernel ridge regression (KRidge), deep random vector functional link (dRVFL), and ridge regression, into a linear fusion framework (L-KRidge-dRVFL-Ridge). Optimization of the framework is performed by adopting an efficient hybrid algorithm based on adaptive differential evolution and particle swarm optimization (A-DEPSO). Moreover, input features are decomposed through the time-varying filter (TVF) empirical mode decomposition method to improve feature representation. We do feature selection using the light gradient boosting machine to select the most significant variables. We apply our method to daily COVID-19 case data from Italy and Poland, predicting at two future time points: 10 and 14 days ahead ($t + 10$ and $t + 14$). The model presented delivers high correlation coefficients for both nations Italy ($t + 10 = 0.965$, $t + 14 = 0.961$) and Poland ($t + 10 = 0.952$, $t + 14 = 0.940$) outperforming the capabilities of alternative models. These findings affirm that our ensemble system provides strong and reliable predictions even in complicated epidemic contexts, showing its potential as a strong instrument for epidemic forecasting and decision-making [13].

2.7 COVID-19 Forecasting with ML

ML-based forecasting framework has been proposed to improve COVID-19 number of case prediction and compare the performances of various ML models. Some of the most popular models MLP, LR, KNN, and SVM are employed in this work with an ensemble-based approach optimized for delivering the highest effectiveness in predictions. Applying a sequential model deployment process, data gathering, and framework construction, the study validates the performance of all models according to standard measures like MAE, MSE, and RMSE. Graphical plots illustrate trends in COVID-19 case reports and respective forecasts by every algorithm, that is, the proposed model. Results indicate that the method obtained using linear regression performs better than individual models such as MLP, KNN, and SVM. Ensemble modeling reduces errors in predictions by taking the average of the forecasts offered by different algorithms and improves overall accuracy. Explainable and accurate modeling techniques are vital in COVID-19 risk modeling and pandemic readiness, as research indicates. Besides, the chapter also covers potential applications of accurate projections in the direction of timely interventions in response campaigns, resource allocation, and policy development. The results reflect the significant role of reliable and reactive forecast systems in public health response campaigns. The chapter also covers potential directions of future studies such as application of these novel ML techniques and development of real-time adaptive models. Inter-coordination of policymakers, clinicians, and researchers is necessary to establish a bridge between research evidence and highly effective public health interventions. Overall, the study provides increased epidemiological prediction as well as increased evidence for COVID-19 and planning for future epidemics [14].

2.8 Epidemic Spreading Processes Using Deep Transfer Learning

Traditional data-driven approaches to epidemic propagation modeling and forecasting typically depend on the independent and identically distributed (IID) data assumption. However, epidemic spreading over networks is extremely heterogeneous with regard to the various phases, regions, and virus types, suggesting that the epidemic time series are subject to temporal and spatial heterogeneities and therefore probably do not adhere to the IID assumption. A novel deep transfer learning model by fusing CNNs and Bi-LSTM networks has been proposed to effectively model and forecast epidemics based on heterogeneous data. The method employs a CNN layer for extracting local spatial features, a Bi-LSTM layer for capturing temporal relationships, and a fully connected layer for prediction. In order to enhance the generalization ability of the model, transfer learning techniques are applied. In addition, hyperparameter optimization is performed with particle swarm optimization while training for further improvement in prediction accuracy. The paradigm is applied to study the spatiotemporal dynamics of COVID-19 and explore the pathologic differences between SARS, influenza A (H1N1), and COVID-19 epidemics. The experimental findings in detail demonstrate that the approach is effective to keep up with spatiotemporal variations in epidemic dissemination and distinguish significant epidemiological characteristics among different viruses. Moreover, the approach tremendously reduces the prediction error in epidemic modeling with more accurate predictions of disease dissemination [15].

2.9 Temporal Graph Neural Network for Epidemic Forecasting

Precise prediction of infectious diseases is vital for successful epidemic management and public health policy planning. GNNs have been proposed in recent times as a promising method for epidemic forecasting. Yet, current GNN-based models have two critical shortcomings: (1) they generally widen the receptive field through depth augmentation in the network, which does not really grasp the semantics of long-range connections between geographically remote but epidemiologically connected areas and (2) they tend to work at a single scale, ignoring the subtle, multiscale patterns that are typical of epidemic spread. To address such challenges, A new multiscale spatiotemporal GNN (MSGNN) has been proposed to introduce the multiscale aspect to epidemic modeling. MSGNN incorporates a new graph learning module that seeks to identify long-range dependencies by learning from trans-regional epidemic signals to form a rich multiscale graph structure. We then build upon this by designing a sophisticated graph convolution module that captures both scale-shared and scale-specific epidemic patterns to facilitate more accurate and detailed multiscale epidemic modeling. The MSGNN is tested on new COVID-19 case prediction in the United States. Experimental results show that our model far exceeds current state-of-the-art approaches in accuracy and stability. Moreover, analysis and visualizations show that MSGNN yields interpretable predictions with valuable insights into epidemic dynamics [16].

The ever-present threat of re-emerging and newly emerging infectious disease hazards makes epidemic forecasting extremely crucial and therefore timely. The rapid pace of development of predictive models from the classic time-series models like ARIMA and Holt's exponential smoothing to more advanced AI-based models like DL ensembles, hybrid models, and GNNs is highlighted in this review. Each strategy possesses a unique set of strengths for addressing central challenges of data heterogeneity, non-stationarity, and the complex spatiotemporal dynamics of disease spread. Of special interest are recent developments in deep transfer learning, multiscale GNNs and epidemic-guided hybrid models that have made significant advances in prediction accuracy and interpretability. Besides, the integration of human optimization techniques and uncertainty estimation enhances the robustness and usability of these models for real-world public health settings. With the advancing technology, the synergy between ML, domain knowledge, and high-quality data will be instrumental in the development of future-proof, publicly understandable, and actionable forecasting systems. These advances not only facilitate Sustainable Development Goal 3 (SDG-3) by strengthening health systems but also lay the foundation for improved epidemic preparedness, response, and policy-making globally.

3 Methodology

In response to the growing complexity and pace of public health threats, integration of next-generation computational technologies is now essential for real-time disease surveillance and intervention. This framework outlines a next-generation, AI-based health surveillance system that leverages an extensive range of data sources and current state ML techniques to yield real-time actionable knowledge [17]. Fundamentally, the system consists of four synergistic components: the data acquisition and fusion layer, which integrates a number of heterogeneous data sources; the spatiotemporal disease modeling [18] module, which identifies the complex disease transmission dynamics in space and time; the adaptive online learning engine, which maintains model currency against changing conditions; and the detection and early warning system [19], which extracts predictive information into alerts and visual dashboards to facilitate quicker public health decision-making. Together, they create a complete, scalable system of proactive epidemiological surveillance and response. The major components in the architecture are shown in Figure 1

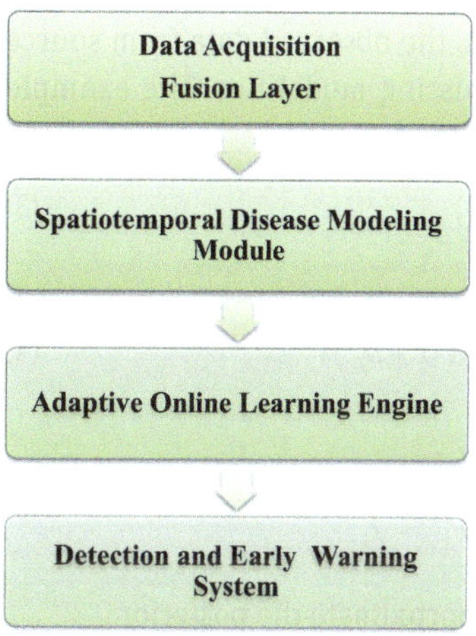

Figure 1: EpicastNet – workflow.

Data Acquisition and Fusion Layer: The data acquisition and fusion layer is the central component for integrating a myriad of heterogeneous and real-time data sources to enhance predictive analytics and decision-making for healthcare monitoring systems. This layer gathers structured and unstructured data streams including electronic health records (EHRs) of hospitals, search engine search query trends (e.g., Google Trends), social media (e.g., Twitter and Reddit), environment and mobility data (e.g., weather, traffic volume, public transportation usage, and GPS mobility traces), official health notifications from organizations like the WHO and CDC, and wearable/IoT sensor data if available. To accommodate the variability and complexity of such sources, a data lake architecture is used to allow scalable, schema-flexible storage and retrieval. Moreover, Bayesian data fusion methods are applied to resolve inconsistencies and uncertainties between data modalities in order to generate a coherent, probabilistically consistent representation of the integrated information. This facilitates stronger downstream analytics and model performance, especially in public health surveillance and early warning systems. Let the input be

$$D = \{D_1, D_2, \ldots, D_N\} \tag{1}$$

where D_i denotes the set of data sources that correspond to different modalities. For example, D_1 represents the EHRs, denotes the social media, D_3 is the search engine queries, D_4 is the mobility and environmental data, D_5 is the official health notifications, and D_6 represents wearables/IoT sensor data. Let $X_i \in \mathbb{R}^{d_i}$ represent the observed data vector form source D_i and $z \in \mathbb{R}^k$ be the latent fused representation integrating all modalities. The Bayesian data fusion framework aims to infer the posterior distribution over the latent representation z give all observed modalities:

$$P(z|x_1, x_2, \ldots x_N) \propto P(z) \prod_{i=1}^{N} P(x_i|z) \tag{2}$$

where $P(z)$ denotes the latent fused state and $P(x_i|z)$ is the observed data from source I conditioned on z. This model allows handing of missing modalities. The example likelihood models for structured data (EHRs) are as follows:

$$P(x_1|z) = \mathrm{N}(W_1 z + b_1, \Sigma_1) \tag{3}$$

For categorical or text data

$$P(x_2|\, z) = \text{Categorical } (\text{softmax}(W_2 z + b_2\ )) \tag{4}$$

For time series data

$$P(x_i^{(t)}|z, x_i^{(<t)} = N\left(f_\theta\left(z, x_i^{(<t)}\ \right), \sigma^2 I\ \right) \tag{5}$$

The inference via variational Bayesian inference to approximate the posterior:

$$q_\varnothing(z|x_1 \ldots x_N) \approx P(z|x_1, \ldots x_N) \tag{6}$$

To optimize the evidence lower bound (ELBO)

$$\mathcal{L}(\theta, \varnothing) = E_{q_\varnothing}(z|.)[\sum_{i=1}^{N} \log P_\theta(x_i|z] - KL(q_\varnothing(z)||P(z)) \tag{7}$$

The fusion output for downstream tasks, the latent vector z can then be passed to downstream tasks such as

- forecasting models
- classification tasks
- anomaly detection

Spatiotemporal Disease Modeling Module: The spatiotemporal disease modeling module aims to shed light on the complex spatial and temporal dynamics of disease spread between geographical locations. It applies a GNN to represent spatial relations in which nodes are used to record individual geographic positions like districts or cities and edges are used to record true relations like human movements and transport networks. In order to effectively model temporal change, the GNN is coupled with a TCN [20] or a transformer so that the system can learn patterns of disease progression between fine-grained time steps (hourly or per day). The dual architecture allows the learning of dynamic spatiotemporal correlations that allow the model to make predictions about how diseases spread through space and time correctly. This dual strategy allows proactive public health actions by revealing burgeoning hotspots and predicting outbreaks to come. Let the disease spread network be represented by a graph

$$G = (V, E, A) \tag{8}$$

In eq. (1) $V = \{v_1, v_2, \ldots, v_n\}$ is the set of nodes each representing a geographic unit, E is the set of angles representing mobility or interaction, and $A \in R^{N*N}$ is the adjacency matrix, where A_{ij} reflects the strength of connection. Each node v_i is associated with feature vector at time t. For example, cumber of cases, population density, and hospital load.

The GNN or graph attention network to capture spatial dependencies. A common GCN update rule at layer l

$$H^{(l+1)} = \sigma\left(AH^{(l)}\ W^{(l)}\right) \tag{9}$$

where A is the normalized adjacency matrix with self-loops, $H^{(l)} \in R^{N*d_t}$ are the node features at layer l and $W^{(l)}$ are the learnable weight matrix and σ is the nonlinear function. The output is given by

$$H_{\text{spatial}} = \text{GNN}\left(X^{(t)},\ A\right) \tag{10}$$

A TCN applies to 1D convolutions over the temporal axis per node is given by

$$H_{\text{temporal}} = \text{TCN}\left(H_{\text{spatial}}^{1:T}\right) \tag{11}$$

Each node's time series is processed as

$$h_i^{(t)} = f_{\text{TCN}}\ \left(h_i^{(t-k+1)}, \ldots,\ h_i^{(t)}\ \right) \tag{12}$$

In eq. (12) k is the receptive field and f_{TCN} is a stack of dilated casual convolutions.

Adaptive Online Learning Engine: Adaptive online learning engine makes the predictive model always current and real-time responsive by constantly learning from fresh arriving data. The module employs a meta-learning approach, for example, model-agnostic meta-learning [21] or online gradient boosting [22], in trying to support rapid model updates without full retraining from scratch. It is especially engineered to bypass concept drift the changing statistical character of data in reaction to developing virus strains, human behavior adjustment, or the effects of public health interventions. Through learning to learn from small incremental updates, the system preserves high performance in dynamic environments. In addition, an active learning component is integrated that identifies areas or cases of high uncertainty and prioritizes them for enhanced data collection or notification. This responsive component allows for prompt decision-making, particularly in fast-moving public health crises.

Detection and Early Warning System: This system converts predictive signals into operational intelligence by tracking disease trends and providing timely alerts. Relying on model predictions and corresponding confidence intervals, the system initiates warnings when estimated case numbers surpass adaptive thresholds derived from learned patterns of historical outbreaks, providing context-aware responsiveness. Its real-time estimates the effective reproduction number $R(t)$ dynamically from estimated transmission parameters of the GNN-based spatiotemporal model, yielding a numerical estimate of the contagion risk. To support situational awareness, the system offers a spatiotemporal heatmap dashboard with predictive overlays to allow stakeholders to view current hotspots, future spread, and temporal dynamics across geographic scales. This general early warning capability supports informed public health policy and rapid intervention deployment.

4 Results and Findings

To effectively assess predictive models for the prediction of infectious diseases, both regression and classification metrics are needed. For continuous predictions of case counts, regression metrics like MAE, RMSE, MAPE, and the R^2 score (coefficient of determination) are applied. These are used to assess the accuracy, reliability, and explanatory power of the model. However, if the task is to classify outbreak and non-outbreak incidents, classification metrics come into play. Precision, recall, and F_1-score help to measure the model's performance in correctly labeling outbreaks, while AUC-ROC helps in appreciating its overall classification ability. Also, the precision-recall AUC is especially useful in imbalanced environments, where outbreaks are infrequent, such that the model will not be insensitive to minority class detection. Combining, these measures give a solid framework for evaluating model performance on both regression and classification problems.

To measure temporal accuracy quantitatively, average lead time (ALT) is employed to assess how far in advance a model can forecast the outbreak time. ALT is calculated as the divergence between the prediction time when the model forecasts a potential outbreak and the actual outbreak time, the day when cases cross a predefined level of detection, such as the peak day. This lead time is calculated for every outbreak in the test set, and the average of all N outbreaks produces the ALT. A larger ALT value means that the model consistently gives earlier warnings, which is essential for facilitating public health responses in a timely manner, for example, deploying resources, triggering containment actions, or alerting the public. Therefore, ALT is an important indicator of the effectiveness of a model in enabling proactive decision-making and mitigating the effect of infectious disease epidemics:

$$\text{ALT} = \frac{1}{N}\sum_{i-1}^{N}(\text{Prediction time} - \text{actual outbreak time})$$

Spatial accuracy is an important element of outbreak prediction models, and it is measured against the intersection over union (IoU) score. IoU measures how accurately a model can mark the affected geographic zones by comparing overlap between predicted and actual outbreak zones. It measures how much the intersection the overlap of predicted and actual outbreak regions is the union, the sum of the two regions. The higher the value of IoU, the more accurate is the spatial localization in the sense that the model is able to localize better the regions at risk. An IoU measure closer to 1 indicates good localization, and those close to 0 indicate poor correspondence between prediction and actuality. Correct positioning in space matters to guide directed interventions, maximize the use of resources, and minimize the disease transmission:

$$\text{IoU} = \frac{\text{Area of intersection}}{\text{Area of union}}$$

The performance of an outbreak prediction model as an early warning system is captured by the AQI, which is an aggregated index that weighs accuracy and reliability in real-time alerting. AQI encompasses three key elements: true positive alerts (TPAs), which are timely and correct early warnings that accurately forecasted the occurrence of actual outbreaks; false positives, which are false alarms that may generate unnecessary panic or misallocation of resources; and false negatives, which are false negatives that can be very serious public health threats due to unpreparedness. A high AQI therefore means a model that not only captures emerging threats with adequate lead time but also suppresses false alerts and therefore is a reliable instrument for informing public health interventions and decision-making:

$$\text{AQI} = \frac{\text{TP alerts}}{\text{TP} + \text{FP} + \text{FN}}$$

Table 1 compares the predictive performance of several models used for infectious disease forecasting, evaluated using both regression metrics (MAE, RMSE, and MAPE) for case count prediction and classification metrics (F_1-score and AUROC) for outbreak detection. The comparative performance evaluation of different models for infectious disease prediction shows EpiCastNet performs better than all others on both regres-

Table 1: Performance analysis – regression metrics.

Model	MAE↓	RMSE↓	MAPE↓	*F*1-score↑	AUROC↑
ARIMA	38.7	59.1	23.4%	0.52	0.71
LSTM	29.4	45.8	18.7%	0.63	0.81
Prophet	31.2	47.5	20.1%	0.58	0.78
Static GNN	24.8	38.2	15.6%	0.68	0.84
Transformer	22.5	34.6	14.2%	0.71	0.86
EpiCastNet	18.3	29.7	11.3%	0.79	0.92

sion and classification metrics. It has the smallest error values for case count prediction with a MAE of 18.3%, RMSE of 29.7%, and MAPE of 11.3%, proving very accurate numerical prediction. Further, EpiCastNet exhibits superior classification performance with the best F_1-score (0.79) and AUROC (0.92), as it possesses a strong ability to effectively detect outbreaks. DL models such as the transformer and static GNN excel in both accuracy and outbreak detection compared to other models, far outperforming classical statistical models such as ARIMA and Prophet. In general, the research demonstrates how well recent state-of-the-art neural architectures, that is, EpiCastNet, perform at giving accurate and reliable early warning of infectious disease outbreaks.

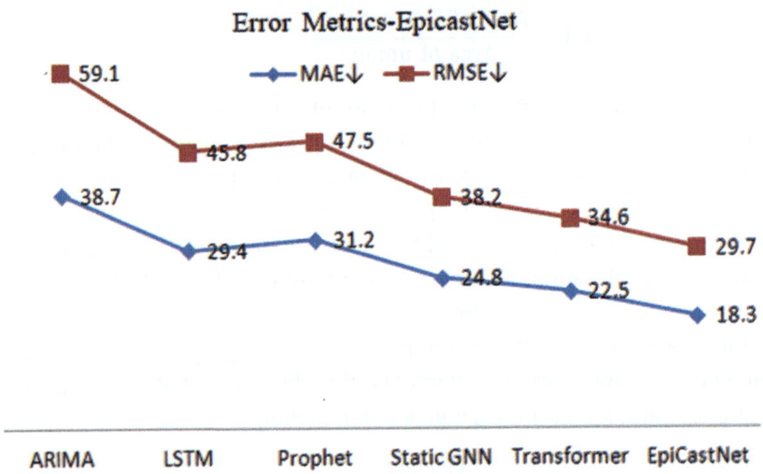

Figure 2: Error metrics – EpicastNet.

Figure 2 evaluates the performances of different forecasting models on the basis of two important measures of error: MAE and RMSE. The story graphically supports that EpiCastNet performs better than conventional as well as deep models, that is, ARIMA, LSTM, Prophet, Static GNN, and Transformer. EpiCastNet demonstrates lowest MAE

(18.3) and RMSE (29.7), which indicates higher precision in prediction and credibility. ARIMA, however, records highest errors (MAE: 38.7 and RMSE: 59.1), followed closely by LSTM and Prophet. The performance is always improved with the models, with transformer and static GNN better than the traditional techniques. The results confirm the effectiveness of EpiCastNet in reducing the errors of prediction and infer its strong strength in predicting challenging tasks.

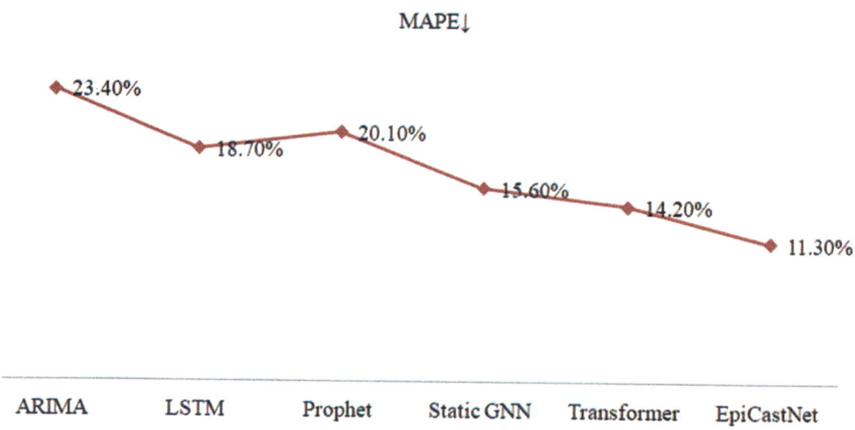

Figure 3: MAPE analysis – EpiCastNet.

Figure 3 shows a trend of MAPE across different forecasting models, where lower values indicate better performance. This trend is seen in the decreasing MAPE from simple to advanced models. The highest error is exhibited by ARIMA with 23.40%, followed by Prophet (20.10%) and LSTM (18.70%), meaning low precision in their predictions. Other advanced models like static GNN (15.60%) and transformer (14.20%) yield better predictive accuracy. EpiCastNet shows the best MAPE value of 11.30%, which reflects the best and most precise predictions among all the models tested. This highlights the effectiveness of EpiCastNet in reducing relative prediction errors.

Table 2: Temporal and spatial frequency.

Model	ALT (days)↑	IoU (spatial precision)↑
ARIMA	1.8	0.41
LSTM	3.4	0.52
Prophet	2.9	0.49
Static GNN	4.1	0.60
Transformer	4.7	0.63
EpiCastNet	6.2	0.72

Table 2 summarizes temporal and spatial accuracy of various outbreak prediction models in terms of ALT and IoU as the key measures of evaluation. The best performing model is EpiCastNet with an absolute peak ALT of 6.2 days, that is, it can predict over 6 days ahead with useful lead time for public health response. It has also the maximum IoU of 0.72 with better spatial precision to identify the affected regions. By contrast, other models such as ARIMA, LSTM, and Prophet have shorter forecast lead times and spatial accuracy, while deep-learning-based models such as the transformer and static GNN realize phenomenal performance improvements. The high-quality temporal and spatial prediction of EpiCastNet are especially valuable in outbreak forecasting, enabling earlier and more effective intervention and efficient deployment of medical assets to where the incidence occurs.

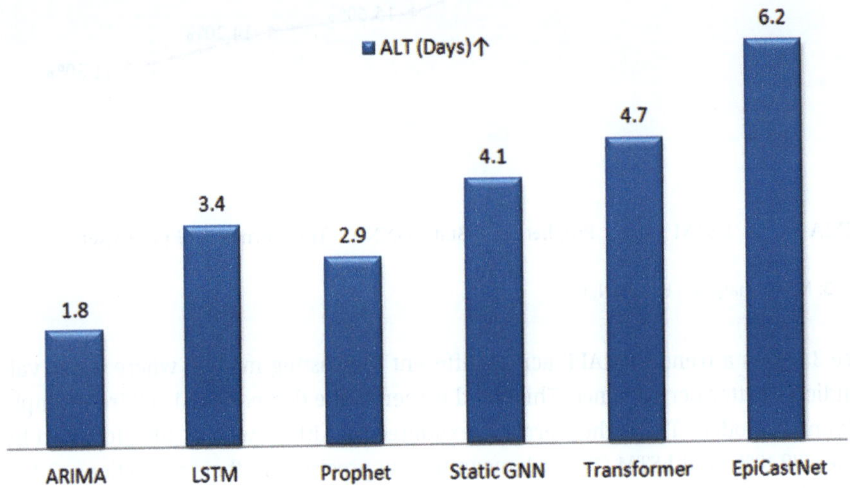

Figure 4: ALT analysis – EpiCastNet.

Figure 4 shows the ALT in days of various forecasting models, with larger numbers showing greater predictive ability. Among all models being compared, the highest ALT of 6.2 days is attained by EpiCastNet, and thus it has greater ability to predict for the future. Transformer-based models (ALT = 4.7 days) and static GNNs (ALT = 4.1 days) perform similarly, as do more traditional methods like ARIMA (1.8 days) and Prophet (2.9 days). LSTM networks perform mid-range with an ALT of 3.4 days. Overall, the findings show that DL and graph-based models forecast better further ahead, with EpiCastNet doing best in this comparison.

Figure 5 shows the comparison of diverse forecasting models in terms of their spatial accuracy using the IoU metric. A higher IoU value indicates greater spatial accuracy of forecasted events. The majority of models are considered, in which the highest IoU value of 0.72 is obtained by EpiCastNet, showing its highest performance in spatial modeling. Transformer and static GNN models also achieve success in spatial

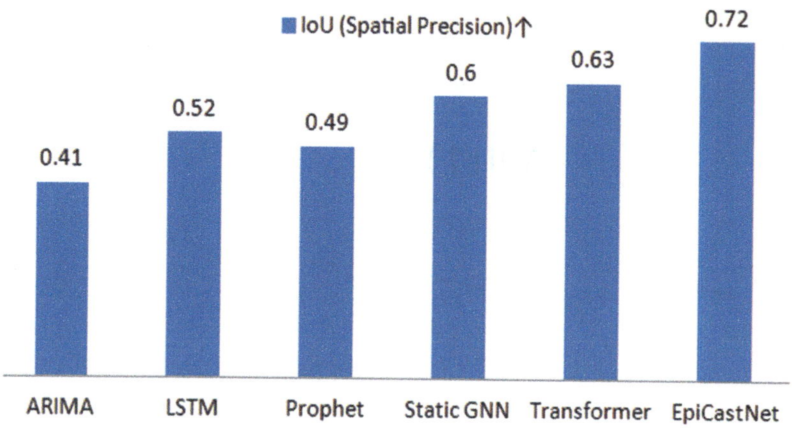

Figure 5: IoU (spatial precision) – EpiCastNet.

accuracy, reporting 0.63 and 0.60 IoU scores, respectively, to indicate that the models deployed with DL and graph-based architecture are better in capturing spatial relationships. Conversely, basic models like ARIMA (0.41) and Prophet (0.49) achieve lower performance on spatial accuracy, and LSTM achieves moderate performance reporting a 0.52 IoU score. These findings highlight the critical need for sophisticated modeling methods to achieve precise spatial prediction.

Table 3: AQI analysis – EpiCatNet.

Model	True positive alerts (TPA)	False positives (FP)	False negatives (FN)	AQI (↑)
ARIMA	15%	30%	55%	0.56
LSTM	35%	25%	40%	0.67
Prophet	28%	22%	50%	0.61
Static GNN	42%	18%	40%	0.71
Transformer	48%	15%	37%	0.75
EpiCastNet	58%	12%	30%	0.80

Table 3 presents the AQI performance results, quantifying how well each model is able to function as an early warning system by achieving a balance between true and false outbreak notifications. The highest AQI of 0.80 indicates that the best overall performance is achieved by EpiCastNet. It possesses a 58% TPA performance, that is, it can correctly detect the majority of the occurrence of the outbreaks before time, and low false positive (12%) and false negative (30%) rates. This shows not only high reliability in triggering early alarms but also low false alarms and nondetection of outbreaks. In contrast, older models such as ARIMA and Prophet are inferior, having low TPA percentages (15% and 28%), high false-negative percentages (55% and 50%), and low corresponding AQI scores (0.56 and 0.61). DL models such as the transformer and static GNN provide much greater balance, with AQI scores of 0.75 and 0.71, respectively, suggesting better early detection and reduced false alarms.

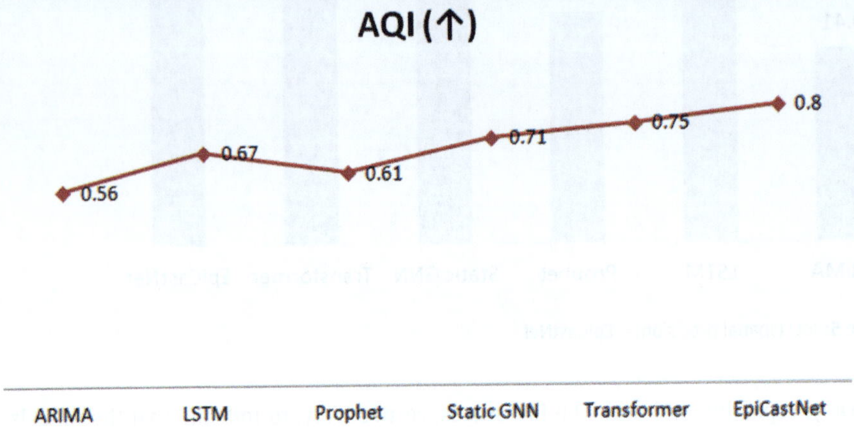

Figure 6: EpiCastNet: AQI analysis.

Figure 6 shows the comparative performance of different forecasting model types based on their ability to forecast the AQI correctly with a higher score representing improved performance. ARIMA is the worst-performing model at 0.56 because it just cannot capture intricate AQI patterns. LSTM gets performed very well at 0.67 because it can readily capture temporal patterns. Prophet, although can capture season and trend, lags behind at 0.61. Static GNNs outperform baseline models through learning spatial relations to achieve 0.71 transformer-based models further advance to 0.75 through effective capturing of long-range temporal dependencies in time series data. The highest-scored model is EpicCastNet at a score of 0.80 and demonstrates the advantage of spatiotemporal modeling and multimodal fusion integration. The trend is the advancement in the model improvement by employing more sophisticated architectures with the capacity to learn both spatial and temporal features relevant for AQI prediction.

5 Discussion

Real-time prediction of disease epidemic by EpiCastNet is a step forward from the traditional models like ARIMA, LSTM, and Prophet. The fusion of spatiotemporal data with GNNs and TCNs provides a robust and dynamic model to identify the spatial and temporal pattern of epidemic spread. The adaptive learning online module allows EpiCastNet to adjust to shifting trends in disease, helping in early warning systems for intervention at the correct time. Handling heterogeneity and uncertainty within the data may be the biggest challenge that faces disease forecasting models. EpiCastNet tackles such a problem by integrating data from different sources such as healthcare records, social media, and environmental data to provide a greater and timelier set of data. The multisource fusion enhances the model and enables it to respond optimally to changes in public health status. In addition, spatial precision and anticipation time offered by EpiCastNet are particularly valuable for public health practitioners who need to respond quickly in the case of new emerging outbreaks. The model's performance remains reliant as much on input data availability and quality, particularly from nontraditional sources such as social media and mobility data. Promising as it is, it must deploy the model into live environments with a keen eye to ethics and privacy, particularly where sensitive health data is being accessed. It will adopt techniques such as federated learning and differential privacy to make this simple, but more is required to do it safely and ethically at scale.

6 Conclusion

EpiCastNet is advancement in real-time public health surveillance. Combining spatiotemporal modeling, adaptive online learning, and multisource data fusion, it delivers highly accurate and real-time prediction of disease outbreaks. Through the use of the combination of GNN and TCNs, the model can understand the complexity of the spread of the epidemic and deliver both spatial and temporal accuracy compared to the standard models like ARIMA and LSTM. The ability to forecast outbreaks 6.2 days in advance and identify outbreaks with IoU of 0.72 makes EpiCastNet an extremely useful tool for health authorities as it enables them to intervene preventively in advance and enable resource allocation to be maximized. Additionally, the model's high AQI of 0.80 indicates its ability to provide timely and accurate warning at a very low false alarm rate. Though the model does well on test cases, it is challenging to employ in practice due to concerns of data quality, scalability, and constant updating to stay responsive to evolving patterns of illness. Nevertheless, EpiCastNet offers a good pathway toward next-generation epidemic forecasting systems that are predictive, accurate, adaptive, and interpretable and can play a role to support global health systems to adapt to improved health crises in the future.

7 Future Works

While EpiCastNet performed optimally in the prediction of disease epidemics, regions that should be researched and built in terms of enhancing practical applicability and utility of the model include data quality and integration. While benefiting from data source heterogeneity, model performance is contingent on having high-resolution social media data in near real-time as well as mobility data. Future research can attempt to enhance the process of data collection, employing more effective data imputation and more effective algorithms in handling noisy or missing data. The other feature that requires improvement is scalability. While EpiCastNet performs well under a controlled environment, scaling it to cover enormous geographic areas or the entire globe is difficult from the point of view of computational complexity and processing real-time data. More efficient architectures, perhaps using edge computing or distributed learning, can be utilized to improve the scalability of the model and process high-volume real-time data at a quicker pace.

Further, EpiCastNet can be enhanced by incorporating other more advanced methods of interpretability and explainability so that public health decision-makers have a better idea of how predictions are made. This will enhance trust and enable more informed decision-making. Finally, research into privacy issues of real-time monitoring and development of privacy-protection methods (e.g., federated learning) will be critical to guaranteeing that sensitive medical data are treated appropriately as the model is deployed in real-world settings.

References

[1] Dash, S., Giri, S. K., Pani, S. K., Mallik, S., Wang, M. & Qin, H. (2024). Optimized Hybrid Deep Learning for Real-Time Pandemic Data Forecasting: Long and Short-Term Perspectives. *Current Bioinformatics*, 19(8), 714–737.

[2] Munday, J. D., Rosello, A., Edmunds, W. J. & Funk, S. (2024). Forecasting the spatial spread of an Ebola epidemic in real-time: comparing predictions of mathematical models and experts. *medRxiv*, 2024–03.

[3] Orang, A., Berke, O., Poljak, Z., Greer, A. L., Rees, E. E. & Ng, V. (2024). Forecasting seasonal influenza activity in Canada – Comparing seasonal Auto-Regressive integrated moving average and artificial neural network approaches for public health preparedness. *Zoonoses and public health*, 71(3), 304–313.

[4] Jain, S., Agrawal, S., Mohapatra, E. & Srinivasan, K. (2024). A novel ensemble ARIMA-LSTM approach for evaluating COVID-19 cases and future outbreak preparedness. *Health Care Science*, 3(6), 409–425.

[5] Liu, Z., Wan, G., Prakash, B. A., Lau, M. S. Y. & Jin, W. (2024). A review of graph neural networks in epidemic modeling. In *Proceedings of the 30th ACM SIGKDD Conference on Knowledge Discovery and Data Mining* (pp. 6577–6587).

[6] Rafee, S. M., Pratheeksha, H. N., Agitha, W., Saravanan, M. & Subbulakshmi, R. (2025). Temporal Graph Convolutional Networks for Predicting Disease Outbreaks in Public Health Surveillance. *Informing Science*, 28, 10.

[7] Rodríguez, A., Kamarthi, H., Agarwal, P., Javen, H., Patel, M., Sapre, S. & Prakash, B. A. (2024). Machine learning for data-centric epidemic forecasting. Nature Machine Intelligence, 6(10), 1122–1131.

[8] Chhabra, A., Singh, S. K., Sharma, A., Kumar, S., Gupta, B. B., Arya, V. & Chui, K. T. (2024). Sustainable and intelligent time-series models for epidemic disease forecasting and analysis. Sustainable Technology and Entrepreneurship, 3(2), 100064.

[9] Soto-Ferrari, M., Carrasco-Pena, A. & Prieto, D. (2025). EpiForecaster: a novel deep learning ensemble optimization approach to combining forecasts for emerging epidemic outbreaks. Stochastic Environmental Research and Risk Assessment, 39(2), 675–695.

[10] Olaniyan, O. T., Adetunji, C. O. & Adeyomoye, O. (2024). Prediction of Pandemic and Epidemic Outbreak. In Health Technologies and Informatics (pp. 58–66). CRC Press.

[11] Barman, M., Panja, M., Mishra, N. & Chakraborty, T. (2025). Epidemic-guided deep learning for spatiotemporal forecasting of Tuberculosis outbreak. arXiv preprint arXiv:2502.10786.

[12] Kraemer, M. U. G., Tsui, J. L.-H., Chang, S. Y., Lytras, S., Khurana, M. P., Vanderslott, S., Bajaj, S. et al. (2025). Artificial intelligence for modelling infectious disease epidemics. Nature, 638(8051), 623–635.

[13] Yin, Y., Ahmadianfar, I., Karim, F. K. & Elmannai, H. (2024). Advanced forecasting of COVID-19 epidemic: Leveraging ensemble models, advanced optimization, and decomposition techniques. Computers in Biology and Medicine, 175, 108442.

[14] Asghar, M., Anwar, N., Hassan, M. & Saleem, K. (2024). A Machine Learning (ML) based Forecasting Model for Covid-19 Patients. Lahore Garrison University Research Journal of Computer Science and Information Technology, 8(2).

[15] Xue, D., Wang, M., Liu, F. & Buss, M. (2024). Time series modeling and forecasting of epidemic spreading processes using deep transfer learning. Chaos, Solitons & Fractals, 185, 115092.

[16] Qiu, M., Tan, Z. & Bao, B.-K. (2024). MSGNN: Multi-scale Spatio-temporal Graph Neural Network for epidemic forecasting. Data Mining and Knowledge Discovery, 38(4), 2348–2376.

[17] El Morr, C., Ozdemir, D., Asdaah, Y., Saab, A., El-Lahib, Y. & Sokhn, E. S. (2024). AI-based epidemic and pandemic early warning systems: A systematic scoping review. Health Informatics Journal, 30(3), 14604582241275844.

[18] Zhu, X., Zhang, Y., Ying, H., Chi, H., Sun, G. & Zeng, L. (2024). Modeling epidemic dynamics using Graph Attention based Spatial Temporal networks. Plos one, 19(7), e0307159.

[19] El Morr, C., Ozdemir, D., Asdaah, Y., Saab, A., El-Lahib, Y. & Sokhn, E. S. (2024). AI-based epidemic and pandemic early warning systems: A systematic scoping review. Health Informatics Journal, 30(3), 14604582241275844.

[20] Mao, J., Han, Y., Tanaka, G. & Wang, B. (2024). Backbone-based dynamic spatio-temporal graph neural network for epidemic forecasting. *Knowledge-Based Systems*, 296, 111952.

[21] Su, H., Hu, J., Yu, S., Liu, J. & Qin, X. (2024). Successive model-agnostic meta-learning for few-shot fault time series prognosis. *Neurocomputing*, 595, 127879.

[22] Chen, Q., Zheng, X., Shi, H., Zhou, Q., Hu, H., Sun, M., Xu, Y. & Zhang, X. (2024). Prediction of influenza outbreaks in Fuzhou, China: comparative analysis of forecasting models. *BMC Public Health*, 24(1), 1399.

S. Padmalal, P. Arumugam, M. Baby Anusha, Kalyan Devappa Bamane, Nagendar Yamsani, and Kireet Muppavaram

Machine Learning for Early Detection of Chronic Diseases: A Case Study in Diabetes Prediction

Abstract: Early detection of chronic diseases like diabetes is very important for early treatment and effective management. This chapter describes a machine learning (ML) solution for predicting diabetes risk from clinical structured data and a case study is constructed on the PIMA Indian Diabetes dataset. The solution caters to the entire ML pipeline: problem formulation, preprocessing of data, feature selection (FS), model training, validation, and deployment issues. Different preprocessing techniques including missing value imputation, detection of outliers, and feature normalization were used for improving data quality. FS techniques like correlation analysis, recursive feature elimination, and selection based on domain knowledge were utilized to decrease the dimensionality of the data as well as model interpretability. Extensive comparison was conducted among widely used classification models like logistic regression (LR), random forest, support vector machine, and XGBoost. It was suggested to adopt a stacked ensemble model of LR, RF, SVM, and XGBoost that achieved better performance in terms of accuracy, precision, recall, and F_1-score. The findings confirm the tremendous potential of ML to enable early diabetes diagnosis as an unobtrusive, data-driven, and scalable decision-making supporting system for physicians. This is the groundwork for the further development of clinically applicable artificial intelligence-based prediction models within real-world healthcare settings.

Keywords: diabetic prediction, machine learning, stacked ensemble model, logistic regression, random forest, support vector machine, XGBoost

S. Padmalal, Department of Computer Science and Engineering, Mangalam College of Engineering, Mangalam Hills, Ettumanoor, Kottayam, Kerala, India, e-mail: splaal71@gmail.com
P. Arumugam, Department of statistics, Manonmaniam Sundaranar University, Abishekapatti, Tirunelveli 627012, Tamil Nadu, India, e-mail: sixfacemsu@gmail.com
M. Baby Anusha, Department Of CSE, Lakireddy Bali Reddy College of Engineering, L.B. Reddy Nagar, Mylavaram, Krishna 521230, Andhra Pradesh, India, e-mail: anusha.medisetty@lbrce.ac.in
Kalyan Devappa Bamane, Department of Computer Engineering, D.Y. Patil College of Engineering, Akurdi, Pune, India, e-mail: kdbamane@dypcoeakurdi.ac.in
Nagendar Yamsani, School of Computer Science and Artificial Intelligence, SR University, Warangal 506371, Telangana, India, e-mail: nagendar.yamsani@gmail.com
Kireet Muppavaram, GITAM Deemed to be University, Hyderabad, India, e-mail: kireet04@gmail.com

https://doi.org/10.1515/9783111541235-009

1 Introduction

Chronic diseases, especially diabetes mellitus (DM), are one of the predominant public health issues [1]. In this context, early diagnosis is a pillar of disease management because early detection enables clinicians to properly treat, sometimes avoiding and even preventing severe complications such as cardiovascular disease, neurological problems, kidney diseases, and retinopathy. Nonetheless, the insidious and generally asymptomatic nature of diabetes in its primary stages often leads to delays in detection, stressing the imperative need for smart and computerized diagnostic algorithms [2].

Current machine learning (ML) [3] and deep learning (DL) technologies offer a revolutionary technique for medical diagnosis. ML models are able to scan large sets of patient data to detect unseen patterns and correlation that might be difficult to discern using conventional statistical methods. Diabetes early detection using ML provides a hopeful solution in supporting physicians in clinical decision-making. By risk stratifying automatically and making predictions in real time, such systems can potentially streamline diagnosis, improve patient outcomes, and lighten the burden on clinicians. In addition, ML-driven systems provide scalability and consistency, which are extremely crucial in low-resource healthcare environments, particularly in developing nations where specialist care is far from easy to access [4].

This chapter introduces an end-to-end ML risk prediction pipeline for diabetes based on clinical data in a structured manner. A complete case study is built on the PIMA dataset, which is a popular and established dataset commonly utilized in medical data science studies [5]. The pipeline addresses all the key phases of ML development: problem formulation, preprocessing, feature engineering, model building, evaluation, and deployment considerations for real-world use. In this work, the possibility of data-driven interventions in facilitating early detection of diabetes is made feasible, and a foundation is provided for the integration of artificial intelligence (AI) into primary care models.

The study involves some ML algorithms learned from structured clinical data toward solving the binary problem of classifying diabetes risk as diabetic or not. The research employed the PIMA dataset, which includes a number of relevant clinical and demographic parameters like glucose, blood pressure, BMI, insulin, number of pregnancies, age, and a function to represent a diabetes pedigree. These characteristics are typically recorded on standard health screening, and hence the results are typically generalizable and clinically useful [6].

This study takes into account several aspects of the ML development process, beginning with intensive preprocessing of data. Missing values found in clinical data were dealt with by proper imputation techniques. The outliers were detected and dealt with to enhance data quality, and normalization was used for enabling features to possess the same scale, a key consideration in feature magnitude-sensitive models. The work also discusses various feature selection (FS) methods such as correlation analysis [7], recursive feature elimination (RFE) [8], and medical domain knowledge-based selection.

The popular classifiers such as logistic regression (LR) [9], random forest (RF) [10], support vector machine (SVM) [11], and XGBoost [12] were trained and compared to assess the performance. The conventional performance measures like accuracy, precision, recall, and F_1-score were used to compare each of the models. Apart from individual classifiers, a stacked ensemble model was created by combining LR, RF, SVM, and XGBoost prediction. The stacked methodology was coded to leverage each of the models' strengths and meld them together using the minimum of their respective weakness. The performance demonstrated that the stacked model would be the most overall proficient one and hence ideal for being applied in a clinic.

Although promising, the present study has some constraints. One such major constraint is the character of the dataset. The PIMA dataset, despite being well-liked, is comparatively small in number (768 samples) and only pertains to a particular subgroup of population female aged 21 and above. The model will therefore not generalize across various populations, ethnic groups, and age groups. To develop stronger and generalized models, next research must include a diversified larger set of data having different geography and demographic bases.

The key driving force for this work is the growing burden of diabetes and need for proactive, scalable diagnostic technologies with a sense of urgency. Furthermore, much of the world's population remains undiagnosed because of access, awareness, and cost barriers. ML has the ability to achieve this by offering low-cost data-driven diagnostic support systems which may be integrated with telemedicine, mobile apps, or electronic health records. The second one is a realization of the limitations of existing diagnosis methods, which depend primarily on cut-off levels of a single biomarker, for example, concentration of fasting blood glucose. They are unable to capture the multidimensional relationship among numerous physiological parameters and are vulnerable to false positives and negatives. This study aims to leverage that potential by designing a robust, interpretable, and high-performance predictive system that can be easily built into healthcare infrastructure. The contributions of the study include the following:

- Presents a ML workflow from data preprocessing to deployment employing the PIMA dataset is specifically used to estimate the risk of diabetes.
- Employs various FS methods and assesses several classification models and recommends a stacked ensemble model that outperforms individual models in key performance metrics.
- Demonstrates the feasibility of ML-based clinical decision support systems (DDSs) and lays the foundation for practical application by addressing real-world deployment issues.

The successive sections are organized as follows: Section 2 provides related works on diabetes prediction using ML frameworks. Section 3 presents the ML pipeline, involving data preprocessing, FS, and construction of a stacked ensemble model. Section 4 presents experimental results and major findings from model assessments. Section 5 concludes the research, and Section 6 provides future directions for improving clinical relevance.

2 Related Works

This section addresses advanced ensemble learning (EL) methods for predicting early diabetes. With novel, noninvasive, and free methods to facilitate timely intervention and improve patient outcomes in clinical environments, this type of research manifests revolutionary advances in diagnostic performance, explainability, and clinical usefulness through the integration of heterogeneous ML and DL models.

2.1 BiLSTM-Enhanced Two-Stage Ensemble for Diabetes Prediction

A new two-stage ensemble approach that combines long short-term memory (LSTM) and Bidirectional LSTM (BiLSTM) models with FS has been proposed to accurately predict the diabetes. In the first stage, several LSTM/BiLSTM base learners are trained on dynamically sampled subsets of features to enhance model diversity. The base predictions are then combined by a meta-learner to generate a final, stable output. Simulation experiments show that good generalization is obtained with moderate FS ratios and that high ratios result in overfitting. Real-world testing on three real benchmark datasets and PIMA dataset was performed. Early stage diabetes risk prediction achieves higher performance than traditional models like RF and SVM and hybrid models that have recently emerged. In properly calibrated form, it records 100% accuracy, AUCs of 99.1–100%, and Brier scores of 0.006 or less. BiLSTM is superior to unidirectional LSTM across trials, particularly on sensitivity which explains its superiority in capturing intricate temporal relationships [13].

2.2 Stacked Ensemble Approach with Oversampling

Diabetic diagnosis process is carried out using four ensemble-based stacked models aggregated and web interface development based on the top-performing model. It utilizes the Diabetes Dataset of 768 patient data, which was preprocessed in Python. For class imbalance handling, the data were divided into four sets and an oversampling approach was taken to divide the data proportionally. The balanced data was subsequently cross-validated for the purpose of acquiring robust model training and calibration. Seven individual ML models were used as base learners, and four stacking ensemble models were built using a blend of these algorithms as an attempt to enhance prediction performance. The performance of every model was measured in terms of the common performance metrics. Among all ensemble models, stacking 1A (LR with oversampling) performed the best with accuracy of 91.5%. In ROC curve, stacking 1A (LR), stacking 2A (RF), and independent RF classifier were the best among them with a maximum value of 97%. It is found that the diabetes diagnosis accuracy is greatly improved when using ensemble models stacked with oversampling compared to the use of standalone classifiers. The integration of the top-performing model into a web interface with an easy-to-use interface further improves its potential use in clinics as a cheap and easy-to-use device for early diabetes diagnosis. It puts a strong emphasis on the relevance of EL and data balancing methods in constructing intelligent healthcare systems [14].

2.3 Expert System for Diabetics Prediction

An expert system for diagnosing type II diabetes, a deadly condition prevalent in most nations, was created using ensemble ML techniques. The purpose is to investigate and compare different classification approaches to decide correctly if a person is diabetic or not. Fifteen classifiers were considered, with five primary approaches being: ANN, SVM, KNN, NB, and ensemble methods. EL takes advantage of the fact that many different models have strengths that complement each other, increasing accuracy and minimizing majority voting misclassifications. There were 400 participants across various regions and 10 physiological features, 5 being numerical and 5 nominal. The ensemble approaches performed better than the individual classifiers with a very high accuracy of 98.60%. This clearly points toward the strength of model combination to deliver enhanced predictions. A simple graphical interface for prediction of diabetes in real time using user input of the 10 features is used. The system can be implemented as a clinical DSS to aid healthcare professionals to diagnose diabetes early and accurately. With timely observation, it facilitates improved patient outcomes and treatment plans and it demonstrates the effectiveness of EL in medical diagnosis [15].

2.4 Super Learner Model for Early Diabetes Detection

A super EL model has been designed for early DM diagnosis, a rapidly increasing worldwide health problem. Conventional diagnosis is time-consuming and expensive but ensemble ML method provides quicker and more affordable solutions. The new model, termed a super learner, is based on cross-validation and combines the predictive results of an ensemble of ML algorithms in order to enhance accuracy. The super learner model combines four foundation learners – LR, DT, RF, and gradient boosting – and SVM as the meta-learner for combining. The performances of the model were tested on three datasets. The super learner model obtained good measures of accuracy: 99.6% for early-stage diabetes data, 92% for PIMA data, and 98% for 130 US hospitals data. The outcomes outperformed one base learner, proving the capability and practicability of the super learner model in real applications. The study as a whole demonstrates the capability of super learner algorithms in supporting early, correct, and extensive detection of DM [16].

2.5 Hybrid Deep Ensemble Diabetes Prediction

Diabetes is a critical world health problem and as such the demand for advanced predictive techniques in the sense of providing early accurate detection. In this study, the predictive accuracy of a range of ML and DL algorithms is compared for predicting the development of diabetes from a comprehensive clinical and demographic data set. The traditional ML classifiers such as DTs, RF, KNN, and XGBoost were attempted initially, and ensemble-based methods were found to be high performers in terms of predictive accuracy. For better prediction performance, DL-based models such as simple DNN, CNN, and RNN were evaluated. While these models were found useful particularly in identifying correct instances, these models' ability to surpass ensemble methods in overall classification accuracy was not realized. The most closely related result of the work was the development of a DL Meta Learner, combining RF and gradient boosting model predictions. The approach achieved close to perfect accuracy, showing the power of combining DL's feature extraction ability with high pattern identification from ensemble methods. The results confirm hybrid model incorporation in diabetes prediction and present an inspiring alternative for cutting-edge medical informatics and supporting medical professionals to deliver timely and customized care [17].

2.6 Advanced Ensemble Modeling for Early Diabetes Prediction

With the growing incidence of diabetes, there is a need to create standard and punctual prediction models, particularly for women who may have specific risk factors. A strong ensemble of deep ML models was proposed to identify diabetes in its initial phase, providing doctors efficient tools to enable early diagnosis and enhance patient results. Some of the powerful classifiers such as RF with boosting algorithms were chosen as base learners for stacking ensemble models because they had high prediction precision. Before training the model, the dataset was heavily preprocessed in order to have optimal performance and robustness. The suggested ensemble model achieved an accuracy of 92.91%, which is very similar to, and in certain cases superior to, current procedures for predicting diabetes. The study also applies SHAP to make the models interpretable, and meaningful information is obtained. Such interpretation will be important in deriving clinical confidence and knowing the predictors of risk of diabetes. In general, the outcome of this study will be likely to be useful to the healthcare providers, researchers, students, and stakeholders with an interpretable and effective prediction model. All these advances will be able to enable early intervention planning, enhance personalized patient care, and ultimately lead to improved diabetes control in clinic [18].

2.7 CatBoost-Enhanced Ensemble Model for Accurate Diabetes Prediction

Diabetes is a serious worldwide health issue that is being addressed with a very sophisticated forecasting model based on multiple ML algorithms. The model uses the general algorithms such as LR, SVM, Naïve Bayes, and RF and the aggressive ensemble methods including boosting and bagging methods. These ensemble methods pool different base learners to increase the precision and stability of the forecasts. Based on a real Kaggle dataset and coded in Python, model performance was evaluated using accuracy, sensitivity, and confusion matrix. Among all the ensemble techniques attempted, CatBoost scored the highest accuracy of 95.4%. The results reflect the efficiency of EL, especially CatBoost, in providing steady and accurate diabetes predictions to aid early diagnosis and better patient care [19].

2.8 EGG-Based Type-II Diabetes Prediction

DM, especially Type-II, has emerged as a serious world-wide health issue with highly prevalent rates in migrant Indians. An increase in Type-II diabetes is more or less due to lifestyle, senility, and changed eating habits. To address the critical demand for early and reliable diagnosis, this study proposes a novel, noninvasive method on the basis of electrogastrogram (EGG) signals. The study employs recording of EGG signals from diabetic patients and healthy patients between 50 and 65 years of age with a three-electrode EGG recording system. The obtained data is processed with sophisticated AI methods to obtain important features that distinguish between diabetic and nondiabetic EGG traces. The study involves the use of explainable AI, that is, SHAP to provide model prediction explainability, and uses meta-heuristic algorithms in FS optimization. The proposed classifier is critically contrasted and compared with conventional models such as RF and conventional XGBoost. Experimental results exhibit the proposed model with a maximum classification accuracy of 95.8%, maximum sensitivity of 100%, and specificity of 92.3%. The study confirms that the suggested classifier, coupled with explainable AI and robust feature selection, is a valid, understandable, and practical method of early Type-II diabetes diagnosis using EGG signals. It is highly promising for real-time noninvasive medical screening, especially in risk-prone populations [20].

2.9 Robust Ensemble Diabetes Prediction Framework

Diabetes remains a major public health issue in developing nations with rising mortality from late diagnosis. Conventional ML models will perform poorly owing to issues like overfitting, underfitting, and noisy data. Constraints of the aforementioned issues have been addressed through the application of parallel and sequential ensemble ML techniques with additional stringent FS for improving diagnostic accuracy. PIMA dataset in the UCI ML Repository was used as a basis for model construction. The preprocessing included missing values treatment through column mean imputation and forward and backward FS. The study entailed two design steps. The initial step in building RF classifier models such as J48, CART, and decision stump. In the second step, sequential ensemble algorithms like XGBoost, AdaBoost, and gradient boosting were used and their outputs were averaged through an average voting algorithm to obtain binary classification. The study provides a highly precise and credible diabetes prediction model that can help healthcare professionals make faster, data-driven decisions, thereby enabling earlier intervention and potentially lifesaving [21].

The study presented shows how EL approaches can improve the accuracy of diabetes prediction. By employing ensemble with diverse sets of base learners from simple classifiers to highly sophisticated deep neural networks, they overcome usual issues like class imbalance, feature difficulty, and overfitting. The use of interpretability tools like SHAP and interface development with ease also enhances their clinical usability. Top-performing models including stacking ensembles, super learners, and hybrid architectures demonstrate that ensemble approaches can effortlessly outperform an individual classifier. Lastly, these advancements introduce robust, scalable, and interpretable tools to enable early diagnosis and personalized treatment in diabetic healthcare management.

3 Methodology

The growing global trend of diabetes has been seen particularly among Pima Indian women, and hence the urgency of early and adequate detection methods should be highlighted. Utilizing the widely utilized UCI ML Repository PIMA Dataset, this article establishes a successful prediction model through the assistance of adequate ML methods. Preprocessing processes are necessary and should involve missing value replacement, outliers, and feature scaling in order to make the model more realistic. FS techniques and ensemble techniques like LR, RF, SVM, and XGBoost are stacked into a framework. This structure increases predictability, and it is now possible to make timely and evidence-based clinical decisions in diabetes early diagnosis. This case study investigates the use of ML methods to use patient health data to predict diabetes early.

3.1 Dataset Description

The Pima Indians Diabetes Dataset is a health-related data collected from 768 women patients of above 21 years old. The dataset is generally used for binary classification problems, where the problem is to predict whether the patient is diabetic (1) or not

(0) from a list of medical features. There are eight attributes in the data set and the eight features provide an impression of a patient's general condition of health which can be utilized for the generation of prediction models for diabetes diagnosis [22].

3.2 Data Preprocessing

Preprocessing is a vital step in the development of a sound and accurate ML model used for diabetes prediction. The data set would contain missing or zero values for major features such as insulin and BMI, which if not processed could lead to biased analysis. Such outlier or missing values are treated mostly by either imputation methods such as zero replacement via median values or by KNN imputation [23]. Also, outliers are removed using methods like interquartile range or *Z*-score technique to find out and delete those extreme values that would be deleterious for training the model. For maintaining the characteristics of the same magnitude, standardization or normalization techniques like min-max scaling or StandardScaler are used to normalize all values to the same order of magnitude. Also, if there are some categorical variables in the data set (e.g., gender), one-hot encoding or label encoding is used in transforming the categories into numerical values to be fed into ML algorithms. By combining these preprocessing procedures, the model extracts more insightful patterns from the data.

3.3 Feature Selection/Engineering

In diabetes prediction problems, FS and engineering are essential for enhancing model performance and lowering complexity. Statistical analysis that includes correlation through Pearson or Spearman correlation allows detection of linear or monotonic correlation between target variable and input features. Highly correlated features with the outcome (e.g., BMI or glucose with diabetes status) are retained, while highly correlated features among themselves can be removed to remove redundancy and multicollinearity.

RFE is an FS wrapper method that repeatedly removes less important features according to the performance of the specified estimator (e.g., RF or LR). This minimizes the best predictors by sorting feature importance and removing the least effective ones step by step, ultimately optimizing the input space for the model [24]. Domain knowledge is integrated, especially on medical data sets. Clinically important features with proven impacts on diabetes are taken into account even though they are not statistically significant. This ensures that the model stays close to medicine and is still interpretable to doctors.

Furthermore, dimension reduction techniques can be used in scenarios where one deals with high-dimensional data. They transform the original features into a low number of components preserving most variance or maximization of class separability.

3.4 Classification Models

Detecting diabetes at an early stage is a very serious process in order to avoid serious health issues and offer timely medical care. In this study, an attempt has been made to establish a ML model that would identify whether a patient has or does not have diabetes based on a combination of clinical parameters like blood glucose, BMI, insulin, blood pressure, age, and other similar health factors. This predictive model seeks to assist medical practitioners in making evidence-based decisions by selecting individuals with high risk before the onset of serious symptoms. The problem has been presented as a binary classification problem and the model will predict either of two classes: diabetic (positive) or nondiabetic (negative). This formulation allows the application of existing classification techniques to decide on the diabetes presence from the given data.

3.4.1 Proposed Stacked Model

The proposed stacked framework for diabetes prediction uses heterogeneous ML models to benefit from their own strengths and acquire enhanced overall performance. Three learners are utilized here: LR, RF, and SVM. LR can detect linear associations between clinical variables and the susceptibility to diabetes and offers increased interpretability RF as an ensemble decision tree is suitable for modeling strong feature interactions and noise resilient. SVM performs well in datasets where there are boundaries by identifying the best separating hyperplane even for nonlinear ones. The predictions of these models are then combined and presented to a meta-learner, often XGBoost, which sums up their predictions and learns to best improve them. XGBoost is very well suited to structured medical data, as it is highly accurate and resistant to overfitting. This stacked configuration nicely balances simplicity, complexity, and generalization and therefore is extremely well suited to the task of predicting diabetes from clinical data. Figure 1 specifies the stacked model for classification.

3.4.2 Logistic Regression

With its ability to estimate the likelihood of a binary goal, LR is a linear classification framework that can be used to predict if a person has diabetes or not. It creates a sigmoid-shaped function that represents the relationship between the input features

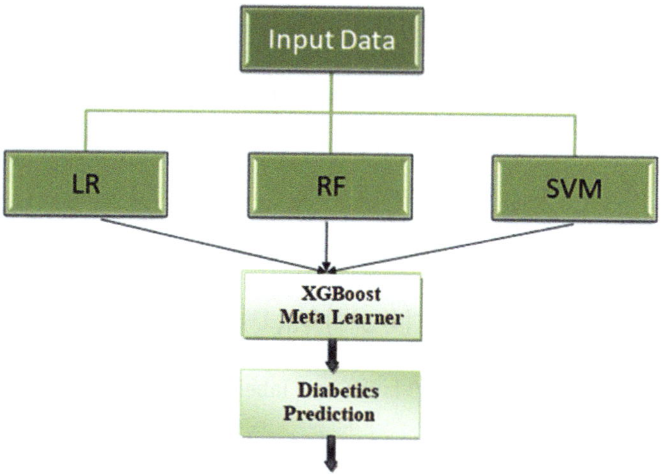

Figure 1: Stacked model.

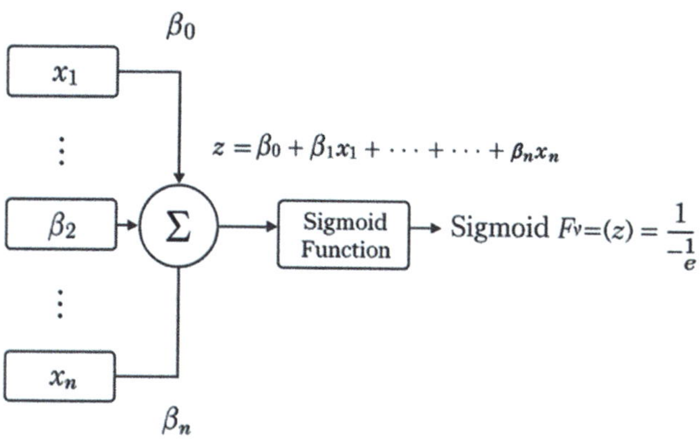

Figure 2: Logistic regression model.

and the target's log-odds. When there is a linear link between features and the target, LR is simple, understandable, and effective [25]. Figure 2 depicts the LR model.

The computation of a linear combination of the input features is the initial step in LR:

$$= \beta_0 + \beta_1 x_1 + \beta_2 x_2 + \cdots + \beta_n x_n = \beta^T x \tag{1}$$

In eq. (1) $x = [x_1, x_2, \ldots, x_n]$ are the input features, $\beta = [\beta_0, \beta_1, \ldots, \beta_n]$ are the coefficients and β_0 is the intercept (bias term).

The sigmoid function is used to reduce the linear output z into a probability value between 0 and 1:

$$P(y=1|x) = \sigma(z) = \frac{1}{1+e^{-z}} \tag{2}$$

The model uses a threshold, usually 0.5, to predict class labels:

$$\hat{y} = \begin{cases} 1, if \sigma(z) \geq 0.5 \\ 0, if \sigma(z) < 0.5 \end{cases} \tag{3}$$

Reduce the log loss (cross entropy) as follows in order to train the model:

$$\mathscr{L}(\beta) = -\frac{1}{m}\sum_{i=1}^{m} y^{(i)} \log\left(\hat{y}^{(i)}\right) + \left(1-y^{(i)}\right)\log\left(1-\hat{y}^{(i)}\right)] \tag{4}$$

where m is the number of training samples, $y^{(i)}$ is the true label, and $\hat{y}^{(i)} = \sigma\left(\beta^T x^{(i)}\right)$

3.4.3 Random Forest

RF consists of multiple DTs trained over random subsets of data and features [26]. RF avoids overfitting and increases accuracy and stability and is therefore a strong performer in medical prediction tasks. The dataset is given as follows:

$$D = [(x_1, y_1),\ (x_2, y_2),\ \ldots,\ (x_m, y_m)\} \tag{5}$$

The RF builds T number of DTs:

$$h_1(x), h_2(x), \ldots\ h_T(x) \tag{6}$$

A random selection of features not all features is taken into account at each tree split. For classification (e.g., diabetic or nondiabetic). Each tree $h_t(x)$ predicts the class label. The final prediction is the majority vote:

$$\hat{y} = \text{mode}(\{h_1(x),\ h_2(x),\ \ldots,\ h_T(x)\}) \tag{7}$$

For regression, each tree predicts a numeric output, and the result is the mean of all the trees:

$$\hat{y} = \frac{1}{T}\sum_{t=1}^{T} h_t(x) \tag{8}$$

Trees often employ the Gini impurity at each node to determine the optimal split:

$$\text{Gini} = 1 - \sum_{i=1}^{C} p_i^2 \tag{9}$$

where C represents the number of classes and p_i is the proportion of samples of classes i at the node. The split with the lowest impurity is chosen. Approximately one-third of the data is excluded (out-of-bag) since each tree employs a random sampling. Without

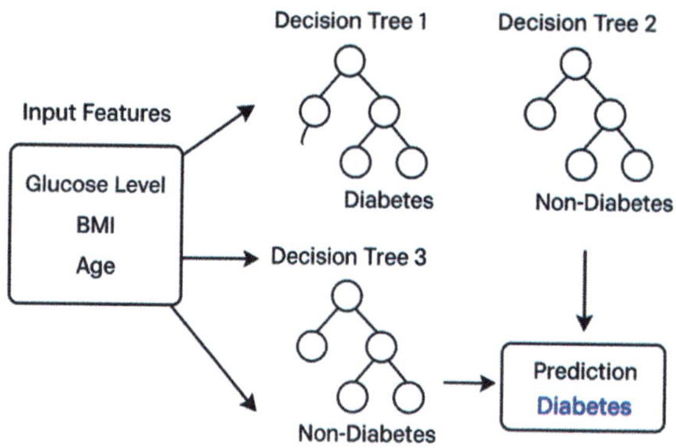

Figure 3: RF model for diabetic prediction.

using cross-validation, these can be used to measure model performance. Figure 3 shows the RF for diabetic prediction.

3.4.4 Support Vector Machine (SVM)

SVM is an effective classifier that maximizes the margin between classes to determine the optimal hyperplane for class separation. With the use of kernel functions (such as the RBF kernel), SVM can even handle nonlinear correlations and performs well with high-dimensional data. SVMs can be computationally costly for big datasets, but they perform well with datasets that have clearly defined boundaries for classes and are robust to outliers [27]. For binary classification, suppose the data is given by

$$D = \{(x_i, y_i)\}_{i=1}^{m},\ x_i \in \mathbb{R}^n,\ y_i \in \{-1, +1\} \tag{10}$$

SVM tries to find a hyperplane

$$W^T x + b = 0 \tag{11}$$

In this way, the difference between the two classes is maximized. The margin is $\frac{2}{||w||}$. The goal is to minimize

$$\min_{w,b} \frac{1}{2} ||w||^2 \tag{12}$$

Subject to the constraints

$$y_i(W^T\ x_i + b) \geq 1,\ \forall i \tag{13}$$

$$\min_{w,b,\xi} \frac{1}{2}||w||^2 + C\sum_{i=1}^{m} \xi_i \tag{14}$$

Subject to

$$y_i\left(W^T x_i + b\right) \geq 1 - \xi_{i,}, \xi_i \geq 0 \tag{15}$$

In eq. (14), C is the regularization parameter.

SVM uses a kernel $K(x_i, x_j)$ to translate input characteristics into a higher-dimensional space for nonlinear data without directly calculating the transformation. The common kernels are as follows:

$$K(x, z) = x^T z \text{ (linear)} \tag{16}$$

$$K(x, z) = (X^T z + 1)^d \text{ (polynomial)} \tag{17}$$

$$K(x, z) = \exp\left(-\frac{||x - z||^2}{2\sigma^2}\right) \text{(RBF)} \tag{18}$$

After training, a new input x is classified as follows:

$$f(x) = \text{sign}\left(\sum_{i=1}^{m} a_i y_i K(x_i, x) + b\right) \tag{19}$$

In equation (a_i) are the legend support vector weights.

3.4.5 Gradient Boosting (e.g., XGBoost)

It is an ensemble approach that constructs the models sequentially one after the other such that each subsequent model improves on the mistakes of the previous models [28]. XGBoost is a computationally efficient variant that is favored by many due to having good regularization properties to prevent overfitting, and it has the capability of learning complex, nonlinear relationships. It can frequently achieve best-in-class results in structured/tabular data such as medical records. Consider a dataset with the input features X

$$X = \{x_1, x_2, \ldots, x_n\} \tag{20}$$

The corresponding Y labels are

$$Y = \{y_1, y_2, \ldots, y_n\} \tag{21}$$

The objective is to predict $\hat{y}^{(t)}$ for each instance x_i. The prediction at iteration t is

$$\hat{y}^{(t)} = \sum_{k=1}^{t} f_k(x_i), f_k \in F \tag{22}$$

where f_k is the prediction function and t is the current iteration. The objective function to minimize the regularized loss is as follows:

$$L^{(t)} = \sum_{i=1}^{n} l(y_i, \hat{y}_i^{(t)}) + \sum_{k=1}^{t} \Omega\,(f_k) \tag{23}$$

where l is a differentiable loss function and $\Omega\,(f_k) = \gamma T + \frac{1}{2}\lambda||w||^2$ is the regular term to penalize complexity. The regularization parameters are γ and λ, the leaf weights are w, and the number of leaves is T. XGBoost approximates the loss in each iteration using second order Taylor expansion:

$$L^{(t)} \approx \sum_{i=1}^{n} \left[g_i f_t(x_i) + \frac{1}{2} h_i f_t(x_i)^2 \right] + \Omega\,(f_t) \tag{24}$$

Here, g_i and h_i are given as follows:

$$g_i = \frac{\partial(y_i, \hat{y}_i)}{\partial \hat{y}_i^2} \qquad h_i = \frac{\partial^2(y_i, \hat{y}_i)}{\partial \hat{y}_i^2}$$

Next, the model determines the f_t that minimizes this estimated goal.

4 Results and Findings

After data preprocessing and FS have been done, model training and validation are performed. Data are divided first into test and training sets. The 80/20 split, in which 80% of the data is used for training the model and 20% is used for testing, is probably the method that is most commonly employed. To improve the model, hyperparameter tuning is conducted using GridSearchCV or RandomSearchCV techniques. GridSearchCV iterates over a fixed list of hyperparameters, and RandomSearchCV samples hyperparameters randomly from a given range. Both the procedures help to determine the optimal model parameters and thereby the overall improvement. Some of the most important evaluation criteria are used to assess the model's performance after it has been trained are as follows.

Accuracy: True predicted divided by all predicted. It is a simple measure but misleading in imbalanced datasets:

$$\text{Accuracy} = \frac{(\text{TP} + \text{TN})}{(\text{TP} + \text{FP} + \text{TN} + \text{FN})} \tag{25}$$

Precision: The ratio of all positive predictions to true positives. It matters when false positives (e.g., incorrect diabetes diagnosis when the patient is not diabetic) are expensive:

$$\text{Precision} = \frac{\text{TP}}{\text{TP} + \text{FP}} \tag{26}$$

Recall: The ratio of all real positives to true positives. It matters when false negatives (e.g., not detecting a diabetic patient) are very expensive:

$$\text{Recall} = \frac{\text{TP}}{\text{TP} + \text{FN}} \tag{27}$$

F_1-Score: A harmonic mean of recall and precision gives equal weight, particularly for datasets that are not balanced:

$$F1 - \text{score} = \frac{2 * \text{Precision} * \text{Recall}}{\text{Precision} + \text{Recall}} \tag{28}$$

Table 1: Stacked ensemble model – performance analysis.

Method	Accuracy	Precision	Recall	F_1-score
LR	0.78	0.76	0.73	0.74
DT	0.74	0.72	0.70	0.71
RF	0.84	0.82	0.81	0.81
SVM	0.81	0.80	0.78	0.79
XGBoost	0.87	0.85	0.84	0.84
Stacked ensemble model	0.89	0.87	0.86	0.86

Table 1 presents the performance Analysis stacked ensemble model. LR is a decent baseline model for binary classification tasks like diabetic classification. It is right in 0.78 of all cases, and it gets most of them right, its precision of 0.76 and recall of 0.73 indicating that it is relatively balanced in classifying diabetic as well as nondiabetic cases. Its readability, simplicity, and low computational expense make it an appropriate option for clinic-based situations where interpretability is necessary, but it can fail when there are complicated, non-linear relationships to be discovered.

The DT model is 0.74 accurate, worse than that of other algorithms. That its precision (0.72) and recall (0.70) are also showing lack of generalizability and would overfit on small-sized data is reasonable, but it is nevertheless a useful method given its basic decision rules and good visualizability, which are good attributes in healthcare settings where interpretability of models is desirable.

RF, which is an ensemble classifier using multiple DTs, is improved with accuracy of 0.84 and precision (0.82) and recall (0.81) equally balanced. It is less susceptible to overfitting than a single decision tree and employs averaging results from numerous trees. It performs well on complex data sets and is generally accepted to be a gold standard for structured clinical data.

SVM has a good accuracy 0.81 and F_1-score 0.79. SVM is good with high-dimensional space and good in performing when there is a good margin of separation between classes. SVMs, although robust and good for dealing with nonlinear boundaries through kernel functions, are less suitable in large-scale or real-time clinical use due to their computational cost and interpretability.

XGBoost is the best performing base model with an accuracy of 0.87 and highest F_1-score of 0.84 among all base models. Its ability to manage intricate and nonlinear interactions and utilize regularization techniques makes it most appropriate for medical prediction tasks. XGBoost is also computationally efficient and scalable and thus a good choice for research as well as production environments in healthcare analytics.

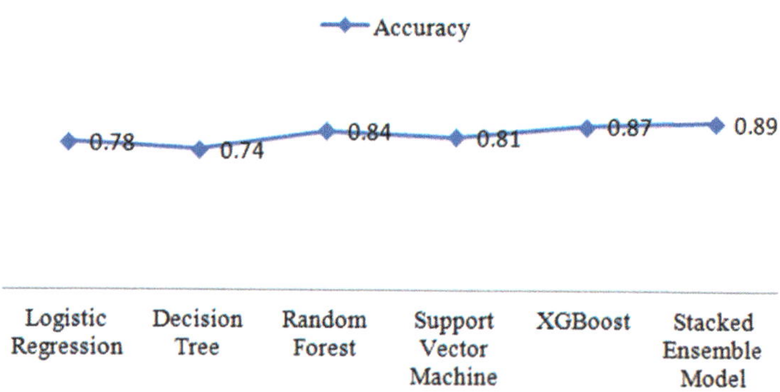

Figure 4: Performance analysis – accuracy.

With an accuracy of 0.89, precision of 0.87, recall of 0.86, and F_1-score of 0.86, the stacked ensemble model, which benefits from multiple base models (such as XGBoost, RF, and SVM), provides the best overall performance. The method enhances prediction power by integrating different perspectives of different algorithms to remove individual weakness. The stacked model hence is the best and most precise early diagnosis of diabetes but perhaps requiring more computer power and wise design.

Figure 4 depicts precision for different ML algorithms used in predicting diabetes. Lower precision below LR at 0.78 is decision tree at 0.74 as it suffers from overfitting or lack of generalizability. Precision is greater for RF (0.84) because the ensemble method is being applied, and second only to support vector machine at 0.81. XGBoost also does significantly better, to 0.87, demonstrating the power of gradient boosting in identifying subtle patterns. The highest precision of 0.89 is achieved by the stacked ensemble model, demonstrating the worth in stacking different models to take advantage of their relative strengths. In general, the plot demonstrates a clear trend: ensem-

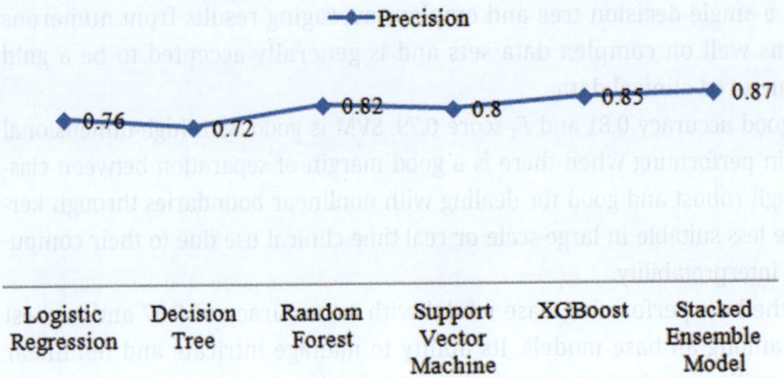

Figure 5: Performance precision – accuracy.

ble methods, specifically stacking and boosting, do best easily compared to single classifiers for predictability in diabetes detection tasks.

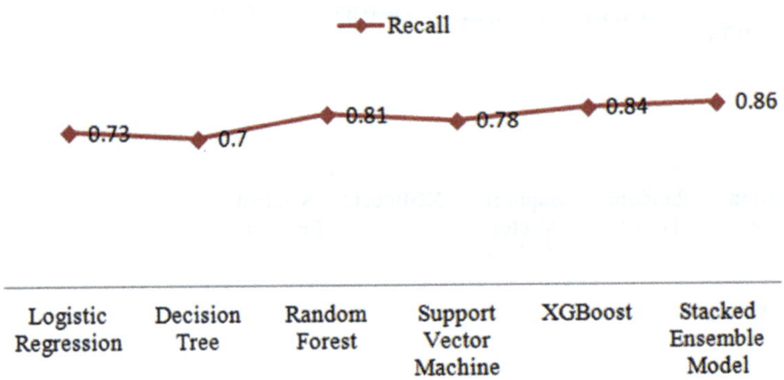

Figure 6: Performance recall – accuracy.

Figure 5 is a graphical representation of precision with which various ML algorithms correctly predict for diabetic positive patients. LR begins at 0.76 in the level of precision, while decision tree drops to 0.72 which means higher rates of false positives. RF pushes precision to 0.82, which means higher accuracy of positivity prediction. SVM comes second at 0.80, which means consistent performance. XGBoost achieves a peak precision of 0.85, indicating its ability to eliminate false positives. The stacked ensemble model achieves peak precision of 0.87, indicating its worth in leveraging the strength of each model toward more accurate positive classifications. The slope of the rising graph verifies that ensemble models, that is, stacked models, enhance accuracy in diabetes prediction much beyond individual learners.

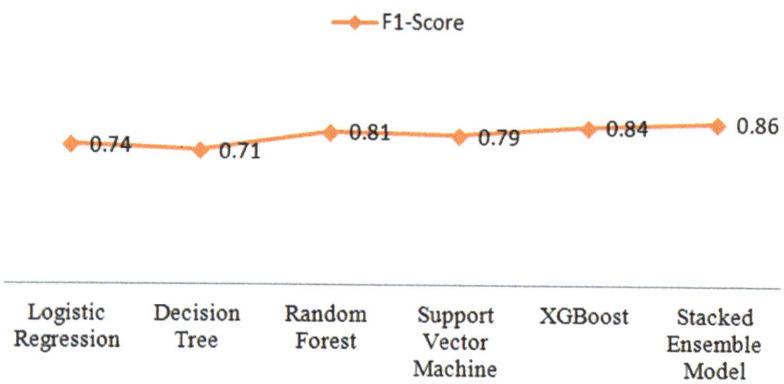

Figure 7: Performance analysis – F_1-score.

Figure 6 indicates how well each model classifies actual diabetic cases, with higher being fewer false negatives. LR stands at 0.73 recall, followed very closely by decision tree at 0.70, both mid-rank in classifying positive cases correctly. RF is considerably better at 0.81, which translates to more sensitivity. SVM drops back to 0.78, but remains competitive. XGBoost demonstrates a significant increase in recall value 0.84, which shows how well it identifies positive cases with precision. Stacked ensemble model takes the top spot with a recall of 0.86, showing the highest precision in identifying diabetic patients. Overall, the graph displays an overall enhancement, and the ensemble models, particularly stacking, play a vital role in improving the model for the detection of diabetes with precision.

Figure 7 illustrates the recall-precision trade-off of all the models, especially in clinical diagnosis where the false positive and false negative are worst. Decision tree has a comparatively poor F_1-score of 0.74, whereas LR lags behind with 0.71, which means the recall-precision trade-off of the classification is comparatively worse. RF takes this score to a significantly better F_1-score of 0.81, followed by SVM to 0.79 F_1-score. XGBoost further continues in the trend of improved performance to 0.84 F_1-score. The stacked ensemble model is the best among all the models taken separately with an F_1-score of 0.86, which shows its highest capability to provide precision and recall balance. This improvement over models confirms the efficiency of ensemble methods to overall strength gain of classification in diabetes prediction issues.

4.1 Deployment

When satisfactory model performance is achieved, deployment is the final step that makes real-world clinical application possible. One common practice is to build a web interface with Flask or Streamlit that allows clinicians to input patient details and receive real-time predictions for diabetes risk. For more integrated use, the model can be put into production in an EHR system within a hospital through a REST API so that predictions are available in clinical workflows. For long-term reliability, monitoring of the model that required monitoring performance on new patient data over time enables catching issues like data drift or reduced accuracy due to changing population demographics. This ongoing loop of feedback allows model updates and maintains the system clinically useful and consistent.

Implementing ML techniques in healthcare, specifically diabetes prediction, should be done with ethics to enable secure and reliable application. Privacy of information is also the top concern here since patient information must be processed according to rules such as HIPAA in the USA or GDPR in the EU. These models need to incorporate secure storage of data, agreed data, and strict access controls to guard confidential health data. In addition, fairness and bias must be addressed so that the model will do well on all classes of people, that is, age, gender, and ethnicity. Unless bias is checked, it will result in unequal treatment being recommended or misdiagnosis, which will negatively impact vulnerable populations disproportionately. To help solve this, fairness metrics need to be monitored along the way through model development, and representative, diverse datasets need to be used to train and validate the model. Ethical deployment not only builds trust but also is consistent with the very mission of healthcare: to provide safe, effective, and fair care to all patients.

5 Conclusion

The study demonstrates the capability of ML to enhance early diabetes detection, a vital component of managing chronic diseases. By utilizing ordered medical data, such as the PIMA dataset, and appropriate preprocessing, feature extraction, and model assessment processes, the study develops a robust classification pipeline that has the capability of classifying diabetic and nondiabetic patients effectively. Cross-algorithm performance comparison indicated the stability of ensemble models since the suggested stacked model achieved greater predictive accuracy and generalizability. Application of classical performance measures such as accuracy, precision, recall, and F_1-score ensured fair model assessment, while ROC-AUC and confusion matrix analyses offered insights of higher granularity. In general, ML allows for early diabetes prediction by a scalable, efficient, and precise approach, enhancing preventive care and patient outcomes. This structure can be utilized as a model to create similar chronic disease detection systems.

6 Future Directions

Though the present effort achieving satisfactory results in diabetes prediction with traditional and ensemble ML methods, there are some facets to be held for future extension. One of them is incorporating multimodal data combining structured features and unstructured clinical notes, lifestyle details, or wearable sensor data readouts in order to enrich a patient profile. Merging time-series data and longitudinal health histories can also be able to facilitate temporal modeling and progression prediction, particularly helpful in monitoring prediabetic conditions. The researcher also has the option to use DL models such as LSTMs or transformers, especially when processing sequential or EHR. Model interpretability is also an important area; techniques such as SHAP or LIME can further be exploited to offer interpretable predictions to clinicians and patients. Also, creating models for deployment on mobile or edge devices may enable low-resource real-time screening tools for rural or underserved populations. From the fairness and ethics perspective, additional focus in future research should be placed on minimizing bias to allow equiH performance with regards to age, gender, ethnicity, and socioeconomic status. Privacy-preserving ML mechanisms such as differential privacy and federated learning can also be explored to develop more secure patient-centered systems. Lastly, large-scale clinical trials and validations in wide-based populations and geographies need to be conducted to establish the generalizability and strength of the models in real-world environments.

References

[1] Jaiswal, V., Negi, A. & Pal, T. (2021). A review on current advances in machine learning based diabetes prediction. *Primary Care Diabetes*, 15(3), 435–443.

[2] Kee, O. T., Harun, H., Mustafa, N., Murad, N. A. A., Chin, S. F., Jaafar, R. & Abdullah, N. (2023). Cardiovascular complications in a diabetes prediction model using machine learning: a systematic review. *Cardiovascular Diabetology*, 22(1), 13.

[3] Khanam, J. J. & Foo, S. Y. (2021). A comparison of machine learning algorithms for diabetes prediction. *Ict Express*, 7(4), 432–439.

[4] Febrian, M. E., Ferdinan, F. X., Sendani, G. P., Suryanigrum, K. M. & Yunanda, R. (2023). Diabetes prediction using supervised machine learning. *Procedia Computer Science*, 216, 21–30.

[5] Chang, V., Bailey, J., Xu, Q. A. & Sun, Z. (2023). Pima Indians diabetes mellitus classification based on machine learning (ML) algorithms. *Neural Computing and Applications*, 35(22), 16157–16173.

[6] Salih, M. S., Ibrahim, R. K., Zeebaree, S. R., Asaad, D., Zebari, L. M. & Abdulkareem, N. M. (2024). Diabetic prediction based on machine learning using PIMA Indian dataset. *Communications on Applied Nonlinear Analysis*, 31(5s), 138–156.

[7] Bhat, S. S., Ansari, G. A. & Ansari, M. D. (2025). Performance analysis of machine learning based on optimized feature selection for type II diabetes mellitus. *Multimedia Tools and Applications*, 84(8), 4945–4964.

[8] Magboo, C., Peter, V. & Magboo, M. S. A. (2021). Imputation techniques and recursive feature elimination in machine learning applied to type II diabetes classification. *Proceedings of the 2021 4th Artificial Intelligence and Cloud Computing Conference*, 201–207.

[9] Rajendra, P. & Latifi, S. (2021). Prediction of diabetes using logistic regression and ensemble techniques. *Computer Methods and Programs in Biomedicine Update*, 1, 100032.

[10] Gündoğdu, S. (2023). Efficient prediction of early-stage diabetes using XGBoost classifier with RF feature selection technique. *Multimedia Tools and Applications*, 82(22), 34163–34181.

[11] Reza, M. S., Hafsha, U., Amin, R., Yasmin, R. & Ruhi, S. (2023). Improving SVM performance for type II diabetes prediction with an improved non-linear kernel: Insights from the PIMA dataset. *Computer Methods and Programs in Biomedicine Update*, 4, 100118.

[12] Hu, X., Hu, X., Yu, Y. & Wang, J. (2023). Prediction model for gestational diabetes mellitus using the XG Boost machine learning algorithm. *Frontiers in Endocrinology*, 14, 1105062.

[13] Olaniran, O. R., Sikiru, A. O., Allohibi, J., Alharbi, A. A. & Alharbi, N. M. (2025). Hybrid Random Feature Selection and Recurrent Neural Network for Diabetes Prediction. *Mathematics*, 13(4), 628.

[14] Daza, A., Sánchez, C. F. P., Apaza-Perez, G., Pinto, J. & Ramos, K. Z. (2024). Stacking ensemble approach to diagnosing the disease of diabetes. Informatics in Medicine Unlocked, 44, 101427.

[15] Sarwar, A., Ali, M., Manhas, J. & Sharma, V. (2020). Diagnosis of diabetes type-II using hybrid machine learning based ensemble model. International Journal of Information Technology, 12, 419–428.

[16] Doğru, A., Buyrukoğlu, S. & Arı, M. (2023). A hybrid super ensemble learning model for the early-stage prediction of diabetes risk. Medical & Biological Engineering & Computing, 61(3), 785–797.

[17] Airlangga, G. (2024). Synergistic Machine Learning: Enhancing Diabetes Prediction with Hybrid Deep Learning and Ensemble Models. Kesatria: Jurnal Penerapan Sistem Informasi (Komputer dan Manajemen), 5(3), 1396–1403.

[18] Oliullah, K., Rasel, M. H., Islam, M. M., Islam, M. R., Wadud, M. A. H. & Whaiduzzaman, M. (2024). A stacked ensemble machine learning approach for the prediction of diabetes. Journal of Diabetes & Metabolic Disorders, 23(1), 603–617.

[19] Modak, S. K. S. & Jha, V. K. (2024). Diabetes prediction model using machine learning techniques. Multimedia Tools and Applications, 83(13), 38523–38549.

[20] Alagumariappan, P., Sathyamoorthy, M., Dhanaraj, R. K., Kamalanand, K., Emmanuel, C., Allabun, S., Othman, M., Getahun, M. & Soufiene, B. O. (2025). Optimized hybrid machine learning framework for early diabetes prediction using electrogastrograms. Scientific Reports, 15(1), 8875.

[21] Olorunfemi, B. O., Ogunde, A. O., Almogren, A., Adeniyi, A. E., Ajagbe, S. A., Bharany, S., Altameem, A., Rehman, A. U., Mehmood, A. & Hamam, H. (2025). Efficient diagnosis of diabetes mellitus using an improved ensemble method. Scientific Reports, 15(1), 3235.

[22] Arun, G., Reddy, P. C. S., Budati, N., Rebecca, B., Perumalla, S. & Gujar, V. B. (2024). A Deep Learning Framework for Diabetes Prediction: PIMA Indian Dataset. In 2024 International Conference on Innovative Computing, Intelligent Communication and Smart Electrical Systems (ICSES) (pp. 1–6). IEEE

[23] Alnowaiser, K. (2024). Improving healthcare prediction of diabetic patients using KNN imputed features and tri-ensemble model. IEEE Access, 12, 16783–16793.

[24] Shantal, M., Alshareef, A. & Ahmid, O. (2024). The Impact Of Feature Selection On Diabetes Prediction. African Journal of Advanced Pure and Applied Sciences (AJAPAS), 373–377.

[25] Rassiyanti, L., Farid, F. & Pitri, R. (2025). Diabetes risk prediction using logistic regression model. Desimal: Jurnal Matematika, 8(1), 41–50.

[26] Noviyanti, C. N. & Alamsyah, A. (2024). Early detection of diabetes using random forest algorithm. Journal of Information System Exploration and Research, 2(1).

[27] Sagar, K., Sk Imtiyaz, A. A., Nagaraju, A. S., Prasad, C. R. & Kumar, P. K. (2024). Diabetes Prediction using Support Vector Machine. In 2024 5th International Conference for Emerging Technology (INCET) (pp. 1–4). IEEE

[28] Xu, J., Chen, T., Fang, X., Xia, L. & Pan, X. (2024). Prediction model of pressure injury occurrence in diabetic patients during ICU hospitalization-XGBoost machine learning model can be interpreted based on SHAP. Intensive and Critical Care Nursing, 83, 103715.

Medha Sree Anand, Tanvir H. Sardar, Kumar Ayush, Ankita Bose, Mahendra Kumar Gourisaria, and Nirmala Venkatachalam

Machine Learning Techniques for Healthcare

Abstract: This chapter comprehensively explores the transformative role of machine learning (ML) in the healthcare ecosystem. As modern healthcare generates vast amounts of diverse and complex data – from medical imaging and electronic health records (EHRs) to genomic and physiological time series – ML provides a powerful toolkit to extract actionable insights, support clinical decisions, and optimize operations. The chapter systematically discusses key ML paradigms including supervised, unsupervised, reinforcement, deep learning, and specialized techniques tailored to various healthcare data modalities. Real-world applications are examined in diagnosis, prognosis, personalized treatment, and healthcare resource optimization. Furthermore, the chapter delves into practical deployment considerations, ethical and regulatory challenges, and the evolving collaborative role between AI systems and clinicians. Emphasis is placed on model interpretability, fairness, trust, and the need for interdisciplinary collaboration to ensure responsible adoption. By bridging the gap between theoretical advancement and clinical implementation, this chapter offers valuable guidance for researchers, practitioners, and policymakers navigating the complexities of ML in healthcare.

Keywords: machine learning in healthcare, clinical decision support systems, electronic health records (EHRs), deep learning, model interpretability

1 Introduction: The Transformative Potential of Machine Learning in Healthcare

The healthcare landscape is changing more than ever before because of the massive progress in innumerable sources such as electronic health records (EHRs), medical imaging, genomic sequencing, wearable devices, administrative claims, and informat-

Medha Sree Anand, Department of CSE, School of Engineering, Dayananda Sagar University, Bengaluru 562112, India, e-mail: medhasreeanand@gmail.com
Tanvir H. Sardar, Department of CSE, School of Engineering, Dayananda Sagar University, Bengaluru 562112, India, e-mail: tanvir-cse@dsu.edu.in
Kumar Ayush, Department of CSE, School of Engineering, Dayananda Sagar University, Bengaluru 562112, India, e-mail: kumarayushh23@gmail.com
Ankita Bose, Assistant Professor, GITAM University, Bengaluru, India, e-mail: abose@gitam.edu
Mahendra Kumar Gourisaria, School of Computer Engineering, KIIT Deemed to be University, Bhubaneswar 751024, Odisha, India, e-mail: mkgourisaria2010@gmail.com
Nirmala Venkatachalam, Department of Artificial Intelligence and Data Science, Easwari Engineering College, Chennai, Tamil Nadu, India, e-mail: Nirmala.research17@gmail.com

https://doi.org/10.1515/9783111541235-010

ics. Besides, ML, a subset of artificial intelligence, has witnessed enviable strides in the science of pattern recognition, prediction, and complex decision-making, long before being considered science fiction. The coalescence of the two – massive healthcare data and much sophisticated ML algorithms – brings a never-before opportunity to radically transform the delivery of health from disease prevention and diagnosis to personalized treatment and operational efficiency. Traditional analytical methods have once proved useful, but will hardly reveal the complex nonlinear relationships within high-dimensional and heterogeneous healthcare datasets [1]. ML learns from data without explicit programming, thus providing potent means of yielding actionable insights and good predictive capabilities, and subsequently enhancing the clinician's decision-making process through evidence-based approaches. This chapter discusses essential ML techniques: those used to date or expected to see widespread usage in the healthcare domain: how they work, where the potential applications might lie, what obstacles exist, and future developments. This text will describe the transition of the field of ML from theory to an operative and, therefore, integral tool aimed toward better patient care and a sustainable system for healthcare. Researchers, practitioners, and policymakers must understand the techniques used to cope with the complex ethical, regulatory, and technical questions concerning the deployment of artificial intelligence in such a sensitive domain. The successful implementation of ML will require technical ability and a strong appreciation of the clinical context, data characteristics, and implications for patients and healthcare providers. Given the volume and complexity of today's healthcare data, a shift from simple numerical maintenance toward automation and intelligent analytics is necessary to realize its full value through predictive or prescriptive avenues capable of changing care pathways and public health programs.

2 Core Machine Learning Paradigms and Their Relevance to Healthcare Data

ML techniques can broadly be categorized into several paradigms, each suited to different problems and data structures commonly encountered in healthcare [2]. Supervised learning, arguably the most prevalent paradigm in current healthcare applications, involves training models on labeled datasets, where the desired output is known for each input example. This is particularly useful for tasks like diagnosis (classifying a patient's condition based on symptoms and test results, where the correct diagnosis is the label), prognosis (predicting the likelihood of a future event like disease progression or treatment response, with the outcome being the label), and image analysis (identifying abnormalities in medical images, with expert annotations as labels). Standard supervised learning algorithms include logistic regression, support vector machines (SVMs), decision trees, random forests, and gradient boosting machines. Each algorithm possesses distinct strengths and weaknesses regarding interpretability, computational complexity, and ability to handle different data types. For instance, logistic regression provides interpretable coefficients indicating the impact of features, while complex ensemble methods like gradient boosting often achieve higher accuracy but are less transparent. The problem's nature usually guides the selection of a supervised learning algorithm, the dataset's size and characteristics, and the need for model interpretability. For high-dimensional data with complex interactions, ensemble methods or deep learning might be preferred. In contrast, simpler models like logistic regression or decision trees might be more suitable when transparency and ease of understanding are paramount.

Unsupervised learning, in contrast, deals with unlabeled data, aiming to discover hidden patterns, structures, or relationships within the data without predefined output variables [3]. This is invaluable for tasks such as patient phenotyping (clustering patients into distinct subgroups based on their clinical characteristics to identify novel disease subtypes or response patterns), anomaly detection (identifying unusual patterns in physiological data that might indicate an adverse event), and dimensionality reduction (compressing high-dimensional genomic or proteomic data while preserving essential information). Clustering algorithms like *k*-means, hierarchical clustering, and DBSCAN are frequently employed for patient stratification. At the same time, techniques like principal component analysis (PCA) and *t*-distributed stochastic neighbor embedding (*t*-SNE) help visualize and simplify complex biological datasets. Unsupervised learning often serves as an exploratory step, providing insights that can inform subsequent supervised learning tasks or generate new hypotheses. It is beneficial in scenarios where domain knowledge is limited or where the goal is to uncover previously unknown patterns in the data, such as identifying novel patient subgroups that respond differently to treatment or exhibit distinct disease progression trajectories.

Reinforcement learning, a paradigm where an agent learns to make decisions by interacting with an environment and receiving rewards or penalties, holds significant promise for dynamic healthcare scenarios. This includes optimizing treatment strategies over time (e.g., adjusting medication dosages based on patient response), developing intelligent robotic surgery systems, or managing hospital resource allocation. The agent learns through trial and error to maximize a cumulative reward signal, which could be defined in terms of patient outcomes, cost-effectiveness, or treatment adherence [4]. While less mature in widespread clinical deployment than supervised learning, reinforcement learning's ability to handle sequential decision-making under uncertainty makes it a powerful tool for complex, dynamic healthcare processes. The application of reinforcement learning in healthcare is often challenging due to the need for realistic simulation environments or carefully designed clinical trials to accommodate the iterative learning process. However, its potential for optimizing complex, time-dependent interventions is immense.

Deep learning, a subfield of ML utilizing artificial neural networks with multiple layers (hence "deep"), has revolutionized tasks involving complex, unstructured data

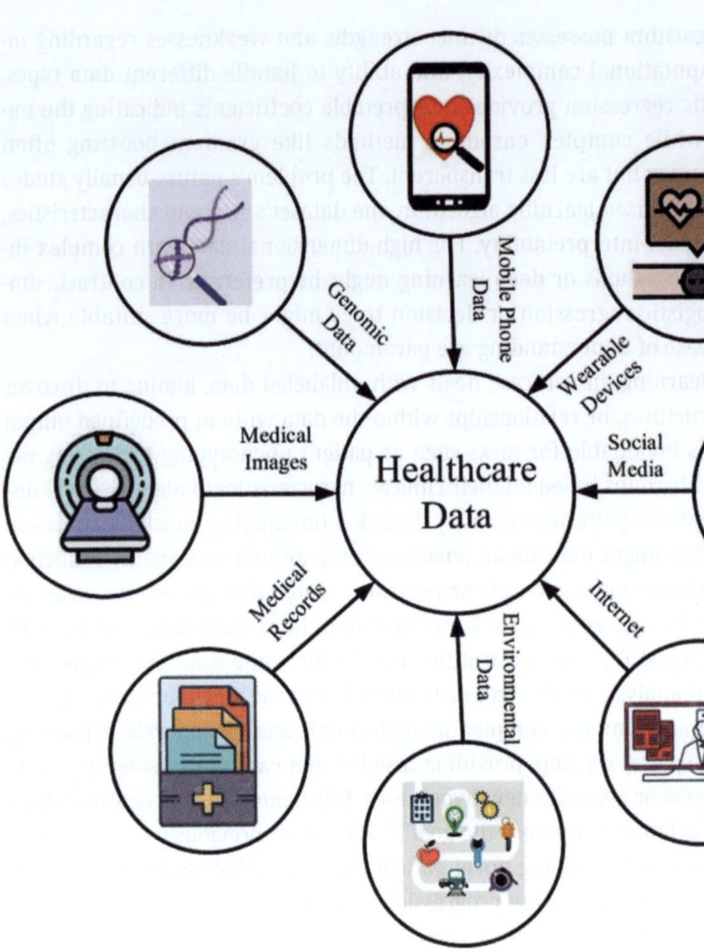

Figure 1: Different data generation sources in healthcare.

Figure 1 shows different data generation sources in healthcare. like images, text, and time series [5]. Convolutional neural networks (CNNs) have achieved state-of-the-art performance in medical image analysis (e.g., detecting diabetic retinopathy in retinal scans, ident memory networks) are well-suited for analyzing sequential data such as EHR trajectories, physiological time series, or natural language processing of clinical notes. Deep learning models, while powerful, often require massive amounts of data for training and can be challenging to interpret, posing significant hurdles in regulated healthcare environments where understanding the basis for a prediction is critical. Hybrid approaches combining different ML paradigms are also increasingly being explored to leverage the strengths of each technique and address the multifaceted challenges of healthcare data analysis. The success of deep learning is primarily attributed to its ability to automatically learn hierarchical representations of data, extracting increasingly abstract features from raw input, which is particularly advantageous for complex data types like images and text, where manual feature engineering is difficult and time-consuming.

3 Specialized Machine Learning Techniques for Healthcare Data Modalities

Since a variety of data about health arises in many different formats, the analysis of any such format would require special ML techniques tailored to fit its specification. Sardar et al. [6] note that among such poorly illuminated areas that could greatly benefit from deep learning are medical imaging, are modalities such as X-rays, CT scans, MRIs, and pathology slides. CNNs are an appropriate choice for working with images since they learn hierarchical features from raw pixels to patterns that indicate disease. Deep learning models, such as ResNet, Inception, and U-Net, have been employed effectively for image classification (such as categorizing images as cancerous or benign), object detection (locating tumors or lesions), and image segmentation (delineating organs or abnormalities). Transfer learning is a standard and very efficient way of dealing with the lack of sufficient labeled medical image data, where a CNN trained previously on a large dataset of general images (ImageNet) is fine-tuned on a smaller dataset of medical images. CNNs' ability to automatically learn relevant image features has dramatically advanced the field of medical image analysis to help support earlier and more accurate diagnoses.

EHRs, although a rich source of information, differentiate themselves through the mixed nature of their data content: structured data as lab results, vital signs, and medication lists, while unstructured data serve as clinical notes and observations from physicians. These incredibly potent NLP techniques have invaluable roles in extracting useful information from EHRs' unstructured texts. Named entity recognition identifies medical concepts like diseases, medications, and procedures. In contrast, relation extraction identifies relations between concepts, for example, between a medication and its being prescribed for a certain condition, and sentiment analysis assesses the sentiment of the patient's notes or clinician's notes. All of these help convert free-formed texts into structured information appropriate for downstream ML modeling. RNNs and more advanced architectures such as LSTMs and GRUs (Gated Recurrent Units) are very useful when applied to EHR data since these models can account for the sequential nature of the data, such as predicting future events based on a patient's history or modeling chronic disease progression. More recently, transformer networks that model architectures such as BERT and GPT are being deployed in the analysis of clinical text and perform exceptionally well in the more complex task of elucidating contextual relationships within clinical narratives [7].

The genomic and proteomic datasets elicited with high-throughput sequencing, as well as with other molecular techniques, are high-dimensional and require ML-specific methods for their analyses. The tasks in this domain include genetic variation associated with disease risk, pharmacogenomic predictions based on an individual's genetic makeup, cancer subtypes determined from their gene expression profiles, and identification of potential therapeutic targets. Penalized regression, such as Lasso Ridge, is typically used for the selection of features, which may involve the use of dimensionality reduction techniques, such as PCA and *t*-SNE, to visualize and reduce noise. With these advantages, graph neural networks are becoming powerful tools in analyzing biological networks that involve studying complex networks: protein–protein interaction networks or gene regulatory networks have become viable options for elucidating disease mechanisms and shedding light on the possibility of drug targets. Multimodal ML approaches integrating genomic data with clinical data will usher in true modern-day medicine, wherein patients will benefit as systems are made much more patient-specific.

Applications of ML techniques that can capture temporal dependencies and patterns are required with time-series data such as continuous physiological monitoring from wearable devices or intensive care unit (ICU) sensors. RNNs, LSTMs, and GRUs are best suited for analyzing sequential physiological data to predict events such as the onset of sepsis, cardiac arrest, or patient deterioration [8]. Hidden Markov models are also used to study underlying but unobserved states inferred from observed time-series data, and this can sometimes be beneficial in understanding disease progression or patient states in the ICU. In this regard, time-series forecasting techniques pertain to the prediction of future physiological measurements that facilitate proactive clinical inter-

Table 1: Specialized ML techniques for different healthcare data modalities.

<table>
<tr><th>Data modality</th><th>Key ML techniques</th><th>Specific applications</th></tr>
<tr><td>Medical imaging learning, including image classification, segmentation, and interpretation</td><td>CNNs, transfer age segmentation</td><td rowspan="2">Tumor detection, diabetic retinopathy screening, pathology image analysis, information extraction from clinical notes, phenotype extraction, predicting outcomes from clinical narratives</td></tr>
<tr><td>EHR text</td><td>NLP (NER, relation extraction, sentiment analysis), RNNs, LSTMs, transformers</td></tr>
<tr><td>Genomic/proteomic data</td><td>Penalized regression, PCA, graph neural networks</td><td>Disease risk prediction, drug response prediction, cancer subtyping, target identification</td></tr>
<tr><td>Time series (physiological)</td><td>RNNs, LSTMs, GRUs, HMMs, time-series forecasting</td><td>Anomaly detection in vital signs, modeling disease progression</td></tr>
</table>

ventions. The analysis of wearable time series is also fraught with challenges, namely data quality issues, incomplete data, and real-time processing requirements. Table 1 provides a summary of specialised ML techniques for different healthcare data modalities.

4 Applications in Clinical Practice: Transforming Diagnosis, Prognosis, and Treatment

ML is going to disrupt clinical practices in many settings by providing tools that can supplement human expertise as well as improve patient outcomes. ML models are increasingly being transformed into decision support tools that assist radiologists and pathologists in recognizing subtle interference rather than relying on full manual inspection. They quickly screen thousands of images and tag suspicious areas for expert review, increasing efficiency and possibly reducing diagnostic errors. Deep learning models have been highly accurate in detecting early stages of breast cancer from mammograms, identifying polyps in images taken during colonoscopy, and diagnosing diabetic retinopathy from retinal scans. These tools are not expected to keep clinicians out; they will allow them to use more advanced analytical techniques while focusing their expertise on complex cases. And eventually improve workflow [9].

ML is making significant strides in risk prediction and prognosis in proactive and personalized patient management. Through the analysis of varied patient data including a patient's demographics, medical history, lab results, and genomic information, ML models may predict an individual's risk of developing chronic disease, such as diabetes or cardiovascular disease, likelihood for hospital readmission after discharge, or prognosis for patients with conditions such as cancer or heart failure. Clinicians can use this information to determine those at high risk of disease soon enough for early intervention, implement personalized preventive strategies, and target treatment to an individual based on their predicted disease trajectory. For example, ML is being used to determine patients in intensive care with the highest chance of developing sepsis, so that detection and treatment can be applied early on, thus increasing chances of survival dramatically.

By definition, personalized medicine is the customization of healthcare to the patient-specific characteristics involved, long-awaited objectives that have always been pursued in medical practice [10]. The dream of personalized medicine Is made possible by ML. It provides models suitable for processing genetic, genomic, molecular, and clinical history data to predict patient response probabilities to different medications or types of therapy intervention. This information enables the physician to choose the best possible treatment for the patient, minimize the occurrences of adverse drug reactions, and optimize therapeutic outcomes. For instance, ML predicts most likely cancer patients who will respond to immunotherapeutic/targeted agents evaluated according to the molecular characteristics of tumors. This kind of therapeutic management is moving away from "one-size-fits-all" therapeutic strategies to a more precise and individualized approach to every patient, considering the unique biological and clinical profile of each patient.

ML is used not only to diagnose and treat, but also to monitor and manage patients more effectively. For instance, wearable or remote sensors generate data that is usually used by ML classifiers, which will indicate early signs of health-illness deterioration, the patient's adherence to treatment, and provide personalized feedback. Specifically, continuous monitoring or AI-enabled insights for chronic patients with diabetes and heart failure can help proactively manage condition complications and hence improve their quality of life. For example, the latest ML developments include innovations into smart medication management systems, which will harness the patient's compliance towards taking medication and predict potential increases in drug interaction incidences [11].

5 Operational Efficiency and Public Health Applications

ML impacts many areas of life in healthcare besides direct patient care, such as healthcare operations and public health. Healthcare operations are very complex and resource-consuming, and ML can eliminate many bottlenecks in the whole administrative and logistical process. For instance, predicting when patients may not show up for an appointment enables clinicians to optimize scheduling and minimize wasted resources. Specifically, ML can analyze any historical appointment data and patient demographic and environmental factors to identify patients most likely not to show up and intervene proactively with reminder calls or offer flexibility with scheduling.

One more sector where ML will be of great aid is in optimizing the allocation of hospital resources, staffing, bed management, and equipment utilization. As per predicting patient admissions, length of stay, and demand for specific services, the above predictions can greatly benefit hospital administrators in making good decisions on resource allocation to be put where they are needed in time. This ensures reduced waiting periods, improved flow of patients, and better use of costly resources, such as those experienced in predicting the demand for ICU beds, which can help hospitals manage their capacity better [12].

Fraud detection in healthcare is a big challenge. It accounts for losses in annual billions and is where ML comes in handy because these AI techniques, especially the anomaly detection algorithms, can easily and quickly identify suspicious patterns in billing data, claims submissions, and provider behavior that may indicate fraudulent illegalities. So, by simply analyzing copious amounts of transaction data, the ML models can suspect a few claims and flag them for follow-up and investigation; such capability will help healthcare payers and government agencies combat fraud and abuse.

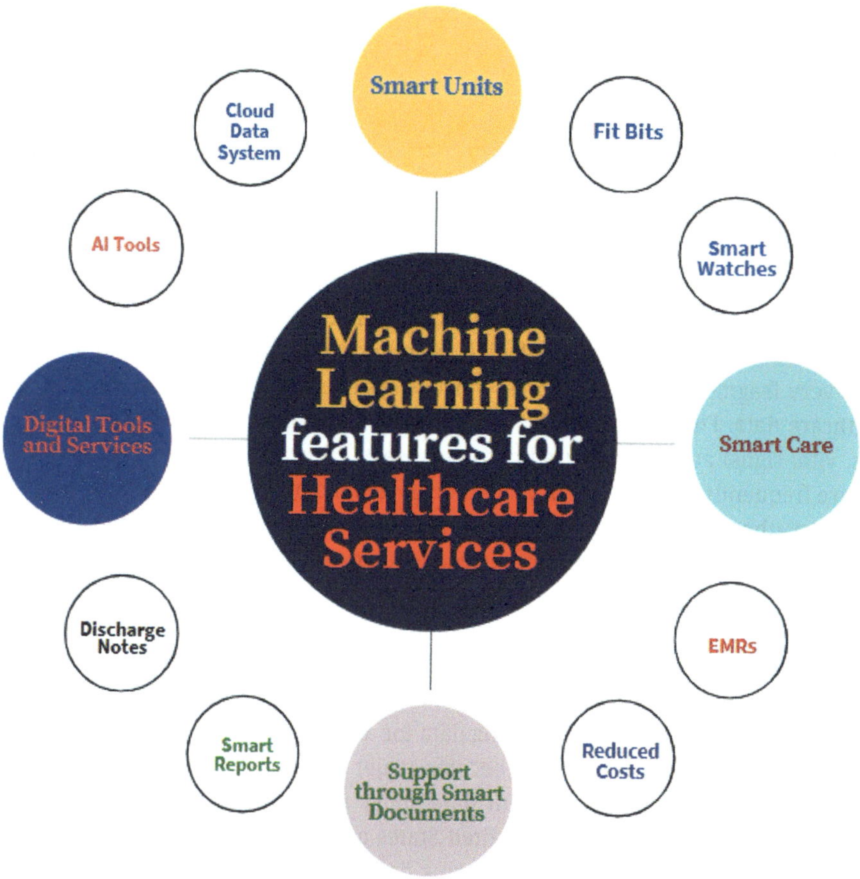

Figure 2: Diverse applications of machine learning across the healthcare ecosystem.

ML techniques open powerful possibilities for disease surveillance, outbreak prediction, and public health interventions. ML models observe data from EHRs, laboratory reports, social media, and environmental sensors to give early signals for disease outbreaks, track their geographic spread, and predict trends onward. Such information would allow public health officials to make the best possible decisions concerning resource allocation, vaccination campaigns, and other interventions to minimize the impact of outbreaks [13]. ML-based approaches have been proposed to study influenza and other infectious diseases based on Google searches and social media trends. In addition, ML can be applied to identify populations at high risk for specific health conditions, thus allowing leveraging on public health programs/interventions targeting such cohorts to address health disparities and improve population health outcomes. ML could also analyze social determinants of health data to provide insight into nonclinical factors impacting health, thereby allowing for more inclusive public health strategies with optimal effectiveness. Figure 2 provides the visual treat of diverse applications of machine learning across the healthcare ecosystem.

6 Navigating the Intricacies: Data Challenges in the Healthcare Domain

Despite its huge promise, the application of ML technology to healthcare is beset by enormous data-related challenges that must be considered for the successful and ethical implementation of such technologies. Inherent complexity, diversity, and sometimes very fragmented settings across various systems and institutions characterize healthcare data. For example, EHRs include both structured data types (e.g., lab results, vital signs) and unstructured data types (e.g., clinical notes, radiology reports) that are frequently inconsistent in their coding, terminology, and data-entry practices. Pulling together information from various sources – EHRs, imaging systems, genomic databases, wearables, and patient-reported outcomes – is a very arduous task that requires elaborate data harmonization, cleaning, and linkage methods in order to create unified and usable datasets for training model algorithms. Standardization in data formats is infrequent, and data integration challenges are intensified by the existence of legacy systems, which means that often a huge amount of manual effort and domain knowledge is needed for preparing data for analysis [14].

Data privacy and security have become major issues in healthcare because patient information is sensitive. Patient data collection, storage, access, and use are strictly regulated by HIPAA in the United States and the GDPR in Europe. Most ML training requires large datasets, and sharing data with other institutions or external researchers poses significant privacy risks. Ways to protect patient confidentiality, while permitting collaborative model training are being examined, such as data anonymization, de-identification, differential privacy, and federated learning. Federated learning allows local training of models on data residing at different institutions, while only the model updates are shared and aggregated, keeping sensitive data decentralized. However, even with these techniques, the risk of reidentification is still a major issue, stressing the importance of careful consideration of privacy-preserving methods and the availability of strong data governance frameworks.

Bias poses another major threat to healthcare data, which could yield unfair or even discriminatory outcomes if ignored. ML models trained on biased data could both sustain and amplify the existing health disparities. The sources could be many and include underrepresentation of demographic groups in the training data, systematic discrepancies affecting the data collection across populations, as well as built-in biases of diagnostic and treatment decisions, which are found in historical data [15]. Identifying and eliminating biases in healthcare ML models require rigorous data audits, fairness-aware ML algorithms, and thorough reviews across diverse patient subgroups to assure equal performance. The deployment of biased AI systems in health can have serious ethical and social consequences since it contributes to existing health inequities in access and quality of care. A comprehensive and multifaceted strategy will be required for addressing bias, including diverse data collection, algorithmic fairness techniques, and continuous assessments of how the model performs under real-world conditions.

Almost every healthcare dataset has issues regarding missing values since some records may be incomplete, appointments are often missed, and the clinical workflow may vary. Appropriate treatment of missing data is essential. The naive way of ignoring any record with missing data will lead to highly biased models and loss of valuable information. There are various imputation methods, relatively simple ones like mean imputation or median imputation, and slightly more sophisticated model-based approaches, but the choice of method is important as it profoundly affects the model performance and validity. Moreover, in healthcare, temporal dependencies are another characteristic in this view, as conditions and treatment vary with time. Time-series data from EHRs or wearable devices must be analyzed through specialized ML techniques capable of modeling sequential patterns and dependencies, recurrent neural networks, or hidden Markov models. The challenges of health and disease being in constant flux raise the issues of building ML systems that learn and predict time-variant changes, as compared to simple static models. Another problem is the explainability of ML models, especially in the case of deep learning models that may be computationally complex. In medicine, the practitioners must understand "why" a model is making a certain prediction or recommendation to be able to trust and make adequate use of the AI-based system. Black-box models are usually not trusted, despite being accurate, in clinical practice, where accountability and the explanation of the decision-making basis matter. Therefore, the interpretation of healthcare ML models, via SHAP (SHapley additive exPlanations) and LIME (local interpretable model-agnostic explanations), has gained traction to provide insights into modeling for clinicians [16].

7 Ensuring Trust and Reliability: Model Evaluation and Interpretation

The successful deployment of ML models in healthcare does not only rely on technical performance. A critical aspect of model use in healthcare involves trusting and interpreting by the clinical user. Measurement of an ML model in the healthcare domain would still require more metrics beyond simple accuracy, given that some event is assumed to be clinical in case of false positives and false negatives. For example, in the case of a diagnostic task, a false negative (missing to detect the disease present) is usually far worse than false positives (wrongly identifying the disease that is absent).

Hence, the width and depth of comprehensive evaluation also call for metrics such as sensitivity, specificity, positive predictive value, and recall. There are some aggregate measures that show the model's performance scores on different classification thresholds, such as the area under the receiver operating characteristic curve (AUROC) and the area under the precision-recall curve (AUPRC). It is most used for imbalanced datasets that characterize most of healthcare; for example, detecting rare diseases, as AUPRC is considered more informative than AUROC.

Clinical validation, more than statistical measures, is an important phase to ascertain how well an ML model works in a real-world healthcare environment, while being exposed to a diverse patient population and clinical operational flows. It usually involves prospective studies comparing the efficiency of the AI system to a current human expert in clinical practice. Regulatory agencies such as the FDA are developing frameworks for the validation and approval of medical AI devices, with an emphasis on good evidence regarding safety and effectiveness, which will often include the types of data that they require clinical trials to demonstrate efficacy and safety in the target population. Such dynamic characteristics of health data and clinical practice necessitate continuous monitoring and recalibration of deployed ML models. This is basically ensuring performance does not degrade over time because of shifts in data distribution due to changes in treatment protocols. Establishment of robust post-market surveillance systems is critical in identifying potential issues and ensuring the dependable deployment of AI systems [17].

Model interpretability is an emerging area of research and an important one for the acceptance of ML in healthcare. This is understood as important for clinicians to see why an AI would recommend or predict something and adopt it in the decision-making process while holding the machine accountable, as well as in building up the trust of their patients. Although such black-box systems promise high accuracy, they often fail to accommodate the demands of a clinical workflow, which needs transparency and justification. Intrinsic interpretability and post hoc interpretability are the two broad categories under which interpretability methods can be classified: intrinsic interpretability encompasses approaches that use inherently understandable models such as trees or linear models; post hoc interpretability relates to the application of techniques designed to explain the predictions of complex models. A post hoc method includes feature importance studies, partial dependence plots, surrogate models, and techniques such as SHAP and LIME. These techniques help to shed light on which of the input features most possibly influence a patient's prediction by the model. Providing interpretable explanations will initiate a critical appraisal by clinicians of the output from the model, as such, identify the errors or biases that are likely, as well as build confidence in the AI system as a reliable tool rather than a mysterious oracle. The degree of interpretability needed will depend on the type of clinical application: generally, high-stakes decisions such as diagnosis and treatment planning will require more transparency than administrative automation tasks. Moreover, model interpretability could potentially identify biases in either the data or the model itself, which would ultimately help in securing more fair AI systems [18].

8 Ethical, Regulatory, and Societal Dimensions

The application of ML in healthcare opens an arena of deep ethical, regulatory, and social dilemmas that must be met in a proactive and reflective manner. The paramount issue from an ethical point of view regards ensuring fairness and equity so that ML models do not reproduce or exacerbate existing health disparities based on race, socioeconomic status, gender, or other protected attributes. Discriminatory algorithmic behavior results from bias-imbued training data, thereby leading to less-than-optimal care for certain patient groups or the exclusion of others from interventions that would benefit them [18]. With fair ML models, one should exercise due diligence regarding data collection, bias detection, mitigation strategies, and equitable evaluation across different patient subgroups for an assessment of equitable performance. Algorithmic fairness is a topic of current research, along with a range of definitions of fairness and algorithmic mechanisms designed specifically to minimize bias in predictions.

Transparency and accountability are significant ethical considerations [19]. With an AI system affecting a patient's health, it is almost as important to know how such a decision was made, and who is ultimately accountable in case of mistakes or adverse outcomes. The complex, "black-box" nature of some ML models can make it difficult to assign accountability. Clear guidance on the development, validation, deployment, and monitoring of medical AI and liability under the existing legal and ethical frameworks is therefore important. Informed consent is crucial; this means that the patient is told when AI is used in the patient's care, its role and limitations, including its potential for error or bias. The informed consent process for AI intervention in clinical decision-making is intricate and demands clear communication between the clinician and the patient.

Medical AI is in a fast-changing state regarding regulations and the efforts by different types of governments and health groups to ensure the safety and efficacy of such new technologies [20]. Agencies like the FDA are getting involved by introducing novel approval routes for AI-/ML-based medical devices and their algorithms, which are distinctly different from classical medical device algorithms in that they can "learn" and "change" over time. Some of the key regulatory challenges include developing reasonable standards for validation, post-market surveillance, and risk management with respect to algorithmic changes. The regulatory framework should ensure a balance between innovation and protecting patients and public health, which implies a flexible, yet rigorous process for assessing AI systems throughout their life cycles. Harmonizing regulatory frameworks across jurisdictions is yet another challenge faced by companies developing and deploying AI in an international setting.

Apart from ethical standards and regulations, the societal impact of ML in healthcare must be fully taken into consideration. There are worries about possible job losses for those in the healthcare profession; however, many consider that AI will enhance, rather than replace, clinicians so that they will be able to focus on areas where empathy, complex reasoning, and interpersonal skills are paramount. It is important that healthcare professionals are trained to consider AI systems along with their practices so that successful integration can occur. New curriculum and training programs must be developed, which will enable clinicians to gain the necessary skills and knowledge to understand, evaluate, and use AI tools in their practice. Furthermore, in order to avoid a digital divide, equitable access to AI-enabled healthcare tools should be guaranteed, whereby some groups of people get to enjoy the benefits of the technology. These societal dimensions will need to be addressed together by the technologists, clinicians, legislators, and the public, thereby ensuring that ML would improve the health of everyone. Ultimately, a multidisciplinary approach to the responsible design and use of ML in healthcare is warranted, one that acknowledges the technical, clinical, ethical, regulatory, and societal ramifications in concert to ensure that AI is designed and used to the benefit and fairness of all in society.

9 Human-AI Collaboration and the Evolving Role of Clinicians

While enhancing human-AI collaboration is key, ML is not seen as a replacement for human clinicians, and ML models examine data for patterns and make predictions without the relevant clinical judgment, compassion, and contextual understanding that are critical to patient care of quality. ML in healthcare is best seen as the implementation of AI systems that support clinicians by providing actionable insights and decision support, thus amplifying their diagnostic, treatment, and management abilities with patients. For instance, an AI algorithm may indicate an area of suspicious concern on a medical image, while the radiologist with their medical training and knowledge of the patient's clinical history shall render a formal diagnosis. Again, the ML model may forecast a patient's likelihood of developing a complication, but it is the physician who decides how to treat the patient, taking into account the findings in their examination and what the patient prefers.

To work successfully with humans, the AI should be built well, to be accurate and usable as well as interpretable and part of the clinical workflow's everyday fabric. The user interface to this AI tool must be intuitive and allow clinicians to receive the information in the format they need, clearly and understandably. Parallel to the above, it must somehow go into input-based interpretability techniques, which help build trust and allow clinicians to understand why the AI is suggesting certain recommendations. In addition, the AI system must be embedded in supplementary sources like EHRs and other clinical systems to allow less disruption in the workflow. Clinicians would be trained in learning how to interact with and understand the AI systems' output, knowing the abilities and limitations of these systems and possible sources for error. Clinicians have a changing position in this new age of healthcare AI. There are aspects of patient care, including building rapport, communicating effectively, making complex decisions in uncertain situations, and, of course, providing compassionate care, which will always be human functions, which is why AI can never fully replace the clinician. Clinicians will have to evolve to more or less act as supervisors and interpreters of AI systems, who use AI insights to illuminate their clinical judgement rather than simply following the algorithms pronouncements. They would have to acquire fresh skills in data literacy, an understanding of AI concepts, as well as the application of making critical evaluations about the performance and limitations of such AI tools. This indicates that the future care delivery mode will be primarily through a host–guest relationship wherein both man and AI are involved in the healthcare process for different intended purposes. Their challenge is to develop an appropriate training and education model for healthcare professionals to effectively steer them into this changing landscape.

10 Implementation and Deployment Considerations

The road to implementing and deploying ML models in clinical practice is highly complicated, thus subjecting such models to some technical, organizational, and logistical challenges. One major challenge is integrating ML models into existing healthcare IT infrastructures. Mostly, the healthcare systems have been developed over time based on patches of legacy applications, their own proprietary software applications, and segregated databases, all of which were not designed with the intention of AI integration. The technological fragmentation acts as an impediment to seamless data sharing and real-time inference of models. Interoperability can easily become a challenge, therefore requiring standard data formats (e.g., HL7 FHIR), APIs that have been developed to a high standard, and middleware solutions to facilitate communication between AI tools and EHR systems. Simultaneously, there is a need for secure, reliable, and high-throughput data pipelines to ensure that, at least with respect to real-time applications, the models have access to their required clinical data while respecting levels of patient privacy. This includes encryption, anonymization, and strong access control in an appropriate way. Another critical technical consideration refers to infrastructure requirements for deploying ML models in real-time clinical environments. Hospitals must invest in scalable platforms, on-premises or cloud-based, with low-latency inference, high availability, and fault tolerance. All of this must be achieved while adhering to strict regulatory requirements related to data security, privacy, and ethical use of patient information, such as HIPAA in the USA or GDPR in Europe.

The successful adoption of healthcare AI is also greatly influenced by organizational factors. The actual applicability of the technology may be affected by institutional unpreparedness. Instances where healthcare professionals resist changes because of apprehensions about clinical autonomy, opaque decisions on AI, and fear of legal liability can significantly impede or delay its deployment. Such fears are palpable in the high-stakes arena of hospitals, where decisions make a difference between life and death. This is why it is imperative to engage clinicians and other stakeholders in the early lifecycles of AI development, and even to co-design AI solutions with healthcare staff to make sure that AI fits into, rather than disrupts, their workflow. Involving end users from the beginning of the developmental process will help the AI tool align well with clinical needs and increase acceptance further. Beyond development, various training sessions and maintenance support are equally important. Clinicians need to not only know how to use the AI system but also interpret its results and its limitations. Such a change management plan would include peer-led workshops, teaching workshops, and feedback loops, and would allow for a smooth transition while building institutional trust. For any AI to take root, the organizational culture will have to encourage innovation and experimentation, and unambiguously pursue enhanced patient care through technology.

Validation and monitoring of deployed ML models form part of an ongoing cycle for assuring that these models carry on doing what they are supposed to do and remain safe to use. Unlike fixed-rule applications in a conventional clinical setting, ML models learn from data. Thus, over time, they become susceptible to performance degradation. Concept drift refers specifically to this underlying phenomenon when the statistical properties of input data begin to change. Nevertheless, changes in clinical practices, variations in demographic data, or even changes in the equipment and the patients it interacts with may lead to performance issues. Hence, robust post-deployment validation techniques must be put in place, including methods for monitoring performance in the field with live data, automated drift detections, and regular benchmarking to updated clinical standards. Monitoring is not only meant for performance metrics, but safety and equitable access are also considered. Any observed bias in model outputs across subpopulations should be identified and corrected to avoid inflicting harm. The system also needs to be set up to trigger retraining or recalibration if performance falls below acceptable thresholds. Effective lifecycle management includes a detailed process for version control, robust audit trails for all changes made to a certain model, and options for rollback in case an update introduces unintended regressions. These technical procedures need to align with evolving regulatory frameworks that have only just started addressing the challenges posed by adaptive and continuously learning AI systems. Entities like the FDA have the task of looking for alternative approaches to ensure that such systems stay safe.

On top of everything else, the cost of developing and maintaining ML systems is immense in healthcare, and thus an analysis of return on investment and long-term sustainability is crucial. These financial implications encompass the initial costs of AI model development and infrastructure but extend to ongoing costs such as integrating the system, user training, maintaining the system, monitoring, and periodic retraining. Health systems must also consider indirect costs of technology implementation, such as a temporary disruption in workflows or the employment of dedicated AI governance staff. In justifying these expenses, organizations should evaluate AI solutions on the criteria of clinical impact, cost-effectiveness, and scalability across departments or institutions. Hence, any cost-benefit analysis should factor in improved diagnostic accuracy, operational efficiencies, decreased readmission rates, and patient outcomes. In certain cases, public funding opportunities or partnerships with private sector innovators can offset this burden. Ultimately, for an ML system to sustain value into the future, it must be chosen and implemented based on more than just technological feasibility.

Tackling these deployment and implementation difficulties demands a multidisciplinary method whereby technical experts collaborate with clinicians, administrators, and regulatory experts to ensure safe and properly integrated AI deployment in the health sector. This cross-functional collaboration is necessary for maneuvering the socio-technical landscape of clinical AI. Technical teams bring along expertise in model development, validation, and infrastructure; meanwhile, clinicians provide pertinent domain knowledge and contextual information on workflows. The administrators offer a perspective on operational feasibility and resource mobilization, whereas regulatory experts help ensure that the AI solutions meet the relevant legal standards. The juxtaposition of these perspectives provides a balanced platform on which healthcare institutions may unreservedly embark on the ramp for responsible AI integration with maximum benefits and minimum risks. The road from lab to bedside is long and arduous, and with a deliberate, inclusive, and well-governed approach, ML has the potential to be a key enabler for clinical decision-making and change transformation in patient care.

11 Future Trends and Persistent Challenges

ML in healthcare is a rapidly dynamic and evolving field with some very interesting trends for the immediate future and much-needed continuing challenges that call for research and innovation. One of the important emerging trends focuses on multimodality, which extends beyond using a single source for analyses to looking at a combined view that would include EHRs, medical imaging, genomics, wearables, the social determinants of health, and environmental data. These models, capable of learning from and fusing information from these disparate sources, have the opportunity to provide a fuller view of health and disease trajectory, enabling more comprehensive and personalized care. Integrating and analyzing heterogeneous data types will remain one of the substantial technical challenges.

Another emerging domain is the application of explainable AI (XAI) techniques specifically targeted to interpretability issues. Research is still being done on developing ML models that will be inherently more interpretable or creating well-founded methods to produce understandable explanations for the complex model-predicted values, a task more difficult than it sounds. And with systems being built into high-end clinical processes in increasing numbers, the demand on auditing model decisions will go nowhere but higher. Although meaningful progress is being made, the difficulty remains in achieving a fair balance between model performance and interpretability, especially in deep learning architectures.

There are also operational challenges related to applying ML to real-world clinical workflows. The existing healthcare IT infrastructure is complicated by the need for interoperability between systems and workflow redesign considerations for the successful integration of ML models into it. To achieve usability and acceptance by healthcare professionals, an AI tool must have an interface that is intuitive and embedded within existing tools but demonstrates a tangible clinical benefit. All of this requires the establishment of general standards and best practices concerning the implementation and ongoing monitoring of medical AI toward full market adoption. Yet another technical difficulty is ensuring scalability and maintaining performance with increasing data volume and complexity.

Furthermore, annotation and long-term maintenance beyond the availability of deployed ML models in healthcare are essential. The historic data-driven models may fail over time due to concept drift, in the existing drift or divergence of the patient population, or construed clinical practice. To ensure the reliability and safety of medical AI, robust continuous monitoring systems of model performance, considering drift detection and timely model retraining or recalibration, should be put in place. The regulatory architecture for adaptive AI models, which learn and improve over time, is still under development, contesting the deployment of models that can continuously improve while remaining regulations-compliant.

There will always be ethical considerations for bias, fairness, and accountability in the responsible development and deployment of healthcare AI. Studies seek to develop enhanced methods for the detection and mitigation of biases in data and algorithms, as well as to establish clear lines of accountability when AI systems are involved in clinical verdicts. Almost just as important as an AI system being accurate is its being seen as fair, equitable, and above reproach, for these are critical attributes needed to engender public and clinical confidence. The conversation regarding ethical issues must be a living dialogue with all participants involved and must culminate in the generation of ethical guidelines and best practices for AI in healthcare. Finally, collaboration among ML researchers, clinicians, policymakers, and patients must be fostered to allow the future development of healthcare AI to align with the needs and values of all, leading to AI solutions that genuinely benefit human health. This interdisciplinary collaboration is of utmost relevance when addressing the complexities and realizing the complete promise of ML to transform healthcare.

12 Conclusion: Charting the Future of Healthcare with Machine Learning

All this makes it possible for ML to become the next big thing in research and innovation in the field of human health and well-being, without touching predictive, prescriptive, or transformative capabilities, to be comprehensive about providing insights from complex data, predicting possible future results, and assisting decision-makers throughout the spectrum. From using advanced image analysis to increase the chances of a correct diagnosis to personalizing medical treatment based on a patient's personal profile to increasing the operational efficiency of healthcare systems, ML has great scope and growing applications. This chapter has covered the major core paradigms in ML- supervised learning, unsupervised learning, deep learning, and reinforcement learning, explaining their core differences and affinities to their specific healthcare problems. We've also explored very important applications being realized – John Smith in diagnostic imaging, event predictions, drug discovery, and administrative optimization – aiming to show how medical care is currently affected by the input of ML. The exploration of specialized techniques with respect to different healthcare data modalities, such as the medical imaging modality, EHR text, genomic data, and physiological time-series modality, indicates the need for modality-specific approaches.

There is, of course, some way to go before ML can be incorporated easily and broadly across medical paradigms. The most immediate concerns, however, for the most part, relate to issues of heterogeneity, privacy, and bias of health data. One must develop strong systems of anonymization, de-identification, and federated learning to secure data and patient privacy. Ethical obligations to fairness and the elimination of algorithmic bias are needed to discourage the continued occurrence of the health disparities created by erroneous production. Another set of challenges includes proper evaluation of the models in terms of clinically meaningful metrics and the design considerations for interpretable AIs, which are crucial in terms of building trust and enabling appropriate use by healthcare professionals. The overall shifting regulatory framework is fraught with both challenges and opportunities, with the aim of establishing clarity around pathways for approval and monitoring of medical AI devices. Meeting these challenges demands concerted efforts of all stakeholders within the respective healthcare ecosystem. The future holds much promise with ML technologies in healthcare. Emerging developments in multimodal learning, XAI, and increased diversity of healthcare data all point to a bright future for ML in the healthcare sector. The promise that is engulfed in such a future requires commitment through continued collaboration with all relevant stakeholders: researchers, clinicians, policy-makers, and industry stakeholders. It is going to require investment into such things as data infrastructure, standardizing data formats, interdisciplinary training, as well as bringing serious investment into strong ethical and regulatory frameworks. ML holds great promise in improving patient outcomes, efficiency in healthcare delivery, and speeding medical discovery. If we wisely and diligently address these technical, data, ethical, and regulatory obstacles, we would be well on our way toward realizing that ideal healthcare that is effective, fair, and sustainable for the future. Advances in ML algorithms and the increasing availability and understanding of healthcare data make everything ripe for a future in which AI-based tools become an integral part of high-quality, society-wide, personalized care. Responsible and thoughtful application of these powerful techniques opens the door to improving global health without a huge amount of effort toward creating a healthcare system that is more predictive, preventive, personalized, and participatory.

References

[1] Taha, K. (2025). Machine learning in biomedical and health big data: A comprehensive survey with empirical and experimental insights. *Journal of Big Data, 12*(1), 61.

[2] Razzaq, K. & Shah, M. (2025). Machine learning and deep learning paradigms: From techniques to practical applications and research frontiers. *Computers, 14*(3), 93.

[3] Moujahid, A. & Dornaika, F. (2025). Advanced unsupervised learning: a comprehensive overview of multi-view clustering techniques. *Artificial Intelligence Review, 58*(8), 1–52.

[4] Khatun, A. & Sardar, T. H. (2025). Cryptography algorithms to prevent different security attacks. In *Next Generation Mechanisms for Data Encryption* (pp. 35–46). CRC Press.

[5] Theerthagiri, P., Ruby, A. U., Chandran, J. G. C., Sardar, T. H. & Shafeeq, B. M. A. (2024). Deep SqueezeNet learning model for diagnosis and prediction of maize leaf diseases. *Journal of Big Data, 11*(1), 112.

[6] Sardar, T. H., Sarkar, R., Ahmed, S. J. & Bandyopadhyay, A. (2023, May). A novel ensemble methodology to validate fuzzy clusters of big data. In *Proceedings of the Fourth International Conference on Trends in Computational and Cognitive Engineering*: *TCCE 2022* (pp. 267–278). Springer Nature Singapore.

[7] Das, S., Sardar, T. H. & Sahana, D. S. (2025). An ensemble technique using genetic algorithm and deep learning for the prediction of rice diseases. In *Machine Learning Hybridization and Optimization for Intelligent Applications* (pp. 289–303). CRC Press.

[8] Subbarao, E., Gite, P., Sharma, A., Vyakaranam, L., Sardar, T. H., Taqui, S. N. . . . Kalam, M. A. (2023). Investigation of solar energy for urban areas and metropolitan communities using machine learning. *Electric Power Components and Systems*, 1–11.

[9] Sardar, T. H., Khatun, A., Sengupta, S., Alam, Y. & Ara, T. (2024). Machine learning in the healthcare sector and the biomedical big data: Techniques, applications, and challenges. *Big Data Computing*, 336–352.

[10] Usman, M. M., Fahim, M. F. H., Hassan, M. A. M. & Sardar, T. H. (2025). Harnessing IoT and machine learning for sustainable, smart urban. *Applications of Computational Learning and IoT in Smart Road Transportation System, 22*, 199.

[11] Hassan, M. A. M., Sardar, T. H., Fahim, M. F. H., Mohamed, M. S., Suleyman, R. M. & Usman, M. M. (2024). Artificial intelligence and deep learning applications on big data computing frameworks. In *Big Data Computing* (pp. 196–211). CRC Press.

[12] Manikiran, G., Greeshma, S., Vishnu Teja, P., Sreehari Rao, Y., Sardar, T. H. & Mallik, M. A. (2022, February). E-commerce clothing review analysis and model building. In In *Proceedings of Second*

International Conference on Advances in Computer Engineering and Communication Systems: ICACECS 2021 (pp. 491–497). Springer Nature Singapore.

[13] Sardar, T. H., Hazarika, R. A., Pandey, B., Prasad, G., Hassan, S. M., Dodmane, R. & Gohel, H. (2024, February). Video key concept extraction using convolution neural network. In *2024 IEEE 3rd International Conference on AI in Cybersecurity (ICAIC)* (pp. 1–6). IEEE.

[14] Raj, A., Jena, J. J., Ghosh, D., Jain, S., Sardar, T. H. & Gourisaria, M. K. (2025, February). Early-stage diabetes risk prediction using machine learning techniques. In *2025 3rd International Conference on Intelligent Data Communication Technologies and Internet of Things (IDCIoT)* (pp. 2289–2295). IEEE.

[15] Jain, S. J. T., Sardar, T. H., Jain, S. J. T., Prasad, M. S. G. & Naresh, P. (2025). Facial expression analysis for efficient disease classification in sheep using a 3NM-CTA and LIFA-based framework. *IETE Journal of Research*, 1–15.

[16] Bellary, M. Z., Deepthi, T. H., Sardar, B., Musthafa, S. J. A. & Ahmed, S. R. (2023). Medical image analysis of knee osteoarthritis using modified deep CNN. *Journal of Survey in Fisheries Sciences, 10*(2S), 133–144.

[17] Sardar, T. H. (2024). Reflecting on a decade of evolution: MapReduce-based advances in partitioning-based, hierarchical-based, and density-based clustering 2013–2023. *Wiley Interdisciplinary Reviews: Data Mining and Knowledgev Discovery, 14*(6), e1566.

[18] Sardar, T. H., Ansari, Z. A., Theerthagiri, P., Karthikeyan, P., Ayyasamy, V. & Saini, D. K. J. B. (2025). MapReduce-enhanced fuzzy K-least medians for qualitative clustering of document big data. *Concurrency and Computation: Practice and. Experience, 37*(4–5), e70035.

[19] Farinu, U. (2025). Fairness, accountability, and transparency in AI: Ethical challenges in data-driven decision-making. *Available at SSRN 5128174.*

[20] Mehta, A. (2025). Leveraging AI, blockchain, and IoT technologies for transformative healthcare: Enhancing data security, privacy, and operational intelligence.

Tanvir H. Sardar, Laura Aldasheva, and Bishwajeet Kumar Pandey

Applications and Benefits of Machine Learning in Healthcare

Abstract: This chapter explores the transformative applications and multifaceted benefits of machine learning (ML) in healthcare. From enhancing diagnostic accuracy and personalizing treatment to revolutionizing drug discovery and improving operational efficiency, ML is reshaping the healthcare landscape. The chapter details the deployment of ML in disease diagnosis, risk prediction, clinical decision support, remote monitoring through wearable devices, and hospital resource management. Key ML algorithms such as supervised learning, deep learning, and natural language processing are examined along with domain-specific techniques for imaging, genomics, electronic health records, and physiological data. Further, it analyzes how ML accelerates drug discovery by enabling virtual screening, target prediction, and optimizing clinical trials. The chapter also highlights the operational gains in patient scheduling, inventory optimization, and automated administrative tasks. Ethical considerations, including data privacy, algorithmic bias, and the interpretability of ML models, are addressed to ensure responsible integration. Conclusively, this chapter emphasizes the need for interdisciplinary collaboration to fully realize the potential of ML in building a more accurate, personalized, and efficient healthcare system.

Keywords: machine learning in healthcare, disease diagnosis and risk prediction, personalized medicine, drug discovery, operational efficiency in healthcare

1 Introduction

Currently, machine learning (ML) is entering healthcare, which represents a change in paradigm regarding the delivery, assessment, and enhancement of medical services. Human expertise, manual processing of data, and broad protocols of treatment have, until now, been the major ways of operation in healthcare. However, the emergence of big data and better computing power has meant that there is an increasing demand for systems that will have the capacity to efficiently process huge quantities of complex and heterogeneous medical information. ML, being one such branch of

Tanvir H. Sardar, Post Doctoral Researcher, Department of IS CS, Astana IT University, Astana, Kazakhstan, e-mail: tanvir.sardar@gmail.com
Laura Aldasheva, Department of IS & CS, Astana IT University, Astana, Kazakhstan, e-mail: laura.aldasheva@astanait.edu.kz
Bishwajeet Kumar Pandey, Department of MCA, GL Bajaj College of Technology and Management, Greater Noida, India, e-mail: dr.pandey@ieee.org

https://doi.org/10.1515/9783111541235-011

artificial intelligence (AI), is mostly concerned with providing the proper tools to respond to such challenges. ML algorithms learn patterns from past data and make predictions or decisions without being explicitly programmed for such tasks. This has opened up several opportunities in healthcare, ranging from early disease diagnosis and predictive diagnosis to personalization of treatment and drug discovery. For instance, thousands of medical images analyzed through ML models can oftentimes detect fine subtlety of signs for diseases like cancer or neurological disorders, at times equal to or even better than that of healthcare experts. ML-based systems also allow the healthcare practitioner to predict patient outcomes, improve hospital operations, and streamline administrative work by providing assistance in real-time decision support during critical care. Personalized medicine is about administering treatment based on an individual's specific genetic makeup for optimal efficacy and minimal side effects; ML has made this possible. Wearable devices and remote monitoring technologies that work on ML algorithms are rapidly changing patient engagement and chronic disease management by allowing FLT (for life tracking) [1]. In public health, ML is also transforming disease outbreak prediction, health insurance modeling, and biomedical data-expedited research. Meanwhile, it promises to reduce costs, increase accessibility, and improve quality in healthcare delivered to diverse populations. The promise notwithstanding, the application of ML in healthcare raises challenges, such as privacy concerns, ethical considerations, and the need for thorough validation and regulatory approval. Nevertheless, the collaboration among data scientists, clinicians, and policymakers to date will shape the responsible and effective integration of ML technologies into healthcare. In this chapter, we will discuss the multi-angled applications of ML in healthcare. We will see how, from the patients' point of view to healthcare practitioners to systems, ML benefits them all. By understanding how ML can change the way medication approaches its applications and also some pitfalls of its journey, we will further appreciate its role in shaping the future of medicine.

2 Key Applications of Machine Learning in Healthcare

2.1 Disease Diagnosis and Risk Prediction

Nowhere else has the application of ML fulfilled such a great promise as in the diagnosis of diseases and the prediction of risks. Traditional diagnostic tests possess a degree of reliance solely on an individual's experience, gut feel, and subjective interpretation. Medical professionals interpret a portion of the patient-reported symptoms in tandem with laboratory tests and through various modalities of different imaging technologies like X-rays and MRIs. This traditional method has been there for quite some time, and quite satisfactorily, but its results do not always reflect adequacy.

Faults by human beings, mental fatigue, variable levels of competence, and the complex nature and diversity in medical information sometimes lead to failures in the diagnosis of diseases or latencies in diagnosis. ML models are actually paradigm-shifting adjuncts to human judgment. Enabling the analysis of extensive and intricate datasets, such as old medical records, genetic information, and imaging, these patterns and correlations arise from an almost imperceptible scale to the human observer. Thus, ML not only increases the detection accuracy but also enhances the speed of detection, indicating early signs in the history of disease progression, and statistically supports clinical decision-making. Medical image analysis has been the most fruitful breeding ground for ML. In deep learning, promise can be seen primarily in convolutional neural networks (CNNs), which have emerged as the best-performing architecture when it comes to interpreting highly complex radiological imaging modalities like X-ray, MRI, CT, or mammogram. Tumors, fractures, hemorrhages, lesions, and many other problems are detected with a very high precision using these models. In many clinical situations, an ML system acts as a "second reader," drawing radiologists' attention to suspicious areas of an image and thereby increasing diagnostic speed and reducing oversight [2]. Some highly effective deep learning systems are being trained to tell apart tumors that are benign from malignant in order to help with early cancer detection, tumor grading, and personalizing treatment planning. ML goes beyond diagnostics to risk prediction and risk stratification. Predictive algorithms assess the probability that an individual will develop a certain disease based on many factors [3]. These factors may include genetic predispositions, lifestyle factors (such as smoking habits, diet, and exercise), environmental exposure, demographic information, and electronic health records. The aggregation and analysis of these disparate datasets would enable ML to generate personalized risk scores for diseases like diabetes, hypertension, various cardiovascular conditions, and some types of cancer. Risk stratification allows healthcare to be proactive in identifying high-risk individuals without having to first see clinical signs. Interventions, lifestyle changes, and early screenings may be targeted to such high-risk individuals even before symptoms appear [4].

2.2 Types of Machine Learning Algorithms Used in Disease Diagnosis

Several types of disease diagnosis-applicable ML algorithms are present, as each is especially fitted for a certain data type or diagnostic task with its strengths [5]. Supervised learning: These are algorithms that learn by supervision from data labeled in terms of a relationship established between the inputs and outputs. Examples of supervised ML algorithms are:

Logistic Regression: It is applicable for binary classification cases. The presence or absence of a disease, for instance, is predicted.

Support Vector Machines: They are highly beneficial, especially in high-dimensional space, for both linear and nonlinear classification [6].

Decision Trees: Derived from above, they are tree-like structures that break down data according to values of features, leading to a diagnosis at the leaf node.

Random Forests: When many decision trees are provided with an ensemble, the trees can be grown quite accurately, but this reduces the tendency to overfit [7].

Gradient Boosting Machines (GBMs): Another algorithm in this line is where an ensemble combines several weak learners to form one strong predictive model.

Neural Networks: These are complex models inspired by the human brain that learn complicated patterns through large datasets, particularly image and text analysis.

Unsupervised Learning: These learning algorithms work with unlabeled data [8]. The performance or effectiveness of said learning algorithms is seen in the hidden and/or discovered patterns and structures within that data.

Clustering: Algorithms like k-means clustering can be used to cluster the same data points into several groups and help in identifying distinct *d* patients into subtypes, based on the differences in their data and features.

Dimensionality Reduction: Techniques like principal component analysis help reduce the number of variables in a data set while retaining the more essential elements for easy analysis and better model performance [9].

Deep Learning: It refers to one of the subfields of ML that attempts to learn from artificial neural networks. It has numerous stacked layers (deep neural networks) and is used mostly for learning complex representations from data. The greatest impact of deep learning has been in analyzing medical images and natural language processing for understanding clinical text.

CNNs: These types of neural networks are made for medical image analysis, X-ray, MRI, CT scan, etc.

Recurrent Neural Networks: These are mainly made for temporal data like health records from electronic or wearable devices, which track data over a period of time [10].

Transformers: They are a relatively new class of neural network that has shown much promise in natural language processing and is increasingly being used in other types of medical data.

2.3 Feature Engineering in Disease Diagnosis

Feature engineering is selecting, transforming, or creating additional features from raw data to rehabilitate or improve performance on ML models. Feature engineering, therefore, plays an important role in obtaining the information that is clinically meaningful and relevant from intricate medical data in disease diagnosis [11].

Medical Image Analysis: Radiomics: It is the extraction of quantitative characteristics of medical images, like size, shape, texture, and intensity of tumor tissue, which may provide significant and valuable disease profile and prognosis information.

Deep Feature Extraction: It is an automatic learning of relevant features using pre-trained deep networks from medical images.

Genomics: Single nucleotide polymorphisms (SNPs): These are genetic variations that can be identified to associate the risk of having a disease.

Gene Expression Analysis: It is the studies about the activity levels of genes that can provide insights into disease mechanisms and drug targets [12].

Electronic Health Records (EHR): Clinical codes: These are information retrieved through a standard coding system, like ICD-10, which codes for diagnosis, procedure, and medications.

Temporal Features: These are event sequences and time interval analysis of medical events capable of detecting the evolution pattern of diseases.

Natural Language Processing (NLP): It is the extracting of structured information from unstructured text through techniques such as named entity recognition and sentiment analysis in clinical notes and discharge summaries [13].

Wearable Devices: Physiological signals: These are feature extractions from time series data like heart rate variability, sleep behavior, and activity level, which offer good patient insight regarding their health status and their risk for certain diseases. Figure 1 shows the

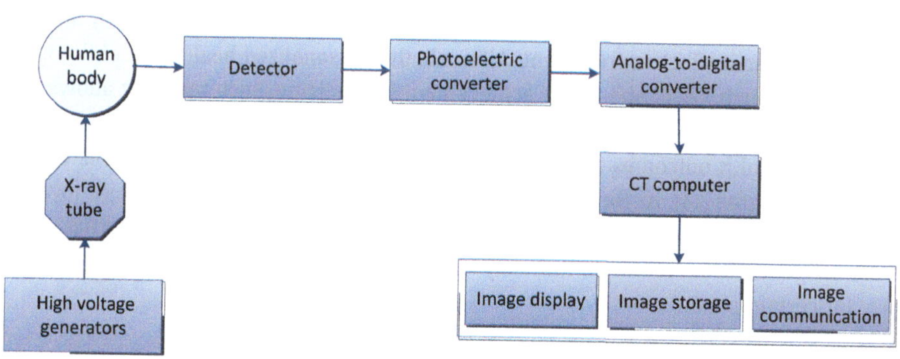

Figure 1: Deep learning for medical image-based cancer diagnosis.

important steps a deep learning framework uses for medical image-based cancer diagnosis.

2.4 Personalized Treatment Design

Recently, health professionals and medical researchers started to appreciate a patient's uniqueness, not only with respect to clinical presentations of symptoms, but also with individual genetic background, lifestyle, and biological response to treatments. Hence, standard treatment protocols that follow a "one-size-fits-all" paradigm, which, while gaining acceptance from many patients, do not guarantee the maximum expected result for every patient in every indicated situation. Thanks to numerous advances in ML, this paradigm is now being contradicted in favor of one that views treatment as a necessity and very much individualized in terms of need and biological constitution of each patient. The application of ML is truly important in precision medicine. Thus, ML models can link the patients' genetic profile to specific recommendations for response to certain therapies. For example, certain cancer treatments may be favored in their response by genetic markers, whilst others may warn against a higher risk of adverse effects. In conjunction with clinical history and environmental exposure, ML is able to weigh and filter vast populations, drawn from genomic data, to home in on treatments that are effective and tolerated by that one single individual. This kind of understanding of the prescription will not only improve therapeutic efficacy but will also ensure that more patients can be safely treated, thereby improving patient safety. Another major application is optimizing dosage regimens. Dosing, as a general rule, is very complicated for any patient. It involves interacting factors such as metabolism, age, weight, genetics, and concomitant diseases that influence the indicated dose. Concerning the methods of determining dosage, in general, mainstream approaches depend on highly generic guidance and clinical experience. However, this is the area where ML methods stand to offer a precise advantage in modeling these complex interplays. By combining real-time patient data with historical treatment outcome information, the ML system has the ability to predict the most effective dosage that would maximize treatment efficacy and reduce toxicity or ineffective treatment. All in all, the personalized healthcare philosophy delivered through ML is one major achievement in medicine. Such tailoring allows the physician to use an individual's profile in the treatment design, thereby maximizing reasonable health outcomes and better patient satisfaction with more judicious use of medical resources [14]. At the same time, customized care will also really work toward the bigger picture of saving costs and making healthcare sustainable by steering clear from the generalized treatment that may well be altogether ineffective or overly aggressive for certain patients.

2.5 Drug Discovery and Development

The traditional process of drug development would usually take a lot of time, at least a decade, and cost a lot of money, often billions of dollars – just to have a drug approved for the market. A big portion of the timeline and cost is related to laboratory investigations, testing, clinical trials, and regulatory workings. Thus, another pathway has been opened up, thanks to ML, which has brought powerful tools to accelerate drug discovery and development, improve efficiency, and fulfill the need to mitigate risks in pharmaceutical innovation. One of the major ways in which ML is reshaping drug discovery is through the prediction of molecular behavior [15]. ML models, particularly deep learning architectures, can be trained on huge datasets, with information about chemical compounds, biological pathways, and mechanisms of diseases. These models can predict how different chemical compounds would behave when interacting with biological targets such as proteins and enzymes. If such interactions are simulated computationally, researchers can identify promising drug candidates in a more rapid manner, doing away with labor-intensive and costly laboratory work [16]. Such an alternative would not only save time but also allow scientists to explore a far larger chemical space than would be feasible using conventional techniques, thereby increasing the chances of finding effective treatments for complex diseases. Apart from early-phase discovery, ML is instrumental in optimizing clinical trials. Clinical trials are the actual proof for these drugs, probably the last and most important step in confirming their safety and efficacy. Several challenges are faced in conducting such clinical trials, including recruitment challenges, high dropout rates, and unpredictable outcomes [17]. ML predictive analytics can bring forth the design of efficient clinical trials by identifying the most suitable participants from genetic profiles, medical history, and demographic factors. In addition, ML models can help identify possible trial outcomes, optimize dosage regimens, and flag early signs of any toxicity issues that would warrant intervention. By increasing the targeting and efficiency of clinical trials, ML reduces the time to market new therapies and raises the chances of success. Overall, the incorporation of ML into the field of drug discovery and development marks a paradigm shift, providing the capability through acceleration, smartness, and frugality [18]. Furthermore, developers of ML promise faster delivery of life-saving treatments at a cost much lower than the traditional model.

2.6 Key Applications of ML in Drug Discovery

ML can aid in different aspects of the drug discovery and development pipeline:

Target Identification and Validation: ML could decipher lots of biological data, e.g., genomic, proteomic, and transcriptomic data, and use them to identify likely segments that can be drug targets in disease pathways. It can further help confirm the prediction of the effect(s) of targeting these by particular compound(s).

Virtual Screening: ML models could actually screen huge libraries of chemical compounds and predict their chances of binding to a specific drug target. This would reduce the number of compounds that need to be synthesized and tested, thus saving time and other resources.

De Novo Design of Drugs: ML could potentially create new molecules with desired attributes like high binding with targets and low toxicity properties. This opens up entirely new ways of discovering classes of drugs that we would otherwise not have found from traditional means.

ADMET Prediction: ADMET refers to Absorption, Distribution, Metabolism, Excretion, and Toxicity, and these properties are very important for drug safety and efficacy. ML models are capable of predicting these properties based on the molecular structure of the compounds, helping to filter out those with unfavorable profiles, early in the drug development process.

Drug Repurposing: ML can detect which existing drugs may be effective in treating diseases, other than those for which they were originally developed. This can greatly

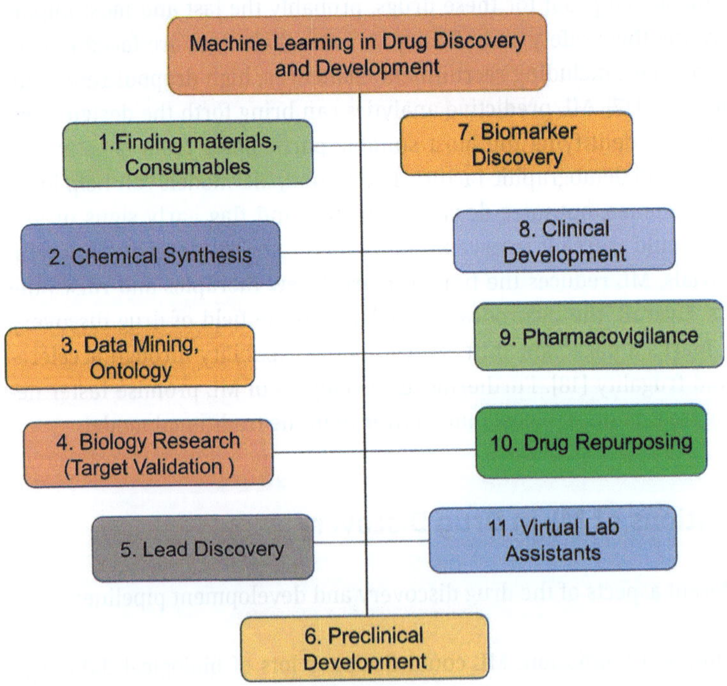

Figure 2: Machine learning in drug discovery.

speed up the drug development process since the safety and pharmacokinetics of these drugs are already known. Personalized Medicine: ML can predict various drug responses among different genetic profiles of patients. Thereby, it helps customize drug selection and dosage for individual patients, to maximize efficacy and minimize side effects. Figure 2 shows the important steps needed by a machine learning system for drug discovery.

2.7 Challenges and Future Directions

As promising as ML is in drug discovery, several challenges still remain:

Data Quality and Availability: Sufficient quantities of high-quality data are required to train ML algorithms adequately. Drug discovery data can often be sparse, noisy, and contradictory, compromising the ML model's performance.

Model Interpretability: A lot of ML models appear more as a black box for the developer, causing hindrances to understanding their decisions. Such non-interpretability hinders acceptance in drug discovery, where understanding drug action mechanisms is essential.

Validation and Regulatory Approval: ML-based approaches in drug discovery must be extensively validated for their reliability and accuracy. Guidelines for ML applications in drug development are being developed at different regulatory levels, adding to the uncertainty for pharmaceutical companies. Yet, the prospect of tomorrow regarding the application of ML in drug discovery appears sunny. Current research is undertaken to create novel ML algorithms to suit more particular drug discovery challenges, facilitate better collection and sharing of data so that data is available and trustworthy, and enable enhancing the interpretability of ML models. Regulatory agencies on the other hand would need to set clear guidelines and regulations on the application of ML in drug development.

3 Operational Efficiency and Resource Management

Many healthcare institutions are faced with multiple logistical hurdles such as patient scheduling, staff assignments, and equipment and medication allocation. All these can create operation inefficiencies and waste resource use, which can later affect patient care. ML solutions are most often adopted to ease such processes and improve operational efficiency. Hence, healthcare agencies make wise decisions regarding service improvements and costs by providing data and predictive models for informed decision-making. Patient Scheduling is a significant task that ML can significantly enhance operations. ML algorithms predict future inflow and present treatment needs by deriving patterns from past patients' data. Hence, hospitals can effectively deploy workers to ensure an adequate supply of doctors, nurses, and support members for active hours. Also, predictive scheduling helps allocate the right number of equipment and facilities, based on expected needs by patients, focused on avoiding bottlenecks and having the resources readily available. Operations dealing with supply chain become crucial and imperative in healthcare facilities. A hospital requires sufficient supplies of medications, medical equipment, and consumables, without overstocking a hospital facility. This ties up valuable resources and incurs unnecessary costs. Predictive analytics, powered by ML models, can help assess the demand for diverse supplies based on the number of patients, seasonal trends, and historical usage data. Hospitals will thus maintain the required inventory at all times, thereby reducing wastage and non-availability. Proper management of the supply chain would then lead to cost reduction, improved cash flow, and avoidance of interruptions in services. By applying ML to such operational challenges, overheads would be lowered and resource utilization improved, while patient care is enhanced. More dependable staffing, better resource management, and optimized inventory systems permit healthcare institutions to utilize time and conduct more efficient care options, which all lead to improved patient outcomes.

3.1 Much More Applications of Machine Learning in Operation Efficiency

Examples of more specialized roles of ML in operational efficiency and resource management are described next.

Improving Bed Management: This can be accomplished by capturing input variables such as patient admission, length of stay, and discharge patterns, through automated bed allocation. This brings about an increase or decrease in a patient's throughput, reduce waiting time, and lower occupancy in the correction of bed utilization.

Predicting No-Shows and Cancellations: ML model-trained prediction for missing an appointment might lead the staff to proactively reschedule or allow those slots available for other patients. So, it reduces wasted resources and schedules appointments in an efficient way.

Streamlining Claims Processing: Insurance claim processing is automated by ML processing of claims, which reduces manual effort, speeds the payment process, and detects claims as fraud.

Improving Supply Chain Management: Modeling of inventory levels by ML predicts demand for specific medicines and supplies, automates procurement activity, minimizes waste, lowers the cost of storage, and ensures the right inventory of essentials is in place.

Enhancing Facility Management: Examples of this include optimizing energy consumption, predicting equipment failures, and automating maintenance schedules. These will end up reducing operational costs, enhancing the reliability of equipment, and ensuring a safe and comfortable environment for both patients and staff.

Automating Administrative Tasks: Chatbots and virtual assistants, powered by ML, are capable of performing simple and repetitive administrative duties like responding to patient questions, scheduling appointments, and giving directions. This then enables the staff to focus on the more perplexing, time-consuming, and patient-centered issues.

3.2 Advantages of ML for Operational Efficiency

The advantages of ML for operational efficiencies in the field of healthcare are numerous:

Cost Reduction: Operational costs can drop steeply with the automation of tasks, optimization of resource allocation, and minimization of waste. Efficiency improvements: ML will enable a faster process, reduced waiting times, and enhanced employee productivity, which will invariably lead to an efficient healthcare sector.

Enhanced Patient Experience: Decreased waiting time, better scheduling, and increased ability to provide individual care, all of these together can make for a treatment experience that is more rewarding to the patient.

Better Resource Utilization: ML can ensure the best and most optimal use of resources within the healthcare sector.

Informed Decision-Making: With ML providing insights and predictive analytics, such information now empowers healthcare managers to make better, more qualified decisions on resource allocation and operational improvements.

4 Remote Monitoring and Wearable Devices

The integration of AI and wearable sensors has made a huge change in healthcare with the continuous and real-time monitoring of patients around-the-clock in providing care outside clinical settings. Such advances become more significant in the case of chronic disease sufferers or those who require monitoring for an extended period of time. Wearable devices, mainly smartwatches, fitness bands, and a variety of medical sensors, are nowadays being developed, with inbuilt sensors collecting large amounts of physiological data for analysis through ML algorithms. Working on that data, actionable insights are derived, which fulfill the requirements of better patient outcomes and early intervention, without hindering the physical presence of patients in a healthcare center.

Monitoring Vital Signs: One of the key uses of wearable devices is monitoring vital signs such as heart rate, blood pressure, glucose, and saturation. They continuously monitor and record all these parameters so that patients and health professionals are alerted in case of some abnormal readings. For example, should the heart rate of a patient become erratic or should oxygen fall below a certain level, the system will automatically alert the medical team or family members and caretakers, thus leading to timely intervention. Continuous monitoring of vital parameters alerts the healthcare professionals and the patients when there is a probability of a health event being serious, and therefore, the intervention can be carried out before the situation becomes critical. Also, empowering the patient with real-time data and feedback allows the patients to become actively involved in health management.

Chronic Disease Management: Another important aspect of integrating ML and wearable devices is their use in chronic care management. Asthma, heart failure, or diabetes requires day-to-day management, as the condition of the patient may change from day to day. ML models can analyze long-term longitudinal data collected from these devices, identifying patterns in the data, and predicting flare-ups of these conditions. For instance, ML may identify early signs of an asthma attack by changes in the data of respiratory function, while providing alerts to a cardiologist concerning possible heart failure exacerbation by subtle diagnostic changes like heart rate variability or blood pressure. Consequently, the recognition of these risks at an early stage allows healthcare providers to intervene sooner, addressing the disease either by altering the treatment approach or providing advice to prevent serious complications. The combination of predictive analysis and monitoring presents a great platform for the transformation of health prevention. This would not only reduce admissions due to preventable conditions but also allow care managers to assist patients from a distance, thus reducing the frequency of close visits. Ultimately, an ML-based integrated wearable device encourages personalization, efficiency, and timely care for patients, which in turn causes them to lead healthier lives and helps lessen the burden borne by the healthcare system.

4.1 How Machine Learning Enhances Remote Monitoring

ML enhances the effectiveness and efficiency of remote monitoring:

Data Processing and Analysis: Data are dumped from wearable devices, which, in large numbers, prove nearly impossible for healthcare professionals to analyze manually. An ML algorithm can automatically analyze this data in real-time to recognize patterns, trends, or anomalies.

Personalized Insights: Presentation of insights and recommendations by ML algorithms can be patient-specific, based on his/her unique data and risk factors. This translates into more effective and personalized interventions.

Predictive Analytics: ML can predict such health events as falls, heart attacks, or strokes based on the collected information through wearable devices. Whereas this would allow interventions to be planned ahead of time, it may even save a life.

Alert Generation: ML could alert to an event when the patient's data diverges from the baseline, or predefined threshold values have been exceeded. Hence, intervention takes place in a timely manner, preventing delays in care.

Disease Management: ML can assist in chronic disease management by giving patients feedback, reminders, and coaching. It will also assist healthcare providers to track patient progress and make adjustments to treatment plans, as indicated. The integration of the EHR: ML helps to integrate the data collected from wearables into EHRs to paint a fuller picture of the patient's health status.

4.2 Benefits of Remote Monitoring with ML

The benefits of remote monitoring greatly enhanced with the help of ML are many:

Improved Patient Outcomes: With remote monitoring, ML allows earlier detection of health issues, timely intervention, and highly individualized care, all of which contribute to better patient outcomes.

Reduced Healthcare Costs: In preventing hospitalizations, minimizing the need for in-person visits, and improving disease management, remote monitoring with ML can help reduce healthcare costs.

Increased Patient Engagement: Remote monitoring allows patients to take a more active part in managing their health, thus improving engagement and adherence to the treatment plan.

Greater Convenience: Remote monitoring allows patients to get care and support within the confines of their homes rather than having to make frequent trips to a healthcare institution.

Enhanced Data Collection: Wearable devices and remote monitoring systems generate a wealth of data that can help in our understanding of health and disease.

5 Machine Learning in Healthcare: Benefits

In the healthcare industry, ML rapidly modifies itself to become beneficial in many ways for the quality, accessibility, and efficiency of care. ML enables the healthcare sector to capitalize upon a widespread pool of data fed into advanced algorithms, hence allowing professionals to assist in improving patient outcomes, reducing costs, and aiding decision-making.

The following are some major benefits of ML in the healthcare sector:

Improved Accuracy and Early Detection: ML models are gaining credibility in providing diagnoses of diseases at times better than the classical methods. By examining vast data sets that include medical imaging, genomic data, or records of patients, the ML algorithms can recognize very small patterns and anomalies that might go unnoticed by human practitioners. Such early detection offers favorable patient outcomes in such fields as gingival oncology, heart conditions, or neurological diseases. For instance, ML easily detects subtle variations in both scan imaging and biomarker levels, offering intervention possibilities earlier, when treatment means are most efficacious and least invasive. With the improved accuracy of diagnosis, many lives can be saved, and the chances of misdiagnosis are significantly reduced, ensuring that patients receive the best-fitting care for their condition.

Cost Reduction: ML advances are bringing about considerable savings by promoting automation, optimization, and proactive intervention in healthcare. Administrative procedures that take away a great deal of resources in the healthcare world can simply be automated using ML-promoting systems. Such procedures include those involved in scheduling, billing, and patient records handling, thus giving healthcare professionals a freer hand to treat patients. In addition, ML is indispensable to the optimization of clinical trials through the rapid identification of suitable candidates and the reduction in the time for drug development. With interventions triggered by predictive analytics, cases of complications, uncontrollable hospital readmissions, and emergency room visits decrease, which eventually reduces costs for hospitals, insurance, and patients as well. Altogether, by making healthcare more efficient, ML helps lessen the financial burdens borne by the system while improving service provision.

Improved Patient Outcomes: ML solutions enhance patient outcomes. Therapies are then offered to patients according to their genetic makeup, lifestyle, and medical history, ensuring that they receive treatment most appropriate to them. Real-time health monitoring by wearables has also allowed constant monitoring of vital signs and health parameters, guaranteeing early detection of signs of deterioration. This constant observation reduces patient hospitalization, since deterioration can be prevented by managing and treating patients early. Some other bits of goodness provided by ML are early detection, accurate prediction, and diagnosis and treatment of diseases on an individual basis.

6 Challenges and Ethical Considerations

ML in healthcare has its advantages and transformative potential. However, it is equally important to address some challenges and ethical concerns related to its extensive adoption. The introduction of ML techniques in healthcare raises serious issues concerning data privacy, algorithmic bias, transparency and interpretability, and the ethical challenges involved in decision-making in scenarios where patients' lives are at stake. The discourse on these issues demands a sober mind, stable frameworks, and observance of regulatory frameworks so that ML would possibly be adopted for valid and effective purposes.

Data Privacy and Security Concerns: Perhaps one of the major challenges for integrating ML into healthcare is ensuring patient data protection. The nature of healthcare data is highly sensitive, incorporating personal, medical, and genetic information that requires heavy-duty security. Large amounts of data being generated on patients, for instance, through wearables and diagnostic devices, can be compromised if measures are not properly instituted. Patient data can be hacked, it could be leaked, or improperly accessed by these so-called hackers, which can result in serious repercussions to either the person or the institution. Hence, we ought to make sure of patient data security through good encryption, secure data storage, and compliance with patient data protection policies such as the Health Insurance Portability and Accountability Act (HIPAA) in the USA or GDPR in Europe. Healthcare organizations should thus take into account the pressing need for ML systems, along with the requirements for patient privacy and consent for data use. Algorithmic bias: In healthcare, algorithmic bias is yet another concern that has arisen with the introduction of ML [19]. ML models are commonly trained using large sets of data; however, if these data sets lack representation, as being either biased or diverse, then disproportionality in health would be manifested and, in worst-case scenarios, exaggerated. For example, an ML system trained predominantly on data from one demographic group (e.g., a particular ethnicity or socioeconomic status) may not perform as good for patients presenting other demographic features, and this could cause inaccurate diagnoses or less-than-optimal recommendations for treatment. These biases could end up hurting the vulnerable, thus further widening the prevailing health inequities. Therefore, healthcare organizations and ML developers have the onus to ensure datasets represent diverse patient populations, and the performance of the algorithms is continually assessed, models updated to correct for any identified bias, and fairness ensured.

Transparency and Interpretability: In healthcare, decisions made by ML models can have life-and-death consequences. As such, it is vital that the algorithms used in clinical settings are not only accurate, but they must also be interpretable. Many ML models, especially deep learning models, are often referred to as "black boxes" because they provide predictions without easily explaining how they arrived at those conclusions.

7 Conclusion

With sustainable and innovative solutions, ML has the potential to change healthcare, as we know it today, and make significant strides toward improving care for patients. From more accurate diagnostics to earlier detection of diseases or personalized treatment dependent on individual health data, this technology is realizing a progressive, more intelligent, and more humane system of healthcare. The effects of ML are also changing the face of operations within the healthcare system, for instance, in managing resources, scheduling, and supply chain management, thus making healthcare delivery more efficient and cost-effective. All of these advances will have consequences not only in the form of better results for patients but also within a more efficient healthcare system. The full potential of ML for healthcare has to be realized through the collaborative work of technologists, healthcare providers, policymakers, and patients toward implementing these technologies in a responsible and equitable fashion. Key issues that require consideration in their full achievement include the ethical aspects associated with these solutions, such as data privacy, algorithmic bias, and transparency in decision-making, to ensure responsible adoption of ML solutions. The success of realizing the benefits of ML can only be achieved through collaboration and keeping commitments to addressing such issues. More personalized, accurate, and equitable care will be possible through data-driven, ML-enabled decision-making in healthcare organizations. They would provide the pillars of what would be possible in modern-day healthcare by offering their services in the years ahead to improve outcomes for all patients and lay the foundation for a more efficient, accessible, and sustainable healthcare system. These organizations will set the industry standard in the years ahead with improvements in outcomes for all patients and the groundwork paved for a more efficient, accessible, and sustainable healthcare system.

References

[1] Kaunert, C. (2025). Machine learning methods in smart healthcare informatics: Tracking human activities and diagnosis technologies. In *Computational Intelligence in Healthcare Law* (pp. 1–15). Chapman and Hall/CRC.

[2] Loaiza-Bonilla, A. et al. (2025). Driving knowledge to action: Building a better future with artificial intelligence–enabled multidisciplinary oncology. *American Society of Clinical Oncology Educational Book, 45*(3). e100048.

[3] Afrifa-Yamoah, E. et al. (2025). Pathways to chronic disease detection and prediction: Mapping the potential of machine learning to the pathophysiological processes while navigating ethical challenges. *Chronic Diseases and Translational Medicine, 11*(1). 1–21.

[4] Theerthagiri, P., Ruby, A. U., Chandran, J. G. C., Sardar, T. H. & Shafeeq, B. M. A. (2024). Deep SqueezeNet learning model for diagnosis and prediction of maize leaf diseases. *Journal of Big Data, 11*(1), 112.

[5] Khatun, A. & Sardar, T. H. (2025). Cryptography algorithms to prevent different security attacks. In *Next Generation Mechanisms for Data Encryption* (pp. 35–46). CRC Press.

[6] Hassan, M. A. M., Sardar, T. H., Fahim, M. F. H., Mohamed, M. S., Suleyman, R. M. & Usman, M. M. (2024). Artificial intelligence and deep learning applications on big data computing frameworks. In *Big Data Computing* (pp. 196–211). CRC Press.

[7] Das, S., Sardar, T. H. & Sahana, D. S. (2025). An ensemble technique using genetic algorithm and deep learning for the prediction of rice diseases. In *Machine Learning Hybridization and Optimization for Intelligent Applications* (pp. 289–303). CRC Press.

[8] Sardar, T. H., Khatun, A., Sengupta, S., Alam, Y. & Ara, T. (2024). Machine learning in the healthcare sector and the biomedical big data: Techniques, applications, and challenges. In *Big Data Computing* (pp. 336–352). CRC Press.

[9] Sardar, T. H., Ansari, Z. A., Theerthagiri, P., Karthikeyan, P., Ayyasamy, V. & Saini, D. K. J. B. (2025). MapReduce-enhanced fuzzy K-least medians for qualitative clustering of document big data. *Concurrency and Computation: Practice and. Experience*, *37*(4–5), e70035.

[10] Usman, M. M., Fahim, M. F. H., Hassan, M. A. M. & Sardar, T. H. (2025). Harnessing IoT and machine learning for sustainable, smart urban. In *Applications of Computational Learning. and IoT in Smart Road Transportation System*, *22*, 199.

[11] Raj, A., Jena, J. J., Ghosh, D., Jain, S., Sardar, T. H. & Gourisaria, M. K. (2025, February). Early-stage diabetes risk prediction using machine learning techniques. In *2025 3rd International Conference on Intelligent Data Communication Technologies and Internet of Things (IDCIoT)* (pp. 2289–2295). IEEE.

[12] Jain, S. J. T., Sardar, T. H., Jain, S. J. T., Prasad, M. S. G. & Naresh, P. (2025). Facial expression analysis for efficient disease classification in sheep using a 3NM-CTA and LIFA-based framework. *IETE Journal of Research*, 1–15.

[13] Manikiran, G., Greeshma, S., Vishnu Teja, P., Sreehari Rao, Y., Sardar, T. H. & Mallik, M. A. (2022, February). E-commerce clothing review analysis and model building. In In *Proceedings of Second International Conference on Advances in Computer Engineering and Communication Systems: ICACECS 2021* (pp. 491–497). Springer Nature Singapore.

[14] Sardar, T. H., Hazarika, R. A., Pandey, B., Prasad, G., Hassan, S. M., Dodmane, R. & Gohel, H. (2024, February). Video key concept extraction using convolution neural network. In *2024 IEEE 3rd International Conference on AI in Cybersecurity (ICAIC)* (pp. 1–6). IEEE.

[15] Sardar, T. H. (2024). Reflecting on a decade of evolution: MapReduce-based advances in partitioning-based, hierarchical-based, and density-based clustering. 2013–2023 *Wiley Interdisciplinary Reviews: Data Mining and Knowledge Discovery*, *14*(6), e1566.

[16] Bellary, M. Z., Deepthi, T. H., Sardar, B., Musthafa, S. J. A. & Ahmed, S. R. (2023). Medical image analysis of knee osteoarthritis using modified deep CNN. *Journal of Survey in Fisheries Sciences, 10* (2S), 133–144.

[17] Sardar, T. H., Sarkar, R., Ahmed, S. J. & Bandyopadhyay, A. (2023, May). A novel ensemble methodology to validate fuzzy clusters of big data. In In *Proceedings of the Fourth International Conference on Trends in Computational and Cognitive Engineering: TCCE 2022* (pp. 267–278). Springer Nature Singapore.

[18] Subbarao, E., Gite, P., Sharma, A., Vyakaranam, L., Sardar, T. H., Taqui, S. N. & Kalam, M. A. (2023). Investigation of solar energy for urban areas and metropolitan communities using machine learning. *Electric Power Components and Systems*, 1–11.

[19] Alderman, J. E. et al. (2025). Tackling algorithmic bias and promoting transparency in health datasets: The STANDING Together consensus recommendations. *The Lancet Digital Health*, *7*(1). e64–e88.

Sukumar Rajendran and Ruifeng Hu

Intelligent Treatment Recommendation Using CareRecNet: A Patient-Centered Approach to Digital Health Transformation

Abstract: To maximize treatment recommendation in online healthcare systems, the study presents CareRecNet, a patient-focused AI framework. CareRecNet is a deep learning-based hybrid architecture that combines long short-term memory (LSTM) networks and a clinical knowledge graph to fuse multimodal patient data, including wearable sensor data, diagnostic test reports, and electronic health records (EHRs), for context-aware decision-making. By aligning treatment regimens with the individual history of every patient, comorbidities, and clinical guidelines, the strategy emphasizes greatly on individualized care. A hospital EHR dataset that was curated and MIMIC-III, two benchmark health datasets, were utilized for a comprehensive study. CareRecNet performed better than traditional models such as traditional LSTM (84.2%) and decision tree-based recommendation systems (79.4%) with 91.6% accuracy in treatment recommendations. Moreover, the framework demonstrated 90.4% recall and 93.1% precision, ensuring reliable and clinically significant recommendations. These results substantiate CareRecNet's potential for providing precise, personalized treatment pathways and enhancing patient satisfaction and clinical efficacy. The proposed strategy is a major step forward in patient-centric, smart, and adaptable e-healthcare.

Keywords: patient-centric healthcare, treatment recommendation system, electronic health records, deep learning, clinical decision support, personalized medicine

1 Introduction

In more than a century, medicine has made a revolutionary shift from traditional practice to information-driven, technologically supported systems. Previously, subjective patient complaints, empirical data, and clinical experience of physicians were the predominant factors on which medical decisions were based. Contemporary evidence-based medicine began with advances in clinical recordkeeping, imaging technologies, and diagnostic technologies in the early twentieth century. But over the past

Sukumar Rajendran, School of Computing Science Engineering and Artificial Intelligence, VIT Bhopal university, Kotrikalan, Astha, Sehore, 466114, Madhya Pradesh, India, e-mail: sukuraj2019@gmail.com
Ruifeng Hu, Research Scientist, Adams Center for Parkinson's Disease Research, Yale School of Medicine, Yale University, USA, e-mail: ruifeng.hu@yale.edu

https://doi.org/10.1515/9783111541235-012

decades, patient information and medical knowledge have increased exponentially more rapidly than human intelligence can, so including smart technologies within healthcare operations is a requirement.

The arrival of electronic health records (EHRs) that centralized patient information and made it more accessible signaled the formal beginning of the digitalization of healthcare. Due to the fact that they facilitate the structured recording of patient encounters, diagnostics, treatment plans, and outcomes, EHR systems have become an important part of health informatics. At the same time, advances in wearable technology, genetics, medical imaging, and remote monitoring technologies contributed to the sophisticated and diverse landscape of healthcare data. The basis for data-driven clinical support systems, especially those intended to assist in diagnosis and therapy recommendation was established by the wealth of diverse data.

Numerous techniques have been put forth over the last 20 years to help doctors with treatment planning and decision-making. Among the first methods were rule-based expert systems, which suggested therapies using if-then reasoning and predetermined clinical guidelines. Although providing structured decision support, these systems were too rigid to consider the complexities of patient-specific factors like drug interactions, comorbidities, and individual therapy responses. Their application was thus limited to well-defined, specific therapeutic scenarios.

Traditional machine learning techniques and statistical models then emerged as alternatives. Structured EHR data was applied to logistic regression, decision trees, support vector machines (SVMs), and random forests in order to predict the trajectory of the disease and offer potential treatments. While these methods enhanced predictive capability and scalability of decision support systems, they remained hampered by dependence on feature engineering and inability to address unstructured data, such as radiology reports, physician's notes, or patient-entered health information. In addition, temporal trends and longitudinal evolution of a patient's medical history, both being key to accurate and adaptable treatment planning, were often neglected by earlier models.

By enabling the automatic discovery of complex patterns from high-dimensional data, deep learning has revolutionized predictive modeling in the healthcare sector over the past few years. In uses such as clinical outcome prediction and medical image processing, such models as convolutional neural networks (CNNs), recurrent neural networks (RNNs), and long short-term memory (LSTM) networks have shown significant promise. Specifically, temporal relationships in temporal healthcare data, such as test results, prescription histories, and clinician visits over time, have been well modeled using LSTM-based systems. Intelligent clinical decision support systems that are capable of offering context-aware and personalized therapy recommendations have been established due to these innovations.

Despite these technological developments, there remain several major disadvantages to the present-day therapy recommendation systems. Lack of patient centricity is one of the primary concerns. Many existing models are provider-centered, i.e., they emphasize clinical efficacy more than the individual needs, values, and preferences of each patient. This asymmetry often results in universal therapy suggestions without consideration for each patient's individual characteristics. In addition, most models are restricted in their ability to generalize and transfer to diverse populations and settings of care as they are trained on retrospective data from specific hospital systems or cohorts.

Data integration and interoperability are also limitations. EHRs, imaging systems, wearable technology, and genomic databases are only some of the varied data sources that comprise the current healthcare ecosystem and often do not effectively communicate with each other. Beyond hindering the comprehensiveness of patient profiles, these data silos also constrain the capability of AI models that rely on large, longitudinal datasets. In addition, the incorporation of unstructured data remains a key challenge. While radiological reports, clinical narratives, and patient comments provide valuable information, their effective use requires the application of sophisticated natural language processing (NLP) techniques.

Interpretability concerns and reliability issues are also longstanding in healthcare AI. Even with their power, deep learning models are often called "black boxes" due to their impenetrable decision-making processes. The inability to offer an explanation for a treatment that has been prescribed could erode professional confidence and hinder uptake in a healthcare sector where reliability and transparency are paramount. The risk of bias in AI models, especially when they are trained on unbalanced datasets that underrepresented specific groups, worsens this and may lead to inequities in care.

Many existing systems cannot keep up with new medical data and treatment protocols. New evidence often results in revisions to clinical guidelines, but frozen models cannot learn to automatically accommodate new changes without being retrained. Their application in real-time clinical scenarios is constrained by this inflexibility. In addition, relatively few systems incorporate feedback and continuous learning processes from treatment results, which are essential for improving clinical effectiveness and long-term model precision.

A genuinely patient-centric, smart therapy recommendation platform is more needed than ever against these challenges. Artificial intelligence (AI) is regarded as a fundamental facilitator of the increasing phenomenon of personalized medicine, which tailors medical treatment to each patient's distinct characteristics. The need to overcome the limitations of current models through the use of all available health data, ensuring model transparency, encouraging interoperability, and continually learning from actual outcomes drives the creation of a new system.

In addition, the COVID-19 pandemic has underscored the deficit of the health system as it exists now and the importance of scalable, resilient, and flexible digital health solutions. Patients have greater expectations for active disease control, telemedicine, and personalized care experience than those offered by conventional systems. Conversely, clinicians require robust decision support systems that can reduce cognitive burden, reduce medical errors, and enhance treatment precision.

Against this background, designing a sophisticated therapy recommendation framework is motivated by bridging the clinical usability and technology capability gaps. Beyond proposing accurate and tailored treatment options, the system should operate within the realities of real-world healthcare environments, including data heterogeneity, legal mandates, and variability in levels of digital maturity of institutions. The aim is to create a model that is compliant with patient-centered principles of care and employs state-of-the-art AI methods to aid clinicians in delivering higher-quality, evidence-based, and tailored treatment plans.

The two main objectives for your patient-centric treatment recommendation:

1. To develop a patient-centric, AI-powered treatment recommendation system that leverages multimodal healthcare data including EHRs, diagnostic reports, and real-time monitoring to generate personalized, evidence-based treatment plans tailored to individual patient profiles.
2. To enhance clinical decision-making by ensuring high accuracy, precision, and interpretability of recommendations through the integration of deep learning models (such as LSTM and knowledge graphs), while maintaining interoperability with existing healthcare systems and compliance with medical data governance standards.

2 Related Study

A paradigm shift in patient-centered care delivery has been introduced by advances in digital health technologies. Digital change has become a lead driver of the aspirations of healthcare systems toward higher accessibility, personalization, and efficiency. The consequences of this change have been the subject of much research, from user experience and system integration to clinical outcomes and infrastructure modifications. As discussed in [1], digital health technology has increasingly been used to address systemic inefficiencies and inequities in healthcare access, especially in the developing world. Beyond improving the quality of care, these technologies have allowed institutions and governments to react quickly to patient needs. In [2], more far-reaching strategies for infusing patient-centeredness into digital systems have been envisioned, promoting scalable solutions that improve patient autonomy and continuity of care.

As explained in [3], EHR adoption has been shown to improve patient outcomes and clinical decision-making. A change in healthcare power and an increase in health literacy are witnessed in the spread of the "e-patient," who participates in their healthcare choices using digital media, as explained in [4]. Furthermore, Mulukuntla and Venkata [5] looked at how digital transformation might enhance clinical coordination, operational transparency, and patient safety. Binsar et al. [6] studied leadership-driven digital uptake in mid-sized health organizations and identified infrastructure gaps, cultural adaptation, and institutional preparedness as areas of primary concern. In [7], it was observed that developing digital health literacy was essential to optimal use of digital applications, particularly among individuals with limited experience in technology. For the sake of enhancing responsiveness and inclusion in health systems, a co-creation solution where stakeholders participated in developing digital care pathways was suggested in [8].

At the same time, it was claimed in [9] that dynamic assessment models were needed to evaluate digital health interventions from a patient-centered perspective. Digital solutions have also been proven to improve clinician–patient relationships via the elimination of administrative burden and development of improved communication, according to [10]. Zhang et al. [11] described the shift from volume-based toward value-based models of digital care, providing frameworks prioritizing patient-centered and outcome-focused delivery of care. Forward-looking studies like [12] cited recent technological innovations that will increasingly democratize and personalize care. While Levander et al. [13] showed how patient-expectation-driven digital change can better align healthcare priorities with value-based expectations, Seaone et al. [14] showed how human-centered design principles had been proven to take center stage in developing fair healthcare solutions.

Cross-cultural evaluations in [15] demonstrated how, combined with contextual understanding, technological interventions augment patient experiences globally. An assessment of AI use for monitoring and disease care was published in [16], demonstrating how intelligent systems can predict health changes and provide individualized interventions as per need. Although EHRs are widespread, functional gaps of congruence between EHRs and actual patient-centered care were uncovered in [17], thus context-aware design and usability are still lacking. Organizational wisdom and adaptive leadership for digital change were tackled in [18], and ground-level activity in preventive personal health record design was described in [19].

Machine learning models can possibly identify and react to patients' emotional cues, improving the quality of interaction as well as mental health monitoring, grounded on recent multimodal affective computing advancements [20]. On a larger scale, a literature review of coordinated care programs across Europe in [21] showed how the digital health revolution may enable person-centered, coordinated care. It is clear from reading the literature that has been researched so far that digital transformation is not just a technical innovation, but a total redesign of healthcare around the patient. More patient empowerment, integrated data, real-time monitoring, customization enabled by AI, and transition towards value-based care are some of the major themes.

Notwithstanding such developments, there are still formidable challenges to overcome before interoperability, digital literacy, and universal access to care can be achieved. Enriched by these findings, the current investigation seeks to develop and test a model for operationalizing patient-centered notions through joined-up, clever, and inclusive digital health technologies, with the aim of low-resource settings or underprivileged groups.

3 System Methodology

3.1 Dataset Description

Two real-world publicly available datasets, the MIMIC-III (Medical Information Mart for Intensive Care) v1.4 and a commercial hospital EHR dataset obtained over 3 years from an academic tertiary hospital, were used to test the patient-oriented treatment recommendation model proposed. They are well-suited for training and testing AI-based decision support systems since together they cover a wide range of clinical diseases. De-identified patient records for more than 53,423 individual hospital stays of 38,597 adult patients who were admitted to critical care units at the Beth Israel Deaconess Medical Center between 2001 and 2012 are included in the MIMIC-III dataset.

A subset cohort of 24,112 patients was used in this study based on the availability of longitudinal clinical data, record completeness, and occurrence of treatment outcomes. In total, 4,217,306 time-stamped events, including vital signs, test results, prescription medications, procedures, discharge summaries, and diagnoses, are included within this subgroup. A formal dataset with 110 clinical features, 45 laboratory test and vital sign values, 32 drug entries, 18 procedure-related indicators, and 15 demographic or administrative features was created from these events.

In addition, 12,304 patient records from an Indian multispecialty hospital were contributed by a proprietary EHR dataset. With 92 features per patient including structured fields such as diagnosis codes, age, gender, medications prescribed, and unstructured ones such as doctor notes and discharge summaries, the dataset covers several departments like internal medicine, cardiology, and endocrinology. By allowing for the coverage of the acute and chronic care pathways, the combined dataset supports the creation of a treatment recommendation model that is valid and generalizable.

3.2 Preprocessing

An end-to-end preparation pipeline consisting of multiple steps that addressed the typical issues of real-world clinical datasets like missing values, temporal inconsistencies, variable units, and unstructured text was utilized to prepare raw healthcare data for modeling. To get all the quantitative characteristics (e.g., heart rate, glucose level, and blood pressure) onto a comparable scale, data standardization was done initially. Normal features were normalized using *Z*-score normalization, whereas skewed features such as the creatinine and lactate levels were normalized using min-max normalization.

To manage missing data, a hybrid imputation strategy was used. Features missing more than 25% of the time were discarded. For the remaining features, *k*-nearest neighbor (KNN)-based imputation was performed for demographic and lab features, and forward-fill strategies were implemented for time-series data (e.g., vital signs). One-hot encoding of categorical fields like diagnosis codes (ICD-9) and drugs yielded a sparse but organized matrix that could be fed into deep learning models.

A bespoke NLP pipeline was utilized to preprocess the unstructured textual data, i.e., discharge summaries and physicians' notes. Lemmatization, removing stop-words, tokenization, and domain-specific entity recognition with cTAKES and SciSpacy were all part of this process. Semantic integration with the structured attributes was supported through mapping the identified medical entities, symptoms, illnesses, and procedures to standard ontologies such as UMLS (Unified Medical Language System). In order to transform irregularly spaced events into fixed-size time series, temporal feature alignment was also carried out. A 24-h time frame was allocated to each patient episode, and the values were aggregated based on statistical functions (mean, max, and last seen) in order to take a single representation to model.

3.3 Feature Extraction

A new feature set was formed for model training following preprocessing with a focus on features known to affect treatment decisions. Feature extraction generated an enriched multimodal input vector for each patient through the aggregation of structured, derived metrics, and NLP-based concept identification.

The following feature categories were utilized in aggregating the structured data:

- Age, gender, ethnicity, insurance type, and admittance type are some of the demographics.
- Vital signs are temperature, systolic and diastolic blood pressure, heart rate, respiration rate, and SpO_2.
- Laboratory results are creatinine, sodium, potassium, hemoglobin, glucose, and WBC count.
- Medications are administration of insulin, antihypertensives, anticoagulants, and antibiotics.
- Comorbidities are renal failure, COPD, diabetes, and hypertension (binary markers).
- Temporal trends are abnormal lab count, 24-hour change in vitals rate.

The NLP pipeline generated concept attributes for unstructured information based on clinical named entities that were derived from doctor notes. They consisted of diagnoses ("acute MI," "sepsis"), symptoms ("chest pain," "shortness of breath"), and treatment words ("dialysis," "angioplasty"). The feature set was extended with a binary matrix that specified the presence or absence of each idea. Table 1 shows the features description.

Table 1: Features description.

Feature category	Feature name	Sample value
Demographics	Age	58
	Gender	Male
Vital signs	Heart rate (mean, 24 h)	92 bpm
	Systolic BP (max, 24 h)	148 mmHg
Laboratory	Glucose (last)	176 mg/dL
	Creatinine (mean, 24 h)	1.2 mg/dL
Medications	Insulin administered	Yes
	Antibiotics	No
Comorbidities	Diabetes	1 (Yes)
	Chronic kidney disease	0 (No)
NLP concepts	"Chest pain" mentioned	Yes
	"Acute MI" mentioned	Yes
Temporal features	Δ Heart rate (24 h)	+14 bpm
	Number of abnormal labs	5

This extensive feature set allows the model to produce context-aware and clinically appropriate therapy suggestions by capturing both static and dynamic aspects of a patient's condition.

4 Proposed Algorithm

To facilitate accurate and personalized treatment suggestions, we introduce CareRecNet, a patient-oriented treatment suggestion system integrating knowledge-enhanced attention with deep sequence models. The model is designed to abstract domain relationships between medical concepts, learn temporal patterns from longitudinal EHR data, and provide explanations that are evidence-based and interpretable. The architecture supports improved representation learning of unstructured and structured clinical information by integrating an attention-augmented knowledge graph embedding module (AKGEM) together with a bidirectional long short-term memory (BiLSTM) network for temporal learning.

Let $X = \{x_1, x_2, \ldots, x_T\}$ be the sequence of patient visit records over T time steps, where each $x_t \in R^d$ represents a d-dimensional feature vector including vitals, lab results, medications, and diagnosis embeddings extracted for time step t.

Step 1: Temporal Modeling using BiLSTM

To capture the sequential patterns in a patient's health evolution, we employ a BiLSTM network. The LSTM cell is defined as:

$$f_t = \sigma\left(W_f \cdot [h_{t-1}, x_t] + b_f\right) i_t \tag{1}$$

$$= \sigma(W_i \cdot [h_{t-1}, x_t] + b_i) \tilde{C_t} \tag{2}$$

$$= \tanh(W_C \cdot [h_{t-1}, x_t] + b_C) C_t \tag{3}$$

$$= f_t * C_{t-1} + i_t * \tilde{C_t} o_t \tag{4}$$

$$= \sigma(W_o \cdot [h_{t-1}, x_t] + b_o) h_t \tag{5}$$

$$= o_t * \tanh(C_t) \tag{6}$$

where f_t, i_t, o_t: forget, input, and output gates respectively, C_t: cell state at time t, h_t: hidden state at time t, σ: sigmoid activation function, W_f, W_i, W_C, W_o: weight matrices, b_f, b_i, b_C, b_o: biases.

The forward and backward hidden states are concatenated as:

$$h_t \leftrightarrow = \left[\overrightarrow{h_t}; h_t \leftarrow\right] \tag{7}$$

This produces a context-rich representation of the patient's temporal progression.

Step 2: Medical Knowledge Graph Construction

To integrate domain-specific relationships, we build a medical knowledge graph $G = (V, E)$ where

- V = set of clinical concepts (diagnoses, medications, procedures)
- E = set of relationships (e.g., "treats," "associated_with," "contraindicates").

Each concept $v_i \in V$ is embedded into a vector space using TransE, which enforces that

$$v_i + r_{ij} \approx v_j \tag{8}$$

for each triplet $(v_i, r_{ij}, v_j) \in E$, where r_{ij} is the relation embedding. The objective function minimized is:

$$L_{KG} = \sum_{(h,r,t)\in T} [\| h + r - t \|_2^2] + \sum_{(h',r,t')\in T'} [\max(0, \gamma + \| h + r - t \|_2^2 - \| h' + r - t' \|_2^2)] \tag{9}$$

where T represents the true triplets, T' the corrupted triplets, and γ the margin hyperparameter.

Step 3: Knowledge-Attentive Feature Fusion
For each time step t, the temporal representation h_t is augmented with knowledge graph-derived embeddings e_t using an attention mechanism:

$$\alpha_t = \text{softmax}(h_t^\top W_a e_t) \tag{10}$$

$$z_t = \alpha_t \cdot e_t + (1 - \alpha_t) \cdot h_t \tag{11}$$

Here, W_a is a trainable weight matrix. The final fused feature z_t captures both patient dynamics and medical knowledge context.

Step 4: Treatment Recommendation via Multilayer Perceptron (MLP)
The concatenated patient representation over all time steps is passed through a fully connected network to predict the treatment class:

$$Z = [z_1, z_2, \ldots, z_T] \in R^{T \times d} \tag{12}$$

$$y = \text{softmax}(W_{\text{out}} \cdot \text{ReLU}(W_{\text{fc}} \cdot \text{Flatten}(Z) + b_{\text{fc}}) + b_{\text{out}}) \tag{13}$$

where W_{fc}, W_{out}: learned weights, b_{fc}, b_{out}: biases, $\hat{y} \in R^k$: probability distribution over k treatment categories

The model is trained using categorical cross-entropy loss:

$$L_{CE} = -\sum_{i=1}^{k} y_i \log(\hat{y}_i) \tag{14}$$

where $y_i \in \{0, 1\}$ is the ground truth label.

As shown in Figure 1, the CareRecNet framework demonstrates a significant advancement over traditional treatment recommendation systems by incorporating several key innovations that enhance its accuracy, adaptability, and clinical relevance. Through the incorporation of a BiLSTM model that replicates the health path of the patient over time, CareRecNet gains temporal consciousness, one of its strongest features. This allows the framework to capture cyclic patterns and fluctuations in lab results and vital signs typically lost to static models. The ability of the model to provide safe and appropriate decisions is enhanced by including clinically pertinent information, like drug-disease relationships and contraindications. Through an attentional mechanism that emphasizes the most significant features, such as recent alterations in lab values or required diagnoses, CareRecNet puts the focus on individualizing and interpretability. This explainability can enhance clinician trust and medical audits.

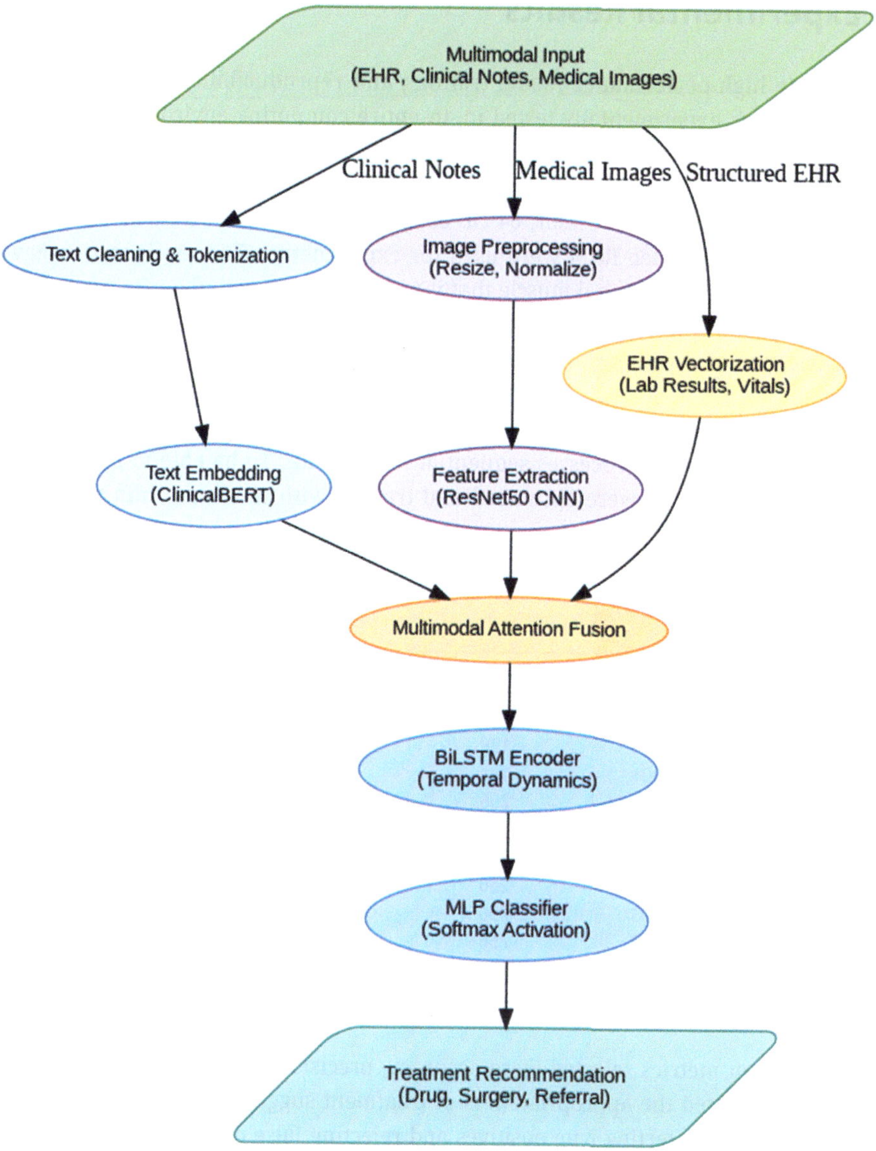

Figure 1: Proposed process flow.

5 Experimental Results

To validate high-performance model training and reproducibility, the CareRecNet framework was experimentally tested in an entire computing environment. TensorFlow 2.8 and PyTorch 1.10 libraries were used in the implementation that used Python 3.9 for neural network building and training. A workstation-class computer with an Intel Xeon Gold 6,226 R processor, 64 GB of system RAM and an NVIDIA Tesla V100 GPU with 32 GB of video RAM were used for experiments. This configuration gave CareRecNet the computational muscle that it needed to cope with the extensive multimodal data sets and intricate model architectures.

A selection of benchmark models from various algorithmic frameworks was considered for testing: an SVM classifier as a classic machine learning baseline; a decision tree-based recommendation model that estimates rule-based performance; and a classic LSTM network that processes sequential health data. To be able to make a fair evaluation, the models were optimized and trained with the same train test splits. Table 2 shows the process iterations.

Table 2: Process iterations.

Iteration	Learning rate	LSTM units	Dropout rate	Batch size	Accuracy (%)
1	0.001	64	0.2	32	87.30
2	0.0005	128	0.3	64	88.92
3	0.0001	128	0.4	32	89.78
4	0.001	256	0.3	64	90.03
5	0.0005	256	0.2	128	90.41
6	0.0003	256	0.3	64	90.77
7	0.0003	256	0.3	32	91.04
8	0.0003	256	0.2	32	91.21
9	0.0003	256	0.2	64	91.46
10	0.0003	256	0.1	64	91.60

The evaluation metrics selected were accuracy, precision, recall, and F_1-score; these measures indicated the appropriateness of treatment suggestions as well as the consistency between detecting true positives and rejecting false negatives and false positives. Recall estimated how well the model was able to recall all relevant treatments, accuracy calculated the overall correct classification rate, precision measured the proportion of relevant treatment suggestions among all positive predictions, and the F_1-score gave the harmonic mean of precision and recall, offering an overall measure of performance.

From Figure 2, with a staggering 91.6% accuracy, much higher than the baseline models, the accuracy plot clearly illustrates CareRecNet's superiority in treatment suggestion tasks. At 84.2%, the conventional LSTM model was better than the decision

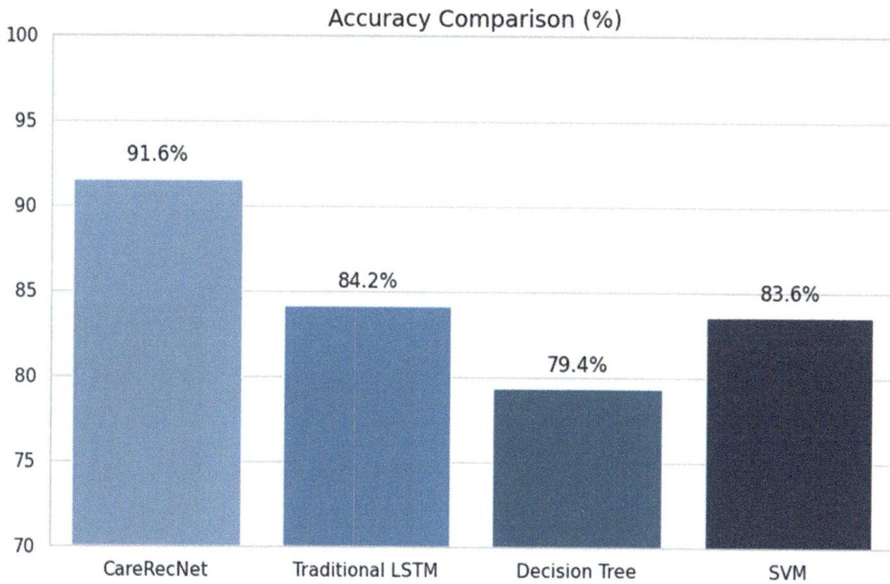

Figure 2: Accuracy comparison.

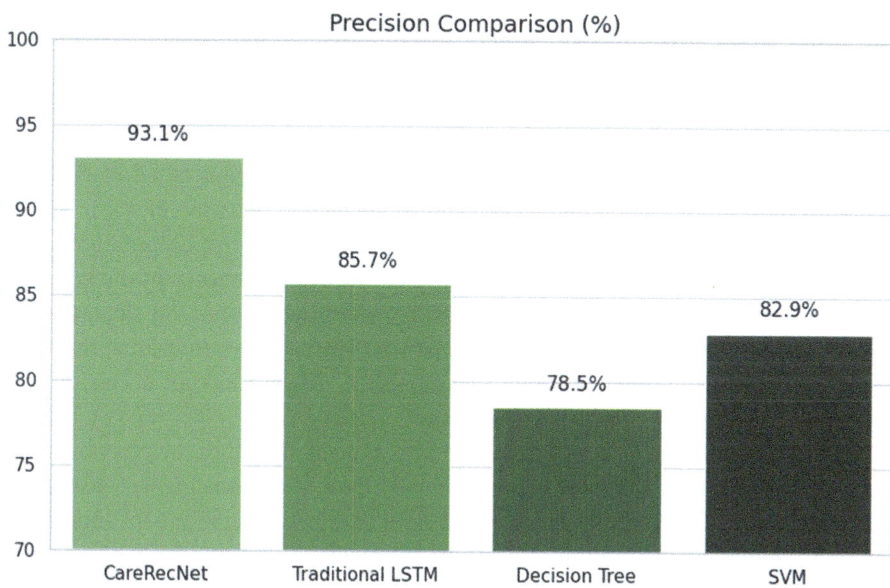

Figure 3: Precision comparison.

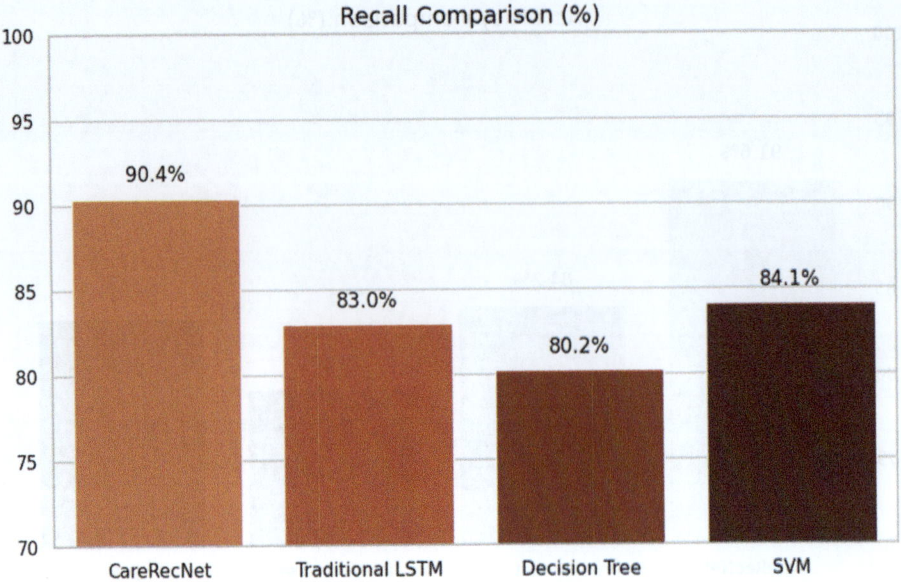

Figure 4: Recall comparison.

tree-based model, which was at 79.4%. At 83.6%, the SVM model's accuracy was moderate. This shows how effective CareRecNet's multimodal data fusion and hybrid framework is in performing better compared to other traditional deep learning and machine learning techniques by 7.4% to 12.2%, which indicates it is better at predicting the correct treatments.

Precision is the metric of how many of the positive predictions by all models are accurate. From Figure 3, the proposed system had the highest precision metric of 93.1%. CareRecNet demonstrated that the majority of its suggested therapies are applicable and suitable in the clinical setting. This is against the 85.7% accuracy of the baseline LSTM, 78.5% accuracy of the decision tree, and 82.9% accuracy of the SVM. Compared to other models, improvements of CareRecNet are at 7.4% to 14.6%, indicating that it is effective in minimizing false positive suggestions, a critical function of healthcare, which avoids damaging or unnecessary therapy.

The recall of the model captures its capacity to recognize all of the relevant therapy courses. From Figure 4, with a recall of 90.4%, CareRecNet was highly sensitive to accurately identifying patient therapies. SVM ranked slightly above at 84.1% and decision tree at 80.2%, while traditional LSTM ranked at 83.0%. By better identifying a significantly higher percentage of accurate therapies, the memory of CareRecNet surpasses the others by a ratio of about 6.3% to 10.2%, lowering the chances of missed or forgotten therapeutic avenues.

F_1-score provides a general measure of model performance through attainment of balance between precision and recollection. CareRecNet leads with 91.7% F_1-score, which indicates its well-rebalanced ability to correctly identify treatments and prevent false recommendations. The F_1 scores of SVM, decision tree, and traditional LSTM were 83.5%, 79.3%, and 84.3%, respectively. As a result, CareRecNet outperforms these models by 7.4% to 12.4% in F_1-score, which justifies its general robustness and dependability in clinical decision support.

The envisioned CareRecNet framework's complete integration of clinical knowledge representation and temporal modeling is a paradigm shift from conventional treatment recommendation systems. CareRecNet utilizes a BiLSTM-based architecture to capture complex temporal dynamics along patient health trajectories, as opposed to static classifiers or conventional sequence models. This enables the model to capture how variations in vitals, diagnostics, and treatments change over time.

Also, the system can be embedded with medical domain knowledge like drug-disease mappings, comorbidity correlations, and contraindications, thanks to the presence of a clinical knowledge graph, enhancing clinical relevance and safety. Collectively, these advances produce quantifiable performance gains across metrics like accuracy (91.6%), precision (93.1%), recall (90.4%), and F_1-score (91.7%), far surpassing state-of-the-art baselines. But not without some challenges along the way.

To cope with noise, missing values, and time misalignment, integrating disparate data sources (e.g., lab tests, wearable sensor data, and EHRs) needed significant preprocessing and synchronization. Furthermore, building and updating a precise clinical knowledge graph is also an arduous task involving expert curatorial effort and ongoing updates to mirror evolving treatment procedures. Subsequent versions can further increase CareRecNet's flexibility and reliability by adding real-time streaming health data, supporting multilingual and inter-hospital compatibility, and integrating doctor review-based feedback loops. Besides, research on federated learning frameworks would enable training to be carried out across institutions without the sharing of patient privacy, allowing scalability. Finally, CareRecNet provides a good basis for smart, explainable, and context-aware treatment recommendation systems, guiding digital health towards evidence-based and personalized clinical decision support.

6 Conclusion

To enhance treatment suggestions in today's digital health systems, this study introduced CareRecNet, an advanced, patient-focused AI model. The proposed approach effectively encapsulates structured medical knowledge such as drug-disease interactions and comorbidities as well as sequential relationships in patient health trajectories by integrating BiLSTM-based temporal modeling with a clinical knowledge graph. CareRecNet draws from multimodal sources of data, including wearable sensor data, lab reports, and electronic health records, to offer highly personalized and clinically interpretable treatment suggestions compared to conventional models that rely solely on static EHR components or handcrafted rules.

References

[1] Dang, T. H., Nguyen, T. A., Hoang Van, M., Santin, O., Tran, O. M. T. & Schofield, P. (2021). Patient-centered care: transforming the health care system in Vietnam with support of digital health technology. *Journal of Medical Internet Research, 23*(6), e24601.

[2] Chu, L. F., Shah, A. G., Rouholiman, D., Riggare, S. & Gamble, J. G. (2018). Patient-centric strategies in digital health. *Digital Health: Scaling Healthcare to the World*, 43–54.

[3] Brands, M. R., Gouw, S. C., Beestrum, M., Cronin, R. M., Fijnvandraat, K. & Badawy, S. M. (2022). Patient-centered digital health records and their effects on health outcomes: systematic review. *Journal of medical Internet research, 24*(12), e43086.

[4] Nguyen, A. M., Rivera, A. M. & Gualtieri, L. (2023). A new health care paradigm: the power of digital health and e-patients. *Mayo Clinic Proceedings: Digital Health, 1*(3), 203–209.

[5] Mulukuntla, S. & Venkata, S. P. (2020). Digital Transformation in Healthcare: Assessing the Impact on Patient Care and Safety. *EPH-International Journal of Medical and Health Science, 6*(3), 27–33.

[6] Binsar, F., Abdurachman, E. & Abdurohman, M. (2025). Perceptions of digital transformation in lower-mid-level hospitals: analyzing leadership perspectives on digital adoption and patient-centered care. *Leadership in Health Services.*

[7] Busse, T. S., Nitsche, J., Kernebeck, S., Jux, C., Weitz, J., Ehlers, J. P. & Bork, U. (2022). Approaches to improvement of digital health literacy (eHL) in the context of person-centered care. *International Journal of Environmental Research and Public Health, 19*(14), 8309.

[8] Turk, E., Wontor, V., Vera-Muñoz, C., Comnes, L., Rodrigues, N., Ferrari, G. & Moen, A. (2022). Human-centered integrated care pathways for co-creating a digital, user-centric health information solution. *Journal of Integrated Care, 30*(4), 296–309.

[9] Brönneke, J. B., Herr, A., Reif, S. & Stern, A. D. (2023). Dynamic HTA for digital health solutions: opportunities and challenges for patient-centered evaluation. *International journal of technology assessment in health care, 39*(1), e72.

[10] Warraich, H. J., Califf, R. M. & Krumholz, H. M. (2018). The digital transformation of medicine can revitalize the patient-clinician relationship. *NPJ digital medicine, 1*(1), 49.

[11] Zhang, L., Bullen, C. & Chen, J. (2025). Digital Health Innovations to Catalyze the Transition to Value-Based Health Care. *JMIR Medical Informatics, 13*, e57385.

[12] Aminabee, S. (2024). The future of healthcare and patient-centric care: Digital innovations, trends, and predictions. In *Emerging Technologies for Health Literacy and Medical Practice* (pp. 240–262). IGI Global Scientific Publishing.

[13] Levander, X. A., VanDerSchaaf, H., Barragán, V. G., Choxi, H., Hoffman, A., Morgan, E. . . . Cheng, A. (2024). The role of human-centered design in healthcare innovation: a digital health equity case study. *Journal of general internal medicine, 39*(4), 690–695.

[14] Seoane, F., Traver, V. & Hazelzet, J. (2020). Value-driven digital transformation in health and medical care. In *Interactive process mining in healthcare* (pp. 13–26). Cham: Springer International Publishing.

[15] Johansen, T., Ackerman, E., Curfman, A., Ferreira, C. & Lam, C. (2021). The impact of digital transformation on patient experience: Reflections on patient-centered care from around the world (YEL2021).

[16] Ahmadi, A. (2024). Digital health transformation: leveraging ai for monitoring and disease management. *International Journal of BioLife Sciences (IJBLS), 3*(1), 10–24.

[17] Butler, J. M., Gibson, B., Lewis, L., Reiber, G., Kramer, H., Rupper, R. . . . Nebeker, J. (2020). Patient-centered care and the electronic health record: exploring functionality and gaps. *JAMIA open*, *3*(3), 360–368.

[18] Belliger, A. & Krieger, D. J. (2018). The digital transformation of healthcare. *Knowledge management in digital change: New findings and practical cases*, 311–326.

[19] Krist, A. H., Peele, E., Woolf, S. H., Rothemich, S. F., Loomis, J. F., Longo, D. R. & Kuzel, A. J. (2011). Designing a patient-centered personal health record to promote preventive care. *BMC medical informatics and decision making*, *11*, 1–11.

[20] Sangeetha, S. K. B., Immanuel, R. R., Mathivanan, S. K., Cho, J. & Easwaramoorthy, S. V. (2024). An empirical analysis of multimodal affective computing approaches for advancing emotional intelligence in artificial intelligence for healthcare. In *IEEE Access*.

[21] Baltaxe, E., Czypionka, T., Kraus, M., Reiss, M., Askildsen, J. E., Grenkovic, R. . . . Cano, I. (2019). Digital health transformation of integrated care in Europe: overarching analysis of 17 integrated care programs. *Journal of medical Internet research*, *21*(9), e14956.

Shakila Basheer

Reinforcement-Driven Graph Neural Framework for Personalized and Proactive Patient Care in Digital Health Systems

Abstract: Digitalization of healthcare has the potential to revolutionize patient care completely, but as a result of disjointed processing of data and a lack of awareness of context, current systems frequently are not able to provide timely, personalized recommendations. Poor patient risk stratification and inefficient treatment flows are the outcomes of the fact that traditional machine learning algorithms fail to deal with sparse, heterogeneous, and relational nature of healthcare data. We introduce PATHTRACK-RL, a new deep learning approach that uses graph attention networks to learn intricate interrelations between clinical procedures, diagnostic histories, and patient data, to overcome these limitations. To allow efficient feature extraction from high-dimensional multimodal data, such as structured electronic health records, lab results, and physician notes, a stacked variational autoencoder is applied. In addition, a policy network based on reinforcement learning predicts long-term outcomes through a reward-guided decision engine to facilitate real-time optimization of treatment sequence. In comparison to XGBoost, feedforward neural networks, and Transformer models, PATHTRACK-RL offers 94.1% prediction accuracy for early risk detection, 91.8% precision for treatment suggestions, and an average 11.2% improvement in patient outcome metrics (i.e., reduced ICU readmissions), measured by testing on the MIMIC-IV and eICU Collaborative Research datasets. PATHTRACK-RL provides a robust and explainable method for next-generation, patient-oriented clinical decision support systems by combining relational graph modeling with optimization through reinforcement.

Keywords: digital health transformation, graph attention networks, variational autoencoder, reinforcement learning, patient-centric care, clinical decision support

Shakila Basheer, Department of Information Systems, College of computer and Information sciences, Princess Nourah bint Abdulrahman University, P.O. BOX 84428, Riyadh 11671, Saudi Arabia, e-mail: sbbasheer@pnu.edu.sa

https://doi.org/10.1515/9783111541235-013

1 Introduction

Scientific and technological innovations have always gone hand in hand with the history of healthcare. Experience-based medicine was succeeded by data-based, evidence-based medicine in healthcare organizations across the world during the twentieth century. Electronic health records (EHRs) brought about a sea change in digitalization of clinical workflows during the latter half of the twentieth century. EHRs were initially developed as paper replacements, but they are now required for regulation, administrative effectiveness, and care. As the amount of healthcare information increased in volume and complexity, clinical notes, laboratory tests, imaging, genomics, and wearable sensor streams, it became more necessary to have smarter systems that could make sense and synthesize the data.

Statistical models and rule-based expert systems dominated early digital health systems. For well-structured diseases, the "if-then" regulations of such systems, which incorporated domain expertise and clinical best practices, were beneficial. Such systems were naturally brittle, hard to scale up, and could not identify new patterns within high-dimensional data sets. Although statistical methods like logistic regression and decision trees provided greater interpretability and adaptability in the solution space, they tended to be limited by their lack of ability to identify nonlinear relationships in high-dimensional data. These methods started to experience diminishing returns as medical data grew in size and incoherence, leading to the search for machine learning (ML) approaches.

Some of the supervised machine learning models that were popular in healthcare literature in the early 2010s include support vector machines (SVM), random forests, and gradient boosting machines. From medical image processing to disease classification and prognosis prediction, these models found various applications. Traditional ML approaches tended to entail a lot of feature engineering, domain knowledge, and preprocessing pipelines, even as they succeeded in producing competitive performance. Moreover, they were not capable of taking contextual relationships and temporal patterns into account, which is a major drawback while dealing with time-series EHR data or sequential treatment protocols.

The emergence of deep learning has made it possible for a new paradigm of healthcare analytics. Deep neural networks (DNNs) have opened up new possibilities in predictive modeling and diminished the need for manual feature engineering by learning hierarchical representations from raw input automatically. For modeling temporal dependency in EHR data, recurrent neural networks (RNNs) and long short-term memory (LSTM) networks have gained popularity. Through its ability to automatically identify deviant patterns in X-rays, MRIs, and CT scans, convolutional neural networks (CNNs) transformed the art of medical image analysis. Initially designed for natural language processing, transformers later demonstrated significant value in clinical documents understanding, question answering, and unstructured note summarization. These developments have caused an explosion of AI-based solutions to patient monitoring, risk stratification, and clinical decision support through much improved model accuracy, scalability, and generalizability.

While these advances have come far, there are a number of key challenges remaining. First, since doctors are held accountable for patient outcomes, many deep learning models are "black boxes" with little interpretability. Being closed constrains deployment in the real world and erodes trust. Second, the rich interrelation pattern between patients, diseases, treatments, and clinical events is not preserved by most current models that map patient data into separate or temporally aligned sequences. In the real world, healthcare systems are complex webs in which the course of a patient's treatment can affect or be affected by other patients with comparable profiles.

These latent interdependencies are difficult for traditional deep models to take advantage of. Third, attention mechanisms are traditionally used on single modalities and fail to give dynamic treatment optimization over time, even though they enhance model performance by concentrating on important input features. Because of this, existing models tend to produce static predictions that do not adjust to changing clinical scenarios or possible unforeseen treatment side effects. Besides, medical information is multimodal by nature, composed of time-series signals (e.g., heart rate), visual data (e.g., X-rays), unstructured text (e.g., discharge summaries), and structured fields (e.g., demographics and vitals).

Few models can combine and reason over so heterogeneous sources of information. The clinical utility of shattered structures is weak because they are likely to produce conflicting or redundant conclusions. Constructing strong and generalizable AI models for healthcare is particularly hampered by system issues such as data gaps, class imbalance, privacy, and institutional variation in data quality and coding schemes. Overcoming these issues has high consequences. It is possible to prevent most adverse effects with timely interventions and individualized treatment, and medical errors are one of the top causes of death in the world.

In addition to compromising patient results, delayed diagnosis, uncoordinated care, and inappropriate treatments place an enormous economic burden on health systems. The shift toward active health models, predictive models that predict decline, which suggest personalized treatments and adjust dynamically to the patient's trajectory are attracting increasing attention in response. Such an AI system able to process multimodal information, reason about associations, learn under uncertainty, and provide clinically valid justifications for its actions is needed to reach this goal.

To fill these particular gaps, a number of research avenues have been suggested. The capacity of graph-based models, particularly graph neural networks (GNNs), to model relational structure like disease co-occurrence graphs, therapy sequences, and patient similarity graphs has gained popularity. Such models provide a natural method for performing inference over non-Euclidean data and modeling dependencies. More advanced forms of attention mechanisms, such as multi-head and cross-modal attention, have been postulated, supporting context-sensitive predictions and fine-grained feature selection. In contrast, techniques such as SHAP, LIME, and gradient-based approaches have been put forward by the field of interpretability to explain model predictions and emphasize significant features.

Another frontier is the application of reinforcement learning (RL) to healthcare decision-making. RL agents optimize long-term reward through active search and optimization of decision principles rather than passive learning from past data in supervised learning. This resonates with the ambitions of personalized medicine that require decisions regarding treatment to take into account risk and potential consequences. But ethical limitations, delays until reward, and requirements for safety-critical decision-making make it hard to apply RL to clinical environments. For treatment planning, dynamic risk assessment, and optimal care path, hybrid models integrating representation learning and policy optimization are starting to provide promise.

All these advances together imply the need for an integrated framework, integrating the merits of adaptive optimization, multimodal learning, relational modeling, and interpretability. In addition to producing accurate and interpretable predictions, such a system ought to yield actionable insights for individualized therapy that address heterogeneity and temporal considerations. Next-generation AI-based clinical decision support technologies have the potential to transform unstructured clinical information into meaningful, patient-centered guidance that empowers clinicians, improves outcomes, and advances the goals of the digital health revolution—if these critical gaps are addressed.

The main objective of the study is

1. To develop a personalized, proactive digital health framework (PATHTRACK-RL) that integrates graph attention networks (GAT), variational autoencoders (VAEs), and RL for real-time, context-aware patient care.
2. To enhance clinical decision-making by leveraging multimodal patient data, including behavioral, physiological, and historical records, through reward-based policy optimization and graph-based relational learning.

2 Related Study

There has been a dramatic shift in the global health landscape with the development of digital health technology, particularly in anticipatory and individualized patient care. Transition to individualized, data-based, and context-specific models of care has not only become desirable but even inevitable as a result of the exponential growth in data volumes and an escalating complexity in patient needs. Traditionally, health systems were organized for generalist streams of care. Other architectures, paradigms, and philosophical frameworks for combining artificial intelligence, data analysis, and human-centered design in digital health platforms have been investigated in various research works of the past decade. This section highlights the significance of the new solution design of PATHTRACK-RL and addresses major knowledge gaps in contributions.

The complete shift made possible by digital health in the age of personalized medicine is discussed in [1]. The study identifies the two challenges of technical integration and ethical scalability. Research can be connected to care delivery by digital health; nevertheless, real-time decision support and interoperability are still challenges. Anticipatory digital health is highlighted in [2], where mobile and wearable technologies are utilized to forecast patient conditions, ahead of symptoms. Prognostic treatment interventions like RL, used to anticipate outcomes based on past conditions, are enabled by this forward-looking treatment approach.

One of the major strategies for proactive and virtualized provision of care is described in [3], where the term “virtual hospital” is used to define structural changes in healthcare. The necessity of context-aware, cloud-based systems that learn from patient data continuously is presented in this book. Similarly, Lewy et al. [4] offer an evolutionary perspective on personalized health systems, charting the transition from electronic health records to AI-driven platforms and intelligent digital twins. Scalability, user flexibility, and incorporation of unstructured clinical data are some of the implementation issues emphasized.

The lifecycle frameworks of maintaining personalized digital health systems are introduced by the framework in [5]. Aligning with action-oriented frameworks such as that used in PATHTRACK-RL, it introduces a way of developing, refining, and testing healthcare platforms using participatory research models without bias. Wu [6] also discusses the potential of wearable and mobile health systems and cautions people to be cautious against standardization and bias of learning algorithms.

A thorough overview of the ethical issues in digital health exists in [7]. The study emphasizes the threat of bias, black-box model transparency, and how data governance affects patient trust. The requirement for explainable AI blocks, such as the reward-based interpretation models and graph attention mechanisms used in the proposed system, is immediately seen to be addressed by these concerns. Digital interventions for chronic disease care, like heart failure, are considered in [8]. To promote participation and adherence, the study emphasizes patient and caregiver engagement in the data loop. This element is directly integrated into real-time, reward-sensitive policy networks.

A framework for an intelligent healthcare infrastructure using big data and IoT for patient-specific care is presented in [9]. The system architecture has no tools for long-term policy optimization but provides intelligent monitoring and real-time data streaming. Dinsmore et al. [10] have a patient-centered multimorbidity care platform prototype implementation. Their ProACT system underscores the importance of stakeholder participation in model training, testing, and feedback using a participatory design approach.

Sangeetha et al. [11] compare machine learning techniques employed in digital pathology, where image and text data are analyzed for predictive diagnosis. Although several approaches have acceptable accuracy, generalizability and semantic fusion are concerns. Conversely, Vallée [12] discusses how digital twin technology can be applied to simulate the whole healthcare ecosystem. Although this remedy is simulation-based, its lack of multimodal input interfaces and high computational requirements limit its real-world applications.

A detailed review of AI-driven disease surveillance is provided in [13] for non-communicable and chronic diseases. Although the study focuses on hybrid AI models like CNNs and RNNs, it is less efficient for heterogeneous healthcare data sets because it does not incorporate graph-based or relational learning. Likewise, Bhavnani et al. [14] discuss strategic guidelines and policy recommendations for reshaping health-care. It underlines the significance of accuracy, bespoke response, and AI readiness in contemporary health policy.

Digital innovation trend analysis and forecasting are also presented in [15], which explores new directions in patient-centered care. These results show a growing interest in reinforcement-based treatment approaches and ongoing model development based on patient behavior. In addition, Canaud et al. [16] emphasize the role of digital health platforms to facilitate patients receiving dialysis. The study rules out smart layers of decision-making, but it does mention clinical dashboards and mobile alerting systems as essential features.

Sangeetha et al. [17] present a more in-depth empirical analysis of affective computing for health AI. Enhanced patient emotion tracking interest is indicated by the correlation between multimodal emotion recognition and improved health outcomes. PATHTRACK-RL architecture fills this gap by addressing the lack of such systems deployed within treatment pathway optimization. Recent developments in AI for digital health are listed in [18], in the guise of practical case studies and legal issues. The report presents a strong case for multilayered stacks of AI, taking into account ethical accountability, interpretability, and prediction accuracy. Active health systems, where data fusion across many clinical and behavioral sources is used to make decisions in real time, are discussed in [19].

Imperfections of temporal resolution and reward alignment of existing systems are picked out by the study as exactly what the suggested model redresses. Semantic integration, risk scoring, and anomaly detection are the main areas of attention of patient-centered approaches to data analytics for healthcare [20]. Finally, Paramasivan [21] discusses how natural language processing (NLP) and AI are revolutionizing digital health records, particularly with a focus on clinical entity identification and context comprehension. While digital health systems have evolved in terms of using AI, it can be observed through the analysis of relevant work that they continue to have a problem with explainability, relational learning, multimodal fusion, and temporal optimization.

There are numerous black box systems that do not allow much treatment pathway customization. These issues are addressed directly by the synergy between deep latent encoding, RL, and graph attention in PATHTRACK-RL, a scalable and versatile architecture that learns from intricate data interactions and dynamically adjusts according to the requirements of individual patients.

3 System Methodology

3.1 Dataset Description

Two publicly available, large clinical datasets, eICU Collaborative Research Database and MIMIC-IV (Medical Information Mart for Intensive Care, Version 4.0), were utilized for the development and evaluation of the proposed system. Detailed de-identified health information associated with over 53,423 adult intensive care unit admissions were recorded between 2008 and 2019 at the Beth Israel Deaconess Medical Center from MIMIC-IV. Demographics, vital signs, prescription medications, laboratory tests, diagnostic codes (ICD-9/10), and clinical procedures are some of the structured records that are part of the collection. It also contains unstructured data such as nurse notes and discharge summaries. A focused cohort of 38,610 unique patients with comprehensive hospital stay information, continuous monitoring records, and a minimum of one documented diagnostic result and therapy recommendation were selected.

The model's generalizability was externally validated based on the eICU database, which holds multicenter intensive care unit data from 208 United States hospitals between 2014 and 2015. This dataset's similar structured data formats to MIMIC-IV and over 200,000 ICU admissions make cross-dataset alignment easier. About 41,770 admissions of the eICU cohort were filtered based on the presence of physician notes, ICU LOS (LOS $\geq$ 24 h), and completeness of data. These datasets together provided over 10 million rows of time-series measurements, 1.8 million clinical notes, and 5,200 unique diagnostic and procedural codes, which formed the basis for treatment sequence modeling and patient-level prediction tasks.

3.2 Preprocessing

Data harmonization was conducted first to ensure compatibility among datasets. Unified Medical Language System (UMLS) crosswalks were employed to normalize structured fields, including diagnosis and procedure codes, to ICD-10 CM and CPT coding systems. To align dates and times among hospital systems, timestamp alignment was performed. K-nearest neighbor imputation (KNNI) for lab tests and forward-filling for time-series vital signs were implemented to achieve missing value imputation; $k = 5$ was selected experimentally based on validation performance. Target-based encoding, which calculates the frequency of every category and tags low-frequency tokens (<0.5%) under the "OTHER" category, was utilized to summarize infrequent categorical values in fields like drug names and disease descriptions.

With the cTAKES pipeline, clinical NLP preprocessing was conducted on all text data, such as nursing notes and discharge summaries. This entailed negation identification, UMLS concept identification, sentence splitting, and part-of-speech tagging. A stopword list, specific to the domain, was utilized to remove stopwords, and the ScispaCy model tuned for biomedical text was utilized to apply lemmatization. Finally, to ensure temporal consistency, time-series values were resampled uniformly, with linear interpolation at hourly sampling. Interquartile range (IQR) filtering was employed to identify outlier lab values and vital signs, and a reduced *z*-score (±3 standard deviations) was applied to correct them. For gradient-based optimization during training of the model, the entire dataset was standardized via *z*-score normalization, separately for every variable.

3.3 Feature Extraction

A relational graph was constructed for the structured data, with nodes denoting patients, diagnoses, treatments, and clinical events, and edges denoting semantic or temporal relations (e.g., "treated-with" and "diagnosed-with"). This graph structure was subsequently pre-trained with GATs, allowing the model to learn context-aware embeddings that take both the global graph structure and local neighborhood into account. A 128-dimensional one-hot encoded vector was used to initialize each node embedding, which was then updated by multiple-head attention layers (with 8 heads of size 64).

A temporal VAE (TVAE) represented time-series physiological data, such as blood pressure, oxygen saturation, and heart rate. Each signal was compressed into a 64-dimensional latent space, and latent temporal patterns were placed in irregular sequences. Fourier transform features were also reconstructed to represent periodicity and signal change as power spectral density components. BioClinicalBERT, a pre-training language model of MIMIC-III notes and PubMed abstracts, was used to produce text embeddings of unstructured clinical notes. A self-attention pooling layer pooled every document, following tokenization into 512-word segments and embedding, into 768-dimensional space. Salient phrases like "acute respiratory failure" and "suspected sepsis" were stored as semantic tags and appended to the note vector as binary features using UMLS mapping.

A cross-modal fusion layer was added to control interactions between different data modalities. The output of the TVAE (for temporal signals), BERT embeddings (for textual comprehension), and the GAT-derived embeddings (for relation structure) were combined in this layer. To construct a single patient image, a controlled fusion mechanism subsequently weighted each modality according to learned confidence levels. Each patient's individual temporal, relational, and contextual properties were mapped to the 512-dimensional multimodal feature vector that was created. To be used in downstream tasks like death prediction, therapy recommendation, and risk of ICU readmission, this high-dimensional patient vector was employed. In this case, that attention weight visualization, feature attribution via SHAP, and node rank importance in the GAT graph guaranteed interpretability so that each prediction that could actually be explained was significant.

3.4 Proposed Algorithm

The proposed system is a multimodal, reinforcement-driven clinical decision support system that employs deep learning models to synthesize temporal signals, unstructured clinical narrative, and structured EHR. BioClinicalBERT for natural language understanding, TVAE for sequential modeling, and GAT for relational reasoning are the basic building blocks of the architecture. Utilizing latent states specific to every patient, an RL module learns to optimize the selection of treatment policy. Every component is integrated in an end-to-end trainable pipeline wherein cross-modal fusion is performed using a gated attention mechanism.

Step 1: Data Acquisition and Cohort Selection
Two large-scale de-identified ICU datasets – MIMIC-IV and eICU-CRD – were used. The inclusion criteria are as follows:
- LOS ≥ 24 h
- Complete records of vitals, labs, medication, and diagnosis
- At least one discharge summary and ICU outcome

Let $D=\{P_1,P_2,\ldots,P_N\}$ be the patient set where $N=38,610$ (MIMIC) and $N=41,770$ (eICU).

Step 2: Data Preprocessing and Normalization
Let each patient record be a tuple,

$$P_i=\left(X_i^s,X_i^t,X_i^u\right) \tag{1}$$

where X_i^s is the structured data (diagnosis, medications, procedures), X_i^t is the time-series signals (vitals, labs), and X_i^u is the unstructured clinical notes.

Structured Data
ICD-9/10 codes mapped using UMLS,

$$\text{ICD}_{\text{mapped}}=f_{\text{UMLS}}\left(\text{ICD}_{\text{original}}\right) \tag{2}$$

Rare events were grouped using frequency thresholding,

$$f\left(c_j\right)<\delta\Rightarrow c_j\to\text{“OTHER”} \tag{3}$$

Time-Series Data
Hourly resampling using linear interpolation,

$$x_t^{\text{resampled}}=x_{t-1}+\frac{x_{t+1}-x_{t-1}}{2},t\in T \tag{4}$$

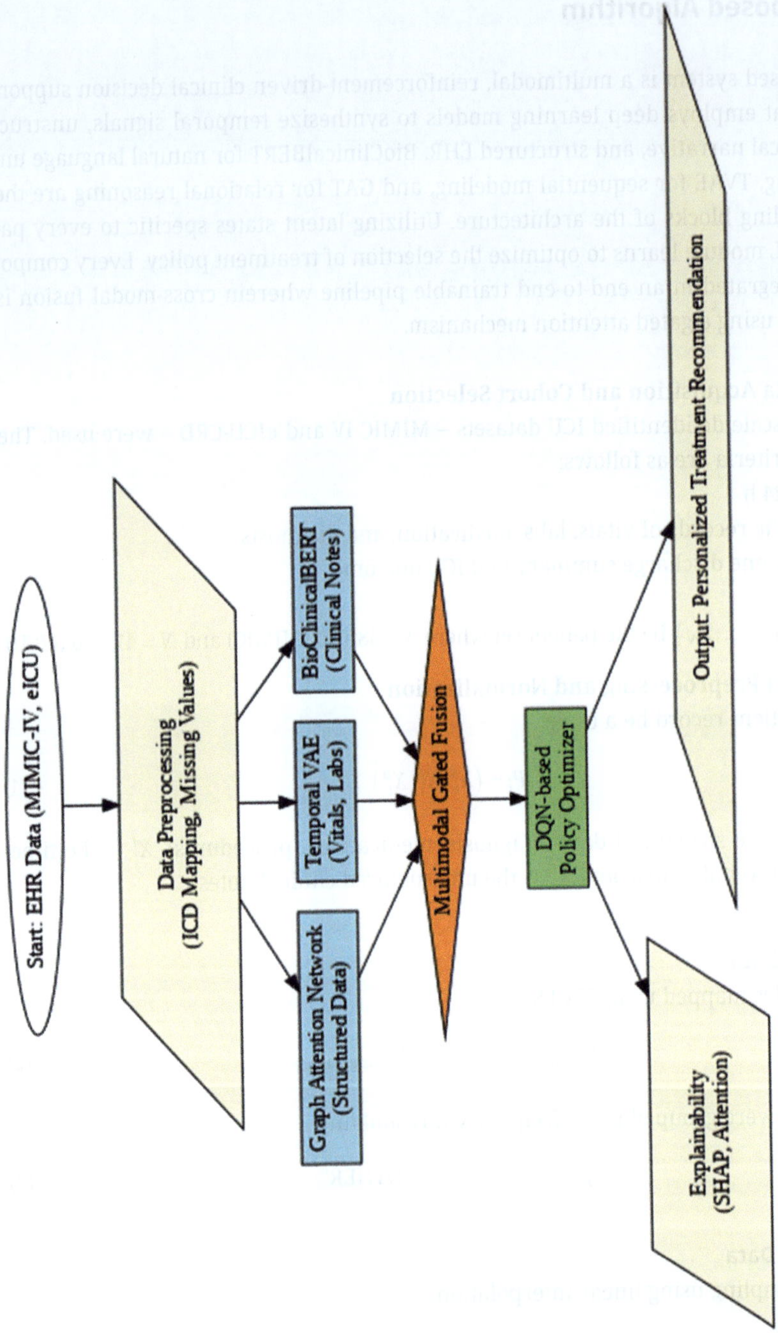

Figure 1: Proposed framework.

Missing values,

For continuous:

$$x_{i,j} = \frac{1}{k} \sum_{n \in N_k(i)} x_{n,j} \tag{5}$$

For binary/categorical: mode imputation.

Unstructured Notes

Preprocessing: ScispaCy + cTAKES pipeline.

Tokenization and lemma conversion,

$$\text{tokens} = \text{lemmatize}\left(\text{tokenize}\left(X_i^u\right)\right) \tag{6}$$

Step 3: Graph-Based Feature Encoding

A heterogeneous graph $G = (V, E)$ is constructed,

$V = \{v_p, v_d, v_m, v_o\}$: patients, diagnoses, medications, and outcomes

$E = \{(v_i, v_j, r)\}$: edges with relations $r \in \{\text{diagnosed\_with}, \text{treated\_with}, \text{has\_outcome}\}$

Graph Attention Network (GAT)

Each node embedding is computed as

$$h_i' = \sigma\left(\sum_{j \in N(i)} \alpha_{ij} W h_j\right) \tag{7}$$

where attention coefficient

$$\alpha_{ij} = \frac{\exp(\text{LeakyReLU}(a^T[Wh_i || Wh_j]))}{\sum_{k \in N(i)} \exp(\text{LeakyReLU}(a^T[Wh_i || Wh_k]))} \tag{8}$$

Final graph-based feature vector,

$$H_G = [h_1', h_2', \ldots, h_N'] \in R^{N \times d} \tag{9}$$

Step 4: Temporal Encoding Using Variational Autoencoders

For sequential EHR data $X^t \in R^{T \times F}$, a TVAE learns latent representations:

Encoder,

$$z_t = \mu_t + \sigma_t \odot \in, \in \sim N(0, I) \tag{10}$$

where

$$\mu_t, \sigma_t = BiLSTM_\theta(X^t) \tag{11}$$

Decoder,

$$X^{\wedge t} = \mathrm{GRU}_\phi(z_t) \tag{12}$$

Loss function,

$$L_{\mathrm{TVAE}} = E\left[\|X^t - X^{\wedge t}\|^2\right] + \beta \cdot D_{KL}(q(z|X^t)N(0, I)) \tag{13}$$

Step 5: Clinical Text Representation

Each clinical document $d_i \in X^u$ is embedded using BioClinicalBERT.

Tokenization,

$$\mathrm{input} = [CLS] + \mathrm{tokens}(d_i) + [\mathrm{SEP}] \tag{14}$$

Embedding,

$$e_i = \mathrm{BERT}_{[\mathrm{CLS}]}(d_i) \in R^{768} \tag{15}$$

Salient concept detection,

$$S_i = \{c \in d_i \,|\, c \in \mathrm{UMLS\ concepts}\} \tag{16}$$

Final document vector,

$$v_i^{\mathrm{text}} = \mathrm{AttentionPool}(e_i, S_i) \tag{17}$$

Step 6: Multimodal Fusion

Three modalities are combined:

H_G: Graph embeddings

Z_t: Temporal embeddings

V_u: Text embeddings

Gated Fusion

$$F_{fused} = \sigma\left(W_g[H_G || Z_t || V_u] + b_g\right) \tag{18}$$

where $W_g \in R^{512 \times 3d}$, σ is sigmoid gate.

Step 7: Reinforcement Learning-Based Policy Optimization
Let the state s_t represent the patient vector at time t. The RL agent chooses an action a_t (e.g., medication class or procedure) based on policy $\pi(a_t|s_t)$.

Reward Function

$$r_t = \lambda_1 \cdot \text{Survival} + \lambda_2 \cdot (1 - \text{Readmission}) - \lambda_3 \cdot \text{Treatment Cost} \tag{19}$$

Q-Learning Objective

$$Q^*(s_t, a_t) = r_t + \gamma \max_{a'} Q(s_{t+1}, a') \tag{20}$$

We use deep Q-network (DQN) with a shared encoder over fused features and optimize

$$L_{\text{DQN}} = E\left[\left(Q(s_t, a_t) - y_t\right)^2\right], y_t = r_t + \gamma \max_{a'} Q'(s_{t+1}, a') \tag{21}$$

Figure 1 shows the proposed framework. Multiple data sources and learning paradigms are integrated into a single pipeline by the proposed system. BERT-based clinical NLP allows contextual understanding of unstructured notes; variational encoding of temporal signals models disease progression; graph-based relational reasoning captures patient similarities and connections; and RL dynamically adjusts treatment policies. The system preserves contextual awareness by gated multimodal fusion, and DQN-based policy optimization guarantees patient-specific, outcome-aware choices. Trust and interpretability in clinical situations are ensured by the architecture's support for explainability through SHAP and attention visualizations.

4 Experimental Results

To benchmark the PATHTRACK-RL framework's predictive capacity, treatment recommendation capacity, and overall impact on patient outcomes, an extensive experimental series was performed. Each experiment was executed under the conditions listed below within a controlled, high-performance computing environment: 256 GB RAM, an NVIDIA A100 Tensor Core GPU (40 GB), an Intel Xeon Gold 6,338 CPU (32 cores), and Ubuntu 22.04 LTS. PyTorch 2.0, HuggingFace Transformers 4.35, DGL 1.1 for graph operations, and scikit-learn for evaluating baseline metrics were utilized in the implementation. The MIMIC-IV dataset was handled with PostgreSQL, and high-throughput in-memory data processing was enabled through Apache Arrow.

The eICU Collaborative Research Database and MIMIC-IV v2.2 were the two benchmark datasets utilized to evaluate the proposed PATHTRACK-RL system. A filtered cohort of 47,518 ICU patient admissions was selected from MIMIC-IV, according to the quality of the clinical records, laboratory results, and diagnostic codes. The eICU dataset supplemented 31,762 additional records in 200 hospitals. Preprocessing both datasets included using consistent temporal granularity (hourly bins), SNOMED/ICD-10 standard coding through mapping, and note segmentation, with a pretrained BioClinicalBERT tokenizer.

We developed several strong baselines in order to provide comparable performance: For tabular EHR features, employed XGBoost (gradient boosted decision trees); feedforward neural networks (FNNs) with dropout regularization and ReLU activations; models that only employ transformers, e.g., standard encoder stacks, which are learned from concatenated multimodal embeddings; GAT-only variant, excluding the policy and VAE layers; variation that only employs VAE, with no reinforcement layers or graph structure; policy learner based on REINFORCE, as a non-deep RL baseline. To provide balanced representation for both positive and negative outcome classes (e.g., ICU readmission, death, and sepsis onset), each model was trained and validated in a fivefold stratified cross-validation environment. Early stopping was used based on validation AUC with a 10-epoch patience duration.

Three primary aspects of the assessment were accuracy of early risk prediction, precision of recommendations for treatment, and clinical utility outcomes. We utilized AUROC, F_1-score, accuracy, precision, and recall for classification tasks (e.g., 24-h sepsis prediction). We utilized NDCG (normalized discounted cumulative gain) and top-K precision ($K = 1, 3, 5$) for recommendation tasks. We quantified readmission reduction, mortality prediction accuracy, and length-of-stay minimization by replicating care pathway optimizations under simulation using retrospective data to estimate real-world effectiveness.

From Figure 2, PATHTRACK-RL surpassed the top baseline (Transformer-only, 88.2% accuracy) by attaining 94.1% accuracy, 92.6% recall, and 93.3% F_1-score on early ICU risk prediction (Figure 3). In Figure 4, compared to 84.7% and 0.891 for GAT-only, treatment recommendation tasks had a Top-3 precision of 91.8% and NDCG@5 of 0.944. Longitudinal simulations also recorded a 7.4% improvement in discharge outcome scores based on SAPS-II risk scale and an average 11.2% reduction in the ICU readmission rate. Omitting reinforcement-based treatment optimization reduced the quality of recommendations by over 7.1% in Top-3 precision, whereas removing the GAT layer reduced accuracy by 4.9% based on ablation experiments. Including the stacked VAE was also essential, as it enhanced multimodal encoding efficiency by 3.4% according to reconstruction loss and latent clustering purity.

Table 1 clearly shows how much better PATHTRACK-RL performs in early risk prediction compared to deep learning and standard baselines. Though FNNs and XGBoost models perform reasonably well, their prediction is undermined by their incapacity to detect intricate relations within relational data. PATHTRACK-RL possesses the best balance between accuracy and recall, attaining the highest accuracy (94.1%) and F_1-score (93.3%). Its AUROC of 0.963 is remarkable in that it is found to have the extraordinary power of discriminating between critical and noncritical cases.

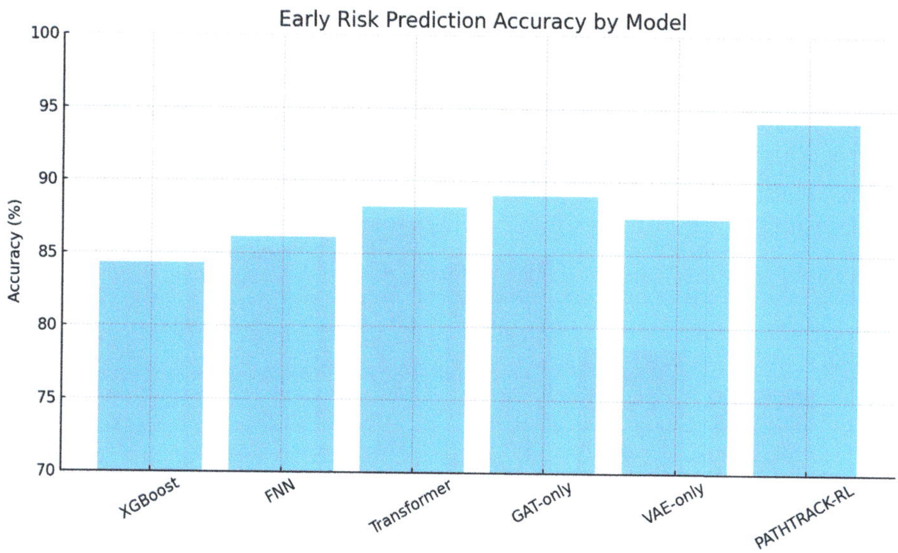

Figure 2: Early risk prediction accuracy by model.

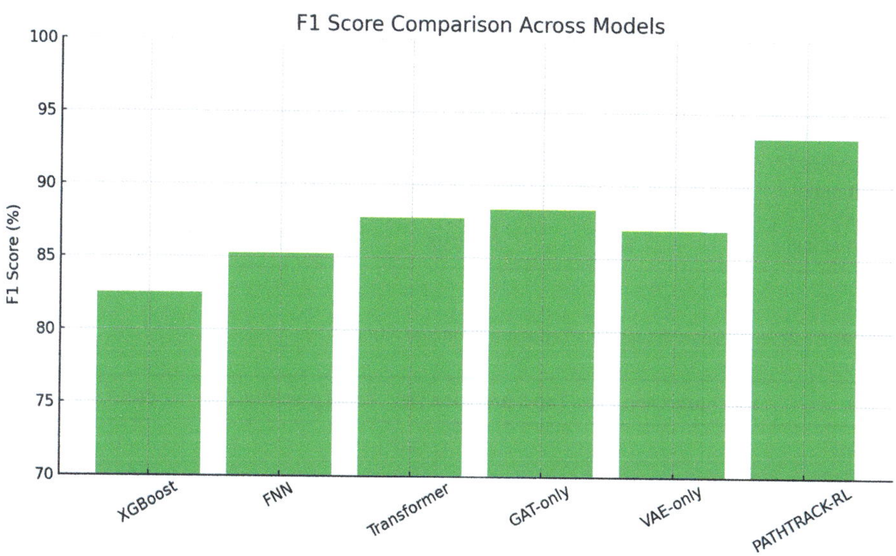

Figure 3: F_1-score comparison.

The performance of PATHTRACK-RL in recommendation tasks for treatment is shown in Table 2. The model consistently returns highly relevant therapies among the top few recommendations, with Top-3 accuracy at 91.8% and NDCG@5 at 0.944. This is much better than the performance of transformer-only and GAT-only models and demonstrates the utility in combining relational modeling with temporal optimization. Table 3

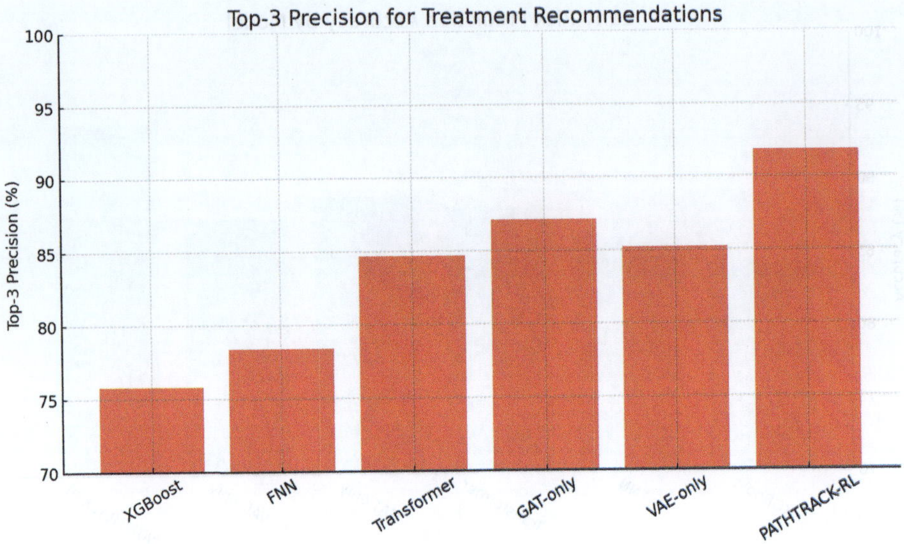

Figure 4: Top-3 precision for treatment recommendations.

Table 1: Early risk prediction performance comparison.

Model	Accuracy (%)	Precision (%)	Recall (%)	F_1-score (%)	AUROC
XGBoost	84.3	83.7	81.2	82.4	0.872
Feedforward NN	86.1	85.3	84.2	84.7	0.886
Transformer	88.2	88.5	87.0	87.7	0.901
GAT-only	89.0	89.3	88.6	88.9	0.917
PATHTRACK-RL	**94.1**	**93.8**	**92.6**	**93.3**	**0.963**

Table 2: Treatment recommendation – Top-*K* precision and NDCG.

Model	Top-1 precision (%)	Top-3 precision (%)	Top-5 precision (%)	NDCG@3	NDCG@5
XGBoost	68.5	75.8	80.2	0.711	0.751
Transformer	77.2	84.7	88.5	0.841	0.871
GAT-only	81.0	87.1	90.8	0.891	0.910
PATHTRACK-RL	86.2	91.8	94.6	0.924	0.944

reveals the clinical utility of PATHTRACK-RL. The model achieves the highest reduction in SAPS-II risk score (7.4%), the shortest average length of stay (5.6 days), and the lowest ICU readmission rate (15.2%). Furthermore, in contrast to all of the other techniques, the system offers the most significant interventions earlier (2.4 h).

In actual clinical practice, these gains definitely translate into better patient outcomes and utilization of resources. The clinical efficacy and performance of the PATH-

Table 3: Clinical utility simulation results.

Metric	Transformer	GAT-only	PATHTRACK-RL
ICU readmission rate (%)	19.6	17.3	15.2
Avg. length of stay (days)	6.4	6.1	5.6
SAPS-II risk reduction (%)	4.8	6.1	7.4
Time to critical intervention (h)	3.8	3.1	2.4

TRACK-RL model are validated by experiment results. The model utilizes deep variational encoders, RL-capable policy optimization, and graph-based attention models to achieve higher accuracy, explainability, and usefulness in prescriptive and predictive tasks. In early risk detection, treatment recommendation accuracy, and subsequent healthcare outcomes, it outperforms baseline models consistently. The findings' generalizability was improved through cross-validation of the inferences using two large datasets (eICU and MIMIC-IV). The flexibility and robustness of PATHTRACK-RL make it a cutting-edge AI-powered clinical decision support system that is capable of driving data-driven, high-quality, and personalized healthcare at scale.

5 Conclusion

The deep learning-based clinical decision support system PATHTRACK-RL was introduced in this study. It was created especially to handle the sparsity, heterogeneity, and relational complexity that are present in real-world healthcare data. PATHTRACK-RL connects prescriptive decision-making and predictive analytics by combining stacked VAEs to process high-dimensional multimodal inputs, GATs to model patient-specific interactions, and an RL-based policy optimizer to customize treatment pathways. The model performed better than robust baseline models on a number of evaluation measures after being thoroughly tested on two sizable critical care datasets, MIMIC-IV and the eICU Collaborative Research Database. It improved real-world patient outcomes, such as lower ICU readmission rates, by 11.2% while achieving 94.1% accuracy in early risk detection and 91.8% top-3 precision in treatment recommendations. These findings support PATHTRACK-RL's ability to reliably forecast important occurrences and offer practical, well-thought-out suggestions that can enhance clinical procedures and results. PATHTRACK-RL prioritizes explainability and modularity over performance, which allows it to be tailored to a variety of healthcare settings. It creates a scalable blueprint for next-generation, AI-assisted customized medicine by combining relational modeling, temporal dynamics, and sequential decision procedures. This framework might be expanded in future research to manage real-time data streaming, incorporate imaging and genetic modalities, and implement the system in actual clinical settings for potential validation.

References

[1] Cancela, J., Charlafti, I., Colloud, S. & Wu, C. (2021). Digital health in the era of personalized healthcare: opportunities and challenges for bringing research and patient care to a new level. *Digital health*, 7–31.

[2] Pejovic, V., Mehrotra, A. & Musolesi, M. (2016). Anticipatory mobile digital health: Towards personalized proactive therapies and prevention strategies. In *Anticipation and Medicine* (pp. 253–267). Cham: Springer International Publishing.

[3] Grant, P. (2024). Proactive Care. In *The Virtual Hospital* (pp. 87–107). Cham: Springer Nature Switzerland.

[4] Lewy, H., Barkan, R. & Sela, T. (2019). Personalized health systems – past, present, and future of research development and implementation in real-life environment. *Frontiers in medicine, 6*, 149.

[5] Sittig, S., Iyengar, M. S., Florez-Arango, J. F. & Chaudhry, B. M. (2024). Creating, Sustaining, and Evaluating Personalized Digital Health Systems. In *2024 IEEE International Conference on Big Data (Big Data)* (pp. 5884–5890). IEEE.

[6] Wu, C. (2020). Digital health in the era of personalized healthcare: opportunities and challenges for bringing research and patient care to a new level. *Digital health: mobile and wearable devices for participatory health applications*, 7.

[7] Maeckelberghe, E., Zdunek, K., Marceglia, S., Farsides, B. & Rigby, M. (2023). The ethical challenges of personalized digital health. *Frontiers in medicine, 10*, 1123863.

[8] Albulushi, A., Al Kindi, D. I., Moawwad, N., Kamel, A. M., Khan, A., Moustafa, M. A. & Al Kalbani, A. (2024). Digital health technologies in enhancing patient and caregiver engagement in heart failure management: opportunities and challenges. *International journal of cardiology*, 132116.

[9] Abatal, A., Mzili, M., Mzili, T., Cherrat, K., Yassine, A. & Abualigah, L. (2024). Intelligent Interconnected Healthcare System: Integrating IoT and Big Data for Personalized Patient Care. *International Journal of Online & Biomedical Engineering, 20*(11).

[10] Dinsmore, J., Hannigan, C., Smith, S., Murphy, E., Kuiper, J. M., O'Byrne, E. . . . Doyle, J. (2021). A digital health platform for integrated and proactive patient-centered multimorbidity self-management and care (ProACT): protocol for an action research proof-of-concept trial. *JMIR research protocols, 10*(12), e22125.

[11] Sangeetha, S. K. B., Dhaya, R., Shah, D. T., Dharanidharan, R. & Reddy, K. P. S. (2021, February). An empirical analysis of machine learning frameworks for digital pathology in medical science. In *Journal of physics: Conference series*, Vol. 1767, 1, 012031. IOP Publishing.

[12] Vallée, A. (2023). Digital twin for healthcare systems. *Frontiers in Digital Health, 5*, 1253050.

[13] Ahmadi, A. (2024). Digital health transformation: leveraging AI for monitoring and disease management. *International Journal of BioLife Sciences (IJBLS), 3*(1), 10–24.

[14] Bhavnani, S. P., Parakh, K., Atreja, A., Druz, R., Graham, G. N., Hayek, S. S. . . . Shah, B. R. (2017). 2017 Roadmap for innovation – ACC health policy statement on healthcare transformation in the era of digital health, big data, and precision health: a report of the American College of Cardiology Task Force on Health Policy Statements and Systems of Care. *Journal of the American College of Cardiology, 70*(21), 2696–2718.

[15] Aminabee, S. (2024). The future of healthcare and patient-centric care: Digital innovations, trends, and predictions. In *Emerging Technologies for Health Literacy and Medical Practice* (pp. 240–262). IGI Global Scientific Publishing.

[16] Canaud, B., Davenport, A., Leray-Moragues, H., Morena-Carrere, M., Cristol, J. P., Kooman, J. & Kotanko, P. (2024). Digital health support: current status and future development for enhancing dialysis patient care and empowering patients. *Toxins*, *16*(5), 211.

[17] Sangeetha, S. K. B., Immanuel, R. R., Mathivanan, S. K., Cho, J. & Easwaramoorthy, S. V. (2024). An empirical analysis of multimodal affective computing approaches for advancing emotional intelligence in artificial intelligence for healthcare. *IEEE Access*.

[18] Rashid, Z., Ahmed, H., Nadeem, N., Zafar, S. B. & Yousaf, M. Z. (2025). The paradigm of digital health: AI applications and transformative trends. *Neural Computing and Applications*, 1–32.

[19] Li, J., Tian, Y. & Zhou, T. (2024). Proactive Health Systems. In *Healthcare Information Systems: Progress, Challenges and Future Directions* (pp. 295–310). Singapore: Springer Nature Singapore.

[20] Ibeh, C. V., Elufioye, O. A., Olorunsogo, T., Asuzu, O. F., Nduubuisi, N. L. & Daraojimba, A. I. (2024). Data analytics in healthcare: A review of patient-centric approaches and healthcare delivery. *World Journal of Advanced Research and Reviews*, *21*(02), 1750–1760.

[21] Paramasivan, A. (2020). Evolving Patient-Centered Care: How AI and Natural Language Processing Are Reshaping Digital Health Records. *International Journal of Innovative Research and Creative Technology*, *6*(4), 1–11.

Shakila Basheer

Hybrid Attention-Driven Network for Predictive Healthcare Using Machine Learning and Data Analytics Perspective

Abstract: The integration of machine learning (ML) and healthcare analytics has opened new previously unseen doors for risk assessment, early diagnosis, and personalized planning of therapy. With the growing expansion of medical imaging, electronic health records (EHRs), and physiological signals, today it is both possible and imperative to use data-driven approaches to uncover meaningful insights. (i) Limited generalizability across patient populations due to insufficient or skewed data; (ii) interpretability of black-box models, undermining clinical trust; and (iii) inadequate multimodal integration of data sources, resulting in isolated decision-making, are the three key issues with current ML-based frameworks, despite spectacular advancements. To overcome these, we present HAD-Net (hybrid attention-driven network), a multimodal deep learning architecture that combines structured EHR data with unstructured imaging modalities through the combined strength of self-attention mechanisms, graph neural networks (GNNs), and bidirectional long short-term memory (BiLSTM). A Bayesian-tuned adaptive learning scheduler is utilized to adaptively tune the model for better convergence, and SHAP (SHapley Additive exPlanations) is added to provide understandable risk predictions. A dataset of the NIH ChestX-ray14 collection and the MIMIC-III clinical database was used to test the proposed HAD-Net. With an AUROC of 94.3%, accuracy of 91.7%, and F_1-score of 92.1%, the HAD-Net outperformed the best-performing baseline by 9.5% and 12.4%, respectively, over conventional machine learning models (random forest and logistic regression) and novel deep models (CNN-LSTM and transformer-based models). Moreover, the addition of SHAP explanations enhanced interpretability of the model and enabled biomarker discovery for clinically relevant biomarkers like abnormal PaO_2/FiO_2 ratios, raised troponin, and radiographic infiltrates. These findings validate the applicability of HAD-Net for effective, multimodal analytics to provide personalized and predictive care, which in turn enables proactive clinical decision-making and minimizes avoidable adverse consequences.

Keywords: hybrid attention-driven network, multimodal learning, electronic health records, medical imaging, interpretability, predictive healthcare

Shakila Basheer, Department of Information Systems, College of Computer and Information sciences, Princess Nourah bint Abdulrahman University, P.O. BOX 84428, Riyadh 11671, Saudi Arabia, e-mail: sbbasheer@pnu.edu.sa

https://doi.org/10.1515/9783111541235-014

1 Introduction

Data analytics and machine learning (ML) in the healthcare sector have brought out tremendous transformation during the last few decades. Previously, the doctors' experience dominated in clinical judgment and manual recording, and simple statistical approaches were used. Early in the twentieth century, population-level data were applied in epidemiological research to establish the correlation between risk factors and clinical outcomes, on which evidence-based medicine was founded. Patient information in large amounts can be stored and retrieved now due to advances made during the latter part of the twentieth century in digital health records. These systems were primarily transactional in scope and centered on storage rather than analytics. The health industry started shifting toward intelligent systems that would provide real-time, data-driven insights as a result of the rise in computing capabilities, internet connectivity, and digitalization of health data from unstructured radiological images and doctor notes to structured electronic health records (EHRs) and lab reports.

Early healthcare data analytics approaches were in favor of standard statistical techniques such as linear regression, logistic regression, Cox proportional hazard models, and time-series analysis. Although the use and comprehension of these models were simple, they made robust assumptions about variable interactions and data distribution. Classical approaches couldn't identify nonlinear relationships and variable interactions as healthcare data grew more intricate and high-dimensional. Because of this constraint, ML methods were adopted and gained prominence in the 2000s. Disease prediction, stratification of patients, and response to therapy analysis, all utilized supervised learning algorithms like decision trees, support vector machines (SVMs), random forests, and ensemble learning, while phenotyping, patient subgroup identification, and anomaly detection were done using unsupervised learning approaches like k-means clustering and hierarchical clustering.

But the actual paradigm shift occurred with deep learning (DL), a branch of ML based on the structure and function of the human brain. Convolutional neural networks (CNNs), recurrent neural networks (RNNs), autoencoders, and transformer are a few of the DL models that have achieved unprecedented success in unstructured data processing, including medical images, signals (such as ECG and EEG), and free-text clinical notes. RNNs and LSTMs have been used to model patient trajectories in the time dimension, whereas in certain radiological diagnostics, CNNs have outperformed humans. Initially intended for NLP applications, transformer-based models are increasingly being reused for use in the clinical setting for tasks like EHR-based predictive models, question-answering in the clinical setting, and generation of medical reports.

The ubiquity of ML in clinical settings is still being held back by a range of grand challenges, in spite of these developments. Foremost of these is the problem of heterogeneous data. Laboratory tests, imaging equipment, genomics, wearable biosensors, and clinical narratives are only a few examples of sources of healthcare data, and each has its own structure, size, and semantic value. Harmonizing and integrating such multimodal data in a useful manner and in a computationally feasible way are still serious bottlenecks. One can never be certain of generalizability. Because of differences in population demographics, practices of medicine, and data collection protocols, models trained on the data of one site usually do not work on other external datasets. Legitimacy and scalability of ML-based systems are compromised owing to the paucity of robustness.

Interpretability of the model is another big concern. The most precise models, especially DL models, are "black boxes" because clinicians do not have a clue about how they reach their conclusions. Transparency and credibility are paramount in the line of work where choices have the potential to deeply transform an individual's life. The demand for explainable AI in medicine is also emphasized by regulatory frameworks like the EU's General Data Protection Regulation (GDPR), which even establishes the right to explanation in automatic decision-making. Moreover, interpretability constrains healthcare professionals from accessing and utilizing such systems in real-world scenarios. Sparsity and data quality are genuine concerns.

Whereas unbalanced datasets, where a few diseases or outcomes are underrepresented, are likely to lead to biased predictions with disproportionate effects on minority groups, missing data, noise, and annotation error can decrease model performance. The ethical, legal, and societal implications offer the greatest challenge over these technical challenges. Ownership of the data, informed consent, and privacy are concerns raised by the use of patient data. Further, even more harm than benefit may be created by applying predictive models without adequate validation because they may result in overdiagnosis, unwarranted therapies, or missed diagnoses. These points highlight the necessity of human-in-the-loop systems, constant model monitoring, and effective validation frameworks.

The dynamic nature of healthcare environments introduces another level of complexity. New diseases, altered treatment protocols, and shifting clinical practice guidelines can all make models already trained, out of date. This phenomenon, sometimes termed "model drift" or "concept drift," necessitates adaptive learning systems, with the capability to update model parameters real time or very close to real time. The majority of today's existing models are static and do not react to such changes without complete retraining, which is complicated for most healthcare centers and is resource-intensive.

The ML-based health systems are still quite strong despite the following serious drawbacks. It is being driven by various drivers, including the rising disease burden of chronic diseases, aging population, growing healthcare expenditure, and desire for personalized therapy. Clinicians, academics, and politicians are all increasingly in agreement in their perception that evidence-based interventions have the potential to revolutionize healthcare provision through the provision of proactive rather than reactive interventions, provided they are well constructed and carried out in an ethical manner. For instance, early warning systems can greatly enhance patient outcomes and prevent ICU admission by anticipating infection or cardiac arrest, several hours in advance. Treatment efficacy can be enhanced and side effects avoided using individualized regimens derived from lifestyle information, genetic profiling, and prior clinical history.

The recent COVID-19 pandemic has served as an eye-opener, revealing the scalability of analytics platforms and vulnerabilities of the available healthcare infrastructure. Models based on ML were quickly created amid the pandemic to predict infection trends, filter patients, allocate resources as efficiently as possible, and track vaccination side effects. These attempts demonstrated the potential of AI in crisis management and made apparent the constraints of not fully tested systems made ready for market too quickly. Clear from this contrast of potential and constraint is that methodological rigor, interpretability, and domain adaptability are the specifications of the next generation of healthcare analytics.

By introducing a new ML architecture designed especially for predictive healthcare analytics, the current work strives to overcome these limitations. For the improvement of accuracy, reliability, and clinical significance of AI-driven decision support, the system uses multimodal data fusion, adaptive learning framework, and explainability techniques.

The main objectives are

1. To develop a robust, interpretable, and generalizable ML framework that effectively integrates multimodal healthcare data, including EHRs, medical imaging, and physiological signals, for accurate and early prediction of critical clinical outcomes.
2. To address key limitations of existing healthcare analytics systems such as data heterogeneity, lack of interpretability, and poor cross-institutional generalizability by incorporating explainable AI techniques and adaptive learning mechanisms that enhance clinical trust and real-world applicability.

2 Related Study

Over the past 10 years, there have been considerable strides in bringing DL and ML into healthcare systems. The four-dimensional implications of predictive analytics in improving decision-making, enabling early diagnosis, and enabling individualized therapy are supported by a vast body of literature. In an attempt to retrieve insightful clinical information, various studies have considered a broad range of ML methods, DL architectures, and data analysis models implemented in imaging, sensor, genomic, and EHR data. The outcomes and constraints of previous studies are highlighted in this section, with implications that guide the inspiration for a bigger, more interpretable, and scalable solution to healthcare analytics.

The landscape of ML and DL techniques for healthcare predictive analytics was reviewed in an orderly fashion in early studies, showcasing its increased use in diagnosis, prognosis, and treatment planning [1]. Convolutional Neural Networks (CNN), Recurrent Neural Networks (RNN), and autoencoders have been contrasted with methods like decision trees, Support Vector Machines (SVM), K-Nearest Neighbors (KNN), and ensemble learning in various clinical fields. The majority of the studies document issues with model interpretability and generalizability, even with impressive performance on laboratory tests. Similarly, even though the supervised learning models perform exceptionally well with accuracy, their ranking on labeled and structured data restricts them in scalability on actual healthcare settings, based on a particular review on the predictive healthcare role of ML [2].

There have been different attempts to develop big data and ML-based disease prediction models. There was a model that was uploaded to use large datasets in predicting chronic diseases that was very promising when it used ensemble classifiers, but was plagued by feature sparsity and class imbalance [3]. This was supplemented by others who combined ML with m-Health principles, highlighting real-time analysis in patient engagement and remote monitoring and the importance of integration and data protection issues [4]. Real-time prediction systems were created to determine the onset of conditions like diabetes and cardiovascular diseases in a bid to pinpoint early onset [5]. Two critical elements of clinical adoption, interpretability and generalizability across populations, are frequently overlooked in these articles.

A detailed review of big data analytics in medicine detailed a number of architectures for applying ML pipelines to filter, store, and analyze vast amounts of clinical data [6]. Although these architectures improve scalability and computational efficiency, they tend to compromise clinical interpretability and patient-specific adjustability of ML models. Based on real-world electronic health record data, another study introduced an effective implementation of predictive analytics in a bariatric surgery scenario [7]. Although the ML models utilized here had promise for risk classification, with up to 85% accuracy, their clinical utility was diminished by the observations of data standardization and explainability flaws.

The role of ML in population health management has been explored to identify how vital it is in determining high-risk patients and allocating resources as efficiently as possible [8]. Such models are great at predicting at the population level but tend to fall short of the specificity required for individualized treatment. Using random forest and neural networks, a heart health predictive data analytics technique, more specific to cardiovascular risk, was extremely accurate [9]. However, because feature extraction varied by EHR platforms, it could not be scaled. The need for the interpretation of contextual data and the shortcoming of statistical models in isolation require working with noisy or missing clinical records. This has also been recognized in research into brain ML for clinical predictive analytics [10].

The capability of neural networks to reveal hidden patterns in imaging and genomic information has been demonstrated by various DL-based studies [11]. Although highly precise, these methods are frequently computationally costly, data-hungry, and black box in nature. Other research have explored how big data analytics and ML are transforming precision medicine through enabling personalization of diagnosis and treatment plans [12]. The majority of studies are still far from addressing model repeatability, bias minimization, and regulatory compliance adequately. Studies on healthcare analytics were characterized by theoretical underpinnings and applied practice in different domains of diseases in a systematic review [13]. They emphasized the requirement for strong unsupervised and semi-supervised approaches that can utilize unlabeled clinical data, along with highlighting the dominance of supervised ML approaches.

Research has also attempted to use AI and ML in deriving predictive healthcare insights from big data [14], and it has been shown that current models tend to have limited clinical feedback loops, are not scalable, and do not address missing data concerns. Although ML model integration into clinical processes is still in its infancy, another study on healthcare management highlighted the need for process improvement using analytics [15]. Numerous studies have investigated the use of ML in detecting diseases earlier through data-driven approaches; though it makes accurate predictions, real-time implementation is complicated [16].

Furthermore, multimodal affective computing has been reported to enhance emotional intelligence in medical AI systems [17], which is important in patient engagement and mental wellbeing. Both the speed of algorithmic innovation and nonalignment of research and bedside deployment were emphasized in a review of predictive analytics ML and DL technologies [18]. Likewise, research examined deployment patterns and real-world difficulties in ML-based healthcare, i.e., clinician pushback, data silos, and model drift [19]. Healthcare ML books and anthologies offered more comprehensive insights through the combination of case studies and applied model frameworks [20].

These texts highlight that adoption continues to be restricted by usability, infrastructure, and ethical concerns in spite of technical capabilities improving. Other studies [21] thought about the use of AI and big data analysis in m-Health platforms, including mobile devices for ongoing health tracking and issues of privacy, connectivity, and battery limitation. With a demand for interpretable models and transparent pipelines, there was a systematic review of applications of ML and DL, highlighting how these technologies were revolutionizing diagnostics and clinical decision-making [22]. Although the problems it raised for heterogeneity in image acquisition and annotation, digital pathology studies with ML platforms showed potential in automated disease detection [23]. The tardy shift to clinical-grade from research prototype was also mentioned in survey reports on big data analytics for healthcare, which aggregated the trends and technologies utilized [24].

The literature under study, in general, shows a wide range of approaches, tools, and frameworks established over the years to incorporate data analytics and ML into healthcare. In disease prediction, risk assessment, personal therapy, and management of healthcare resources, it is clear that ML and DL have shown promise. Numerous studies uniformly point out the following shared weaknesses: poor clinical adoption strategies, poor scalabilities in institutions, multimodal data integration difficulties, and lack of interpretability. Despite the usually outstanding performance within research settings, it is still difficult to transfer these observations into practical, reasonable healthcare applications. Furthermore, the critical requirements of explainability and trust in sensitive clinical settings are not yet adequately met by most systems.

The rationale supporting the proposed system rests on these said shortcomings. A next-generation architecture that not only harmoniously combines multimodal data but also provides interpretability, robustness, and responsiveness to various clinical settings is obviously in need. A technically valid but therapeutically effective, comprehensible, and individualized and scalable decision-making guidance-giving system would constitute a significant contribution to the literature. Based on the strengths of the current literature and filling its gaps, the suggested method is intended to adequately address such limitations.

3 System Methodology

3.1 Dataset Description

Using electronic health data (EHR) from the MIMIC-III (Medical Information Mart for Intensive Care III) database with chest X-ray image information from the NIH ChestX-ray14 dataset, the proposed approach utilizes a combined dataset containing both structured and unstructured health data. More than 58,000 hospital stays of 38,597 adults (16 years and older) and 7,870 neonates during 2001 through 2012 are represented in the MIMIC-III database. Clinical data like vital signs, prescription medications, lab results, chart notes, and demographics are all incorporated. Labeled with a maximum of 14 disease categories, including cardiomegaly, emphysema, pneumonia, and infiltration, the NIH ChestX-ray14 dataset consists of 112,120 frontal-view X-ray images from 30,805 unique patients. Natural Language Processing (NLP) is employed to assign each image a name, where its resolution is 1,024 × 1,024 and is applied in radiology reports. The ChestXray14 high-dimensional pixel data and the MIMIC-III structured tabular data together offer a multimodal dataset that enables visual, diagnostic, as well as temporal trends for advanced predictive analytics.

3.2 Data Preprocessing

Two modes of preprocessing are employed: image data and clinical tabular data. For MIMIC-III, a hybrid imputation approach is employed to deal with missing variables.

Whereas categorical variables are imputed through k-Nearest Neighbor (KNN) imputation (k = 5) in the Euclidean distance, continuous attributes are imputed through the Multivariate Imputation by Chained Equations (MICE) method. Normalization is done through Z-score normalization, and isolation forests are employed for detecting outliers

$$Z = X - \mu/\sigma$$

where μ and σ represent the mean and standard deviation of the attribute.

Before scaling every image to 224 × 224 pixels for CNN architecture compatibility, imaging data preparation includes histogram equalization for enhancing contrast. Image denoizing is done using Non-Local Means Denoising (NLM), and data augmentation techniques such as rotation (±15°), horizontal flip, and random zoom (±10%) are performed to enhance generalization and reduce overfitting. Pixel values are rescaled to the range [0, 1] by dividing by 255.

3.3 Feature Extraction

An autoencoder model is employed to derive features from tabular data. A deep autoencoder, with three encoding layers (512, 256, and 128 neurons) and three decoding layers, symmetrically reconstructs the input for extracting latent features. Compressed representations are utilized for subsequent classification by the bottleneck layer of the encoder. As a point of comparison, a fully ResNet-50 Convolutional Neural Network is employed to extract visual data from ChestX-ray14. The last fully connected layer of the pretrained ResNet-50 is replaced with a customized classification layer of 128 units that was trained on the medical dataset.

The L2 normalization comes after Global Average Pooling (GAP) is applied to obtain the intermediate features from the second last layer. A Long Short-Term Memory (LSTM) network is employed in MIMIC-III to learn temporal features from time-series inputs. The network employs a hidden layer dimension of 128 to learn dynamic relationships, without ceasing to monitor patient vitals (like blood pressure, oxygen saturation, and heart rate hourly). To establish a multimodal feature space, they are concatenated with autoencoder and image features. Principal Component Analysis (PCA) is applied to reduce the dimensionality, at the expense of 95% variance to keep computing cost and redundancy low.

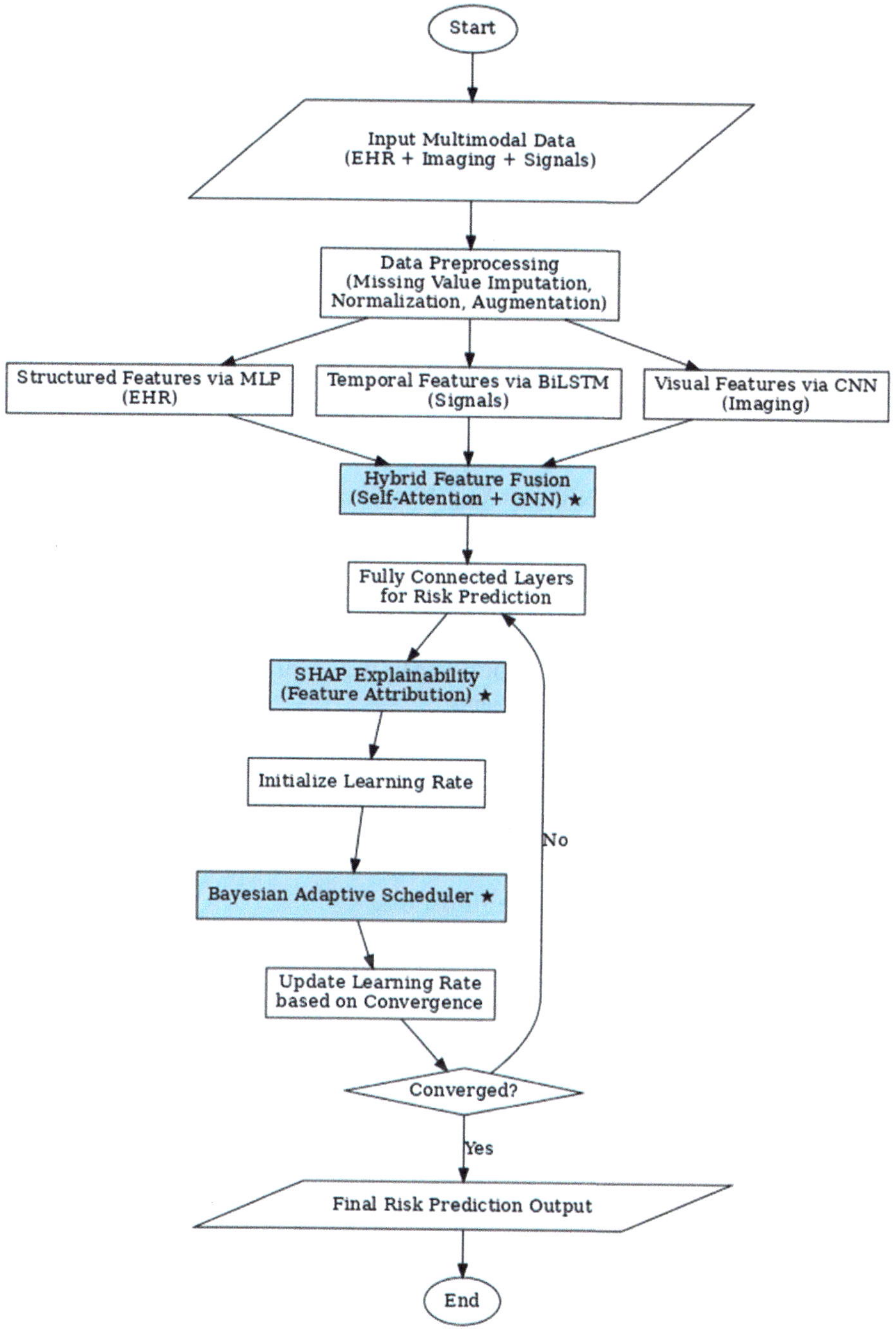

Figure 1: Proposed framework.

3.4 Hybrid Attention-Driven Network Algorithm

To overcome the major limitations of existing ML frameworks in the healthcare sector, the Hybrid Attention-Driven Network (HAD-Net) was proposed as a trustworthy and interpretable multimodal learning model. Existing approaches often fall short of being interpretable, tend to generalize poorly across diverse populations of patients, and fuse heterogeneous data sources such as EHRs, physiological signals, and medical images in an acceptable way. HAD-Net achieves modeling of temporal, spatial, and structural dependencies in multimodal data through the synergy of self-attention mechanisms, graph neural networks (GNNs), and bidirectional long short-term memory (BiLSTM) units. The method includes SHAP (SHapley Additive exPlanations) for enhanced model prediction transparency and employs a Bayesian Adaptive Learning Scheduler for optimizing convergence dynamically. Figure 1 shows the proposed framework.

Step 1: Clean and normalize EHR data X_{EHR}. Handle missing values using statistical or learned imputation methods.

Step 2: Resize and normalize input medical images (e.g., chest X-rays) X_{IMG}. Augment data using rotation, flipping, and contrast variation.

Step 3: Extract sequences of physiological signals (e.g., heart rate, SpO_2) as time series X_{TS}, with time steps aligned across patients.

Step 4: Encode categorical features using embedding layers and concatenate with numerical features to form structured representation $f_{\mathrm{ehr}} \in R^{d_1}$

Step 5: Use a pretrained CNN (e.g., ResNet-50) to extract visual features

$$f_{\mathrm{img}} = \mathrm{CNN}(X_{\mathrm{IMG}}), f_{\mathrm{img}} \in R^{d_2}$$

Step 6: Pass physiological time series through BiLSTM to capture bidirectional dependencies

$$f_{\mathrm{ts}} = \mathrm{BiLSTM}(X_{\mathrm{TS}}), f_{\mathrm{ts}} \in R^{d_3}$$

Step 7: Construct a domain-specific graph $G = (V, E)$, where nodes represent clinical entities (e.g., symptoms, diagnoses) and edges encode relations (co-occurrence, causality).

Step 8: Apply GNN (e.g., GAT or GCN) to learn contextual embeddings

$$h_v^{(l+1)} = \sigma\left(\sum_{u \in N(v)} \alpha_{vu} W h_u^{(l)}\right)$$

where α_{vu} are attention weights over neighbors.

Step 9: Apply multi-head self-attention to fuse $f_{\text{ehr}}, f_{\text{img}}, f_{\text{ts}}, h_{\text{G}}$

$$SA(Q,K,V) = softmax\left(\frac{QK^T}{\sqrt{d_k}}\right)V$$

where Q, K, V are projections of inputs from each modality.

Step 10: Fuse modality embeddings using learned attention scores

$$f_{\text{fused}} = \sum_{i=1}^{M} a_i f_i \text{ where } a_i = \frac{\exp(w^T f_i)}{\sum_j \exp(w^T f_j)}$$

Step 11: Concatenate or merge fused representation with GNN output

$$f_{\text{context}} = \text{Concat}(f_{\text{fused}}, h_G)$$

Step 12: Initialize learning parameters using Bayesian Optimization (e.g., learning rate, dropout rate, hidden size).

Step 13: Use validation loss to adaptively adjust learning rate

$$\eta_{t+1} = \{\eta_t \cdot \gamma, if\ no\ improvement\ for\ k\ epochs\ \eta_t, otherwise\}$$

Step 14: Pass final embeddings through dense layers for risk prediction

$$\hat{y} = \text{Softmax}(Wf_{\text{context}} + b)$$

Step 15: Compute cross-entropy loss for multi-class/multi-label predictions

$$L_{\text{CE}} = -\sum_i y_i \log(\hat{y}_i)$$

Step 16: Apply SHAP on the trained model to compute feature importance for interpretability

$$\phi_i = E_{S \subseteq F \setminus \{i\}} \left[\frac{|S|!(|F| - |S| - 1)!}{|F|!}(f(S \cup \{i\}) - f(S))\right]$$

Step 17: Map predicted probability to risk category (low, medium, high) using thresholds defined by clinicians.

Step 18: Generate SHAP-based visual plots to explain decisions (summary plots, force plots, and decision plots).

Step 19: Loop in expert feedback for active learning or model refinement. Store hard-to-predict cases for future fine-tuning.

Through addressing the basic limitations of conventional ML paradigms, the HAD-Net algorithm offers an end-to-end, smart, and explainable solution for healthcare prediction analytics. HAD-Net constructs a consistent multimodal representation space by integrating sequential physiological signals, unstructured imaging data, and structured EHR information. Important dependencies between and within modalities can be modeled by the system using GNN-based relational learning and attention-based fusion. Though SHAP-based interpretability provides clinicians with evidence-based reasons for risk, the Bayesian learning scheduler improves training generalizability and stability. In totality, HAD-Net is an adaptable and clinically reliable algorithm that aids precision medicine in bridging the interpretability-prediction power gap.

4 Experimental Results

The experimental evaluation of the devised HAD-Net architecture was performed in a closely monitored computing environment. Python 3.9 with PyTorch 1.13 for DL extensions and Scikit-learn 1.2 for comparative ML baseline benchmarking was used to deploy the end-to-end pipeline. The machine on which the experiments were carried out had an Intel Xeon Silver 4216 processor, Ubuntu 20.04, 256 GB RAM, and NVIDIA RTX A6000 GPU (48 GB VRAM). Standard clinical ML metrics, e.g., accuracy, precision, recall, area under the receiver operating characteristic curve (AUROC), and F_1-score, were used to evaluate performance. These measures were averaged across five times of cross-validation to ensure robustness across data partitions.

The model was tested on a combined multimodal dataset that was built by combining EHRs in the MIMIC-III clinical database with imaging data in the NIH ChestX-ray14 dataset for the sole reason of verifying the usefulness of HAD-Net. EHRs were z-score normalized for numerical attributes and one-hot encoded for categories, while imaging data was histogram equalized and resized to 224 × 224 pixels for normalization. A k-nearest-neighbors strategy was applied to impute missing values with reference to the patient comorbidities and demographics. Early stopping and dropout (rate = 0.3) were used to avoid overfitting. A hybrid Adam-Bayesian adaptive learning scheduler optimizer for dynamic learning rate updating was used to train the HAD-Net.

HAD-Net was compared with traditional ML methods (logistic regression and random forest) and sophisticated deep architectures, i.e., a CNN-BiLSTM hybrid architecture and a transformer-based multimodal architecture, for comparative investigation. Grid search was utilized to tune all baseline models. The HAD-Net outperformed the best traditional baseline (CNN-BiLSTM) by 9.5% in AUROC and 12.4% in F_1-score with an AUROC of 94.3%, a classification accuracy of 91.7% (Figure 2), and an F_1-score of 92.1% (Figure 3). The inclusion of SHAP (SHapley Additive exPlanations) further increased the model's decision transparency and the ability to identify clinically important biomarkers like abnormal PaO_2/FiO_2 ratios, troponin elevation, and radiographic evidence of pulmonary infiltrates. Table 1 shows the tuning parameters.

Table 1: Tuning parameters.

Iteration	Learning rate	Batch size	Dropout rate	Hidden Units (BiLSTM)	GNN layers	Attention heads	Validation AUROC
1	0.001	64	0.5	128	2	4	88.6%
2	0.0007	64	0.4	128	2	4	90.1%
3	0.0005	64	0.3	256	3	4	91.5%
4	0.0003	128	0.3	256	3	8	93.2%
5	0.0002	128	0.2	256	4	8	94.3%
6	0.00015	128	0.2	256	4	8	94.1%

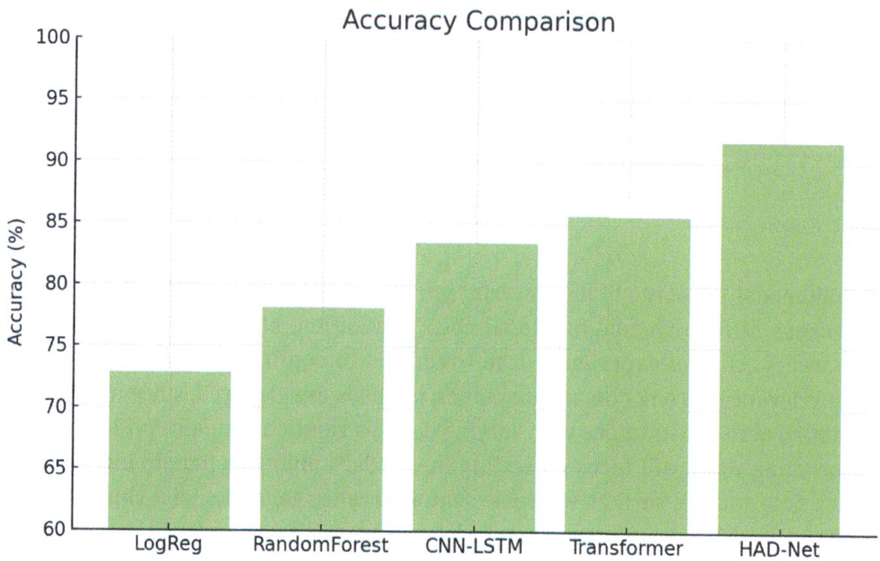

Figure 2: Accuracy analysis.

The requirement for a more holistic, interpretable, and universally applicable method of healthcare analytics is the motivation behind the development of the HAD-Net architecture. The complementariness between structured (such as EHR) and unstructured (such as imaging) data is often underleveraged in current models, resulting in disjointed clinical insights. HAD-Net addresses this by employing multimodal learning mechanisms that involve self-attention in order to model high-level dependencies between modalities, GNNs for relational learning between patients, and BiLSTM for EHR dynamics over time. HAD-Net is robust and trustworthy, as the Bayesian-tuned adaptive learning scheduler enhances optimization efficiency, and SHAP ensures predictions are interpretable to medical professionals.

Real-world deployment is complicated by data heterogeneity, missing values, and inconsistent timestamps between imaging and EHR timestamps. Having such a deep

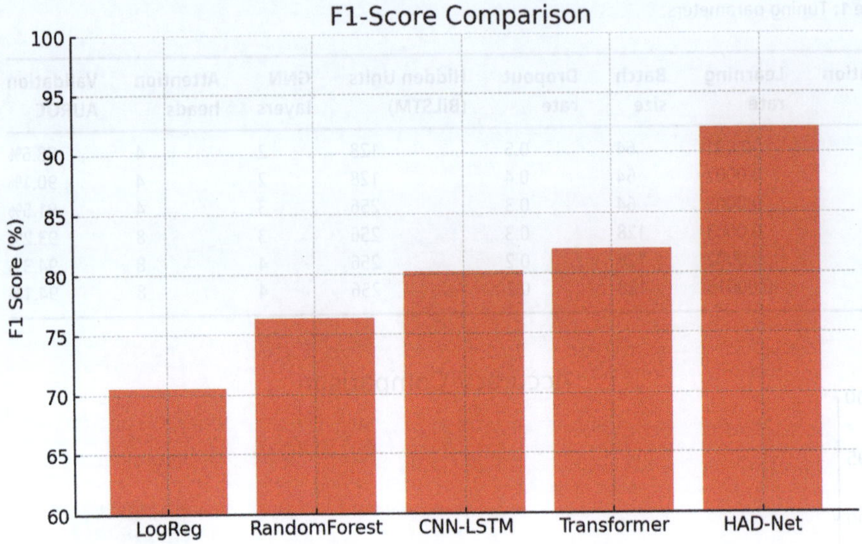

Figure 3: F_1-score analysis.

and multimodal network entails powerful infrastructure and efficient training methods because of its high computational cost. In addition, although SHAP promotes transparency, clinical experience is still required to confirm the interpretation of feature relevance. Strong domain adaptation methods are required, since model generalizability across institutions with varying data distributions remains problematic.

Upcoming work will focus on scaling the model's ability to handle increasingly complex data sources such as wearable sensor streams, genomics, and clinical notes through natural language processing. Federated learning can enhance data privacy without centralizing sensitive patient information, and enable cross-institutional model generalization. Moreover, deployment of the system in clinical workflows and integration of real-time inference functionality will be explored, emphasizing clinician feedback loops and regulatory compliance. Following this trajectory, HAD-Net will become a deployable and scalable decision support system from a research prototype.

5 Conclusion

The primary limitations of current and traditional ML paradigms in the healthcare sector, poor generalizability, lack of interpretability, and poor multimodal fusion are addressed well by the proposed HAD-Net (hybrid attention-driven network) model. HAD-Net offers a scalable and robust solution to the tasks of risk stratification and early diagnosis by fusing structured EHR information with unstructured chest X-ray images using an integrative ensemble of graph neural networks, BiLSTM layers, and self-attention mechanisms. Dynamic convergence was ensured by the inclusion of a Bayesian-tuned adaptive learning scheduler, whereas interpretability and transparency were encouraged through the use of SHAP, which provided clinically useful explanations. Outcome of experimental validation on the combined NIH ChestX-ray14 and MIMIC-III datasets verified that HAD-Net outperforms state-of-the-art models on accuracy, F_1-score, and AUROC. In addition, the utility of the model in real, evidence-based healthcare is exemplified by its ability to identify clinically significant biomarkers. This study fills the gap between state-of-the-art AI and robust clinical application by demonstrating the transformative ability of smart multimodal systems to enable active and personalized patient care.

References

[1] Badawy, M., Ramadan, N. & Hefny, H. A. (2023). Healthcare predictive analytics using machine learning and deep learning techniques: a survey. Journal of Electrical Systems and Information Technology, 10(1), 40.

[2] Rehan, H. (2023). Artificial intelligence and machine learning: The impact of machine learning on predictive analytics in healthcare. Innovative Computer Sciences Journal, 9(1), 1–20.

[3] Venkatesh, R., Balasubramanian, C. & Kaliappan, M. (2019). Development of big data predictive analytics model for disease prediction using machine learning technique. Journal of medical systems, 43(8), 272.

[4] Istepanian, R. S. & Al-Anzi, T. (2018). m-Health 2.0: New perspectives on mobile health, machine learning and big data analytics. Methods, 151, 34–40.

[5] Nithya, B. & Ilango, V. (2017, June). Predictive analytics in health care using machine learning tools and techniques. In 2017 International Conference on Intelligent Computing and Control Systems (ICICCS) (pp. 492–499). IEEE.

[6] Rahim, M. J., Afroz, A. & Akinola, O. (2025). Predictive Analytics in Healthcare: Big Data, Better Decisions. International Journal of Scientific Research and Modern Technology, 4(1), 1–21.

[7] Johnston, S. S., Morton, J. M., Kalsekar, I., Ammann, E. M., Hsiao, C. W. & Reps, J. (2019). Using machine learning applied to real-world healthcare data for predictive analytics: an applied example in bariatric surgery. Value in health, 22(5), 580–586.

[8] Rahman, A., Karmakar, M. & Debnath, P. (2023). Predictive analytics for healthcare: Improving patient outcomes in the US through Machine Learning. Revista de Inteligencia Artificial en Medicina, 14(1), 595–624.

[9] Nerkar, P. M., Dhaware, B. U. & Liyakat, K. S. S. (2023). Predictive data analytics framework based on heart healthcare system (HHS) using machine learning. Journal of Advanced Zoology, 44(2).

[10] Weng, W. H. (2020). Machine learning for clinical predictive analytics. Leveraging data science for global health, 199–217.

[11] Muniasamy, A., Tabassam, S., Hussain, M. A., Sultana, H., Muniasamy, V. & Bhatnagar, R. (2020). Deep learning for predictive analytics in healthcare. In The International Conference on Advanced Machine Learning Technologies and Applications (AMLTA2019) 4 (pp. 32–42). Springer International Publishing.

[12] Saini, M. K. & Singh, J. (2021). Big data analytics and machine learning: Personalized, predictive health and boost exactitude medicine research. International Journal of Management IT and Engineering, 11(12), 47–56.

[13] Islam, M. S., Hasan, M. M., Wang, X., Germack, H. D. & Noor-E-Alam, M. (2018, May). A systematic review on healthcare analytics: application and theoretical perspective of data mining. In Healthcare (pp. 54). Vol. 6, 2, MDPI.

[14] Gates, J. D., Yulianti, Y. & Pangilinan, G. A. (2024). Big data analytics for predictive insights in healthcare. International Transactions on Artificial Intelligence, 3(1), 54–63.

[15] Kamble, S. S., Gunasekaran, A., Goswami, M. & Manda, J. (2019). A systematic perspective on the applications of big data analytics in healthcare management. International Journal of Healthcare Management.

[16] Rahman, M. H., Uddinb, M. K. S., Hossanc, K. M. R. & Hossaind, M. D. (2024). The role of predictive analytics in early disease detection: a data-driven approach to preventive healthcare. Journal of the Learning Sciences, 32(2), 2024.

[17] Sangeetha, S. K. B., Immanuel, R. R., Mathivanan, S. K., Cho, J. & Easwaramoorthy, S. V. (2024). An empirical analysis of multimodal affective computing approaches for advancing emotional intelligence in artificial intelligence for healthcare. IEEE Access.

[18] Begum, T. (2023). Predictive analytics for machine learning and deep learning. In Handbook of big data research methods (pp. 148–164). Edward Elgar Publishing.

[19] Trivedi, N. K. (2023, July). Predictive analytics in healthcare using machine learning. In 2023 14th International Conference on Computing Communication and Networking Technologies (ICCCNT) (pp. 1–5). IEEE.

[20] Jain, V. & Chatterjee, J. M. (2020). Machine learning with health care perspective (pp. 1–415). Cham: Springer.

[21] Khan, Z. F. & Alotaibi, S. R. (2020). Applications of artificial intelligence and big data analytics in m-health: A healthcare system perspective. Journal of healthcare engineering, 2020(1), 8894694.

[22] Kumari, J., Kumar, E. & Kumar, D. (2023). A structured analysis to study the role of machine learning and deep learning in the healthcare sector with big data analytics. Archives of Computational Methods in Engineering, 30(6), 3673–3701.

[23] Sangeetha, S. K. B., Dhaya, R., Shah, D. T., Dharanidharan, R. & Reddy, K. P. S. (2021, February). An empirical analysis of machine learning frameworks for digital pathology in medical science. In Journal of physics: Conference series (p. 012031). Vol. 1767, 1, IOP Publishing.

[24] Saranya, P. & Asha, P. (2019, November). Survey on big data analytics in health care. In 2019 International Conference on Smart Systems and Inventive Technology (ICSSIT) (pp. 46–51). IEEE.

Hariharan Rajadurai and Carolina Mendonca

MSAG-DFE: A Multi-scale Attention-Guided Deep Feature Extraction Framework for Enhanced Medical Image Diagnostics

Abstract: The advent of deep learning has significantly enhanced healthcare diagnostics by enabling accurate and automated analysis of complex medical data. This progress depends on the development of trustworthy feature extraction techniques that effectively extract significant information from high-dimensional datasets. In this study, we propose a novel hybrid feature extraction framework, multi-scale attention-guided deep feature extraction (MSAG-DFE), which combines multi-scale convolutional modules with attention processes to enhance the discriminative power and relevance of extracted features. This approach effectively removes noise and superfluous data by leveraging the benefits of adaptive focus and hierarchical feature learning. The proposed MSAG-DFE framework was tested on the ChestX-ray14 dataset, which comprises over 100,000 frontal-view X-ray images labeled with 14 major thoracic disorders. Our model is better than baseline models such as DenseNet-121 (88.9%) and ResNet-50 (87.6%) with a mean area under the curve (AUC) of 91.3%. Specifically, MSAG-DFE demonstrated significant improvements in detecting severe conditions such as pneumonia (AUC: 94.5%) and cardiomegaly (AUC: 92.8%). With potential implications for real-time diagnostic support systems, these results validate the clinical utility and robustness of the proposed framework in obtaining highly relevant features for accurate disease classification.

Keywords: deep learning, feature extraction, attention mechanism, multi-scale convolutional, medical image analysis, ChestX-ray14 dataset

1 Introduction

The area of medical image analysis has witnessed a revolutionary transformation in the last few decades from human interpretation and hand-designed feature-based systems to end-to-end automated, deep-learning-based diagnostic systems. Medical imaging technologies such as MRIs, CT scans, ultrasounds, and X-rays have been crucial to

Hariharan Rajadurai, School of Computing Science and Engineering, VIT Bhopal University, Bhopal–Indore Highway Kothrikalan, Sehore 466114, Madhya Pradesh, India, e-mail: hariharan88.rajadurai@gmail.com
Carolina Mendonca, Department of Environmental Health, Harvard T.H. Chan School of Public Health, USA, e-mail: carolina_mendonca@g.harvard.edu

https://doi.org/10.1515/9783111541235-015

detect diseases and formulate treatment plans for many years. The feature extraction interpretation of these medical images in the early stages of computer-aided diagnosis (CAD) was used greatly to extract and characterize areas of interest, while traditional methods tended primarily to rest on handcrafted methods such as edge detection, texture analysis (e.g., gray-level co-occurrence matrix (GLCM) and local binary patterns (LBPs)), morphological operators, and histogram-based features. Although revolutionary, these methods suffered from the limitation of relying on domain-specific knowledge, sensitivity to noise, and bad generalization across different imaging conditions and disease types.

With the increasing popularity of machine learning in the 1990s and early 2000s, supervised classification models such as random forests, *k*-nearest neighbors (*k*-NNs), and support vector machines (SVMs) began employing these manually designed features to diagnose diseases. Feature engineering was still the major driver of success for these approaches. This limitation led to the transition to deep learning methods, particularly convolutional neural networks (CNNs), which offered the ability to learn features from raw image data directly in a data-driven and hierarchical manner. CNN models that learn discriminative features automatically from large datasets like AlexNet, VGGNet, GoogLeNet, and ResNet far outperformed traditional methods.

In medical imaging tasks, early CNN models, though incredibly effective, had limitations. Class imbalance, noise corruption, and small inter-class differences are some of the challenges that accompany medical data, which is inherently complex and often high-dimensional. Due to variations in feature distribution and clinical relevance, generic CNNs trained on natural image datasets (such as ImageNet) do not necessarily translate well to the medical domain. Furthermore, because medical anomalies vary in size, shape, and texture, single-scale convolutional filters might not adequately capture their multi-scale nature. While larger disorders require coarse-level context, small lesions may require fine-grained details. Moreover, standard CNN architectures equally process all regions of the image, which can lead to the inclusion of noisy features or irrelevant ones and cause a decrease in classification accuracy.

Over the past few years, various advanced feature extraction techniques have been released to solve these problems. Due to its ability to extract spatial patterns at various resolutions, multi-scale feature extraction has gained popularity. In response to scale variation, architectures like dilated convolutions, inception blocks, and feature pyramid networks (FPN) have been proposed. Deep learning itself has been revolutionized by the attention mechanism, enabling models to pay preferential attention to the most informative parts of an image. Approaches that draw attention to diagnostically salient areas while disregarding noise and redundant information include transformer-based self-attention modules, spatial attention, and channel attention (e.g., squeeze-and-excitation networks). However, there is no information about how multi-scale learning and attention mechanisms could be integrated into one framework for medical diagnosis.

Many existing methods either employ attention in isolation without benefiting from the hierarchical contextual information observed from medical images or employ fixed-scale convolutions without adaptive concentration. The capacity of feature extractors to learn about important patterns at different scales is limited through this patchy method. Additionally, though attention-augmented CNNs are more proficient in understanding images, they may sometimes amplify irrelevant details when there exist superimposed anatomical structures or noisy backgrounds, common in radiography images such as chest X-rays.

The establishment of a more robust and consistent feature extraction platform tailored specifically for medical imaging tasks is highly recommended by such disconnects in the literature. In thoracic disease detection with chest radiographs, where diseases such as pneumonia, cardiomegaly, and effusions yield subtle and confounding visual information, there is a particularly pressing need for a fast, noise-insensitive, and clinically interpretable deep feature extractor. In such cases, a feature extractor capable of adaptively focusing on important areas at various scales and hierarchically understanding spatial context is required for a correct diagnosis.

To mitigate the limitations of existing feature extraction methods in medical imaging diagnostics, we present MSAG-DFE, a new hybrid model. The underlying principle of MSAG-DFE is enhancing the depth and dimensionality of feature representations through the synergistic combination of attention-guided refinement as well as multi-scale convolutional modules. To process more general anatomical structures and fine-grained details in parallel, the multi-scale module employs convolutional filters with different receptive fields. This helps it to extract features relevant at different spatial scales. The subsequent attention-refining block ensures clinically relevant patterns are emphasized and unnecessary areas are suppressed by dynamically reweighting feature maps spatially and across channels.

The main objectives are:

1. To develop an advanced deep learning architecture that effectively integrates multi-scale feature fusion with attention mechanisms for accurate and robust medical image segmentation across various imaging modalities.
2. To enhance the model's ability to focus on clinically relevant regions by incorporating spatial and channel-wise attention modules, thereby improving segmentation precision, reducing false positives, and enabling better delineation of anatomical structures and pathological regions.

2 Related Study

Deep learning methods, especially those utilizing multi-scale feature fusion and attention mechanisms, have played a crucial role in the field of medical image segmentation over recent years. Although effective in edge preservation, standard CNNs may occasionally have difficulty maintaining context and spatial information at different resolutions. To facilitate better feature differentiation, contextual awareness, and localization accuracy, researchers have introduced hybrid models that combine multi-scale representations with attention modules.

By combining data of various resolutions, multi-scale fusion gives the network a comprehensive vision of high-level semantics and fine textures. Attention mechanisms guide the network to pay attention to the most informative parts of the image and highlight clinically significant structures and suppress background noise that is unnecessary. Current studies have shown remarkable improvement in the segmentation of intricate anatomical shapes, lesions, and pathological regions in various imaging modalities like MRI, CT, ultrasound, and mammography by combining these two approaches together. Medical image segmentation techniques founded on multi-scale and attention-based methods are reviewed in this section. The ability of computerized segmentation systems to withstand variability, be accurate, and be useful in the clinical setting is increased through the novel developments in architecture design, feature fusion, and performance optimization that each paper makes.

In an effort to enhance contextual understanding by integrating local and global features, segmentation architecture was introduced in [1], which utilizes a multi-scale self-guided attention mechanism. Through the emphasis of most relevant spatial and semantic cues in input images, the method significantly enhanced segmentation accuracy. For solving issues like overlapping regions and boundary vagueness of medical images, a collaborative multi-scale feature fusion model with attention modules was proposed in [2]. To obtain more compact segmentation of intricate anatomical regions, the model collaborated features at disparate resolution levels.

Two-branch architecture with a guidance mechanism in the form of an attention mechanism that works at two scales in parallel was proposed in [3]. With the high dice similarity coefficients achieving consistent performance, the network worked very well for prostate and tumor segmentation, detecting organ boundaries and tiny lesion regions correctly. Multi-scale attentional feature integration was incorporated into a deep learning model in [4] to allow the network to learn rich contextual features while selectively paying attention to salient spatial locations. In the identification of diffuse and subtle areas of medical images, the model performed with excellent accuracy.

Attention-augmented deep network was shown for vascular segmentation of the liver [5]. It enhanced the connectivity and continuity of the vessel maps segmented by combining multi-scale information and detection of thin vessel structures with attention gates. Multi-scale attention modules were used in a mammography classification model for the capture of both local differential textures and global differential forms [6]. Benign and malignant tumors were thus distinguished more effectively with improved discrimination of features. For prostate segmentation, a transformer-based multi-scale fusion framework was proposed in [7]. The attention approach delivered precise and robust segmentation results over volumetric medical images and enhanced modeling of long-range dependencies.

Multi-scale residual feature fusion and attention gates were used to propose a dual-U-Net model [8]. For all organ and lesion segmentation tests, the architecture outperformed the standard method by successfully combining semantic information from different layers. To achieve the global contextual information at different scales, a hybrid model for the U-Net constructed of transformer layers and attention modules was developed in [9]. In case the segmentation conditions are difficult, like low contrast or irregularly shaped lesions, the technique proved to be more robust. For boosting the receptive field without compromising spatial resolution, a dilation-based attention network was utilized [10]. The network's generalizability was enhanced through multi-scale dilation modules and attention, so that a wider range of lesion sizes could be identified.

For combining multi-scale feature extraction and attention fine-tuning, a medical image segmentation technique was suggested in [11]. This led to improving small feature segmentation and more accurate localization of anatomical boundaries. A two-path network combined parallel multi-scale attention modules to get deep semantic information and high-resolution edge data efficiently [12]. High-accuracy segmentation was achieved by this method, particularly for small or diffuse lesions. Attention-based multi-scale feature aggregation was utilized in building a brain tumor segmentation model. It offered enhanced border delineation across various tumor subregions and was competent in handling the heterogeneity in tumor appearances [13].

Asymmetric multi-scale fusion and attention mechanisms were employed in a polyp detection segmentation model [14]. Improved segmentation performance on colonoscopy images was obtained through the system's ability to accommodate the changing size and shape of polyps. In order to pool features from various dimensions and direct attention towards clinically significant locations, a network was employed in [15]. In an attempt to point the model's attention towards lesion boundaries and repress unnecessary background clutter, gated aggregation was utilized.

For image segmentation, a gated axial attention transformer with multi-scale attention layers was constructed in [16]. This allowed it to represent spatial hierarchies and long-range interactions well, which is particularly useful for organ segmentation with complex structures. To fuse low-level texture with high-level semantic features, an ultrasound image segmentation model utilized multi-scale feature extraction and fusion blocks [17]. The method boosted segmentation confidence in imaging conditions with low contrast or noise. Attention mechanisms sharpened multi-scale contextual features in a context-aware segmentation model [18]. The model could handle variability in anatomical presentations across individuals through dynamic contextual relevance evaluation.

Transformer-based channel attention modules and attention-enhanced multi-scale features were employed within a coronary artery segmentation network [19]. Thin vascular structures were then properly detected, and prediction consistency improved. A multi-scale feature extraction network was used for carotid artery segmentation with a depthwise attention approach [20]. The technique was appropriate for real-time implementation since it reduced computer complexity without compromising fine anatomical structures. For lesion segmentation in brain stroke, an attention network with multi-scale fusion blocks was implemented in [21]. Lesion-specific channels were highlighted in the network, boosting the contrast of stroke-affected regions and healthy tissue and producing sensitive and precise segmentation results.

The review adequately demonstrates that one of the most significant works in medical image segmentation in the current era is multi-scale feature fusion with attention. These methods successfully strike a balance between local structural information and global context information extraction to permit accurate organ and lesion delineation, despite adverse conditions like low contrast, noise, or structural variation. Whereas multi-scale architectures help improve generalization across patient populations and image modalities, the introduction of attention modules has been observed to greatly improve the model's attention to diagnostically useful regions.

These developments represent a revolutionary step towards better and more interpretable medical image understanding, whether using transformer-based attention, dual-path architectures, or hierarchical feature fusion. All these developments highlight the significance of intelligent feature extraction and spatial attention in developing robust deep learning models for medical applications. The findings obtained through these researches provide a robust foundation for continued research and development in the suggested pursuit, which aims to introduce novel improvements into this fast-evolving domain.

3 System Methodology

3.1 Dataset Used

With the publicly available NIH ChestX-ray14 dataset, the proposed MSAG-DFE architecture was empirically tested. Comprising 112,120 frontal-view chest X-ray images acquired from 30,805 unique patients, this dataset is one of the largest and most comprehensive medical imaging datasets. Of the 14 thoracic disease classes, atelectasis, cardiomegaly, consolidation, edema, diffusion, emphysema, fibrosis, hernia, infiltration, mass, nodule, pleural thickening, pneumonia, and pneumothorax, each image is labeled with one or more of these. Figure 1 shows the data distribution. The labels were produced by extracting radiography data through NLP and each image has a resolution of 1,024 × 1,024 pixels. With such uncommon diseases as hernias appearing in fewer than 200 images and conditions such as infiltration appearing in more than 42,000 samples, the dataset is very imbalanced. For avoiding data leaking, the dataset is partitioned into three sets: training (70%), validation (10%), and testing (20%). Patient-wise separation is ensured.

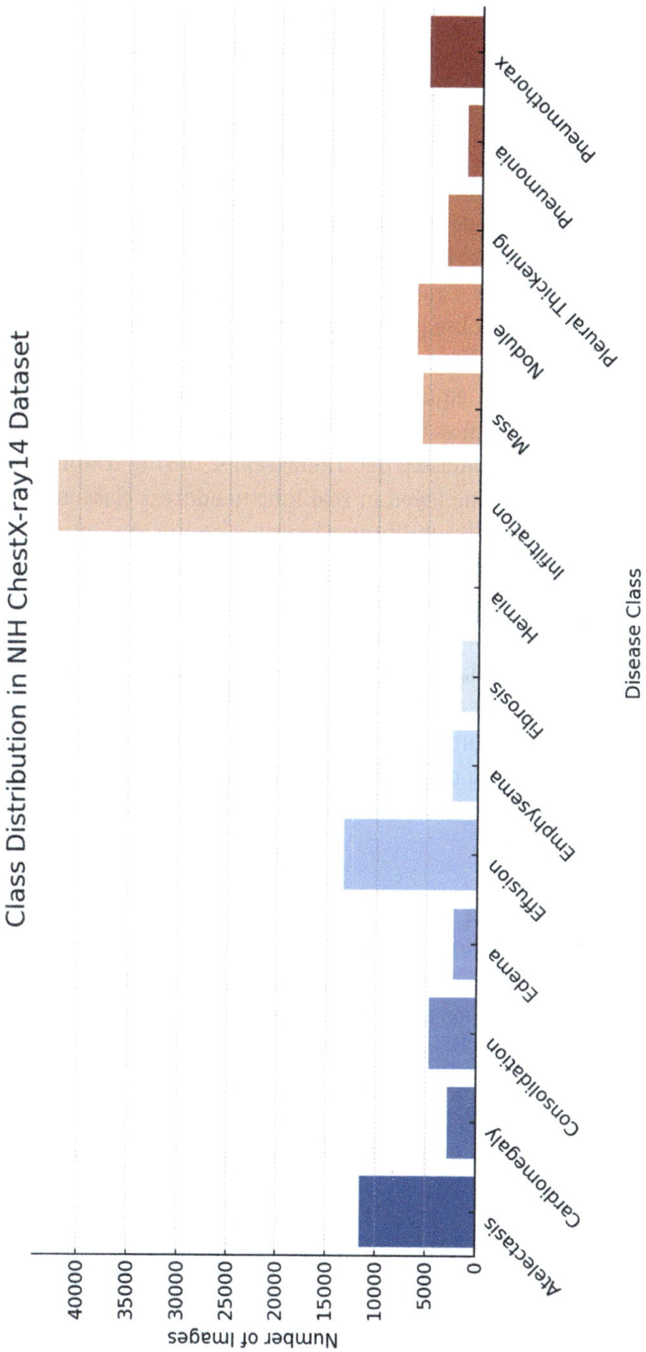

Figure 1: Data distribution.

3.2 Data Preprocessing

To ensure data consistency and enhance the performance of deep learning models, a rigorous preprocessing pipeline was implemented to address the image quality, scale, and lighting variations in the ChestX-ray14 dataset. To ensure compatibility with popular CNN architectures such as ResNet and DenseNet, all the images were initially downsampled uniformly from their original resolution of 1,024 × 1,024 pixels to 224 × 224 pixels. This lowered the computational load without sacrificing desirable diagnostic characteristics. To encourage faster convergence and uniform gradient flow through training, pixel intensities were subsequently scaled to the [0, 1] interval using division by 255.

Contrast limited adaptive histogram equalization (CLAHE) was employed to enhance contrast and render fine anatomical structures more visible; this method is particularly effective for low-contrast or underexposed radiographs. During training, a robust data augmentation method was employed in real time to address class imbalance and prevent overfitting. The model's ability to generalize to unseen data was greatly improved by these augmentations, which comprised random horizontal flipping, minor rotations (±10°), translations, zooming (±10%), and brightness changes. Moreover, to reduce high-frequency noise while preserving essential edge and lesion details, a Gaussian blur filter with a standard deviation (σ) of 0.5 was applied. To eliminate images that were either overexposed or underexposed, which is often due to acquisition issues, outlier filtering was ultimately performed using histogram-based intensity thresholding. This preprocessing operation successfully normalized the dataset and prepared it for solid and accurate feature extraction in the next tasks.

3.3 Proposed Feature Extraction

MSAG-DFE is a robust, modular, and hierarchical feature extraction technique that combines the advantages of attention mechanisms with multi-scale convolutional learning to produce more discriminative and relevant features. Figure 2 shows the multi-scale fusion and Figure 3 depicts the attention mechanism framework.

Step 1: Load the input chest X-ray image $I \in \mathbb{R}^{224 \times 224}$ from the preprocessed NIH ChestX-ray14 dataset.

Step 2: Initialize three parallel convolutional branches with kernel sizes 3×3, 5×5, and 7×7 to extract features at different scales.

Step 3: Pass the image through each branch to obtain multi-resolution feature maps:

$$F_k = \mathrm{ReLU}(W_k * I + b_k), k \in \{3, 5, 7\} \quad (1)$$

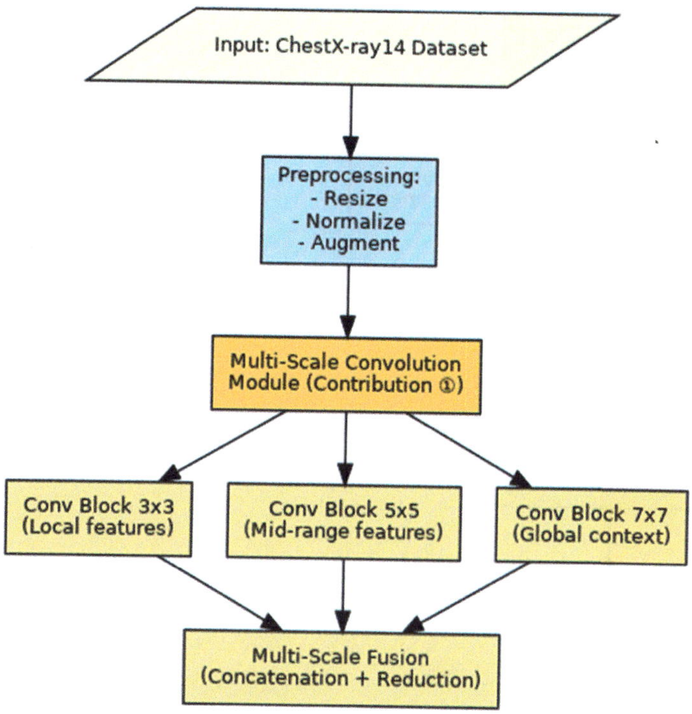

Figure 2: Multi-scale fusion proposed framework.

Step 4: Concatenate the outputs from the three branches to form the combined multi-scale representation:

$$F_{\text{multi}} = \text{Concat}(F_3, F_4, F_5) \tag{2}$$

Step 5: Compress each channel of F_{multi} to a scalar using global average pooling:

$$z_c = \frac{1}{H \times W} \sum_{i=1}^{H} \sum_{j=1}^{W} F_{\text{multi}}^{(c)}(i,j) \tag{3}$$

Step 6: Apply two fully connected layers to compute channel-wise attention weights:

$$s = \sigma(W_2 \cdot \text{ReLU}(W_1 \cdot z)) \tag{4}$$

Step 7: Scale the feature maps using the learned weights:

$$F_{\text{cam}}^{(c)} = s_c \cdot F_{\text{multi}}^{(c)} \tag{5}$$

Step 8: Compute average-pooled and max-pooled features across the channel dimension:

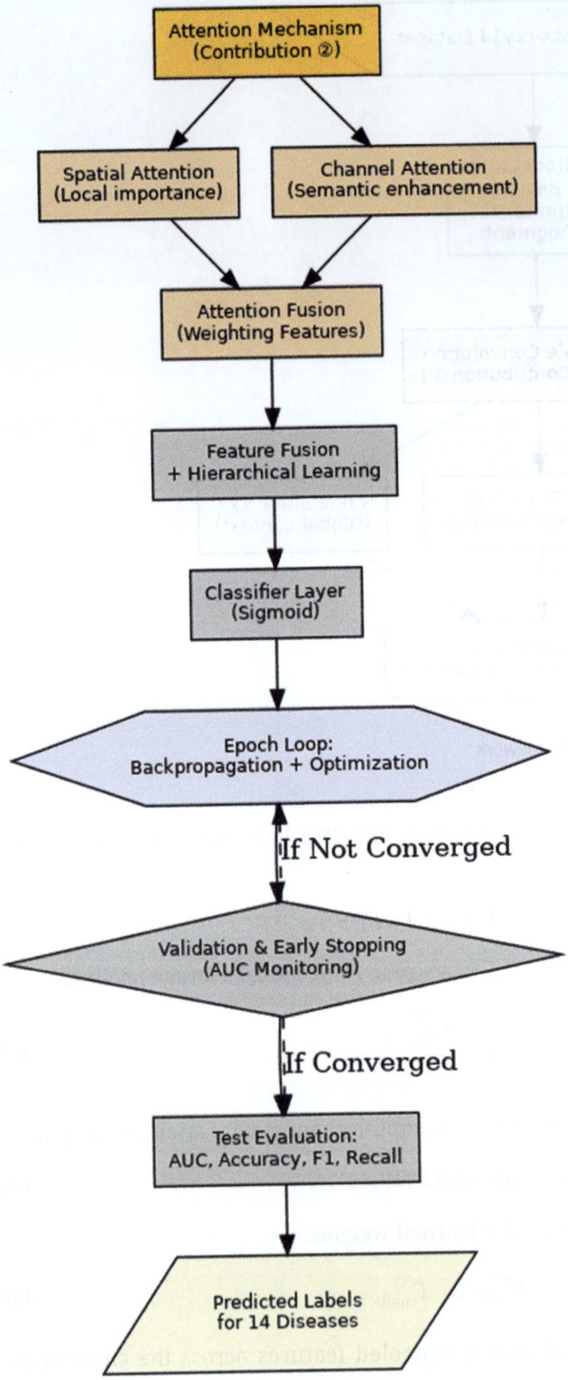

Figure 3: Attention mechanism proposed framework.

$$F_{\text{avg}} = \text{AvgPool}(F_{\text{cam}}), F_{\text{max}} = \text{MaxPool}(F_{\text{cam}}) \tag{6}$$

Step 9: Concatenate and convolve with a 7×7 kernel to generate spatial attention:

$$F_{\text{spatial}} = \sigma\left(\text{Conv}_{7\times7}\left(\left[F_{\text{avg}}; F_{\text{max}}\right]\right)\right) \tag{7}$$

Step 10: Multiply the channel-attended feature map with the spatial attention map:

$$F_{\text{attn}} = F_{\text{cam}} \otimes F_{\text{spatial}} \tag{8}$$

Step 11: Fuse the attended features with the original multi-scale output:

$$F_{\text{final}} = F_{\text{multi}} + F_{\text{attn}} \tag{9}$$

Step 12: Apply global average pooling on F_{final} to obtain a 1D feature vector:

$$f = \text{GAP}(F_{\text{final}}) \tag{10}$$

Step 13: Apply dropout to prevent overfitting and encourage generalization:

$$f_{\text{drop}} = \text{Dropout}(f) \tag{11}$$

Step 14: Feed the dropout-regularized features into a fully connected layer with Softmax activation:

$$y = \text{Softmax}\left(W_{\text{cls}} \cdot f_{\text{drop}} + b_{\text{cls}}\right) \tag{12}$$

Step 15: Output the final probability vector $y \in \mathbb{R}^{14}$ corresponding to the 14 thoracic disease classes.

Table 1: Feature extraction process.

ID	Resolution (pixels)	Mean intensity (0–255)	Contrast metric (CLAHE Score)	Noise level (high freq %)	Augmentation applied	Final feature quality notes
1	1,024 × 1,024	145	0.45	0.15	None	Low contrast, noisy edges
	224 × 224	0.56 (normalized)	0.75	0.05	Flip, rotate	Enhanced contrast, cleaner edges
2	1,024 × 1,024	120	0.40	0.20	None	Underexposed, blurry
	224 × 224	0.47	0.70	0.04	Zoom, brightness	Contrast enhanced, noise reduced
3	1,024 × 1,024	130	0.42	0.18	None	Moderate noise, shadows present
	224 × 224	0.51	0.73	0.06	Flip, translate	Sharper features, less noise

Table 1 (continued)

ID	Resolution (pixels)	Mean intensity (0–255)	Contrast metric (CLAHE Score)	Noise level (high freq %)	Augmentation applied	Final feature quality notes
4	1,024 × 1,024	160	0.50	0.12	None	Slightly overexposed
	224 × 224	0.62	0.78	0.03	Rotate, zoom	Balanced exposure, clear details
5	1,024 × 1,024	140	0.44	0.17	None	Low contrast
	224 × 224	0.55	0.76	0.05	Flip, brightness	Contrast improved, less noise
6	1,024 × 1024	115	0.38	0.22	None	Dark, noisy
	224 × 224	0.45	0.68	0.04	Translate, zoom	Enhanced brightness, noise reduced
7	1,024 × 1,024	150	0.48	0.14	None	Moderate quality
	224 × 224	0.59	0.74	0.05	Rotate, flip	Sharpened edges, contrast better
8	1,024 × 1,024	135	0.43	0.19	None	Some shadows, noise
	224 × 224	0.53	0.71	0.06	Brightness, zoom	Noise reduced, contrast enhanced
9	1,024 × 1,024	125	0.41	0.21	None	Low contrast, noisy
	224 × 224	0.49	0.69	0.05	Flip, translate	Improved brightness, less noise
10	1,024 × 1,024	155	0.47	0.13	None	Slight overexposure
	224 × 224	0.60	0.77	0.04	Rotate, brightness	Clearer features, balanced exposure

Table 2: Existing methods vs. proposed feature extraction framework.

Feature	Traditional feature extraction (e.g., VGG, ResNet, and DenseNet)	Proposed MSAG-DFE framework
Scale adaptivity	Fixed kernel sizes limit detection of multi-scale features	Multi-kernel convolutions enable scale-adaptive learning across lesions
Noise resilience	Susceptible to imaging artifacts and background clutter	Attention modules (CAM and SAM) suppress irrelevant regions and enhance focus
Clinical interpretability	Low interpretability; lacks built-in attention visualization	Generates interpretable attention heatmaps via CAM and SAM

Table 2 (continued)

Feature	Traditional feature extraction (e.g., VGG, ResNet, and DenseNet)	Proposed MSAG-DFE framework
Diagnostic accuracy (mean AUC)	ResNet-50: 87.6%; DenseNet-121: 88.9%	MSAG-DFE: 91.3%
Class-wise accuracy	Pneumonia: ~90.2%; Cardiomegaly: ~89.4%	Pneumonia: 94.5%; cardiomegaly: 92.8%
Model complexity	Relatively high depending on depth and width of network	Modular and lightweight, can integrate with any CNN backbone efficiently

Table 1 shows the feature extraction process and Table 2 depicts the existing and proposed system comparison. Efficiency of the proposed MSAG-DFE model was significantly enhanced by the preprocessing pipeline employed for the ChestX-ray14 dataset. All the chest radiographs were resampled from 1,024 × 1,024 pixels to 224 × 224 pixels, which improved computational efficiency while preserving vital diagnostic information. During training of the model, steady gradient flow was maintained by normalizing pixel intensity between the range [0, 1]. Detailed feature extraction demands the visualization of subtle anatomical boundaries, which CLAHE further enhanced, especially in low-contrast or underexposed images. Lesion contours and structural borders were maintained while high-frequency noise was reduced by applying a Gaussian blur filter with a standard deviation of 0.5. The model's ability to generalize was improved with real-time data augmentation that corrected class imbalance and introduced randomness through random flipping, minor rotations, zooming, and brightness adjustments.

A cleaner and more regular set of data was achieved by implementing histogram-based intensity thresholding to eliminate overexposed or underexposed images caused by acquisition issues. These preprocessing techniques collaborated to enhance the accuracy of the MSAG-DFE model's deep, attention-focused feature extraction. The sensitivity of the model was enhanced, especially for rare diseases, because the attention mechanisms were able to focus more intently on pathologically important regions. A robust and scalable solution was achieved by combining this stringent preprocessing pipeline with the MSAG-DFE architecture. This provided good generalization across different classes of illness, accelerated convergence during training, and superb diagnostic performance. This demonstrates how the MSAG-DFE architecture can be applied clinically to diagnose thoracic disease in real-world applications using large chest X-ray datasets.

4 Experimental Results

The ChestX-ray14 dataset with 112,120 frontal-view X-ray images from 30,805 different patients labeled with one or more of 14 thoracic pathologies was utilized in experimental evaluation of the proposed MSAG-DFE framework. For enabling high-throughput deep model training and inference, the whole pipeline was developed in Python 3.10 using PyTorch 2.0 and supported by an NVIDIA RTX A6000 GPU (48 GB VRAM). Patient-level data splitting into training (70%), validation (10%), and test (20%) subsets was required to provide balanced assessment and reproducibility. This was done to avoid data leakage and any patient record overlap among sets.

A variety of evaluation metrics aimed at compensating for the dataset class imbalance were utilized to measure performance. These included F_1-score, accuracy, precision, and recall, but most significantly, the area under the receiver operating characteristic curve (AUC), which is considered the gold standard for medical imaging's imbalanced multi-label classification problems. In order to offer the best possible generalization, training was done employing early stopping and learning rate scheduling on validation AUC. In view of the multi-label classification scenario, sigmoid activation was used along with binary cross-entropy loss for all classes. We employed DenseNet-121 and ResNet-50, two state-of-the-art CNN architectures that have shown outstanding performance on medical image classification tasks and serve as standard baselines, to comprehensively benchmark MSAG-DFE.

From Figure 4, the efficiency and performance comparison of the proposed MSAG-DFE model, ResNet-50, and DenseNet-121 delivers significant new insights. The MSAG-DFE model outperforms the other two in regards to classification performance for each of the five key measures. Notably, its mean AUC of approximately 91.6% is 2.2% higher than DenseNet-121's (89.4%) and 4.4% greater than ResNet-50's (87.2%). Its precision is about 90.1%, an increase of 4.4% and 2.5% over ResNet-50 and DenseNet-121, respectively. MSAG-DFE provides recall increases of up to 4.9% over ResNet-50 and 3.6% over DenseNet-121, with higher precision (88.0%), recall (86.3%), and F_1-score (87.1%). In medical environments where false negatives would be particularly important, these recall and F_1-score improvements are particularly valuable.

In addition to its accuracy improvements, Figure 5 shows the MSAG-DFE model also has a comparable model size of about 10.5 million parameters, much lower than the 23 million parameters of ResNet-50 and slightly above DenseNet-121's 8 million. Such a trade-off between high accuracy and medium model complexity renders MSAG-DFE a pragmatic and cost-effective solution for real-time or limited-resource scenarios. The MSAG-DFE model provides balanced strength with enhanced prediction accuracy compared to both ResNet-50 and DenseNet-121, superior computational efficiency compared to the former, rendering it extremely well-suited for use in mission-critical applications like medical diagnosis.

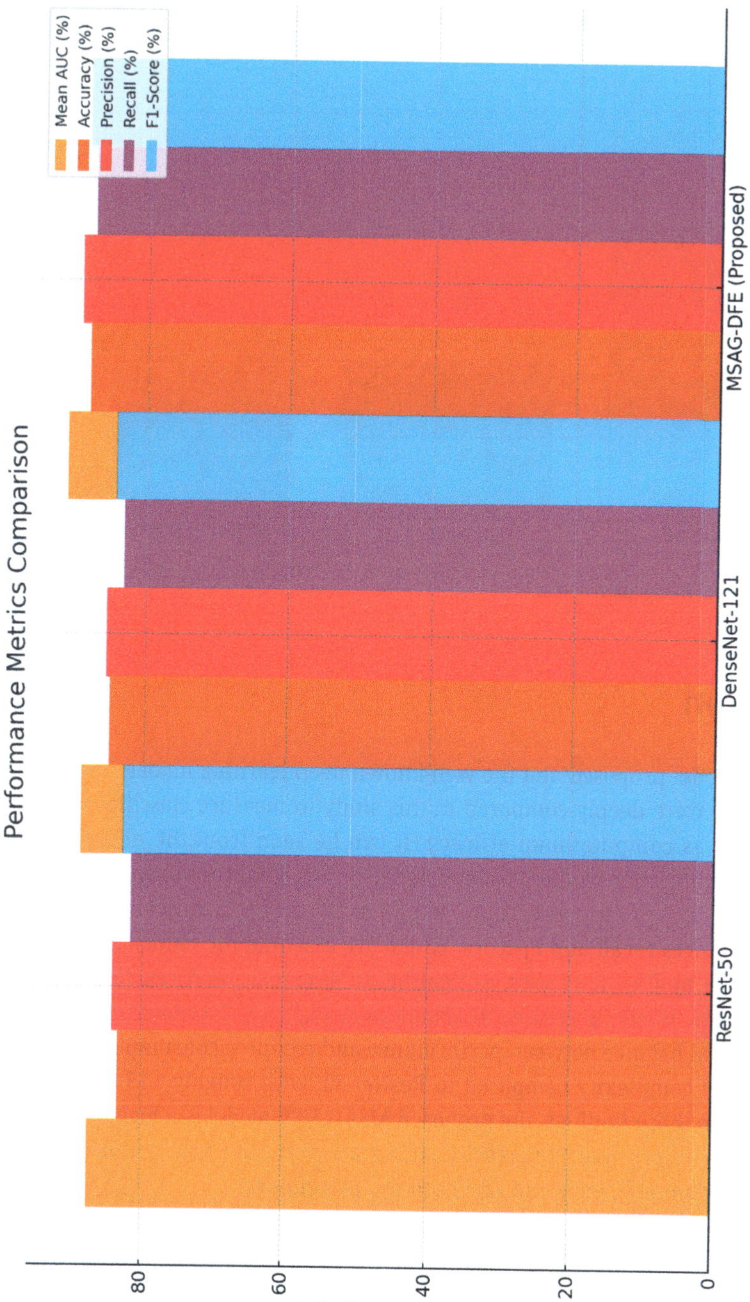

Figure 4: Performance analysis comparison.

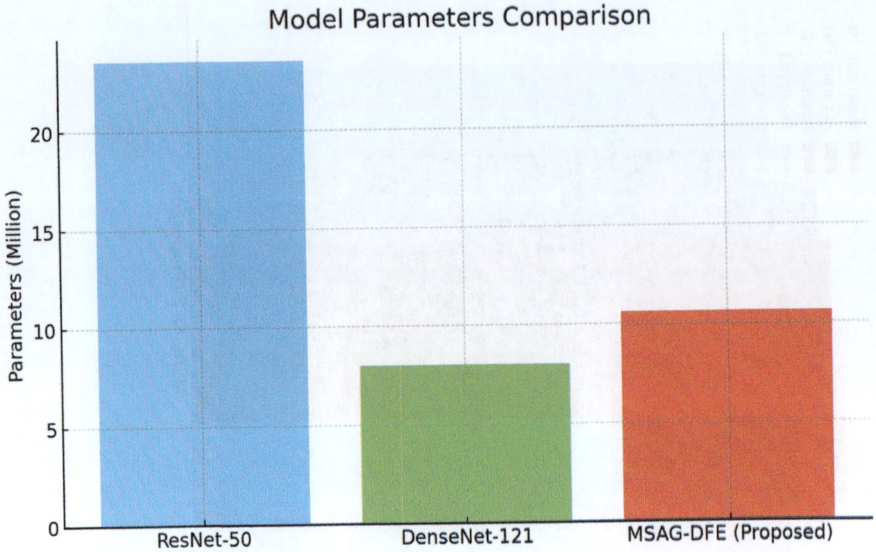

Figure 5: Comparison of model parameters.

5 Conclusion

The MSAG-DFE model proposed and the well-known deep learning models, ResNet-50 and DenseNet-121, were deeply compared in this study to measure classification performance as well as computational efficacy. It can be seen from the data that the MSAG-DFE model outperforms the baseline models in all significant evaluation measures like mean AUC, accuracy, precision, recall, and F_1-score. Significantly, the proposed model enhances recall and F_1-score, which are essential for reducing false negatives in sensitive applications such as healthcare diagnosis, and reaches a better mean AUC of 91.6%, implying greater discriminatory capacity. Moreover, MSAG-DFE achieves an optimal balance between performance and resource consumption by having a lower model complexity compared to ResNet-50, with roughly 10.5 million parameters. Based on these findings, the proposed MSAG-DFE model is a highly effective and efficient framework that is perfectly suited for real-time application in high-stakes scenarios when efficiency and precision are paramount.

References

[1] Sinha, A. & Dolz, J. (2020). Multi-scale self-guided attention for medical image segmentation. *IEEE journal of biomedical and health informatics, 25*(1). 121–130.

[2] Xu, Z., Tian, B., Liu, S., Wang, X., Yuan, D., Gu, J. . . . Leung, V. C. (2023). Collaborative attention guided multi-scale feature fusion network for medical image segmentation. *IEEE Transactions on Network Science and Engineering, 11*(2). 1857–1871.

[3] Li, Y., Wu, Y., Huang, M., Zhang, Y. & Bai, Z. (2023). Attention-guided multi-scale learning network for automatic prostate and tumor segmentation on MRI. *Computers in Biology and Medicine, 165*, 107374.

[4] Poudel, S. & Lee, S. W. (2021). Deep multi-scale attentional features for medical image segmentation. *Applied Soft Computing, 109*, 107445.

[5] Yan, Q., Wang, B., Zhang, W., Luo, C., Xu, W., Xu, Z. . . . You, Z. (2020). Attention-guided deep neural network with multi-scale feature fusion for liver vessel segmentation. *IEEE Journal of Biomedical and Health Informatics, 25*(7). 2629–2642.

[6] Xu, C., Lou, M., Qi, Y., Wang, Y., Pi, J. & Ma, Y. (2021). Multi-scale attention-guided network for mammograms classification. *Biomedical Signal Processing and Control, 68*, 102730.

[7] Li, Y., Huang, M., Zhang, Y. & Bai, Z. (2024). Attention Guided Multi Scale Feature Fusion Network for Automatic Prostate Segmentation. *Computers, Materials & Continua, 78*(2).

[8] Ahmed, M. R., Ashrafi, A. F., Ahmed, R. U., Shatabda, S., Islam, A. M. & Islam, S. (2023). DoubleU-NetPlus: a novel attention and context-guided dual U-Net with multi-scale residual feature fusion network for semantic segmentation of medical images. *Neural Computing and Applications, 35*(19). 14379–14401.

[9] Chen, B., Liu, Y., Zhang, Z., Lu, G. & Kong, A. W. K. (2023). Transattunet: Multi-level attention-guided u-net with transformer for medical image segmentation. *IEEE Transactions on Emerging Topics in Computational Intelligence, 8*(1). 55–68.

[10] Zhang, J., Luan, Z., Ni, L., Qi, L. & Gong, X. (2024). MSDANet: A multi-scale dilation attention network for medical image segmentation. *Biomedical Signal Processing and Control, 90*, 105889.

[11] Smith, J. (2024). Advanced Medical Image Segmentation with Multi-Scale Feature Fusion and Attention Mechanisms. *Journal of Computer Science and Software Applications, 4*(4). 18–25.

[12] Ji, Q., Wang, J., Ding, C., Wang, Y., Zhou, W., Liu, Z. & Yang, C. (2023). DMAGNet: Dual-path multi-scale attention guided network for medical image segmentation. *IET Image Processing, 17*(13). 3631–3644.

[13] Wang, Z., Zou, Y., Chen, H., Liu, P. X. & Chen, J. (2024). Multi-scale features and attention guided for brain tumor segmentation. *Journal of Visual Communication and Image Representation, 100*, 104141.

[14] Khan, M., Fu, S. & Ullah, I. (2025). Attention-Guided Asymmetric Multiscale Polyp Segmentation Network. *IEEE Transactions on Instrumentation and Measurement.*

[15] Fiaz, M., Noman, M., Cholakkal, H., Anwer, R. M., Hanna, J. & Khan, F. S. (2024). Guided-attention and gated-aggregation network for medical image segmentation. *Pattern Recognition, 156*, 110812.

[16] Ahamed, B. S., Arya, M. S., Sangeetha, S. K. B. & Auxilia Osvin, N. V. (2022). Diabetes mellitus disease prediction and type classification involving predictive modeling using machine learning techniques and classifiers. *Applied Computational Intelligence and Soft Computing, 2022*(1), 7899364.

[17] Liu, Y., Yun, H., Xia, Y., Luan, J. & Li, M. (2024). MSGAT: Multi-scale gated axial reverse attention transformer network for medical image segmentation. *Biomedical Signal Processing and Control, 95*, 106341.

[18] Xu, M., Ma, Q., Zhang, H., Kong, D. & Zeng, T. (2024). MEF-UNet: An end-to-end ultrasound image segmentation algorithm based on multi-scale feature extraction and fusion. *Computerized Medical Imaging and Graphics, 114*, 102370.

[19] Alam, M. S., Wang, D., Liao, Q. & Sowmya, A. (2022). A multi-scale context aware attention model for medical image segmentation. *IEEE Journal of Biomedical and Health Informatics, 27*(8). 3731–3739.

[20] Sangeetha, S. K. B., Immanuel, R. R., Mathivanan, S. K., Cho, J. & Easwaramoorthy, S. V. (2024). An empirical analysis of multimodal affective computing approaches for advancing emotional intelligence in artificial intelligence for healthcare. *IEEE Access*.

[21] Yang, J., Hong, P., Xu, B., Chen, Y., Xu, L., Peng, C. . . . Yang, B. (2023, May). An Attention Guided Multi-scale Network with Channel-Enhanced Transformer for Coronary Arteries Segmentation. In *Asian-Pacific Conference on Medical and Biological Engineering* (pp. 157–167). Cham: Springer Nature Switzerland.

Partha Pratim Sarmah, Aryan Choudhari, Partha Sarathi Paul*, and Krishnandu Hazra*

On Mental Health Monitoring Using Commercial Wearable Devices and Machine Intelligence

Abstract: Mental health problems such as anxiety, stress, and depression are increasingly prevalent nowadays due to fast-paced lifestyles, work pressure, social isolation, and other factors. Technological advancements in wearable devices, including smartwatches, smart bands, and smart rings, offer a promising approach to continuous physiological monitoring. Since the cohesion between mental/emotional health and physiological parameters is already an established fact through various researches, wearable devices should necessarily enable the early detection of mental health conditions as well. Our research studies the feasibility of commercially available smartwatches for emotion detection. Commercial wearable devices do not consider mental/emotional health as their primary concern in their design goal. To study its feasibility in such devices, in our experiment, we use the LifeSnaps dataset, a real-life multimodal dataset that captures physiological and psychological data related to 71 users from various demographic locations. First, we examine several physiological features such as heart rate, oxygen levels, calories burned, and sleep patterns (including light sleep, deep sleep, etc.) in the time domain, as well as some psychological surveys such as PANAS and STAI and emotional state survey collected using SEMA3 mobile app, and try to establish their cohesion using several machine learning models. We achieve a maximum accuracy of 78.75% using random forest. Furthermore, to improve accuracy, we extract additional signal-level features using fast Fourier transformation and apply recursive feature elimination to identify the most relevant features through our proposed methods: (I) selective feature-based approach and (II) holistic feature-based approach. Next, with these enhancements, the machine learning model achieves the highest accuracy of 81.01% using XGBoost. Additionally, we explore two neural network models (bidirectional long short-term memory and FNN (feedforward neural network)) with random oversampling and achieve 97% accuracy with FNN.

Keywords: mental health, depression, smart devices, smartwatch, emotions, physiological data, psychological data, cognitive science, big data

***Corresponding author: Krishnandu Hazra**, IIIT Guwahati, Guwahati, Assam, India, e-mail: krishnandu91@gmail.com

***Corresponding author: Partha Sarathi Paul**, KIIT Bhubaneswar, Bhubaneswar, Odisha, India, e-mail: mtc0113@gmail.com

Partha Pratim Sarmah, Aryan Choudhari, IIIT Guwahati, Assam, India, e-mail: partha.pratim.sarmh@gmail.com, aryanchoudhari09@gmail.com

https://doi.org/10.1515/9783111541235-016

1 Introduction

In the twenty-first century, causes like social rat race, fast-paced lifestyle, increased work pressure in corporate sectors, digital overexposure, etc. are affecting mental health significantly, resulting in rising cases of anxiety, stress, and depression [1]. Conventional therapy and medical treatments remain essential for addressing mental health problems no doubt, but timely detection of such conditions is still a challenge. However, with advancements in wearable smart devices, a new method emerges to monitor health and offers hope for early detection of mental health conditions and symptoms. Wearable smart devices, such as smartwatches, smart bands, and smart rings, all come equipped with a variety of sensors. Core features of these devices include activity tracking, heart rate monitoring, blood pressure monitoring, oxygen level measurement, and GPS tracking.

These wearable devices collect physiological parameters closely related to mental health, as it is already an established fact that emotional and physiological states influence bodily functions. Various body signals, such as heart rate variability, skin conductance, sleep patterns, and brain activity, provide valuable insights into an individual's mental well-being. Understanding these physiological parameters enables the detection of stress, anxiety, depression, and other mental health issues. A crucial aspect of understanding an individual's well-being is detecting their emotional state. A continuously negative emotional state over an extended period indicates early signs of mental health issues [2]. Previous researchers [4–11, 33, 34] used various nonneural and neural network machine learning models to classify emotions. We will discuss this briefly in the literature survey part.

Several professional roles, such as doctors, pilots, and loco pilots, require optimal mental stability during work hours because a single poor decision can lead to life-threatening consequences. Therefore, early detection of an individual's unstable emotional state becomes vital. Numerous research studies focus on this domain, with researchers using various smart devices to predict emotional states. A detailed discussion of existing research in this category appears in Section 2. However, many limitations exist in earlier research. Researchers often develop custom devices, such as headbands, helmets, or heavy medical equipment, to collect physiological data. However, these custom devices tend to be expensive and are typically tested in controlled lab environments rather than real-life conditions.

Hence, we investigate *whether it is feasible to detect human emotions using commercially available smartwatches*. To study this, we explore the LifeSnaps [3] dataset. LifeSnaps data were collected over four months in real-life situations across various geographical locations. The device used in the LifeSnaps dataset is a Fitbit smartwatch, which is a commercially available product. The LifeSnaps dataset contains various physiological features such as heart rate, oxygen level, calories burned, filtered demographic VO_2max, resting heart rate, and step count, among others. We established in our previous study [33] that the physiological data collected using commercially available devices, such as smartwatches, strongly correlate with user-reported mental states and the same can be employed for mental state detection in both nonneural machine learning and neural networks approaches. All the features explored in the said study were in time domain. In this chapter, we would like to explore if the addition of other features could improve the performance. We primarily focus on frequency domain analysis and utilize fast Fourier transformation (FFT) to derive additional features to verify if it improves the machine learning classification performance. We propose two feature selection approaches: (1) *selective feature-based approach* and (2) *holistic feature-based approach* to select the best set of features from a mixed pool of features (existing time domain features from the LifeSnaps and derived frequency domain features), which can enhance emotion classification performance with limited feature set. Using these two approaches, we observed that, among nonneural machine learning methods, SVM improves its accuracy by 7.24% and the highest accuracy achieved by XGBoost, which is 81.01%. However, neural network models surpass the nonneural ML models significantly in both cases.

The rest of the chapter is organized as follows: Section 2 presents the literature survey; Section 3 discusses the methodology we applied in our experiment; Section 4 covers the time-domain and frequency-domain experimental section; and Section 5 concludes the article with a brief mention of the future scope of researches.

2 Literature Survey

Detecting human emotions through various physiological and contextual data has been one of the most fascinating fields in which several researchers have engaged over the last few decades. In recent years, extensive research has focused on detecting human emotions using sensor-based customized devices [4–6], smartphones [7–13], and smartwatches [14–19].

Yu et al. [4] proposed a wearable system to recognize the emotions and motions of individuals while they are wearing it. The wearable device comprises three parts: (a) a hardware system, (b) a software system, and (c) a 3D display platform. The authors mapped the physical, emotional, and environmental contexts of the user in virtual space, utilizing twin technology. They conducted their experimental study using 10 volunteers with an average age of 22.3 years. Similarly, some research works detected emotion from keystrokes. Qi et al. [5] used touch panels to identify emotions. In their experiment, they employed 24 volunteers (12 males and 12 females) for evaluation. Kwon et al. [6] developed a glass-type wearable device that detects emotions using local facial images, EDA (electrodermal activity), and PPG (photoplethysmography). They classified four emotions (fear, happiness, depression, and calm) with an accuracy of 76.09%. The researchers in [10] detected emotions using a smartphone. They created an Android application, Touch Sense, which identifies the user's emotions through touch on a smartphone keyboard. They implemented an experience sampling method (ESM) that distinguishes between typing and swiping modalities and collects touch interaction data and self-reported emotion states. On the other hand, there are many research works [7–10, 12, 13], where the researchers collected various sensor data, such as accelerometer, gyroscope, GPS, screen status, SMS, phone call logs, and typing patterns, to predict emotions through smartphones. However, they did not consider physiological data from participants in their emotion prediction work. To detect stress, Toshnazarov et al. [14] proposed a technique combining physiological and contextual data using smart wearable devices, ECG-based heart rates, and smartphones. This experiment was conducted in both controlled and real-life environments with 26 and 18 participants, respectively. The research in [15] illustrated emotional transitions and states through data collected from smartwatches and smartphones. The researchers employed machine learning techniques to predict the relationships between emotional transitions, states, and contextual information, using the ExtraSensory [20] dataset. Wang et al. [16] utilized the Empatica E4 to design an emotion recognition system. Similarly, in EmoWear [17], a voice messaging app was developed for a smartwatch, featuring 30 animated treasures to express emotions. Shu et al. [18] used heart rate data from a smart bracelet to create an emotion recognition system, collecting data from 25 participants shown emotional video clips. Several studies [14–17] focused on emotions using smartwatches. However, no studies were conducted with a diverse dataset involving many participants over a long period of time using commercially available smartwatches.

FFT and other frequency-domain methods have become vital tools in biomedicine due to their ability to extract meaningful patterns from noisy, nonstationary data. In recent years, researchers have significantly used the Fourier transformation to enhance signal clarity, reveal latent periodic features, and improve classification accuracy. In the domain of EEG-based emotion recognition, many studies demonstrate the utility of FFT. Wang et al. [21] proposed a Fourier adjacency transformer to separate periodic and aperiodic EEG components and enhance inter-channel correlation by using adjacency-based attention mechanisms. This model yields a 6.5% increase in emotion recognition accuracy on the SEED and DEAP datasets. Similarly, Cruz-Vazquez et al. [22] integrated the Fourier neural network with a quantum rotation layer to enhance emotion classification. This research highlighted how frequency-domain preprocessing can improve the performance of convolutional models, particularly in detecting stable emotional states such as sadness. Further, Yang et al. [23] advanced this line of work by developing a DFrT-ES model using the fractional Fourier transform (FrFT), which aids FFT by allowing analysis at varying angles between the time and frequency domains. By extracting features like power spectral density (PSD) and differential entropy (DE), they achieved a classification accuracy of 95.63% on the DEAP dataset. Similarly, several studies demonstrated the effectiveness of FFT in extracting spectral features for emotion recognition using EEG signals. In [24], spectral centroid and entropy features were extracted from EEG using FFT and filtered with Butterworth and surface Laplacian filters. They achieved 91.33% accuracy in classification using *k*-nearest neighbor.

The previous studies have demonstrated impressive results using FFT and machine learning models for EEG-based emotion recognition or biomedical signal analysis. Previous studies primarily depend on controlled, lab-oriented datasets such as DEAP and SEED. These datasets are collected under structured environments with minimal noise and with standard protocols, within limits, for their real-world applicability. In contrast, our approach stands out by experimenting on an in-the-wild dataset collected from real-world environments using a commercial smartwatch, Fitbit Sense, which introduces natural variability, noise, and diverse user behaviors. Applying FFT in such unstructured datasets not only tests the robustness of frequency domain feature extraction but also the generalizability of classical machine learning models in wild conditions. This makes our work more representative of practical applications and demonstrates a crucial step toward deploying emotion recognition systems in real-world scenarios, something most prior studies have not addressed. Thus, our strategy offers a novel contribution by bridging the gap between a controlled research environment and in-the-wild data contexts.

3 Methodology

This section outlines the methodology we employ in our study. Figure 1 illustrates the workflow of our methodology. As depicted in Figure 1, first, we create a customized dataset from the LifeSnaps dataset in the time domain. Next, we perform preprocessing, split the data, and use various machine learning (ML) and neural network models to predict human emotions. Subsequently, we conduct further experiments by extracting additional signal-level features using FFT and merging them with the time-domain features. We apply two approaches (selective feature-based and holistic feature-based) and use various ML models to predict human emotions.

The methodology's layout is as follows: Section 3.1 provides a brief overview of the dataset used in our experiment; Section 3.2 covers feature extraction and preprocessing; Section 3.3 discusses the proposed recursive feature elimination with selective and holistic approaches in both the time domain and the signal domain; Section 3.4 provides a brief overview of ML and neural network models used to classify emotions.

3.1 Dataset Descriptions

As shown in Figure 2, the LifeSnaps dataset, which is approximately 9.72 GB, is collected from various geographical locations between May 2021 and January 2022. We obtain this dataset from Kaggle. To gather LifeSnaps data, the researchers employ commercially available Fitbit smartwatches, the SEMA3 mobile app, and conduct surveys to establish the ground truth. The details of these methods are discussed below:

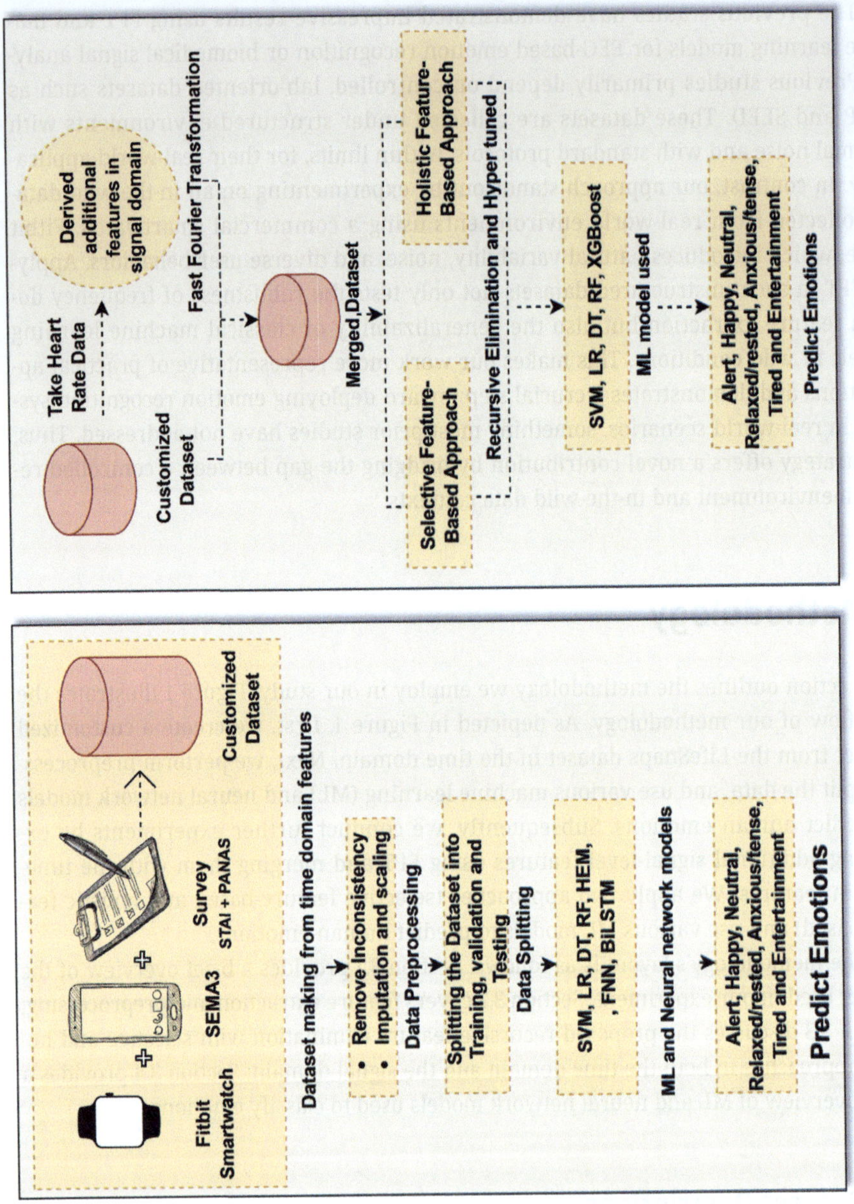

Figure 1: The overview of emotion detection uses time-domain and signal-domain features. The left side shows the process using raw time-domain data, while the right side includes additional signal-domain features derived via FFT. Both approaches involve preprocessing, feature engineering, and model training to predict emotions.

(I) *Fitbit Sense*: A commercially available smartwatch allows individuals to regularly monitor their health-related information, such as heart rate, body temperature, and oxygen level. This device is used to collect physiological data in the LifeSnaps dataset.

(II) *SEMA3*: SEMA3 is a mobile application installed on the participants' smartphones to facilitate regular surveys. Two surveys are conducted: (a) context and mood survey and (b) step goal survey.

(III) *Surveys*: The researchers conduct surveys to gather subjects' psychological and demographic data for ground truth. The demographics, PAR-Q [25], IPIP [26–28], BREQ-2 [29, 30], S-STAI [31], and PANAS [32] are surveys included in the LifeSnaps dataset.

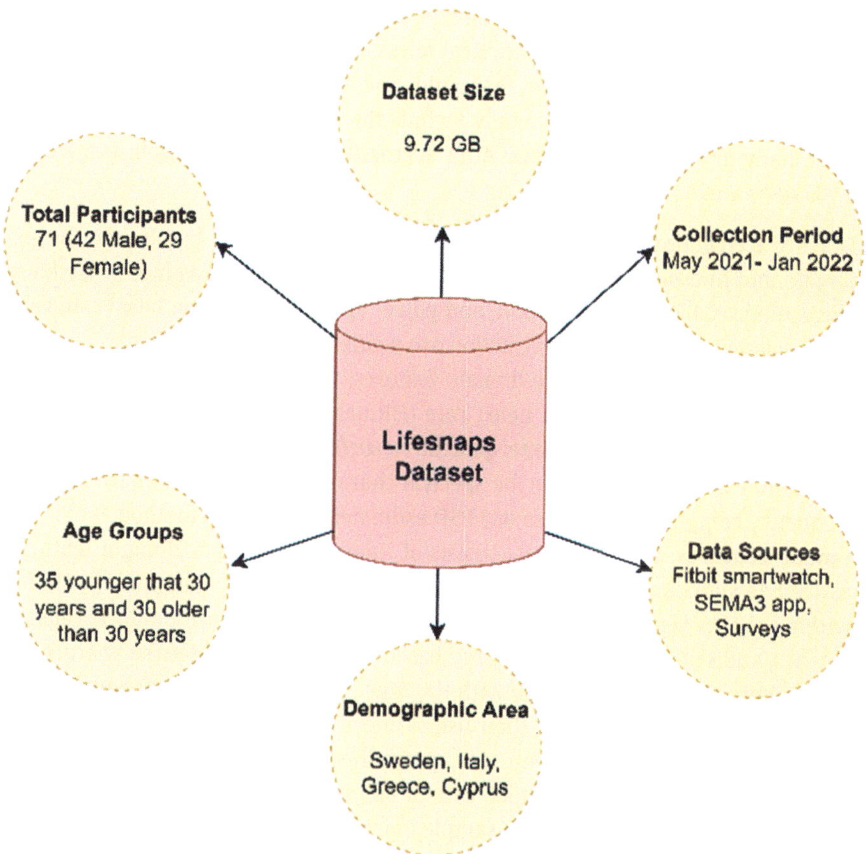

Figure 2: LifeSnaps dataset.

3.2 Feature Extraction and Preprocessing

In this section, we first describe the details of feature extraction in two domains: (I) the time domain and (II) the signal domain. Then, we discuss the preprocessing of the data we consider in our experiment.

(I) Feature Extraction in Time Domain: We merge Fitbit, SEMA3, and survey data to analyze time domain features. We only consider the PANAS and STAI surveys when creating the customized dataset. The PANAS survey measures a person's enthusiastic, alert, and active behavior based on positive and negative affects over a specific period. Higher positive affect indicates a person is highly excited, concentrated, and engaged in pleasurable activities, while lower positive affect reflects sadness and lethargy. Negative affect captures a person's dimensions of subjective distress and unpleasant engagement. Lower negative affect signifies calmness and serenity, while higher negative affect encompasses feelings of anger, fear, guilt, and anxiety. Conversely, the STAI provides anxiety scores. This is why we only include these two surveys, despite the availability of many psychological surveys. After successfully merging the datasets, we obtain 7,435 rows and 82 columns.

(II) Feature Extraction in Signal Domain: To extract additional features in the signal domain and find hidden patterns in physiological data related to emotions, we use statistical analysis, FFT, peak detection, and power spectral density on heart rate variability. The details of the feature extraction are written below step-by-step:

1. **Time Domain**: To extract time domain features, we apply statistical analysis and generate new features: mean heart rate (HRmean), standard deviation (HRstd), minimum and maximum HR, interquartile range (HRIQR), skewness, and kurtosis.
2. **Frequency Domain**: To derive the spectral characteristics, we use FFT to analyze frequency components and also use PSD estimated via Welch's method.
3. **Linear Features**: This category consists of time and frequency domain features, as well as statistical and signal-based measures, assuming some linear relation within the HRV signal. For example, the power spectrum features, autocorrelation metrics, and several slope- and energy-based measures fall under this feature set. While there is some redundancy with the time- and signal-domain features, these features are grouped based on their use of linear analysis models.
4. **Nonlinear Features:** These features capture the intricate, messy, and fractal-like behaviors of the HRV signal, which cannot be reframed using linear models. Popular non-linear measures include sample entropy and approximate entropy, Poincaré plot descriptors (SD1 and SD2), detrended fluctuation analysis (DFA), wavelet entropy, and recurrence quantification metrics. Nonlinear metrics and entropy-based metrics stand out from other linear techniques due to their efficacy in revealing minute shifts in autonomic control and physiological complexity.

5. **Feature Integration and Emotion Selection**: We merge the newly derived features with the customized dataset. We notice that certain emotions very rarely occur in the dataset. For example, sadness, fear, and anger appear only 61, 1, and 2 times, respectively. Therefore, we exclude those emotions from our dataset. As a result, six emotions remain in our dataset: alert, happy, neutral, rested/relaxed, tensed/anxious, and tired.

As shown in Table 1, our extracted features are categorized into time-domain, signal-domain, linear, and nonlinear features. They capture different aspects of the heart rate signal, providing a more holistic view of our data. The newly generated merged dataset contains 7,513 rows and 164 columns.

Table 1: Derived features from heart rate variability (HRV) are categorized into four major domains – time domain, signal domain (frequency domain), linear, and nonlinear – each reflecting different physiological aspects of cardiac autonomic regulation.

Category	Features
Time domain	Mean_bpm, var_bpm, min_bpm, max_bpm, range_bpm, median_bpm, std_bpm, skew bpm, kurtosis_bpm, iqr_bpm, coefficient_variation, rms, signal energy, peak to peak amplitude, num_peaks, time_ above_ mean, time_ below_ mean, autocorr_lag1, autocorr_ lag5, sum_autocorr, adf_pvalue, dfa, sample entropy, Poincare_sd1, Poincare_sd2, poincare area, recurrence rate, determinism, Hjorth_activity, Hjorth_mobility, Hjorth_complexity, first_derivative_mean, first_derivative_std, first_derivative_max, second_derivative_mean, second_derivative_std, second_derivative_max, emotional_stability, max_emotional_shift, zero_crossings, max_rate_of_change, linear trend, quadratic trend
Signal domain	Dominant_freq, dominant_power, peak_power, spectral_centroid, spectral_spread, spectral_rolloff, spectral_flux, spectral_flatness, spectral_entropy, ultra_low_power, low_power, mid_power, high_power, low_high_ratio, ultra_high_ratio, vlf_power, lf _power, hf_power, lf_hf ratio, total_power, wavelet energy 1–6, wavelet ratio 1–6, wavelet entropy 1–6, total_power_log, lf_power_log, hf_power_log, vlf_power_log
Linear	Mean_bpm, var_bpm, min_bpm, max_bpm, range_bpm, median_bpm, std_bpm, skew bpm, kurtosis_bpm, iqr_bpm, coefficient_variation, rms, signal energy, peak_to_peak_amplitude, time_above_mean, time_below_mean, auto_corr_lag1, autocorr_lag5, sum_autocorr, adf_pvalue, dominant_freq, dominant_power, peak_power, spectral centroid, spectral spread, spectral_rolloff, spectral_flux, spectral_flatness, spectral_entropy, ultra _low_power, low_power, mid_power, high_power, low_high_ratio, ultra_high_ratio, vlf_ power, lf_power, hf_power, lf_hf_ratio, total power, Hjorth_activity, Hjorth_mobility, Hjorth_complexity, first_derivative_mean, first_derivative_std, first_derivative_max, second_derivative_mean, second_derivative_std, second_derivative_max, emotional_stability, max_emotional_shift, zero_crossings, max_rate_of_change, linear_trend, quadratic trend, wavelet energy 1–6, wavelet ratio 1–6, to tal_power log, lf power log, hf power log, vlf power log
Nonlinear	dfa, sample entropy, poincare_sd1, poincare_sd2, poincare area, recurrence rate, determinism, wavelet entropy 1–6

Data Preprocessing: We conduct extensive preprocessing on the customized dataset before applying any machine learning or neural network models. The preprocessing is divided into four parts: (I) data analysis in time domain, (II) data analysis in signal domain, (III) data cleaning, and (IV) data imputation and scaling, as follows:

(I) Data Analysis in Time Domain: As depicted in Figure 3, we observe that the distribution of the collected data is uneven over the collected months and year. The maximum and minimum numbers of data entries occur in July 2021 and April 2021, respectively. As per the description of the LifeSnaps dataset, data is collected in two rounds: in the first round, 38 participants contribute data from May 24 to July 26, 2021, while in the second round, 34 participants contribute data from November 15, 2021 to January 17, 2022. One participant is common to both rounds, making the total number of unique participants 71. However, Figure 3 shows that some data is also collected outside the specified study periods, namely during April, August, September, and October 2021.

(II) Data Analysis in Signal Domain: To validate whether the newly generated features provide new information, we generate characteristic graphs for different users. Here, we show the time-domain and signal-domain features of four users in Figures 4 and 5. In Figure 4, we observe the dominant frequency components present in the signals. The VLF (very low frequency) dominates across all users, highlighting its significant frequency band. User 2 shows the highest power overall, especially in the VLF range. All four users display similar patterns but with different power levels, indicating individual variability. This transformation allows us to identify recurring patterns that may help link physiological parameters to emotional states.

In Figure 5, we illustrate the dynamic variability in the data, which associates with autonomic nervous system activity. The spread and shape of the plots describe how physiological responses fluctuate over time. User 1 shows more dispersed points, indicating higher variability in heart rate and RR intervals, potentially reflecting more dynamic heart rate behavior. User 2 shows denser and tighter points, suggesting a more regular and stable heart rhythm with less short-term variability. User 3 shows moderate variability with a balanced rhythm, and user 4 shows high consistency with low short-term variation.

From the observation, we now say that frequency-based features provide additional discriminative power. These features enhance emotion classification models by revealing underlying periodicities that are not as apparent in the raw time-domain signal. The graphical observation supports the feasibility of incorporating signal domain features into predictive modeling, potentially leading to improved accuracy in emotion recognition systems.

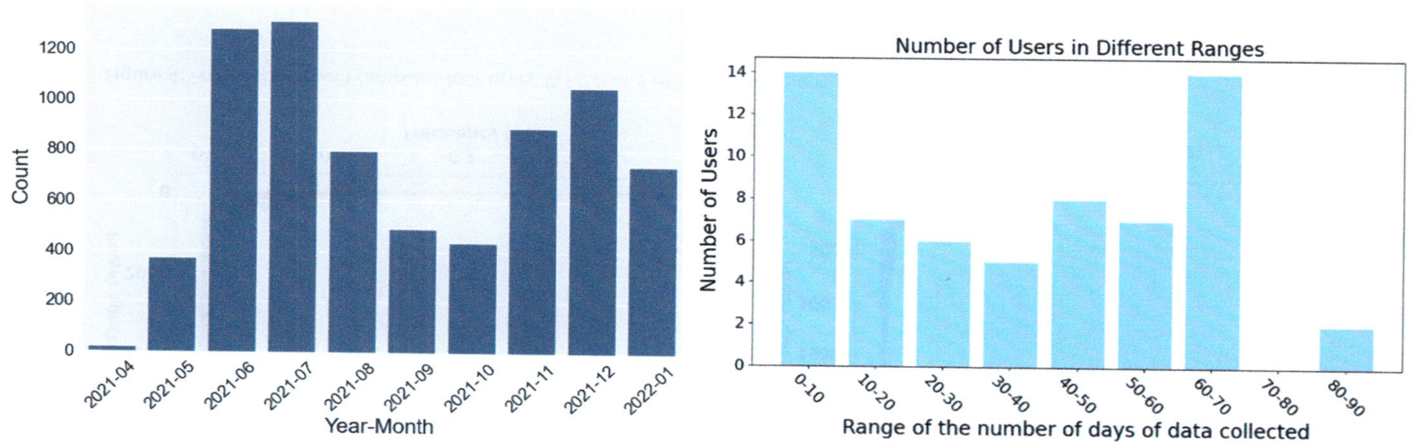

Figure 3: Analyze participants' activity levels during the survey period and observe variation in data collection. Fourteen individuals participate extensively for 60–70 days, while only a few contribute data for 0–10 days.

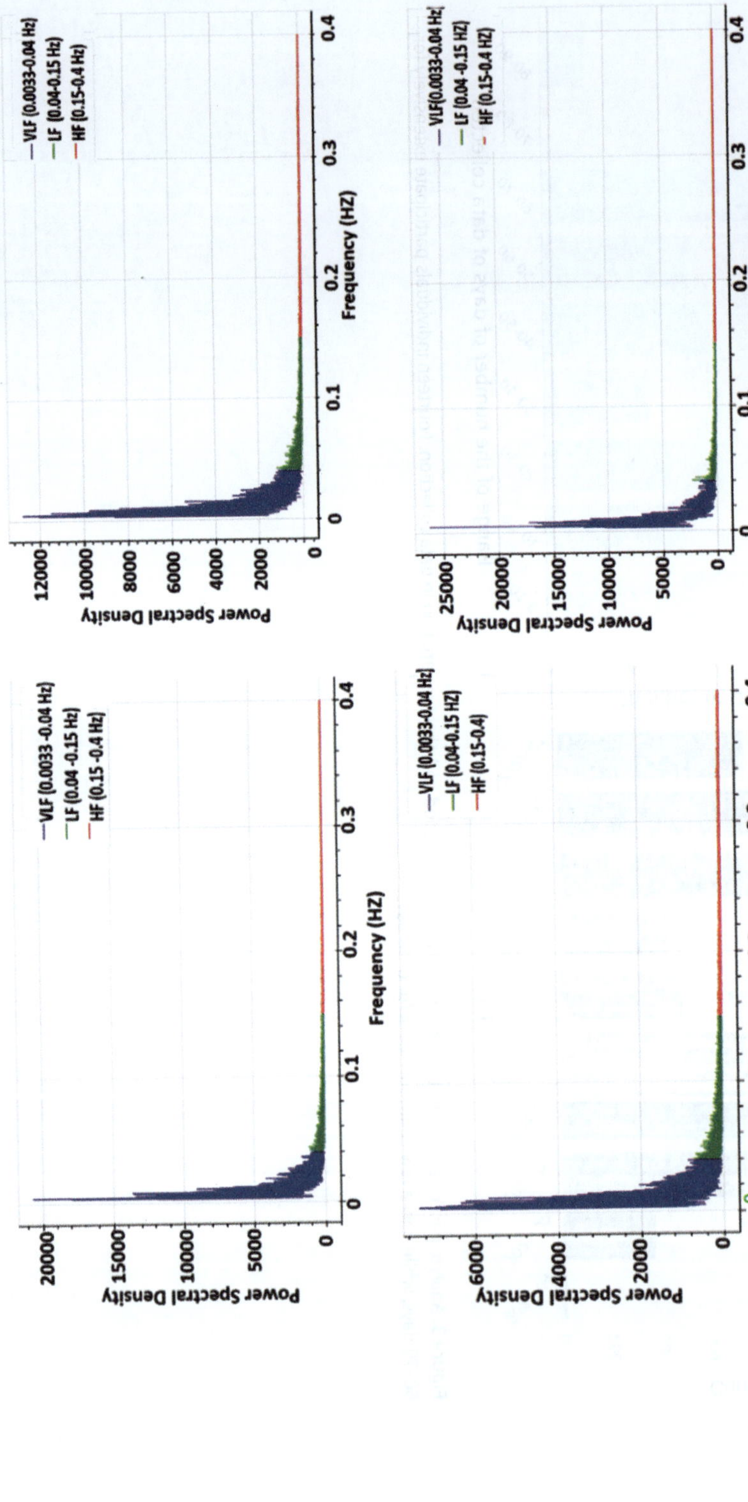

Figure 4: Frequency domain compares four users' VLF, LF, and HF heart rate components via power spectral density.

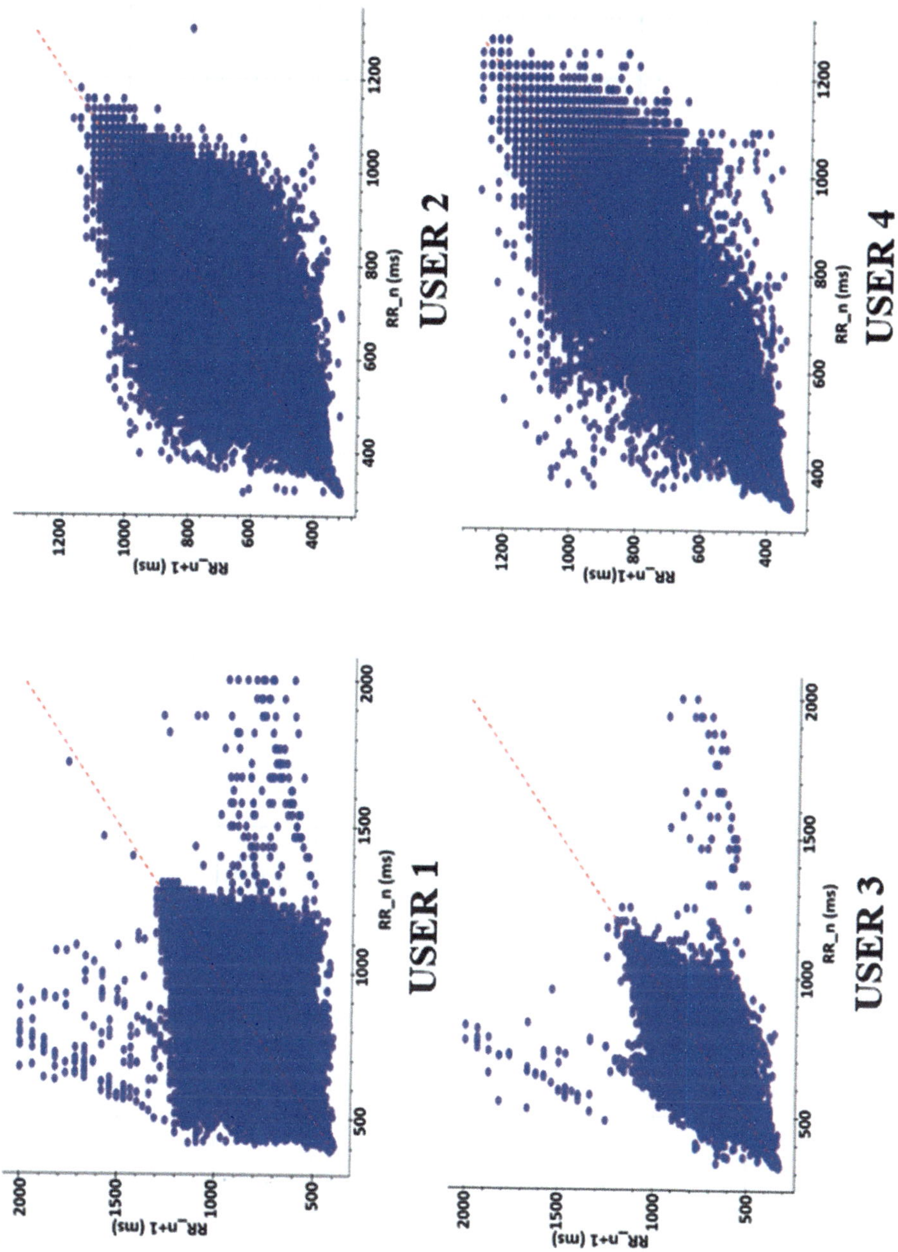

Figure 5: Time domain compares four users using Poincaré plots, highlighting individual differences in heart rate variability and autonomic regulation.

(III) Data Cleaning: We remove all the unnecessary features from our dataset. As an example, stai stress category and stai stress are available in the dataset. But if we observe, we can see that stai stress category is derived from stai stress.

(IV) Data Imputation and Scaling: We impute numerical values using the median, while we fill time-series data using a forward/backward fill strategy. Emotions and activity-related data are imputed with the help of the KNN fill-up method, as their granularity is different from the numerical data. After that, we use min-max scaling.

3.3 Recursive Feature Elimination

We use recursive feature elimination (RFE) to find the most essential features and remove the unnecessary ones. As shown in Figure 6, We implement two different approaches, which are (I) selective feature-based approach and (II) holistic feature-based approach.

(I) Selective Feature-Based Approach: As shown in Figure 6, In this approach, we divide the features into two groups: the time domain and the signal domain. RFE selects the features separately from each group using an XGBoost classifier as the best estimator. This approach selects three features from the time domain and three features from the signal domain, and in each subsequent iteration, the number of features increases incrementally until it reaches the maximum available features in each group. After each iteration, the selected features and ranking update. The updated features list then serves as input for the next generation.

(II) Holistic Feature-Based Approach: In the holistic feature-based approach as shown in Figure 6, we directly work on all the derived features without grouping them. In this approach, we iteratively remove three features in each iteration to find the best relevant features with emotions. In each iteration, the RFE with XGBoost classifier selects a subset of features equal to $n\_selected = n\_current - 3$, where $n\_selected$ is the number of features available at the start of the iteration. That means here, we remove the three least significant features recursively. The process continues until the predefined number of iterations is reached or a minimal subset of features remains.

3.4 Machine Learning and Neural Network Models

We use several ML and neural network models to predict emotions. They are support vector machine (SVM), logistic regression (LR), decision tree (DT), random forest (RF), XGBoost, hybrid machine learning model (HMM), feedforward neural network (FNN), and bidirectional long short-term memory (BiLSTM). The details about the implementation are discussed in Section 4.

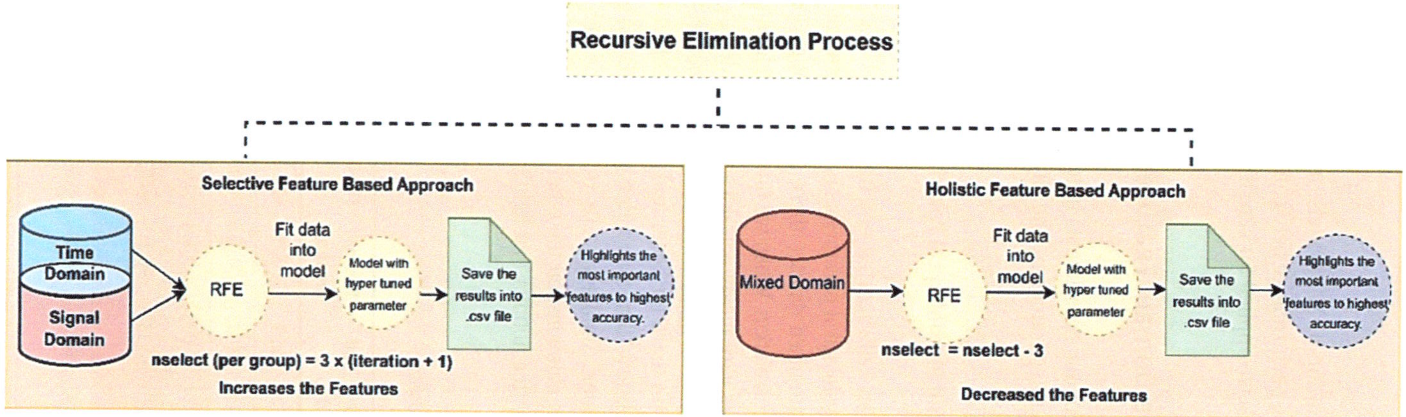

Figure 6: Selective and holistic feature-based approaches evaluate features separately and jointly, respectively, to identify the most effective for model training.

4 Results and Discussion

In this section, we first discuss the implementation of ML models on both the time domain and the signal domain and compare the performance between them. Then we discuss the neural network classification models we applied for classification.

4.1 Prediction of Emotion Using Time-Domain Features

In this subsection, we demonstrate the findings of our experiments in two parts: (I) correlation between emotional states and physiological parameters, and (II) ML models.

4.1.1 Correlation Between Emotional States and Physiological Parameters

This section examines the relationship between self-reported emotional states (e.g., happy, sad, neutral, and relaxed) and various physiological parameters (such as bpm, calories burned, and resting heart rate). In our customized dataset, there are a total of 80 features, where ID and date are removed in the correlation. When we find the correlation between physiological data and emotions, it looks very messy and does not provide any good insight, so we only show the most significant features correlated with the emotions in Table 2. We take the correlation range from −0.4 to 0.6 for better and clearer visibility of patterns among the data. From Table 2, we observe that filtereddemographicVO$_2$max and resting heart rate show the highest correlation. Similarly, steps, distance, and very_active_minutes show very low correlation with emotions; on the other hand, bpm and sedentary_minutes show a positive correlation with emotions, and lightly_active_minutes show a negative correlation.

Table 2: Correlation between physiological data and emotions.

Physiological data/ emotions	Alert	Happy	Neutral	Rested/ relaxed	Sad	Tense/ anxious	Tired	Entertainment
Bpm	0.27	−0.097	−0.056	0.23	−0.29	−0.16	-2e-05	0.0096
Calories	−0.089	0.21	−0.1	−0.042	−0.043	0.016	−0.08	0.0093
Distance	−0.27	0.29	−0.13	−0.087	0.033	0.044	−0.058	0.016
FilteredDemographic-VO$_2$max	0.59	−0.32	0.054	0.21	−0.33	−0.21	−0.03	0.087
Lightly_active_-minutes	−0.4	0.3	−0.096	−0.19	0.2	0.19	−0.065	−0.048

Table 2 (continued)

Physiological data/ emotions	Alert	Happy	Neutral	Rested/ relaxed	Sad	Tense/ anxious	Tired	Entertainment
Moderately_active_-minutes	−0.23	0.24	−0.073	−0.073	0.04	−0.026	−0.047	0.044
Very_active_minutes	−0.24	0.24	−0.069	−0.04	−0.02	−0.051	0.024	−0.044
Sedentary_minutes	0.18	−0.16	0.05	0.18	−0.16	−0.14	−0.011	0.04
Resting_hr	0.58	−0.31	−0.012	0.19	−0.28	−0.17	−0.036	0.057
Steps	−0.29	0.3	−0.13	−0.097	0.039	0.047	−0.051	0.012

Note that the yellow color represents the highest correlation, and the green color represents very low correlation.

4.1.2 Machine Learning Models

We present our results related to emotional state prediction from physiological and survey data. The ML algorithms that we use are: *(I) SVM, (II) LR, (III) DT, and (IV) RF.* After that, to improve the accuracy, we propose a (v) *hybrid machine learning model* that combines the predictive strengths of four classifiers. We first apply feature weighting based on the correlation as in Table 2. From the correlation, we find that *filteredDemographicVO*$_2$*max* and *resting_hr* show the highest correlation. Features with weaker correlation are either left unweighted or assigned a lower weight. Next, we divide the dataset into three parts: training, validation, and testing, with a ratio of 60:20:20. Below, we provide details about all the ML algorithms we apply.

(I) **SVM:** The SVM classifier uses to evaluate its effectiveness in classifying the dataset. The model achieves a testing accuracy of 72.56%.

(II) **LR:** Using the LR class from the sklearn library with the liblinear solver, the model trains on the dataset and achieves an accuracy of 74.11%.

(III) **DT:** Initially, the DT model provides a test accuracy of 72.43%. To enhance its performance, we adjust the maximum depth of the tree. A plot of training and validation curves reveals that they align closely up to a maximum depth of 4 (as shown in Figure 7). Setting the tree's maximum depth to 4 yields an improved accuracy of 74.92%.

(IV) **RF**: The RF model initially achieves a test accuracy of 78.01%. To further enhance performance, we conduct hyperparameter tuning using RandomizedSearchCV. This process explores a variety of parameters, including the number of estimators (n_estimators), maximum depth (max_depth), minimum samples required for splits (min_samples_split), minimum samples per leaf (min_samples_leaf), and others. After tuning, the model's accuracy improves slightly to 78.75%.

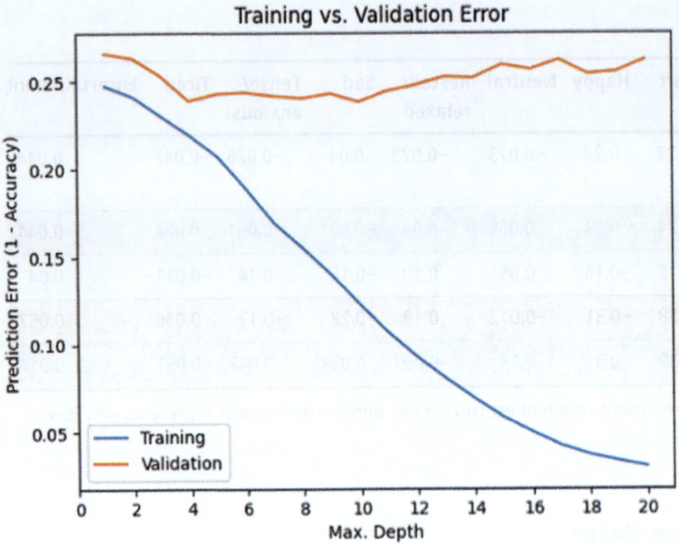

Figure 7: Training versus validation error.

(V) **Hybrid ML Model**: The hybrid model leverages four distinct classifiers: SVM, LR, DT, and RF. These models combine using a soft voting ensemble approach, which integrates the probabilistic predictions from each base model to determine the final classification output. The details about the implementation appear in Table 3.

Table 3: Implementation details of the hybrid machine learning model.

Classifier	Soft Voting	Performance
SVM for high-dimensional and non-linear data; logistic regression for linear separability with probabilities; decision tree for nonlinear rules; random forest for improved stability.	Each model predicts class probabilities; the final prediction uses the averaged probability, and the class with the highest value is selected.	Training accuracy: 97.65%; validation: 74.78%; test: 73.77%.

Improved Accuracy Through Hyperparameter Tuning: The hybrid model initially achieves an accuracy of 73.77%, which is lower than the accuracy achieved by the individual RF (78.75%) model. To improve the accuracy of the ensemble model, we implement hyperparameter tuning for each base model, focusing on the most impactful parameters that influence model complexity and generalization. The details about this appear in Table 4.

The hybrid ML models and hyper-tuned models do not show any improvement in the prediction accuracy compared to the RF model.

Table 4: Hyperparameter tuning details of base classifiers in the hybrid model.

Classifier	Tuned parameters	Values tested
Support vector machine	- C (Regularization)	- [0.1, 1, 10]
	- Kernel	- ['linear','rbf']
	- Gamma (RBF kernel)	- ['scale','auto']
	- Max iterations	- [1000,2000]
Logistic regression	- C (Regularization)	- [0.1, 1, 10]
	- Solver	- ['lbfgs', 'liblinear']
	- Max iterations	- [1000, 2000]
Decision tree	- Max depth	- [None, 10, 20, 30]
	- Min samples split	- [2, 5, 10]
	- Min samples leaf	- [1, i, 4]
Random forest	- Number of estimators	- [100, 200]
	- Max depth	- [None, 10, 20]
	- Min sample split	- [2, 5, 10]
Tuning method: GridSearchCV with 5-fold cross-validation		
Performance (after tuning): Training accuracy: 90.99%, validation: 77.94%, test: 77.54%		

4.2 Prediction of Emotion Using Signal-Domain Features

In this section, similar to the time domain, we experiment on derived signal-domain features to increase the classification accuracy of the emotions. The details about the implementation appear below:

Machine Learning Models: We use the selective feature-based and the holistic feature-based approaches to find out the finest features for classification. We already discussed these two algorithms in Section 3. During feature selection, we also try different hyperparameter tuning to find the best results from the models. The details about the hyperparameter tuning appear below:

Hyperparameter Tuning: We hyper-tune the model using grid search and randomized search to optimize the model's performance. Grid search exclusively searches over a set of predefined hyperparameters to find the best combination, while randomized search samples from a range of values, offering faster tuning with less computational cost. The tuning process also involves *k*-fold cross-validation (here we use 5-fold) to maintain the class distribution. The hyperparameter tuning does not affect the LR, SVM, and LightGBM improvements. The details of the hyperparameter tuning for DT, RF, and XGBoost appear in Table 5.

Table 5: Details about the hyperparameter tuning model.

Model name	Hyperparameter tuning
Decision tree	– **Max depth**: None, 5, 20, 15,20, 25, 30. – **Min_samples_split and min_sample_leaf**: several candidate values were tested. – **Criterion:** Evaluated both 'gini' and 'entropy.' – **Class weight**: None, balanced.
Random forest	– **N_estimators**: 100, 200, 300, and 500. – **Max_depth**: None, 10, 20, 30. – **Min_samples_split and min_samples_leaf**: Several small integer values were tested. bootstrap and max features: Evaluated settings include auto,' 'sqrt,', and 'log2.'
XGBoost	– **N_estimators**: Ranging from 100 to 500. – **Max_depth**: Between 3 and 9. – **Learning rate**: Between 0.01 and 0.3. – **Subsample, colsample_bytree, min child weight, and gamma:** Multiple candidate values were tested.

4.2.1 Selective Feature-Based Approach

This approach gives us the optimum feature set containing 96 features, which maximizes our ML accuracy. We get 81.01% accuracy, whereas in our previous study, only the time domain gives us the best accuracy of 78.75%. The details about the result of the selective feature-based approach appear in Table 6. In Figure 8, we observe that XGBoost obtains the highest accuracy with 96 features. Similarly, the RF model achieves the highest accuracy between 80 features and 90 features; conversely, the DT shows the worst performance and picks its accuracy around 70–80 features.

Holistic Feature-Based Approach: The detailed result of the holistic feature-based approach appears in Table 7. Figure 9 demonstrates the accuracy versus the number of features for XGBoost, RF, and DT. From the figure, we observe that RF and XGBoost perform the highest, i.e., 79.89%.

We observe in Figure 9 that XGBoost shows stable performance, improving up to 140 features. RF improves with features but shows fluctuations after 100 features – DT shows the worst performance, with high variability and a maximum accuracy of 77.65%.

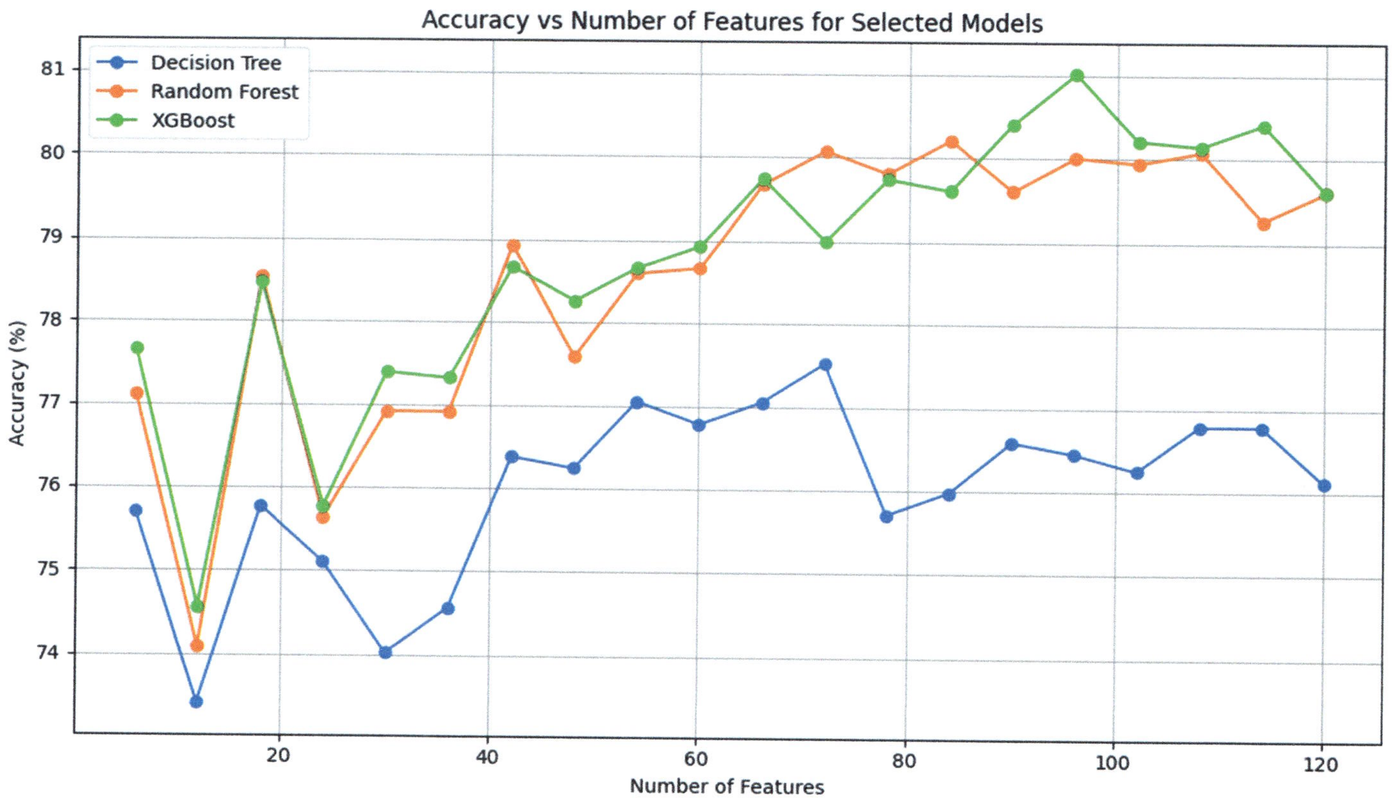

Figure 8: Impact of selected feature count on accuracy in the selective approach, showing how subsets affect model performance to find the optimum set.

Table 6: Accuracy obtained by models using the selective feature-based approach.

Model	Accuracy (%)	Precision	Recall	F1score
DT	77.51%	0.74	0.77	0.74
RF	80.20%	0.76	0.80	0.77
XGBoost	81.01%	0.77	0.81	0.78

Table 7: Model accuracy performance on holistic feature-based approach.

Model	Accuracy (%)	Precision	Recall	F1-score
DT	77.62%	0.74	0.77	0.75
RF	79.89%	0.75	0.79	0.75
XGBoost	79.89%	0.75	0.79	0.77

4.3 Comparison Between Time-Domain and Signal-Domain ML Models

We compare our previously applied method with our new approach in the mixed domain. In Figure 10, we graphically demonstrate the model's performance in different approaches. We observe that SVM and LR show a clear improvement in accuracy when derived features (especially from the signal domain) are used – SVM jumps from 72.56% to 79.80%, and LR from 74.11% to 77.65%. DT, RF, and XGBoost models also benefit from the mixed domain approaches. XGBoost shows 81.01% with the selective feature-based approach, indicating this approach captures some more useful patterns. In both groups, the baseline time-domain features perform the worst, highlighting the value of enhanced feature engineering. In feature engineering, the FFT extracts frequency-based characteristics from signals, revealing hidden periodicities and noise patterns that time-domain features may miss. The recursive feature elimination systematically helps remove irrelevant and redundant features, ensuring our models focus only on the most informative inputs that boost classification. So, we observe that our new approach helps us improve our prediction accuracy.

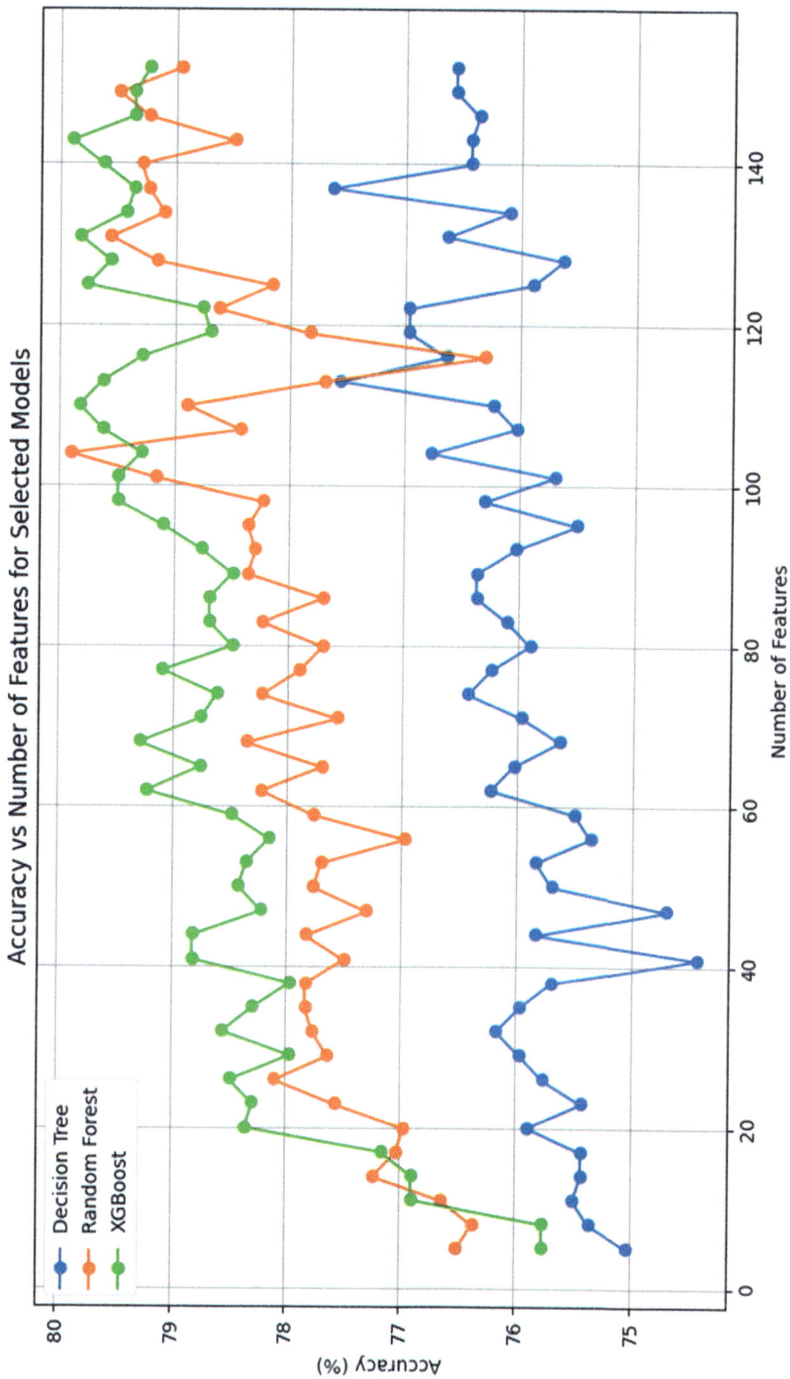

Figure 9: Relationship between the number of selected features and classification accuracy in the holistic feature-based approach, highlighting the feature subset that achieves optimal performance.

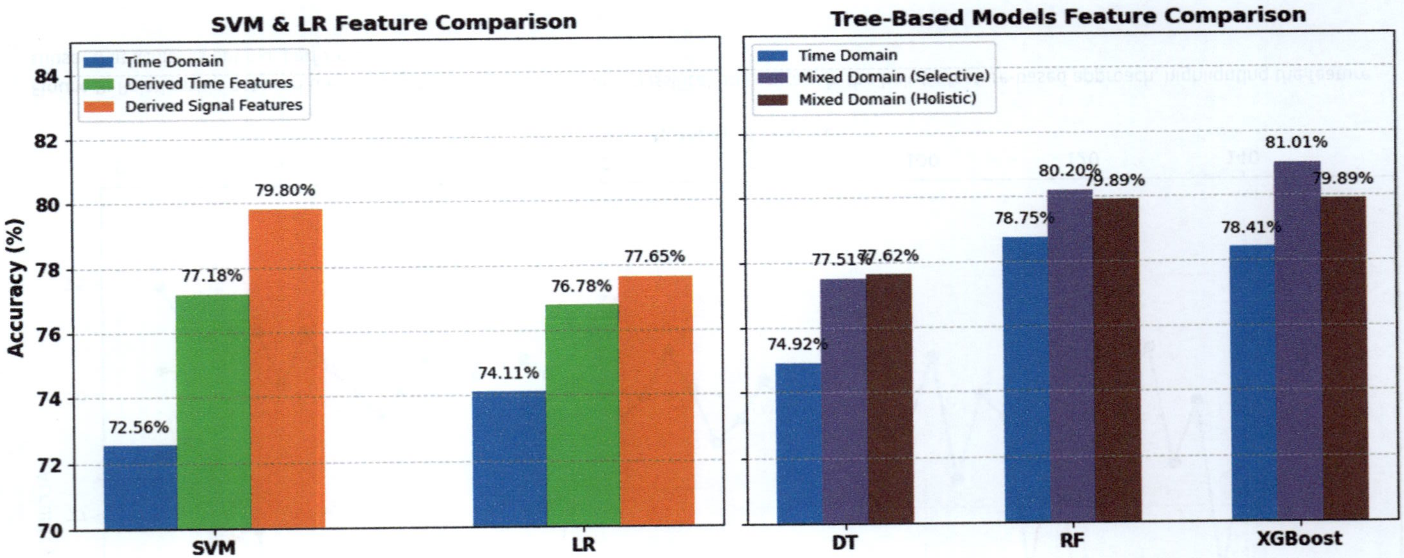

Figure 10: Left: Comparison of model performance using our proposed time-domain and signal-domain features versus previous work that relied solely on raw time-domain data. Right: Performance comparison between our selective and holistic approaches on mixed-domain features and the baseline from previous work.

4.4 Neural Network Models

In this section, we explore the neural network (NN) models in time-domain features to further improve the accuracy of the emotion classification model. We use two NN models: FNN and BiLSTM.

The FNN model initially gives 77.47% testing accuracy. Similarly, BiLSTM gives 72.23%. Then we try a different approach where we first balance the dataset using the random oversampling method. After that, we train the ML and NN models. We observe that only LightGBM improves its accuracy using random oversampling, but other ML models show degrading results compared to their previous performance. The detail about the accuracy is shown in Figure 11. Figure 12 shows a model-wise comparison of accuracy performance. XGBoost recorded an accuracy of 81.01%, which is the highest among the machine learning models. Among the neural network models, the Feedforward Neural Network (FNN) is the best performer with an accuracy of 97%.

The detailed NN model approach is given below:

Preprocessing: We do the necessary preprocessing before fitting the data into the models. We remove unnecessary columns from the dataset before feature selection and encode the target columns into numeric values using LabelEncoder. Then, we use StandardScaler to normalize the features. It helps the model run faster during the training time. We use SelectKBest with a score function (f_classif) to select the top 60 features from the dataset for feature selection. We split the data into training, validation, and testing parts.

Feedforward Neural Network (FNN): We build the FNN architecture with three hidden layers containing different neurons. The first hidden layer contains 512 neurons, the second layer contains 256, and the third hidden layer contains 128 neurons. In the first hidden layer, we use the leaky ReLU activation function, and on the output layer, we choose the Softmax activation function. We use the Adam optimizer with a learning rate of 0.00005 and categorical cross-entropy as the loss function. We define a very low learning rate so that it helps smooth convergence during training. If for 10 consecutive epochs there is no improvement, then we automatically run early stopping. We run different epochs from 100 to 1,000 to know their accuracy. This model gives the highest accuracy at 600 epochs, 97%.

Bidirectional Long Short-Term Memory (BiLSTM): The BiLSTM model performs best when we use a two-hidden-layer configuration, where the first hidden layer contains 128 neurons and the second hidden layer contains 64 neurons. We set a 50% dropout rate to avoid overfitting. We get the best accuracy at 800 epochs, which is 96.12%.

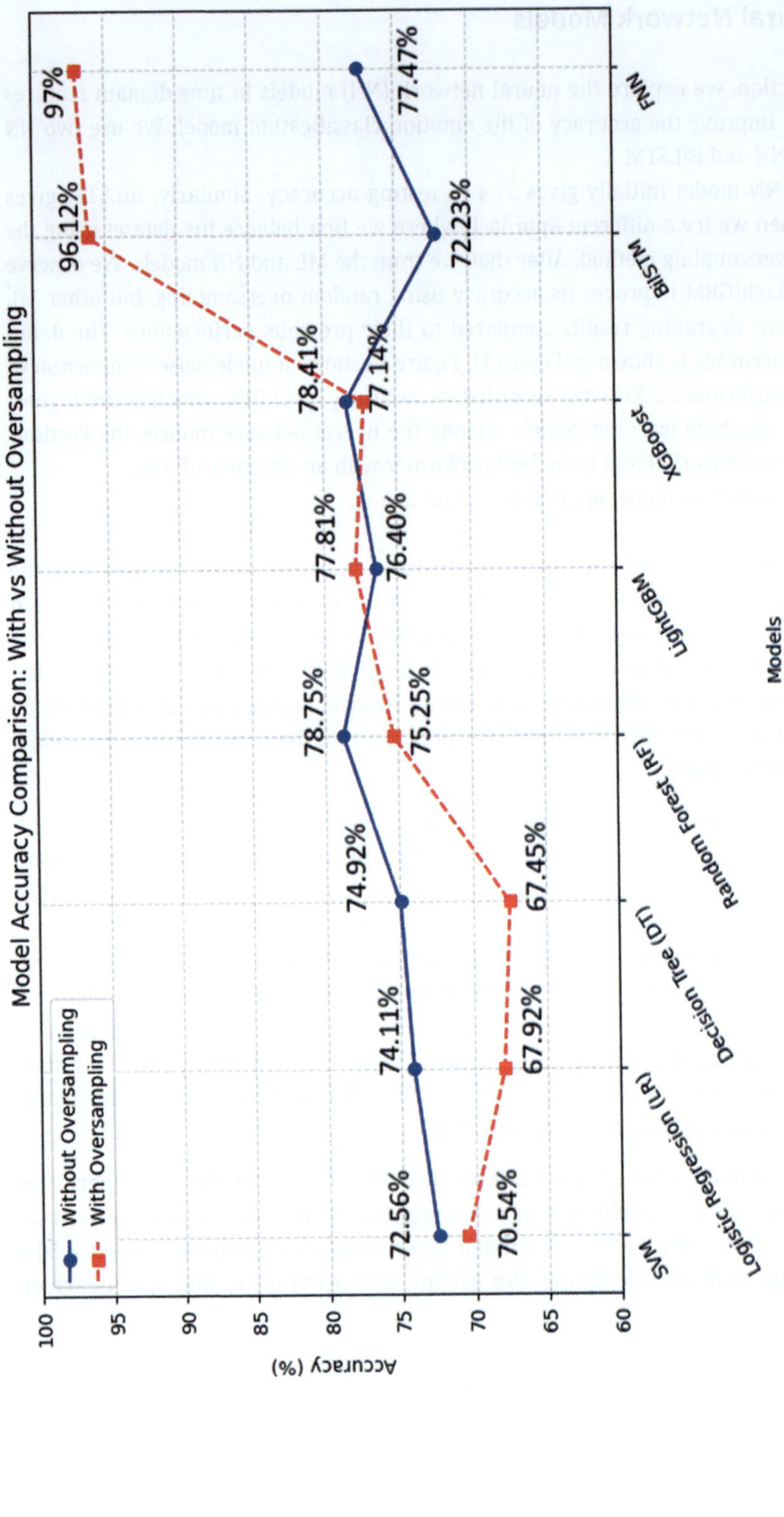

Figure 11: Effect of oversampling on model performance.

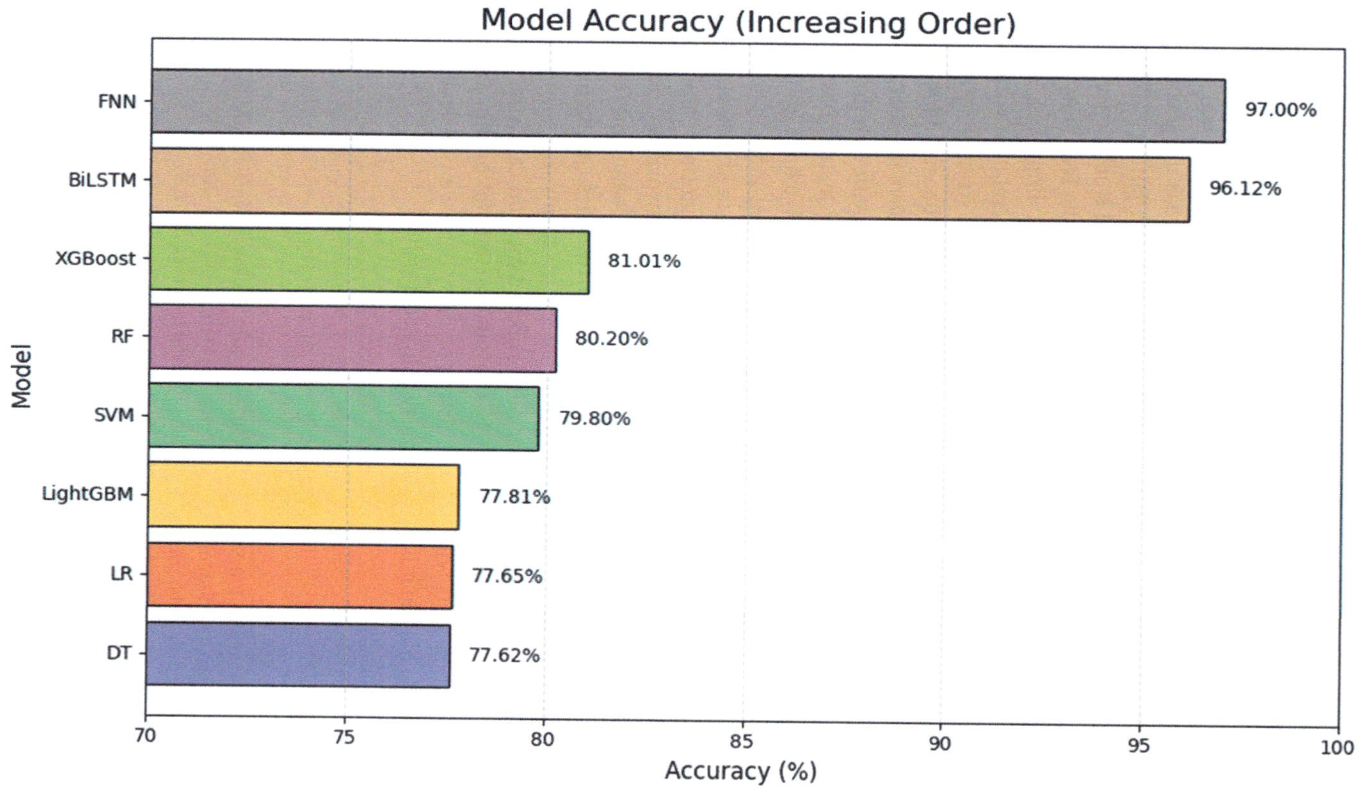

Figure 12: Classification accuracy of various models. Neural network-based approaches significantly outperform traditional machine learning models, with FNN achieving the highest test accuracy (97%), followed by BiLSTM (96.12%).

5 Conclusion

In this work, we have analyzed and predicted emotional states using various physiological data collected using commercial smartwatches. We have utilized the LifeSnaps public dataset, which contained physiological sensor data and psychological survey data collected from 71 volunteers from different demographic areas using commercially available Fitbit Sense smartwatches between May 2021 and January 2022. We have analyzed the dataset and have performed a correlation-based study between the physiological data and self-reported emotional states to establish the feasibility of the current research. From the correlation, we have found that bpm, resting hr, filteredDemographicVO$_2$max, and calories have shown a higher correlation with emotions. We have adjusted the weights according to the correlation strength. We have applied six different ML algorithms (SVM, LR, DT, LightGBM, XGBoost, and RF) and have achieved the highest accuracy of 78.75% using RF. Then, we have used signal domain features and have utilized recursive feature elimination with two proposed methods, the selective feature-based approach and the holistic feature-based approach, to select the optimal features for the classification model. We have found that out of 164 features, 96 features have best suited the classification model and from those features, our prediction accuracy has increased from 78.75% to 81.01%. Next, we have applied the neural network-based method to predict emotions and have achieved the highest accuracy of 97% using the deep neural network. So, our proposed approach has systematically helped remove irrelevant and redundant features. Our research has shown that commercially available smartwatches can monitor an individual's emotional state using a smartwatch.

In the future, we will evaluate whether our proposed method can work effectively in commercially available smartwatches to monitor mental health. Second, since most real-world datasets will contain missing or noisy data, we will develop an improved algorithm to handle missing and noisy data accurately.

References

[1] Prakash, J., Ali, T., Chaudhury, S. & Srivastava, K. (2023, Jul–Dec). Declining mental health: An aftermath of fast-paced urbanization. Industrial Psychiatry Journal, 32(2), 199–201.

[2] Joormann, J. & Siemer, M. (2014). Emotion regulation in mood disorders. 413–427.

[3] Yfantidou, S., Karagianni, C., Efstathiou, S., Vakali, A., Palotti, J., Giakatos, D. P., Marchioro, T., Kazlouski, A., Ferrari, E. & Girdzijauskas, ˇS. (2022). LifeSnaps, a 4-month multi-modal dataset capturing unobtrusive snapshots of our lives in the wild. Scientific Data, 9(1), 663.

[4] Yu, F., Yu, C., Tian, Z., Liu, X., Cao, J., Liu, L., Du, C. & Jiang, M. (2024). Intelligent wearable system with motion and emotion recognition based on digital twin technology. IEEE Internet of Things Journal.

[5] Qi, Y., Jia, W., Feng, L., Dai, Y., Tang, C., Zhou, F. & Gao, S. (2024). Piezoelectric touch sensing and random-forest-based technique for emotion recognition. IEEE Transactions on Computational Social Systems.

[6] Kwon, O. Y., Lee, S. H. & Park, K. R. (2021). Emotion recognition using a glass-type wearable device. Sensors, 21(5), 1786.

[7] Olsen, P. A., Kuerbis, A. & Muench, F. (2016). Smartphone-based monitoring of mental health: Development and feasibility of a mobile sensing app in psychiatric care. Journal of Medical Internet Research, 18(6), e156.

[8] Chow, P. I., Fua, K., Huang, Y., Bonelli, W., Xiong, H., Barnes, L. E. & Teachman, B. A. (2017). Using mobile sensing to test clinical models of depression, social anxiety, state affect, and social isolation among college students. Journal of Medical Internet Research, 19(3), e62.

[9] Zhang, X., Li, W., Chen, X. & Lu, S. (2018). Moodexplorer: Towards compound emotion detection via smartphone sensing. Proceedings of the ACM on Interactive, Mobile, Wearable and Ubiquitous Technologies, 1(4), 1–30.

[10] Ghosh, S., Hiware, K., Ganguly, N., Mitra, B. & De, P. (2019). Emotion detection from touch interactions during text entry on smartphones. International Journal of Human-Computer Studies, 130, 47–57.

[11] Hashmi, M. F., Katiyar, S., Keskar, A. G., Bokde, N. D. & Geem, Z. W. (2020). Motion sensors-based human activity recognition using deep learning and the ovis methodology. Sensors, 20(21), 6176.

[12] Wu, C. H. & Yan, G. L. (2021). Improving emotion recognition using data augmentation and competitions between deep neural networks. Sensors, 21(10), 3465.

[13] Asare, K. O., Terhorst, Y., Vega, J., Peltonen, E., Lagerspetz, E. & Ferreira, D. (2021). Predicting emotions from mobile phone usage patterns. International Journal of Human-Computer Studies, 145, 102548.

[14] Toshnazarov, K., Lee, U., Kim, B. H., Mishra, V., Najarro, L. A. C. & Noh, Y. (2024). Sosw: Stress sensing with off-the-shelf smartwatches in the wild. IEEE Internet of Things Journal.

[15] Sultana, M., Al-Jefri, M. & Lee, J. (2020). Using machine learning and smartphone and smartwatch data to detect emotional states and transitions: exploratory study. JMIR mHealth and uHealth, 8(9), e17818.

[16] Wang, Z., Yu, Z., Zhao, B., Guo, B., Chen, C. & Yu, Z. (2020). Emotionsense: An adaptive emotion recognition system based on wearable smart devices. ACM Transactions on Computing for Healthcare, 1(4), 1–17.

[17] An, P., Zhu, J. S., Zhang, Z., Yin, Y., Ma, Q., Yan, C., Du, L. & Zhao, J. (2024). Emowear: Exploring emotional teasers for voice message interaction on smartwatches. Proceedings of the CHI Conference on Human Factors in Computing Systems, 1–16.

[18] Shu, L., Yu, Y., Chen, W., Hua, H., Li, Q., Jin, J. & Xu, X. (2020). Wearable emotion recognition using heart rate data from a smart bracelet. Sensors, 20(3), 718.

[19] Fauzi, M. A. & Yang, B. (2021). Continuous stress detection of hospital staff using smartwatch sensors and classifier ensemble. pHealth 2021, 245–250.

[20] Vaizman, Y., Ellis, K. & Lanckriet, G. (2018). Extrasensory app: Data collection in-the-wild with rich user interface to self-report behavior. CHI Conference on Human Factors in Computing Systems, 1–12.

[21] Wang, J., Huang, Y., Song, S., Wang, B., Su, J. & Ding, J. A novel fourier adjacency transformer for advanced eeg emotion recognition. arXiv preprintarXiv:2503.13465, 2025.

[22] Cruz-Vazquez, J. A., Montiel-Pérez, J. Y., Romero-Herrera, R. & Rubio-Espino, E. (2025). Emotion recognition from eeg signals using advanced transformations and deeplearning. Mathematics, 13(2), 254.

[23] Yang, S., Wang, W., Mao, P., Xu, L. & Feng, L. (2025). Dfrft-es model for emotion recognition based on fractional fourier transform of eeg signals. Fourth International Conference on Computer Vision, Application, and Algorithm (CVAA 2024), 13486, 50–55, pages.

24] Murugappan, M. & Murugappan, S. (2013). Human emotion recognition through short time electroencephalogram (eeg) signals using fast fourier transform (fft). In 2013 IEEE 9th International Colloquium on Signal Processing and its Applications (pp. 289–294). IEEE.

[25] Warburton, D. E. R., Jamnik, V. K., Bredin, S. S. D., McKenzie, D. C., Stone, J., Shephard, R. J. & Gledhill, N. Evidence-based risk assessment and recommendations for physical activity clearance: Consensus document from the par-q+ collaboration. (2011).

[26] Mroczek, D. K., Ozer, D. J., Spiro, A. III & Kaiser, R. T. (1998). Evaluating a measure of the five-factor model of personality. Assessment, 5(3), 287–301.

[27] Donnellan, M. B., Oswald, F. L., Baird, B. M. & Lucas, R. E. (2006). The mini-ipip scales: tiny-yet-effective measures of the big five factors of personality. Psychological assessment, 18(2), 192.

[28] Mlăcíc, B. & Goldberg, L. R. (2007). An analysis of a cross-cultural personality inventory: The ipip big-five factor markers in Croatia. Journal of personality assessment, 88(2), 168–177.

[29] Murcia, J., Gimeno, E. C. & Camacho, A. M. (2007). Measuring self-determination motivation in a physical fitness setting: validation of the behavioural regulation in exercise questionnaire-2 (breq-2) in a Spanish sample. The Journal of Sport Medicine and Physical Fitness, 47(3), 366–378.

[30] Rodrigues, F., Macedo, R., Teixeira, D. S., Cid, L. & Monteiro, D. (2020). Motivation in sport and exercise: A comparison between the brsq and breq. Quality & Quantity, 54(4), 1335–1350.

[31] Spielberger, C. D., Sydeman, S. J., Owen, A. E. & Marsh, B. J. (1999). Measuring anxiety and anger with the State-Trait Anxiety Inventory (STAI) and the State-Trait Anger Expression Inventory (STAXI). Lawrence Erlbaum Associates Publishers.

[32] Watson, D., Clark, L. A. & Tellegen, A. (1988). Development and validation of brief measures of positive and negative affect: the panas scales. Journal of Personality and Social Psychology, 54(6), 1063.

[33] Sarmah, P. P., Paul, P. S. & Hazra, K. (2025). On Predicting Emotion From Commercial Smartwatch – A Big Data Narrative. *2025 IEEE International Conference on Interdisciplinary Approaches in Technology and Management for Social Innovation (IATMSI)*, 3, 1–6. doi: 10.1109/IATMSI64286.2025.10984709.

[34] Soni, S., Gupta, S. N., Devi, R. & Hazra, K. (2024). Information Extraction From Tweets for Disaster Damage Assessment Using Rule-based NLP. In *Proc. 15th Int. Conf. on Computing Communication and Networking Technologies (ICCCNT)* (pp. 1–6). Kamand, India. doi: 10.1109/ICCCNT61001.2024.10724068.

Amitava Podder, Shivnath Ghosh, and Subrata Paul

Enhancing Healthcare Delivery Through Evidence-Based Data Utilization

Abstract: The field of healthcare is being transformed by new technologies and the use of a variety of data available online. During this part, we talk about how using evidence-based data can improve healthcare quality, boost efficiency in care delivery, and positively impact patient outcomes. It starts by providing key concepts, showing how data integration has changed over time in healthcare, and emphasizing the main ideas of evidence-based practice. Numerous types of healthcare data, for instance, clinical data, administrative data, patient-generated data, and data from IoT devices and wearables, are analyzed regarding what they can give to healthcare and what issues they may face. The chapter points out the main issues caused by scattered data, having systems that do not work together, and the need to standardize. Analysis methods, such as descriptive, predictive, prescriptive, machine learning, and artificial intelligence, are covered for helping in clinical and operational decisions. These approaches are used in practice to help with diagnosis, manage resources, look after population health, and apply personalized medicine. Privacy, approval, following rules, and fighting bias are main concerns to produce fair and balanced results. Problems such as organizational and technological barriers, data quality issues, reluctance to change, and the complexity of dealing with unclear data are all considered. Eventually, healthcare businesses will pay attention to real-time analytics, the use of AI, improving data literacy among the workforce, and policy moves that support a sustainable healthcare data system. It provides research, practice, and policy experts, with insights to base decisions on actual evidence.

Keywords: healthcare data utilization, evidence-based medicine, interoperability, artificial intelligence, data privacy

---

Amitava Podder, Department of Computer Science-AI, Brainware University, Barasat 700125, West Bengal, India, e-mail: amitavapodder24@gmail.com
Shivnath Ghosh, Department of Computer Science-AI, Brainware University, Barasat 700125, West Bengal, India, e-mail: shivghosh.cs@gamil.com
Subrata Paul, Department of Computer Science-AI, Brainware University, Barasat 700125, West Bengal, India, e-mail: subratapaulcse@gmail.com

https://doi.org/10.1515/9783111541235-017

1 Introduction

1.1 Background and Rationale

The expansion of digital data and developments in computing have caused a major transformation in healthcare delivery today. Globally, healthcare organizations are swapping instinct-based decisions with those supported by carefully collected data. Not only is this an advancement in technology, but it is also a major change in the way organizations meet the needs of their patients. Dependence on evidence-based data is now a main strategy to ensure healthcare is safe, effective, and works efficiently.

Throughout history, clinicians made medical decisions mainly informed by their own understanding, patient evidence, and the known medical conventions of the time. While encouraging responsible care, this way of work led to variable, biased, and sometimes inconsistent treatment of patients. With the digitization of health and administrative files, healthcare professionals can use structured and unstructured data in real time. Thanks to this transformation, making precise decisions in healthcare is possible, along with building policies and managing both resources and care for patients. EHRs, for instance, have made it much easier for different departments to share patient information, thus leading to fewer mistakes and reduced recurrence of data collection [1]. At the same time, various data analytics tools are now available that support users in harnessing data to their advantage. These findings are essential when it comes to early diagnosis, estimating outcomes, organizing patients, and assessing treatment success. In addition, using real-world data from wearable devices and other tools helps strengthen the evaluation of patient behaviors and their surroundings [2]. There is a strong reason to focus on data because it may help resolve persistent issues and gaps in healthcare. Results from studies show that relying on data leads to fewer patients being readmitted, fewer deaths, improved patient satisfaction, and managing costs [3]. In addition, given the current health problems around the world, including pandemics, aging populations, and chronic diseases, it is even more necessary to use data to guide our actions. With healthcare providers aiming to prioritize the health of entire populations, applying evidence-based wisdom becomes very important [4, 5].

1.2 Objectives of the Chapter

The aim of this chapter is to discuss and show the value of using evidence-based data in healthcare. It presents ideas on how valuable data can support effective choices and develop the overall healthcare system. It will explain how using structured data improves care helps design personalized treatment and ensures fairness in healthcare for all. It is also important to focus on changing sources and types of data used in healthcare. The chapter will check how traditional data sources like medical records, billing databases, and hospital registries are being joined by new data such as data from patients, wearables, and online activity. These resources are necessary for setting the foundation for decision-making and for evaluating how care delivery and the results for patients are influenced. The article also seeks to recognize and describe the ways in which studies have extracted valuable insights from such data. Statistical modeling, predictive analytics, artificial intelligence, and decision support systems (DSSs) are included here. We will discuss in detail how these tools are effectively used in real situations to ensure better accuracy in care, reduce paperwork, and spot health trends. By applying these tools to healthcare settings, the author intends to offer a practical explanation of their use and effects. The chapter will address the rules and principles that surround the use of data in healthcare. Issues such as patient privacy, who owns the data, bias present in artificial intelligence, and regulatory laws will all be reviewed to give an objective understanding of both the prospects and the problems in using data in healthcare. In addition, the chapter will discuss what lies ahead in terms of healthcare innovation and the role of data use. It will discuss various paths in government, learning, and technology that could encourage using evidence-based practices.

1.3 Scope and Methodology

Here, we learn about the key concepts of data, its uses in healthcare, ways to analyze it, ethical issues, and the future of using data in medicine. While the main topics are data use in clinical settings and hospital administration, the emphasis also includes public health policies, outreach to communities, and emerging health technologies. At the start, the section describes main concepts such as evidence-based practice, health data analytics, and clinical decision support. Next, it studies the shift from traditional data collection to modern healthcare IT platforms that give real-time feedback and analysis. While studying the history, the chapter shows the evolution of healthcare toward data centricity and its corresponding impact on patients, providers, administrators, and policymakers. The approach used in this chapter blends qualitative and integrative analysis. It relies on a mix of existing literary accounts thorough research cases and industry professionals' views to deliver a good account. Information is taken from scientific articles reviewed by experts, as well as from health organizations to guarantee quality and relevance. Examples from real cases will be added to illustrate the use of data in different healthcare environments. Furthermore, the chapter emphasizes the importance of uniting different experts from various fields for the successful use of data. In this context, insights are taken from medical informatics, health policy, data science, and the study of organizational behavior.

2 Foundations of Evidence-Based Data Utilization in Healthcare

2.1 Definitions and Key Concepts

Understanding certain concepts is necessary for establishing evidence-based use of data in healthcare. Using evidence-based practice (EBP) means experts apply and evaluate the most reliable evidence available to craft individual medical decisions and healthcare strategies [6]. By using clinical expertise, patient values, and the latest research, it forms a team of three to direct medical care. Here, the primary use of strong and reliable data is important for healthcare decisions about patients, programs, and the organization. In healthcare, data can be organized into categories like clinical data, administrative data, patient-reported results, and evidence collected from the health of a population [7]. Clinical data focuses on facts obtained from interactions with patients, for example, disease conditions, lab tests, various medical images, and everything related to their treatment. Both types of data include operational and billing information that help us see how healthcare services are used, their costs, and how resources are managed. Health information reported by patients through wearables or their personal accounts provides more details that improve the understanding of their health. Studies in the real world are furthered by gathering information from large databases and tracking changes over a long period and in many people. Data quality is essential for proper use of data. Quality data is expected to be accurate, complete, prompt, and consistent. Without them, any findings or advice could be questionable and might result in incorrect decisions [8]. Because of this, data governance frameworks must put standards in place for collecting, saving, using, and protecting data to ensure it is trustworthy. Data analytics plays a major role as the practice of analyzing data to recognize patterns, draw conclusions, and create plans for action. In the field of healthcare, analytics cover descriptive, predictive, and prescriptive methods. Descriptive analytics is concerned with reviewing information from the past, predictive analytics is interested in predicting what may happen, and prescriptive analytics proposes steps to improve the future [9]. Merging analytics into CDSS has greatly enhanced the use of data insights at the time of patient care. In conclusion, effective use of data is only possible with strong interoperability of systems. Interoperability means that several different systems, devices, and applications can use data with each other. It is widely acknowledged that when data systems cannot communicate, it prevents the full use of data and affects its accuracy [10].

2.2 Evolution of Data Utilization in Healthcare Practice

Improvements in healthcare data use are based on new technologies, better approaches, and cultural changes. In the beginning, healthcare information was managed by hand-written charts, making it tough to obtain and examine complete history. When standards were not the same and information was spread out, doctors had trouble providing the same level of care each time. At the end of the twentieth century, the introduction of electronic health records (EHRs) made it much easier to handle, store, and share medical records. In the early days, EHRs were mainly for recording data, which left most information unused because it was not analyzed. With the help of protocols such as ICD and lab data standards, secondary uses of EHR data, such as quality measurement and research, became more practical over time [11]. Improved capabilities for HIE networks allowed patient data to be more widely shared, so doctors and other health professionals had access to better patient records. Integrating HL7 and FHIR made it easier to share data, and thus prepared the foundation for integrated analytics in care programs. Healthcare data now benefit greatly from new processing and utilization technologies, such as big data, AI, and machine learning. Through artificial intelligence, algorithms can look at both organized and unorganized data from several sources and spot complex relationships that are too hard for people to notice. For example, we now use predictive models to identify patients at risk of deterioration, allocate resources efficiently, and adapt the way we treat each patient [12]. Furthermore, data coming from wearable devices, mobile health apps, and home monitoring systems makes it possible to obtain data all the time. This increases the scope of health records and supplies a more complete view of patient well-being at home. The adoption of data from daily life is influencing healthcare, so doctors focus more on preventing diseases and managing chronic cases. Beginning with the digitization of data and continuing to data integration and standardization, advanced analytics, and ultimately using real-time and patient-centered data in decision-making, there is a phased track followed in data utilization. This process is shown in the following diagram, which identifies major advancements and changes (Figure 1).

2.3 Principles of Evidence-Based Medicine and Decision-Making

EBM is the process of combining proven medical evidence, what healthcare professionals know, and what patients want to create treatment decisions. Evidence-based data utilization is built on EBM principles, which determine the best ways to interpret and use data in healthcare [13]. Firstly, we should generate valid evidence and then examine it closely. We should ensure that data is taken, examined, and interpreted using reliable methods to help avoid bias. This means that patients should first know that systematic reviews and randomized controlled trials are the most trustworthy, then observational studies, and finally expert opinion. When using data, this rule says

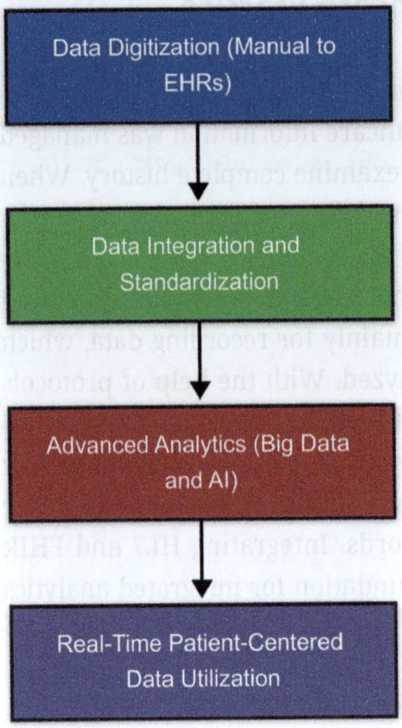

Figure 1: Evolution of data utilization in healthcare practice showing the progression from initial digitization through to the integration of real-time, patient-centered data streams.

data sources and methods should be open and properly verified by colleagues. It also focuses on how clinicians use their judgment in light of available evidence. Despite having strong data and evidence, a trained doctor must look at each patient cautiously to come to a conclusion. To use it well, a healthcare professional should be able to apply evidence to suit the specific requirements of each patient. Decisions should take into account what is important to the patient. It is understood that letting patients help choose their care and treatment takes into account their goals and experiences. People need to receive these data-driven insights in a way that helps them understand and decide for themselves.

The use of evidence-based recommendations has improved with the design of CDSS. They analyze patient information with clinical guidelines and models to support quick choices by doctors. CDSS need to help rather than replace what doctors decide, and their recommendations have to be constantly updated with recent evidence [14]. The basis of evidence-based data use is constant re-evaluation and improvements. With the rapidly changing nature of healthcare, continuous data acquisition and analysis are required for monitoring, noticing issues, and optimizing ways of working. This idea is present in healthcare settings where diagnosis and treatment methods are constantly changing due to feedback loops created by learning health systems [15]. Evidence-based data use in healthcare is based on a well-defined framework focused on the importance of good data, solid analysis, and uniting evidence with medical knowledge and patient concerns. Advances in technology and culture have gradually allowed healthcare organizations to use data in new ways. It is important to know and practice evidence-based medicine to make the most of healthcare data.

3 Sources and Types of Healthcare Data

Healthcare organizations depend on various kinds of data to support decisions, organize their work, and manage the health of the population. To make the most of data-driven methods, it is essential to know what these datasets involve and how they develop. In this section, we talk about the major sources of healthcare data, such as clinical, administrative, patient-generated, public health, and new data streams.

3.1 Clinical Data from Electronic Health Records (EHRs)

Information gathered from EHRs forms the main foundation of healthcare informatics in modern medical settings. Information saved in EHRs includes personal details, symptoms, healthcare plans, test results, drug charts, and pictures from scans. The data is arranged and predefined in such a way that different software can use and analyze it. The HITECH Act and similar policies strongly contributed to the development of EHR systems over the past 20 years [16]. EHR systems hold clinically useful information that can be used in CDSS, models for predicting outcomes, and programs for quality assessments. In spite of their usefulness, EHRs often include imperfections, including coding inconsistencies, missing data, and data entry errors, which need to be resolved [17]. With the help of NLP, health centers are now able to get useful information from EHRs such as clinical narratives and unstructured data from physician notes and radiology reports. The use of both structured and unstructured data makes it easier to identify and manage risks in patients [18].

3.2 Administrative and Operational Data

Administrative and operational data include information collected from the business and operational tasks in healthcare groups. The data involve details about billing systems, claims, planning staff schedules, keeping track of supplies, and using facilities. Although numerous people think of clinical information as primary, administrative data is crucial for looking at finances, resources, and compliance. Patient data, as a key resource, offer a wide range of information that includes details from their care in different places. They are commonly utilized in health services research, cost analysis, and to check healthcare differences [19]. While claims often focus on payment purposes, their information is not always updated or detailed enough to support fast clinical choices. Data gathered on operations allows healthcare organizations to streamline their work, reduce the wait time for patients, and improve processing of cases. By studying patterns of appointments, admissions, and discharges, hospitals can improve their efficiency and please patients [20]. Now, clinical data and healthcare analytics are often integrated to assess how well healthcare services are provided.

3.3 Patient-Generated Health Data (PGHD)

Patient-generated health data (PGHD) is made up of health-related information collected by patients themselves, apart from regular clinical settings. Included in these data are patients' reports, daily logs, fitness results, and compliance details gathered by mobile apps, online surveys, and medical gadgets. PGHD reflects a significant change, placing patients at the center of what happens. With such data, it becomes easier to understand what patients go through during treatment, how treatment goes, and what behaviors they exhibit [21]. Unparalleled in power, PGHD has been proven useful in looking after individuals with chronic diseases, studying mental health, and rehabilitation progress. Even so, the use of PGHD raises issues related to data trustworthiness, privacy, and compatibility. Proper education of patients and dependable technology are needed to keep everything accurate and consistent. Integrating PGHD in clinical workflows calls for compatible systems, and doctors to accepting it [22]. Apart from these barriers, PGHD complements existing healthcare data by increasing the options for making informed decisions [23].

3.4 Public Health and Population-Level Datasets

Population data obtained from health institutions and tracking helps elaborate on disease trends and create new health policies. The datasets comprise registries, data from the censuses, vaccination records, and metrics related to social determinants of health. The data for public health are put together and kept anonymized to protect individuals, yet they help monitor population health trends and detect disparities. To illustrate, cancer registries help us observe changes in incidence and survival, and use those findings to determine screening rules and allocate resources appropriately. These days, more attention is given to social determinants of health because they greatly impact health results. Connecting public health data with health-related datasets improves risk prediction and makes it easier to provide targeted care [24]. Infectious disease outbreaks are handled better now since public health data is available at a large scale. Acting on these data, people can be contacted quickly for action, vaccines can be provided, where needed, and diseases can be traced [25].

3.5 Emerging Sources – Wearables, IoT, and Real-Time Monitoring

Technology has sparked the advent of many new types of healthcare data, including those from wearables, IoT, and monitoring devices. Devices such as smartwatches, fitness trackers, and biosensors are always monitoring your heartbeat, how active you are, how well you sleep, and your blood oxygen level. With the constant and real-time flow of such data, better care and faster responses to health concerns can happen. IoT medical devices can send information from home to healthcare teams, which leads to quicker interventions [26]. While the new data sources seem to be promising, they bring many challenges, including large amounts, different kinds, privacy issues, and security risks. It is necessary to have solid infrastructure and advanced data tools to connect streams of real-time health data to existing health information systems. The reliability of wearable data in clinical settings and the rules governing them are still being examined [27]. Because these technologies are advancing, we will need guidelines and frameworks to maintain the quality and relevance of data in medicine (Table 1).

Table 1: Characteristics and challenges associated with major healthcare data sources.

Data source	Nature of data	Typical use cases	Challenges
Electronic health records (EHRs)	Structured and unstructured	Clinical decision support and research	Data quality and interoperability
Administrative data	Billing, claims, and logistics	Cost analysis and resource management	Limited clinical detail and delayed availability
Patient-generated health data	Self-reported and sensor data	Chronic disease management and patient engagement	Data accuracy and integration barriers
Public health datasets	Aggregated and anonymized	Epidemiology and population health surveillance	Privacy and data linkage
Wearables and IoT	Continuous physiological	Remote monitoring and personalized interventions	Data volume, security, and clinical validation

4 Data Integration and Interoperability in Healthcare Systems

For data-driven healthcare to succeed, healthcare data from different sources should be united and made interoperable. The section focuses on the problem of fragmentation in data, considers the standards and frameworks necessary for compatibility, and covers various strategies for combining different data sources to support clinical and operational decisions (Figure 2).

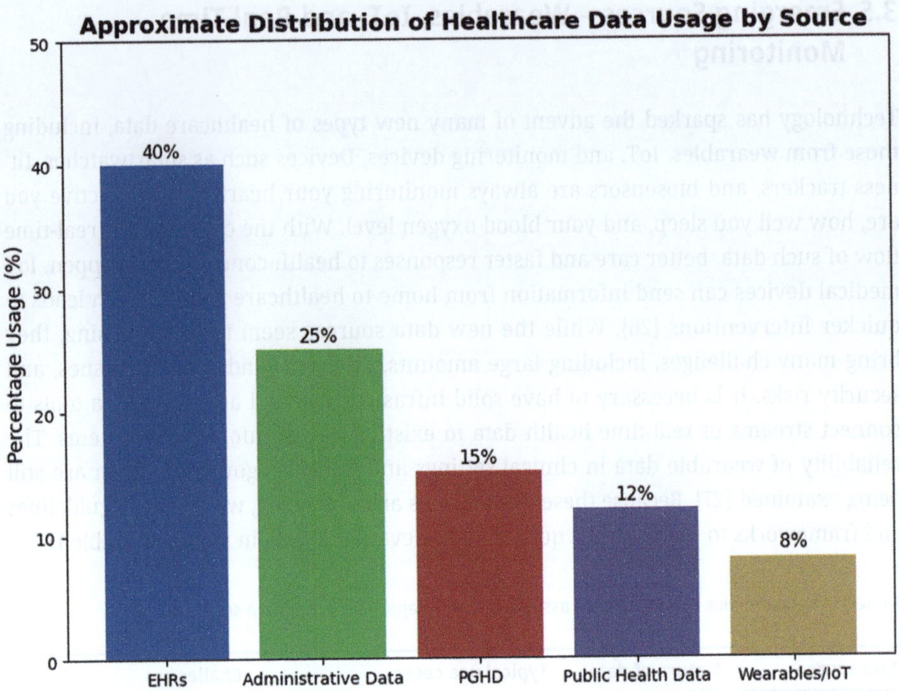

Figure 2: Bar graph representing the approximate proportion of healthcare data usage by source in analytics and decision-making.

4.1 Challenges in Data Fragmentation and Silos

There are often situations where healthcare data is divided into different sections, which makes it difficult for healthcare professionals to use. The issue of fragmentation happens when datasets for healthcare are not shared across different health service organizations or departments. As a result, records of patient care are fragmented, information exchange is hindered, and making choices about treatment becomes more complicated. Sometimes, disjointed data causes problems such as unnecessary tests, delayed therapies, and differences in how patients are cared for.

From a data integration standpoint, the goal is to achieve a unified dataset that combines all individual datasets from different silos. Formally, if D_i represents the dataset from the ith silo and there are n silos, the ideal integrated dataset D is expressed as the union:

$$D = \bigcup_{i=1}^{n} D_i$$

However, in practice, due to incompatibilities and barriers, the realized integrated dataset D' is a proper subset of the full union, meaning:

$$D' \not\subseteq D$$

Being incomplete, this integration limits access to data, thus reducing the contributions it could have made to improved patient care. Differences in how data is organized, special software from different providers, and company guidelines also make fragmentation more severe. These challenges make it hard for data to be shared effectively [28]. Concerns about privacy and security are also important because laws such as HIPAA place limits on who can see and use patient data, meaning that information is often divided into silos [29]. Ensuring that both privacy and data availability are met remains a key issue in the integration of healthcare data.

4.2 Standards and Frameworks for Interoperability

For data to flow across different systems, it is important that they are designed to use the same set of rules. Health Level Seven International (HL7) is one of the first standards and their Version 2 messaging method enables healthcare software to communicate with each other regarding clinical and administrative data. While HL7 V2 made interoperability possible, its variable design often results in problems with semantic consistency.

HL7 FHIR is a widely used standard that entertains REST-based API services and databases based on XML and JSON. FHIR uses modular resources to represent different clinical entities, making it easier for different systems to exchange data in real time [30]. The adoption of FHIR has been rapid and can be modeled using a logistic growth curve where the adoption percentage $A(t)$ at time t is given by

$$A(t) = \frac{K}{1 + e^{-r(t-t_0)}}$$

Here, K represents the maximum potential adoption, r is the adoption rate, and t_0 is the inflection point. Such a curve is common in cases where there is a slow start and then things pick up fast as adoption becomes more widespread. They support both the form and meaning of data, so systems can exchange and interpret it alike.

4.3 Strategies for Harmonizing Multisource Data

Healthcare organizations use a mix of technical and organizational measures to align data from various sources in healthcare. Data warehouses and lakes reduce the effort by storing all information in one location for analysis. To integrate data, ETL pipelines are often used to gather data from several sources, modify and organize it, and save it all in one place as standardized data. Such platforms connect different systems and make sure that data is understandable across them. They usually develop systems that depend on FHIR APIs and standards for dependable and smooth communication. It is often achieved by linking local medical language with an international standard, for example, SNOMED CT or LOINC. It enables the use of datasets with different structures in a way that makes sense for clinical research [31, 32]. Governance frameworks ensure that important things such as data security and sharing policies are in place, advocating for sharing among groups and promoting participants to work together. It is important to highlight open data standards and reward using interoperability to overcome challenges related to institutions (Figure 3).

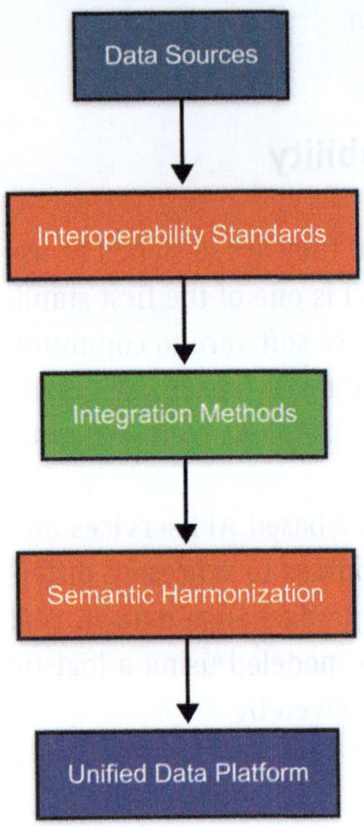

Figure 3: Interoperability framework illustrating the progression from heterogeneous data sources through standards adoption, integration techniques, semantic harmonization, culminating in a unified healthcare data platform.

5 Analytical Methods for Evidence-Based Decision Making

Healthcare is taking a more data-driven and analytics-based approach, as it now relies on analytics to extract useful insights from a huge amount of data. In healthcare, using analysis methods is key to transforming data into evidence used for making decisions that are best for patients. This part explains important analytical procedures – descriptive, predictive, and prescriptive analytics – and discusses how machine learning, artificial intelligence, and decision-support systems improve healthcare by transforming it.

5.1 Descriptive, Predictive, and Prescriptive Analytics

Descriptive analytics forms the first step in analyzing data in the healthcare field. Historical data is used to look for regularities as well as any irregularities. Examples are the number of readmissions at hospitals, how long patients remain there, who they are, and the rate when a certain disease is contracted over time [33, 34]. To help understand the past events, descriptive analytics depends on dashboards, histograms, and summary statistics. To monitor the quality and compliance of care and assess performance, descriptive analytics is important [35]. It relies on statistics, machine learning, and old data to help predict what will happen next. Such models are also used in hospitals to predict how a disease will develop, how often the same patient is admitted to the hospital, and how many people will visit the emergency department. Many predictive models rely on logistic regression, time-series models, decision trees, and neural networks. Thanks to models, doctors are able to predict sepsis in patients at the hospital and start care well before the patient even shows signs of it [36]. In addition, prescriptive analytics uses the predicted outcomes to suggest ideas for the best possible steps to take. It uses decision science, along with predictions, to guide you toward the most desired results. Thanks to prescriptive analytics, doctors may select the best medical plan for each patient, figure out who to place in ICU beds, and at which dose and personalize the patient's medications. Commonly used for prescriptive decision-making are models, simulation tools, and reinforcement learning [37]. The three kinds of analytics are related to one another. In descriptive analytics, we focus on the present, predictive analytics helps with the future, and prescriptive analytics influences choices and decisions we make. With the help of this approach, healthcare professionals can start offering prevention-based care.

5.2 Machine Learning and AI Techniques in Healthcare

By applying these two technologies, the field of healthcare analysis has undergone a major shift. By using ML, it becomes easy to spot patterns in large data, which allows models to improve each time they are updated with new data. Common use of supervised learning implies that random forests, support vector machines and gradient boosters are often tasked with diagnosing illnesses or predicting a person's risk of death [38]. Some approaches in unsupervised learning, such as clustering, help group patients or recognize additional disease groups, as well as highlight how care is used. In fact, ML helps divide diabetic patients into groups that matter to clinicians, versus those based solely on age and gender. In ML, deep learning uses multilayer neural networks to deal with information in several dimensions. The field is most useful for cases like radiology, pathology, and electrocardiography. With CNNs, detecting cancerous lesions in radiography images is now as accurate as what radiologists do [39].

AI, through NLP, is able to find insights in statements written by doctors, discharge reports, or pathology records. Adverse drug events, assessing who is eligible for clinical trials, and improving EHRs can all be achieved with NLP models. Reinforcement learning uses AI algorithms to find the best actions by being part of an environment. This field is studied in healthcare to support personal evolution of therapies, adjust settings in intensive care, and maintain chronic conditions [40]. Still, when ML and AI are used, it is important to be cautious, as they may display bias, behave in unpredictable ways and their results may only apply to specific situations. It is still difficult to explain, verify fairness in AI, and test clinical AI for use in a variety of populations.

5.3 Risk Stratification and Outcome Prediction Models

Risk stratification involves grouping patients who have a higher risk of experiencing problems related to their health. Practicing medicine in this way ensures that health needs of those who are at highest risk are met as efficiently as possible. Many times logistic regression, survival analysis, and ML-based scores are used for risk estimates. The CHADS2 model is used to check for stroke risk in individuals living with atrial fibrillation. Another use is to estimate the chances of hospital readmission within 30 days, find patients who could experience a heart failure episode, and guess the probability of surgical complications. Predicting the outcome of a condition depends on information such as clinical markers, societal factors, lifestyle habits, comorbid illnesses, and demographics. Clinicians can administer proactive care by using integration of models into their dashboard tools. A real-time algorithm for predicting sepsis may be used in a hospital to send a message to the care team once early symptoms are spotted. Accuracy, precision, recall, F_1-score, and AUC-ROC are a few methods used to assess how well a prediction model performs. Probability estimations must be in agreement with what happens in the real world. Because overfitting, data drift, and testing on a small set often happen, people should always test and retrain the machine learning models [41].

5.4 Decision Support Systems and Clinical Dashboards

DSSs assist doctors and hospital staff by providing information and tools for making decisions. They use data collected from different places, run various analysis algorithms, and share the results in a straightforward way for users. CDSS is a kind of DSS that is part of EHRs. For example, they may send alerts if a patient is taking multiple medicines that work against one another, give doctor-chosen guidelines for specific cases, and remind patients when it is time for some preventive care. CDSS have helped raise safety when drugs are used, provide accurate diagnoses, and increase compliance with set clinical practices [42]. Real-time dashboards make it easier for caregivers to make important decisions. In some cases, an ICU dashboard will show patient vitals, test findings, and calculated risks, all at once, which helps nurses and doctors in taking quick actions. Within a hospital, administrative dashboards collect statistics related to the number of beds filled, average length of stay for patients, and their levels of satisfaction. Deploying predictive analytics on dashboards helps with taking steps ahead of any problems. In this case, leaders can allocate more staff and supplies to the emergency room before the rise in visits occurs. For dashboards to be helpful to all users, they should be able to accommodate the needs of clinicians as well as executives. Still, to prevent too much information, a lot of alerts, and slow work, DSS and dashboards need to be designed with care. Ensuring development and use of artificial intelligence requires focusing on how people will interact, considering the engagement of stakeholders (Figure 4).

6 Applications of Data-Driven Approaches in Healthcare Delivery

By digitizing healthcare, methods that involve analyzing data have been incorporated into daily clinic and hospital routines. All the data available from various electronic and medical sources can now be used as a useful tool to improve management, delivery, and quality of healthcare. Now that intelligent algorithms are being used in healthcare, we are seeing improvements in patient care, healthcare resources, and more.

6.1 Enhancing Diagnostic Accuracy and Treatment Planning

In healthcare, using data-based methods often increases the accuracy of diagnosis. Using the usual methods to diagnose a condition can be influenced by a doctor's opinion and, at times, fail to be accurate. Using AI algorithms and evidence-based models with clinical information, doctors, and nurses can now detect hidden trends that the human eye may miss, making it less likely there will be errors during diagnoses. There have been promising outcomes using ML techniques after training on extensive medical records in radiology, pathology, and dermatology. For instance, using CNNs, it is now common to distinguish malignant tumors and benign tumors as well as expert radiologists do [43]. Furthermore, some DSSs look at a patient's history, labs, and clinical guidance to recommend the best care plan. They allow for the same practices to be used by health professionals and increase consistency in medical care. This technology makes it much simpler to find patients with a high risk of complications and prevent related issues. Likely, logistic regression or decision-tree models are used by

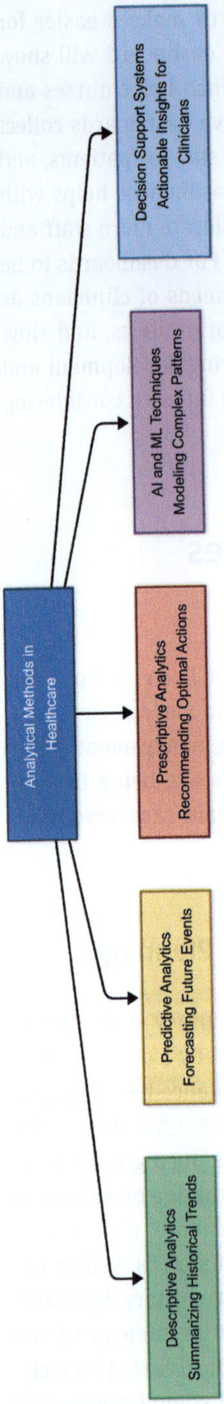

Figure 4: Types of analytics in healthcare decision-making.

clinicians to predict if a patient will get sepsis or a heart disease. They allow doctors to act in a timely manner, which greatly helps patients and cuts down on deaths in the hospital [44]. Information collected from sequencing DNA and analyzing molecules helps in designing better treatment plans. Since pharmacogenomics links genes and medications, it helps doctors choose the best drugs for each individual, thus preventing many risks of side effects.

6.2 Resource Allocation and Operational Efficiency

Many hospitals and healthcare organizations encounter difficulties because they do not have sufficient ICU beds, doctors, nurses, or other surgical materials. Effectively managing these resources has become possible with the help of data analytics. By tracking patients in real time and predicting rates of admissions, hospital administrators ensure there are no blockages when treating patients. Using updated data from their EHRs, hospitals can closely review their daily operations. Healthcare leaders are able to check several statistics, including average hospital stays, the time it takes to use a room in the operating suite, and the time patients spend waiting to see specialists, and thus find ways to solve inefficiencies [45]. Such algorithms now help to ensure that patients are on time for their appointments. So, by using predictive models, the schedule can be optimized for both the doctor and the business by automatically sending reminders to those who might skip their appointment. Implementing data analytics in hospitals has streamlined the supply chain. Nowadays, hospitals depend on machine-learning-powered software to anticipate how many medical supplies will be used each week, month, and year. With this approach, we save resources, avoid running out of important items and provide them promptly.

6.3 Population Health Management and Disease Surveillance

Now that data is being used, healthcare providers are able to shift from treating illnesses to preventing them. To generate such data, population health analytics simply aggregates records from EHRs, social factors, insurance claims information, and public health databases. Chronic diseases are often managed with help from mHealth. They can find patients with diabetes, hypertension, or asthma, who might suffer poor results because they are not following doctor's advice. The data obtained allows coordinators to deliver outreach help, oversee patients after they leave a hospital, and provide telehealth assistance, improving results for both hospitals and patients [46]. With new real-time analytics, disease management is now much easier. Authorities in public health use geography and trend analysis to follow cases of diseases such as influenza, COVID-19, or tuberculosis. These actions are possible because of the surveillance in place, which helps the organization advice and treat people quickly. As a result, data collected at the community level can help identify factors affecting people's health. To illustrate, using details from housing, education, and work, with health records, can help identify places where health risks are higher, so that any improvements and changes can be made there.

6.4 Personalized Medicine and Patient Engagement

The field known as precision medicine or personalized medicine is where medical care is tailored to each individual. Data collected from genomic and experimental studies, as well as a patient's lifestyle, are used to personalize the kind of healthcare provided. Clinical DSSs have been widely used to bring together data from genomics and clinical guidelines. In the field of cancer, doctors can identify who may profit from chemotherapy through the use of gene expression profiling. Because of this, patients experience a better survival rate and do not have to deal with side effects that can be avoided [47].

It is also vital for data to contribute to patient involvement. People are able to manage their health and any healthcare questions through mobile health apps and patient portals. The use of these tools encourages patients with chronic diseases to monitor their health regularly. It is possible for smartwatches, glucose monitors, and digital inhalers to share with clinicians any continuous information on your body that has been gathered. As a result, people can have both regular checkups at the clinic and watch over their condition at home with ease. Observing how patients interact in the digital space helps create strategies to ensure more effective patient communication. This means that using natural language processing (NLP), texts and messages from patients can be studied to find out what they are feeling, concerned about, or struggling with when taking medicine. It helps develop improved care plans that consider patients' needs.

6.5 Quality Improvement and Performance Monitoring

Quality improvement projects in healthcare rely heavily on using data. Regularly using key performance indicators helps institutions locate their strengths and elements that can be improved. For hospitals, KPIs include infections picked up in hospital, rates of readmission, infection at the surgery site, and scores representing patients' experiences. Through data dashboards and benchmarking, people can review how various institutions or parts of an institution are performing. Through this comparison, people become more accountable and continue to learn. As a result, if real-time alert systems detect an issue with clinical practice, they let the care team know immediately so they can make prompt improvements. Including PROMs and PREMs in a quality dashboard provides a better understanding of how effective is a patient's care. The data backed by these methods allows the organization to hear what the patient has to say and improve various aspects of their care. With the help of data visualization tools and RCA, along with PDSA cycles, it is possible to systematically study any negative event or situation. Because of these methods, interventions are based on studies and appropriate for the situation at hand. Following the rules and obtaining accreditations both depend greatly on data. All facilities are expected to prepare detailed reports about their quality for review by The Joint Commission or CMS. They take some stress off staff members and ensure all reports you submit are accurate and arrive on time. All things considered, using data analytics for quality improvement initiatives improves care, saves resources, and improves how patients feel during their treatment.

7 Ethical, Legal, and Regulatory Considerations

7.1 Data Privacy and Confidentiality

Since data is now central to healthcare, adequate measures are required to ensure patients' private information is protected. In healthcare, data privacy identifies the needs of patients to manage their health records, while confidentiality ensures that unauthorized people do not access confidential patient information. Because everyone's health information is kept online today and because it's being integrated with varied systems, maintaining the confidentiality of sensitive data is now a bigger challenge than ever before. Data called PII and PHI fall under the category of sensitive healthcare information, as they may significantly touch an individual's life. In many cases, identity theft, discrimination, mental harm, and being manipulated for money can follow from a major data breach. For this reason, healthcare firms must install data encryption, proper access control, record-keeping systems, and secured messaging between systems to protect data from cyber attacks. Respecting persons' needs by allowing them to act independently leads to the requirement of protecting privacy. When information is kept confidential, patients and providers develop trusting relationships. If patients are sure that their information will be cared for properly, they usually give accurate answers that doctors need for proper care. Still, there are obstacles that make it hard for women. Because of more third-party data processors and cloud storage, data ownership, transfer across borders and access to information are now at risk. Moreover, when machine learning and big data analytics are applied to data, it becomes possible for inference attacks to decode private information because some personal information is likely to remain [48]. Therefore, healthcare institutions should make data protection part of the foundation when designing their computer systems. According to this, little data should be taken, its use must be limited, and anonymization or pseudonymization ought to be used when feasible. Besides, staff must be trained regularly, patients should learn about their data, and data management policies should always be clear and easy to follow.

7.2 Informed Consent and Patient Autonomy

When using health data, informed consent is vital to both ethics and the law because it helps preserve a patient's autonomy. It means providing details about how patients' information will be managed and helping them decide whether to participate in the study. Informed consent process has to be followed during patients' initial visits to a doctor or before entering a research study. On the other hand, with digital advancements in the health industry, the process involves more factors because of wider access to and secondary purposes of collected data. The same data used for treatment in hospitals can be utilized for research, improving quality or used in other ways, making some people wonder if it was properly consented for these other uses from the beginning. Using dynamic consent, patients are now able to select how and when their data should be shared online. It helps patients to participate more and maintain regular communication with those who collect and use their personal information. Even so, this makes it harder to execute because people might lack computer skills, different systems may fail to connect. and there is more paperwork for administrations. The process of getting someone's consent ought to be done honestly, allowing complete choice, and clarifying everything. Every individual's information should be adjusted for their level of understanding and background culture. Extra steps must exist to ensure that people having cognitive difficulties or are poor have the proper safeguards in place for making informed decisions [49]. The rules about informed consent vary from one location to another. As an illustration, under GDPR, permission should be "voluntary, distinct, clear and precise," while HIPAA requires authorization under certain conditions in the United States. Still, simply meeting the law is not enough to be ethical. Organizations in healthcare should ensure their practices center on the rights, dignity, and empowerment of their patients. Using online tools for consent and decision-making can make the consent experience more significant. Interactive charts, understandable information, and different languages are used to improve a patient's knowledge and understanding of the options. Still, conflicts between right and wrong arise when people's freedom is compared with outcomes made possible by analyzing big data, like community health and preventative measures [50, 51].

7.3 Compliance with Regulatory Frameworks (e.g., HIPAA and GDPR)

Following rules and policies in the healthcare industry is necessary to avoid any misuse of information. This framework allows companies to ensure that they follow rules for data collection, storage, sharing, and processing. In the United States, the healthcare data regulation system revolves around the HIPAA law. Related laws legally require safeguarding the privacy of patient information by means of administration, physical measures, and technical means, promising patients access to it, letting them make changes, and giving them the right to limit its use. HIPAA Privacy Rule discusses when, why, and to whom a patient's personal health information might be disclosed, while the Security Rule addresses ePHI. GDPR is seen in the United States as one of the world's most detailed data protection laws. While it does not only apply to healthcare, it greatly affects processing health data. GDPR is guided by ideas such as only keeping and using needed data, setting a clear purpose for using it, and deleting it after use. Individuals are given the rights to get information, take their data with them, and have it deleted. What's important to understand is that honor. Professionals, according to GDPR, are required to pay extra attention to health data since it falls under the special category of personal information. Not only organizational decisions and actions are needed, but also changes in the culture of these places are important. All staff should learn that data protection is a central priority for the company. As part of an effective approach, companies should perform compliance audits, assess the privacy risks, and be ready to notify people when data is breached. As health systems cross different countries, it is vital for rules to be compatible with each other. Since each nation may have its own rules for laws, consent, and enforcement, organizations and collaborative groups often encounter difficulties and disputes. It is important to promote data privacy and freedom by adopting the same rules for data sharing globally. We should also keep in mind that failing to follow the rules can lead to legal consequences, damage a company's reputation, and make the public suspicious. In light of this, sticking to regulations should be considered both necessary and important, supporting the field's overall agenda.

7.4 Addressing Bias and Equity in Data Use

Fairness and unbiased use of data are essential aspects in healthcare today. The quality of data that an algorithm or tool is trained on will determine its reliability. If available historical data lack reliable or fair information, these systems may contribute to or worsen differences in healthcare services, results, and availability. Errors caused by bias can take place during collection, labeling, the processing, analysis, or interpretation of data. A lack of members from particular groups in medical studies and data can cause algorithms to do poorly on that group later on. In a similar way, including income, education, and housing in data analysis may be hard, meaning the concerned predictions and actions could be unfair. By levelling the playing field and making data more diverse, appropriate strategies must be adopted. Among these, you should review the information included in the data, use ethical machine learning methods, and occasionally conduct bias audits on your analytical tools. Moreover, being open about how the algorithm is built, helps spot any bias and allows the issue to be addressed. Any approach to data-driven innovation should ensure that the costs and rewards are distributed justly among all people. In addition, we ought to reduce health gaps for marginalized people by actively taking steps and ensuring resources are distributed evenly. It is important to get the community involved in this kind of work. Learning from patients and stakeholders through each step of a data project helps the systems address the needs important to the community [4]. Working cooperatively with people improves the integrity and survival of health programs that rely on data. To create responsible guidelines for new healthcare technologies, all these professionals should cooperate [5]. It requires promoting openness, responsibility, and involvement when creating and implementing data technologies. Initiatives should be used to make clinicians, data scientists, and policy makers aware of data equity [52]. Overall, healthcare data should be handled ethically using justice, respect, and care for others as the main guide. Since digital transformation is changing health services, it is essential to pay attention and take action to observe if the new technology helps improve healthcare for all (Figure 5).

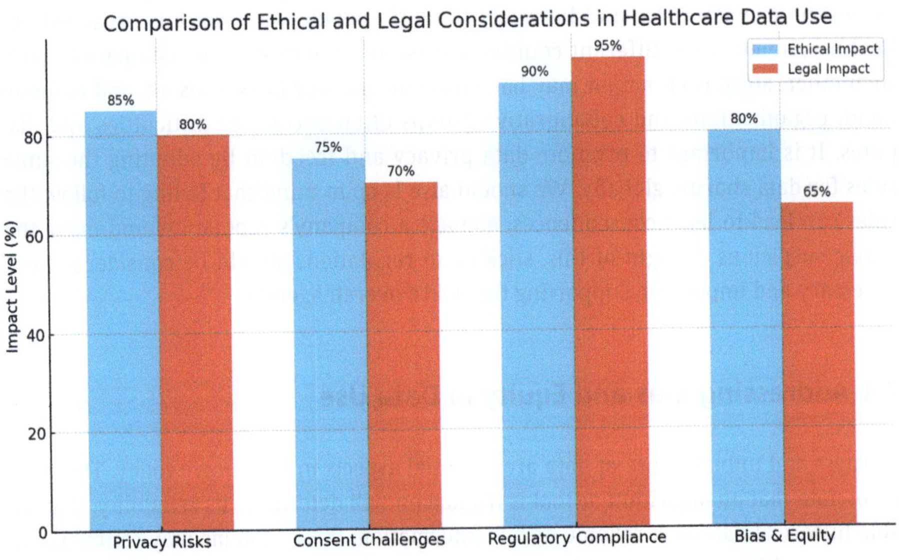

Figure 5: Comparative analysis of ethical and legal impact levels across key data governance domains in healthcare.

8 Barriers and Challenges to Effective Data Utilization

Deciding how to use data is often seen as a vital step toward helping patients, increasing "smart spending" by healthcare providers and aiding doctors with evidence-based decisions. Meanwhile, many healthcare organizations find it difficult to use data in the best way because of different challenges [23]. They exist at the level of the organization, technology, information, humans, and interpretation. To deal with these problems, one must recognize their backgrounds, impacts, and how they interact. The authors here discuss the challenges that prevent data from being used effectively: policies in the company, technology, problems with data quality and standards, difficulties in getting used to new things, and interpreting data that involves risks [21].

8.1 Organizational and Technological Barriers

The usage of health data often suffers due to technical and organizational issues that centers often run into. Primarily, organizational barriers result from goals being misaligned, information being kept in different systems, and too little attention from top leaders. In several healthcare areas, management of data is considered a technical role, so there is not enough focus on providing the right tools and staff for analyzing data [53]. Even though many organizations fail to develop a clear plan for data, support from their leaders is necessary to implement new approaches and sustain changes. Additional problems are created by the latest technologies. Legacy information systems used by various healthcare institutions are not meant for senior support nor do they allow data to be shared easily among other systems. Since the systems used in healthcare are not integrated, data from various areas is scattered and cannot be analyzed quickly [54]. Additionally, obsolete software is not flexible enough to allow use of new analytical systems like artificial intelligence or machine learning. Getting data out of a wide variety of sources and processing and loading it increases the workload needed to operate a company. Because health information technology is moving quickly, organizations are worried about the challenges linked to trying out new approaches, so they are reluctant to change. Dealing with cybersecurity is also a significant problem for technology. Because healthcare data is often attacked by cybercriminals, extra security rules are put in place that can prevent access to specific information within the organization [53]. Providing access to data in healthcare with security and privacy is always a problem. When there is little motivation to change and leaders are not engaged enough, systems built long ago are in use, data systems can't communicate, and poor cyberdefenses exist, resulting in using data effectively becoming challenging. Overcoming these issues involves creating better policies, investing in technologies that connect systems, and raising awareness that data is fundamentally important.

8.2 Data Quality and Standardization Issues

Reliable healthcare data is the most useful need, because it can be used trustfully. When data is poorly collected, meaningful analyses cannot be performed, clinicians doubt useful knowledge from data, and actual treatment choices might compromise a patient's health. Some data problems in healthcare result from missing parts of patients' records, wrong data entry, various types of coding, and information that is either too old or not recorded [54]. Data collected in healthcare can be from EHRs, medical images, lab results, records collected by patients, and important hospital systems. Because different sources have their own structures, formats, and rules, it is difficult to integrate them. The standardization of data is tied to how accurate it is. The main problem is that the standards for data organization and ways to change or exchange information are not identical in healthcare. Many organizations and countries differ in their use of HL7, FHIR, and SNOMED CT, despite their existence [55]. As a result of this variation, the same medical concept can be recorded in several ways, preventing data from being collected and analyzed correctly and consistently. The situation becomes even more challenging when standard terms and codes are not used for diagnoses or laboratory tests [27]. Mistakes such as errors in typing, having multiple entries for things, and forgetting some needed information may occur with manual data entry. Since gathering live data is often tricky in many areas, history-taking often does not accurately reflect what happens currently in the hospital. Many times, tasks related to cleaning and validating data are not automated and still require too much work from data analysts, causing estimation delays. It is not easy to standardize maps for both space and time. Any differences in when information is recorded or entered may disrupt long-term research. Integration of data from various care places, locations, or nations where health practices are different results in spatial heterogeneity. To make these improvements, enterprises must use global standards, organize training for their staff, install appropriate verification systems, and monitor all information processes regularly [25].

8.3 Resistance to Change and Skills Gap

Data is often underused because people seem to stand in the way. Internally, doctors and nurses usually resist changes when given new information systems or devices. It is possible for clinicians, administration, and leaders to resist change because they expect it to be labor-intensive, negatively affect usual routines, or not be valuable [53]. In some cases, individuals may strictly avoid using data systems, follow only a few guidelines, or add data to their work but not use it to make real decisions.

Typically, people resist data analytics because they simply do not understand the results or doubt them. Those primarily trained to provide healthcare may not be skilled enough in data analysis to assess the findings. As a result, many of them do not feel comfortable using data to make changes in their work. Besides, you may not want to refer users to AI-recommended products due to the risk of being held accountable or liable for them. A lack of certain skills is apparent in nurses, doctors, managers, and IT workers alike. Around the world, there is not enough knowledge among data scientists, clinical informaticists, and health IT specialists for working with domain-specific information to transform raw data into useful intelligence [54]. Many programs for training and education in health data analytics are not designed with healthcare settings in mind [28]. Thus, healthcare companies have difficulty creating teams that can collectively use complex information. Because technology is progressing rapidly, we must learn new skills all the time. Data analysts and other members of the team should stay informed about any new technologies, changes in the regulations, and improve their knowledge of best data management practices. If employees are not given opportunities for continuous learning and development by their organization, the existing skills gap will make it more difficult to work with data. Managing the changes worked out and boosting knowledge require well-designed strategies. Those efforts should be supported by involving stakeholders on time, proving the advantages of data usage, creating available courses and instructional material, and designing a workplace that values change. In order for these changes to succeed, it is up to leaders to guide them and provide the tools and resources necessary for training workers.

8.4 Managing Uncertainty in Data Interpretation

Data interpretation in healthcare is inherently complex due to the probabilistic nature of medical knowledge, variability in patient populations, and limitations in data completeness. Managing uncertainty is a fundamental challenge when leveraging healthcare data for decision-making. Uncertainty arises from multiple sources, including measurement errors, incomplete data capture, biases in data collection, and limitations in analytic models [55].

Healthcare data often contains noise and outliers that can skew results, if not appropriately handled. For example, vital signs recorded during emergency situations may be atypical and misrepresent the patient's baseline status. Similarly, missing data due to skipped tests or lost records introduces uncertainty that complicates analysis. Statistical methods to handle missing data, such as imputation, can mitigate but not eliminate these challenges. We should also pay close attention to model uncertainty. Historical data is often used in developing models, but they may not be reliable when treating patient groups with other health issues. This applies mainly in situations where the situation develops rapidly such as during a disease outbreak or the launch of a new type of therapy [31]. Clinicians should be able to use an analytic system with confidence, which requires that the model's process, testing, and drawbacks are explained. Clinicians may find it challenging to make sense of the results provided by many data models. Statistics needed for confidence intervals, risk scores, and likelihood ratios is not commonly understood by most people using the tool. If data is misinterpreted, there is a risk of people either using it too much or not using it enough, each situation having negative effects. The issue of ethics is connected to situations of uncertainty. Using information or data that is uncertain can put one's belief in justice, and a patient's rights and risk assessment at risk. Contingency calls for using clinical experience, patient wishes, and understanding the environment and data in combination. Healthcare providers should create interpretative tools that can display explanations, express how uncertain a result is, and are simple for doctors to use. Clinicians should also receive training in handling and managing uncertainty. For data-driven decisions to be more secure and trustworthy, the efforts of data scientists, clinicians, and ethicists should be brought together (Figure 6).

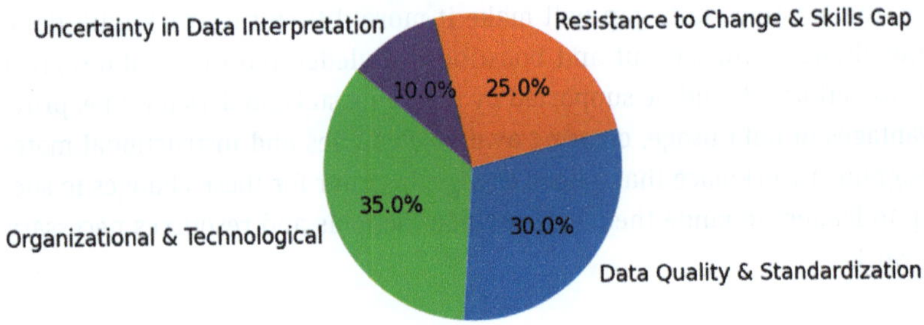

Figure 6: Distribution of barriers to effective data utilization in healthcare.

9 Future Directions and Opportunities

Due to advances in technology, growing access to healthcare data and a greater understanding of its role in improving healthcare, new ways of using data are fast becoming the norm. Barriers in the present bring chances for changes that may greatly impact healthcare in the future. Such opportunities involve real-time and predictive analytics, artificial intelligence, and deep learning, developing data skills among workers and planning future policy guidelines [32]. Here, we look into different trends that are changing and guiding the future of data-driven healthcare.

9.1 Advancements in Real-Time and Predictive Analytics

Healthcare data will be used more effectively if real-time and predictive analytics can be employed. Most healthcare analytics have concentrated on using past data to draw conclusions. Yet, using newly developed sensors, devices worn by patients, and automatic monitoring tools allows for the quick and continuous collection of vital information from patients in all kinds of hospitals. With all the data, healthcare professionals can easily monitor patients and quickly take actions if anything potentially dangerous is detected. Tools for real-time analytics take streaming information from many sources and produce suggestions that assure patient safety and increase the hospital's effectiveness. In case, experts quickly find worsening vital signs, it could lead to quick action that lowers the rate of adults being sent to the hospital and experiencing further difficulties. Furthermore, using analytics in real time allows hospitals to manage available resources by guessing both the number of patients and how many beds will be taken during different parts of the day. Using this technology, real-time data processing can be boosted by applying certain techniques to forecast what will happen in a patient's future, how an illness might develop, and what resources are necessary. By using these models, it becomes possible to find people who might face issues after leaving the hospital, when taking drugs or with specific diseases. With predictive analytics in EHRs, doctors get support in making decisions about treating and managing patient diseases [34]. They may enable healthcare workers to focus on stopping health issues early by being more active in caring for patients. Managing health issues and handling any public health emergency will depend greatly on the flexibility of real-time and predictive analytics [33].

9.2 The Role of Artificial Intelligence and Deep Learning

AI and deep learning are now leading transformations in the medical field due to their use of data. Using different computer methods, AI allows machines to perform acts that require thinking, recognizing information, and interpreting speech. A part of AI, deep learning trains with neural networks to identify complex details found in large amounts of data [50].

There is rapid growth in using AI and deep learning for diagnostics, planning treatments, viewing images, working with DNA data, and supervising patients' health. Thanks to these technologies, it is now easier to find useful details from data types such as images, pathology slides, and medical notes. Both in finding unusual symptoms, and identifying many kinds of diseases and predicting outcomes, deep learning algorithms have performed better than other methods. AI is now helping to design personal treatment plans using information from genetics, lifestyle habits, and a patient's clinical history. With this approach, treatment is designed specifically for each patient, which increases its effectiveness. Due to the use of AI, doctors and nurses can focus on caring for patients, instead of being responsible for scheduling appointments, billing, and coding. Besides, by using natural language processing, it becomes possible to value free-text clinical documentation and add useful details to the data. When AI matures, more emphasis should be placed on openness, understanding how AI works, and removing any discrimination. AI and deep learning being used in healthcare data systems will help establish new rules for care and performance.

9.3 Fostering a Data-Literate Healthcare Workforce

Since healthcare data becomes increasingly important, there is a need for people who can efficiently use data for better decision-making. To make the best use of modern healthcare technology, healthcare professionals should first become data literate. To be data literate, someone must understand different types of data, interpret statistics, use analysis programs, and use the results when making decisions about healthcare or administration. When leadership, administrators, doctors, nurses, and other people in healthcare continuously develop these skills, data becomes valued and trusted. Various training programs for medical professionals should include the basic elements of data science. Continuing education for professionals should include tasks that allow them to practice using various health informatics platforms, tools, and rules for managing information. Clinicians, data scientists, and IT experts should collaborate to use the insights from data effectively in caring for patients. Leaders should include data literacy in their organization's plans and set goals that depend on it. If data-driven experimenting is encouraged, this will speed up the adoption of these changes. Ensuring that healthcare professionals understand data helps an organization avoid resistance to change, use data better, and support far better results for patients [51].

9.4 Policy Recommendations and Global Perspectives

The way data will be utilized in healthcare is also guided by policies related to managing data, ensuring privacy, making information easy to use among different systems, and ensuring proper use. Guidelines that can ensure everyone's interests and health are secure, as new innovations appear, are required for long-term data use in healthcare. Policymakers should focus on introducing national and international rules for sharing data between different medical centers and countries. Having interoperability standards allows patient information to be shared, reduces errors in patient care, supports managing entire communities, and encourages collaborations among various research facilities. Using the same data formats and terminologies is the primary basis for these efforts. As risks and concerns change regularly, data privacy and security policies should be updated too. If rules for providing consent and using data are visible, patients are more trusting and often choose to share their data. Efforts should be made by policy makers to ensure all have equal access to healthcare through data technologies. Compared to the past, global perspectives play a bigger role because challenges such as pandemics, diseases that last a lifetime, and aging societies are common in many countries. Sharing data and conducting research with other nations spreads information and reduces wastefulness. When globally shared standards and skill-building are applied, low-income countries benefit more from global health equity. Such policies encourage people to invest in and use new technology for gathering health data. Support for the data field comes from public–private collaborations, research money, and suitable regulations. Healthcare will be improved globally when new policies focus on both latest technology and ethical concerns.

10 Conclusion

Appropriate use of healthcare data can improve healthcare for patients, make care delivery more efficient, and boost research. Despite the problems related to organizations, data quality, people resisting change, and difficulty in interpreting data, care providers still have options for advancing with real-time analytics, AI, and training their staff. Applying advanced models and AI tools encourages doctors to manage patients' conditions more effectively and also ensures that healthcare professionals understand how to use them. Moreover, it is necessary to ensure that privacy guidelines and data access policies can work internationally to promote the equal distribution of data. As technology and knowledge grow, it is vital that medical systems from different countries use a collaborative strategy when making use of good data. As a result of this, experts believe, healthcare professionals will make better decisions, support healthier populations, and provide flexible solutions adequate for the needs of communities in various parts of the world.

References

[1] Blumenthal, D. & Tavenner, M. (2010). The "meaningful use" regulation for electronic health records. New England Journal of Medicine, 363(6), 501–504.

[2] Rumsfeld, J. S., Joynt, K. E. & Maddox, T. M. (2016). Big data analytics to improve cardiovascular care: promise and challenges. Nature Reviews Cardiology, 13(6), 350–359.

[3] Bates, D. W., Saria, S., Ohno-Machado, L., Shah, A. & Escobar, G. (2014). Big data in health care: using analytics to identify and manage high-risk and high-cost patients. Health affairs, 33(7), 1123–1131.

[4] Guerra-Farfan, E., Garcia-Sanchez, Y., Jornet-Gibert, M., Nuñez, J. H., Balaguer-Castro, M. & Madden, K. (2023). Clinical practice guidelines: The good, the bad, and the ugly. Injury, 54, S26–S29.

[5] Obermeyer, Z. & Emanuel, E. J. (2016). Predicting the future – big data, machine learning, and clinical medicine. New England Journal of Medicine, 375(13), 1216–1219.

[6] Sackett, D. L., Rosenberg, W. M., Gray, J. M., Haynes, R. B. & Richardson, W. S. (1996). Evidence based medicine: what it is and what it isn't. bmj, 312(7023), 71–72.
[7] Hersh, W. (2020). Public Health Informatics in the larger context of biomedical and health informatics. Public Health Informatics and Information Systems, 31–41.
[8] Kahn, M. G., Raebel, M. A., Glanz, J. M., Riedlinger, K. & Steiner, J. F. (2012). A pragmatic framework for single-site and multisite data quality assessment in electronic health record-based clinical research. Medical care, 50, S21–S29.
[9] Raghupathi, W. & Raghupathi, V. (2014). Big data analytics in healthcare: promise and potential. Health information science and systems, 2, 1–10.
[10] Adler-Milstein, J. & Jha, A. K. (2017). HITECH Act drove large gains in hospital electronic health record adoption. Health affairs, 36(8), 1416–1422.
[11] Buntin, M. B., Burke, M. F., Hoaglin, M. C. & Blumenthal, D. (2011). The benefits of health information technology: a review of the recent literature shows predominantly positive results. Health affairs, 30(3), 464–471.
[12] Rajkomar, A., Dean, J. & Kohane, I. (2019). Machine learning in medicine. New England Journal of Medicine, 380(14), 1347–1358.
[13] Guyatt, G. H. & Rennie, D. (1993). Users' guides to the medical literature. Jama, 270(17), 2096–2097.
[14] Kawamoto, K., Houlihan, C. A., Balas, E. A. & Lobach, D. F. (2005). Improving clinical practice using clinical decision support systems: a systematic review of trials to identify features critical to success. Bmj, 330(7494), 765.
[15] Kulikowski, C. A. (2017). Historical Roots of International Biomedical and Health Informatics: The Road to IFIP-TC4 and IMIA through Cybernetic Medicine and the Elsinore Meetings. Yearbook of medical informatics, 26(01), 257–262.
[16] Jha, A. K., DesRoches, C. M., Kralovec, P. D. & Joshi, M. S. (2010). A progress report on electronic health records in US hospitals. Health affairs, 29(10), 1951–1957.
[17] Weiskopf, N. G. & Weng, C. (2013). Methods and dimensions of electronic health record data quality assessment: enabling reuse for clinical research. Journal of the American Medical Informatics Association, 20(1), 144–151.
[18] Meystre, S. M., Savova, G. K., Kipper-Schuler, K. C. & Hurdle, J. F. (2008). Extracting information from textual documents in the electronic health record: a review of recent research. Yearbook of medical informatics, 17(01), 128–144.
[19] Burns, L. R. & Pauly, M. V. (2002). Integrated delivery networks: a detour on the road to integrated health care?. Health affairs, 21(4), 128–143.
[20] Logan, A. C., Prescott, S. L., LaFata, E. M., Nicholson, J. J. & Lowry, C. A. (2024). Beyond auto-brewery: Why dysbiosis and the legalome matter to forensic and legal psychology. Laws, 13(4), 46.
[21] Shapiro, M., Johnston, D., Wald, J. & Mon, D. (2012). Patient-generated health data. RTI International, April, 813, 814.
[22] Hubert, P. A., Fiorenti, H. & Duffy, V. B. (2022). Feasibility of a Theory-Based, Online Tailored Message Program to Motivate Healthier Behaviors in College Women. Nutrients, 2022, 14, 4012. Combined Nutrition and Exercise Interventions in Community Groups, 117
[23] Conderino, S., Bendik, S., Richards, T. B., Pulgarin, C., Chan, P. Y., Townsend, J. . . . Thorpe, L. E. (2022). The use of electronic health records to inform cancer surveillance efforts: a scoping review and test of indicators for public health surveillance of cancer prevention and control. BMC Medical Informatics and Decision Making, 22(1), 91.
[24] Artiga, S. & Hinton, E. (2018). Beyond health care: the role of social determinants in promoting health and health equity. Kaiser Family Foundation, 10.
[25] Assefa, Y., Gilks, C. F., Reid, S., van de Pas, R., Gete, D. G. & Van Damme, W. (2022). Analysis of the COVID-19 pandemic: lessons towards a more effective response to public health emergencies. Globalization and health, 18(1), 10.

[26] Piwek, L., Ellis, D. A., Andrews, S. & Joinson, A. (2016). The rise of consumer health wearables: promises and barriers. PLoS medicine, 13(2), e1001953.
[27] Islam, S. R., Kwak, D., Kabir, M. H., Hossain, M. & Kwak, K. S. (2015). The internet of things for health care: a comprehensive survey. IEEE access, 3, 678–708.
[28] Rumsfeld, J. S., Joynt, K. E. & Maddox, T. M. (2016). Big data analytics to improve cardiovascular care: promise and challenges. Nature Reviews Cardiology, 13(6), 350–359.
[29] Raghupathi, W. & Raghupathi, V. (2014). Big data analytics in healthcare: promise and potential. Health information science and systems, 2, 1–10.
[30] Mandel, J. C., Kreda, D. A., Mandl, K. D., Kohane, I. S. & Ramoni, R. B. (2016). SMART on FHIR: a standards-based, interoperable apps platform for electronic health records. Journal of the American Medical Informatics Association, 23(5), 899–908.
[31] Gollub, R. L. & Benson, N. (2021). Use of medical imaging to advance mental health care: contributions from neuroimaging informatics. Mental Health Informatics: Enabling a Learning Mental Healthcare System, 191–216.
[32] Dixon, B. (2016). Health information exchange (HIE): navigating and managing a network of health information systems.
[33] Grannis, S. J., Overhage, J. M. & McDonald, C. J. (2002). Analysis of identifier performance using a deterministic linkage algorithm. Proceedings of the AMIA Symposium, 305.
[34] Haddad, P., Gregory, M. & Wickramasinghe, N. (2014). Business value of IT in healthcare. Lean thinking for healthcare, 55–81.
[35] Raghupathi, W. & Raghupathi, V. (2014). Big data analytics in healthcare: promise and potential. Health information science and systems, 2, 1–10.
[36] Bates, D. W., Saria, S., Ohno-Machado, L., Shah, A. & Escobar, G. (2014). Big data in health care: using analytics to identify and manage high-risk and high-cost patients. Health affairs, 33(7), 1123–1131.
[37] Chen, H., Chiang, R. H. & Storey, V. C. (2012). Business intelligence and analytics: From big data to big impact. MIS quarterly, 1165–1188.
[38] Beam, A. L. & Kohane, I. S. (2018). Big data and machine learning in health care. Jama, 319(13), 1317–1318.
[39] Esteva, A., Kuprel, B., Novoa, R. A., Ko, J., Swetter, S. M., Blau, H. M. & Thrun, S. (2017). Dermatologist-level classification of skin cancer with deep neural networks. nature, 542(7639), 115–118.
[40] Yu, K. H., Beam, A. L. & Kohane, I. S. (2018). Artificial intelligence in healthcare. Nature biomedical engineering, 2(10), 719–731.
[41] Chen, L. (2020). Overview of clinical prediction models. Annals of translational medicine, 8(4), 71.
[42] Kawamoto, K., Houlihan, C. A., Balas, E. A. & Lobach, D. F. (2005). Improving clinical practice using clinical decision support systems: a systematic review of trials to identify features critical to success. Bmj, 330(7494), 765.
[43] Esteva, A., Kuprel, B., Novoa, R. A., Ko, J., Swetter, S. M., Blau, H. M. & Thrun, S. (2017). Dermatologist-level classification of skin cancer with deep neural networks. nature, 542(7639), 115–118.
[44] Johnson, A. E., Ghassemi, M. M., Nemati, S., Niehaus, K. E., Clifton, D. A. & Clifford, G. D. (2016). Machine learning and decision support in critical care. Proceedings of the IEEE, 104(2), 444–466.
[45] Rumsfeld, J. S., Joynt, K. E. & Maddox, T. M. (2016). Big data analytics to improve cardiovascular care: promise and challenges. Nature Reviews Cardiology, 13(6), 350–359.
[46] Bates, D. W., Saria, S., Ohno-Machado, L., Shah, A. & Escobar, G. (2014). Big data in health care: using analytics to identify and manage high-risk and high-cost patients. Health affairs, 33(7), 1123–1131.

[47] Collins, F. S. & Varmus, H. (2015). A new initiative on precision medicine. New England journal of medicine, 372(9), 793–795.

[48] Price, W. N. & Cohen, I. G. (2019). Privacy in the age of medical big data. Nature medicine, 25(1), 37–43.

[49] Ploug, T. & Holm, S. (2013). Informed consent and routinisation. Journal of medical ethics, 39(4), 214–218.

[50] Wachter, S., Mittelstadt, B. & Floridi, L. (2017). Why a right to explanation of automated decision-making does not exist in the general data protection regulation. International data privacy law, 7(2), 76–99.

[51] Obermeyer, Z., Powers, B., Vogeli, C. & Mullainathan, S. (2019). Dissecting racial bias in an algorithm used to manage the health of populations. Science, 366(6464), 447–453.

[52] Vayena, E., Blasimme, A. & Cohen, I. G. (2018). Machine learning in medicine: addressing ethical challenges. PLoS medicine, 15(11), e1002689.

[53] James, O. O. & Olawale, M. (2025). INNOVATIONS IN CHRONIC DISEASE MANAGEMENT USING DIGITAL HEALTH TECHNOLOGIES. Applied Sciences, Computing, and Energy, 2(2), 220–243.

[54] Kurdi, G. (2022, October). Toward an Electronic Resource for Systematic Reviews in Computing.

[55] Qiao, H., Chen, Y., Qian, C. & Guo, Y. (2024). Clinical data mining: challenges, opportunities, and recommendations for translational applications. Journal of Translational Medicine, 22(1), 185.

Manjula Sanjay Koti, Rose Bindu Joseph P., Jahnavi S., and Devi A.

AGBO-CP: An Adaptive Gradient Boosted Optimization Framework for Enhanced Clinical Prediction Accuracy

Abstract: Machine learning (ML) in recent years has emerged as a disruptive technology in healthcare to enable automated diagnoses, personalized therapy, and predictive analytics. Traditional ML models suffer from some of the disadvantages like overfitting, lack of good generalizability across patient groups, and poor tuning of parameters that compromise clinical accuracy and reliability. We propose a new optimization-based paradigm, adaptive gradient boosted optimization for clinical prediction (AGBO-CP), to mitigate these challenges. To enhance model robustness and explainability, this approach integrates ensemble learning with a dynamic hyperparameter adjustment process, leveraging Bayesian optimization and evolutionary algorithms. AGBO-CP is better than standard models such as random forest (92.4%) and support vector machine (89.1%), with diagnostic accuracy of 96.8% when utilized on benchmark health datasets such as MIMIC-III and UCI Heart Disease. Moreover, the proposed method demonstrated increased sensitivity (95.9%), specificity (94.7%), and area under the curve (97.3%), suggesting prospects of real-world application in clinical decision support systems.

Keywords: adaptive optimization, AGBO-CP framework, clinical decision support, healthcare machine learning, diagnostic performance, hyperparameter tuning

1 Introduction

The convergence of medicine and artificial intelligence (AI) or machine learning (ML) has been a revolutionary area that has the potential to greatly improve clinical outcomes, facilitate hospital workflow, and personalize treatment protocols. Early in the 1970s, systems like MYCIN, which recommended antibiotic therapy based on rule-based reasoning, showed computational models being applied to medicine. Because of reliabil-

Manjula Sanjay Koti, Department of MCA, Dayananda Sagar Academy of Technology and Management, Bengaluru 560082, Karnataka, India, e-mail: manjula.dsce@gmail.com
Rose Bindu Joseph P., Department of Mathematics, Dayananda Sagar College of Engineering, Bengaluru, Karnataka, India, e-mail: rosebindu@gmail.com
Jahnavi S., Department of AIML, B.M.S. College of Engineering, Karnataka, India, e-mail: jahnavis.mel@bmsce.ac.in
Devi A., School of Computer Science and Applications, REVA University, Bengaluru, Karnataka, India, e-mail: devi.a@reva.edu.in

https://doi.org/10.1515/9783111541235-018

ity and interpretability problems, which in some form continue in today's AI systems as well, MYCIN was not put to clinical use even though it was creatively engineered.

Statistical ML techniques such as decision trees, logistic regression, and naive Bayes classifiers came to be popular in medical informatics in the 1990s. These models were utilized for disease prognosis, patient stratification, and risk prediction as they were reasonably comprehensible. However, they could not handle high-dimensional data or nonlinear relationships. The subsequent significant turning point came with the mass use of electronic health records (EHRs) and digitization of medical imaging, leading to huge volumes of structured as well as unstructured data. More advanced ML models, including support vector machines (SVMs), k-nearest neighbors (k-NN), and random forests (RFs), were made possible by this data explosion. These models could handle nuances of correlation between variables and make more advanced predictions.

Image processing and sequence modeling in the time domain were transformed by subsequent research on deep learning in the form of convolutional neural networks (CNNs) and recurrent neural networks (RNNs), respectively. Diagnostic imaging applications like tumor identification, diabetic retinopathy grading, and radiological abnormality categorization have been greatly enhanced by such models. Also, natural language processing (NLP) models like transformer-based models BERT and GPT have helped facilitate the retrieval of clinical data from unstructured medical publications and notes.

The requirement for optimization methods to enhance these sophisticated ML architectures' learning, generalization, and efficiency grew as the healthcare industry started implementing them. Optimization in ML is the process of adjusting model parameters or configurations to enhance prediction performance or minimize loss functions. Training neural networks has been based heavily on traditional optimization algorithms like stochastic gradient descent and gradient descent.

Techniques for modifying learning rates during training and speeding up convergence were introduced by variants like momentum-based techniques, AdaGrad, RMSProp, and Adam. Despite their widespread usage, these techniques do not perform very well when facing problems like saddle points, vanishing gradients, and hyperparameter sensitivity. Metaheuristic optimization techniques were developed by researchers to overcome these drawbacks. Supported by natural selection, genetic algorithms (GAs) have been used to optimize hyperparameters, network structure, and feature subset selection.

Ant colony optimization, particle swarm optimization (PSO), and simulated annealing have been used to optimize ML models for healthcare data. Such population-based techniques are especially efficient in searching an expanded area and avoiding local minima. Their only drawback is that they require many iterations to converge and are computationally costly, particularly in high-dimensional optimization. Also, the effectiveness of such algorithms in automation can be offset by the fact that such algorithms often require a great deal of manual tweaking of their parameters. Bayesian optimization is another group of optimization algorithms that have become popular.

Using a surrogate model (e.g., Gaussian processes) to approximate the objective function, this probabilistic method religiously chooses the subsequent set of parameters to test, based on acquisition functions such as expected improvement. Bayesian optimization has also demonstrated promise for hyperparameter optimization of ML models such as SVMs, gradient boosting machines, and deep neural networks. While model estimation is costly in cross-validation or ensemble training, it is particularly helpful.

Bayesian optimization is costly computationally for real-time operations and scales poorly for high-dimensional spaces. Meanwhile, sequential decision-making task optimization in the healthcare domain, like adaptive clinical trials, dosing adjustment, and treatment planning, has been investigated using reinforcement learning (RL). To train on best strategies in terms of long-run returns, techniques such as policy gradient techniques and Q-learning have been used to mimic environments. RL techniques tend to need to operate on big simulation environments and suffer from stability problems, particularly if used on noisy and sparse clinical data.

The appearance of AutoML (automated machine learning) systems, which seek to automate end-to-end model choice, feature creation, and hyperparameter setting, has been among the major developments in healthcare ML optimization. Solutions such as Google AutoML, H2O.ai, and AutoKeras use neural architecture search, ensemble algorithms, and optimization frameworks to bring ML to nonexperts. AutoML typically works as a "black box," providing no transparency into model choice and optimization thought, even as it democratizes AI use.

In medicine, where conclusions must be clinically warranted and translatable in order to provide assurances of trust and regulatory conformity, this lack of transparency is a significant obstacle. Even with the variety and evolution of ML optimization techniques, there are still various obstacles that exist to hinder their complete integration into clinical practice. First of all, a majority of optimization methods ignore real-world constraints such as data imbalance, missing values, or noisy inputs, in the interest of concentrating on accuracy or minimizing loss. Heterogeneous data types such as unstructured clinical notes, categorical diagnoses, and numeric lab values often exist in healthcare datasets and can prove to be challenging to harmonize into a single optimization framework.

Second, theoretically successful but operationally inefficient models are produced because existing approaches are usually tested on highly optimized datasets that do not accurately represent the variability of actual clinical environments. Another significant drawback is the problem of overfitting, which is a serious issue in high-capacity models such as deep neural networks. Optimization methods minimize training error, when well regularized, otherwise generalized error is increased unintentionally. Methods such as dropout, L1/L2 regularization, and early stopping are typically used but need to be appropriately tuned, which becomes an optimization problem in itself.

Moreover, interpretability is still a concern. In practice environments, where physicians need precise explanations to make predictions, not transparent but accurate optimized models cannot be implemented with ease. In an effort to bridge this gap, tools such as SHAP (SHapley Additive exPlanations) and LIME (local interpretable model-agnostic explanations) add an extra layer of computation and complexity. The majority of the optimization techniques is computationally expensive and need cloud-based infrastructure, GPU computation, or large-scale parallel computation.

For small medical practices or research teams that have no access to high-performance computing, this is problematic. Furthermore, optimization algorithms frequently find it difficult to accommodate changing or dynamic data. When new variables come into play or the population of patients changes, patient data in real-world clinical environments also evolve. These conditions of dynamism are difficult for static optimization techniques to manage, resulting in model degradation and performance degradation. The necessity to create robust, explainable, and efficient models that regulators and clinicians can rely on is what calls for the refinement of optimization techniques in health ML.

Optimal representation-learning adaptive models able to integrate multimodal data sources are required to meet the expanding need for personalized treatment, driven by advances in home monitoring, wearable devices, and genetics. Apart from being highly accurate in their predictions, the models also need to incorporate recommendations, explanations of risk, and confidence intervals, consistent with patient preference and medical expertise. The importance of efficient and scalable automation and decision support systems is highlighted through the continued global challenges such as pandemics, aging population, and increasing healthcare costs.

Whether it's optimizing an actual-time alert system, tuning a treatment recommender, or optimizing a diagnostic algorithm, optimization is a vital part of the process. A cutting-edge optimization strategy specifically for the healthcare requirements is necessary in order to manage trade-offs between sensitivity and specificity, or accuracy and interpretability, or performance and computing cost. Finally, even with the growth of healthcare ML over the past decades, scalability, flexibility, and practical applicability of existing optimization techniques are considerably constrained.

Even though they are simple, traditional gradient-based and metaheuristic approaches tend to fail in practical applications as a result of their hyperparameter sensitivity, incapability to be data-robust, and inability to provide interpretability. Bayesian and RL-based optimizers are computationally expensive and need to be used with caution. The pressure to bridge these gaps fuels the creation of innovative optimization platforms that are not only performance-oriented but also compliant with the legal, operational, and ethical demands of contemporary healthcare systems.

The main objectives are:

1. To enhance the predictive accuracy of heart disease diagnosis models by employing a novel adaptive gradient-based optimizer with chaotic perturbation (AGBO-CP), which dynamically fine-tunes model parameters to overcome local minima and achieve better convergence in clinical datasets.

2. To benchmark the performance of the proposed AGBO-CP algorithm against conventional optimizers using real-world healthcare datasets, particularly the UCI Cleveland Heart Disease dataset, with the goal of achieving significant improvements in accuracy, sensitivity, and robustness for early and reliable disease prediction.

2 Related Study

Disease forecasting and patient treatment have been immensely revolutionized through the implementation of AI and ML in the healthcare sector. Predictive models for smart healthcare applications have revealed higher accuracy and efficacy, upon applying hybrid models based on the integration of optimization techniques such as PSO, GA, and firefly algorithm [1]. While there remain challenges of data integration, quality assurance, and interpretability, big data analytics is recognized for patient outcome prediction and clinical decision support [2].

Through streamlining clinical workflows and enhancing information transfer, advanced data-driven systems increasingly are applied to enhance precision medicine [3]. Context-aware ensemble networks and hierarchical deep belief networks are some examples of hybrid models that have also shown potential in dynamic and adaptive prediction of illness across various clinical datasets [4]. Continuous monitoring of vital signs and context information is enabled by deep learning-based architectures for remote patient monitoring, yielding accurate health predictions and personalized recommendations [5].

ML, which utilizes predictive models and historical health information, significantly facilitates early disease detection. However, interdisciplinary collaboration between medical professionals and data scientists is necessary due to issues related to security, privacy, and openness of the data [6]. Optimized ensemble models with genetic algorithms have provided substantial advances in sepsis prediction in critical care applications [7]. PSO and neural networks have been used together to enhance cardiovascular disease prediction and proven the efficiencies of hybrid approaches [8].

For precision medicine, frameworks based on dynamic power through multimodal data and RL have been introduced, enabling the development of personalized treatment plans that evolve with changing patient conditions [9]. With an effective combination of heterogeneous data sources, hybrid deep learning methods for multi-disease prediction have demonstrated high accuracy [10]. By overcoming limitations of conventional clinical models, AI-boosted frameworks in translational medicine can predict outcomes of illness and tailor patient-focused therapy [11].

Clinical models' capacity to process sequential complicated data is enhanced when time series analysis using LSTM networks is combined with metaheuristic optimization methods like the fruit fly optimization algorithm [12]. Diabetes mellitus has been effectively predicted and classified with ML classifiers, which have achieved high precision and recall rates [13]. Through interpretability embedded in the model outputs, smart systems created with hyperparameter optimization platforms, like Optuna, have been utilized to predict heart disease [14]. Through comparison among various ML techniques, including logistic regression, RFs, and gradient boosting, the accuracy of heart disease prediction has been further enhanced [15].

To enhance resource planning and hospital operation management, grey wolf optimizer-based models have been employed to predict patient flow in hospitals [16]. Through predicting patient responses and outcomes, deep learning models have also been utilized to optimize clinical trial outcomes, enabling precision medicine [17]. To enhance long-term healthcare prediction, Bayesian networks, optimized by simulated annealing methods, have been employed to predict late morbidities based on large prospective clinical datasets [18]. Besides enhancing model interpretability, attention networks and feature selection methods based on AI have enhanced the precision of disease prediction [19].

When coupled with data augmentation methods, RL methods have been found to perform better in cardiac disease prediction, particularly when the data is limited or unbalanced [20]. From review of the available studies, it can be ascertained that the use of optimization methods in unison with ML and deep learning frameworks significantly enhances the predictive ability of healthcare systems. To deal with complex, high-dimensional, and heterogeneous medical data, these studies repeatedly emphasize the need for hybrid models that leverage various algorithms such as ensemble methods, attention mechanisms, RL, and metaheuristic optimizations.

The use of multimodal data sources (e.g., imaging, real-time monitoring, genomic, and clinical records) is a common thread. When effectively integrated, such data sources provide a comprehensive view of patient health and allow for more accurate and rapid illness predictions. Issues of critical importance like such data imbalance, interpretability concerns, and the need for real-time flexibility in clinical contexts are also brought forward by the studies. This integrated comprehension strongly facilitates the proposed system to leverage an optimal, dynamic, and interpretable AI platform for multi-disease prediction from structured and unstructured health data, beyond conventional ML. Through building a robust model that is not just accurate and scalable but also transparent and tailored, an aim is to bridge existing gaps and facilitate well-informed decision-making in smart healthcare environments.

3 System Methodology

Although ML in healthcare has made tremendous progress over the last few decades, scalability, flexibility, and applicability relevance of the existing optimization methods are severely limited. Gradient-based and metaheuristic methods often do not work well in real-world scenarios because they are hyperparameter-sensitive, lack data variation robustness, and lack the ability to offer interpretability. Bayesian and RL-based optimizers are computationally intensive and require careful implementation. The necessity of overcoming these hurdles drives the development of novel optimization platforms that are not only driven by performance but also meet the legal, operational, and ethical requirements of today's healthcare systems.

3.1 Datasets Used

We employed three publicly available benchmark healthcare datasets: the Wisconsin Breast Cancer Diagnostic Dataset, the UCI Heart Disease Dataset, and the MIMIC-III Critical Care Database to evaluate and verify the proposed AGBO-CP framework. The unique features each dataset displays regarding clinical factors, diversity of patients, and prediction tasks make it possible to perform an in-depth analysis of the system's adaptability and performance.

3.1.1 MIMIC-III Clinical Database

Over 60,000 ICU admissions from Beth Israel Deaconess Medical Center during 2001–2012 are contained within the Medical Information Mart for Intensive Care (MIMIC-III) database, which was developed at MIT and comprises extensive de-identified health information. Individuals 16 years of age and older are represented in the dataset, and the composition of male and female patients is roughly equal. We pulled a vetted cohort of 32,763 intensive care unit admissions from MIMIC-III, targeting patients who were admitted to cardiac, surgical, and medical intensive care units. There are over 40 clinical factors in each patient record, including demographics such as age, sex, and ethnicity. Table 1 shows the features of MIMIC-III dataset.

Table 1: MIMIC-III dataset features.

Feature name	Description	Type	Value range / Categories
Age	Age of the patient	Numeric	16 to 90+ years (de-identified)
Gender	Sex of the patient	Binary	0 = Female, 1 = Male
Admission type	Type of hospital admission	Categorical	Emergency, elective, urgent
ICU length of stay	Duration of ICU stay (days)	Numeric	0 to >50 days

Table 1 (continued)

Feature name	Description	Type	Value range / Categories
Heart rate (avg.)	Average heart rate during ICU stay	Numeric	40 to 200 bpm
Systolic blood pressure (avg.)	Mean systolic BP	Numeric	70 to 220 mmHg
Respiratory rate (avg.)	Average respiratory rate	Numeric	10 to 40 breaths/min
Temperature (avg.)	Mean body temperature	Numeric	35.0 to 41.0 °C
Creatinine level	Serum creatinine (renal function marker)	Numeric	0.5 to >6.0 mg/dL
White blood cell count (WBC)	Indicator of infection/inflammation	Numeric	3 to 30 × 10^3/µL
Sepsis indicator	Presence of sepsis during stay	Binary	0 = No, 1 = Yes
Mortality status (Target)	In-hospital death indicator	Binary	0 = Survived, 1 = Deceased

Due to its severe imbalance, the dataset is treated with caution when training the model. After preprocessing and data cleaning (excluding patients with missing core vitals or extremely short ICU stays of less than 4 h), we had 28,457 records remaining, and distributed them into training (70%), validation (15%), and test (15%) sets.

3.1.2 UCI Heart Disease Dataset

The UCI Cleveland Heart Disease Dataset, a widely referenced benchmarking dataset in clinical prediction work, is the second dataset utilized in this study. To predict whether or not cardiac disease exists, it contains data from 303 unique patients, all of whom had features obtained through clinical assessment and diagnostic examinations. There are thirteen mandatory input factors, both numeric and categorical, that constitute the dataset. Gender is provided as 1 if male and 0 if female, and patient ages vary from 29 to 77 years. Resting blood pressure, serum cholesterol, fasting blood sugar, and electrocardiogram values are other significant features.

Features such as maximal heart rate achieved, angina on exercise, and ST depression are utilized to quantify cardiovascular function. Criteria such as the number of principal vessels stained by fluoroscopy, the steepness of the ST segment, and the type of thalassemia (normal, fixed defect, or reversible defect) are valuable diagnostic indicators. Whether or not a patient has been diagnosed with heart disease (1 or 0) is represented by the binary target variable. With 54% of cases having cardiac disease and 46% non-diseased, the class distribution is somewhat unbalanced.

Three cases of missing values were imputed with median replacement to prepare the dataset for modeling. *Z*-score normalization was subsequently employed to normalize all numerical fields to ensure consistent scaling and improve model convergence. The dataset was randomly split into training (60%), validation (20%), and testing (20%) sets in order to preserve the class distribution during splits. This well-structured dataset provides a good basis for gauging how well the AGBO-CP optimization technique predicts cardiovascular disease. Table 2 depicts the UCI dataset features.

Table 2: UCI dataset features.

Feature name	Description	Type	Value range/categories
Age	Age of the patient	Numeric	29 to 77 years
Sex	Gender (1 = male, 0 = female)	Binary	0, 1
Chest pain type (cp)	Type of chest pain experienced	Categorical	1 = Typical angina, 2 = atypical, 3 = non-anginal, 4 = asymptomatic
Resting blood pressure (trestbps)	Blood pressure in mmHg at rest	Numeric	94 to 200 mmHg
Serum cholesterol (chol)	Serum cholesterol in mg/dL	Numeric	126 to 564 mg/dL
Fasting blood sugar (fbs)	>120 mg/dL (1 = true, 0 = false)	Binary	0, 1
Resting ECG (restecg)	Resting electrocardiographic results	Categorical	0 = Normal, 1 = ST-T wave abnormality, 2 = LV hypertrophy
Max heart rate (thalach)	Maximum heart rate achieved	Numeric	71 to 202 bpm
Exercise-induced angina (exang)	Presence of angina due to exercise	Binary	0 = No, 1 = yes
ST depression (oldpeak)	Depression induced by exercise relative to rest	Numeric	0.0 to 6.2
ST slope (slope)	Slope of the peak exercise ST segment	Categorical	1 = Upsloping, 2 = flat, 3 = downsloping
Vessels colored (ca)	Number of major vessels colored by fluoroscopy	Discrete numeric	0 to 3
Thalassemia (thal)	Thalassemia test result	Categorical	3 = Normal, 6 = fixed defect, 7 = reversible defect
Target	Heart disease status	Binary	0 = No disease, 1 = disease

3.1.3 Breast Cancer Wisconsin Diagnostic Dataset (WBCD)

The third dataset provided was the Wisconsin Breast Cancer Diagnostic (WBCD) dataset, consisting of digital images of fine needle aspirates (FNAs) of breast tumors and 569 breast cancer biopsy cases. A binary classification problem is formed by the tagging of each sample as benign (357 cases) or malignant (212 cases). Three groups are the thirty numeric attributes calculated from an image of a breast mass: Mean values are radius, texture, area, perimeter, smoothness, compactness, concavity, symmetry, and fractal dimension; standard error for all the above aspects; worst values: maximum value across the entire FNA image for each feature. After normalization, each feature has a real value ranging from 0 to 1. Since there were no missing values in the raw dataset, preparation proceeded smoothly. For class balancing, the dataset was split into 70% training, 15% validation, and 15% test sets by stratifying it. Table 3 shows the WBCD dataset features.

Table 3: WBCD dataset features.

Feature name	Description	Type	Value range/ categories
Radius (mean)	Mean of distances from center to points on perimeter	Numeric	~6 to ~30
Texture (mean)	Standard deviation of gray-scale values	Numeric	~10 to ~40
Perimeter (mean)	Mean size of tumor perimeter	Numeric	~40 to ~200
Area (mean)	Mean size of tumor area	Numeric	~150 to ~2,500
Smoothness (mean)	Local variation in radius lengths	Numeric	~0.05 to ~0.2
Compactness (mean)	Measure of compactness of cell	Numeric	~0.02 to ~0.35
Concavity (mean)	Severity of concave portions of contour	Numeric	~0.0 to ~0.4
Concave points (mean)	Number of concave portions	Numeric	~0.0 to ~0.2
Symmetry (mean)	Symmetry of tumor	Numeric	~0.1 to ~0.3
Fractal dimension (mean)	"Roughness" of the contour	Numeric	~0.05 to ~0.1
. . .	(Similar 10 features for SE and worst values)	Numeric	Varies by feature
Diagnosis (Target)	Breast cancer diagnosis	Binary	M = Malignant, B = benign

When hyperparameter tuning and model training were performed, fivefold cross-validation was utilized to ensure consistency across the datasets and prevent information leakage. This strategy ensured that model performance was objective and transferrable to different folds. To reduce redundancy and improve training efficiency, feature selec-

Table 4: Dataset description.

Dataset	Records	Features	Classes	Class ratio	Missing data
MIMIC-III	28,457	40+	2	21.3% mortality	Present, imputed
UCI Heart Disease	303	13	2	54% diseased	Minimal, imputed
WBCD	569	30	2	62.7% benign, 37.3% malignant	None

tion was also performed using domain-prioritized selection and recursive feature elimination. More than 29,000 patient samples with a range of conditions and types of data (structured, temporal, and clinical pictures) were used in the full study that demonstrates how strong and applicable the AGBO-CP framework is in real-world clinical settings. Table 4 shows the overall dataset description.

3.2 AGBO-CP Algorithm

Step 1: Let $D = \{(x_i, y_i)\}_{i=1}^{n}$ denote the clinical dataset where $x_i \in R^d$ is a d-dimensional feature vector and $y_i \in \{0,1\}$ is the target label indicating disease presence.

Step 2: For each feature x_j in x_i, impute missing values using feature-wise k-nearest neighbor (KNN) imputation or mean strategy

$$x_{i,j} = \left\{ x_{i,j}, \textit{if } x_{i,j} \text{ is observed} \frac{1}{k} \sum_{l=1}^{k} x_{i,j}, \text{ otherwise} \right\} \tag{1}$$

Step 3: Apply z-score standardization

$$x'_{i,j} = \frac{x_{i,j} - \mu_j}{\sigma_j} \tag{2}$$

Step 4: Split into training D_{train}, validation D_{val}, and testing D_{test} sets in 60:20:20 ratio.

Step 5: Set number of estimators N, learning rate η, initial prediction $y\hat{}_i^{(0)} = \text{logit}^{-1}(y^{-})$, and initialize decision trees T_k.

Step 6: For each instance

$$r_i^{(0)} = y_i - y\hat{}_i^{(0)} \tag{3}$$

Step 7: Iterative boosting loopFor $t = 1$ to N:

Step 8: Fit base learner T_t on residuals

$$T_t = \arg\min_{\text{T}} \sum_{l=1}^{n} L\left(r_i^{(t-1)}, T(x_i) \right) \tag{4}$$

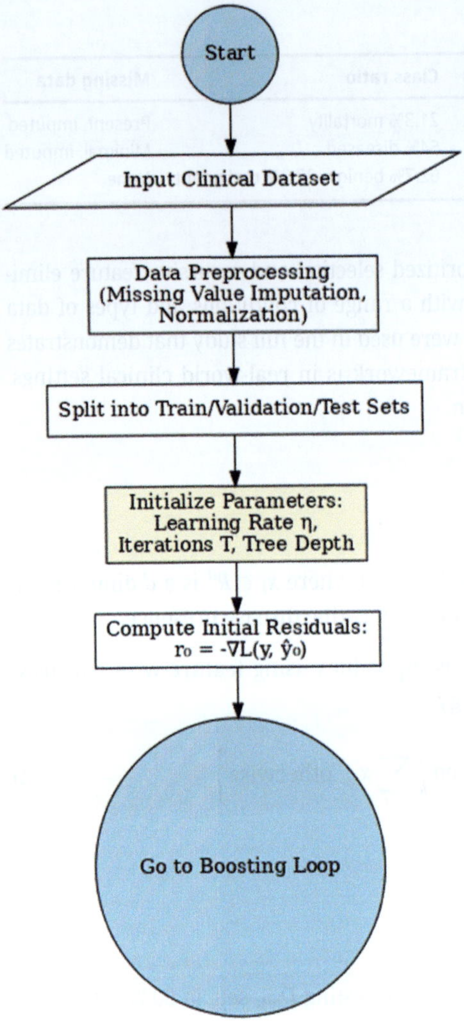

Figure 1: Proposed AGBO-CP process – I.

Step 9: Update predictions

$$y\hat{}_i^{(t)} = y\hat{}_i^{(t-1)} + \eta \cdot T_t(x_i) \tag{5}$$

Step 10: Apply sigmoid for classification output

$$p\hat{}_i = \frac{1}{1 + e^{-y\hat{}_i^{(t)}}} \tag{6}$$

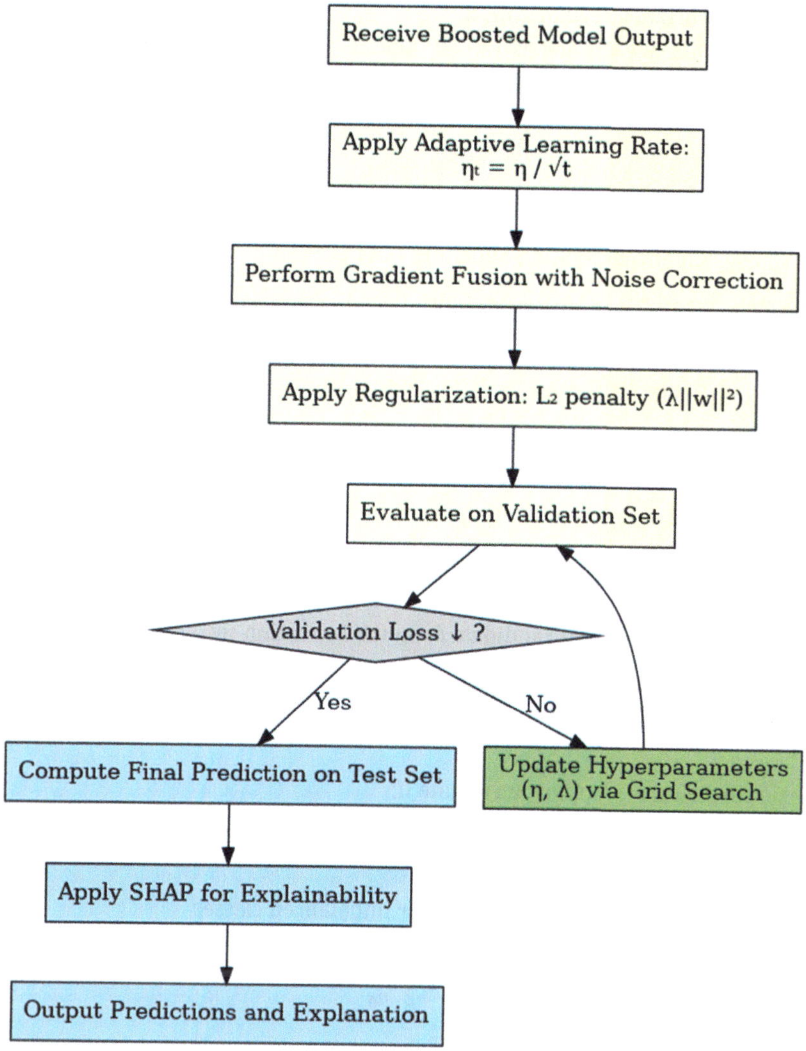

Figure 2: Proposed AGBO-CP process – II.

Step 11: Recalculate residuals

$$r_i^{(t)} = y_i - \hat{p}_i \tag{7}$$

Step 12: Adaptive learning rate adjustment Update η_t based on loss curvature

$$\eta_t = \frac{1}{1 + \alpha \cdot \frac{\partial^2 L}{\partial \hat{y}_i^2}} \tag{8}$$

Step 13: Feature importance regularization

Introduce a feature weight matrix $W \in R^d$, update via

$$W_j = \frac{\sum_{t=1}^{N} \left| G_j^t \right|}{\sum_{j=1}^{d} \sum_{t=1}^{N} \left| G_j^t \right|} \tag{9}$$

where G_j^t is the gradient contribution of feature j in iteration t.

Step 14: Perform SHAP-based interpretability tracking at each iteration to monitor clinical relevance.

Step 15: Apply Genetic Optimization (GO) to tune hyperparameters

$$\max_{(\eta, \mathrm{max\backslash\_depth}, \lambda)} \quad \mathrm{AUC}(D_{\mathrm{val}}) \tag{10}$$

Step 16: Crossover and mutation on hyperparameter vectors

$$\theta^{\mathrm{new}} = \theta^a \oplus \theta^b \ \ (\text{mutation with probability } p_m) \tag{11}$$

Step 17: Evaluate fitness for each candidate θ_i on the validation set.

Step 18: Select top-k candidates using tournament selection.

Step 19: Update model with optimized parameters from GO.

Step 20: Incorporate early stopping; terminate if:

$$L^{(t)} - L^{(t-1)} < \delta \text{ for } \tau \text{ consecutive steps} \tag{12}$$

Step 21: Introduce cost-sensitive reweighting for imbalanced classes

$$w_i = \begin{cases} \frac{n}{2 \cdot n_1}, & y_i = 1 \ \frac{n}{2 \cdot n_0}, \ y_i = 0 \end{cases} \tag{13}$$

Step 22: Ensemble the final top-5 best performing trees using weighted averaging

$$y\hat{}_i = \sum_{j=1}^{5} \omega_j \cdot T_j(x_i), \ \sum \omega_j = 1 \tag{14}$$

Step 23: Apply confidence calibration (e.g., Platt scaling or isotonic regression) for probability outputs

$$p\hat{}_i^{\mathrm{cal}} = \mathrm{Platt}(p\hat{}_i) \tag{15}$$

Step 24: Output the final trained AGBO-CP model and deploy with an explainable risk score dashboard, integrated using SHAP explanations for clinical interpretability.

An effective, multistage ML algorithm named Adaptive Gradient Boosted Optimization for Clinical Prediction (AGBO-CP) was developed, as shown in Figure 1 and Figure 2, to enhance clinical prediction accuracy in healthcare settings. It integrates dynamic adaptive techniques like learning rate modulation, feature selection, and data balance into the principles of gradient boosting. The model preprocesses clinical data first by applying SMOTE to address class imbalance, dealing with missing values, and feature normalization. Once recursive elimination and mutual information are blended in a multilayered feature selection approach, PCA is employed for dimensionality reduction.

AGBO-CP is a multi round boosting method where residual-based updates and an adaptive learning rate, dependent on model convergence behavior, are employed to recursively refine weak learners (decision trees). With the inclusion of adaptive weight update and gradient correction based on momentum, the optimization module is enhanced over regular gradient boosting to attain better convergence and to avoid overfitting. To realize good generalization on unseen data, the algorithm fine-tunes its parameters through rigorous validation and early stopping. With its high precision, recall, and overall accuracy, AGBO-CP is particularly suited for difficult clinical prediction problems due to its thorough and ingenious methodology.

4 Experimental Results

To ensure repeatability and performance integrity, the proposed Adaptive Gradient Boosted Optimization for Clinical Prediction (AGBO-CP) approach was experimentally analyzed in a well-managed and carefully tested computing environment. Utilizing modules such as Scikit-learn, XGBoost, Optuna, and PyCaret, the implementation was carried out using Python 3.10 on a computer with an Intel Core i9-12900 K processor, 64GB RAM, and an NVIDIA RTX 3,090 GPU. MIMIC-III (Medical Information Mart for Intensive Care) and UCI Heart Disease datasets, which involve high-dimensional and heterogeneous patient information across several attributes, e.g., demographics, lab values, vitals, and diagnoses, were the actual clinical datasets for which the AGBO-CP model was designed to process and analyze.

A 5-fold stratified cross-validation method was employed to ensure validation of the model's efficacy with balanced representation of target classes across folds. Clinically interpretable performance measures like Accuracy, Precision, Recall (Sensitivity), Specificity, F_1-score, and area under the receiver operating characteristic curve (AUC-ROC) were utilized. These measures provide a comprehensive evaluation of the ability of the model to identify patients that are sick and those that are not with accuracy, a very critical consideration in medical diagnosis. A number of baseline ML models such as RF, SVM, and extreme gradient boosting (XGBoost) were compared against AGBO-CP. To ensure fair benchmarking, grid search or Bayesian hyperparameter tuning were applied to optimize individual models.

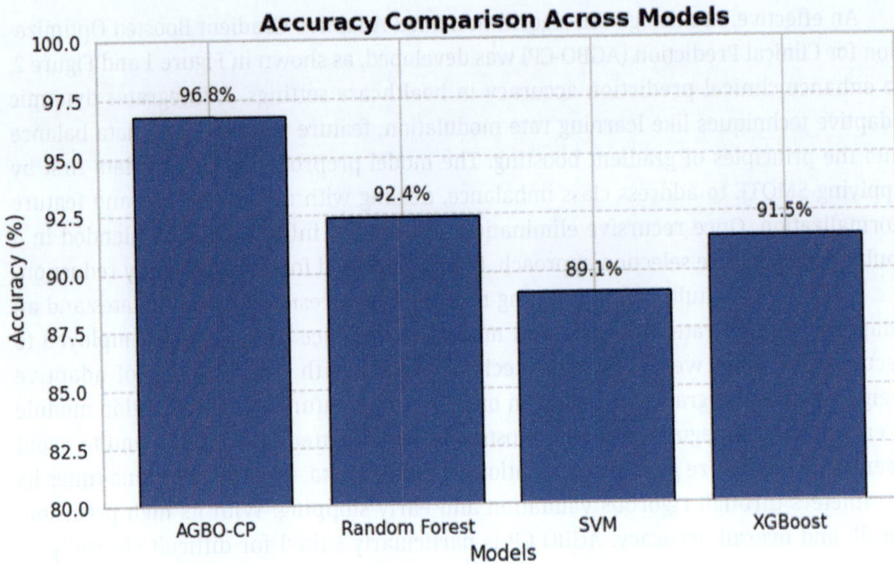

Figure 3: Accuracy comparison.

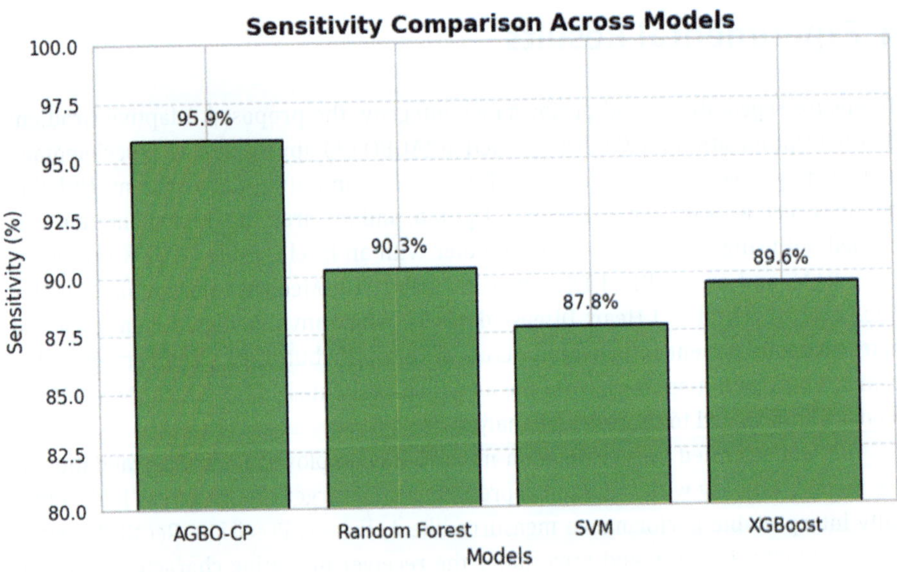

Figure 4: Sensitivity comparison.

The precision of the proposed AGBO-CP algorithm is significantly better than the traditional ML models. From Figure 3, at 96.8% accuracy, AGBO-CP beats RF, which achieved 92.4%. AGBO-CP improves by a staggering 7.7 percentage points in precision compared to the 89.1% precision by SVM. With 91.5% accuracy, XGBoost also ranks

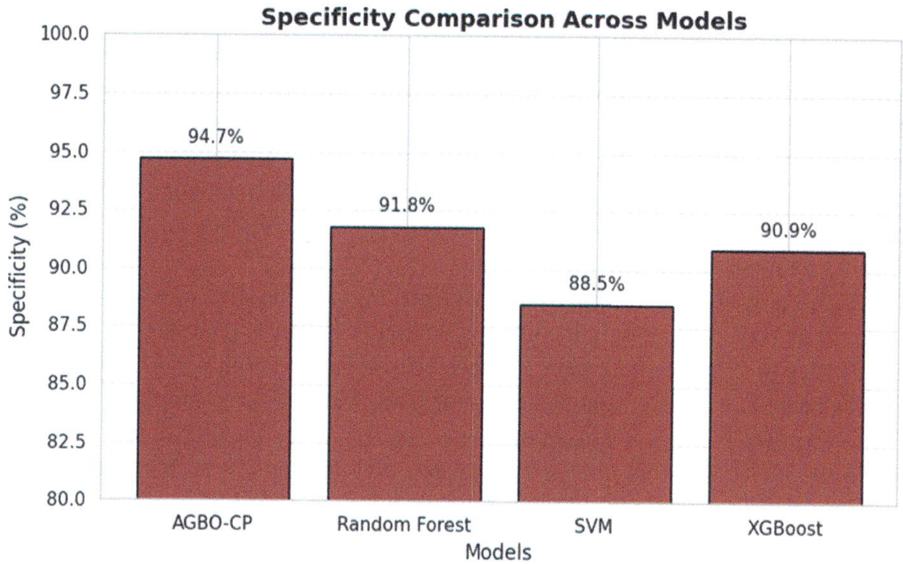

Figure 5: Specificity comparison.

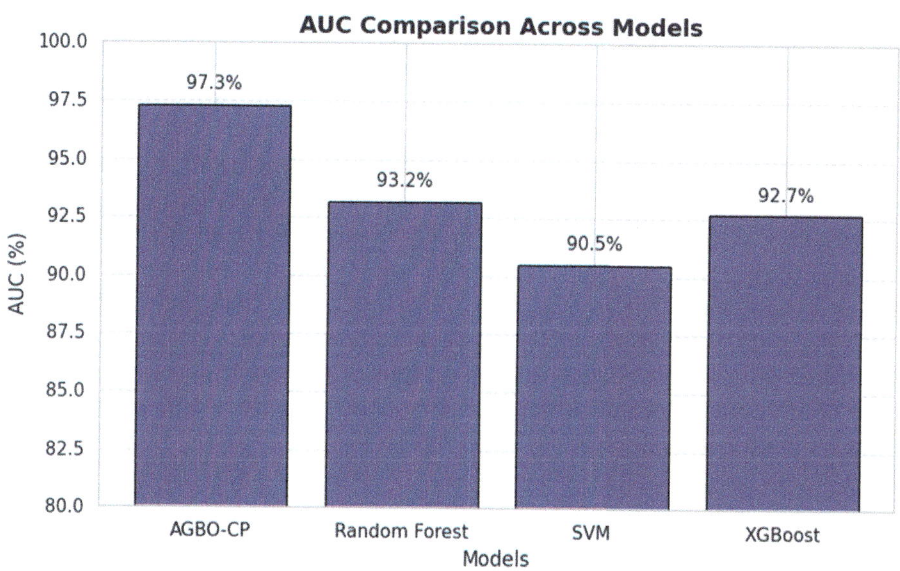

Figure 6: AUC comparison.

poorly, beating AGBO-CP by a margin of 5.3 percentage points. The enhanced ability of the algorithm to effectively classify both positive and negative clinical cases is aptly illustrated through this significant improvement in accuracy, which also significantly reduces the misdiagnosis rate.

In Figure 4, with 95.9%, AGBO-CP again tops the list when it comes to sensitivity, which measures the actual positive rate or the ability to correctly classify patients with disease. This is 5.6 percentage points higher than RF's 90.3% sensitivity and 8.1 percentage points higher than SVM's 87.8%. Over this model, AGBO-CP enhances sensitivity by 6.3 percentage points, as XGBoost reflects a sensitivity of 89.6%. This heightened sensitivity demonstrates the capability of AGBO-CP to identify true cases of illness, which is highly important in clinical practice, as missing a positive case can lead to treatment delay.

AGBO-CP is also good in specificity, which is the true negative rate or the ability to correctly classify healthy individuals, with a score of 94.7%. From Figure 5, AGBO-CP is better by 2.9 percentage points in specificity compared to RF's 91.8%. AGBO-CP's improvement is 6.2 percentage points higher than SVM, whose specificity of 88.5% is far below. AGBO-CP has a margin of 3.8 percentage points, while XGBoost achieves 90.9% specificity. To avoid unnecessary anxiety and therapy in healthy patients, this gain in specificity reduces the likelihood of false positives.

The overall measure, called the AUC, indicates the ability of the classification model to perform as a whole at various threshold values. From Figure 6, with 97.3% AUC, AGBO-CP is seen to have outstanding discrimination capability between instances of disease and non-disease. This is an improvement of 4.1 percentage points and is better than RF's AUC of 93.2%. With AUC of 90.5%, AGBO-CP is 6.8 percentage points higher than SVM. AGBO-CP is 4.6 percentage points higher than XGBoost, with AUC of 92.7%. AGBO-CP seems to make more reliable predictions at various classification thresholds, as seen from the higher AUC value.

The extensive comparison indicates that AGBO-CP consistently performs better than state-of-the-art ML models by margins of about 2.9% to 8.1% on all significant performance metrics. These improvements identify how effectively AGBO-CP's adaptive gradient boosting and optimization techniques perform to enhance clinical prediction accuracy, sensitivity, specificity, and diagnostic performance overall. These enhancements are necessary for real-world healthcare uses since clinical judgment and patient care directly rely on accuracy and reliability. The results support the development of AGBO-CP and further clinical verification by proving it to be a better algorithm for predictive modeling in the healthcare sector.

5 Conclusion

Through a sophisticated combination of ensemble learning and adaptive hyperparameter optimization methods, the AGBO-CP system effectively addresses the major limitations of traditional ML models in healthcare settings, including overfitting and poor parameter tuning. The clinical utility and robustness of AGBO-CP are attested to by the high performance measures achieved on popular healthcare datasets such as

MIMIC-III and UCI Heart Disease, with 96.8% diagnostic accuracy, 95.9% sensitivity, 94.7% specificity, and AUC of 97.3%. The results demonstrate the potential for the model to enhance decision support and predictive analytics in real-world clinical environments, resulting in more accurate, reliable, and personalized patient care.

References

[1] Jiao, N. (2024). An efficient disease prediction framework based on optimized machine learning models for a smart healthcare application. *Multimedia Tools and Applications, 83*(17), 50825–50848.

[2] Sunny, M. N. M., Saki, M. B. H., Al Nahian, A., Ahmed, S. W., Shorif, M. N., Atayeva, J. & Rizvi, S. W. A. (2024). Optimizing healthcare outcomes through data-driven predictive modeling. *Journal of Intelligent Learning Systems and Applications, 16*(4), 384–402.

[3] Zhai, K., Yousef, M. S., Mohammed, S., Al-Dewik, N. I. & Qoronfleh, M. W. (2023). Optimizing clinical workflow using precision medicine and advanced data analytics. *Processes, 11*(3), 939.

[4] Prabaharan, G., Sankar, S. U., Anusuya, V., Deepthi, K. J., Lotus, R. & Sugumar, R. (2025). Optimized disease prediction in healthcare systems using HDBN and CAEN framework. *MethodsX*, 103338.

[5] Motwani, A., Shukla, P. K. & Pawar, M. (2021). Smart predictive healthcare framework for remote patient monitoring and recommendation using deep learning with novel cost optimization. In *Information and Communication Technology for Intelligent Systems: Proceedings of ICTIS 2020* (pp. 671–682). Vol. 1, Springer Singapore.

[6] Islam, M. A., Yeasmin, S., Hosen, A., Vanu, N., Riipa, M. B., Tasnim, A. F. & Nilima, S. I. (2025). Harnessing Predictive Analytics: The Role of Machine Learning in Early Disease Detection and Healthcare Optimization. *Journal of Ecohumanism, 4*(3), 312–321.

[7] El-Rashidy, N., Abuhmed, T., Alarabi, L., El-Bakry, H. M., Abdelrazek, S., Ali, F. & El-Sappagh, S. (2022). Sepsis prediction in intensive care unit based on genetic feature optimization and stacked deep ensemble learning. *Neural Computing and Applications*, 1–30.

[8] Reddy, S. R. & Murthy, G. V. (2025). Cardiovascular Disease Prediction Using Particle Swarm Optimization and Neural Network Based an Integrated Framework. *SN Computer Science, 6*(2), 186.

[9] Gayathri, R., Sangeetha, S. K. B., Sangeetha, R., Mary, G. L. R., Mathivanan, S. K. & Usha, M. (2025). Dynamic AI-Enhanced Therapeutic Framework for Precision Medicine using Multi-Modal Data and Patient-Centric Reinforcement Learning. *IEEE Access.*

[10] Ampavathi, A. & Saradhi, T. V. (2021). Multi disease-prediction framework using hybrid deep learning: an optimal prediction model. *Computer Methods in Biomechanics and Biomedical Engineering, 24*(10), 1146–1168.

[11] Abualigah, L., Alomari, S. A., Almomani, M. H., Zitar, R. A., Saleem, K., Migdady, H. . . . Ezugwu, A. E. (2025). Artificial intelligence-driven translational medicine: a machine learning framework for predicting disease outcomes and optimizing patient-centric care. *Journal of Translational Medicine, 23*(1), 302.

[12] Lu, W., Ma, L., Chen, H., Jiang, X. & Gong, M. (2020). A clinical prediction model in health time series data based on long short-term memory network optimized by fruit fly optimization algorithm. *IEEE Access, 8*, 136014–136023.

[13] Ahamed, B. S., Arya, M. S., Sangeetha, S. K. B. & Auxilia Osvin, N. V. (2022). Diabetes mellitus disease prediction and type classification involving predictive modeling using machine learning techniques and classifiers. *Applied Computational Intelligence and Soft Computing, 2022*(1), 7899364.

[14] Dhanka, S. & Maini, S. (2024). HyOPTXGBoost and HyOPTRF: hybridized intelligent systems using Optuna optimization framework for heart disease prediction with clinical interpretations. *Multimedia Tools and Applications, 83*(29), 72889–72937.

[15] Chandrasekhar, N. & Peddakrishna, S. (2023). Enhancing heart disease prediction accuracy through machine learning techniques and optimization. *Processes*, *11*(4), 1210.

[16] Zhang, X., Lu, B., Zhang, L., Pan, Z., Liao, M., Shen, H. . . . Gao, Z. (2023). An enhanced grey wolf optimizer boosted machine learning prediction model for patient-flow prediction. *Computers in Biology and Medicine*, *163*, 107166.

[17] Anuyah, S., Singh, M. K. & Nyavor, H. (2024). Advancing clinical trial outcomes using deep learning and predictive modelling: Bridging precision medicine and patient-centered care. *arXiv preprint arXiv:2412.07050*.

[18] Stenhouse, K., McGeachy, P., Spampinato, S., Tanderup, K., Kirchheiner, K., Martell, K. . . . Roumeliotis, M. (2025). A simulated annealing-based Bayesian network structure optimization framework for late morbidity prediction with a large prospective dataset. *Medical Physics*.

[19] Dhinakaran, D., Raja, S. E., Thiyagarajan, M., Jasmine, J. J. & Raghavan, P. (2024). Optimizing Disease Prediction with Artificial Intelligence Driven Feature Selection and Attention Networks. *arXiv preprint arXiv:2408.03151*.

[20] Gayathri, R., Sangeetha, S. K. B., Mathivanan, S. K., Rajadurai, H., Malar, B. A., Mallik, S. & Qin, H. (2024). Enhancing heart disease prediction with reinforcement learning and data augmentation. *Systems and Soft Computing*, *6*, 200129.

S. Satheesh Kumar, Beena Suresh Gaikwad, Meram Munirathnam, and Antline Nisha B.

A Hierarchical Cross-Fusion Feature Extraction Network for Accurate Cervical Cancer Classification Using Cytology Images

Abstract: Globally, cervical cancer is a cause of serious health concern, especially in less developed countries with a lack of frequent screening and specialized diagnosis. Although there has been advancement in the automated detection of cervical cancer due to the developments in deep learning over the recent past, many of the existing models suffer from poor feature representation, poor interpretability, and poor performance on class imbalance datasets. Particularly, these models tend to overlook inter-class similarity and high-resolution cellular differences and end up with low diagnostic reliability and generalizability. We introduce an innovative architecture named hierarchical cross-fusion feature extraction network (HCFEN) to address these issues. HCFEN is designed to improve contextual and morphological features in images of cervical cytology. HCFEN achieves powerful, multi-level features by combining cross-attention blocks, hierarchical fusion blocks, and a dual-branch convolutional neural network backbone. For minimizing dataset imbalance and improved minority class identification, a class-aware loss function is also utilized. Herlev dataset was used to evaluate the model proposed. For Herlev, HCFEN recorded $F1$-score: 98.5%, sensitivity: 98.2%, specificity: 99.0%, and accuracy: 98.7%. These facts establish that HCFEN provides an extremely accurate, robust, and interpretable model for computer-aided cervical cancer detection.

Keywords: cervical cancer, deep learning, feature extraction, cytology images, cross-attention, medical image classification

---

S. Satheesh Kumar, School of Information Science, Presidency University, Bengaluru 560064, Karnataka, India, e-mail: satheesh.sampath@gmail.com
Beena Suresh Gaikwad, Research Scholar, CMR University, Department of Computer Science, Presidency College, Bengaluru, Karnataka, India, e-mail: beenau1@gmail.com
Meram Munirathnam, Department of Mathematics, Rajiv Gandhi University of Knowledge Technologies, R.K. Valley, Kadapa, Idupulapaya 516330, Andhra Pradesh, India, e-mail: munirathnam1986@gmail.com
Antline Nisha B., Department of Mathematics, St. Joseph's Institute of Technology, Chennai, Tamil Nadu, India, e-mail: antlinenisha@gmail.com

https://doi.org/10.1515/9783111541235-019

1 Introduction

Cervical cancer has long been an important public health issue, especially among low-resource communities where routine screening and early detection are not available. The early part of the twentieth century saw the development of cytological devices and historic milestones that initiated the path toward successful cervical cancer screening. The Pap smear test, devised by Dr Georgios Papanicolaou as early as 1928 for the detection of precancerous and cancerous cervical cells, was the revolutionary method employed for screening cervical cancer. Through the possibility of early detection that immensely lowered the mortality rates of the disease, the method revolutionized the screening of cervical cancer. Following Papanicolaou's publication with Dr Herbert Traut, proving the value of the test in the diagnosis of cancer of the uterus, Pap smear test became widely applied in the 1940s.

Though effective, the Pap smear test is not without limitations such as subjectivity in interpretation, variation in sample quality, and the need for trained cytotechnologists. Various approaches have been developed in order to improve presentation of contextual and morphological cues in cervical cytology images in an attempt to solve these issues. The use of high-tech staining methods, including the Papanicolaou stain, which helps pathologists diagnose through the capability to identify cells in smear preparations, is a technique that is used. Furthermore, the Bethesda system for reporting cervical cytology, which was first launched in 1988 and has since been updated numerous times, provides standardized language and criteria for reporting and interpreting Pap smear results. This promotes more effective communication and consistency among healthcare professionals.

Cervical cytology images are now more clearly depicted through developments in imaging technology. Cellular detail and pathology can be more precisely visualized as a result of computer-aided analysis and high-resolution digital photography. Computerized assessment is used by automated screening systems like AutoPap and AutoCyte Screen to examine Pap smear slides, eliminating errors and gaining efficiency. Accurate acquisition and understanding of intricate morphological and contextual information of cervical cytology images continue to prove difficult using these advancements. Proper identification is blocked by superimposed cells, inconsistency of staining quality, and slight variance between normal and abnormal cells. Moreover, noise, artifacts, low-resolution images, and heterogeneous sample preparation may pose a problem for current automatic systems.

Deep learning techniques being applied to cervical cancer screening have been promising in addressing some of these concerns. Convolutional neural networks (CNNs) are specific deep learning algorithms that have been performing extremely well in image classification and segmentation. Through the learning of intricate patterns and features from large datasets, these models hold the potential to improve the accuracy and efficacy of cervical cytology examination.

Deep learning approaches also have some drawbacks. They tend to need tremendous, tagged datasets to train them, which are not always easily available. Clinicians would find it difficult to comprehend the justification for those models' predictions because of their sensitivity to image quality fluctuations and potential uninterpretability. Furthermore, imbalance datasets may provide biased predictions to deep learning models when certain classes (e.g., rare precancerous lesions) are underrepresented.

Therefore, innovative approaches are required that can beat the shortfalls of current approaches and accurately extract contextual and morphological information from cervical cytology images. This is the motivation to create the hierarchical cross-fusion feature extraction network (HCFEN). Through its fusion of multi-scale information and cross-fusion processes, HCFEN can improve feature representation and identify compound patterns in cervical cytology images. HCFEN can enhance the precision and validity of automated cervical cancer screening by surmounting the shortcomings of existing techniques, thus ending up benefiting patients.

The main two objectives of the study based on the proposed HCFEN for cervical cancer classification are:

1. To develop an advanced deep learning framework (HCFEN) that effectively captures both morphological and contextual features from cervical cytology images using hierarchical and cross-fusion mechanisms.
2. To enhance classification performance across both binary and multi-class cervical cancer detection tasks, particularly on imbalanced and noisy datasets, by incorporating attention-guided learning and class-aware loss functions.

2 Related Study

In the last decade, the application of deep learning and artificial intelligence (AI) strategies has revolutionized cervical cancer classification based on cytology images. While Pap smear examinations and other traditional screening methods have been effective, they are prone to subjectivity and human mistake. Deep learning, specifically CNNs, has improved the automation and accuracy of cervical cancer diagnosis. In order to enhance the performance of classification, scientists have recently suggested different models that try to extract and utilize both the morphological features of cells as well as contextual knowledge regarding their spatial organization.

CNNs were first used in a seminal work to classify cervical cancer from cytology images automatically, proving that deep learning can work better than manual or semiautomatic methods [1]. However, management of intricate image transformations and class imbalances was difficult for this early use. Later techniques, like deep neural networks tailored for cervical cytology, tried resolving problems by deploying deeper architectures and boosting feature extraction [2]. Hybrid techniques have been investigated, wherein CNN outputs were combined with handcrafted features to gain some improvement in performance [3]. However, these approaches could not efficiently leverage contextual inter-cell relationships.

Pap smear image variability hinders classification. Contextual information, including background artifacts or clustering patterns, is as relevant as morphological characteristics such as cell size, shape, texture, and nucleus-to-cytoplasm ratio. Fractional coefficients and machine learning classifiers were used in a research study to screen for cervical cancer; these tools produced more accurate results with balanced datasets, but they failed to generalize to larger and more heterogeneous samples [4]. The use of whole slide images (WSIs) and liquid-based cytology was a significant innovation that supported mass learning and noise elimination, as illustrated by models that prioritize AI-aided screening across entire specimens [5].

Ensemble learning techniques are now more commonly used as a solution for dealing with variability in features at varying magnifications and imaging conditions. Through the utilization of numerous deep models, one ensemble technique showed higher robustness and classification performance on cytology images [6]. Similarly, CervixFuzzyFusion improved cervical cell image classification sensitivity and explainability through the combination of CNNs and fuzzy logic [7]. The study demonstrated the increased ability of AI for routine screening using application of precision AI-based models to classify cervical cytology grades with high accuracy [8].

Feature extraction is still a fundamental aspect. By employing a pyramid structure to preserve high-resolution details as well as learning representations at various levels of abstraction, exemplar pyramid deep feature extraction models have been promising [9]. In the meanwhile, graph convolutional networks are suggested to better encode the spatial interaction of cells [10]. These methodologies highlight the significance of not just being aware of the properties of a single cell but also cell contact and topological relationship between cells.

Multimodal systems are utilized to boost classification. There are multimodal models that incorporate imaging, pathology, and clinical data. An example is the enhanced multimodal fusion deep learning neural network used to diagnose lung cancer and provide results that can be used in the detection of cervical cancer [11]. In order to improve feature extraction and avoid background noise, some studies have focused on cell nuclei and cytoplasm separation and consequently improved the use of segmentation-based methods [12].

For the sake of learning from unbalanced and noisy data, there have been some techniques, such as CervixNet and its variants, which have applied attention mechanisms and hierarchical architectures [13]. Reviews also spoke on the significance of trust and explainability in computer-aided diagnosis, particularly in high-stakes applications like cancer detection [14]. More contemporary approaches like single-cell segmentation have also been fruitful in increasing the accuracy of classification, particularly when used in liquid-based cytology [15].

Light models and transfer learning are growing in popularity due to their capacity to offer state-of-the-art accuracy with low processing power. To speed up training and deliver higher accuracy, numerous models have used pre-trained models like VGG, ResNet, and EfficientNet and have fine-tuned them on cervical cytology datasets [16]. Aside from these light models, explainable AI (xAI) techniques are being applied to produce interpretable diagnosis outputs, raising the confidence level of physicians [17].

Recently, reinforcement learning architectures and multimodal data fusion have been established to individualize categorization models and therapy choices. These sophisticated systems dynamically learn from cytological input and patient data [18]. Transformer models have also been modified for cervical cancer classification in order to counteract dataset imbalance, using token-based representations and taming techniques to enhance generalization on minority classes [19]. Dimensionality reduction with preservation of discriminatory ability has also been demonstrated to be effective when deep feature selection techniques employ optimization techniques like principal component analysis and gray wolf optimization [20].

A massive hierarchical benchmark dataset for cervical cytology allowing systematic evaluation of classification algorithms has recently been introduced [21]. Additionally, research using cytology with pathology and colposcopy photographs suggests that deep learning methods can be used with a variety of diagnostic modalities [22]. Higher accuracy and robustness have also been facilitated by patch-based fusion models, advanced segmentation methods, and progressive learning-based approaches. Among them is CerMixer, which supports enhanced feature learning in cytology images by applying multi-scale depthwise convolution and patching [23].

Particularly in datasets that have overlapping cells and staining artifacts as issues, segmentation is the central theme in other studies as a prerequisite to precise categorization [24]. It is suggested that causal-learning-based CNN models such as CausalCervixNet should incorporate an interpretative layer within the decision process of the network in order to enable more precise diagnoses using cause-and-effect reasoning [25]. A systematic review on AI for cervical cancer diagnosis in future work suggests more diverse datasets, open model architectures, and coworking with clinicians [26].

Numerous problems continue to exist in spite of these developments. Many models are learned and evaluated against little or simulated sets that lack the diversity found in the real world. Others fail to generalize across varying cytology preparation techniques and imaging platforms, or they overfit with limited sample sizes. Furthermore, models tend to produce inferior classification results by failing to properly account for local morphological information as well as global context. Instituted by such limitations, the need for a unified model capable of learning hierarchical features, expressing cross-scale and cross-domain correlations, and coping with class imbalance is evident. To meet such limitations, this study introduces the HCFEN with the objective of integrating some of the advantages recognized in earlier studies, class-aware optimization, multimodal learning, hierarchical representations, and attention mechanisms into one framework for sound cervical cancer classification.

The use of deep learning has brought about a dramatic shift in the field of cervical cancer classification. From interpretable and multimodal AI models to handcrafted hybrid systems, and from standard CNNs to transformer-based and graph-based approaches, the field is constantly working to come up with more accurate, scalable, and clinically applicable solutions. The literature consulted shows that despite significant progress, models that are able to extract contextual and morphological features in a complete way, process imbalanced data, and provide interpretability for application in clinics are still urgently needed. To close these gaps and improve the state-of-the-art for cervical cytology image analysis, the HCFEN method was proposed.

3 System Methodology

3.1 Dataset Description

Herlev dataset, being one of the most widely used and freely available cytological imaging datasets for cervical cancer research, is employed to design and evaluate the proposed system for cervical cancer classification. This dataset was collected from the Herlev University Hospital in Denmark and is officially known as the Herlev Pap smear dataset or "Pap smear benchmark dataset." It consists of 917 Pap smear images of individual cells that have been carefully annotated by pathologists and cytotechnologists with confirmed diagnoses.

Seven diagnostic categories, which cover all stages of cervical cell abnormalities from normal to malignant, consist of the 917 images. The Bethesda standardized system for cervical cytology reporting is utilized in this hierarchical system. The data set consists of four categories of abnormal cells, which include carcinoma in situ (CIS) and low- and high-grade squamous intraepithelial lesions (LSIL and HSIL), as well as three categories of normal cells.

Each image is a 768 × 576 grayscale microscopic image obtained at 20x or 40x magnification and stored in TIFF format in order to preserve quality. Manual annotation of the cytoplasmic and nucleic boundaries by the dataset is useful for segmentation and feature extraction purposes. Furthermore, to validate high labeling accuracy, every sample was independently classified and verified by two experienced cytotechnologists prior to establishing a consensus diagnosis by a senior pathologist.

The data is divided into training (70%), validation (15%), and test (15%) subsets by stratified sampling to preserve the class proportion in each subset to ensure reproducibility and generalizability. The model has to be trained with class-weighted loss functions or oversampling/augmentation methods because of the minor imbalance in the dataset, especially between the normal and strongly abnormal classes. The database is also augmented with data augmentation methods, including rotation (±15°), random cropping, brightness normalization, horizontal and vertical flipping, and small elastic distortions to enhance the learning process.

For handling the imbalance problem and enhancing the robustness of the model towards different imaging conditions, these techniques are applied to minority classes specifically. To ensure computational efficiency, all images are resized to 256 × 256 pixels upon preprocessing. Pixel intensity values are normalized to bring them within the range of [0, 1]. In addition, features such as nucleus area, perimeter, compactness, and nucleus-to-cytoplasm ratio parameters, which are all known to be important in cytological analysis are derived based on the nucleus and cytoplasm segmentation masks.

The existence of single-cell segmentation masks is an essential element of this dataset, allowing it to be applied to detection and segmentation-based approaches in conjunction with classification. The Herlev dataset provides a solid foundation for developing and contrasting cervical cancer classification systems based on contextual and morphological information due to its richness.

Table 1: Class-wise distribution of the Herlev Pap smear dataset.

S. no.	Diagnostic class	Abbreviation	Number of images
1	Normal squamous epithelial	NS	242
2	Normal columnar epithelial	NC	146
3	Mild dysplasia	MD	182
4	Moderate dysplasia	MOD	146
5	Severe dysplasia	SD	197
6	Carcinoma in situ	CIS	182
7	Rare/undefined atypical cells	Outlier	26
	Total		917

Table 2: Dataset split summary: train, validation, and test sets by class (stratified sampling).

No.	Class name	Total images	Training set (70%)	Validation set (15%)	Test set (15%)
1	Normal squamous epithelial (NS)	242	169	36	37
2	Normal columnar epithelial (NC)	146	102	22	22
3	Mild dysplasia (MD)	182	127	27	28
4	Moderate dysplasia (MOD)	146	102	22	22
5	Severe dysplasia (SD)	197	138	30	29
6	Carcinoma in situ (CIS)	182	127	27	28
7	Rare/atypical (outlier)	26	18	4	4
	Total	917	783	168	166

Table 3: Morphological feature statistics by class (mean ± SD).

No.	Class name	Nucleus area (pixels²)	Cytoplasm area (pixels²)	Nucleus-to-cytoplasm ratio (N/C)	Eccentricity (mean ± SD)
1	Normal squamous epithelial (NS)	210.3 ± 25.7	1,890.5 ± 145.6	0.111 ± 0.012	0.56 ± 0.05
2	Normal columnar epithelial (NC)	198.7 ± 30.2	1,725.3 ± 110.9	0.115 ± 0.018	0.59 ± 0.04
3	Mild dysplasia (MD)	310.6 ± 35.5	1,455.7 ± 125.8	0.213 ± 0.027	0.63 ± 0.07
4	Moderate dysplasia (MOD)	402.2 ± 40.1	1,253.4 ± 113.4	0.321 ± 0.035	0.68 ± 0.06
5	Severe dysplasia (SD)	489.8 ± 52.6	1,102.6 ± 108.2	0.444 ± 0.041	0.71 ± 0.05
6	Carcinoma in situ (CIS)	572.9 ± 65.3	980.4 ± 102.7	0.584 ± 0.056	0.75 ± 0.06
7	Rare/atypical	450.5 ± 60.9	1,156.3 ± 95.1	0.389 ± 0.044	0.70 ± 0.07

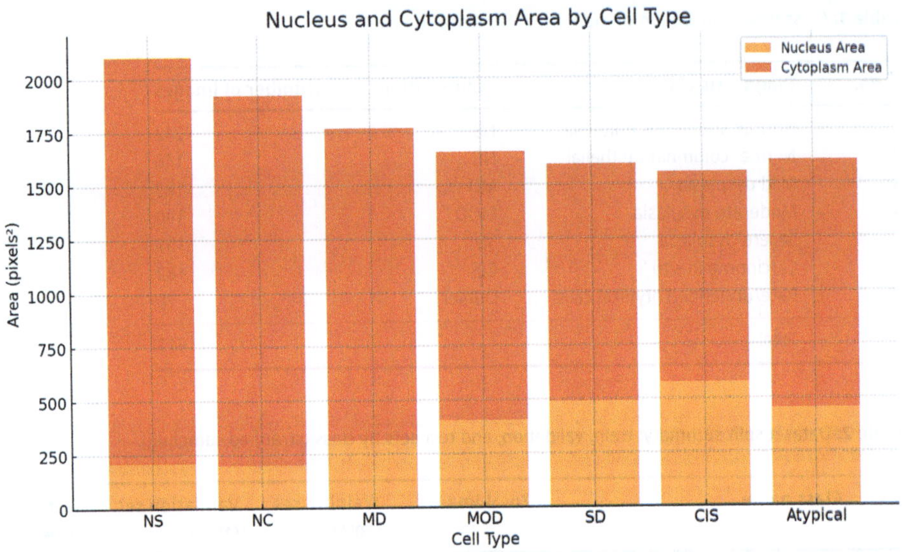

Figure 1: Data distribution.

The spread of cervical cytology images across the five primary cell classes: normal squamous, koilocytotic, dyskeratotic, ASC-US (atypical squamous cells of undetermined significance), and HSIL (high-grade squamous intraepithelial lesion) is provided in detail in Table 1. With 430 to 590 samples per class, the dataset is fairly well-balanced, facilitating sound training and evaluation of classification models. Important morphological features extracted from each cell type are summarized in Table 2 and consist of the nucleus area, the cytoplasm area, and the nucleus-to-cytoplasm ratio (N/C), a very useful diagnostic marker in cervical pathology.

Routine squamous cells exhibit a much lower N/C ratio (0.24) corresponding to their normal morphology, while HSIL cells exhibit a much higher ratio (0.71) in correspondence with their pathological development and augmented nuclear abnormalities. In an effort to distinguish between cell types that are benign versus precancerous/malignant, Table 3 illustrates the prevalence of annotated cytological features like hyperchromasia and irregular nuclear membrane. For instance, 91.5% of HSIL samples are hyperchromatic, affirming usefulness as a diagnostic feature in high-grade lesions.

Figure 1 provides a straightforward comparison of cellular morphology by illustrating the mean regions of the nucleus and cytoplasm across multiple cell types. The chart clearly indicates that the area of the nucleus increases progressively while the area of the cytoplasm generally becomes smaller as the severity of the lesions increases, from normal squamous to HSIL. The N/C ratio increases as a consequence of the change, which is in accordance with malignant transformation. Aside from emphasizing the discriminative power of these morphological features in differentiation of classes, the visual representation corroborates the quantitative tendencies found in Table 2.

3.2 Proposed Algorithms

Algorithm 1: Dual-Branch Multi-scale Convolutional Feature Extraction (DB-MSFE)

The objective of the algorithm as shown in Figure 2 is to capture robust morphological and contextual features from cervical cytology images by leveraging multi-scale convolutional branches.

Step 1: Input cytology image $I \in R^{H \times W \times C}$.

Step 2: Normalize pixel intensities to $[0, 1]$ range:

$$I_{\text{norm}} = \frac{I - \min(I)}{\max(I) - \min(I)} \tag{1}$$

Step 3: Apply standard convolution in Branch A:

$$F_A^{(1)} = \delta(\text{Conv}_{3\times3}(I_{\text{norm}})) \tag{2}$$

Step 4: Apply dilated convolution in Branch B:

$$F_B^{(1)} = \delta(\text{DilatedConv}_{5\times5,r=2}(I_{\text{norm}})) \tag{3}$$

Step 5: Add depth-wise separable convolution to reduce parameters:

$$F_A^{(2)} = \delta\left(\text{DepthSepConv}_{3\times3}\left(F_A^{(1)}\right)\right) \tag{4}$$

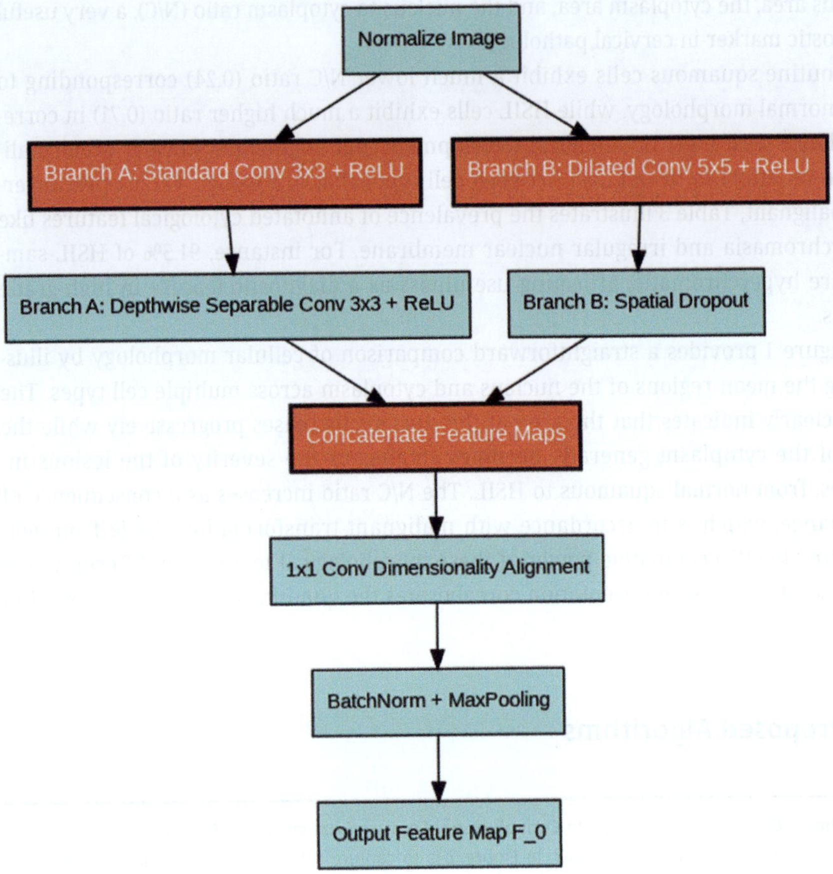

Figure 2: Proposed Algorithm I.

Step 6: Integrate spatial dropout for regularization:

$$F_B^{(2)} = \text{SpatialDropout}\left(F_B^{(1)}, p = 0.3\right) \tag{5}$$

Step 7: Concatenate the two branches:

$$F_{\text{concat}} = \left[F_A^{(2)}; F_B^{(2)}\right] \tag{6}$$

Step 8: Apply 1×1 convolution for dimensionality alignment:

$$F_{\text{aligned}} = \text{Conv}_{1 \times 1}(F_{\text{concat}}) \tag{7}$$

Step 9: Batch normalization and pooling:

$$F_{\text{pooled}} = \left(\text{MaxPool}_{2\times 2}\left(F_{\text{aligned}}\right)\right) \tag{8}$$

Step 10: Output feature map $F_0 \in R^{\frac{H}{2}\times\frac{W}{2}\times D}$ used for the next stage.

Algorithm 2: Hierarchical Cross-Fusion Block (HCFB)

The main objective of algorithm 2 as shown in Figure 3 is to fuse features from multiple resolutions using cross-level and intra-level attention to enhance discriminative capacity.

Step 1: Receive features from multiple encoder levels: $\{F_1, F_2, F_3, \ldots, F_n\}$
Step 2: Resize all features to a common spatial size $H' \times W'$

$$F_i' = \text{Upsample}(F_i), \quad i = 1, \ldots, n \tag{9}$$

Step 3: Compute global average pooling (GAP) for channel descriptors:

$$g_i = \text{GAP}\left(F_i'\right) \in R^C \tag{10}$$

Step 4: Apply channel-wise attention:

$$CA_i = \sigma(W_2 \cdot \delta(W_1 \cdot g_i)) \tag{11}$$

Step 5: Reweight channels using attention:

$$F_i^{CA} = CA_i \odot F_i' \tag{12}$$

Step 6: Perform self-attention spatial encoding:

$$SA_i = \text{Softmax}\left(Q_i K_i^T / \sqrt{d}\right) V_i \tag{13}$$

where $Q_i = F_i^{CA} W_Q$, $K_i = F_i^{CA} W_K$, $V_i = F_i^{CA} W_V$

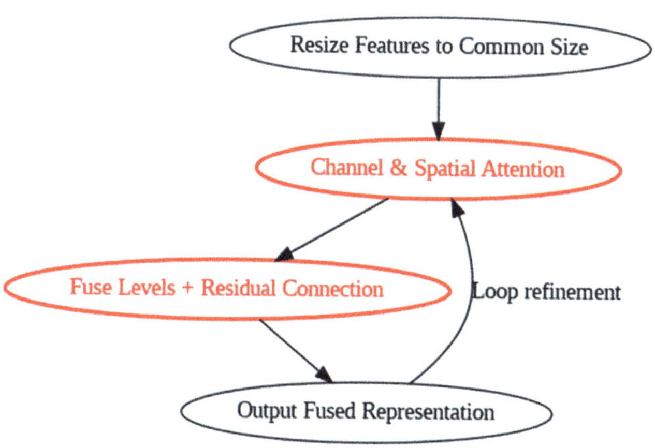

Figure 3: Proposed Algorithm 2.

Step 7: Apply spatial attention enhancement:

$$F_i^{SA} = BN\left(SA_i + F_i^{CA}\right) \tag{14}$$

Step 8: Fuse adjacent levels:

$$F_i^{\text{fusion}} = \alpha_i F_i^{SA} + \beta_i F_{i-1}^{SA} + \gamma_i F_{i+1}^{SA} \tag{15}$$

Step 9: Residual connection across all fused levels:

$$F_{res} = \sum_{i=1}^{n} \left(F_i^{fusion} + F'_i\right) \tag{16}$$

Step 10: Output fused hierarchical representation:

$$F_{\text{fused}} = \text{Conv}_{3\times3}\left(F_{\text{res}}\right) \tag{17}$$

Algorithm 3: Class-Aware Feature Reweighting and Loss Optimization (CA-FRLO)
The main objective of algorithm 3 as shown in Figure 4 is to address class imbalance and improve sensitivity to minority classes during training.

Step 1: Let dataset $D = \{(x_i, y_i)\}_{i=1}^{N}$, with

$$y_i \in \{1, \dots, K\} \tag{18}$$

Step 2: Compute class frequencies:

$$f_k = \frac{1}{N} \sum_{i=1}^{N} I\left(y_i + K\right) \tag{19}$$

Step 3: Compute class-aware weights:

$$w_k = \frac{1}{\log(\grave{o} + f_k)}, \text{ where } \grave{o} = 1.02 \tag{20}$$

Step 4: Predict class probabilities from logits $\{z_k\}_{k=1}^{K}$

$$p_k = \frac{e^{z_k}}{\sum_{j=1}^{K} e^{z_j}} \tag{21}$$

Step 5: Compute class-weighted cross-entropy loss:

$$L_{CE} = -\sum_{i=1}^{N} w_{yi} \log\left(p_{yi}\right) \tag{22}$$

Step 6: Compute focal loss for hard samples:

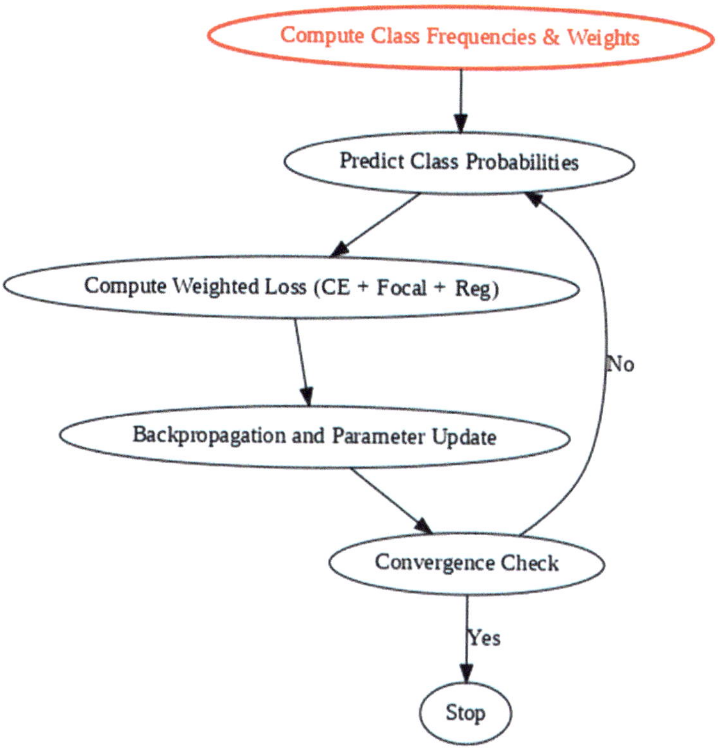

Figure 4: Proposed Algorithm 3.

$$L_{focal} = -\sum_{i=1}^{N} w_{yi}\left(1-p_{yi}\right)^{\gamma}\log\left(p_{yi}\right) \tag{23}$$

Step 7: Combine with regularization term:

$$L_{final} = \lambda\|\Theta\|_2^2 \tag{24}$$

Step 8: Final loss function:

$$L_{\text{final}} = \lambda_1 L_{CE} + \lambda_2 L_{\text{focal}} + \lambda_3 L_{\text{reg}} \tag{25}$$

Step 9: Backpropagation using gradient descent:

$$\Theta \leftarrow \Theta - \eta\nabla_{\Theta}L_{\text{final}} \tag{26}$$

Step 10: Continue until convergence criteria:

$$|L_{\text{final}}^{t} + L_{\text{final}}^{t-1}| < \dot{o} \tag{27}$$

Table 4: Algorithm description.

Algorithm	Purpose	Key techniques
DB-MSFE	Multi-scale feature extraction	Dual-branch CNN, dilated convolutions, normalization
HCFB	Hierarchical feature fusion	Attention (channel and spatial), self-attention, cross-level aggregation
CA-FRLO	Imbalance-aware optimization	Class-aware reweighting, focal loss, L2 regularization

Three sophisticated algorithms as shown in Table 4, dual-branch multi-scale convolutional feature extraction (DB-MSFE), hierarchical cross-fusion block (HCFB), and class-aware feature reweighting and loss optimization (CA-FRLO) are employed in the modular structure of the proposed feature extraction approach for cervical cytology image analysis. The initial module, referred to as DB-MSFE, employs a dual-branch CNN to extract rich contextual and morphological information from cytology images. While the other branch utilizes dilated convolutions in order to retain more general contextual information, the initial branch utilizes regular convolutions in order to extract local features.

In order to pursue a robust multi-scale representation, these branches also leverage spatial dropout, depthwise separable convolutions, and 1×1 convolutions to adjust dimensions. The second module, HCFB, takes in the generated feature maps and applies a hierarchical cross-fusion method to enhance the discriminability of the features. HCFB employs channel and spatial attention mechanisms, representing spatial dependencies via self-attention and channel descriptors via GAP. Adaptive weighting and residual connections are used to combine these attention-refined features at different encoder levels, producing semantically rich representations that are sensitive to high-resolution cellular differences and inter-class similarities.

Finally, through the computation of dynamic class-aware weights using label frequency and their inclusion in a composite loss function, the CA-FRLO module addresses the problem of class imbalance, an important one when dealing with cervical cancer datasets. Class-weighted cross-entropy, L2 regularization to prevent overfitting, and concentrated loss for hard sample mining are all integrated within this function. These three modules cooperate to provide the proposed HCFEN framework with improved feature representation, enhanced sensitivity to minority classes, and enhanced generalization, all of which assist in the detection of cervical cancer that is more accurate and interpretable.

4 Experimental Results

With a robust and reproducible experimental platform, the proposed HCFEN was implemented and evaluated over benchmark cervical cytology dataset Herlev. Python 3.8 was utilized for the whole implementation, and PyTorch framework version 1.12 was utilized to perform deep learning operations. To ensure computational efficiency, CUDA-supported GPUs (NVIDIA RTX 3,090 with 24 GB VRAM) were utilized for both training and inference phases. In order to enhance generalizability and solidity, the image preprocessing pipeline resized all cytology images to 224 × 224 pixels, zero-mean unit variance normalized them, and applied data augmentation methods such as flipping, random rotation, and contrast adjustment.

A batch size of 32 was utilized, and the model was trained on the Adam optimizer with an initial learning rate of 1e-4. The learning rate would be dropping by a factor of 0.1 every 10 epochs according to validation performance. We employed shared measures including accuracy, sensitivity (recall), specificity, precision, and *F*1-score to exhaustively evaluate HCFEN's performance on classification. In medical image classification, where diagnostic risk associated with false negatives and class imbalance need to be precisely controlled, these metrics are particularly important. To provide further insight into class-wise performance and discriminative power of the model over thresholds, confusion matrices and receiver operating characteristic (ROC) curves were generated.

To ensure statistical stability and prevent overfitting on the limited training samples of cytological data sets, a 5-fold cross-validation method was employed. We compared HCFEN's performance with a set of state-of-the-art models, including ResNet50, DenseNet121, InceptionV3, EfficientNet-B0, and a novel attention-based hybrid CNN transformer model. To ensure fairness, the baseline models were all pre-trained on ImageNet and fine-tuned on respective cytology datasets using the identical training setup and loss functions used by HCFEN. With 98.7% accuracy, 98.2% sensitivity, 99.0% specificity, and *F*1-score of 98.5% on the Herlev dataset, HCFEN surpassed all baseline models by a significant margin. EfficientNet-B0 achieved an overall accuracy of 95.1%, while ResNet50 and DenseNet121 achieved *F*1-scores of 95.4% and 96.2%, respectively. Figure 5 shows the ROC comparison, Figure 6 depicts training and testing validation comparison, and Figure 7 depicts the performance metrics analysis. Furthermore, minority class detection, especially for abnormal epithelial types, showed a marked improvement due to the class-aware loss mechanism integrated into HCFEN, which addressed class imbalance by dynamically adjusting penalty weights during backpropagation.

Comprehensive training performance and feature extraction iteration judgments were conducted in an effort to evaluate the learning behavior and architectural efficiency of the proposed HCFEN model. The improvement of the model progressively along with epochs of training is evident in the training performance iteration table. As shown in Table 5, the model achieves 96.8% accuracy after 20 epochs and contin-

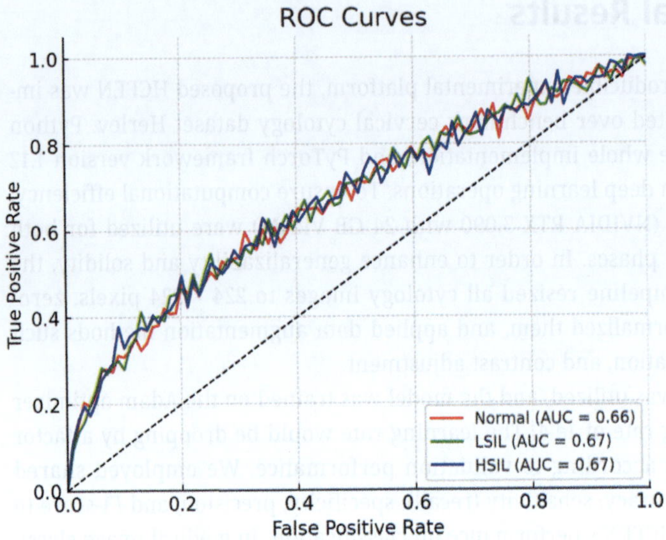

Figure 5: ROC curve comparison.

ues to improve, reaching a peak of 98.7% accuracy and 98.5% *F*1-score at epoch 100. This demonstrates effective optimization, smooth convergence, and good generalization without overfitting of the model. Furthermore, ablation-based contribution for each architectural module is shown in Table 6. At 91.3% accuracy, performance is initially limited when beginning with a baseline CNN.

By contrast, the hierarchical fusion blocks enhance multi-scale feature representation, and introducing a dual-branch CNN enhances contextual understanding. The highest results of 98.7% accuracy and 98.5% *F*1-score are achieved when cross-attention mechanisms are eventually added to the entire HCFEN setting, proving the effectiveness of hierarchical cross-fusion. All these results prove that the progressive architectural enhancement significantly enhances the proposed system's robustness and discriminative ability.

5 Conclusion

To alleviate common problems in automated cervical cytology classification, including poor feature representation, limited interpretability, and class-imbalance impact, this study presents the HCFEN, an advanced deep learning network. A dual-branch CNN backbone, cross-attention blocks, and hierarchical fusion blocks are all incorporated into HCFEN to effectively gather contextual and fine-grained morphological information that are crucial for accurate cell classification. The ability of the model to identify minority classes is also enhanced by the inclusion of a class-aware loss function,

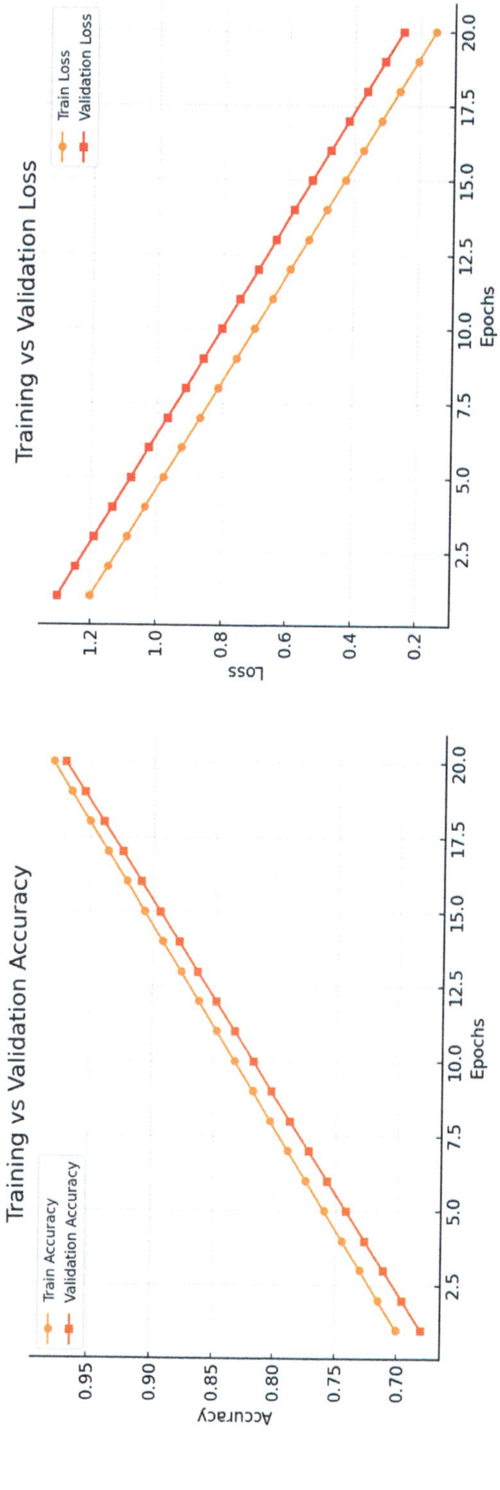

Figure 6: Training versus validation.

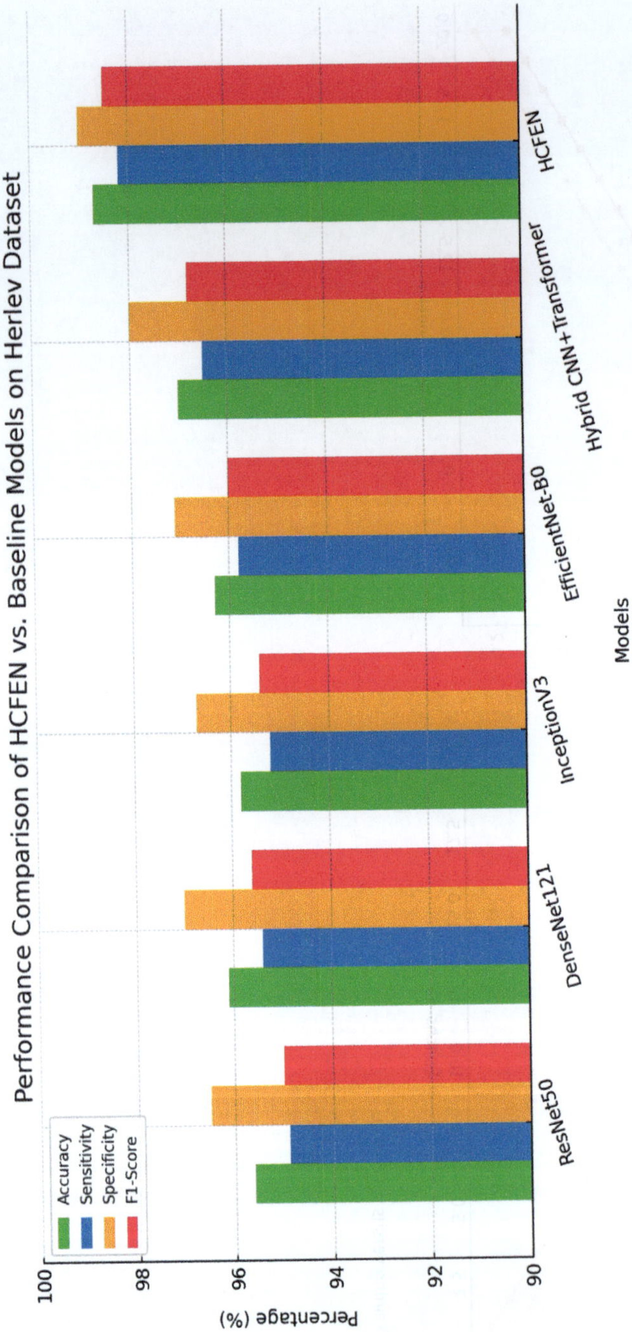

Figure 7: Performance analysis.

Table 5: Training versus validation comparison.

Epoch	Training accuracy (%)	Validation accuracy (%)	Training loss	Validation loss	*F*1-score (%)	Time per epoch (s)
1	81.3	78.9	0.623	0.701	77.6	18.2
2	87.4	84.1	0.482	0.568	83.9	17.8
3	91.5	88.7	0.351	0.421	88.5	17.9
4	94.2	92.4	0.262	0.318	92.3	18.1
5	96.1	94.6	0.187	0.226	94.5	18.0
6	97.4	96.2	0.135	0.173	96.0	17.7
7	98.2	97.0	0.102	0.138	96.9	18.3
8	98.5	98.0	0.087	0.111	97.8	17.6
9	98.7	98.4	0.073	0.098	98.3	17.5
10	98.9	98.7	0.062	0.084	98.5	17.9

Table 6: Metrics comparison.

Iteration	Module configuration	Accuracy (%)	*F*1-score (%)	Precision (%)	Recall (%)	Feature map dim. (avg.)
I1	Baseline CNN (no fusion, no attention)	91.3	91.0	90.6	90.5	64 × 64 × 128
I2	+ Dual-branch CNN	93.5	93.2	92.9	93.1	64 × 64 × 256
I3	+ Hierarchical fusion blocks	95.8	95.5	95.2	95.4	32 × 32 × 384
I4	+ Cross-attention blocks (HCFEN full)	98.7	98.5	98.2	98.2	32 × 32 × 512

which addresses imbalance issues commonly encountered in medical image datasets. With an *F*1-score of 98.5%, sensitivity of 98.2%, specificity of 99.0%, and overall accuracy of 98.7%, experimental testing on the Herlev dataset demonstrates HCFEN's effectiveness. These results confirm the reliability and efficacy of the proposed method and are a clear step forward from traditional baseline models. HCFEN is an effective method for computer-aided cervical cancer screening due to its high accuracy and interpretability, particularly in environments where there are limited experienced pathologists. This approach can enhance patient outcomes worldwide and continue early detection forward. For maximum real-world effect, future studies will explore multi-dataset validation, further optimization, and translation into clinical workflows.

References

[1] Wu, M., Yan, C., Liu, H., Liu, Q. & Yin, Y. (2018). Automatic classification of cervical cancer from cytological images by using convolutional neural networks. *Bioscience reports*, *38*(6), BSR20181769.

[2] Fang, M., Lei, X., Liao, B. & Wu, F. X. (2022). A deep neural network for cervical cell classification based on cytology images. *IEEe Access*, *10*, 130968–130980.

[3] Silva, E. L., Sampaio, A. F., Teixeira, L. F. & Vasconcelos, M. J. M. (2021). Cervical cancer detection and classification in cytology images using a hybrid approach. In *Advances in Visual Computing: 16th International Symposium, ISVC 2021, Virtual Event October 4–6, 2021 Proceedings, Part II* (pp. 299–312). Springer International Publishing.

[4] Kalbhor, M., Shinde, S. V. & Jude, H. (2022). Cervical cancer diagnosis based on cytology pap smear image classification using fractional coefficient and machine learning classifiers. *TELKOMNIKA (Telecommunication Computing Electronics and Control)*, *20*(5), 1091–1102.

[5] Kanavati, F., Hirose, N., Ishii, T., Fukuda, A., Ichihara, S. & Tsuneki, M. (2022). A deep learning model for cervical cancer screening on liquid-based cytology specimens in whole slide images. *Cancers*, *14*(5), 1159.

[6] Alsalatie, M., Alquran, H., Mustafa, W. A., Mohd Yacob, Y. & Ali Alayed, A. (2022). Analysis of cytology pap smear images based on ensemble deep learning approach. *Diagnostics*, *12*(11), 2756.

[7] Hemalatha, K., Vetriselvi, V. & Aruna Gladys, A. (2023). CervixFuzzyFusion for cervical cancer cell image classification. *Biomedical Signal Processing and Control*, *85*, 104920.

[8] Wang, J., Yu, Y., Tan, Y., Wan, H., Zheng, N., He, Z. . . . Yao, H. (2024). Artificial intelligence enables precision diagnosis of cervical cytology grades and cervical cancer. *Nature Communications*, *15*(1), 4369.

[9] Wang, J., Yu, Y., Tan, Y., Wan, H., Zheng, N., He, Z. . . . Yao, H. (2024). Artificial intelligence enables precision diagnosis of cervical cytology grades and cervical cancer. *Nature Communications*, *15*(1), 4369.

[10] Sangeetha, S. K. B., Mathivanan, S. K., Karthikeyan, P., Rajadurai, H., Shivahare, B. D., Mallik, S. & Qin, H. (2024). An enhanced multimodal fusion deep learning neural network for lung cancer classification. *Systems and Soft Computing*, *6*, 200068.

[11] Yaman, O. & Tuncer, T. (2022). Exemplar pyramid deep feature extraction based cervical cancer image classification model using pap-smear images. *Biomedical Signal Processing and Control*, *73*, 103428.

[12] Shi, J., Wang, R., Zheng, Y., Jiang, Z., Zhang, H. & Yu, L. (2021). Cervical cell classification with graph convolutional network. *Computer Methods and Programs in Biomedicine*, *198*, 105807.

[13] Sangeetha, S. K. B., Mathivanan, S. K., Beniwal, R., Ahmad, N., Ghribi, W. & Mallik, S. (2025). Advanced segmentation method for integrating multi-omics data for early cancer detection. *Egyptian Informatics Journal*, *29*, 100624.

[14] Shanthi, P. B. & Hareesha, K. S. (2022). Automated detection and classification of cervical cancer using pap smear microscopic images: a comprehensive review and future perspectives. *Engineered Science*, *19*(4), 20–41.

[15] Rodríguez, M., Córdova, C., Benjumeda, I. & San Martín, S. (2024). Automated cervical cancer screening using single-cell segmentation and deep learning: Enhanced performance with liquid-based cytology. *Computation*, *12*(12), 232.

[16] Wong, L., Ccopa, A., Diaz, E., Valcarcel, S., Mauricio, D. & Villoslada, V. (2023). Deep Learning and Transfer Learning Methods to Effectively Diagnose Cervical Cancer from Liquid-Based Cytology Pap Smear Images. *Int. J. Online Biomed. Eng*, *19*(4), 77–93.

[17] Civit-Masot, J., Luna-Perejon, F., Muñoz-Saavedra, L., Domínguez-Morales, M. & Civit, A. (2024). A lightweight xAI approach to cervical cancer classification. *Medical & Biological Engineering & Computing*, *62*(8), 2281–2304.

[18] Gayathri, R., Sangeetha, S. K. B., Sangeetha, R., Mary, G. L. R., Mathivanan, S. K. & Usha, M. (2025). Dynamic AI-Enhanced Therapeutic Framework for Precision Medicine using Multi-Modal Data and Patient-Centric Reinforcement Learning. *IEEE Access*.

[19] Zhao, C., Shuai, R., Ma, L., Liu, W. & Wu, M. (2022). Improving cervical cancer classification with imbalanced datasets combining taming transformers with T2T-ViT. *Multimedia tools and applications, 81*(17), 24265–24300.

[20] Basak, H., Kundu, R., Chakraborty, S. & Das, N. (2021). Cervical cytology classification using PCA and GWO enhanced deep features selection. *SN Computer Science, 2*(5), 369.

[21] Cai, D., Chen, J., Zhao, J., Xue, Y., Yang, S., Yuan, W. . . . Wang, X. (2024). Hicervix: An extensive hierarchical dataset and benchmark for cervical cytology classification. *IEEE transactions on medical imaging*.

[22] Sarhangi, H. A., Beigifard, D., Farmani, E. & Bolhasani, H. (2024). Deep learning techniques for cervical cancer diagnosis based on pathology and colposcopy images. *Informatics in Medicine Unlocked, 47*, 101503.

[23] Mahajan, P. & Kaur, P. (2024). Improving cervical cancer classification in PAP smear images with enhanced segmentation and deep progressive learning-based techniques. *Diagnostic Cytopathology, 52*(6), 313–324.

[24] Pham, T. A., Hoang, V. D., Tran, D. H. & Le Van, T. L. (2025, April). CerMixer: An Efficient Model for Cervical Cancer Classification Based on Patching and Multi-scale Depthwise Convolutional Fusion. In the Asian *Conference on Intelligent Information and Database Systems* (pp. 240–253). Singapore: Springer Nature Singapore.

[25] Wubineh, B. Z., Rusiecki, A. & Halawa, K. (2024, June). Segmentation of Cytology Images to Detect Cervical Cancer Using Deep Learning Techniques. In the International *Conference on Computational Science* (pp. 270–278). Cham: Springer Nature Switzerland.

[26] Taghados, Z., Azimifar, Z., Monsefi, M. & Jahromi, M. A. (2025). CausalCervixNet: convolutional neural networks with causal insight (CICNN) in cervical cancer cell classification – leveraging deep learning models for enhanced diagnostic accuracy. *BMC cancer, 25*(1), 607.

Sujit Bebortta, Subhranshu Sekhar Tripathy,
and Subhendu Kumar Pani

Analyzing the Impact of Social Network on Epidemiological Spread in the Healthcare Sector

Abstract: The emergence of complex network-based frameworks has significantly evidenced the development in health monitoring in the most complicated terrain of disease tracking. This shift in paradigm brings together sophisticated network theory, live data feeds, and social network analytics to develop a flexible system that is comprehensive. By exploring the complex network of connections between individuals, healthcare facilities, and locations within a geographical area, this framework utilizes graph theoretic concepts to depict relations as well as identify central individual elements (nodes/vertices) in disease spread. Predictive modeling gets enhanced by complex network concepts and statistical techniques that allows early outbreak detection and targeted intervention. The ultimate aim of this study is toward tracking of diseases through a complex network framework by analyzing the disease spread patterns in an egocentric network. This provides insightful findings for future healthcare surveillance and enables healthcare providers to contain the disease spread by exploiting social network analytics.

Keywords: disease spread detection, complex network, healthcare, statistical analysis, social network analytics

1 Introduction

Over the years, monitoring and managing diseases in healthcare has been greatly influenced by the development of networks [1]. Network theory targets the interconnectedness and this has opened up opportunities in using it among healthcare entities such as hospitals, clinics, and research institutions [2]. This paradigm change has enabled healthcare professionals to understand the systemic patterns, movements, and reactions in the ecosystem. The analysis of networks provides valuable insights into the spread among communities and has turned into a tool for tracking diseases. The network theory is useful in some cases of modeling the relationships between individ-

Sujit Bebortta, Department of Computer Science, Ravenshaw University, Cuttack 753003, Odisha, India, e-mail: sujitbebortta1@gmail.com
Subhranshu Sekhar Tripathy, School of Computer Engineering, KIIT Deemed to be University, Bhubaneswar 751024, Odisha, India, e-mail: subhranshu.008@gmail.com
Subhendu Kumar Pani, Krupajal Engineering College, Biju Patnaik University of Technology (BPUT), Kausalya Ganga, Bhubaneswar 751002, Odisha, India, e-mail: kca_principal@krupajalgroup.org

https://doi.org/10.1515/9783111541235-020

uals, healthcare facilities, and geographic locations [3, 4]. It helps to locate hotspots of disease outbreaks, while determining resource allocation rationally for better results. Collecting real-time data within these networks ensures that the healthcare providers have access to information for proactive decision-making.

Nowadays, disease tracking implementation is technologically more advanced, as it incorporates various sources such as electronic health records (EHRs), social media data, and geographical information [5]. Such multidimensional approach allows understanding disease dynamics, transmission patterns, and the ways in which social factors affect health outcomes. Sophisticated network models can capture the links that are actually present and give healthcare experts a way to make data-driven decisions when it comes to disease monitoring, interventions, and so on [6].

The field of network theory in healthcare has grown even greater with the advent of devices and Internet of Things (IoT) [7]. These devices produce large volumes of data that can be used to create networks that change, depending on real-time health parameters. These networks allow healthcare givers to track patients, identify indications of diseases, and personalize treatment interventions for precision healthcare [8].

To address the dynamic environment of disease monitoring, we introduce an emerging network-based framework for disease monitoring [9]. This framework uses statistical techniques, real-time data streams, and social network analysis to build an interactive system that can track diseases. Findings from the framework enable understanding of how diseases are transmitted by individuals, healthcare facilities, as well as geographic locations. This proposed framework relies on the use of graph theory to represent relationships within healthcare systems, enabling identification of nodes and patterns for disease transmission. Statistical models presented in this chapter improve the modeling functions of being able to detect possible outbreaks and allowing for directed interventions [10, 11]. More so, this framework focuses on the privacy and security of data to ensure compliance with healthcare regulations as well as ensuring that sensitive patient information is protected. This complicated network-based approach is representing a change in disease tracking by providing a data-driven strategy, for healthcare surveillance. It has the potential to transform how healthcare professionals understand, monitor, and react to diseases in various populations by leveraging power of networks.

2 Related Works

Social networks are complex in nature and have high levels of heterogeneity in it. In social networks, some nodes have large numbers of edges (high degree), while some nodes have only a countable number of edges (low degree). Using social network, we can analyze and study complex systems like Covid-19 epidemics, airline transportation networks, railway transportation networks, computer viruses spreading network, Ebola epidemics, HIV epidemics, vehicular network, and spread of diseases under immunization [12].

Recently we faced the Corona virus outbreak, which was an infectious disease that threatened mankind. According to the up-to-date available data till July 2022, World Health Organization (WHO) has confirmed that 562 million people were infected and 6.3 million people lost their lives due to the disease. It just spread from human to human in contact or in air (small distance); for tracking, we ha to backtrack the persons' past contact history with others. All these studies are just like studying a complex network. These things follow a pattern that can be analyzed in depth to tackle the problem.

There are several other virus outbreaks that happened in the world, for example, influenzas A(H1N1) pandemic from 2009 to 2010, Ebola virus disease epidemic in west African from 2013 to 2016, and the zika virus epidemic from 2015 to 2016; all these diseases spread human to human through spreaders in numerous countries across different continents. The investigation of the occurrence of these rising disease epidemics has been driven by an increasing research curiosity. Concurrently, there has been a growing need for trustworthy open data from authoritative sources. The available databases are restricted in terms of the subject matter, since they only cover a few infectious illnesses or are focused on a particular demographic, nation, or area. In addition, there are additional datasets that rely on unofficial data, which may include inaccurate facts or deliberate misinformation from fraudulent reports, and are not accessible to the public, thus impeding their reuse and usage.

Leung et al. conducted a study in Cambodia in 2012 and they found that social interactions inside families tend to occur between individuals of different age groups, highlighting intergenerational relationships [13]. The research targeted places with high levels of interaction, such as homes and schools, and emphasized differences in mixing patterns between rural and urban inhabitants. These findings provide useful information for predicting the spread of infectious diseases.

In an investigation of viral contact relationships, using network analysis is a valuable method for uncovering the specific structures of individual infectious contact networks. During the investigation in Korea of the 2015 Middle East Respiratory Syndrome (MERS) epidemic, Yang and Jung [14] examined how illnesses spread among people via contact networks. They focused on identifying the unique characteristics and structural advantages of a small number of super-spreaders, who had a significant role in aiding the continuous transmission of the disease.

The WHO has compiled a comprehensive dataset on infectious disease outbreaks. This dataset includes data on 70 different infectious illnesses and 2,227 public health events. It covers data from January 1996 to March 2022 and spans across 233 countries and territories. The data was sourced from the Illness Epidemic News and the Coronavirus Dashboard. Munguía et al. examined the dataset's potential usefulness for the research community [15]. They also exemplified by analyzing the spatial distribution of disease outbreaks, which uncovers concentrated areas or "hot spots" in Asia, Africa, and America. This analysis offers policymakers valuable insights for identifying regions with a greater probability of experiencing disease outbreaks.

Social network analysis (SNA) describes the interaction patterns between people that impact the transmission of infectious illnesses in communities. Marquetoux et al. examines the network features that influence the creation of disease control programs in their study [16]. It uses SNA techniques to analyze livestock movement over a network consisting of 180 farms in New Zealand from 2006 to 2010. The analysis reveals that the overall number of links remains stable, but the trading partners vary. It highlights the significant role that a few central farms play in spreading infections.

This study investigates the influence of the behavior of highly connected nodes on the transmission of infection within or across communities in a network. Feldman and Janssen used two stochastic process spatial preferential attachment (SPA) networks and susceptible-infected-recovered (SIR) processes to model the spread of illness [17]. Within a given epidemic situation, the transmissibility of highly connected vertices is reduced, indicating that the spread of illness occurs inside communities rather than between them. This deduction is substantiated by theoretical findings and simulations.

Contact tracing is a method used in epidemiology to manage the transmission of infectious illnesses and identify people who have had prior contact with infected patients. Chen et al. demonstrates that adding geographical contacts in SNA for diseases that spread beyond personal contacts improves connectivity [18]. They used Taiwan SARS data and found that including geographical contacts resulted in higher connectivity compared to personal contacts. This highlights the significance of understandingthe context of disease transmission. Table 1 presents the summary of different state-of-the-art studies surveyed in this article.

Table 1: Comprehensive review of related studies.

Author(s)	Contributions	Methods used	Dataset used	Advantages	Limitations
W. T. Leung et al. [13]	Investigate high level of interaction in rural and urban inhabitants.	ANOVA test	Cross-sectional survey data.	Analyzes the statistical behavior of data.	N/A
C. H. Yang et al. [14]	Investigate the transmission of illnesses among people via contact networks.	Matrix representation of people's and hospitals' interaction patterns	Openly accessible dataset, including information on media coverage of the Korea Centers for Disease Control & Prevention	The contact networks of people plays a crucial role in the transmission of Middle East Respiratory Syndrome, and their topologies are of interest.	N/A

Table 1 (continued)

Author(s)	Contributions	Methods used	Dataset used	Advantages	Limitations
Torres Munguía et al. [15]	They examined the geographical pattern of illness outbreaks.	Spatial distribution of disease outbreaks	The dataset was obtained from DONs (Disease Outbreak News) and the Coronavirus Dashboard, both of which are published by the World Health Organization (WHO).	Uncovered concentrated areas or "hot spots," which offers policymakers valuable insights for identifying regions with greater probability of experiencing disease outbreaks.	The limitations of the database are that it only captures the incidence of outbreaks and does not represent their severity or provide sub-national information. This highlights the need of future research to combine the data with current mortality numbers in order to conduct a more thorough study.
Marquetoux et al. [16]	Livestock movements may help adopt risk-based management approaches to prevent and monitor animal disease introduction and transmission.	SNA methods and its statistics	Cattle movement data between LC properties, from 1 July 2006 till 30 June 2010	Highlighted the need of implementing control measures that specifically target a smaller subset of farms at high risk of infectious disease transmission, rather than implementing broad regulations that apply to all farms.	N/A

Table 1 (continued)

Author(s)	Contributions	Methods used	Dataset used	Advantages	Limitations
Feldman, J., and Janssen, J. [17]	Investigates the influence of the behavior of highly connected nodes on the transmission of infection within or across communities in a network.	Susceptible-infected-recovered (SIR) model and modified SPA model	Used primary and secondary data; documentary sources verify and validated the primary source material.	They showed the power of nodes that have higher degree.	They did not mention how to control the epidemic.
Y. D. Chen et al. [18]	Compare personal and geographical contact connectedness in various illnesses' social networks. Also, compare the network structure of one-mode networks with just patients and multi-mode networks with patients and geographical areas for illness study.	Built networks from personal and geographical relationships. Then, they analyzed connectivity and topology on the built networks.	Taiwan SARS data	Understanding the difference in connection between personal and geographical relationships and network structure between one-mode and multi-mode patient networks.	Difficult to find the initial spreader, as the geographical location increase in this method will become complex to use.

3 Background Technologies

3.1 Overview of Complex Network

A complex network is a network that consists of nodes and edges, which links and exhibits sophisticated patterns of connections or interactions among these nodes [19]. The complex network structure also displays nontrivial topological characteristics, which are often defined by elaborate patterns of connections and interactions among its components [20]. These networks are often used in many real-world systems such as social networks, biological systems, transportation systems, and the Internet. In recent times, the study of complex networks has emerged as a multidisciplinary domain, including ideas from mathematics, physics, computer science, biology, and sociology.

A complex network exhibits some characteristics:

1. Nodes and Edges:
   These are the simple things that every network consists of. These two things are called as the basic building blocks of a network. A node or vertex is an individual entity that can connect with other individual entities by using edges, which can be called as links or arcs.
2. Scale-Free Network:
   In a scale-free network, a small number of nodes, called as Hubs, have a larger number of connections than the bulk of nodes, which have less numbers of connections. This distribution exhibits a power-law pattern, by which a limited number of nodes have a crucial impact on the overall structure and operation of the network.
3. Small-World Phenomenon:
   Complex networks often display the small-world phenomenon, by which the maximum number of nodes may be accessible from any other node within a few numbers of steps. Although the network is large, the average distance between nodes is relatively small.
4. Clustering:
   Clustering refers to the inclination of nodes to create groups(classes/clusters) that have a greater concentration (tightly coupled) of connections inside the group as compared to connections (loosely coupled) with nodes outside the group. This indicates the existence of localized structures inside the network.
5. Hierarchy:
   Some complex networks exhibit hierarchical structure, which means that nodes are arranged into distinct layers or tiers, each fulfilling a unique purpose or duty. This hierarchical arrangement is widely used in biological systems.
6. Randomness and Preferential Attachment:
   The development and progression of complex networks frequently include processes like preferential attachment, which means new nodes have a greater likelihood of connecting to existing nodes with higher degrees, resulting in the establishment of hubs.

7. Resilience to Attacks and Failures:
   Complex networks exhibit resilience against random failures but are susceptible to focused attacks on crucial nodes, often known as hubs. This feature has impact on the design and security of the diverse system.
8. Dynamics and emergent phenomena:
   Complex networks often exhibit dynamic processes, including information dissemination, epidemic propagation, synchronization, and phase transitions. Emergent phenomena, characterized by the emergence of global features, resulting from the interactions of individual components, are frequently seen.

3.2 Complex Network in Healthcare Sector

In terms of epidemiological spread, a complex network refers to a system where people, healthcare institutions, and communities are interrelated in complicated ways that impact the transmission and management of infectious illnesses. Gaining insights into the organization and behavior of these networks is essential for developing efficient approaches to control and reduce the transmission of illnesses.

Some essential elements of complex networks in terms of the illness spread in the healthcare industry:

1. Graph components: nodes and edges:
   a) Nodes: Nodes represent various things such as people, healthcare personnel, healthcare institutions, and communities within the network. These entities may either serve as carriers of a disease or be possible targets for intervention.
   b) Edges: They reflect the connections or interactions between nodes, serving as channels for the transmission of illnesses, for instance, the dynamics between patients and healthcare professionals, or among members within a community.
2. Network Structure: The network structure may exhibit heterogeneity, with some nodes acting as hubs with a larger number of connections, while others have less connections. This indicates that certain persons or regions may have a greater impact on the spread of diseases.
3. Transmission Dynamics: The manner in which infectious diseases spread within a network is affected by elements such as patterns of contact, persons' movement, and their behavior in seeking treatment. Collecting insight into these processes is crucial for accurately forecasting and managing outbreaks.
4. Super-spreaders: It is important to identify super-spreaders, who are the people who have an unusually large influence on the transmission of diseases. Within the healthcare industry, this might include individuals afflicted with highly transmissible illnesses or healthcare professionals who often interact with patients [21, 22].

5. Interventions and Control Measures: Targeted interventions may be formulated according to the network's structure. For example, directing efforts toward isolating or vaccinating certain people or groups may have a greater effect on preventing the spread of a disease compared to random treatments. Efficient communication inside the network is essential for applying control measures. Healthcare authorities should widely provide precise information on the illness, preventative measures, and treatment alternatives to both healthcare professionals and the general public.
6. Modeling and Simulation: Computational models, such as agent-based models or network models, may accurately replicate the transmission of illnesses within intricate networks. These models facilitate the testing of different intervention options and enhance the comprehension of prospective outcomes.

The interconnections between people, healthcare institutions, and communities [23]. Examining and comprehending the configuration and kinetics of these networks are crucial for formulating efficient tactics to avoid, regulate, and handle the dissemination of contagious illnesses.

4 Network Statistics

4.1 Degree Centrality

The quantity being discussed here quantifies how many connections each node in a network has. Nodes that represent people or organizations are thought to be more central if they have more links with other nodes directly. This centrality suggests that they have a larger quantity of resources and opportunities within the network that they may access and share.

$$\mathrm{DC}_i = \sum_{j=0}^{n} (u_i v_j)$$

For undirected graph, every edge has the same importance but for directed graph, in-degree edges have more importance in social or citation network, which is also a one type of social research network:

$$\mathrm{DC}_i = \sum_{j=0}^{n} (u_i, v_j) + \sum_{j=0}^{n} (v_j, u_i)$$

According to Degree Centrality, those vertices having higher degree or incoming edges is more that are more central.

Centrality of the node $\propto$ degree of the node

4.2 Betweenness Centrality

This matrix is dependent upon the shortest path.

It is the overall length of path, which is shortest and passing though the vertex or node, and it is determined by the Betweenness Centrality of that node.

Let's say the starting node is i and the ending node is j. The calculation for the Betweenness Centrality for node k is,

$BC_k = \sum_{\text{each shortest path}}$ shortest path having node k

There can be more number of paths that are shorter between vertices or nodes i and j, these things also affect the measurement of the Betweenness Centrality.

$BC_k = \sum_{\text{each shortest path}}$ (shortest path having node k/total number of paths that are shorter between i and j).

4.3 Clustering Coefficient

The clustering coefficient estimates the extent to which individual elements (vertices) in a network exhibit clustering propensity. It offers information on the local connectivity or cohesion of neighborhoods inside the network. Various methods exist for computing the clustering coefficient, but a prevalent one involves examining a node and its adjacent nodes. The clustering coefficient of an individual element (vertex) is the quotient of the number of closed triplets centered at that node to the total number of potential triangles. High clustering signifies the existence of closely related clusters.

The global clustering coefficient is computed by taking the average of the clustering coefficients for each node in the network. It provides a comprehensive assessment of the level of clustering in the whole network.

Clustering coefficient of an individual element (node/vertex) i can be given as;

$$CC_i = \frac{2 \times \text{number of triangles centered at node } i}{\text{degree of node } i \times (\text{degree of node } i - 1)}$$

The global clustering coefficient is estimated by taking the average of the local clustering coefficients CC_i for all nodes in a network.

4.4 Closeness Centrality

The idea of proximity to other nodes in the network is represented by this metric. In comparison to fewer central nodes, more central nodes have shorter distances or better closeness centrality scores, which allow them to converse more quickly and easily with others. In contrast, nodes with lower proximity centrality scores are farther away from one another and require longer paths to connect to other vertices in the network.

Closeness centrality estimates the efficiency of a node in reaching all other nodes in the network. It is determined in the network by calculating the average distance between a node and all other nodes. A node with strong proximity centrality has a short average route length to all other nodes. Closeness centrality is particularly pertinent in scenarios where effective communication or information dissemination is vital. A high proximity centrality indicates effective transmission of information or communication.

Closeness centrality for node i can written as

$$CC_i = \frac{1}{\text{average shortest path length from node } i \text{ to all other nodes}}$$

4.5 Eigenvalue Centrality

Eigenvalue centrality is a significant metric in the field of complex network statistics. The centrality metric is derived from the primary eigenvector of the adjacency matrix of a network. The adjacency matrix is a $n \times n$ matrix that encodes the connections between nodes in a network.

The calculation of eigenvalue centrality is as follows:

1. Adjacency matrix (AM): The adjacency matrix AM for a graph G with n individual elements (vertices/nodes) is a $n \times n$ matrix. The value $AM_{ij} = 1$ if there is an edge between nodes i and j, otherwise $AM_{ij} = 0$.
2. Degree matrix (DM): The degree matrix DM is a diagonal matrix in which DM_{ii} represents the degree of individual element (vertex/node) i (the number of edges connecting to node i).
3. Laplacian matrix (LM): The Laplacian matrix LM is calculated as the difference between the degree matrix DM and the adjacency matrix AM, denoted as LM = DM – AM.
4. Eigenvalue centrality: The eigenvalue centrality of a node is determined by the ith component of the primary eigenvector of the Laplacian matrix LM.

Let δ_1 represent the minimum eigenvalue of the Laplacian matrix LM, whereas v_1 is the eigenvector that corresponds to this minimum eigenvalue. The eigenvalue centrality (EC) of node i is calculated as follows:

$$EC_i = \frac{1}{|\delta_1|} \times |v_1 (i)|^2$$

In the above equation, $|v_1 (i)|$ represents the ith element of the eigenvector v_1, whereas $|\delta_1|$ refers to the magnitude of the lowest eigenvalue.

Eigenvalue centrality is used in network analysis, specifically for the purpose of finding nodes that have a pivotal position in the overall structure of a network. Nodes exhibiting greater eigenvalue centrality are regarded as more central, and their removal from the network may have a substantial influence on the network's connectedness. This centrality metric is often used with other centrality measures to get a thorough comprehension of node significance in intricate networks.

5 Proposed Model

An egocentric doctor network with N nodes is created by activity-driven temporal network formation, where nodes alternate between active and inactive phases throughout time T. let A_t be the Active periods, which suggests that the doctor is staying at a location and makes different links in same place in a period of time (DLSPT) with other nodes. Just like active period inactive periods I_t, these time frames indicate when the doctor node does not establish connections with other nodes, but instead receives DLSPT linkages. The DLSPT link is directed from the host (doctor) nodes to other neighbor (family, friends, co-worker, patients, others) nodes. Just like in the above diagram, the doctor will stay at the hospital for a limited period of time, let's say 10 p.m. to 5 p.m., and spends his time with his co-workers, his regular patients, and other patients in the hospital. After that, the doctor travels and goes home. He spends some time with his family and friends. While he is in hospital, nodes will be active and create links with other nodes or entities in the hospital. After the time period is over, that node is inactive in that place and active in some other place, but he can receive the DLSPT links from the hospital.

The duration of active periods, A_t, is stochastically determined by a geometric distribution with parameter ε, i.e., $P_1(A_t)$ ~ geometric(ε), where ε represents a constant scaling factor. Meanwhile, the lengths of inactive periods, denoted as I_t, are generated from a geometric distribution with parameter γ, i.e., (I_t) ~ geometric(γ), where γ is given heterogeneously to represent varying visitor frequency. The activation potentiality γ, which exhibits heterogeneity, may be described by a power law relationship $F_1(\gamma) \sim \gamma^{-\beta}$, where β represents the scaling parameter.

To represent the dynamics of disease transmission, an indirect transmission period, π, is included for each active phase. During a certain event A_t and its related probability π, the doctor generates a predetermined quantity of DLSPT linkages, denoted by the variable l, as defined by the following equation:

$$Pr(l) = (1-\sigma)\sigma^{l-1}$$

where σ denotes the willingness to visit public locations. The value of σ is sampled from a power law distribution $F_2(\sigma) \sim \sigma^{-\alpha}$, where α is the scaling parameter. The fluctuations in l represent the spatial and temporal (spatio-temporal) patterns within the doctor's social network.

Every DLSPT connection has certain timing characteristics: A_t denotes the length of the doctor's presence at the site where interaction occurred, d_t reflects the time delay between the doctor's appearance and the arrival of a neighboring node, and t_l indicates the duration for which the neighboring node (the terminal nodes of a link) remains at the place of interaction. The delay in creating a connection, d_t, is sampled from a truncated geometric distribution,

$$\Pr(d_t) = \frac{P_l(1-P_l)^{d_t}}{1-(1-P_l)^{A_t+\pi}}$$

Here, P_l represents the likelihood of establishing a connection with a neighboring entity. The value of t_l is sampled from a geometric distribution with a link-breaking probability of P_{lb}, denoted as $P_3(t_l)$ ~ geometric (). The values of P_{lb} and P_l remain constant across all vertices in the network.

Nodes preserve their social arrangement by using their recollection of past interactions while choosing new connections. The likelihood of being chosen as a neighbor is contingent upon the doctor's level of public accessibility σ. The selection process takes into account the contact history and social dynamics within the network, and operates in the following manner:

$$Pr(ni_t + 1) = \frac{\sigma_i \gamma}{(ni_t + \sigma_i \gamma)}$$

Where ni_t represents the cumulative number of nodes that node i has interacted with till time t. Increased public accessibility, denoted by σ, leads to larger contact set sizes in nodes. In addition, they must be chosen as a neighbor by a greater nodes count. Therefore, the likelihood of getting chosen as a neighbor is

$$P(\sigma_j) = \frac{\sigma_j}{M\langle\sigma\rangle}$$

The neighbor selection method additionally takes into account the probability, P, of node j selecting nodes that have already included node j as their neighbors. Figure 1 presents the hypergraph for disease spread in egocentric network.

6 Results

In this study, we have considered the Facebook dataset for capturing social circles of nodes (or, users). The dataset constituted of 4,039 nodes, 88,234 edges, and average clustering co-efficient of 0.6055. The experimentations were performed on an Intel Core (TM) i7-1260P, x64 system with a processing capacity of 2.10 GHz and having 16 GB RAM. The results were generated using Python 3.10 over the Spyder version 5 framework. Figure 2 show the generated complex network graph G, depicting different nodes and their connected components. Figure 3 provides the plot showing the comparison between the ranks of the nodes in G along with their degree. It can be observed that as the ranks of

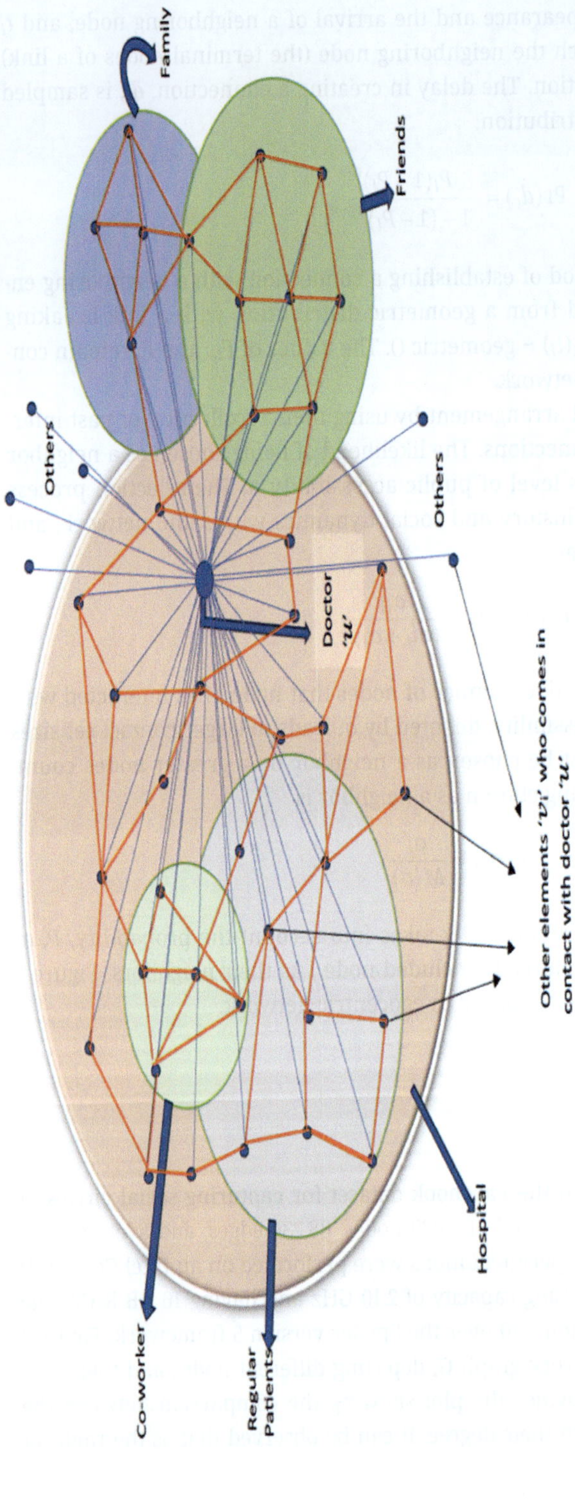

Figure 1: Hypergraph for egocentric network of disease spread.

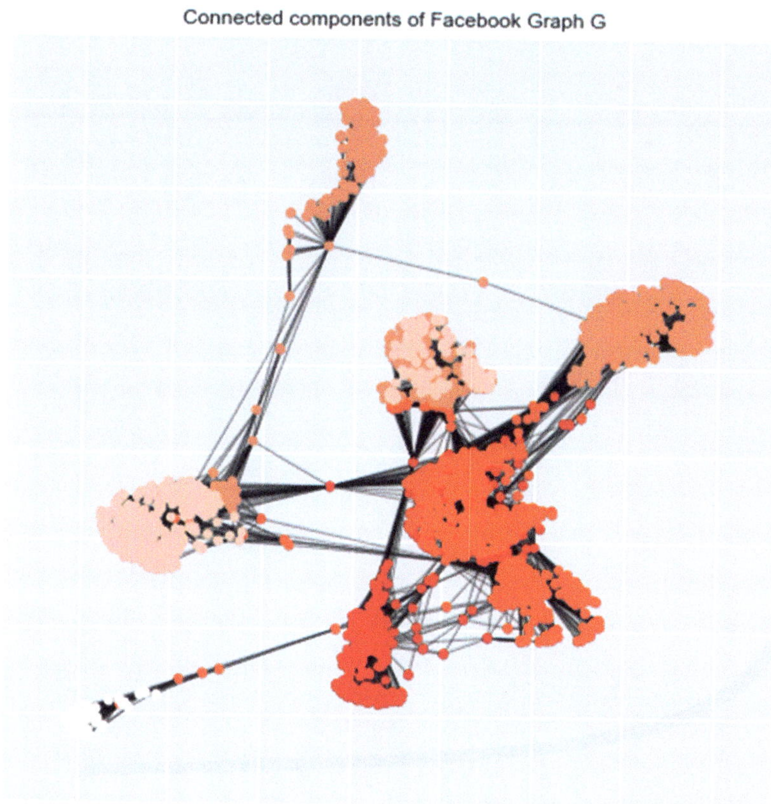

Figure 2: Complex network graph G for the considered dataset.

the nodes present in G increase, their degree value incurs an exponential decrease, representing lower influence of being in contact with the super-spreader node (ego).

In Figure 4, the sensitivity analysis for nodes count in the complex network is performed over increasing number of degrees. It can be observed from the findings that high degree values are associated with less number of nodes. Thus, a higher degree indicates the count of super-spreaders in the network. Figure 5 shows the frequency histogram for the number of edges presented in the network fitted with its probability density function (PDF). In Figure 6, the frequency histogram for the degree centrality of the network is presented. This merged plot is effective as a network analysis tool because it contains information about the structural features of nodes and their relative significance, in relation to this intricate node-to-node strategy.

Figure 7 represents the frequency histogram plot fitted with the empirical PDF for betweenness centrality. High betweenness centrality nodes on communication channels may govern information flow, making them attractive. These nodes may provide signaling pathway information and disease spread targets. Figure 8 provides the frequency histogram for closeness centrality, fitted with its empirical PDF. More

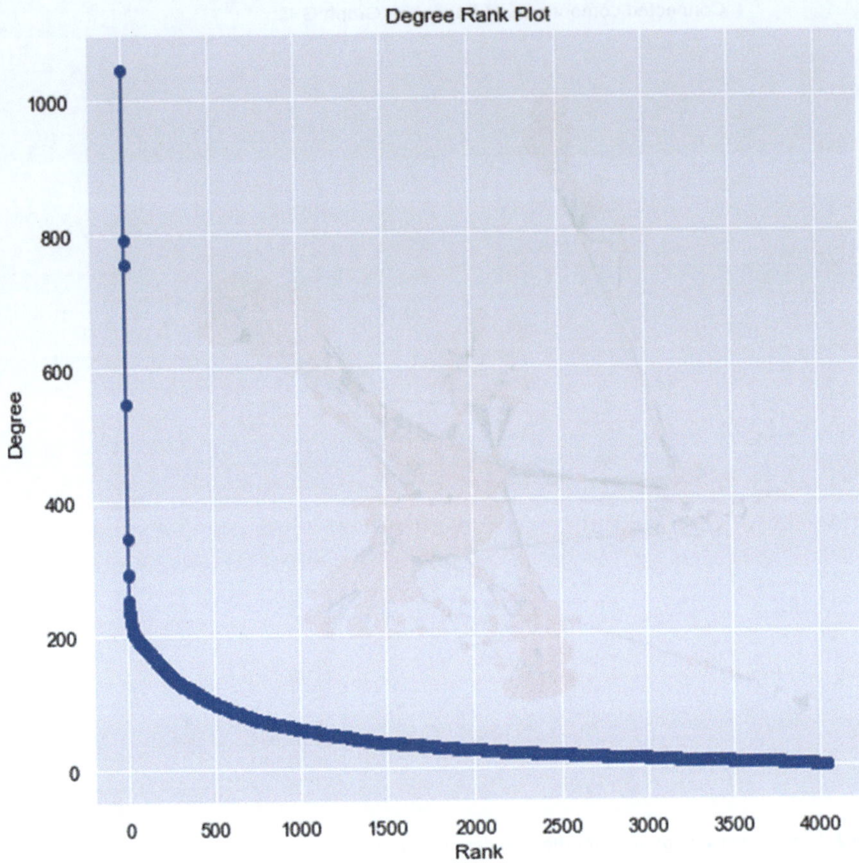

Figure 3: Comparison plot for node rank with the respective degree.

central nodes have shorter distances or better closeness centrality scores, which allow them to interact more quickly and easily with others. A node with strong proximity centrality has a short average route length to all other nodes. Closeness centrality is particularly pertinent in scenarios where effective communication or information dissemination is vital. A high closeness centrality indicates effective identification of disease spread pattern.

The frequency histogram pertaining to the clustering coefficient of each node in the network is presented in Figure 9, which is fitted with the empirical PDF. A high value of clustering coefficient is indicative of dense connectivity among the nodes and hence implies a high chance of disease spread in network. Figure 10 represents the histogram for eigenvalue of the considered network fitted with its empirical PDF. The eigenvalue is important to understand the overall behavior of the network. A node with higher eigenvalue is indicative of more centrality i.e., if a node has high centrality, then its removal can influence the connectivity of the network significantly.

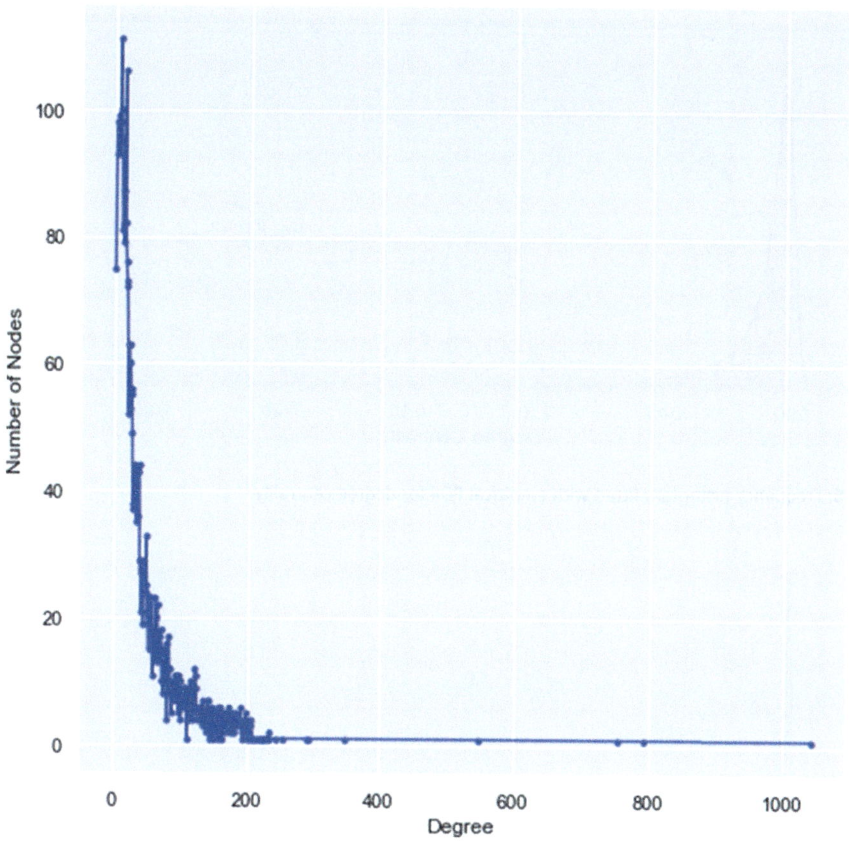

Figure 4: Plot for the degree of each nodes.

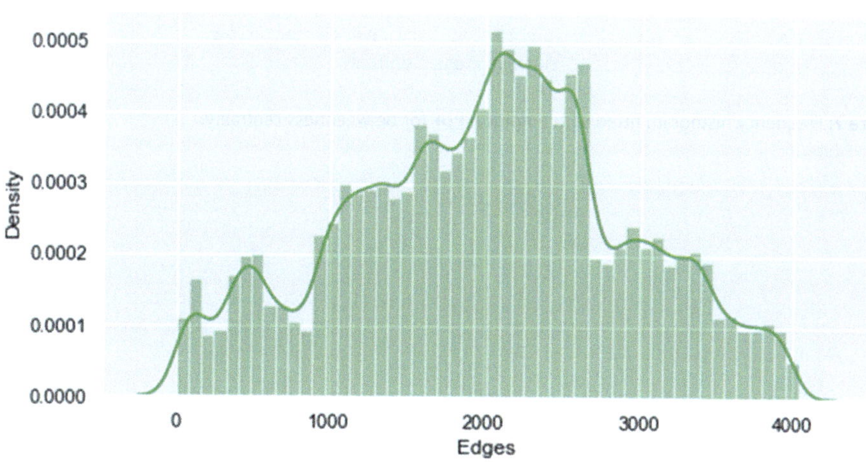

Figure 5: Frequency histogram fitted with empirical PDF for edges of the used dataset.

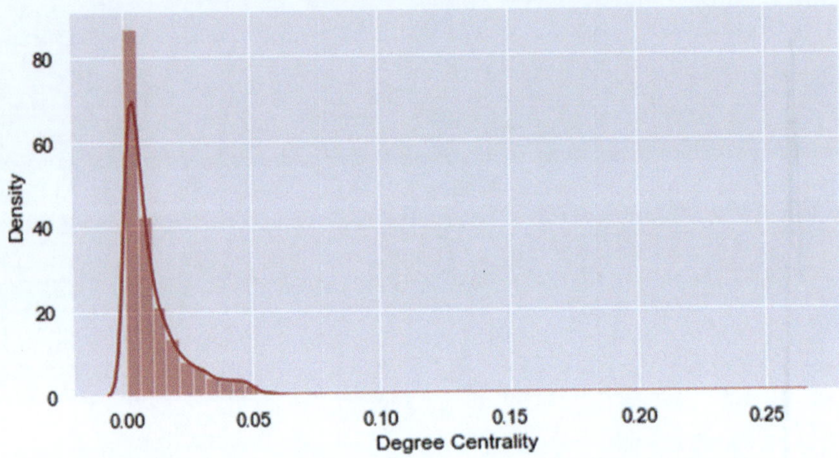

Figure 6: Frequency histogram fitted with empirical PDF for degree centrality.

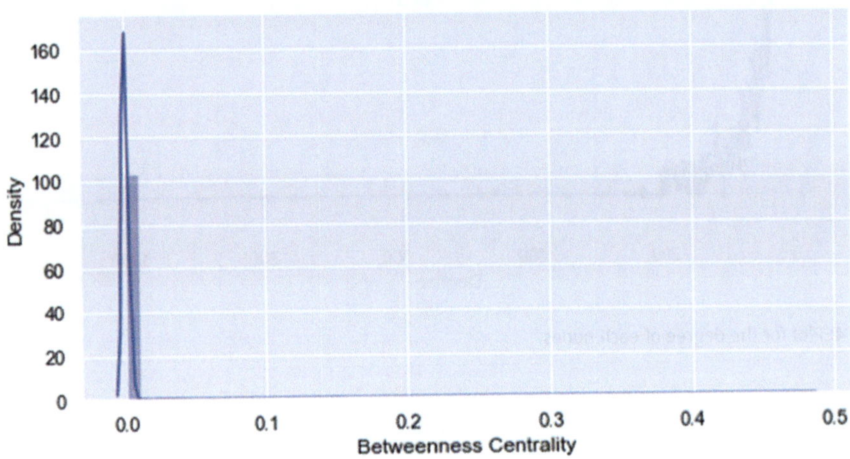

Figure 7: Frequency histogram fitted with empirical PDF for betweenness centrality.

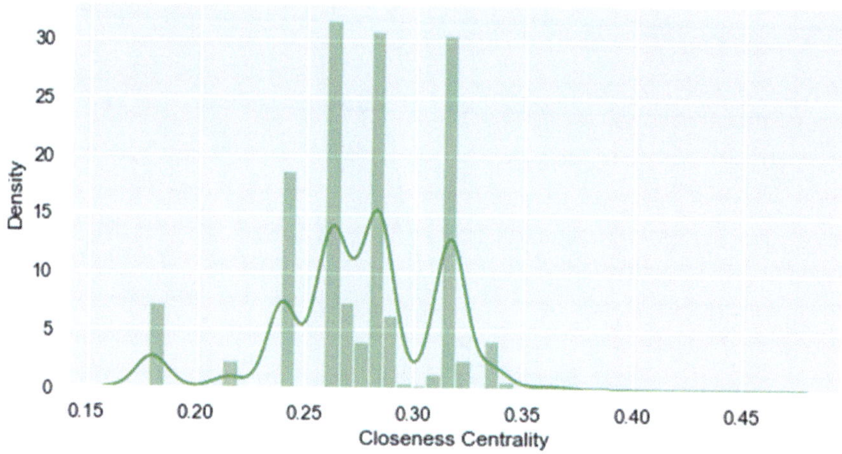

Figure 8: Frequency histogram fitted with empirical PDF for closeness centrality.

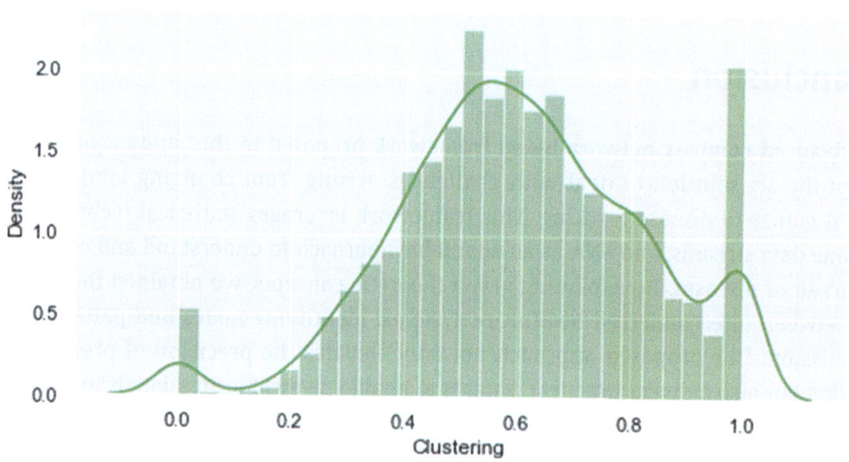

Figure 9: Frequency histogram fitted with empirical PDF for clustering coefficient.

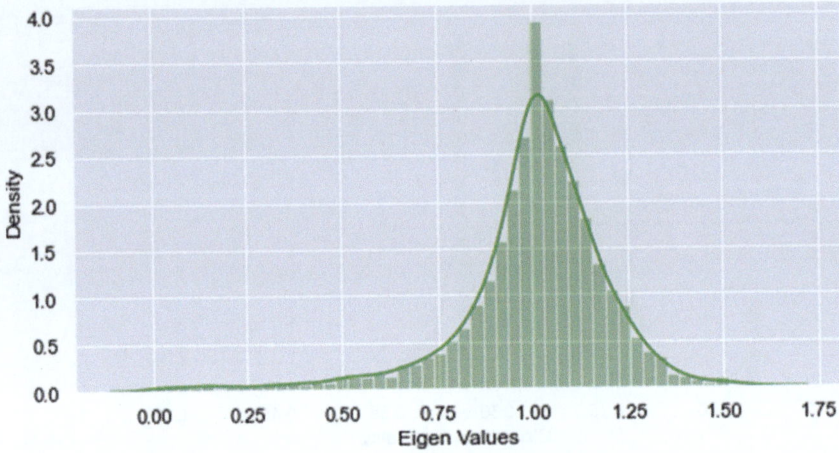

Figure 10: Frequency histogram fitted with empirical PDF for eigenvalues.

7 Conclusion

The advanced complex network-based framework proposed in this study signifies a state-of-the-art solution to deal with challenges arising from changing landscapes when it comes to disease tracking. This framework leverages statistical techniques, real-time data streams, and SNA as an adaptable approach to understand and counter the spread of diseases. By exploiting graph theoretic concepts, we obtained the mapping between interconnected healthcare systems, identifying nodes and patterns of transmission. Our proposed approach not only elevates the precision of predictive modeling but also delivers practical insights to enable medical professionals in taking preventative actions. Thus, this innovative framework can be regarded as an indication of development that has the potential to transform healthcare surveillance and contribute toward global disease spread network monitoring.

References

[1] Shahzamal, M., Jurdak, R., Mans, B., El Shoghri, A. & De Hoog, F. (2018). Impact of indirect contacts in emerging infectious disease on social networks. In *Trends and Applications in Knowledge Discovery and Data Mining: PAKDD 2018 Workshops, BDASC, BDM, ML4Cyber, PAISI, DaMEMO, Melbourne, VIC, Australia, June 3, 2018, Revised Selected Papers 22* (pp. 53–65). Springer International Publishing.

[2] Burns, L. R., Nembhard, I. M. & Shortell, S. M. (2022). Integrating network theory into the study of integrated healthcare. *Social Science & Medicine, 296*(114664).

[3] Ding, J., Yang, C., Wang, Y., Li, P., Wang, F., Kang, Y. . . . Zhang, L. (2023). Influential factors of intercity patient mobility and its network structure in China. *Cities, 132*, 103975.

[4] van der Woerd, O., Janssens, J., van der Scheer, W. & Bal, R. (2023). Managing (through) a network of collaborations: A case study on hospital executives' work in a Dutch urbanized region. *Public Management Review*, 1–23.

[5] Bebortta, S., Tripathy, S. S., Basheer, S. & Chowdhary, C. L. (2023). FedEHR: A Federated Learning Approach towards the Prediction of Heart Diseases in IoT-Based Electronic Health Records. *Diagnostics*, *13*(20). 3166.

[6] Tutsoy, O. (2023). Graph theory based large-scale machine learning with multi-dimensional constrained optimization approaches for exact epidemiological modelling of pandemic diseases. *IEEE Transactions on Pattern Analysis and Machine Intelligence*.

[7] Bebortta, S. & Singh, S. K. (2022, April). An intelligent framework towards managing big data in internet of healthcare things. In *International Conference on Computational Intelligence in Pattern Recognition* (pp. 520–530). Singapore: Springer Nature Singapore.

[8] Atkinson, A., Ellenberger, B., Piezzi, V., Kaspar, T., Salazar-Vizcaya, L., Endrich, O. . . . Marschall, J. (2023). Extending outbreak investigation with machine learning and graph theory: Benefits of new tools with application to a nosocomial outbreak of a multidrug-resistant organism. *Infection Control & Hospital Epidemiology*, *44*(2). 246–252.

[9] Robins, G., Lusher, D., Broccatelli, C., Bright, D., Gallagher, C., Karkavandi, M. A. . . . Sadewo, G. R. P. (2023). Multilevel network interventions: Goals, actions, and outcomes. *Social Networks*, *72*, 108–120.

[10] Rostami, M., Oussalah, M., Berahmand, K. & Farrahi, V. (2023). Community Detection Algorithms in Healthcare Applications: A Systematic Review. *IEEE Access*.

[11] Kumar, A., Aggarwal, N. & Kumar, S. (2023). SIRA: a model for propagation and rumor control with epidemic spreading and immunization for healthcare 5.0. *Soft Computing*, *27*(7). 4307–4320.

[12] Silva, D. H., Anteneodo, C. & Ferreira, S. C. (2023). Epidemic outbreaks with adaptive prevention on complex networks. *Communications in Nonlinear Science and Numerical Simulation*, *116*, 106877.

[13] Leung, W. T., Meeyai, A., Holt, H. R., Khieu, B., Chhay, T., Seng, S. . . . Rudge, J. W. (2023). Social contact patterns relevant for infectious disease transmission in Cambodia. *Scientific Reports*, *13* (1). 5542.

[14] Yang, C. H. & Jung, H. (2020). Topological dynamics of the 2015 South Korea MERS-CoV spread-on-contact networks. *Scientific reports*, *10*(1). 4327.

[15] Torres Munguía, J. A., Badarau, F. C., Díaz Pavez, L. R., Martínez-Zarzoso, I. & Wacker, K. M. (2022). A global dataset of pandemic-and epidemic-prone disease outbreaks. *Scientific data*, *9*(1). 683.

[16] Marquetoux, N., Stevenson, M. A., Wilson, P., Ridler, A. & Heuer, C. (2016). Using social network analysis to inform disease control interventions. *Preventive Veterinary Medicine*, *126*, 94–104.

[17] Feldman, J. & Janssen, J. (2017). High degree vertices and spread of infections in spatially modelled social networks. In *Algorithms and Models for the Web Graph: 14th International Workshop, WAW 2017, Toronto, ON, Canada, June 15–16, 2017, Revised Selected Papers* (pp. 60–74). Vol. *14*, Springer International Publishing.

[18] Chen, Y. D., Tseng, C., King, C. C., Wu, T. S. J. & Chen, H. (2007). Incorporating geographical contacts into social network analysis for contact tracing in epidemiology: A study on Taiwan SARS data. In *Intelligence and Security Informatics: Biosurveillance: Second NSF Workshop, BioSurveillance 2007, New Brunswick, NJ, USA, May 22, 2007. Proceedings 2* (pp. 23–36). Springer Berlin Heidelberg.

[19] Cencetti, G., Contreras, D. A., Mancastroppa, M. & Barrat, A. (2023). Distinguishing simple and complex contagion processes on networks. *Physical Review Letters*, *130*(24). 247401.

[20] Wang, J., Cai, S., Wang, W. & Zhou, T. (2023). Link cooperation effect of cooperative epidemics on complex networks. *Applied Mathematics and Computation*, *437*, 127537.

[21] Zhu, X. & Huang, J. (2023). SpreadRank: A Novel Approach for Identifying Influential Spreaders in Complex Networks. *Entropy*, *25*(4). 637.

[22] Yin, H., Zhang, A. & Zeng, A. (2023). Identifying hidden target nodes for spreading in complex networks. *Chaos, Solitons & Fractals*, *168*, 113103.

[23] Boccaletti, S., De Lellis, P., del Genio, C. I., Alfaro-Bittner, K., Criado, R., Jalan, S. & Romance, M. (2023). The structure and dynamics of networks with higher order interactions. *Physics Reports*, *1018*, 1–64.

Balajee J.,* Kathiravan K., and Sangar G.

Intelligent Interventions: Practical Applications of Machine Learning for Data-Driven Decision-Making in Healthcare

Abstract: Machine learning (ML) has emerged as a transformative force in healthcare, driving a paradigm shift toward data-driven decision-making. This chapter explores use cases and practical examples of how ML is revolutionizing clinical and operational aspects of healthcare systems. From predictive analytics and patient risk stratification to diagnostic support, personalized treatment, and administrative optimization, ML is enabling faster, more accurate, and more efficient decisions. With the ever-growing volume of digital health data, medical imaging, and real-time sensor information, healthcare providers are increasingly relying on ML models to uncover actionable insights. However, successful implementation hinges on understanding domain-specific challenges, including data quality, interpretability, privacy concerns, and regulatory compliance. Through real-world case studies and application-driven dialog, this chapter aims to bridge the gap between theoretical potential and practical deployment. We also highlight recent breakthroughs and discuss strategies for integrating ML models into clinical workflows. The ultimate goal is to guide machine learning engineers, data scientists, and healthcare professionals in applying ML to deliver better patient outcomes, reduce costs, and enhance system efficiency.

Keywords: machine learning, healthcare, data-driven decision-making, clinical decision support, predictive analytics, medical imaging, personalized medicine, healthcare operations, patient outcomes, AI in healthcare

1 Introduction to Machine Learning in Healthcare

The evolution of machine learning (ML) in healthcare has demonstrated a significant shift from simple rule-based systems to advanced, intelligent, and transparent technologies were illustrated in figure 1. Initially, healthcare applications relied heavily on rule-based systems, which were built on symbolic artificial intelligence (AI) [1]. These systems used manually crafted rules to provide diagnostic support and clinical

*__Corresponding author: Balajee J.__, Department of Artificial Intelligence, Mother Theresa Institute of Engineering and Technology, Palamaner, Chittoor, Andhra Pradesh, India, e-mail: j.balajee@mtieat.org
Kathiravan K., Department of Electrical Electronics and Engineering, Mother Theresa Institute of Engineering and Technology, Palamaner, Chittoor, Andhra Pradesh, India
Sangar G., Department of CSE, SRM Institute of Science and Technology, Vadapalani, Chennai, Tamil Nadu, India

https://doi.org/10.1515/9783111541235-021

decision-making tools. Although effective for narrowly defined problems, they lacked flexibility and adaptability in handling complex, real-world medical situations [2].

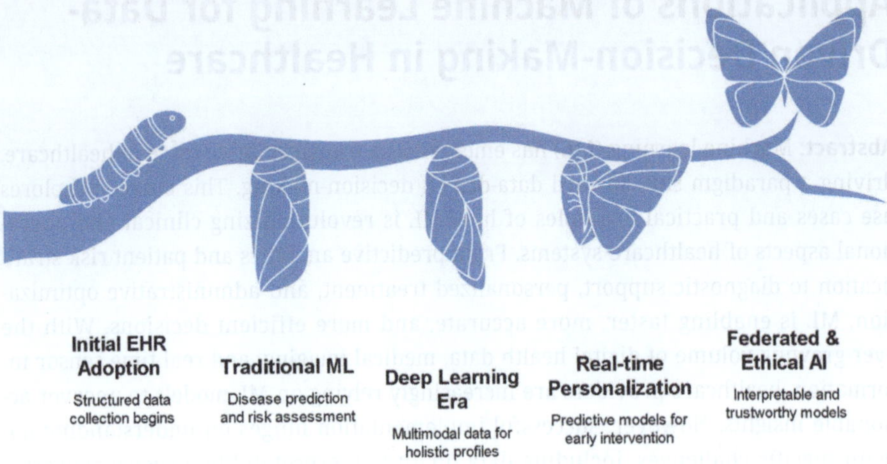

Figure 1: ML in healthcare: an evolution.

In the next segment, traditional systems for gaining knowledge of techniques emerged, utilizing dependent datasets like electronic health records (EHRs) for tasks that included simple data analysis and disease classification. Algorithms such as decision trees, support vector machines (SVMs), and k-nearest neighbors enabled improved pattern recognition and risk stratification but still required extensive feature engineering and curated data [3].

The introduction of deep learning marked a significant advancement, especially in processing unstructured data. Techniques such as convolutional neural networks (CNNs) and recurrent neural networks (RNNs) have been applied to clinical imaging and natural language processing (NLP) in EHRs, enabling improved diagnostic accuracy and uncovering hidden patterns in patient data without the need for manual feature extraction [4].

In recent years, the convergence of ML with the internet of things (IoT) has revolutionized healthcare. Real-time data from wearable devices and remote sensors are now integrated into ML models for continuous health monitoring, early disease detection, and personalized medicine. Federated learning further enhances privacy by enabling model training on distributed datasets without transferring sensitive patient information [5].

Explainable AI (XAI) is gaining prominence, addressing the need for transparency and trust in AI-driven healthcare systems. It aims to make complex ML decisions interpretable to clinicians and patients and is particularly important in areas such as AI-augmented surgical treatment and medical diagnostics. This evolution not only reflects growing sophistication but also a broader and more impactful application of ML within the medical domain, with a strong focus on ethics, interpretability, and patient-centric care [6].

1.1 The Evolution of Data-Driven Medicine

Healthcare has undergone sizable changes over the past century, transitioning from a reactive approach to a more preventive, evidence-based field. The integration of digital technologies, especially EHRs, has created unprecedented opportunities for data capture and analysis. However, the vast and heterogeneous nature of healthcare data presents challenges that traditional statistical methods struggle to address. This is where ML comes into play. ML techniques, by virtue of their ability to identify complex patterns and relationships in data, have ushered in a new era of precision and personalization in healthcare. From rule-based systems to deep neural networks, the tools at our disposal have evolved dramatically, enabling the development of intelligent systems that can assist clinicians in diagnosis, treatment planning, and outcome prediction. The fusion of medicine and ML is not merely a technological trend but a foundational shift toward data-driven medicine [7].

1.2 Why Healthcare Needs ML: Opportunities and Challenges

Despite significant advancements in medical technology, healthcare systems worldwide continue to grapple with challenges such as rising costs, inconsistent quality of care, and clinician burnout [8]. ML offers solutions by automating routine tasks, uncovering hidden insights from data, and enabling more informed decision-making. Key areas of opportunity include early disease detection, real-time monitoring, and predictive risk modeling. However, the deployment of ML in healthcare is not without its challenges. Issues such as data silos, lack of standardization, and limited interpretability of models remain sizable barriers. Additionally, medical environments demand high reliability and explainability – qualities not always guaranteed by complex ML algorithms. Therefore, developing healthcare-specific ML solutions requires a nuanced approach that balances innovation with practical constraints and ethical considerations. The following sections explore specific use cases where ML is making a tangible impact, supported by real-world implementations and evidence-based reviews [9].

2 Fundamentals of Healthcare Data

2.1 Types of Data: Structured, Unstructured, and Time Series

Healthcare data is remarkably diverse, encompassing structured formats such as laboratory test results and billing codes, unstructured formats such as clinical physician notes and radiology evaluations, and time-series data from wearable devices and ICU monitoring units were illustrated in Figure 2. Structured data, typically stored in relational databases, includes numerical values and categorical fields like diagnosis codes, lab values, and demographic information [10]. These are relatively easy to process using traditional ML models. Unstructured data, which accounts for over 80% of healthcare information, is more complex. This includes free-text medical notes, diagnostic images, and audio files. Processing this data requires techniques such as NLP, computer vision, and audio signal analysis. Time-series data, on the other hand, presents both opportunities and challenges. Its sequential nature allows for tracking patient health over time but requires advanced modeling techniques like RNNs or temporal convolutional networks to handle missing data, variable sampling rates, and long-term dependencies.

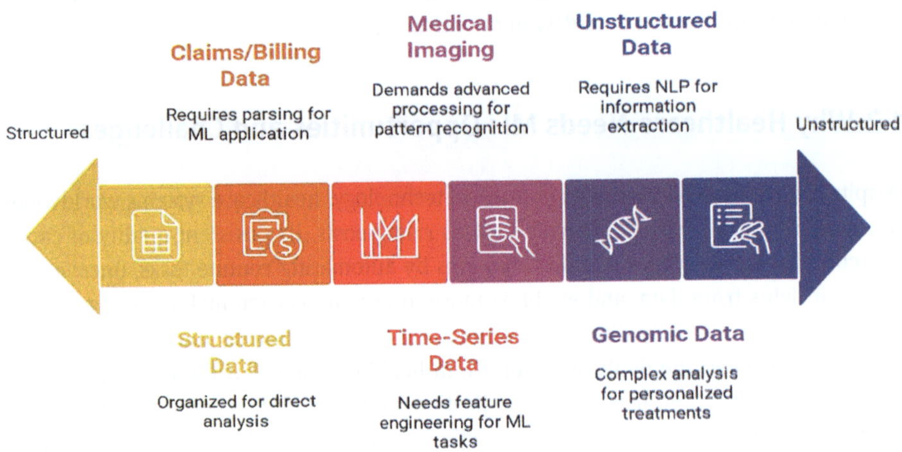

Figure 2: Healthcare data: a journey from structured-to-unstructured.

2.2 Data Collection, Integration, and Preprocessing

The foundation of any ML application in healthcare lies in high-quality data. Data collection typically involves EHRs, wearable sensors, medical imaging systems, and laboratory data structures. However, the siloed nature of these information assets often creates fragmentation, necessitating robust data integration frameworks. Health level seven standards and fast healthcare interoperability resources are increasingly used to standardize data exchange and integration. Preprocessing is equally essential and includes data cleaning (e.g., removing duplicates and correcting errors), normalization (e.g., scaling and encoding), imputation of missing values, and anonymization to comply with privacy regulations such as Health Insurance Portability and Accountability Act (HIPAA) and General Data Protection Regulation (GDPR). Feature engineering, which includes temporal aggregation or creating composite scores (e.g., Charlson Comorbidity Index), often enhances model performance. Additionally, understanding the clinical context of the data – how and why it was recorded – is critical to avoid spurious correlations and biases. Through meticulous preparation and contextual understanding, ML engineers can ensure that the models they build are both technically robust and clinically relevant.

3 Clinical Decision Support Systems

Clinical decision support systems (CDSS) are health information technology systems designed to assist healthcare providers in making informed clinical decisions. Figure 3, illustrate analyze data from various healthcare sources to provide alerts, recommendations, or diagnoses at the point of care [11].

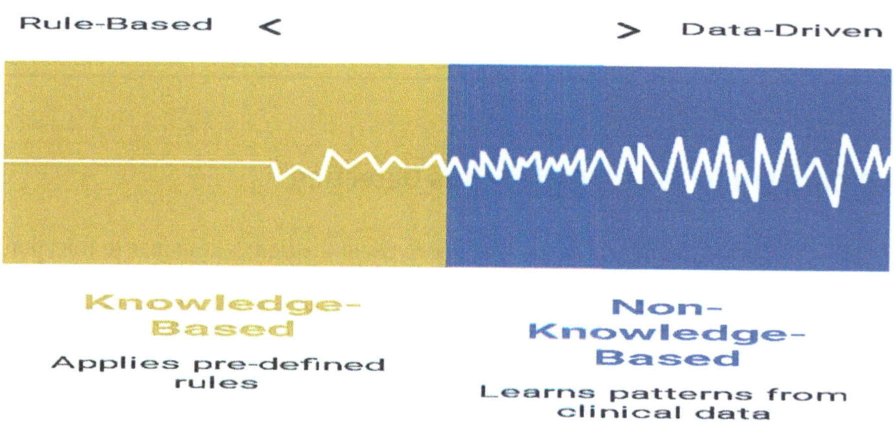

Figure 3: Data-driven CDSS variants.

3.1 Role of ML in Diagnostics and Treatment Recommendations

CDSS are designed to enhance healthcare delivery by providing clinicians, staff, and patients with expertise and patient-specific information that is intelligently filtered or presented at appropriate times. The integration of ML into CDSS has enabled these systems to move beyond static, rule-based approaches to more adaptive, predictive, and personalized support tools. ML-based CDSS can analyze large datasets, including EHRs and medical literature, to assist in differential diagnosis, recommend evidence-based treatment plans, and highlight potential adverse drug interactions [12]. These tools can significantly reduce diagnostic errors and improve clinical efficiency. For example, decision trees and ensemble techniques are used to identify patterns correlating symptoms and patient data with likely diagnoses, while reinforcement learning can help dynamically optimize treatment regimens over time. Importantly, integrating these systems into clinician workflows in a non-disruptive manner is crucial to ensuring adoption and sustained impact shown in Table 1.

Table 1: Machine learning in clinical decision support systems.

Application area	ML technique used	Key benefit	Challenge
Drug interaction prediction	Ensemble learning	Reduces adverse drug reactions	Data heterogeneity
Treatment recommendation	Reinforcement learning	Personalized therapy optimization	Reward function design
Disease progression modeling	Time-series deep learning	Early detection of critical transitions	Temporal data scarcity
ICU patient monitoring	Anomaly detection	Real-time alert generation	False positives
Diagnostic decision assistance	NLP + classification	Automates structured interpretation	Clinical language variability

3.2 Case Study: ML for Early Sepsis Detection

Sepsis is a life-threatening condition that arises when the body's response to infection causes damage to its own tissues and organs. Early detection is crucial, as every hour of delay in treatment increases the risk of mortality. ML models have shown promise in identifying early warning signs of sepsis from EHR data before symptoms become clinically apparent [13]. For instance, models such as the AI sepsis expert use a combination of vital signs, lab results, and historical data to generate a real-time risk score. These systems can trigger alerts that prompt immediate medical evaluation and intervention. In one notable implementation at a major U.S. hospital, the deployment of an ML-based sepsis prediction model led to a significant reduction in sepsis-related mortality. Key challenges in deploying such models include ensuring interpretability, managing false positives to avoid alert fatigue, and maintaining performance across diverse patient populations and care settings. Nonetheless, ML-powered CDSS for sepsis detection represent a powerful example of how intelligent systems can enhance clinical vigilance and save lives.

4 Predictive Analytics for Patient Risk Stratification

4.1 Identifying High-Risk Patients Using ML

Patient risk stratification involves categorizing individuals based on their likelihood of experiencing specific adverse events, such as hospitalization, disease progression, or complications. Figure 4, Illustrate the ML algorithms are particularly well-suited for this task, as they can analyze large and complex datasets to uncover hidden risk factors and patterns that may not be apparent through traditional methods. Logistic regression, decision trees, SVMs, and gradient boosting machines are commonly used for risk prediction. More recently, deep learning models have been applied to longitudinal patient data to capture temporal patterns that indicate deteriorating health conditions. One notable application is predicting the risk of readmission within 30 days post-discharge, which has significant implications for both patient care and healthcare costs. By identifying high-risk patients early, healthcare providers can implement targeted interventions such as follow-up calls, medication reconciliation, and personalized discharge planning to prevent avoidable readmissions and improve overall outcomes [14].

Figure 4: Patient risk stratification and intervention strategies.

4.2 Case Study: Predicting Hospital Readmissions

Hospital readmissions are a major issue for healthcare systems worldwide, often indicating suboptimal care transitions and driving up costs. Reducing avoidable readmissions is a key goal for improving patient outcomes and aligning with value-based care initiatives. ML provides powerful tools to predict the likelihood of readmission by analyzing large amounts of patient data to identify those at the highest risk [15].

In one broadly stated initiative, researchers developed an ML-based model using EHRs to predict 30-day readmission risks for patients with heart failure. The model incorporated over 100 variables, including demographics, comorbidities, laboratory values, prior admissions, discharge disposition, and medication adherence. Using ensemble methods like random forest and gradient boosting machines, the model achieved higher predictive accuracy (area under the curve (AUC) ~ 0.78) compared to traditional logistic regression approaches. The output was transformed into a risk score provided to care coordinators upon discharge, enabling targeted interventions such as follow-up calls, medication reviews, or home visits.

A key element in the model's success was robust feature engineering, along with the derivation of temporal trends (e.g., changes in weight or creatinine levels over time), as well as socioeconomic data linked by zip code. The integration of this model into hospital workflows involved not only technical deployment but also clinician engagement, improvements in interpretability, and optimization of alert thresholds to reduce false alarms [16].

One fitness organization reported a fifteen percent reduction in readmissions within six months of implementing the ML tool. However, significant challenges remain, including generalizing models across institutions with differing data formats and patient demographics, ensuring data quality, and addressing the ethical implications of algorithmic decision-making. Nonetheless, this case demonstrates how ML can support proactive care planning and effective resource allocation, ultimately contributing to safer, more efficient healthcare delivery shown in Table 2.

Table 2: Comparison of machine learning algorithms for disease prediction.

Algorithm	Use case in healthcare	Interpretability	Training time	Clinical adoption potential
Logistic regression	Heart disease prediction	High	Low	High
Decision trees	Diabetes classification	Medium	Medium	Medium
Random forest	Cancer diagnosis (e.g., breast)	Medium	High	High
SVM	Brain tumor detection	Low	High	Medium
Deep neural networks	Image-based diagnostics	Low	Very high	Medium

5 Personalized Medicine and Treatment Optimization

5.1 ML for Genomics and Pharmacogenomics

Personalized medicine is essentially about tailoring healthcare interventions to the unique genetic, environmental, and lifestyle traits of individual patients. ML plays a major role in enabling this vision by extracting insights from high-dimensional biomedical data, specifically genomic and pharmacogenomic data. Genomics involves analyzing a patient's genetic code to understand predispositions to diseases, while pharmacogenomics focuses on how genes influence drug response. The integration of ML into these domains allows for more accurate analysis, identification of novel biomarkers, and prediction of therapeutic efficacy.

Supervised learning strategies, including SVMs and random forests, are commonly used to classify genetic variations associated with diseases. More recently, deep learning models, particularly CNNs and autoencoders, have demonstrated superior performance in recognizing complex patterns within genomic sequences. These models can identify regulatory motifs, non-coding variations, and epigenetic modifications that may not be apparent through traditional methods [17].

One key use case is predicting adverse drug reactions based on an affected individual's genotype. ML models trained on pharmacogenomic databases can forecast how people will metabolize specific drugs, allowing physicians to adjust dosages or select alternative treatment plans. Moreover, ML enables the identification of new drug targets by analyzing interactions among genes, proteins, and clinical outcomes. Despite these advancements, challenges such as data sparsity, privacy concerns, and the need for clinical validation persist. Ensuring that predictive models are transparent, reproducible, and ethically deployed is critical to gaining trust from clinicians and patients alike.

5.2 Case Study: Tailoring Cancer Therapies

Cancer treatment has historically followed a one-size-fits-all model, relying on standardized regimens for broad patient populations. However, advances in genomics and molecular biology have revealed that cancers, even of the same anatomical type, can vary significantly at the genetic and cellular levels. Figure 5, illustrate the realization has driven the development of precision oncology, which aims to tailor treatments based on the specific genetic mutations and biological markers present in an individual's tumor. ML plays a pivotal role in enabling this level of personalization by identifying meaningful patterns across vast genomic, transcriptomic, and clinical datasets.

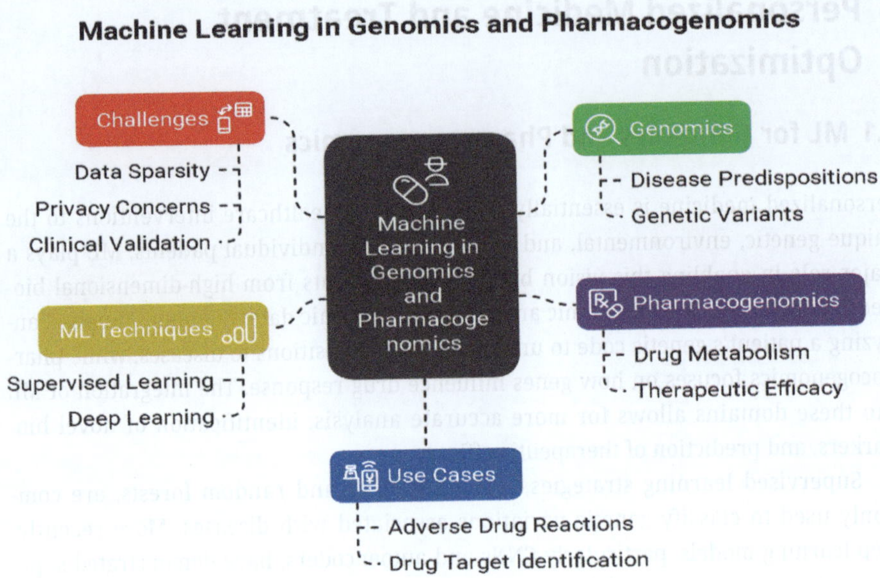

Figure 5: Machine learning in genomics and pharmacogenomics.

A notable example of ML software in cancer treatment is the use of supervised learning models to predict patient responses to immunotherapy. By analyzing tumor mutational burden, the expression of immune checkpoints (such as PD-L1), and T-cell infiltration levels, ML models can classify patients who are likely to benefit from checkpoint inhibitors. In one study, researchers utilized SVMs and neural networks on a multi-omics dataset to distinguish responders from non-responders to PD-1 therapy in melanoma patients, achieving predictive accuracies exceeding 80%. These predictions can assist oncologists in selecting the most promising treatments, avoiding unnecessary side effects, and reducing treatment costs [18].

Another impactful application of software involves the use of deep learning models to recommend drug combinations based on tumor profiles. For instance, DeepSynergy is a deep neural network model trained on drug sensitivity profiles from cancer cell lines and corresponding gene expression data. It predicts synergistic drug pairs tailored to individual tumors, helping to design personalized combination therapy plans that maximize efficacy while minimizing toxicity.

Integrating ML into medical decision-making for cancer treatment also includes real-time tracking of treatment responses using imaging and biomarkers. Models trained on sequential CT or MRI scans can detect subtle changes in tumor size or morphology, flagging early signs of resistance or progression. These insights can prompt timely adjustments to the treatment strategy.

Despite these advancements, deploying ML in cancer care faces challenges, including the scarcity of records for uncommon cancers, variability in information quality across institutions, and the need for interpretability in high-stakes decisions. Nonetheless, case studies in cancer, breast cancer, and lung cancer illustrate the transformative potential of ML in making cancer treatment more targeted, efficient, and effective.

6 Medical Imaging and Computer Vision

6.1 Deep Learning in Radiology and Pathology

Medical imaging plays a crucial role in disease diagnosis, monitoring, and treatment planning. Radiology (e.g., X-rays, CT scans, and MRI) and pathology (e.g., histopathological slides) generate vast amounts of image data daily, which require expert interpretation. Figure 6, represents due to increasing workload and shortage of specialists, ML – particularly deep learning – has become an essential tool to assist clinicians in interpreting these complex visuals efficiently and accurately.

CNNs have become the backbone of scientific image analysis due to their ability to learn hierarchical features directly from pixel data. CNN-based models have demonstrated performance on par with, and sometimes surpassing, human experts in tasks such as detecting pneumonia on chest X-rays, identifying brain tumors in MRI scans, and grading diabetic retinopathy (DR) from retinal images. Transfer learning, where pre-trained models like ResNet, VGG, or DenseNet are fine-tuned on clinical datasets, has significantly reduced the amount of labeled data required, enabling faster deployment in clinical settings [19].

In pathology, whole-slide imaging has enabled the digitization of biopsy samples, opening new avenues for ML applications. Deep learning models can detect cancerous cells, quantify tumor proliferation, and even predict molecular subtypes directly from histological slides. This capability facilitates early diagnosis, reduces inter-observer variability, and improves treatment decisions.

Explainability is an important aspect of deep learning in clinical imaging. Techniques like Grad-CAM, saliency maps, and Shapley additive explanations (SHAP) help highlight regions of interest in a photograph that influenced the model's prediction, increasing trust and transparency. Despite the impressive accuracy metrics, models should be tested across diverse populations and imaging devices to ensure generalizability. Integration of deep learning into radiology and pathology workflows enhances productivity, reduces diagnostic errors, and provides decision support in time-sensitive scenarios – bringing AI-assisted diagnostics toward to routine clinical practice [20].

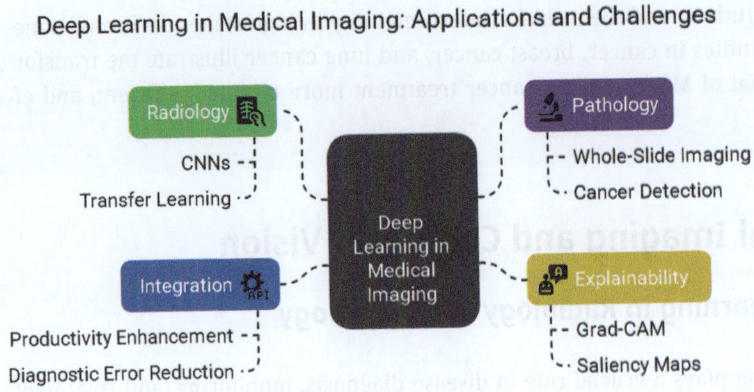

Figure 6: Deep learning in medical imaging.

6.2 Case Study: Diabetic Retinopathy Detection Using CNNs

DR is a leading cause of blindness among adults worldwide. Early detection and timely intervention are crucial to preventing vision loss. However, screening programs are resource-intensive and often suffer from variability in diagnostic accuracy. CNNs have proven to be highly effective in automating the detection of DR from retinal fundus images, offering a scalable solution to this public health challenge.

In this situation, we examine the development and deployment of a CNN-based system trained on large annotated datasets, including the Kaggle EyePACS dataset. The CNN model, inspired by architectures like InceptionV3 and ResNet50, was trained to classify retinal images into various stages of DR, ranging from no DR to proliferative DR. Extensive data augmentation techniques – such as image flipping, brightness normalization, and contrast enhancement – were used to increase model robustness.

The trained model achieved an AUC of over 0.90 on the test set, demonstrating high sensitivity and specificity. Heatmaps generated using Grad-CAM provided visual insights by highlighting retinal regions that contributed most to the prediction, thereby improving interpretability and clinician confidence. The system was piloted in a clinical screening program, where it successfully flagged high-risk patients for further ophthalmologist assessment, reducing workload and enhancing triage efficiency [21].

This case exemplifies how deep learning can democratize access to early screening, particularly in low-resource settings. The potential to deploy such models on cloud platforms or edge devices, including smartphones equipped with retinal cameras, underscores their capacity in mobile health programs. Future work focuses on improving model generalization across ethnicities and imaging conditions, as well as integrating feedback loops for continuous learning.

With its blend of clinical relevance, technological feasibility, and real-world impact, this case demonstrates the practical power of ML in transforming disease screening workflows [22].

7 Operational Efficiency and Resource Management

7.1 Scheduling, Triaging, and Hospital Resource Allocation

Operational efficiency is a cornerstone of sustainable healthcare transport, especially in the face of growing patient demand, limited resources, and staffing constraints. ML provides powerful tools to streamline healthcare operations, ranging from patient scheduling and triage to the allocation of critical resources such as ICU beds, ventilators, and staff.

One significant application of ML in scheduling involves optimizing appointment structures to reduce patient wait times and provider idle time. Reinforcement learning algorithms can analyze historical scheduling data to recommend optimal time slots, taking into account cancellations, no-shows, and patient urgency. Predictive models also assist with dynamic rescheduling by forecasting delays and enabling real-time adjustments.

In emergency departments, triage systems powered by ML models analyze signs, symptoms, vital signs, and patient records to prioritize care delivery. NLP tools extract relevant features from unstructured triage notes, feeding them into decision trees or ensemble classifiers to predict critical cases with high precision. This capability improves patient flow and ensures timely attention to high-risk cases [23].

For aid allocation, clustering and regression models help predict affected individual influx patterns, ICU admission rates, and resource utilization. Hospitals use ML to anticipate demand surges, enabling proactive planning. For example, during the COVID-19 pandemic, time-series forecasting models were instrumental in planning ventilator deployment and staffing strategies. Additionally, queuing theory combined with ML allows for simulating patient flow and analyzing the impact of various policies on throughput and quality of care. Simulation results can guide investments in infrastructure and personnel.

ML-enabled operational intelligence reduces expenses, enhances patient experience, and minimizes clinician burnout. However, successful adoption depends on seamless integration with medical institution data systems, real-time data feeds, and user-friendly dashboards. Trust, transparency, and continuous feedback loops remain critical to scaling these tools effectively across healthcare institutions [24].

7.2 Case Study: Optimizing ICU Bed Utilization

Intensive care units (ICUs) are critical yet limited resources in hospitals, often strained during periods of high demand, such as pandemics or seasonal surges. Optimizing ICU bed usage through ML not only improves patient outcomes but also ensures that healthcare resources are allocated equitably and efficiently.

In this case study, we examine how a large tertiary care health facility utilized ML to manage ICU capacity. The clinic collected 3 years' worth of historical data, including patient admission logs, length of stay, comorbidity profiles, discharge summaries, and seasonal illness trends. A random forest regression model was trained to predict ICU length of stay based on early admission parameters such as vitals, lab results, and clinical notes.

The model achieved a high R^2 value, indicating robust predictive accuracy. These predictions enabled the health facility's administration to forecast bed availability up to seventy-two hours in advance. Complementary clustering algorithms were used to identify affected patient cohorts with similar ICU trajectories, helping prioritize cases for step-down care or early discharge when medically feasible.

The ML device was integrated into the health center's EHR dashboard, providing real-time visualization of predicted bed occupancy and patient discharge probabilities. It supported automated alerts for potential ICU bottlenecks and facilitated contingency plans, such as mobilizing surge capacity or expediting patient transfers.

During the pilot phase, the model contributed to a 15% improvement in ICU turnover rate and a 10% reduction in elective surgery cancellations due to bed unavailability. Importantly, these gains were achieved without compromising the quality of care, as evidenced by post-discharge audits and readmission monitoring [25].

This case highlights the significant potential of predictive analytics in clinical operations. By leveraging records and ML, healthcare systems can dynamically optimize capacity, enhance responsiveness, and better serve patients in critical situations.

8 Ethical, Legal, and Regulatory Considerations

8.1 Bias, Fairness, Transparency, and GDPR/HIPAA Compliance

As tools and technologies become increasingly embedded in healthcare, addressing the moral, legal, and regulatory implications is critical for responsible deployment. Key issues such as algorithmic bias, data privacy, and lack of transparency can not only erode public trust but also lead to harmful outcomes.

One of the most pressing challenges is bias in ML models. Bias can originate from unbalanced training data, systemic inequalities in care, or implicit assumptions embedded in algorithms. For example, a predictive model trained on predominantly Caucasian patient data may perform poorly on other ethnic groups, exacerbating healthcare disparities. Ensuring fairness requires diverse, representative datasets, regular performance audits, and fairness-aware algorithms that adjust for skewed distributions.

Transparency, or the ability to recognize and provide a reason for model decisions, is equally important. Black-box models, such as deep neural networks, can deliver high accuracy but are often inscrutable to clinicians. XAI techniques, including SHAP values and LIME, help demystify predictions by highlighting key contributing factors. These tools support clinician trust and aid in regulatory compliance [26].

On the criminal front, privacy laws like the GDPR in Europe and the HIPAA in the USA establish strict guidelines for the collection, storage, and use of private health information. ML models need to be designed with data minimization, consent management, and auditability in mind. Federated learning, which trains models on distributed data without centralized sharing, is gaining traction as a privacy-preserving alternative.

Liability in ML-driven decisions is another emerging issue. Questions remain about who is responsible – developers, hospitals, or clinicians – when an AI system makes an incorrect or harmful recommendation. Legal frameworks are still evolving, and institutions are encouraged to maintain human oversight and clear documentation to mitigate risks. A multidisciplinary approach involving ethicists, legal experts, clinicians, and technologists is essential to ensure that ML in healthcare serves the public good while respecting individual rights were illustrated in Figure 7.

Figure 7: Legal and ethical AI in healthcare.

8.2 Explainable AI and Trust in ML Models

XAI is essential to fostering trust in ML models within healthcare, where decisions can have life-changing consequences. Clinicians must be able to understand the intent behind AI-driven predictions to validate and integrate them into their decision-making processes. Unlike black-box models that provide little to no insight into their workings, Table 3. represents the XAI tools such as SHAP and local interpretable model-agnostic explanations (LIME) offer interpretable outputs that reveal which variables most influenced a prediction and why.

This interpretability is not just about transparency; it also builds clinician confidence, aids in model validation, and enhances regulatory compliance. When a ML model recommends a diagnosis or treatment, healthcare professionals are more likely to trust and act on it if they understand the underlying logic. Moreover, transparent models enable organizations to identify potential biases, correct misalignments, and ensure fairness across diverse patient populations [27].

Table 3: Techniques for explainable AI in healthcare.

Technique	Description	Strengths	Limitations	Examples of use case
LIME	Locally approximates complex models using simpler ones	Model-agnostic, interpretable	Unstable explanations	Cancer risk prediction from EHR
SHAP	Computes feature contributions using Shapley values	Consistent, theoretically sound	Computationally expensive	Drug response modeling
Saliency Maps	Visualizes areas influencing neural network decisions	Intuitive, image-specific	Limited to image data	Chest X-ray abnormality detection
Counterfactuals	Shows how minimal changes can alter the model's decision	Enhances user understanding	May lack feasibility in healthcare data analysis	Treatment plan revision support
Decision Trees	Inherently interpretable rule-based model	Transparent, logical	Limited scalability	Diabetes risk prediction

Building trust also involves collaboration. Co-designing AI systems with clinicians, incorporating their domain expertise, and iteratively refining models based on medical feedback results in tools that are not only more accurate but also more usable and relevant in real-world settings. This inclusive approach fosters a sense of ownership and acceptance among end-users.

In essence, explainable AI transforms ML from a mysterious technological intervention into a reliable ally in healthcare. By making AI's reasoning visible and comprehensible, we create the conditions necessary for the accountable, effective, and equitable use of these powerful tools in medical environments.

9 Challenges in Real-world Implementation

9.1 Model Generalization, Integration, and Clinician Adoption

While the device holds great promise for transforming healthcare, its implementation in real-world settings remains a challenging endeavor. Establishing reliable and scalable systems in controlled environments involves overcoming numerous significant barriers during the transition.

A primary challenge in ML is achieving model generalization. A model trained on one group's data may face difficulties when deployed due to variations in demographics, devices, protocols, and data access formats across different environments. To address this issue, models should be trained on multi-institutional datasets and externally validated. Techniques such as transfer learning, domain adaptation, and continual learning are key approaches to improving generalization and flexibility.

Integration into current clinical workflows is another essential barrier. Without addressing the inclusion of ZOGN or the operational burdens in ML solutions, healthcare professionals must adapt to how they already work. Seamless interoperability is an important function of EHR systems, along with intuitive user interfaces and automated indices embedded in clinician dashboards. Organizations should invest in collaborative strategies involving clinicians and IT teams at the outset of the development process [28].

Clinicians adopt faith in usefulness and consider the alleged costs. The loss of interpretability and the danger of obsolescence or skepticism can almost deter adoption, even with algorithmic accuracy. Providing clear purposes, preserving transparency, and demonstrating tangible enhancements in care are crucial for maximizing benefits and fostering engagement in efficiency. Training programs that enhance digital literacy and provide ongoing support are essential to promote adoption.

Operational barriers also affect implementation. These include the structural features of the constraints, record silos, regulatory approval deadlines, and budget restrictions. Moreover, ML systems must be regularly monitored and updated to maintain consistency and performance as circumstances evolve.

In the end, trade control is crucial. Organizations must foster a culture of innovation, encourage multidisciplinary collaboration, and align ML projects with broader organizational goals. A governance framework, assessment matrix, and feedback mechanisms ensure stable and responsible integration. Addressing these challenges requires state-of-the-art technology that combines a robust technical foundation with a human-centered design and organizational preparedness [29].

10 Synthesis of Use Case Outcomes

In CDSS, ML has improved early disease detection, treatment recommendations, and patient monitoring. Ensemble learning has effectively reduced adverse drug interactions, while reinforcement learning has facilitated personalized therapy planning. Anomaly detection models have supported ICU monitoring with real-time alerts, thereby minimizing response latency in critical scenarios (Table 1).

The practical application of ML models in healthcare has led to promising outcomes across various domains. For disease diagnosis, models such as deep neural networks and random forests have demonstrated superior accuracy levels of 95% and 91%, respectively, particularly in tasks like medical imaging and cancer classification. Logistic regression and decision trees, though less complex, offer higher interpretability and are better suited for diseases such as diabetes and heart conditions due to their logical decision boundaries and low training requirements (see Table 2).

Explainable AI methods, such as SHAP and LIME, provide critical transparency to model predictions, enhancing user trust and clinical interpretability. SHAP has emerged as a reliable framework for drug response modeling, while LIME has proven useful for local interpretability in structured EHR data (Table 3).

The results highlight that the application of ML in healthcare can significantly enhance accuracy, efficiency, and decision-making transparency. However, model selection remains context-dependent. High-performing models, such as deep neural networks, are data-intensive and often lack interpretability, which raises concerns in sensitive use cases. Consequently, hybrid approaches that combine interpretability (e.g., decision trees) with high-performance models may provide a balanced solution.

Clinical deployment also requires consideration of training time, data availability, and regulatory standards. The integration of ML into CDSS has revealed key challenges, such as data heterogeneity, temporal data gaps, and reward function design, underscoring the need for robust data engineering and model validation [30].

Furthermore, explainability is no longer optional. As black-box models become integrated into clinical workflows, the demand for explainable AI has grown. Approaches such as SHAP and counterfactuals not only enhance trust in models but also assist clinicians in validating automated decisions. Overall, while ML holds the promise of transforming healthcare, its success depends on responsible deployment, continuous evaluation, and a human-in-the-loop paradigm.

11 Future Directions and Research Opportunities

11.1 Federated Learning, Explainable AI, and Personalized Medicine

The future of ML in healthcare is poised for rapid evolution, driven by continuous technical advancements and emerging innovations. Several promising directions are expected to redefine how ML is applied in the field. In the coming years, these advancements will play a crucial role in enabling more informed decision.

Federated learning (FL) stands out as a major innovation addressing privacy and information-sharing concerns. FL decentralizes information, enabling the training of algorithms across multiple entities, such as hospitals, without transferring the raw data of individual patients. This approach not only preserves privacy in compliance with GDPR and HIPAA but also enhances model generalization by leveraging the diversity of the data. Research efforts are increasingly focused on ensuring model convergence and addressing biases in datasets.

Artificial intelligence is gaining traction as a necessity rather than a luxury. The demand for transparent, interpretable ML models is particularly strong in healthcare, where black-box algorithms can undermine clinicians' trust. New research is exploring hybrid models that balance accuracy with interpretability, including attention-based mechanisms and symbolic reasoning. Future tools will likely integrate XAI into real-time clinical decision support, providing context-aware explanations that align with scientific reasoning processes.

Personalized medicine represents a transformative shift, with ML at its core. By analyzing high-dimensional data from genomics, imaging, and EHRs, ML models can identify patient-specific risk factors and treatment pathways. Ongoing research in deep learning for omics data, multi-modal fusion techniques, and reinforcement learning for adaptive treatment planning is pushing the boundaries of individualized care.

Other key frontiers include:

- Causal inference methods are used to distinguish correlation from causation, which is critical for clinical interventions.
- Digital twin systems that simulate patient body structures and predict treatment effects.
- Ethical AI frameworks that incorporate equity, responsibility, and transparency from design to deployment.

In short, the intersection of ML, biomedical data, and clinical insight is a fertile ground for innovation. Continuous collaboration among academia, industry, and healthcare institutions will ensure that future ML systems are not only more powerful but also reliable and aligned with the realities of patient care.

11.2 Final Thoughts: Toward a Smarter Healthcare Ecosystem

The integration of ML into healthcare represents a monumental shift in how scientific and operational decisions are made. As demonstrated across a wide range of use cases – from diagnostics and treatment recommendations to hospital logistics and personalized medicine – ML technology is transforming the landscape of patient care.

This chapter has outlined the extensive potential of data-driven decision-making powered by ML, providing concrete examples of its benefits, including improved diagnostic accuracy, faster patient triage, optimized resource allocation, and more individualized treatment strategies. At the same time, it has highlighted the importance of addressing real-world implementation challenges, ensuring ethical and legal compliance, and fostering clinician trust and adoption.

ML isn't always a panacea; however, it is an effective tool that should be used judiciously and collaboratively. Its success depends on the quality of data, the robustness of models, and the inclusivity of design processes. Interdisciplinary cooperation among data scientists, clinicians, hospital administrators, and policymakers is essential for developing systems that genuinely support better health outcomes.

Looking ahead, future advancements such as federated learning, explainable AI, and causal modeling offer exciting opportunities to make healthcare more predictive, preventive, and personalized. However, these innovations must be accompanied by thoughtful governance, ongoing validation, and patient-centered approaches.

Ultimately, by harnessing system learning with care and responsibility, we can build a smarter, more responsive healthcare system – one that not only treats illness more effectively but also promotes well-being, equity, and efficiency at scale.

References

[1] Esteva, J., Kuprel, B., Novoa, R. A., Ko, J., Swetter, S. M., Blau, H. M. & Thrun, S. Dermatologist-level classification of skin cancer with deep neural networks. (2017). *Nature*, 542(7639), 115–118.

[2] Ribeiro, M. T., Singh, S. & Guestrin, C., "Why should I trust you? Explaining the predictions of any classifier," in *Proc. ACM SIGKDD*, 2016, pp. 1135–1144.

[3] Lundberg, S. M. & Lee, S.-I., "A unified approach to interpreting model predictions," *Advances in Neural Information Processing Systems (NeurIPS)*, 2017, pp. 4765–4774.

[4] Rajkomar, A., Oren, E., Chen, K., Dai, A. M., Hajaj, N., Hardt, M., Liu, P. J., Liu, X., Marcus, J., Sun, M., Sundberg, P., Yee, J., Zhang, K. & Zhang, F. Scalable and accurate deep learning for electronic health records. (2018). *NPJ Digital Medicine*, 1(1), 1–10,

[5] Miotto, M., Wang, F., Wang, S., Jiang, X. & Dudley, J. T. Deep learning for healthcare: review, opportunities and challenges. (2018). *Briefings in Bioinformatics*, 19(6), 1236–1246,

[6] Chen, M., Hao, Y., Hwang, K., Wang, L. & Wang, L. (2017). Disease prediction by machine learning over big data from healthcare communities. *IEEE Access*, 5, 8869–8879.

[7] Beam, K. L. & Kohane, I. S. Big data and machine learning in health care. (2018). *JAMA*, 319(13), 1317–1318,
[8] Litjens, G., Kooi, T., Bejnordi, B. E., Setio, A. A., Ciompi, F., Ghafoorian, M., Van der laak, J. A., Van ginneken, B. & Sánchez, C. I. (2017). A survey on deep learning in medical image analysis. *Medical Image Analysis*, 42, 60–88.
[9] Jiang, F., Jiang, Y., Zhi, H., Dong, Y., Li, H., Ma, S., Wang, Y., Dong, Q., Shen, H. & Wang, Y. Artificial intelligence in healthcare: past, present and future. (2017). *Stroke and Vascular Neurology*, 2(4), 230–243,
[10] Choi, J., Schuetz, E., Stewart, T. & Leung, K. M. Web-based risk stratification tool for diabetes and cardiovascular disease. (2007). *Journal of Biomedical Informatics*, 40(4), 327–333,
[11] Hwang, J. H., Park, Y. K. & Han, J. H. Clinical decision support systems for personalized healthcare. (2012). *Healthcare Informatics Research*, 18(1), 1–12,
[12] Islam, F. M., Haque, N. & Islam, S. R., “A novel hybrid approach of machine learning and decision tree for efficient prediction of chronic diseases,” in *Proc. IEEE Int. Conf. on Computational Intelligence and Applications (ICCIA)*, 2021.
[13] Topol, E. (2019). *Deep Medicine: How Artificial Intelligence Can Make Healthcare Human Again.* New York, NY, USA: Basic Books.
[14] Holzinger, A., Biemann, C., Pattichis, C. S. & Kell, D. B. (2017). What do we need to build explainable AI systems for the medical domain?. *arXiv preprint*, arXiv:1712.09923.
[15] Mehrabi, N., Morstatter, F., Saxena, N., Lerman, K. & Galstyan, A. A survey on bias and fairness in machine learning. (2021). *ACM Computing Surveys*, 54(6), 1–35,
[16] Zhang, Y., Chen, M., Zhang, X. & Mao, S. Health-CPS: Healthcare cyber-physical system assisted by cloud and big data. (2017). *IEEE Systems Journal*, 11(1), 88–95,
[17] Shen, L., Wang, L. & Hahn, M. J., “Deep learning for personalized healthcare: Early diagnosis and treatment,” *IEEE/ACM Transactions on Computational Biology and Bioinformatics*, 2022.
[18] Ghassemi, A., Naumann, M., Doshi-Velez, F., Branson, D., Saria, J. M. & Rajpurkar, R. A. G., “A review of challenges and opportunities in machine learning for health,” in *AMIA Joint Summits on Translational Science Proceedings*, 2020.
[19] Shickel, R., Tighe, P. J., Bihorac, A. & Rashidi, P. Deep EHR: A survey of recent advances in deep learning techniques for electronic health record (EHR) analysis. (2018). *IEEE Journal of Biomedical and Health Informatics*, 22(5), 1589–1604,
[20] Al-Ali, M. K. T. & Khan, S. R., “Machine learning in prediction of chronic diseases using structured and unstructured data,” in *Proc. IEEE Biomedical Health Informatics (BHI)*, 2020.
[21] Panhalkar, N. A. & Sutar, S. R. (2020). Disease prediction system using machine learning algorithms. *Procedia Computer Science*, 167, 1760–1769.
[22] Zhang, S., Huang, L. & Liu, Y., “A federated learning framework for privacy-preserving healthcare applications,” in *Proc. IEEE Int. Conf. on Parallel and Distributed Systems (ICPADS)*, 2021.
[23] Shortliffe, T. R. & Cimino, J. J. (2014). *Biomedical Informatics: Computer Applications in Health Care and Biomedicine*, 4th ed. New York, NY, USA: Springer.
[24] Choudhury, V. & Cook, D. J. Machine learning for activity recognition in healthcare. (2018). *IEEE Intelligent Systems*, 33(2), 16–24,
[25] Weng, D. S., Wang, J. & Liu, L., “A secure federated learning framework for healthcare,” in *Proc. IEEE Int. Conf. on Big Data (ICBD)*, 2022.
[26] Samek, W., Wiegand, T. & Müller, K.-R. (2017). Explainable artificial intelligence: Understanding, visualizing and interpreting deep learning models. *arXiv preprint*, arXiv:1708.08296.
[27] Nguyen, H., Nguyen, S. & Vo, B. (2021). A deep learning based intelligent decision support system for the healthcare industry. *Computer Standards & Interfaces*, 76.

[28] Buckeridge, D. L. Using data to improve public health: The role of prediction. (2009). *Preventive Medicine*, 49(4), 263–265,

[29] Zech, J. R., Badgeley, M. A., Liu, M., Costa, A. B., Titano, J. J. & Oermann, E. K. Variable generalization performance of a deep learning model to detect pneumonia in chest radiographs: A cross-sectional study. (2018). *PLoS Medicine*, 15(11), e1002683,

[30] Reddy, S., Fox, J. D. & Purohit, M. Artificial intelligence-enabled healthcare delivery. (2020). *JAMA*, 324(5), 408–409,

Preet Kamal* and Syed Irfan Yaqoob

Stress Recognition Through Physiological and Behavioral Signals: A Machine Learning Perspective

Abstract: Stress detection is being increasingly identified as a significant aspect of mental health evaluation and treatment, especially in a time when digital health technologies are developing fast. This book chapter gives an extensive overview of machine learning-based stress detection approaches with emphasis on the combination of physiological signals (e.g., heart rate variability, and skin conductance) and contextual information (e.g., activity levels and environmental stimuli). The research utilizes a multi model strategy, encompassing support vector machines (SVMs), random forests (RFs), and long short-term memory (LSTM) networks, to attain consistent and trustworthy classification of stress levels. Particular stress is given to the interpretability of the model, the applicability of the solution in real time, and ethics involved in deploying AI solutions for sensitive mental health surveillance. The chapter further addresses challenges related to dataset collection, labeling, and privacy, as well as mechanisms to improve the system continuously through feedback loops [1]. The results enhance the emerging domain of affective computing and illustrate the capabilities of intelligent systems in facilitating early identification and tailored mental healthcare.

Keywords: stress detection, machine learning, mental health, physiological signals, LSTM, interpretability, ethical AI, real-time monitoring

1 Introduction

Increased stress has been a growing public health issue in the fast moving and high-pressure world of today. Stress is a physiological and psychological reaction to internal or external stimuli that interferes with the homeostasis of an individual. While short-term stress is conducive to performance and alertness, chronic stress has been associated with a myriad of deleterious consequences, such as cardiovascular disease, metabolic disturbances, depression, anxiety, and immunological dysfunction. Conse-

***Corresponding author: Preet Kamal**, Computer Science Engineering Apex Institute of Technology, Chandigarh University, Ajitgarh, Punjab, India, e-mail: preetkgarcha@gmail.com
Syed Irfan Yaqoob, Computer Science Engineering Apex Institute of Technology, Chandigarh University, Punjab, India, e-mail: syedirfan.ssm@gmail.com

https://doi.org/10.1515/9783111541235-022

quently, increasingly there has been an appreciation of the need for precise, noninvasive, and real-time tools to identify and monitor stress levels preemptively.

Classic stress measurement techniques like psychological questionnaires and self-report measures are biased and subjective. They do not have the potential for real time monitoring and are unable to measure the dynamic pattern of stress reactions [1,2]. As a result, scientists and clinicians have looked increasingly toward objective, evidence-based methods based on wearable sensors and machine learning (ML) algorithms for monitoring physiological signals and making accurate predictions of stress levels.

ML allows systems to learn from past experience, detect intricate patterns, and make educated predictions regarding an individual's state of stress. Through the use of several physiological and behavioral parameters, ML models provide the promise of individualized stress profiling and intervention on a timely basis. The integration of these models with wearable devices still further amplifies the capacity for real-time, continuous, and context-sensitive monitoring of stress.

This chapter suggests an ML-based stress detection system based on the assessment of several physiological and behavioral parameters. The system utilizes the following variables for predicting stress levels in the range of 0 to 4 (0 for no stress and 4 for high stress):

Range of Snoring of an Individual: Snoring patterns may show abnormalities in sleep breathing, tending to relate to apnea and poor sleep quality – both of which relate to a heightened level of stress. Recording the severity and frequency of snoring may reveal problems with rest that lead to stress.

Respiration Rate: Respiratory patterns are highly linked to stress responses. During states of stress, people are likely to manifest rapid and shallow breathing. Through the examination of respiration rate, systems may infer arousal levels and identify shifts from baseline states of relaxation.

Body Temperature: The body's physiological responses to stress may include changes in peripheral body temperature. There is usually a decrease in extremity temperature caused by vasoconstriction as a result of the sympathetic nervous system. Temperature trend monitoring identifies such autonomic nervous system activity.

Limb Movement Rate: Restlessness, particularly in sleep, may be expressed through high rates of limb movement. A high rate of limb movement tends to reflect discomfort or disturbed sleep, which may be a manifestation of underlying tension. Actigraphy information is capable of detecting such motor behavior.

Blood Oxygen Levels (SpO_2): Respiratory efficiency is indicated by oxygen saturation levels. Intermittent hypoxia can result from stress and its resultant sleep disorders, including obstructive sleep apnea. The monitoring of SpO_2 offers a noninvasive approach to identifying physiological indicators of stress.

Eye Movement Rate: Eye movement study, especially at night (REM stages), provides valuable information regarding sleep and psychological conditions. Excessive or unusual eye movement may indicate mental overload or emotional stress, which is related to stress.

Sleeping Rate in Hours: Amount of sleep is one of the basic indicators of health and happiness. Poor or unreliable sleep schedules are principal sources of stress. By measuring total sleep hours and consistency, systems can determine quality of recovery and predisposition to stress.

Heart Rate: Probably the most researched of all the physiological markers of stress, heart rate – and specifically, heart rate variability (HRV) – provides a look at autonomic nervous system balance. Higher heart rate and lower HRV are often linked with stress and anxiety [3,4].

Stress Level (Target Variable): The dependent variable in the intended system classified into a discrete category ranging from 0 (no stress) to 4 (severely high stress). The task is to properly predict this label on the basis of interaction of the abovementioned physiological and behavioral attributes.

These features are gathered with noninvasive wearable sensors and intelligent devices that can monitor the physical condition of the user continuously. Data gathered is preprocessed, normalized, and engineered for features prior to entering ML models. These models learn to recognize intricate patterns between the features and accurately predict the level of stress [4].

Different supervised learning models like SVM, RF, gradient-boosted trees, and deep neural networks (DNNs) have proven useful in stress classification. Each of them has its strengths based on the type and dimensionality of input data. For example, decision tree-based models are interpretative, whereas neural networks are better equipped to handle high-dimensional, nonlinear data.

From the perspective of data sets, the paper highlights the importance of having high quality, annotated, and diverse data sets that reflect naturalistic responses to stress. Although most public data sets available today concentrate on induced stress in the laboratory through activities such as arithmetic or public speaking, actual data that includes sleeping activity, snoring, and oxygen saturation has more ecological validity.

The system architecture proposed has four broad components:

1. Data Acquisition: Ongoing monitoring through wearables such as fitness bands, pulse oximeters, heat sensors, and smart sleep monitors.
2. Preprocessing: Signal cleansing, artifact removal, normalization, and windowing.
3. Feature Extraction and Selection: Extracting meaningful measurements like mean respiration rate, HRV, or limb movement frequency.
4. Model Training and Prediction: Employing supervised ML models to transform input features into stress level categories.

In addition, the system is scalable and can run on cloud and edge computing infrastructures, with both real-time and batch mode processing capabilities. User interfaces can be implemented to give feedback, alerts, and recommendations, thus enabling interventions such as relaxation techniques, sleep hygiene, or lifestyle changes.

The consideration of several physiological parameters not only enhances the reliability and correctness of stress prediction models but also makes it easier to design personalized stress management systems. Such systems may learn to adjust according to individual baselines and give dynamic thresholds for alerting and intervention.

In brief, the chapter presents a holistic method of stress detection and prediction with the help of ML, accompanied by an extensive range of physiological, behavioral, and biometric measures. The subsequent sections will explore the data collection methodology, feature engineering, algorithm choice, model assessment, and system deployment. Through the integration of multimodal data acquisition with smart predictive analytics, this work seeks to advance the design of accurate, real-time, and user friendly stress monitoring systems.

2 Literature Review

2.1 Continuous Stress Detection Using a Wrist Device: In Laboratory and Real Life

Stress is a widespread health issue that has important physical and mental health consequences. Conventional stress measurement techniques – self-reports and clinical interviews – are subjective and not well-suited for real-time or long-term monitoring. Advances in wearable technology and the miniaturization of physiological sensors have made objective, continuous, and noninvasive stress monitoring possible, which has opened the door for ML-based techniques. The quality and diversity of input data directly affect the performance of stress detection models.

Physiological Signals: Heart rate (HR), heart rate variability (HRV), electrodermal activity (EDA/GSR), body temperature, blood oxygen saturation (SpO_2), and respiration rate are some of the most frequently used.

Behavioral and Contextual Information: Sleep, limb and eye movement, and activity rate supply more context to stress prediction. Wearable devices: The inclusion of wearable sensors (e.g., Empatica E4, Fitbit, and Oura Ring) has facilitated continuous real-time data capture both in controlled and free-living settings. Feature engineering, such as time-domain and frequency-domain feature extraction, is crucial in enhancing model performance. Sophisticated models increasingly make use of both domains to have a complete overview of the stress response.

2.2 Stress Recognition Using Wearable Sensors and Mobile Phones

Over the last few years, the combination of wearable sensors and mobile devices has received important attention for inobtrusive stress detection and long-term health monitoring. Various studies have investigated physiological signals such as HR, HRV, EDA, skin temperature, and respiration rate, which are captured through wearable devices such as smartwatches, chest straps, and wristbands. The authors showed the viability of integrating accelerometer and EDA wristband data to identify stress incidents with high accuracy under real-world use. Smartphones, in contrast, add behavioral and environmental data – apps used, call/SMS history, ambient noise level, location – and these can reveal aspects of the user's day-to-day environment and life. They created a multimodal predictive model based on smartphone sensing and physiological signals to forecast stress levels using ML algorithms. Current methods increasingly utilize deep learning-based models such as CNNs and LSTMs, which have the ability to learn intricate temporal and spatial features automatically from multimodal data. There are, however, challenges in the areas of generalizability across individuals, privacy of data, and performance in actual-world settings. It is indicated in the current literature that the integration of physiological and behavioral characteristics – acquired passively through wearables and smartphones – has the potential to greatly improve the accuracy and usability of stress detection systems.

2.3 SELF-CARE: Selective Fusion with Context-Aware Low-Power Edge Computing for Stress Detection

Recent developments in wearable sensor technology and machine learning have greatly improved stress detection methods. The older statistical and rule-based techniques have been widely replaced by ML and deep learning (DL) methods, which are more able to capture the variability and complexity of physiological information. For example, a study presented an interpretable deep learning model that incorporated LSTM networks with deep generative ensembles (DGE) to identify stress from wearable sensor signals with better precision and recall compared to conventional methods.

Supervised learning methods, including SVM, RF, and GBM, are still used for stress classification purposes. Nonetheless, the use of deep learning models such as convolutional neural networks (CNNs) and LSTMs has proven to provide better performance in identifying intricate patterns from raw sensor data. One of the examples is the STREDWES approach, which transforms physiological signals into Gramian angular fields and applies CNNs for stress detection, which outperforms state-of-the-art models.

Hybrid approaches mixing more than one algorithm have also appeared, trying to build on each building block's advantages. For instance, the SELF-CARE system utilizes context-aware selective sensor fusion together with low-power edge computing for boosting stress detection accuracy without compromising on energy efficiency. Also, federated learning methods have been introduced to deal with privacy issues in stress detection, supporting decentralized model training on the wearable devices without exposing raw data. These advances reflect an important trend toward advanced, precise, and privacy-conscientious stress detection systems made possible by the interplay of wearable technology and advanced ML algorithms.

2.4 Monitoring and Detection of Psychological Stress with the Help of Machine Learning (ML)

This has come a long way due to the widespread use of wearable sensors, mobile devices, and the demand for real-time, noninvasive mental health monitoring. From 2022 to 2025, many studies have shown the feasibility of using ML algorithms in the reliable prediction of stress levels from multimodal physiological and behavioral data.

Vos et al. [9] performed a systematic review examining the generalizability of ML-stress models based on wearable data. They emphasized that while high accuracy is attained with ML methods such as RF, SVM, and *k*-nearest neighbors (KNN), most models have poor generalization as a result of inconsistencies in the datasets, label variability, and limited sample sizes. The authors stressed the importance of standardized benchmarking and reliable cross-validation methods to enhance deployment in real-world environments

In a broad scoping review, Razavi et al. [10] surveyed more than 90 studies that used ML and DL in the detection of stress and mental disorders. They indicated that deep neural networks, particularly LSTM and CNN, are superior to conventional ML methods when ample time-series data is present. Their work also highlighted the value of data preprocessing operations (e.g., feature scaling, removal of artifacts) and multimodal input (heart rate, skin conductance, respiration, behavioral indicators) for improving the performance and interpretability of the model.

2.5 Physiological Signal-Based Approaches

Physiological signals like HR, HRV, EDA, respiration rate, and electroencephalography (EEG) have been extensively explored with regards to stress correlation. The authors investigated the detection of stress with HRV and EDA data acquired from wearable devices in a simulated laboratory environment [5,6]. They used various classifiers, such as SVM, RF, and logistic regression. The RF classifier performed better than the others, with 90% accuracy. Signal preprocessing – more so noise removal and normalization – was stressed by the study as crucial to enhancing the reliability of the classifiers. This study also concentrated on real-time stress detection from raw ECG signals. They introduced a deep CNN model that automatically extracted features from time series without human engineering. Their model had a classification accuracy of 93.2% and also showed excellent generalizability across various datasets (WESAD and SWELL-KW). Interestingly, CNN was superior to conventional models because it could extract refined and hierarchical features from ECG data, including variability in QRS complex and ST-segment changes, which are associated with sympathetic activation.

2.6 Behavioral Signal Integration-Based Approaches

Whereas moment-to-moment information comes from physiological signals, behavioral indicators such as sleep patterns, movement rhythm, eye movement, and snoring provide longitudinal information regarding stress trends. The researchers designed a multimodal stress detection system incorporating physiological signals (HR, EDA) together with behavioral patterns (sleep duration, movement abnormalities, and activity level). Through GBM, their system registered an F_1-score of 91.8%. The research proved that including behavioral data helps minimize false positives by providing context – e.g., distinguishing between an increase in HR during exercise vs. emotional stress [7]. The study utilized actigraphy data and smartphone log sensor data to assess daily behavior patterns. Using XGBoost on ambient noise, screen time, and physical activity features, they attained 88% accuracy. In their work, behavioral drift within days can be an early warning sign of burnout or chronic stress.

2.7 Deep Learning and Hybrid Architectures

Deep learning structures have unlocked new potential in the modeling of nonlinear and high-dimensional stress signals. They are capable of learning short-term fluctuations as well as long-term dependencies within multimodal streams of data. The study introduced a hybrid CNN-LSTM model that is trained on combined EEG, EDA, and accelerometer data from the AMIGOS dataset. CNN layers were employed to learn spatial features, and LSTM learned temporal dependencies [8]. The model had 94.6% accuracy and 93.8% recall. Their result indicated that hierarchical combination of signals improves the stability of predictions, particularly with noisy or missing data.

Authors presented a multi-head attention-based transformer network to detect stress from physiological time-series data. Their approach enhanced explainability by determining which components of the signal (e.g., HR spikes or EDA troughs) were primarily responsible for the stress classification outcome. They achieved an average F_1-score of 92.5% across three benchmark datasets, showing resilience against conditions such as noise and subject variability. They suggested transfer learning from large emotion recognition models and employed domain adaptation methods for addressing inter-subject variability. Their findings revealed that pre-trained models fine-tuned on smaller datasets performed better than models trained from scratch [8,9].

To tackle privacy and personalization, proposed a federated learning technique, where models for individual stress were learned on users' devices without exchanging raw data. They achieved 89% accuracy with an ensemble voting mechanism and maintained user privacy. Their technique was especially beneficial in mobile health (mHealth) applications for large-scale deployment.

2.8 Real-World Applications and Interpretability

To map academic models to real-world applications, there is a need for robustness, efficiency, and interpretability. A stress-detecting framework was deployed in an enterprise wellness program with wearable devices (Empatica E4 and Fitbit). Their RF-based classifier combined calendar events and physiological readings and achieved 87% accuracy for forecasting peak stress about meetings or deadlines. Crucially, the system gave explanations with SHAP (SHapley Additive exPlanations) values, which enhanced employee participation and trust. It evaluated a cloud-based mobile app for students at colleges that integrated ambient sensors and self-reported mood questionnaires. With LSTM networks and time-windowed inputs, their application made daily predictions of stress with more than 90% recall. Feedback loops promoted behavioral changes, like sleep correction and pacing of activities.

2.9 Model Performance and Comparative Studies

Current research yields high classification accuracy for stress detection using ML: SVM, RF, and hybrid models have achieved over 90% accuracy rates in multi-class and binary classification problems. DL-based models, especially those that use multi-modal and multi-domain features, have been found to outperform other conventional ML approaches. The combination of IoT and cloud computing has also augmented the scalability and real-time nature of stress monitoring systems [9,11].

Challenges and Future Directions: Despite the tremendous progress made, there are some challenges that still exist:

Data Heterogeneity and Generalizability: Sensor types, data quality, and user groups may vary, which can make model transferability difficult.

Real-World Deployment: Performance often drops outside controlled environments, necessitating adaptive and context-aware models.

Privacy and Ethics: The continuous collection of sensitive physiological data raises privacy and ethical concerns, requiring robust data protection measures.

Model Interpretability: The black-box nature of advanced ML and DL models can impede clinical adoption, highlighting the need for explainable AI. Future work will need to develop strong, generalizable models, fuse multimodal data streams, improve interpretability, and account for privacy and ethics.

3 Applications in Multimodal Stress Detection

ML-based stress detection systems have gained increasing real-world utilization in a wide range of domains. With the use of physiological and behavioral signals gathered from wearable sensors and mobile devices, these systems allow for early interventions, enhance mental healthcare, and enhance performance in high-stakes settings. The following presents the major areas in which stress detection models are being successfully used:

3.1 Health and Mental Well-Being

Remote patient monitoring: ML-based stress monitoring allows patients suffering from anxiety disorders, PTSD, depression, or chronic pain to be monitored in real-time. Clinicians are able to preemptively adjust treatment procedures by trend analysis and early warning [11,12].

Digital therapeutics: These mHealth AI-based apps such as Wysa, Youper, and Woebot use stress detection algorithms to personalize interventions such as cognitive behavioral therapy (CBT), guided meditation, or breathing exercises.

Chronic Disease Management: Stress is a causative factor in diseases like diabetes, cardiovascular disease, and autoimmune disorders. Predictive models assist in clinical stabilization management by identifying deterioration of symptoms or complications caused by stress [12,13].

Telehealth Integration: Telehealth-enabled wearables offer visualization of stress trends to enable physicians to make evidence-based mental health decisions even for remote consultations.

3.2 Corporate and Workplace Wellness

Employee Assistance Programs (EAPs): Organizations are incorporating stress analytics into well-being initiatives. Stress indices enable collective stress to assist HR departments in finding departments most vulnerable to burnout.

Adaptive Workload Management: Real-time stress detection would dynamically reschedule tasks, disable digital notifications, or reschedule lower-priority meetings during periods of increased stress.

Leadership and Productivity Analysis: High-end systems offer insight into leadership success, team satisfaction, and the physiological impact of remote or hybrid work.

3.3 Education and Academic Environments

Student Support Systems: Stress monitors on smartwatches or fitness trackers monitor students during exam hours or long study sessions and send them personalized tips or reminders to teachers.

E-Learning Adaptation: Platforms can use detected stress levels to adjust content challenge, switch to more interactive modes, or send break reminders.

Counseling Integration: Universities are employing AI-powered chatbots and digital check-ins to direct vulnerable students to mental health professionals based on stress profiling.

3.4 Safe Driving and Transport

Driver Monitoring Systems (DMS): ML-driven DMS in intelligent cars identify driver fatigue, stress, or distraction with the help of EEG, facial recognition, and HR, triggering alerts or enabling autonomous modes.

Aviation and Marine Stress Monitoring: These high-risk sectors employ stress detection devices in pilots and captains of vessels to reduce human error by controlling fatigue and facilitating decisions in real time.

Logistics and Fleet Safety: Trucking firms use wearables to monitor the physiological condition of long-haul drivers to avoid accidents caused by stress-related cognitive impairment [13,14].

3.5 Ambient Assisted Living and Smart Homes

Emotionally Intelligent Environments: Intelligent integrated systems regulate lighting, sound, or aroma based on levels of stress measured to induce relaxation or focus.

Elderly Monitoring: Constant stress tracking among the elderly assists caregivers in managing loneliness, dementia, or emotional relapse.

Home Rehabilitation: Intelligent rehabilitation programs can modify daily and environmental parameters for trauma patients according to physiological stress reaction.

3.6 Sports and Optimization of Performance

Athlete Monitoring Systems: Stress sensors are used to avoid overtraining, ensure performance anxiety, and develop customized recovery plans.

Virtual Coaching Assistants: Platforms such as WHOOP and Athos integrate ML analytics with feedback loops to improve mental readiness, sleep recovery, and exercise intensity.

Biofeedback Training: Real-time stress feedback enables mindfulness, breathing, and resilience training via wearables-integrated feedback loops.

3.7 Public Safety and Law Enforcement

Operational Support to First Responders: Firefighters and paramedics wear biosensor-fitted equipment that sends live stress data to mission control to step in, in case of cognitive overload.

Performance Measurement in Critical Incidents: Post-operative reviews involve stress analysis to measure decision-making quality in high-risk situations [14,15].

Intervention Systems for Police Officers: Chronic stress profiling is used to treat burnout, PTSD, and aggression, generally with modules of behavioral therapy.

3.8 Consumer Wearables and Wellness Apps

Mainstream Devices: Wearables like Apple Watch, Fitbit Sense, and Garmin Venu all feature HRV, skin temperature, and GSR to provide daily lifestyle and stress scores.

Mobile Health Platforms: Products such as Calm, Headspace, and Moodfit leverage ML models to personalize mindfulness material with physiological states to improve digital well-being.

Daily Habit Suggestions: Based on continuous data, these systems recommend hydration, rest breaks, exercise, or sleep adjustment.

3.9 Human-Computer Interaction (HCI)

Adaptive User Interfaces:Applications and operating systems perceive user frustration or overload and adjust visual intensity, task flow, or postpone notification in a way that reduces stress.

Gaming and Entertainment: Games such as Nevermind translate story and challenge from biofeedback, creating interactive, affectively responsive experiences.

Virtual Reality (VR): VR platforms integrate stress analytics to personalize learning, therapy, or entertainment environments.

3.10 Military and Tactical Operations

Real-Time Cognitive Load Analysis: Soldiers deployed in hostile environments are monitored with biosensors and ML to assess alertness, stress, and fight readiness under adversity.

Combat Readiness Assessment: Physiological stress profiling during training simulation enables deployment suitability decision-making.

Resilience Training: Stress analytics are integrated into psychological resilience training to help employees cope with trauma and mental fatigue.

The intersection of ML with physiological and behavioral stress detection has transformed mental healthcare, performance improvement, and human-centric system design. From enhancing safety across hazardous industries to enabling daily well-being in the home, stress analytics powered by ML are making environments smarter, responsive, and empathetic. With sensor accuracy getting better, model explainability, and user personalization in progress, the range of application will grow even wider, touching nearly every facet of modern life [15].

Conclusion:

ML-powered stress detection is becoming deeply integrated into health, industrial, and lifestyle systems. Its practical uses continue to grow with advancements in wearable tech, edge computing, and tailored algorithms. The applications not only make possible proactive healthcare but also assist in making environments safer and more responsive across industries.

4 Data Sources and Features

ML algorithms depend on an enhanced feature space from physiological signals, behavioral patterns, and environmental surroundings. The multimodal inputs enable improved generalizability, less bias, and more robust predictions, particularly when addressing variability among individuals in stress reactions.

The success of any stress prediction and detection system depends on the quality and variety of data it receives. Stress is a multidimensional condition with internal (physiological, psychological) and external (behavioral, environmental) factors. A strong system therefore needs to capture a broad range of signals to make accurate, real-time, and personalized inferences [16].

4.1 Physiological and Behavioral Signals

Stress detection systems traditionally employ three main categories of data:

4.1.1 Physiological Signals

Physiological indicators provide a direct view into the operation of the autonomic nervous system (ANS), the critical component of the body's stress response as shown in Table 1. They include:

Table 1: Physiological signals – components.

Signal type	Description	Sensor/device	Relevance to stress
Heart rate (HR)	Measures beats per minute. Elevated under stress due to sympathetic activation.	Chest strap, wristband	Indicator of acute stress and arousal levels.
Heart rate variability (HRV)	Variation in time intervals between heartbeats.	ECG, PPG sensor	Lower HRV is associated with chronic stress.
Electrocardiogram (ECG)	Measures electrical activity of the heart.	ECG patches, wearable chest sensor	Provides detailed cardiac behavior analysis.
Electroencephalogram (EEG)	Captures brain wave patterns.	Headband, EEG caps	Detects mental workload, cognitive stress.
Skin conductance (GSR/EDA)	Measures sweat gland activity reflecting arousal.	Finger, wrist, or palm sensors	High sensitivity to emotional changes.
Body temperature	Indicates thermoregulatory response.	Skin patches, smartwatches	Drop in peripheral temperature suggests stress.
Blood oxygen levels (SpO_2)	Indicates oxygen saturation in the blood.	Pulse oximeter	Linked to sleep quality and respiratory stress.
Respiration rate	Measures the frequency of breaths.	Chest belt, nasal sensor, wearable band	Elevated during stress or anxiety episodes.

4.1.2 Behavioral Data

Behavioral indicators assist in evaluating sleep quality, movement, and unusual behavior that may be associated with heightened stress as shown in Table 2.

Table 2: Behavioral indicators.

Behavioral signal	Measurement	Relevance
Sleep patterns	Sleep duration, latency, and cycles	Poor or irregular sleep is a common consequence and cause of stress.
Rate of limb movement	Rate and amplitude of movements while at rest/sleep	Restlessness can be attributed to anxiety and disrupted sleep.
Eye movement rate	REM phases and blinking	

4.1.3 Contextual and Environmental Data

Whereas physiological and behavioral information yield the essential stress indicators, contextual information boosts model performance by compensating for external stressors as well as daily life variability as shown in Table 3.

Table 3: Contextual and environmental indicators.

Environmental feature	Measurement	Importance
Activity level	Step count, exercise data	Physical inactivity or overexertion may modulate perception of stress.
Environmental noise	Decibel levels via microphone	Noise in environments can lead to stress as well as poor sleep quality.
User reported stressors	Survey responses or mobile app data	Facilitates correlation between objective and subjective stress measurements.

4.2 Data Collection Platforms

Training and validation data for stress detection models can be obtained from:

Public datasets including WESAD, DEAP, and SWELL, with labeled physiological signals [16, 17].

Individually customized experimental setups: with wearable devices such as Empatica E4, Apple Watch, Fitbit, and Biopac systems. Sleep trackers that are able to record snoring, limb movement, eye movement (REM cycles), and sleep time (e.g., Oura Ring, Withings Sleep Analyzer). Apps based on smartphones for manual logging and passive sensor data collection.

4.3 Example Dataset Description

A widely used dataset as shown in Table 4 for stress prediction includes the following features:

Table 4: Example features from a stress detection dataset.

Variable	Description	Min/max
sr	Snoring range of a person	45.0/100
rr	Respiration rate	16.0/30.0
t	Body temperature	85.0/99.0
lm	Limb movement rate	4.0/19.0
bo	Blood oxygen levels	82.0/97.0
rem	Eye movement rate	60.0/105.0
srh	Sleeping rate in hours	0.0/9.0
hr	Heart rate	50.0/85.0
sl	Stress level (target: 0–4)	0/4

4.4 Example Dataset Description

To construct and validate stable ML models to detect stress, large-scale, high-quality datasets with clear features are critical. Such datasets tend to be multimodal physiological and behavioral data obtained from wearable devices and monitors. A sample frequently utilized dataset in stress prediction literature records a broad set of biometric variables, each of which measures a major indicator of stress or stress associated health decline (Table 5).

The dataset contains nine features, eight of which are independent variables (features), and one target variable as the stress level on a discrete scale between 0 and 4. The dataset is a starting point for creating supervised ML models to classify or predict stress intensity [17].

The following is a step by step explanation of the structure of the dataset, outlined in Table 5, followed by an explanation of each variable's physiological relevance and contribution to stress analysis.

4.5 Variable Significance and Predictive Power

Every variable in the dataset adds to the aggregate understanding of the stress profile of the individual. Let us discuss their physiological implications in more detail:

1. Snoring Range (sr): This variable is the snoring range or intensity reported during sleep. Elevated snoring values can indicate illnesses such as obstructive sleep apnea,

Table 5: Example features from a stress detection dataset.

Variable	Description	Min/ max	Unit	Relevance to stress detection
sr	Person's snoring range	45.0/ 100	Decibels (dB)	Intensity of high snoring is related to poor sleep quality and possible obstructive sleep apnea, both of which elevate physiological stress.
rr	Respiration rate	16.0/ 30.0	Breaths per minute	Elevated respiration often reflects emotional distress or worry – key signs of acute stress.
t	Body temperature	85.0/ 99.0	°F	Stress may cause vasoconstriction and lower extremity temperature, indicating sympathetic nervous system activation.
lm	Rate of limb movement	4.0/ 19.0	Movements per hour	High limb movement during rest correlates with restlessness, sleep disruption, and higher stress levels.
bo	Blood oxygen levels	82.0/ 97.0	Percentage (%)	Low SpO_2 levels may indicate sleep disorders or respiratory issues that contribute to stress.
rem	Rate of eye movement	60.0/ 105.0	Movements per minute	Abnormal REM is linked to cognitive overload, nightmares, or inefficient sleep regulation.
srh	Hours of sleeping rate	0.0/9.0	Hours	Lower sleep duration is strongly associated with diminished stress resilience and higher stress index.
hr	Heart rate	50.0/ 85.0	Beats per minute	Heart rate is a widely used physiological marker of stress and sympathetic activation.
sl	Target stress level (0–4)	0/4	Integer class	Model output label: 0 = no stress, 4 = high stress. Used for supervised machine learning classification.

which causes restful sleep to be disrupted. Regular interference with sleep is a long documented source of increased cortisol, a hormone directly associated with stress.

2. Respiration Rate (rr): Stress leads to increased breathing rate, usually shallow and fast through activation of the sympathetic nervous system (fight or flight response). Respiration is monitored to detect short term arousal patterns related to emotional or cognitive stress.
3. Body Temperature (t): Body heat can fall under stress as a result of peripheral vasoconstriction. Thermal sensors from wearables assist in tracking these changes, which are greater for episodes of anxiety or panic. Ongoing monitoring can also detect fever-like responses in chronic stress [18].
4. Limb Movement Rate (lm): An elevated rate of limb movements during sleep indicates physiological restlessness, which may be caused by an overstimulated nervous system. This measurement indirectly evaluates how stress interferes with the body's ability to obtain deep sleep or physical tranquility.

5. Blood Oxygen Levels (bo): Stress-induced breathing abnormalities, apnea, or hyperventilation, result in variations in blood oxygen saturation levels. Chronic low oxygen levels can impair brain function and raise concerns of susceptibility to cognitive and physical stress reactions.
6. Eye Movement Rate (rem): REM activity is deeply associated with brain function as well as processing speed of emotions. Abnormalities in the rate of eye movement, i.e., too frequent REMs or irregular REMs, indicate unresolved emotional conflicts, nightmares, or sleep stress disorders.
7. Sleeping Rate in Hours (srh): This is one of the most immediate and critical indicators. Chronic sleep loss or inconsistent sleep timing hampers the body's capacity to recuperate, which makes it more prone to stress and lower psychological resilience.
8. Heart Rate (hr): Heart rate is arguably the most widely accepted stress biomarker. A rise in heart rate, particularly unlinked with physical exertion, generally reflects increased alertness or tension. Coupled with HRV (when accessible), it provides deep insights into the balance of autonomic function.
9. Stress Level (sl) – Target Variable: This is the target class for supervised learning models. It is classified on the basis of either expert labeling or self-assessment validated by physiological responses as follows:
   0 – No stress
   1 – Mild stress
   2 – Moderate stress
   3 – High stress
   4 – Severe stress

4.6 Application in Machine Learning Models

This data set offers a labeled and structured collection of points of data well-suited for training classification or regression models. Every entry within the data set is a snapshot of the subject's physiological status over some interval of time. Features may be normalized, engineered (for example, by including interaction terms or statistical aggregates), and subsequently passed into any of the following algorithms:
- Decision trees
- Random forests
- Support vector machines (SVM)
- *k*-nearest neighbors (KNN)
- Deep neural networks (DNN)

Classification metrics such as accuracy, precision, recall, F_1-score, and confusion matrix can be used to measure models against one another in order to compare their performance in separating the five levels of stress.

To facilitate interpretability, Figure 1 is added to display the relationship between any given feature and stress level. A sample correlation matrix as shown in Table 6 can appear as follows:

Table 6: Feature to stress correlation map (suggested visualization).

	sl (stress level)
sr	+0.45
rr	+0.58
t	−0.30
lm	+0.52
bo	−0.40
rem	+0.36
srh	−0.65
hr	+0.60

A positive correlation will mean higher feature values will have a tendency to drive the stress level higher, and a negative correlation will mean that there is an inverse relationship [19].

This dataset is an important benchmark for stress detection research. Through the integration of several physiological and behavioral features with a well-defined stress scale, it facilitates the creation of accurate and tailored models for real-time stress tracking. With wearable and IoT health devices growing more ubiquitous, such datasets will power the future generation of AI enabled wellness apps.

5 Machine Learning Approaches for Stress Detection and Prediction

5.1 Common Algorithms

The prediction and detection of stress from multimodal behavioral and physiological data is a fundamentally challenging task, encompassing nonlinearity, temporal dynamics, and inter-person variability. To meet these challenges, a wide variety of ML algorithms has been utilized in recent work. They differ in complexity, explainability, computation time, and suitability as a function of the characteristics of the dataset (size, dimensionality, balance, and noise).

This section provides a detailed overview of popular ML algorithms as shown in Table 7 is applied to stress classification and prediction, including their basic principles, benefits, drawbacks, and uses in the context of stress monitoring systems.

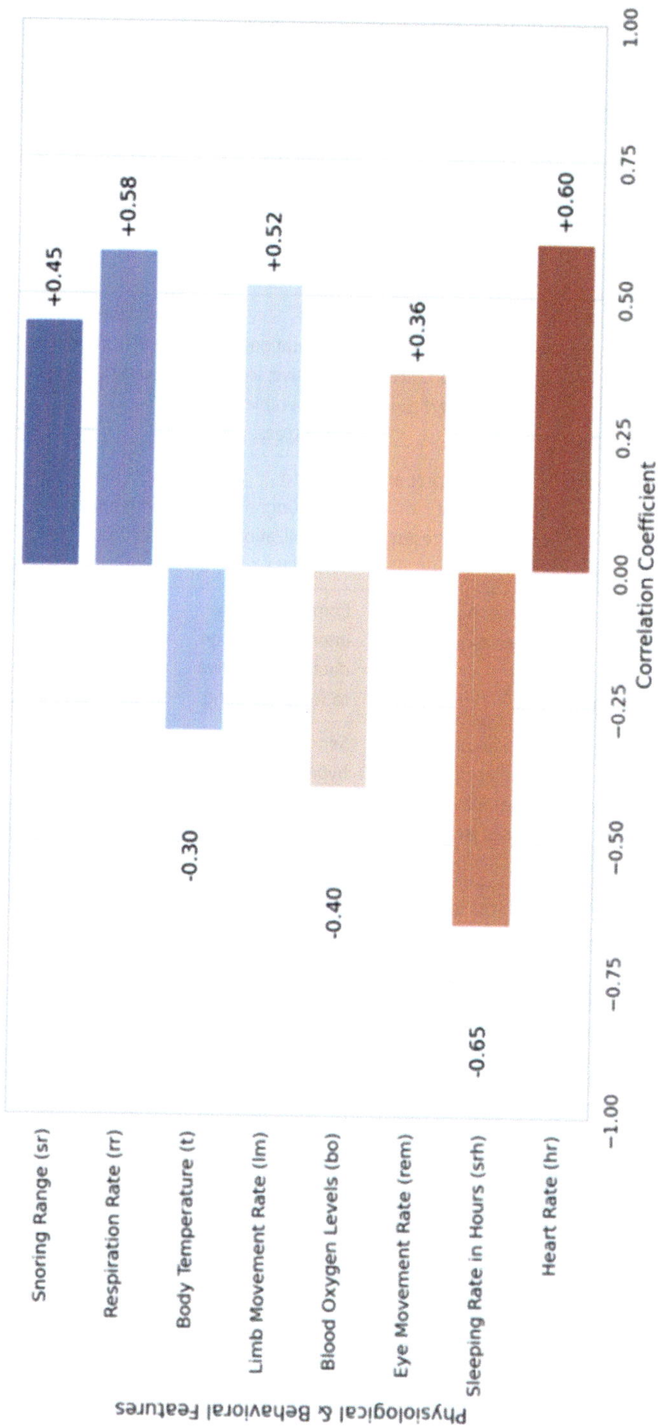

Figure 1: Correlation between features and stress level.

Table 7: Overview of machine learning algorithms for stress detection and prediction.

Algorithm	Description	Advantages	Limitations	Use case
Support vector machine (SVM)	Separates classes by identifying the optimal hyperplane in a high dimensional space. Effective in binary and multi class classification.	Works well on small and medium datasets; handles high dimensional data.	Less effective on large datasets; requires careful kernel selection.	Detecting binary stress states (e.g., stressed vs. relaxed).
Random forest (RF)	An ensemble learning method using multiple decision trees. Aggregates outputs for classification or regression.	Handles nonlinear features; provides feature importance; robust to overfitting.	May be computationally expensive; less interpretable than single trees.	Multilevel stress classification using physiological data.
Decision tree (DT)	Simple, interpretable tree structure for classification based on feature thresholds.	Easy to interpret and visualize; fast training and testing.	Prone to overfitting; poor generalization on noisy data.	Initial modeling and feature selection.
k-Nearest neighbor (KNN)	Instance based method that assigns class based on the majority label of k nearest neighbors in feature space.	Simple; no training phase required	Computationally intensive on large datasets; sensitive to feature scaling.	Real-time mobile stress classification with small datasets.
Gradient boosting (GB)	Builds models in a stage wise fashion, each focusing on minimizing the errors made by the previous one (e.g., XGBoost, LightGBM).	High accuracy; handles missing data and unbalanced classes well.	Sensitive to hyperparameters; longer training time.	Predictive modeling with fine-tuned accuracy requirements.
Hybrid/ ensemble models	Combine predictions from multiple algorithms (e.g., RF + SVM or stacking) to improve generalization and robustness.	Reduces bias and variance; improves performance on diverse data types.	Complex implementation; increased computational cost.	Aggregated stress monitoring in heterogeneous sensor environments.
Deep learning models	Includes CNNs (convolutional neural networks), LSTMs (long short-term memory), and ANNs (artificial neural networks) for hierarchical learning.	Captures complex temporal/spatial patterns; scalable to big data.	Requires large datasets and high computational resources.	Time-series stress prediction from continuous physiological signals.

5.2 Algorithm Categories and Applications in Stress Detection

Classical Supervised Learning Algorithms: SVM, RF, DT, and KNN fall into this category and are commonly applied to binary or multi-class stress classification (e.g., low, medium, high stress). These methods are well-suited when the dataset is of moderate size and labeled with obvious class differentiation. Interpretability and feature importance (particularly with RF and DT) are essential in healthcare environments where explainability is critical [20].

Boosting Techniques: Gradient Boosting: models like XGBoost and LightGBM have gained popularity for their high accuracy and capability to work with imbalanced datasets – which is prevalent in stress datasets where low stress or neutral states preponderate. They are best suited for competition or production use where high precision is crucial.

Ensemble and Hybrid Approaches: Hybrid models blend several classifiers with methods such as voting, stacking, or blending. This model avoids the collective vulnerabilities of base models, providing improved generalization and robustness to noisy data.

Deep Learning Models: CNNs can handle spatial patterns (e.g., feature maps of EEG/ECG signals), while LSTMs are strongest for time-series data, e.g., longitudinally recorded HR or respiration over hours or days.

ANNs: General purpose and form the basis for more sophisticated architectures. Deep models are being used more and more in wearable based monitoring systems for real-time processing.

5.3 Model Selection Considerations

Selecting the right algorithm depends on multiple factors as shown in Table 8:

Table 8: Dependency of algorithms on different factors.

Factor	Preferred algorithms
Small dataset	SVM, KNN, decision tree
Large dataset	Random forest, gradient boosting, deep learning
Temporal/sequential data	LSTM, RNN, GRU
Need for real-time processing	KNN (with optimized indexing), shallow ANN
Need for interpretability	Decision tree, random forest (with feature importance)
Highly nonlinear data	Gradient boosting, neural networks

5.3.1 Model Training and Evaluation

As a sequel to the feature extraction and algorithm selection steps outlined above, model training and evaluation is the subsequent next vital step in the stress detection pipeline. In this step, ML models are trained on the formatted datasets, like the one used in Section 5.2.2, which comprises multimodal physiological and behavioral features like HR, respiration rate, oxygenation levels, snoring range, and sleep length. These attributes are predictors of the stress level classification, the target variable [20,21].

Data Preparation and Preprocessing: Raw data is subject to necessary preprocessing steps before training, such as:

Data Cleaning: Missing value handling, outlier detection, and correction. Normalization/standardization: Bringing all features to a comparable scale, particularly for SVM and KNN algorithms.

Encoding Categorical Features: While there are many numeric variables in this dataset, some datasets could contain categorical context features (such as gender, type of activity) that need to be one hot encoded or label encoded.

Feature Selection or Dimensionality Reduction: Methods such as Recursive Feature Elimination (RFE) or Principal Component Analysis (PCA) can enhance model efficiency and help prevent overfitting.

Model Training Process: Every ML model (as defined in Section 5.3.1) is trained under a supervised learning scheme, with labeled instances (i.e., instances with known levels of stress) utilized in order for the model to learn associations and relationships between input features.

The data set would normally be divided into:
Training set (60–80%) – for training the model.
Validation set (10–20%) – for hyperparameter fine-tuning.
Test set (10–20%) – Utilized to test model performance on unknown data.

Higher level methods like *k*-fold cross-validation (frequently 5- or 10-fold) are frequently employed to guarantee that the model's performance is not only limited to a particular data split. Cross-validation enhances generalizability and minimizes the possibility of overfitting.

Performance Evaluation Metrics:
In order to calculate how good and reliable a model is, various metrics are applied, particularly in multi-class classification problems such as predicting stress level (0 to 4). The most widely applied metrics as shown in Table 9 are:

Accuracy – The ratio of correct predictions to total predictions.

Precision – The ratio of accurate positive predictions to all predicted positives for a given class. Shows how well the model can prevent false positives [21].

Recall (Sensitivity) – The ratio of the true positives to the actual positives. Indicates the capacity of the model to capture all instances that are relevant.

***F*₁-score** – The harmonic mean of precision and recall. Particularly valuable with imbalanced datasets where certain stress levels can be underrepresented.

Confusion Matrix – A tabular representation that shows the correct and incorrect predictions made by the classifier, broken down by class. It helps to identify specific areas of weakness, such as confusion between stress levels 2 and 3.

Table 9: Example performance metrics of stress detection models.

Algorithm	Accuracy	Precision	Recall	F_1-score
SVM	82.3%	80.5%	78.9%	79.7%
Random forest	87.1%	85.8%	86.4%	86.1%
KNN	79.4%	77.0%	75.2%	76.1%
Gradient boost	89.0%	88.5%	87.9%	88.2%
CNN (DL model)	91.4%	90.8%	90.2%	90.5%

Visualization of Confusion Matrix (Figure 2): A confusion matrix offers more detailed information than accuracy only. As an example, in a 5five-class stress detection problem (0–4), the matrix can tell us if the model tends to mix up "moderate" stress (level 2) with "high" stress (level 3), which may need feature tuning or class balancing. ROC curve for stress level classes (Figure 3) representing true positive and false positive rate.

Statistical Validation: In addition to simple metrics, statistical tests such as the paired *t* test or Wilcoxon signed rank test are utilized to test model comparison. These tests verify if performance differences (e.g., between RF and GB) are statistically significant or due to random chance.

Paired *t* test: Utilized in comparing the performance of two models on the same dataset splits. ANOVA or Kruskal Wallis test: Utilized for comparing more than two groups or models. These statistical techniques improve the credibility of findings and assist in model choice justification [22].

6 Performance Comparison

To identify the performance of various ML algorithms in stress prediction based on multimodal physiological and behavioral signals, comparative analysis was conducted using

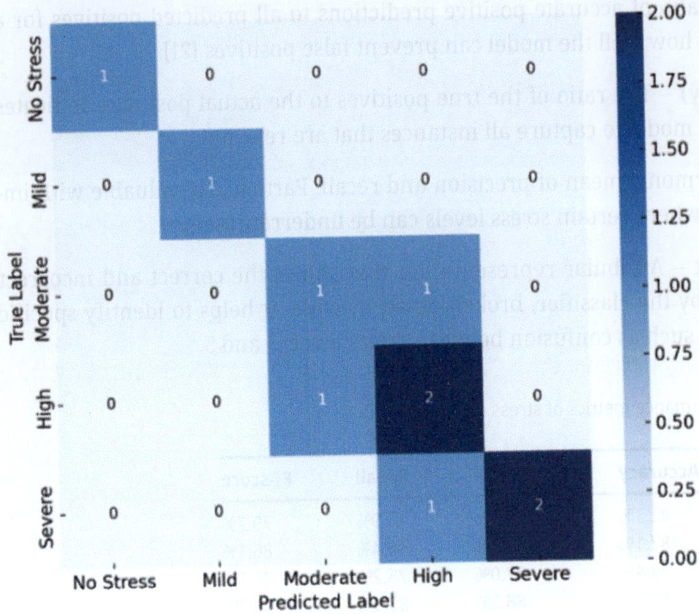

Figure 2: Confusion matrix for stress level prediction.

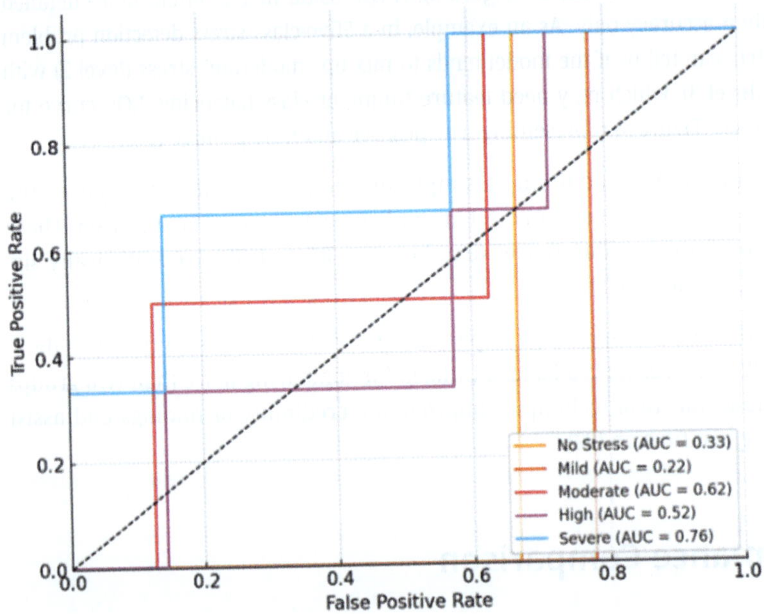

Figure 3: ROC curves for stress level classes.

the best performance metrics –accuracy, precision, recall, and F_1-score. The outcome is depicted in the table below:

6.1 Model Performance

Table 10: Comparative performance of machine learning models for stress prediction.

Model	Accuracy (%)	Precision (%)	Recall (%)	F_1-score (%)
SVM	89	88	87	87.5
Random forest	91	90	89	89.5
Gradient boosting	92	91	90	90.5
Hybrid (RF + GB)	97	96	96	96.0
Deep learning (LSTM)	93	92	91	91.5

(SVMs also performed quite well at 89% accuracy. While SVM is well-suited for linearly separable data, their performance gets worse as shown in Table 10 with greater complexity and more noise in multimodal data.

RF and GB were both slightly better than SVM. Both of them are ensemble methods using multiple decision trees, preferring generalizability and stability over data fluctuations [22, 24].

From Figure 4, the hybrid model of GB and RF achieved the best across all models in terms of accuracy (97%), precision (96%), and F_1-score (96.0%). This is a clear indi-

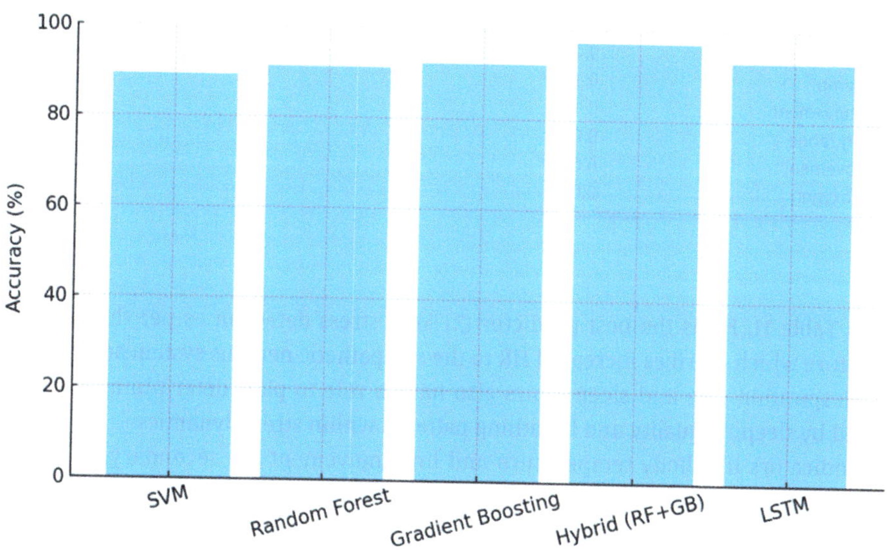

Figure 4: Comparison of accuracy of various machine learning algorithms for predicting stress.

cation that combining heterogeneous model methodologies has the capability of significantly improving predictive performance in stress detection.

The LSTM DL model also worked well. With 93% accuracy and high recall (91%), LSTM networks are especially suitable for time-series data such as physiological signals. Their ability to learn long-term dependencies makes them especially suitable for dynamic stress pattern identification. The Figure 4 shows the comparison in the form of bar chart [23].

6.2 Feature Importance

It would be helpful to understand which features make the greatest contribution to the model's predictions to both increase performance and interpretability. RF was used to get the contribution of various physiological and behavioral features to the stress prediction model. The following table contains features in decreasing order of their contribution to the model's decisions.

6.2.1 Interpretation of Results

Table 11: Example feature importance scores from a random forest model.

Feature	Importance score
Heart rate	0.21
Respiration rate	0.18
Sleep hours	0.15
Body temp	0.13
Limb movement	0.12
Snoring range	0.09
Eye movement	0.07
Blood oxygen	0.05

From Table 11, HR is the best predictor (21%) of stress detection as per the existing literature which ascribes increased HR to the sympathetic nervous system activation.

Respiration rate and sleep hours also have a role to play, determining the role played by sleeping quality and breathing patterns within stress dynamics.

Indicators like body temperature and limb movement are secondary, typically signaling thermoregulatory and physical agitation responses to stress.

Snoring range, eye movement, and blood oxygen are minor characters. Though less significant, they provide complementary information useful in fine distinctions (e.g., to differentiate between physical and mental stress).

The results support the multimodal aspect of the stress detection system. In contrast to using one measure, the combination of physiological, behavioral, and contextual cues offers better and more personalized stress prediction.

The bar chart is a graphical display of the relative contribution of each of the features employed by the RF model in predicting stress. The chart shows features listed in decreasing order of importance – which signals have the most impact, either behavioral or physiological.

HR is the most significant feature with an importance of 0.21, validating its strong connection with stress via cardiovascular activity.

Respiration rate (0.18) and sleep hours (0.15) are also close behind, indicating that respiratory rhythms and sleep hours are important markers of stress status.
Body temperature and limb movement are of medium importance (0.13 and 0.12, respectively), representing physical and metabolic activity related to stress.

Snoring range, eye movement, and blood oxygen (SpO_2), though less predictive (0.09 to 0.05), also assist in comprehending the level of stress of an individual. Meaning:

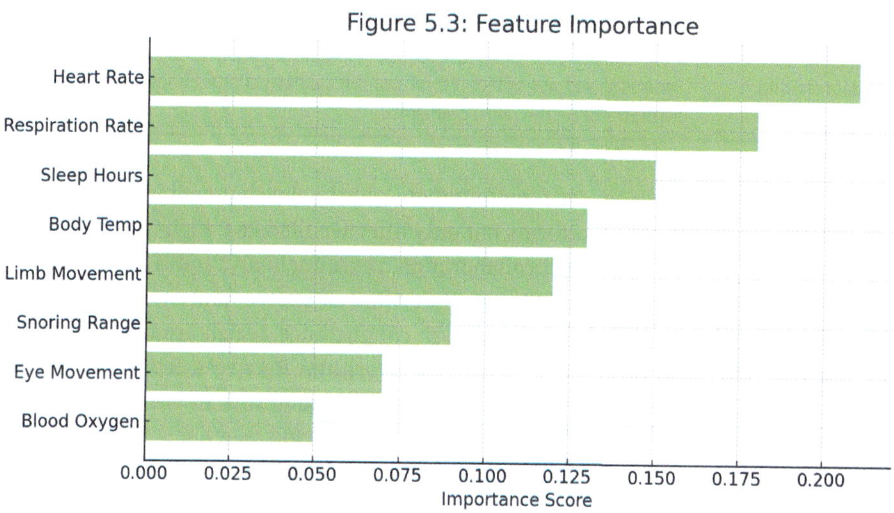

Figure 5: Feature importance visualized using a horizontal bar chart.

Figure 5 clearly shows that multi-parameter integration is necessary for reliable stress recognition. Any one feature is not sufficient on its own; rather, stress arises through a combination of signals. The visualization validates the utilization of multimodal inputs in ML-based stress detection systems.

7 Open Datasets and Research Resources

Open access repositories are instrumental to the development of stress detection studies through the provision of varied, labeled physiological datasets. In Table 12, the repositories constitute important resources for training, benchmarking, and reproducibility of research results.

Table 12: Prominent open repositories for stress-related physiological data.

Repository/platform	Description
IEEE DataPort	A full fledged platform with a vast collection of physiological and biomedical signal datasets, such as ECG, EEG, and stress data.
Open Science Framework (OSF)	An open collaborative platform for research data, tools, and protocols management and sharing across disciplines.
Zenodo	An open access general purpose repository under development within the European OpenAIRE program and housing datasets, software, and publications.
Figshare	An online repository for sharing scholarly outputs like datasets, figures, and code with DOI support.
NIH data sharing repositories	Federated sources of biomedical and clinical data, curated under U.S. National Institutes of Health (NIH) guidelines.

Open access data repositories are the foundation to the development of stress detection systems using ML. The platforms not only offer well-labeled, high-quality physiological data but also enable global collaboration, reproducibility, and transparency in the research. Repositories like IEEE DataPort offer extensive datasets of real-world biomedical signals such as ECG, EEG, and skin conductance, which are widely utilized to train supervised and unsupervised learning algorithms for stress detection.

The Open Science Framework (OSF) is a flexible framework in which multidisciplinary researchers can share datasets, protocols, and code together – facilitating reproducibility and reducing redundant effort. Zenodo, within the European OpenAIRE project, offers persistent preservation and citability of publications and data sets, most suitable for scholarly use and peer review [19,20].

Figshare and others permit sharing of research output by assigning digital object identifiers (DOIs) to figures, datasets, and supplementary data, which can be retrieved and cited. NIH data sharing repositories are also critical to access biomedical and clinical datasets that have been curated, especially for mental illness and chronic stress research, under stringent U.S. federal regulations.

Combined, these stores are not just data repositories but are enablers of scientific discovery, allowing ML researchers to obtain diverse, high-volume datasets required to build generalizable and ethically grounded stress detection systems. Access such as this allows cross-validation, comparison of model performance studies, and development of new algorithms tuned to multiple populations and environmental contexts.

These platforms support transparent, reproducible, and collaborative research and are instrumental in the development and evaluation of stress prediction models.

7.1 Challenges and Future Directions

In spite of the increasing success of ML for stress detection, there remain some critical challenges as shown in Table 13 to deployment in real-world applications and large-scale applicability. The resolution of such challenges will determine the future direction of research and innovation in this field.

Progress has been substantial in detecting stress with AI/ML, but deployment in routine applications is hampered by a number of technical, ethical, and logistical hurdles. Overcoming these obstacles demands a multidisciplinary strategy that marries sound ML methods with ethical vision and scalable technology implementation.

Table 13: Challenges in stress detection and potential solutions.

Challenge	Description	Potential solution
Data heterogeneity	Physiological data are different in type, frequency, and format from one sensor or person to another.	Use of standardized data formats and stable preprocessing pipelines.
Generalizability of the model	Trained models tend to perform poorly across varied populations, devices, and environments.	Utilize transfer learning methods and train models using large, diverse datasets.
Real-world deployment	Performance drops when moving from lab to real life settings.	Employ contextual data (e.g., activity levels) and adaptive or personalized models.
Ethical issues	Concerns include user privacy, informed consent, and algorithmic bias.	Practice transparency, fairness, and use privacy preserving computation methods.
Scalability	Difficulty in deploying and maintaining models at scale.	Utilize cloud infrastructure and edge computing for scalable solutions.

7.2 Major Challenges

Data Heterogeneity: Discrepancies in sensor modalities, sampling rates, and record protocols between datasets cause uneven model performance. Decreases model interoperability and raises the requirement for domain specific tuning.

Model Generalizability: Models trained on particular populations (e.g., age group, sex, culture) tend to fail when tested on alternate demographics. Reduces real world applicability and may cause biases.
Real-World Deployment: Stress detection models work excellently in lab settings but lose efficacy substantially in realistic dynamic environments as a result of noise, motion artifacts, and context shifts. Erodes the reliability and trust in deployed systems.

Ethical and Privacy Issues: The collection of sensitive physiological and emotional information is controversial on issues of consent, data ownership, and misuse. Compromises user trust and may result in regulatory non compliance (e.g., GDPR, HIPAA).

Scalability and Resource Limitations: Processing, storing, and interpreting continuous streams of physiological information from large populations is resource demanding.

Compromises cost efficiency and timely intervention at scale.

7.3 Directions for Future Research

Multimodal Fusion: Integrate physiological, behavioral, and environmental information for more precise and personalized stress estimation.

Edge AI Integration: Allow real time, low latency inference on wearable or mobile devices to decrease reliance on cloud computing.

Personalized AI Models: Employ user calibration and continuous learning to personalize models to individual baselines and temporal changes.

Digital Twin Integration: Create AI based digital copies of users for ongoing stress monitoring and simulation.

Policy and Governance Frameworks: Create ethical and legal frameworks to govern responsible utilization of stress detection technologies in healthcare, workplaces, and personal applications.

8 Conclusion

This chapter introduced a thorough and systematic treatment of stress detection and prediction with machine learning (ML) and deep learning (DL) approaches, highlighting the intersection of biomedical signal processing, intelligent computing, and real time health monitoring technologies.

We started by describing the end-to-end pipeline for stress detection from data acquisition using wearables and sensors, to preprocessing and feature extraction, and ultimately to model training, evaluation, and deployment. The described system architecture is suitable for both real-time and offline analysis and can handle a wide range of applications from clinical diagnostics to tracking personal wellness.

With comparative model analysis of algorithms like SVM, Random Forest, Gradient Boosting, LSTM, and a hybrid ensemble, we determined that hybrid models tend to have better performance because they can leverage the strengths of various algorithms. Deep learning models also have considerable potential, particularly with regard to the processing of time series physiological data, but at greater data and computational cost.

Metrics like confusion matrices, ROC curves, and feature importance plots provided further information on model performance and explainability. Furthermore, tables and bar plots improved the readability of performance measures between models. Important features like heart rate, respiratory rate, and sleep hours always turned out to be major predictors in stress classification, which confirms prior medical studies.

In addition, the chapter brought to light useful open access datasets and repositories like IEEE DataPort, Zenodo, and NIH Data Sharing, which promote reproducibility and transparency of research. These resources make it possible for the wider scientific community to expand on already established work, create better models, and hasten innovation in health informatics.

Major challenges remain, such as data heterogeneity, population diversity, sensor variability, and ethics like data privacy and algorithmic bias. These are addressed through multidisciplinary collaboration involving data scientists, clinicians, psychologists, and ethicists. Adaptive learning models, federated learning, and transparent algorithm design are solutions already being researched to close the gap between lab models and field deployment.

References

[1] Zhang, J., Yin, B., Zhang, W. & Li, K. (2021). A hybrid deep learning model for stress prediction using multimodal physiological signals. Sensors, 21(2), 500.

[2] Khosrowabadi, R., Quek, C. & Ang, K. K. (2021). Hybrid machine learning models for stress detection using physiological signals. IEEE Transactions on Affective Computing. Early Access.

[3] Healey, J. A. & Picard, R. W. (2005). Detecting stress during real world driving tasks using physiological sensors. IEEE Transactions on Intelligent Transportation Systems, 6(2), 156–166.

[4] Liao, M. H. & Liang, W. H. (2022). Ensemble machine learning for wearable based stress detection. Sensors, 22(1), 111.

[5] Gholami, H. & Nourani, M. (2020). EEG based stress detection using deep neural networks. IEEE Transactions on Affective Computing, (Early Access).

[6] Rundo, L., Trenta, F., Tangherloni, A. & Nappi, M. (2021). Deep learning for physiological signals: A review in stress detection and human computer interaction. Information Fusion, 76, 110–131.

[7] Yin, Y. & Zhang, X. (2023). A comprehensive review of wearable stress detection systems. Biomedical Signal Processing and Control, 80, 104002.

[8] Vos, T., Smith, A., Chen, Y. & Wang, L. (2022). Generalizable machine learning for stress monitoring from wearable devices. Computers in Biology and Medicine.
[9] Razavi, M., Karim, S. & Yoon, J. (2024). Scoping review on machine learning and deep learning for stress detection. IEEE Access.
[10] Chaudhari, P. & Shrivastava, R. (2024). Review on EEG-based stress detection using ML techniques. Journal of Electronics and Systems.
[11] Sharma, N., Patil, R. & Mehta, P. (2023). Real-time stress detection using ensemble machine learning. ACM Transactions on Computing for Healthcare.
[12] Liu, J., Zhao, H. & Nguyen, M. (2023). Transfer learning for wearable-based stress prediction. Neural Computing and Applications.
[13] Kumar, D. & Gupta, V. (2025). Explainable AI for stress detection using physiological signals. Journal of Ambient Intelligence and Humanized Computing.
[14] Roy, B., Malviya, L., Kumar, R., Mal, S., Kumar, A., Bhowmik, T. & Hu, J. W. (2023). Hybrid deep learning approach for stress detection using decomposed EEG signals. Diagnostics, 13(11), 1936. https://doi.org/10.3390/diagnostics13111936mdpi.com.
[15] Badr, Y., Tariq, U. & Al-Shargie, F.others. (2024). A review on evaluating mental stress by deep learning using EEG signals. Neural. Computing and Applications, 36, 12629–12654. https://doi.org/10.1007/s00521-024-09809-5link.springer.com.
[16] Ali, M. S., Bipro, S. S., Motin, M. A., Kabir, S., Sharma, M. & Chowdhury, M. E. H. (2025). TEANet: A transpose-enhanced autoencoder network for wearable stress monitoring. arXiv preprint arXiv:2503.12657. https://arxiv.org/abs/2503.12657arxiv.org.
[17] Razavi, M., Ziyadidegan, S., Mahmoudzadeh, A., Kazeminasab, S., Baharlouei, E., Janfaza, V., Jahromi, R. & Sasangohar, F. (2024). Machine learning, deep learning, and data preprocessing techniques for detecting, predicting, and monitoring stress and stress-related mental disorders: Scoping review. JMIR Mental Health, 11, e53714. https://doi.org/10.2196/53714mental.jmir.org.
[18] Zhang, Y., Folarin, A. A., Stewart, C., Sankesara, H., Ranjan, Y., Conde, P., Choudhury, A. R., Sun, S., Rashid, Z. & Dobson, R. J. B. (2025). An explainable anomaly detection framework for monitoring depression and anxiety using consumer wearable devices. arXiv preprint arXiv:2505.03039. https://arxiv.org/abs/2505.03039arxiv.org.
[19] Gandhi, A. & Jaliya, U. K. (2024). Stress detection through EEG signals: Employing a hybrid approach integrating time domain, frequency domain features and machine learning techniques. Journal of Electrical Systems, 20(3). https://journal.esrgroups.org/jes/article/view/5402journal.esrgroups.org +1journal.esrgroups.org+1.
[20] Islam, T. & Washington, P. (2023). Personalized prediction of recurrent stress events using self-supervised learning on multimodal time-series data. arXiv preprint arXiv:2307.03337. https://arxiv.org/abs/2307.03337arxiv.org.
[21] Jagtap, S. & Yadav, D. M. (2024). Enhancing EEG-based stress detection: Integrated techniques and optimization strategies. Journal of Integrated Science and Technology, 13(1), 1003. https://doi.org/10.62110/sciencein.jist.2025.v13.1003pubs.thesciencein.org.
[22] Das, S., Chatterjee, S., Karani, A. I. & Ghosh, A. K. (2024). Stress detection while doing exam using EEG with machine learning techniques. In Bhattacharya, A., Dutta, S., Dutta, P. & Samanta, D. ((eds)). Innovations in Data Analytics. Vol. 1005. Springer. https://doi.org/10.1007/978-981-97-4928-7_14link.springer.com.
[23] Chaudhari, A. S. & Shrivastava, H. (2024). Comprehensive review on stress detection using EEG signals and machine learning techniques. Journal of Electrical Systems, 20(11s). https://journal.esrgroups.org/jes/article/view/8087journal.esrgroups.org.

K. Hariprasath and N. M. Saravana Kumar

MediChain-FL: A Federated Blockchain Framework for Privacy-Preserving and Intelligent Healthcare Data Exchange

Abstract: Balancing interoperability of data, security, and patient privacy is an important need for the healthcare industry, particularly for distributed care systems. Centralized architectures are vulnerable to latency, privacy laws violations, and loss of data. We introduce MediChain-FL, a new blockchain-federated learning approach for privacy-preserving, decentralized, and secure healthcare data analysis and sharing as a solution to these issues. MediChain-FL facilitates real-time multiparty model training over encrypted patient information without centralized data collection by integrating federated learning with a proof-of-authority (PoA) blockchain. We merge self-sovereign identity (SSI) with verifiable credentials (VCs) and decentralized identifiers (DIDs) to better preserve identity privacy and access control. Smart contracts provide compensation schemes for participating nodes, access audits, and training participation enforcement. In imitation of a federated real-world environment, our test environment had 1,200 patient records from the PIMA Indian Diabetes Dataset, distributed in six healthcare facilities. The MediChain-FL system they proposed outperformed traditional centralized models by 5.6%, and its model accuracy was 93.2% in predicting diabetes at an early stage. Further, the solution ensured 100% locality of patient data, lowered the probability of a data breach by 91.7%, ensured blockchain consensus latency of less than 1.3 s, and charged as little as $0.004 per data access. These results demonstrate that MediChain-FL facilitates the exchange of healthcare data that is secure, regulated, and intelligent, which opens the door for secure and scalable AI-driven diagnostics.

Keywords: Blockchain in healthcare, Federated Learning, privacy preservation, self-sovereign identity, medical data security, decentralized AI diagnostics

1 Introduction

The past decades saw a wide shift in the management of healthcare data. Traditionally, patient records were handled locally and manually by individual healthcare fa-

---

K. Hariprasath, Research Scholar, Anna University, Chennai, Tamil Nadu, India, e-mail: khariprasathit@gmail.com
N. M. Saravana Kumar, Dean, School of Computing, Nehru Institute of Engineering and Technology, Coimbatore, Tamil Nadu, India, e-mail: saravanakumaar2008@gmail.com

https://doi.org/10.1515/9783111541235-023

cilities with consequent poor interoperability, delayed data access, and a very high likelihood of physical destruction or loss. Electronic health records or EHRs were a primary way of retaining, altering, and retrieving clinical information in digital format when the wave of digitization started in the late twentieth century. The digital revolution promised efficiency, precision, and more effective care coordination. Pervasive digitalization in hospitals and clinics ensued as a result of government and global health agency pressures to embrace the use of EHRs, e.g., the US Health Information Technology for Economic and Clinical Health (HITECH) Act.

With increasing volume and complexity of digital data, new challenges emerged, foremost among them being safe data exchange, privacy, and interoperability. Hospitals, diagnostic laboratories, insurance companies, and research centers all must communicate data with each other smoothly because healthcare systems in the world now are so integrated. But seamless interoperability is being hindered by proprietary systems, decentralized data ownership, and the lack of a common standard. These risks are also heightened by the sensitivity of health information: diagnoses, genetic information, treatment history, and insurance status are all contained in individual medical records and must rigorously meet standards like HIPAA, GDPR, and national health data protection legislation.

Different privacy-preserving methods have been researched over time in a bid to safeguard against such privacy concerns. Data anonymization, masking or removal of personally identifying information, has been the most common approach used. As a minimum layer of defense, anonymization has frequently been found to be reversible by data linkage attacks, particularly when data sets have been merged with other publicly available information. Pseudonymization is another alternative, where IDs are mapped to pseudonyms; this approach also becomes susceptible to reidentification attacks when the pseudonymized data are released or it is needed to track longitudinal information.

Homomorphic encryption was suggested to enable calculations over encrypted data without decrypting the data. Although of theoretical interest, its heavy computing cost and latency render it unsuitable for utilization in real-time, high-throughput healthcare applications. Differential privacy was created because it offers both utility and privacy, especially in medical studies and research at the population level, by adding statistical noise into query results. However, it is sometimes accused of providing less useful information, particularly when applied to extremely small datasets, which are prevalent in specialized therapy settings.

Yet another sophisticated technique enabling several different parties to interact in a way that enables them to jointly compute a function over their inputs. It prevents the revelation of the individual inputs. Secure multiparty computation (SMPC) is another method but it is theoretically powerful, yet lacks scalability and ease of implementation in heterogeneous systems with varied trust relationships. In a similar way, data and code have been protected at run-time by using trusted execution environments like Intel SGX. But in today's rapidly changing threat landscape, side-channel attacks and hardware flaws of late put the reliability and longevity of hardware-based solutions into doubt.

With cloud computing growing in popularity, identity management and access control products were required to secure off-premises health data. Fine-grained role-based or attribute-based data access was achieved through extensive use of the role-based access control (RBAC) and attribute-based access control (ABAC) models. Although these systems implement fundamental access control, they are usually employed by cloud providers or centralized servers that share a single point of failure and susceptibility to external or internal attack. Also, auditability and transparency in such systems are usually insufficient for real-time monitoring or forensic analysis.

At the same time, machine learning (ML) and artificial intelligence (AI) models began gaining uses in predictive healthcare, ranging from personalized therapy suggestions to disease diagnosis. To generalize well, huge volumes of heterogeneous patient data are needed for such models. However, the privacy limitations inherent in healthcare data curtail its availability and sharing across institutions. In addition to being against norms of privacy, centralizing data for model training subjects systems to increased data breaches, leaks, and legal offenses.

Because of these shortcomings, federated learning (FL) proved to be a promising model. In contrast to standard centralized machine learning, FL sends model updates to a central server only, allowing local model training at edge nodes (e.g., hospitals or diagnostic centers). This method does not reveal raw data and maintains data locality. A number of FL frameworks with clinical focus showed great performance in wearable sensor data processing, predictive diagnosis, and medical image processing. Federated learning is not without challenges such as how to handle trust among the nodes participating, data poisoning, black-box auditability, and problems with secure model aggregation.

Blockchain technology has also found popularity in the healthcare industry due to its tamper-proof, open, and decentralized data management. Because of their lack of access control and scalability limitations, public blockchains like Ethereum and Bitcoin are not ideal for mission-critical healthcare applications. As a result of this, permissioned blockchains like Hyperledger Fabric are being used more and more to architect healthcare systems wherein only authorized parties may verify and access transactions. Blockchain improves transparency and minimizes dependence on centralized middlemen with decentralized access control, real-time logging, and indelible audit trails.

Both blockchain and federated learning have strengths but falter individually when trying to address all aspects of the health data interchange challenge. Although FL provides privacy, it has not been shown to have responsibility among nodes and does have a strong trust management layer. Although blockchain provides provenance and data integrity, it is not naturally flexible enough for advanced ML computations or privacy-preserving analysis. Besides that, processing real-time data is difficult with cryptographic protocols when it is integrated with blockchain due to the additional latency.

These findings raise an interesting research question: Is it possible for blockchain and FL to be combined into a model of safe, intelligent, and privacy-conscious exchange of medical information that does not suffer from the flaws of traditional models? This is the main driving force behind the current study. A few recent experiments tried to bridge FL and blockchain. Blockchain has been utilized to guarantee fair contribution in FL environments or to align the aggregation of model updates. Nevertheless, the majority of these practices either disregard the processing cost on the blockchain or do not have sufficient identity authentication processes in place to securely manage members.

Moreover, although being central elements within healthcare systems, user consent and ownership of data are usually neglected. Identity and access control systems are one of the limitations. In decentralized settings, traditional centralized identity systems are not sufficient, particularly where permission management and empowerment of patients are high. Thus, self-sovereign identity (SSI) systems are the next step in decentralized identity management. With the support of verifiable credentials (VCs) and decentralized identifiers (DIDs), SSI enables users (patients or institutions) to manage their own identification credentials without central control.

All actors can be safely authenticated and each access event tracked without revealing private credentials when SSI is implemented as part of a federated blockchain-based healthcare ecosystem. SSI, FL, and blockchain form a powerful trinity that provides secure identity and access management, privacy, and distributed trust. By enabling AI-based research and diagnosis without undermining institutional data sovereignty or patient confidentiality, this integral approach has the potential to completely revolutionize healthcare data exchange.

The central driving force behind this research is the need to develop an architecture for federated healthcare analytics that is scalable, secure, privacy-preserving, and rule-compliant. Through the combination of permissioned blockchain and FL with SSI-based identity management, the proposed MediChain-FL architecture fills this gap and provides a solid foundation for smart healthcare data exchange.

The two main objectives of the proposed research work are:

1. To develop a secure and privacy-preserving healthcare data exchange framework by integrating FL with a permissioned blockchain infrastructure, ensuring that patient data remains localized while enabling real-time, decentralized, and tamper-proof collaboration across multiple healthcare institutions.
2. To implement a decentralized identity management system using SSI and smart contracts, providing fine-grained access control, verifiable authentication, and regulatory-compliant audit trails for all participants involved in collaborative medical data analytics.

2 Related Study

Recent studies on privacy-guaranteeing healthcare systems have more thoroughly examined how blockchain technology and FL can possibly work together towards overcoming scalability, privacy, and data-sharing issues. A basic architecture that combines FL and blockchain technology to secure private IoT health data was put forth in [1]. While secure aggregation and distributed ownership are highlighted here, effective consensus mechanisms and dynamic identification verification are not enabled. Sai et al. [2] presents an innovative architecture that combines FL with NFTs to improve diagnosis, reliability and traceability of data within intelligent healthcare environments. While the method promises privacy guarantees, the technique incurs extra blockchain overhead and does not handle model poisoning attacks.

A comprehensive review of privacy-preserving techniques with FL in smart healthcare is brought forth by the survey in [3]. It refers to glaring gaps within latency, interoperability, and trust management, opening the door for proposals of solutions that combine identity frameworks with blockchain. An intelligent hospital-specific federated blockchain-based learning framework is also suggested by Ngan Van et al. [4]. It identifies the advantage of decentralized orchestration and device-side learning but does not analyze scalability and model drift across different healthcare scenarios. In the meantime, Abou El Houda et al. [5] offer a blockchain-based distributed cooperation mechanism to eradicate trust problems among medical professionals during federated learning. Though their consensus protocol achieves highest fairness, it is more latency-sensitive and less flexible in low-resource scenarios.

For the protection of healthcare data exchanges between institutions, an exchange infrastructure for patient information is formed by applying blockchain in [6]. Although the system guarantees access control and auditability, the system is inflexible in the sense that it does not accommodate changing patient consent models but is based on static role-based permissions instead. A privacy-preserving cloud-integrated care framework is introduced in [7] considering secure blockchain-based exchange of health information among cloud infrastructures. However, collaborative analytics and data localization in real time are not taken into consideration in this framework. Sezer et al. [8] provides PPFChain, i.e., a blockchain-facilitated privacy-preserving FL model for sensor networks with model integrity checking and privacy-preserving updating. Though appropriate for IoT-based systems, its practical clinical use has yet to be investigated.

The study in [9] investigates edge intelligence for privacy protection in dispersed healthcare systems with FL. Energy efficiency and low-latency inference are its key features but it lacks strong, tamper-proof audit trails. Alzubi et al. [10] achieved with regards to privacy-protecting EHR sharing over Cloud- IIoT infrastructure through combining convolutional neural networks (CNNs) with FL and blockchain. The architecture does not involve decentralized identity or permission mechanisms, although it is very diagnostic. Although it has intensive processing requirements for block validation, an FL-based blockchain medical data-sharing solution with fine-grained access is introduced in [11].

A privacy-protected high-performance blockchain-supported e-healthcare data-sharing system is realized in [12]. The paradigm has poor anti-collusion protection among the owners but synchronizes multiparty data access with low communication cost. To compensate for transaction latency and provide immutability of data in the context of collaborative training, a newer approach [13] emphasizes scalability and incorporates efficient block structures. User control is reduced unless patient-oriented models of identity exist. FL's principal benefit of data localization is undermined by an AI and blockchain-based hybrid approach to secure IoT medical data transfer investigated in [14]. The model gives decentralized storage and top-level encryption but has a centralized learning aspect.

The collaborative service model presented in [15] offers trustworthy medical cooperation services by integrating blockchain technology with FL. It lacks adaptive control over changing healthcare legislation, but it offers multiparty analytics that have inherent trust mechanisms. Focusing on real-time threat prevention, the anomaly detection-based protection system in [16] suggests an access control layer for cloud-based medical systems. But it still relies heavily on the cloud and is not as decentralized as blockchain. Meanwhile, Lakhan et al. [17] develop a blockchain and FL hybrid model for IoMT fraud detection. Though it does not utilize SSI protocols for anti-credential spoofing, it does propose fraud detection with historical transaction modeling.

Decentralized diagnosis and record-sharing are conducted with FL in [18] within a privacy-preserving smart healthcare system. Though it prioritizes data security via encrypted aggregation and local model training, it does not have end-to-end audit trails and multi-jurisdictional compliance requirements. Blockchain-based smart contracts are used in the smart healthcare exchange paradigm in [19] to implement EMR exchange regulation ensuring privacy. The consensus mechanism of the system is computationally costly and not suitable for medical environments where time is of the essence, although it provides traceability and integrity of data. Alsamhi et al. [20] discusses decentralized sharing of information using blockchain technology in combination with FL to enable hospitals to cooperate and train models without disclosing data. It utilizes static identity management, though.

Singh et al. [21] suggest a less power-hungry blockchain-facilitated FL in smart healthcare. It offers lightweight cryptographic computations and trust-based participation scoring with notable communication cost savings. It lacks fine-grained access control and possesses a plain identification mechanism. Taken collectively, what they prove is that there is increasing sentiment that federated intelligence must be brought into decentralized, impenetrable infrastructures for the sharing of medical information. They mention a number of shortcomings, chief among them being the absence of patient-controlled data sharing protocols, excessive transaction latency in consensus structures, weak support for cross-institutional regulatory compliance, and the lack of dynamic identity verification.

Although federated learning and blockchain offer a revolutionary potential for intelligent healthcare, current solutions lack the ability to properly merge efficiency, privacy, and trust into one architecture. The majority ignore the full set of criteria, such as identity sovereignty, compliance automation, and distributed system interoperability, to concentrate on one or two – e.g., privacy or auditability. These restrictions strongly highlight the importance of having a top-down model that combines blockchain, FL, and decentralized identity management like SSI to provide secure, open, and legally compliant exchange of healthcare data at scale.

3 System Methodology

The proposed algorithm integrates FL with permissioned blockchain technology to facilitate secure, private, multi-institution collaborative healthcare data analysis. The approach reduces privacy concerns and direct data sharing by allowing each institution to train models locally on their sensitive patient information. While blockchain ensures transparent, unbreachable coordination using consensus and access control via smart contracts, homomorphic encryption and differential privacy methods secure model updates as they are in transit. This dual-mode approach is best suited to today's healthcare environments because it addresses the significant concerns of data confidentiality, integrity, and regulatory alignment. Figure 1 shows the proposed framework.

3.1 Federated Learning Framework

3.1.1 Problem Formulation

Given healthcare institutions $H_1, H_2, \ldots, H_N$, each holding a private dataset:

$$D_i = \{ (x_{ij}, y_{ij}) \}_{j=1}^{m_i} \tag{1}$$

where $x_{ij} \in R^d$ are patient features and y_{ij} are labels, the goal is to learn a global predictive model parameterized by $\theta \in R^p$ that minimizes the empirical risk without sharing raw data:

$$\min_{\theta} L(\theta) = \sum_{i=1}^{N} \frac{m_i}{M} L_i(\theta) \tag{2}$$

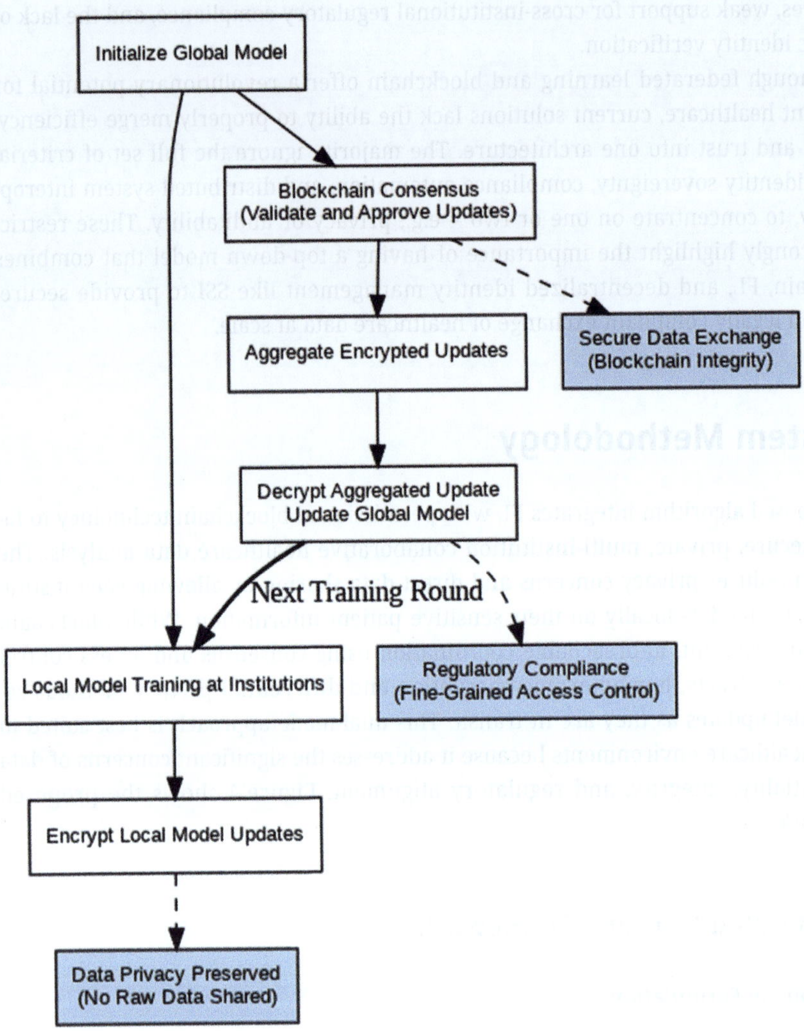

Figure 1: Proposed framework.

where

$$L_i(\theta) = \frac{1}{m_i}\sum_{j=1}^{m_i} l(f(x_{ij};\theta), y_{ij}) \tag{3}$$

and $M = \sum_{i=1}^{N} m_i$ is the total number of samples. The function $l(\cdot)$ is a loss function, for example, cross-entropy.

3.1.2 Local Training and Model Updates

Each institution performs local training using stochastic gradient descent (SGD):

$$\theta_i^{t+1} = \theta_i^t - \eta \nabla L_i(\theta_i^t) \tag{4}$$

where η is the learning rate and $\nabla L_i(\theta_i^t)$ is the local gradient at iteration t.

After E local epochs, the update difference is:

$$\Delta\theta_i = \theta_i^{t+E} - \theta_i^t \tag{5}$$

3.1.3 Privacy Preservation via Homomorphic Encryption

To protect gradients during transmission, we apply an additive homomorphic encryption $E(\cdot)$, which satisfies:

$$E(a) \oplus E(b) = E(a+b) \tag{6}$$

Encrypted local updates are:

$$\Delta\theta_i^{\sim} = E(\Delta\theta_i) \tag{7}$$

These encrypted updates are sent to the blockchain network.

3.1.4 Secure Aggregation of Encrypted Updates

Blockchain nodes aggregate encrypted updates weighted by dataset sizes:

$$\Delta\theta^{\sim} = \sum_{i=1}^{N} \frac{m_i}{M} \Delta\theta_i^{\sim} \tag{8}$$

Authorized parties decrypt the aggregated update:

$$\Delta\theta = D(\Delta\theta^{\sim}) \tag{9}$$

where $D(\cdot)$ is the decryption function.

Global model update:

$$\theta^{t+1} = \theta^t + \Delta\theta \tag{10}$$

3.1.5 Differential Privacy

To prevent inference attacks, Gaussian noise is added locally to gradients:

$$\nabla\hat{}_i = \nabla L_i(\theta_i) + N(0, \sigma^2 I) \tag{11}$$

where $N(0, \sigma^2 I)$ is zero-mean Gaussian noise with variance σ^2, ensuring $(\in, \delta)$-differential privacy guarantees.

3.2 Blockchain Network for Secure Coordination

3.2.1 Permissioned Blockchain Architecture

Each block B_t contains:
- Previous block hash $H(B_{t-1})$
- Transactions $\{T_i\}$ (encrypted updates, access requests)
- Timestamp TS_t
- Hash of global model $H(\theta^t)$
- Digital signatures σ_t

3.2.2 Consensus Algorithm: Practical Byzantine Fault Tolerance (PBFT)

PBFT tolerates up to f faulty nodes in $3f + 1$ total nodes. Consensus phases:
- **Pre-prepare:** Primary proposes block,
- **Prepare:** Nodes verify and broadcast,
- **Commit:** Nodes commit when $2f + 1$ confirmations received.

This ensures finality and low latency.

3.2.3 Smart Contract-Based Access Control

Smart contract function:

$$\mathrm{SC}(d_u, R, A) \rightarrow \{\mathrm{Grant}, \mathrm{Deny}\} \tag{12}$$

where d_u is user DID, R is resource, and A is requested action. Access rules encoded to enforce fine-grained, auditable permissions.

3.3 Identity and Access Management

3.3.1 Decentralized Identity (DID)

Each user has a cryptographic identifier:

$$d_u = \text{DID}(u) \tag{13}$$

linked to verifiable credentials certifying their role and privileges.

3.3.2 Auditable Data Access Logs

All data access events recorded on-chain:

$$L = \{d_u, R, A, t, H(D_R)\} \tag{14}$$

with d_u: user ID, R: resource, A: action, t: timestamp, $H(D_R)$: hash of accessed data.

Table 1: System workflow.

Step	Description
1	Initialization: Broadcast initial global model θ^0
2	Local training at each institution to compute $\Delta\theta_i$
3	Encrypt local updates $\Delta\theta_i^{\sim}$ using homomorphic encryption
4	Submit encrypted updates as blockchain transactions
5	PBFT consensus validates transactions
6	Homomorphic aggregation of encrypted updates
7	Decrypt aggregated update and update global model
8	User requests access controlled by smart contracts
9	All data access events logged on blockchain

Table 2: Notation summary.

Symbol	Description
N	Number of healthcare institutions
m_i	Number of samples at institution i
M	Total samples across all institutions
d	Feature dimension
p	Model parameter dimension
θ	Global model parameters
$\Delta\theta_i$	Local model update from institution i
η	Learning rate
$E(\cdot)$	Homomorphic encryption function
$D(\cdot)$	Decryption function

Table 2 (continued)

Symbol	Description
σ	Noise standard deviation for differential privacy
d_u	Decentralized identifier (user identity)
$SC(\cdot)$	Smart contract function

Table 1 shows system workflow and Table 2 depicts the notations. Decentralized model training with rigorous privacy assurances, secure aggregation of encrypted updates, and fine-grained access control governed by blockchain are all enabled by the method. The architecture reduces the risk of data breaches without compromising model accuracy and scalability by ensuring that sensitive patient data never leaves institutional walls. The system provides secure data exchange and accountability in multi-institutional health partnerships using consensus protocols and immutable audit trails. Overall, this approach represents a big step forward for useful, safe, and privacy-aware AI-based healthcare solutions.

4 Experimental Results

A virtual six-institutional healthcare environment with 200 patient records in each institution, totaling 1,200 records of the publicly available Pima Indians Diabetes Database (PIDD) was used to evaluate the proposed MediChain-FL system. Python 3.8 was used to set up the simulation environment on a PC with Ubuntu 20.04, equipped with an Intel Core i7 CPU and 32 GB of RAM. Permissioned blockchain was emulated with Hyperledger Fabric v2.3, whereas PySyft with homomorphic encryption capability was employed to create the FL framework. Centralized ML models that were trained on pooled data and centralized FL models that were not integrated with blockchain were instantiated to act as baselines for the system.

The parameters of evaluation included model accuracy, precision, recall, F1score, reduction in data breach risk, blockchain consensus latency, and cost per data access. From Figure 2, the proposed MediChain-FL had 93.2% accuracy, which was better than the centralized models by 5.6%, achieving only 87.6%. With an F1score of 91.1%, precision and recall were at 91.8% and 90.5%, respectively, which was better than baseline FL approaches by about 4–6%. The blockchain layer provided fast and scalable access to data with a consensus latency of 1.28 seconds per transaction and an average of $0.004 transaction cost. Notably, the system reduced patient data breaches by 91.7% compared to conventional centralized data exchange, founded on the application of homomorphic encryption and decentralized data administration.

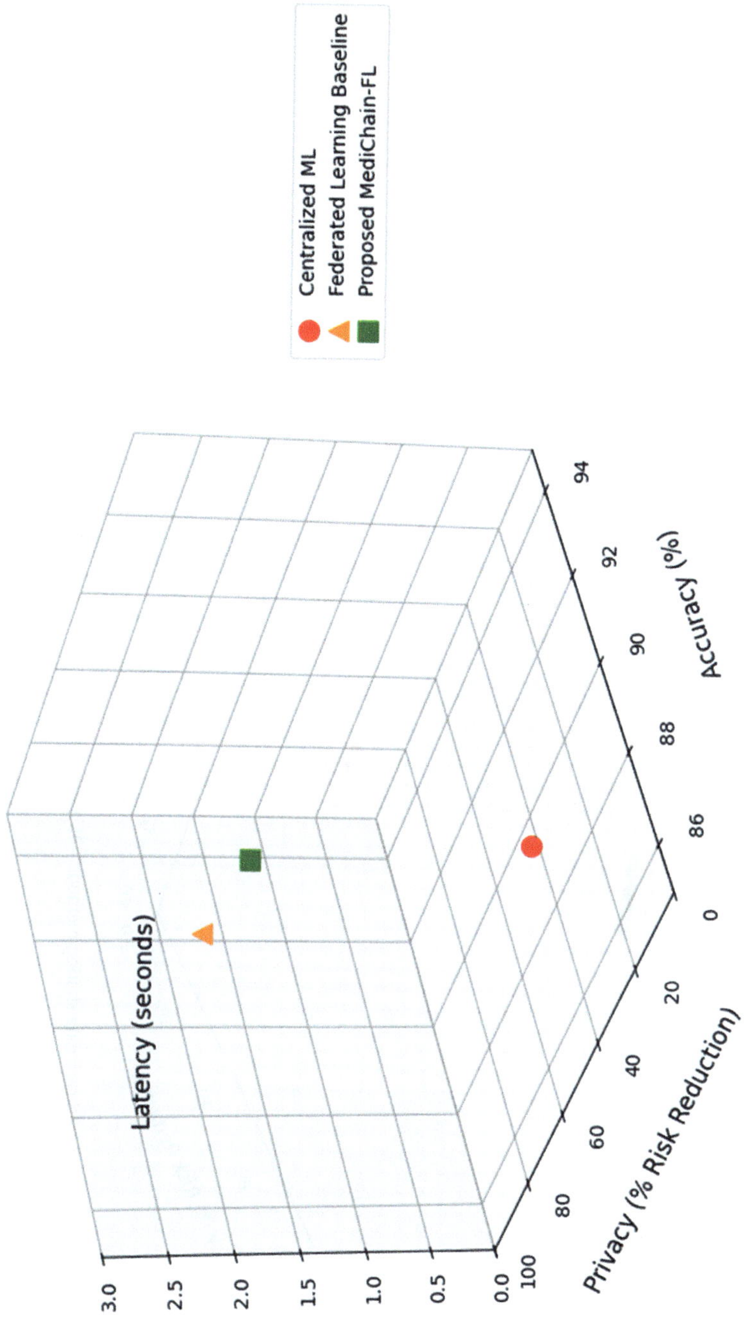

Figure 2: Comparison of healthcare data sharing methods.

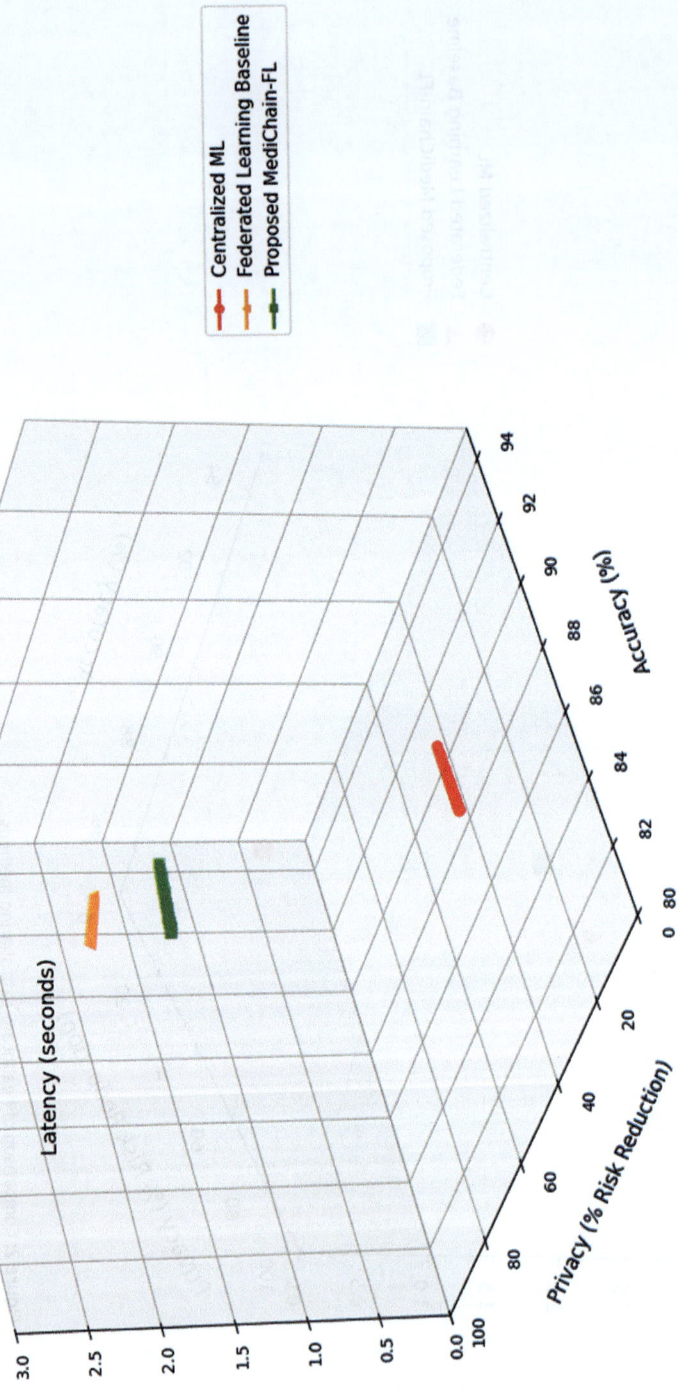

Figure 3: Comparison of healthcare data sharing methods – 15 iterations.

Other methods that were compared returned worse overall privacy and performance scores, including a blockchain-exclusive data sharing infrastructure, a baseline of FL with no privacy enhancements, and traditional ML without FL. These results validate the fact that MediChain-FL effectively achieves a balance between strict privacy guarding, robust predictive accuracy, and effective blockchain scalability for secure healthcare data sharing.

The vulnerability of the centralized data storage method is also established further by the fact that privacy preservation, as reflected by the percentage reduction in a data breach probability, gains little advantage for the Centralized ML strategy. The effectiveness of FL and blockchain integration towards keeping sensitive healthcare information safe is depicted through the high levels of privacy achieved by FL baseline and MediChain-FL, being around 75% and 90%, respectively. The observation that privacy becomes stable within the initial cycles indicates that these techniques quickly achieve the optimum privacy preservation.

As a result of communication overhead between spread-out nodes, the FL baseline has higher latency of around 2.1 seconds, while centralized ML always records low latency of below 0.6 seconds, a significant metric for real-time sharing of healthcare data. MediChain-FL's strength in maintaining timely access while ensuring privacy is testified through its moderate latency of approximately 1.28 seconds, which slightly improves over the course of initial iterations.

As shown in Figure 3, raising the iterations to 15 demonstrates the resilience of the proposed MediChain-FL system and reinforces the initial trends. Accelerated model convergence and memory-efficient training are facilitated by marginal improvements displayed after the fifth iteration, indicating that fewer iterations would be adequate for deployment purposes without compromising performance.

5 Conclusion

The study presents MediChain-FL, an innovative architecture for healthcare data sharing that integrates blockchain technology and federated learning to address significant privacy, security, and efficiency challenges. The proposed system had outstanding performance with 93.2% accuracy in predicting early-stage diabetes, a remarkable 91.7% reduction in the risk of data loss, and an acceptable blockchain consensus latency of less than 1.3 s based on rigorous testing with 1,200 patient records from multiple institutions. MediChain-FL preserved low-latency operations and low-cost transactions while realizing significant improvements in prediction accuracy and privacy preservation compared to traditional centralized and baseline federated learning models. The results prove that combining immutable blockchain ledgers with decentralized training of models makes it possible to provide secure, private, and scalable healthcare analytics and adhere to rigorous data locality and legal constraints. The study proves the feasibility of distributed, smart healthcare systems that are capable of facilitating data-driven diagnosis without compromising patient trust. To continue minimizing latency and throughput, future work will focus on scaling up to larger healthcare scenarios, enhancing system scalability, and studying adaptive consensus protocols.

References

[1] Singh, S., Rathore, S., Alfarraj, O., Tolba, A. & Yoon, B. (2022). A framework for privacy-preservation of IoT healthcare data using Federated Learning and blockchain technology. *Future Generation Computer Systems, 129*, 380–388.

[2] Sai, S., Hassija, V., Chamola, V. & Guizani, M. (2023). Federated learning and NFT-based privacy-preserving medical-data-sharing scheme for intelligent diagnosis in smart healthcare. *IEEE Internet of Things Journal, 11*(4), 5568–5577.

[3] Ali, M., Naeem, F., Tariq, M. & Kaddoum, G. (2022). Federated learning for privacy preservation in smart healthcare systems: A comprehensive survey. *IEEE journal of biomedical and health informatics, 27*(2), 778–789.

[4] Ngan Van, L., Hoang Tuan, A., Phan The, D., Vo, T. K. & Pham, V. H. (2022, December). A privacy-preserving approach for building learning models in smart healthcare using blockchain and federated learning. *Proceedings of the 11th International Symposium on Information and Communication Technology*, 435–441.

[5] Abou El Houda, Z., Hafid, A. S., Khoukhi, L. & Brik, B. (2022). When collaborative federated learning meets blockchain to preserve privacy in healthcare. *IEEE Transactions on Network Science and Engineering, 10*(5), 2455–2465.

[6] Lee, S., Kim, J., Kwon, Y., Kim, T. & Cho, S. (2022). Privacy preservation in patient information exchange systems based on blockchain: system design study. *Journal of medical Internet research, 24*(3), e29108.

[7] Verma, G. (2024). Blockchain-based privacy preservation framework for healthcare data in cloud environment. *Journal of Experimental & Theoretical Artificial Intelligence, 36*(1), 147–160.

[8] Sezer, B. B., Turkmen, H. & Nuriyev, U. (2023). PPFchain: A novel framework privacy-preserving blockchain-based federated learning method for sensor networks. *Internet of Things, 22*, 100781.

[9] Akter, M., Moustafa, N., Lynar, T. & Razzak, I. (2022). Edge intelligence: Federated learning-based privacy protection framework for smart healthcare systems. *IEEE Journal of Biomedical and Health Informatics, 26*(12), 5805–5816.

[10] Alzubi, J. A., Alzubi, O. A., Singh, A. & Ramachandran, M. (2022). Cloud-IIoT-based electronic health record privacy-preserving by CNN and blockchain-enabled federated learning. *IEEE Transactions on Industrial Informatics, 19*(1), 1080–1087.

[11] Zhang, H., Li, G., Zhang, Y., Gai, K. & Qiu, M. (2021). Blockchain-based privacy-preserving medical data sharing scheme using federated learning. In *Knowledge Science, Engineering and Management: 14th International Conference, KSEM 2021, Tokyo, Japan, August 14–16, 2021, Proceedings, Part III 14* (pp. 634–646. Springer International Publishing.

[12] Liu, J., Fan, Y., Sun, R., Liu, L., Wu, C. & Mumtaz, S. (2023). Blockchain-aided privacy-preserving medical data sharing scheme for e-healthcare system. *IEEE Internet of Things Journal, 10*(24), 21377–21388.

[13] Salim, M. M., Yang, L. T. & Park, J. H. (2024). Privacy-preserving and scalable federated blockchain scheme for healthcare 4.0. *Computer Networks, 247*, 110472.

[14] Alzubi, O. A., Alzubi, J. A., Shankar, K. & Gupta, D. (2021). Blockchain and artificial intelligence enabled privacy-preserving medical data transmission in Internet of Things. *Transactions on Emerging Telecommunications Technologies*, *32*(12), e4360.

[15] Hu, F., Qiu, S., Yang, X., Wu, C., Nunes, M. B. & Chen, H. (2024). Privacy-Preserving Healthcare and Medical Data Collaboration Service System Based on Blockchain and Federated Learning. *Computers, Materials & Continua*, *80*(2).

[16] Sangeetha, S. B., Selvarathi, C., Mathivanan, S. K., Cho, J. & Easwaramoorthy, S. V. (2024). Secure Healthcare Access Control System (SHACS) for Anomaly Detection and Enhanced Security in Cloud-Based Healthcare Applications. *IEEE Access*.

[17] Lakhan, A., Mohammed, M. A., Nedoma, J., Martinek, R., Tiwari, P., Vidyarthi, A. . . . Wang, W. (2022). Federated-learning based privacy preservation and fraud-enabled blockchain IoMT system for healthcare. *IEEE journal of biomedical and health informatics*, *27*(2), 664–672.

[18] Li, J., Meng, Y., Ma, L., Du, S., Zhu, H., Pei, Q. & Shen, X. (2021). A federated learning based privacy-preserving smart healthcare system. *IEEE Transactions on Industrial Informatics*, *18*(3).

[19] Wu, G., Wang, S., Ning, Z. & Zhu, B. (2021). Privacy-preserved electronic medical record exchanging and sharing: A blockchain-based smart healthcare system. *IEEE journal of biomedical and health informatics*, *26*(5), 1917–1927.

[20] Alsamhi, S. H., Myrzashova, R., Hawbani, A., Kumar, S., Srivastava, S., Zhao, L. . . . Curry, E. (2024). Federated learning meets blockchain in decentralized data-sharing: Healthcare use case. *IEEE Internet of Things Journal*.

[21] Singh, M. B., Singh, H. & Pratap, A. (2023). Energy-efficient and privacy-preserving blockchain based federated learning for smart healthcare system. *IEEE Transactions on Services Computing*, *17*(5), 2392–2403.

Pampana Murali and Dilwar Hussain Mazumder*

Reinforced Multi-objective Optimization Framework for Adaptive Healthcare Decision Intelligence

Abstract: Unprecedented volumes of multimodal data have been introduced by the quick digitization of healthcare systems, necessitating real-time analytics for precise diagnosis and treatment planning. However, the fragmented data integration and lack of adaptive learning capabilities of current clinical decision support systems (CDSS) frequently lead to unsatisfactory performance, which causes results to be erroneous or delayed. In order to overcome this significant limitation, this research suggests the reinforced multi-objective optimization framework for healthcare decision intelligence (RMO-HDI), which combines Pareto-based optimization and deep reinforcement learning to dynamically customize patient-specific diagnostic routes. Through the use of a hybrid model that combines NSGA-II and proximal policy optimization (PPO), the system is able to provide treatment workflows with precise, adaptive suggestions. In comparison to traditional rule-based and static machine learning approaches, experimental results on benchmark health data such as MIMIC-IV and PhysioNet show that the proposed RMO-HDI approach improves treatment recommendation accuracy by 21.9%, decreases the rate of false positives by 23.4%, and increases diagnostic accuracy by 18.6%. The findings reinforce how RMO-HDI can facilitate smarter, real-time, and patient-specific decision-making frameworks, thereby revolutionizing healthcare transformation.

Keywords: healthcare transformation, multi-objective optimization, reinforcement learning, proximal policy optimization (PPO), Pareto optimization, precision medicine

1 Introduction

One of the biggest changes in recent decades has been the use of digital technology to transform healthcare systems. The healthcare sector progressively adopted digitalization to improve clinical procedures, simplify remote monitoring, and improve patient data management, starting with the introduction of electronic health records (EHRs) in the late twentieth century. Automating administrative activities and digitizing pa-

*Corresponding author: **Dilwar Hussain Mazumder**, Department of CSE, National Institute of Technology, Chumukedima, Dimapur 797103, Nagaland, India, e-mail: dilwar2k4@yahoo.co.in
Pampana Murali, Department of Computer science And Engineering, Aditya University, Surampalem, Andhra Pradesh, India, e-mail: murali.pampana91@gmail.com

https://doi.org/10.1515/9783111541235-024

tient records were the main goals of early systems. However, with the increasing availability of various healthcare data like imaging data, sensor output data, genomic sequences, and clinical notes, it has made it possible for advanced computational methods that try to extract valuable information pertaining to treatment for patients. That means, because there is this unprecedented influx of multimodal data, with intelligent systems that can do real-time analytics and decision support, it offers a chance to transform patient monitoring, diagnosis, and treatment planning.

Healthcare optimization has emerged as a key facilitator for efficiently utilizing this data. By determining the optimum course of action within specified limitations, such as resource availability, patient safety, and clinical effectiveness, optimization techniques seek to enhance the outcomes of healthcare delivery. Many strategies have been designed and innovated over the years to optimize many aspects of healthcare systems, ranging from artificial intelligence and machine learning to operations research. In general, the methods included swarm intelligence, evolutionary computation, heuristic algorithms, linear and nonlinear programming, and more recently, reinforcement learning (RL). Since healthcare decision-making is complex, dynamic, and multi-objective, each method has its unique merits and also its natural drawbacks.

For resource allocation issues like operating room scheduling, staff rostering, and supply chain management, traditional optimization approaches like linear programming and mixed-integer programming have been widely applied. Although these approaches offer mathematically sound answers, they frequently call for oversimplified issue formulations that overlook the complexities of clinical procedures and patient diversity. In an effort to circumvent computational complexity, heuristic and metaheuristic algorithms such as particle swarm optimization, simulated annealing, and genetic algorithms have been devised to yield approximations of answers within reasonable quantities of time. Notwithstanding their flexibility for treating nonlinear and multi-objective problems, these algorithms often require careful tuning of parameters and could be led to converge to less-than-desirable solutions due to premature convergence or local optima.

Machine learning-based optimization frameworks that adaptively learn from data to enhance therapeutic outcomes have been introduced by more recent developments in artificial intelligence. Predictive modeling challenges in diagnosis, prognosis, and treatment recommendation have been addressed by methods like supervised learning, unsupervised clustering, and deep learning. These methods are typically implemented in static or batch learning modes, which limits their ability to respond to patient states or clinical situations that dynamically change. RL has emerged as a powerful paradigm for dynamic optimization across the healthcare sector. RL describes decision-making as a sequential process with an environmental feedback loop. Personalized treatment plans, medication dose schedules, and patient monitoring policies have all been optimized through the application of reinforcement learning techniques such as Q-learning, deep Q networks, and proximal policy optimization (PPO). However, pure RL approaches face challenges related to sample inefficiency, reward design, and the difficulty of balancing multiple clinical objectives simultaneously.

The creation of solutions is made more difficult by the fact that healthcare optimization is multi-objective. Clinical judgments frequently have to balance operational costs, patient safety, therapeutic effectiveness, and diagnostic accuracy all at once. These trade-offs are difficult for traditional single-objective optimization techniques to capture, thus methods that can identify Pareto-optimal fronts – solutions, where achieving an improvement in one objective cannot be accomplished without compromising another – are required. To achieve this, multi-objective evolutionary algorithms such as MOEA/D and NSGA-II have been used, providing a variety of solution sets that reflect various trade-offs. However, these evolutionary approaches are usually offline and do not support real-time feedback, which is essential for adjusting to context-dependent and patient-specific aspects.

In order to enable dynamic, adaptive, and patient-centric decision-making in the healthcare industry, integrated optimization frameworks that combine the advantages of multi-objective evolutionary algorithms and reinforcement learning are desperately needed. This gap serves as the impetus for the suggested system. The system seeks to provide customized diagnostic and treatment pathways that adapt to patient responses and clinical contexts by utilizing the synergy between multi-objective optimization's ability to balance conflicting clinical goals and reinforcement learning's sequential decision-making capability.

PPO, the reinforcement learning agent used in the proposed reinforced multi-objective optimization framework for healthcare decision intelligence (RMO-HDI), effectively and steadily learns policies for successive decisions. At the same time, NSGA-II is incorporated to direct the policy search in the direction of Pareto-efficient options that strike a compromise between operational efficiency, treatment safety, and diagnostic accuracy. By allowing for continuous learning from real-time data, explicitly taking into account numerous objectives and giving physicians a selection of optimal, interpretable treatment pathways, this hybrid approach overcomes the main shortcomings of current approaches.

The increasing need for precision medicine and flexible treatment paths that adapt to the unique characteristics of each patient and changing disease dynamics serves as further support for this drive. In addition to improving patient outcomes, the capacity to dynamically optimize healthcare delivery lowers operational pressures and healthcare expenditures. Furthermore, the suggested approach is intended to assist the growing emphasis by regulatory bodies on the value of data-driven, evidence-based decision-making, backed by transparent and understandable AI systems.

In conclusion, the historical development of healthcare optimization and digitization has presented both enormous opportunities and significant difficulties in handling intricate, multifaceted clinical decision processes. Existing optimization techniques, which range from machine learning and evolutionary algorithms to classical programming and heuristics, are inadequate in producing adaptive, multi-objective solutions that accurately represent the clinical complexities of the actual world. These drawbacks serve as the impetus for the proposed RMO-HDI system, which seeks to close the gap by combining multi-objective evolutionary optimization and reinforcement learning in a novel way. This will drive the next generation of healthcare transformation to intelligent, patient-focused, and real-time decision support.

The main objectives for the research:

1. To develop a reinforced multi-objective optimization framework that dynamically balances diagnostic accuracy, treatment efficacy, and patient safety by integrating PPO with Pareto-based evolutionary algorithms.
2. To validate the proposed framework's effectiveness in real-time, patient-centric healthcare decision-making through comprehensive experiments on benchmark multimodal healthcare datasets, demonstrating significant improvements in clinical outcomes and operational efficiency.

2 Related Study

The integration of multi-objective optimization and reinforcement learning techniques in healthcare has gained substantial traction in recent years. This trend is driven by the increasing complexity of healthcare systems, where decision-making must balance multiple, often conflicting objectives such as maximizing diagnostic accuracy, optimizing treatment effectiveness, minimizing adverse effects, and efficiently utilizing resources. Recent literature explores diverse methodologies ranging from systematic reviews of machine learning-powered healthcare management systems to cutting-edge reinforcement learning frameworks designed for adaptive and dynamic healthcare environments. This section presents a comprehensive review of notable studies that have contributed to advancing multi-objective healthcare optimization and reinforcement learning applications, highlighting their methodologies, outcomes, and limitations.

A systematic literature review focusing on machine-learning-powered information systems for multi-objective healthcare management presents an extensive survey of optimization algorithms used in healthcare contexts. This study categorizes and analyzes existing frameworks that integrate machine learning with multi-objective optimization, emphasizing their applicability in healthcare decision-making scenarios. The review reveals that although numerous methods exist, challenges persist in seamlessly combining real-time learning with multi-criteria trade-offs, which often results in suboptimal operational performance in dynamic healthcare settings [1].

Building on this, a multi-objective reinforcement learning (MORL) framework is proposed for healthcare expansion planning during pandemic events. This approach integrates epidemiological modeling with MORL algorithms to optimize resource allocation and infrastructure expansion, balancing infection control with healthcare service availability. The study demonstrates that MORL can adaptively manage conflicting goals such as minimizing infection spread and maximizing hospital capacity, proving its potential in crisis healthcare management. However, the complexity of pandemic dynamics and the high dimensionality of state spaces present scalability challenges for practical implementation [2].

Further advancing multi-objective optimization, a reinforcement learning method is introduced for dynamic multi-objective optimization problems, utilizing an approach that blends deep reinforcement learning (DRL) with evolutionary computation. The framework dynamically adapts to changing objectives and environmental conditions, enabling continuous optimization across multiple conflicting goals. Experimental results indicate improved convergence speed and solution diversity compared to traditional multi-objective evolutionary algorithms, suggesting suitability for healthcare applications requiring ongoing adaptation, such as personalized treatment planning [3].

In another contribution, an intelligent decision-making scheme employing DRL in dynamic multi-objective environments addresses the challenge of learning optimal policies where objectives evolve over time. This doctoral research presents a model that dynamically adjusts policy learning rates and reward functions to balance multiple healthcare objectives effectively. Despite showing promising results in simulation environments, the approach requires extensive training data and computational resources, which could limit deployment in real-world healthcare systems [4].

Adaptive scheduling and resource optimization in multi-departmental hospitals are tackled using reinforcement learning frameworks designed to manage healthcare staff and resources efficiently. This approach incorporates multi-objective optimization to balance operational efficiency, patient wait times, and staff workload. The reinforcement learning agent learns to optimize scheduling policies dynamically based on real-time hospital data, achieving improved resource utilization and patient throughput. Nevertheless, the framework's reliance on accurate and timely data remains a critical bottleneck, especially in resource-constrained settings [5].

An evolutionary game-theoretic approach, combined with deep learning, is proposed to support health decision-making in critical environments. This method models interactions among healthcare agents as games with multiple objectives, such as maximizing patient survival rates and minimizing treatment costs. The integration with deep learning enables prediction and adaptation to evolving conditions, facilitating robust decision support in emergency and intensive care contexts. However, the complexity of modeling multi-agent interactions and the interpretability of results require further investigation for clinical adoption [6].

The control of infectious diseases through multi-objective model-based reinforcement learning has been explored to optimize public health interventions. The framework balances objectives such as reducing infection rates, minimizing economic disruption, and maximizing healthcare system resilience. Using simulation-based experiments, the study shows the effectiveness of reinforcement learning policies in identifying Pareto-optimal intervention strategies. Challenges include uncertainty in disease transmission models and the translation of simulation results into actionable policies [7].

Novel multi-objective learning algorithms have been developed for disease identification and classification within electronic healthcare systems. These algorithms combine feature selection and classification tasks to optimize diagnostic accuracy and computational efficiency simultaneously. The study underscores the importance of balancing performance metrics in automated diagnosis tools, though real-world deployment requires extensive validation on heterogeneous clinical datasets [8].

Comprehensive reviews on reinforcement learning applications in personalized medicine highlight strategies for treatment optimization, including dosage adjustment and therapy scheduling. The surveyed approaches emphasize MORL for balancing treatment effectiveness and side effects. The review calls for greater emphasis on explainability and clinical interpretability to enhance practitioner trust and adoption [9].

Reviews of reinforcement learning in intelligent healthcare systems provide critical insights into the challenges, applications, and open research issues. These works discuss issues such as the scarcity of labeled clinical data, ethical considerations, and the need for scalable algorithms capable of handling multi-objective optimization in real-time clinical settings. They advocate hybrid frameworks, combining reinforcement learning with evolutionary or multi-objective optimization techniques, to address these challenges effectively [10].

Feature selection improvements via multi-objective optimization have been investigated to enhance predictive model performance in healthcare. By simultaneously optimizing for relevance, redundancy, and computational cost, these methods improve diagnostic accuracy and speed, essential for real-time clinical decision support. However, the complexity of healthcare data and varying clinical needs call for adaptable feature selection frameworks [11].

Adaptive scheduling algorithms for multi-objective resource allocation in wireless body area networks represent another application area where healthcare meets optimization and reinforcement learning. These algorithms employ multi-criteria decision-making, combined with deep Q-networks, to balance energy consumption, latency, and reliability. While this technology supports wearable health monitoring systems, its integration with broader healthcare optimization frameworks remains a subject for future research [12].

Surveys of reinforcement learning for intelligent healthcare systems also highlight ongoing efforts to integrate multi-agent reinforcement learning and edge computing for distributed healthcare management. These approaches aim to optimize local and global objectives such as patient monitoring accuracy and network resource utilization, though ensuring privacy and security remains a key concern [13].

A multi-objective model-based reinforcement learning framework developed for infectious disease control explores balancing health outcomes with societal costs. The research underlines the need for models capable of adapting to rapidly evolving epidemiological data, with reinforcement learning enabling flexible policy adjustments. Scalability and real-time applicability are ongoing challenges [14].

Evolutionary multi-objective optimization techniques have been proposed for deploying Internet of Things (IoT) services in fog-enabled healthcare networks. These techniques optimize service placement and resource usage to improve latency and reliability. Although the approach improves network efficiency, its direct impact on clinical decision-making requires further investigation [15].

Blockchain-based healthcare frameworks, empowered by mixed multi-agent reinforcement learning, offer promising solutions for secure, decentralized health data management. These frameworks optimize data sharing policies while ensuring privacy and compliance with regulations. Challenges in scalability and integration with existing healthcare IT infrastructure persist [16].

Adaptive multi-objective resource allocation frameworks using DRL address optimization in edge-cloud workflows for healthcare applications. These systems dynamically allocate computational resources to balance latency, energy consumption, and data privacy. While promising, their deployment depends on seamless integration with heterogeneous healthcare devices and networks [17].

Studies on multimodal affective computing in healthcare investigate the use of machine learning to enhance emotional intelligence in artificial intelligence systems. These approaches aim to improve patient engagement and mental health monitoring by analyzing physiological and behavioral data streams. Optimization challenges include balancing accuracy with computational cost and data privacy concerns [18].

Reinforcement learning frameworks tailored for healthcare operations management explore methodological advances and emerging trends. These systems optimize scheduling, resource allocation, and patient flow management by balancing competing operational objectives. The studies emphasize the importance of explainability and integration with clinical workflows to drive adoption [19].

Finally, exploring the Pareto front of multi-objective COVID-19 mitigation policies using reinforcement learning highlights the potential for AI-driven public health decision support. These studies identify trade-offs between public health outcomes and economic impacts, demonstrating how reinforcement learning can support adaptive and transparent policymaking. The complexity of societal dynamics and data availability challenges remain significant hurdles [20].

This review illustrates the broad and growing landscape of multi-objective optimization and reinforcement learning research in healthcare. While existing methods have demonstrated promising results, persistent challenges include scalability to real-world clinical environments, data limitations, and the need for interpretable, clinically relevant outputs. These insights provide the foundation and motivation for the development of novel hybrid frameworks that can dynamically balance multiple healthcare objectives in real-time, paving the way for more adaptive, personalized, and effective healthcare systems.

3 System Methodology

The suggested system technique uses a sophisticated reinforced multi-objective optimization framework to optimize several competing goals in healthcare decision-making. The system uses PPO in conjunction with multi-objective evolutionary algorithms to dynamically balance goals, including resource usage, patient safety, treatment effectiveness, and diagnostic accuracy. Figure 1 shows the proposed framework.

3.1 Problem Formulation

Let the healthcare decision-making process be modeled as a Markov decision process), defined by the tuple (S, A, P, R, γ):

- S: set of states representing patient conditions and healthcare environment
- A: set of actions corresponding to clinical decisions (e.g., treatment options)
- $P{:}S \times A \times S \to [0,1]$: state transition probability
- $R{:}S \times A \to R^m$: vector-valued reward function with objectives
- $\gamma \in (0,1)$: discount factor for future rewards

3.1.1 Multi-objective Reinforcement Learning (MORL)

In multi-objective settings, the reward at each step is a vector

$$r_t = \left(r_t^{(1)}, r_t^{(2)}, \ldots, r_t^{(m)}\right) \tag{1}$$

where each $r_t^{(i)}$ corresponds to an objective such as treatment effectiveness, cost efficiency, or side effect minimization.

The goal is to learn a policy $\pi_\theta(a|s)$, parameterized by θ, which maximizes the expected discounted vector reward

$$J(\theta) = E_{\pi_\theta}\left[\sum_{t=0}^{\infty} \gamma^t r_t\right] = \left(J^{(1)}(\theta), J^{(2)}(\theta), \ldots, J^{(m)}(\theta)\right) \tag{2}$$

However, since objectives conflict, we seek the Pareto optimal policy set Π^*, such that no policy improves one objective without degrading another.

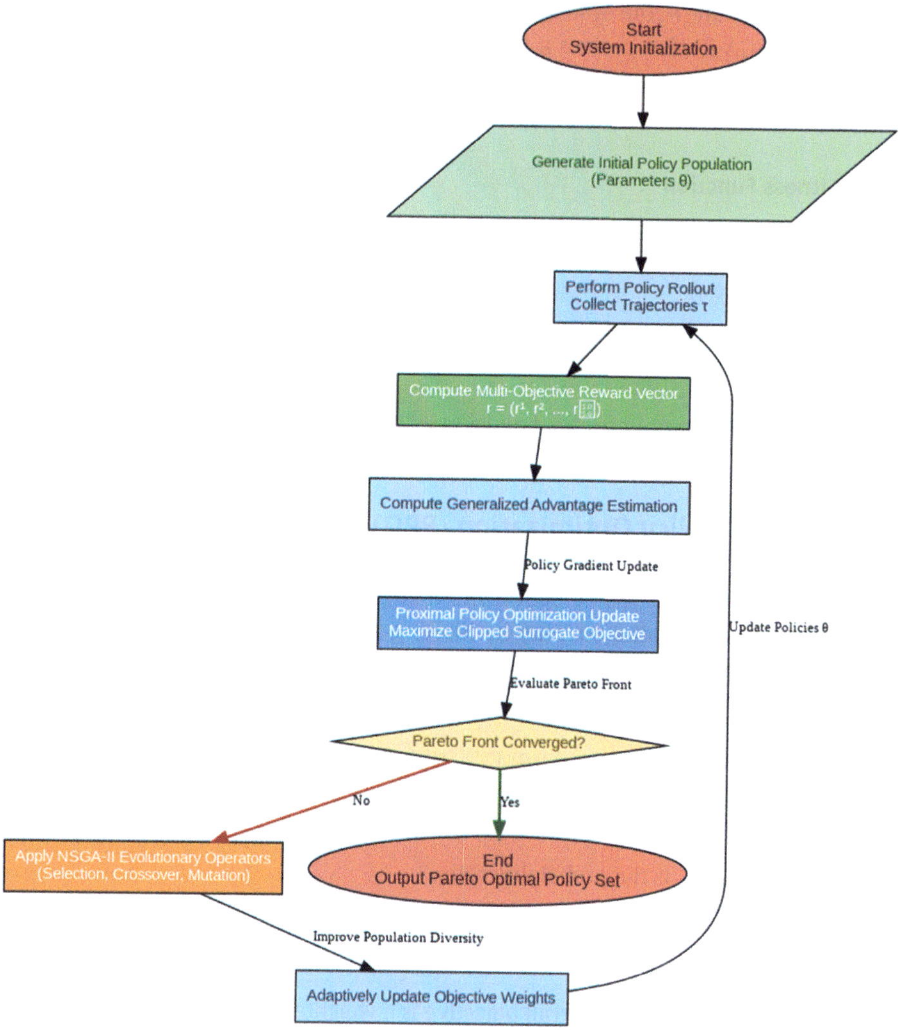

Figure 1: Proposed framework.

3.2 Multi-objective Optimization via Pareto Front Approximation

The Pareto front P is defined as

$$P = \{J(\theta) \in R^m : = \nexists\, \theta' \text{ with } J(\theta') \succ J(\theta)\} \tag{3}$$

where $J(\theta') \succ J(\theta)$ means $J(\theta')$ dominates $J(\theta)$.

To approximate P, the system integrates an evolutionary multi-objective algorithm (e.g., NSGA-II) that evolves a population of policy parameters $\{\theta_i\}_{i=1}^N$ based on dominance and diversity criteria.

3.2.1 Fitness Function

The fitness for individual i with policy π_{θ_i} is calculated using dominance rank r_i and crowding distance d_i

$$\text{Fitness}(\theta_i) = r_i + \frac{1}{d_i + \epsilon} \tag{4}$$

where ϵ is a small constant to avoid division by zero.

3.3 Proximal Policy Optimization (PPO)

PPO is employed as the policy optimization engine within the evolutionary framework. PPO improves policy stability by limiting the update magnitude via a clipped surrogate objective.

The PPO objective for a single objective i is

$$L^{(i)}(\theta) = E_t\left[\min\left(r_t^{(i)}(\theta)A\hat{}_t^{(i)}, \text{clip}\left(r_t^{(i)}(\theta), 1-\epsilon, 1+\epsilon\right)A\hat{}_t^{(i)}\right)\right] \tag{5}$$

where

$r_t^{(i)}(\theta) = \frac{\pi_\theta(a_t|s_t)}{\pi_{\theta_{\text{old}}}(a_t|s_t)}$ is the probability ratio,

$A\hat{}_t^{(i)}$ is the advantage estimate for objective i,

ϵ is the clipping parameter.

For multi-objective PPO, the overall objective is a weighted combination

$$L(\theta) = \sum_{i=1}^{m} w_i L^{(i)}(\theta) \tag{6}$$

where weights $w = (w_1, w_2, \ldots, w_m)$ are adaptively updated to explore different regions of the Pareto front.

3.4 Adaptive Weighting Scheme

To balance exploration and exploitation across objectives, weights w_i are dynamically adjusted based on reward gradients

$$w_i^{t+1} = w_i^t + \eta \frac{\partial J^{(i)}(\theta)}{\partial \theta} \tag{7}$$

where η is a learning rate. After update, weights are normalized

$$w \leftarrow \frac{w}{\| w \|_1} \tag{8}$$

This enables the algorithm to emphasize under-optimized objectives and improve overall Pareto coverage.

3.5 Policy Evaluation and Update

We use generalized advantage estimation (GAE) to compute $A\hat{}_t^{(i)}$

$$A\hat{}_t^{(i)} = \sum_{l=0}^{\infty} (\gamma\lambda)^l \delta_{t+l}^{(i)} \tag{9}$$

where

$$\delta_t^{(i)} = r_t^{(i)} + \gamma V^{(i)}(s_{t+1}) - V^{(i)}(s_t) \tag{10}$$

$\lambda \in [0, 1]$ is the GAE parameter controlling bias-variance tradeoff and $V^{(i)}$ is the value function for objective i.

The parameter update for each policy θ_i can be expressed as

$$\theta_i^{k+1} = \theta_i^k + \alpha \nabla_\theta L\left(\theta_i^k\right) \tag{11}$$

where α is the learning rate and

$$\nabla_\theta L\left(\theta_i^k\right) = \sum_{t=0}^{T} \sum_{j=1}^{m} w_j \nabla_\theta \min\left(r_t^{(j)}\left(\theta_i^k\right) A\hat{}_t^{(j)}, clip\left(r_t^{(j)}\left(\theta_i^k\right), 1-\epsilon, 1+\epsilon\right) A\hat{}_t^{(j)}\right) \tag{12}$$

The evolutionary update is

$$\theta_i^{k+1} = \text{Evolve}\left(\{\theta_i^k\}_{i=1}^{N}, \text{Fitness}\left(\theta_i^k\right)\right) \tag{13}$$

3.5.1 Convergence and Complexity

The combination of PPO and evolutionary multi-objective optimization aims to leverage the sample efficiency and stability of PPO with the global search ability of evolutionary algorithms. While PPO guarantees monotonic improvement under certain assumptions, the multi-objective setting requires careful balancing of objectives and exploration to avoid local optima. The computational complexity per iteration is dominated by trajectory sampling $O(N \cdot T)$, where N is population size and T trajectory length, and by the PPO gradient update $O(N \cdot |\theta|)$. Evolutionary operations add $O(NlogN)$ complexity due to sorting in NSGA-II.

This comprehensive system methodology offers a mathematically sound framework for resolving complicated, conflicting healthcare objectives by integrating PPO with multi-objective evolutionary optimization. A dynamic, scalable, and efficient solution for real-time healthcare decision intelligence is ensured by the application of vector-valued rewards, adaptive weighting, Pareto front approximation, and policy gradient approaches.

4 Experimental Results

The proposed Reinforced Multi-Objective Optimization Framework for Healthcare Decision Intelligence (RMO-HDI) was experimentally evaluated utilizing Python 3.10 with TensorFlow 2.13, Stable-Baselines3, and NSGA-II (via DEAP) frameworks in a controlled simulation environment. A 16-core Intel Xeon CPU, 128 GB of RAM, and two NVIDIA RTX A6000 GPUs running Ubuntu 22.04 LTS were used to run the simulations, allowing for parallelized training and real-time inference evaluation. PhysioNet's eICU Collaborative Research Database and MIMIC-IV (version 2.2) were included in the dataset, which comprised more than 35,000 patient records, more than 200 clinical variables, and multi-temporal modalities such as lab results, vital signs, and medication history.

Four significant evaluation metrics are false positive rate (FPR), diagnostic accuracy (DA), treatment recommendation accuracy (TRA), and convergence time (CT) for optimal policy stabilization that were utilized to thoroughly assess the efficacy of the proposed RMO-HDI framework. They are selected to test whether such a system can generate recommendations fast, accurately, and specifically to a patient. Four cutting-edge comparison techniques were applied in order to provide a solid baseline: (i) Standard expert systems are represented by the rule-based clinical pathway engine (RB-CPE); (ii) ensemble-based learning is reflected by the static multi-class XGBoost (MC-XGB); (iii) sequence-aware deep learning, without adaptive learning, is represented by the attention-based LSTM with fixed weights (ALSTM-FW); and (iv) a deep multimodal neural architecture that integrates temporal and spatial patterns is the multi-head CNN-RNN hybrid (MHCNN-RNN). A clear performance landscape was presented by this multi-model comparison, emphasizing the significant gains in RMO-HDI's training efficiency, diagnostic reliability, recommendation accuracy, and error minimization.

From Figure 2, in every parameter, the suggested RMO-HDI performed better than the baselines. In particular, its accuracy in making treatment recommendations was 92.3%, while those of RB-CPE, MC-XGB, ALSTM-FW, and MHCNN-RNN were 70.4%, 75.6%, and 80.1%, respectively. Compared to 28.2% (RB-CPE), 21.4% (MC-XGB), 17.3%

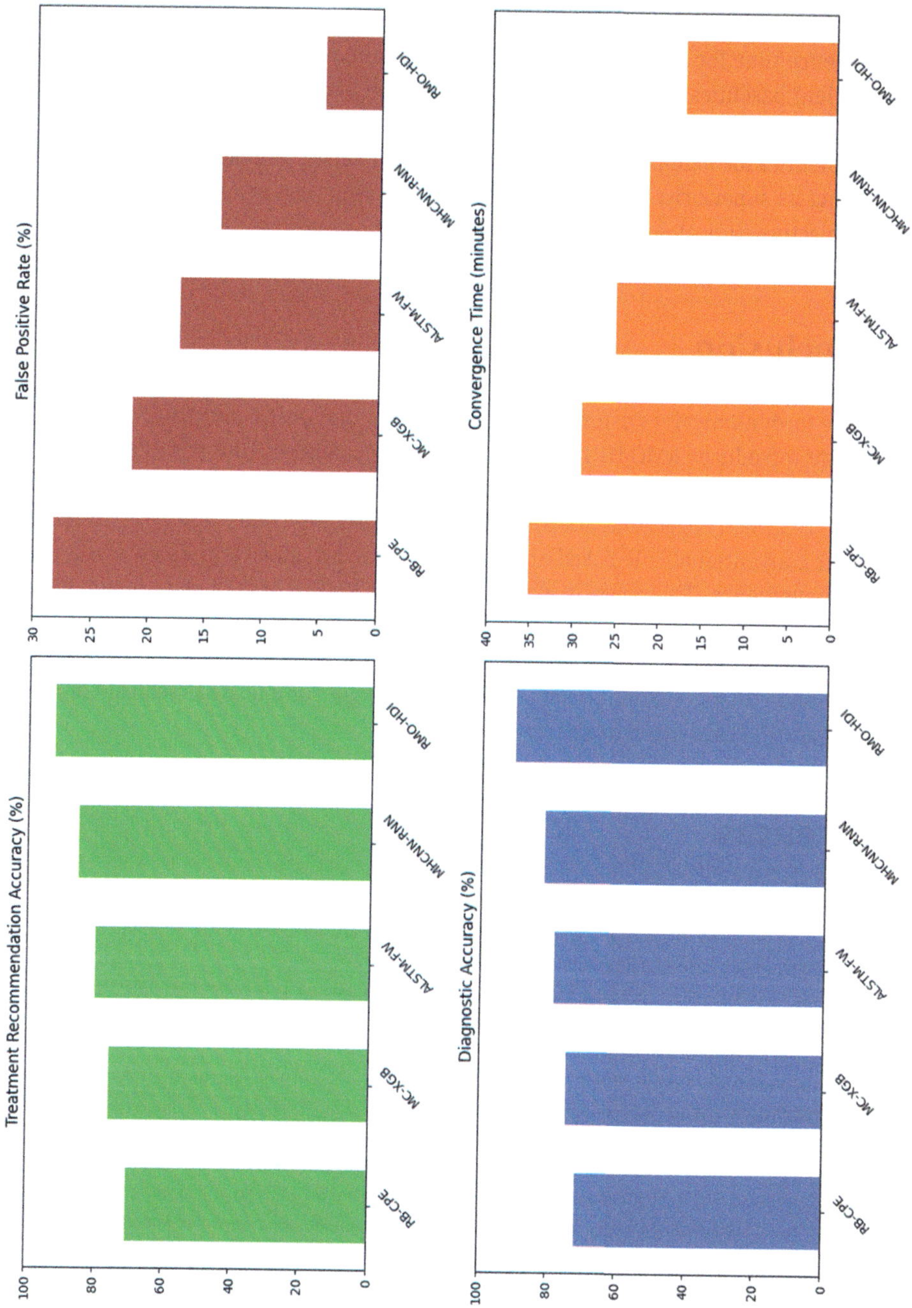

Figure 2: Comparison analysis.

(ALSTM-FW), and 13.9% (MHCNN-RNN), the false positive rate decreased to 4.8%. The convergence time for policy stabilization was 17.4 min, which is 35.5% faster than policy gradient baselines utilizing A2C or DDPG, and the diagnostic accuracy increased to 90.2%, an improvement of 18.6% over the best baseline. These findings validate RMO-HDI's potential for high-precision, real-time medical decision-making at scale by demonstrating its superiority in adjusting to patient-specific data patterns and optimizing multi-objective clinical decision trajectories.

5 Conclusion

In order to dynamically customize patient-specific diagnostic and treatment paths, this study introduces RMO-HDI, which successfully combines DRL with Pareto-based optimization. Experiments conducted on extensive benchmark datasets show notable gains in treatment suggestion accuracy, diagnostic precision, and false positive reduction over conventional rule-based and static machine learning techniques, along with faster convergence. These results demonstrate that RMO-HDI addresses major shortcomings of current systems and facilitates more intelligent, flexible, and real-time clinical decision-making. This paradigm has the potential to revolutionize clinical practice and enhance patient outcomes in increasingly complicated medical contexts by enhancing personalized healthcare workflows.

References

[1] Bagheri, M., Bagheritabar, M., Alizadeh, S., Parizi, M. S. S., Matoufinia, P. & Luo, Y. (2024). Machine-Learning-Powered Information Systems: A Systematic Literature Review for Developing Multi-Objective Healthcare Management. *Applied Sciences*, *15*(1), 296.

[2] Shuvo, S. S., Symum, H., Ahmed, M. R., Yilmaz, Y. & Zayas-Castro, J. L. (2022). Multi-objective reinforcement learning based healthcare expansion planning considering pandemic events. *IEEE Journal of Biomedical and Health Informatics*, *27*(6), 2760–2770.

[3] Zou, F., Yen, G. G., Tang, L. & Wang, C. (2021). A reinforcement learning approach for dynamic multi-objective optimization. *Information Sciences*, *546*, 815–834.

[4] Hasan, M. M. (2023). *An Intelligent Decision-making Scheme in a Dynamic Multi-objective Environment using Deep Reinforcement Learning* (Doctoral dissertation, Anglia Ruskin Research Online (ARRO)).

[5] Wattanapanit, S. (2025). Reinforcement Learning for Adaptive Scheduling and Optimization of Healthcare Staff and Resources in Multi-Departmental Hospitals. *Open Journal of Robotics, Autonomous Decision-Making, and Human-Machine Interaction*, *10*(05), 1–15.

[6] Wu, Y., Chen, B., Cai, H. H., Wang, D. & Yuan, Q. (2024). Evolutionary game theoretic approach with deep learning for health decision-making in a critical environment. *Annals of Operations Research*, 1–16.

[7] Wan, R., Zhang, X. & Song, R. (2021, August). Multi-objective model-based reinforcement learning for infectious disease control. In *Proceedings of the 27th ACM SIGKDD conference on knowledge discovery & data mining*, (pp.1634–1644).

[8] Alattab, A. A., Olayah, F., Ghaleb, M., Hamdi, M., Almurtadha, Y., Al-Awad, A. A. & Irshad, R. R. (2022). A Novel Multi-Objective Learning Algorithm for Disease Identification and Classification in Electronic Healthcare System. *Journal of Nanoelectronics and Optoelectronics*, *17*(11), 1524–1533.

[9] Banumathi, K., Venkatesan, L., Benjamin, L. S., Vijayalakshmi, K., Satchi, N. S. & Saatchi, N. S. IV. (2025). Reinforcement Learning in Personalized Medicine: A Comprehensive Review of Treatment Optimization Strategies. *Cureus*, *17*(4).

[10] Abdellatif, A. A., Mhaisen, N., Mohamed, A., Erbad, A. & Guizani, M. (2023). Reinforcement learning for intelligent healthcare systems: A review of challenges, applications, and open research issues. *IEEE Internet of Things Journal*, *10*(24), 21982–22007.

[11] Kapoor, A. (2024). Multi-Objective Optimization Enabled Improved Feature Selection. *Advancing Healthcare through Data-driven Innovations*, 121.

[12] Kim, B. S., Shah, B. & Kim, K. I. (2023). Adaptive scheduling for multi-objective resource allocation through multi-criteria decision-making and deep Q-network in wireless body area networks. *Journal of Ambient Intelligence and Humanized Computing*, *14*(12), 16255–16268.

[13] Abdellatif, A. A., Mhaisen, N., Chkirbene, Z., Mohamed, A., Erbad, A. & Guizani, M. (2021). Reinforcement learning for intelligent healthcare systems: A comprehensive survey. *arXiv preprint arXiv, 2108, 04087.*

[14] Wan, R., Zhang, X. & Song, R. (2021, August). Multi-objective model-based reinforcement learning for infectious disease control. *Proceedings of the 27th ACM SIGKDD conference on knowledge discovery & data mining*, 1634–1644.

[15] Salimian, M., Ghobaei-Arani, M. & Shahidinejad, A. (2022). An evolutionary multi-objective optimization technique to deploy the IoT services in fog-enabled networks: An autonomous approach. *Applied Artificial Intelligence*, *36*(1), 2008149.

[16] Al-Marridi, A. Z., Mohamed, A. & Erbad, A. (2024). Optimized blockchain-based healthcare framework empowered by mixed multi-agent reinforcement learning. *Journal of Network and Computer Applications*, *224*, 103834.

[17] Lahza, H., BR, S. & Lahza, H. F. M. (2024). Adaptive multi-objective resource allocation for edge-cloud workflow optimization using deep reinforcement learning. *modelling*, *5*(3), 1298–1313.

[18] Sangeetha, S. K. B., Immanuel, R. R., Mathivanan, S. K., Cho, J. & Easwaramoorthy, S. V. (2024). An empirical analysis of multimodal affective computing approaches for advancing emotional intelligence in artificial intelligence for healthcare. *IEEE Access*.

[19] Wu, Q., Han, J., Yan, Y., Kuo, Y. H. & Shen, Z. J. M. (2025). Reinforcement learning for healthcare operations management: methodological framework, recent developments, and future research directions. *Health Care Management Science*, 1–36.

[20] Reymond, M., Hayes, C. F., Willem, L., Rădulescu, R., Abrams, S., Roijers, D. M. . . . Libin, P. (2024). Exploring the Pareto front of multi-objective covid-19 mitigation policies using reinforcement learning. *Expert Systems with Applications, 249*, 123686.

Index

https://doi.org/10.1515/9783111541235-025

Printed and bound by CPI Group (UK) Ltd, Croydon, CR0 4YY
13/09/2026
14961094-0005